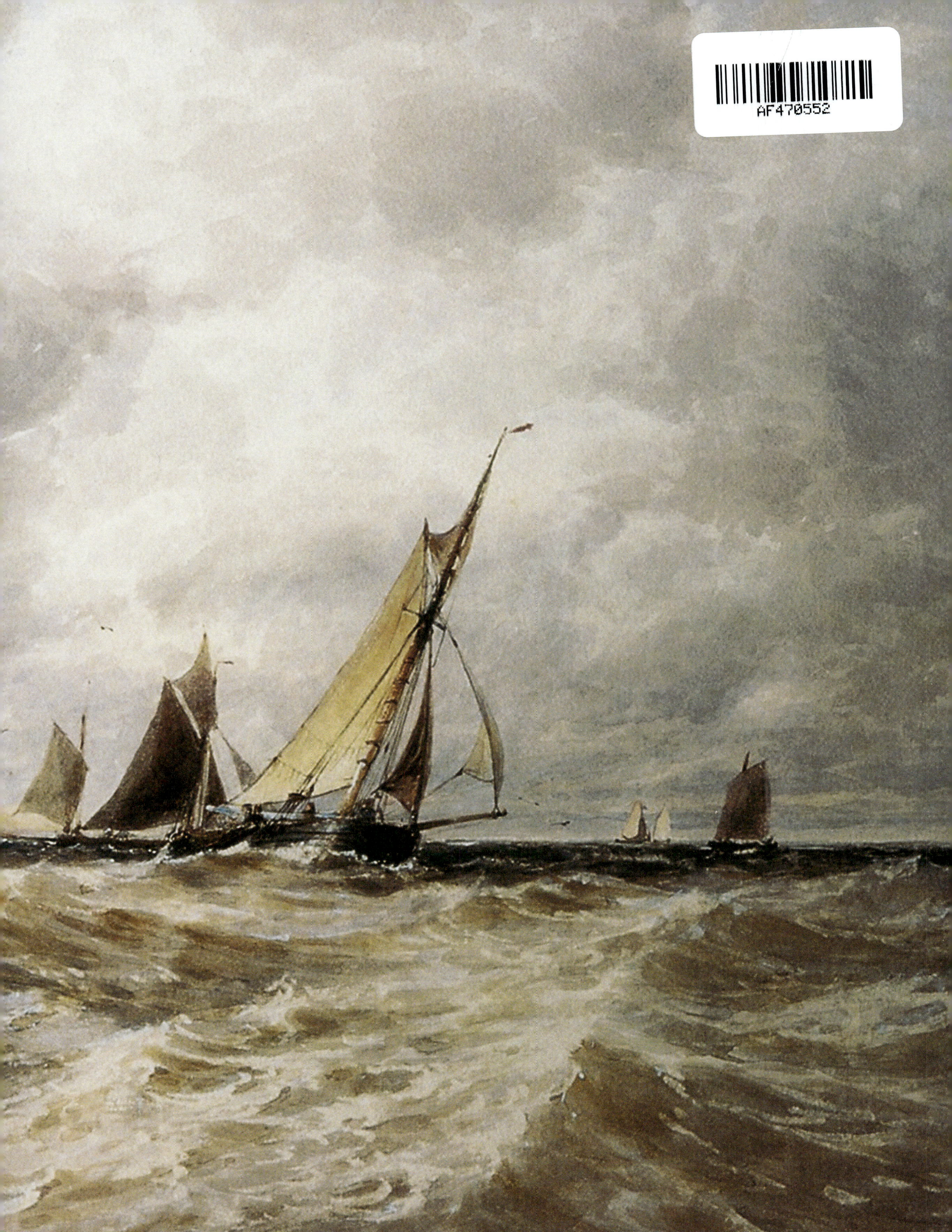
AF470552

THOMAS BUSH HARDY RBA

1842-1897

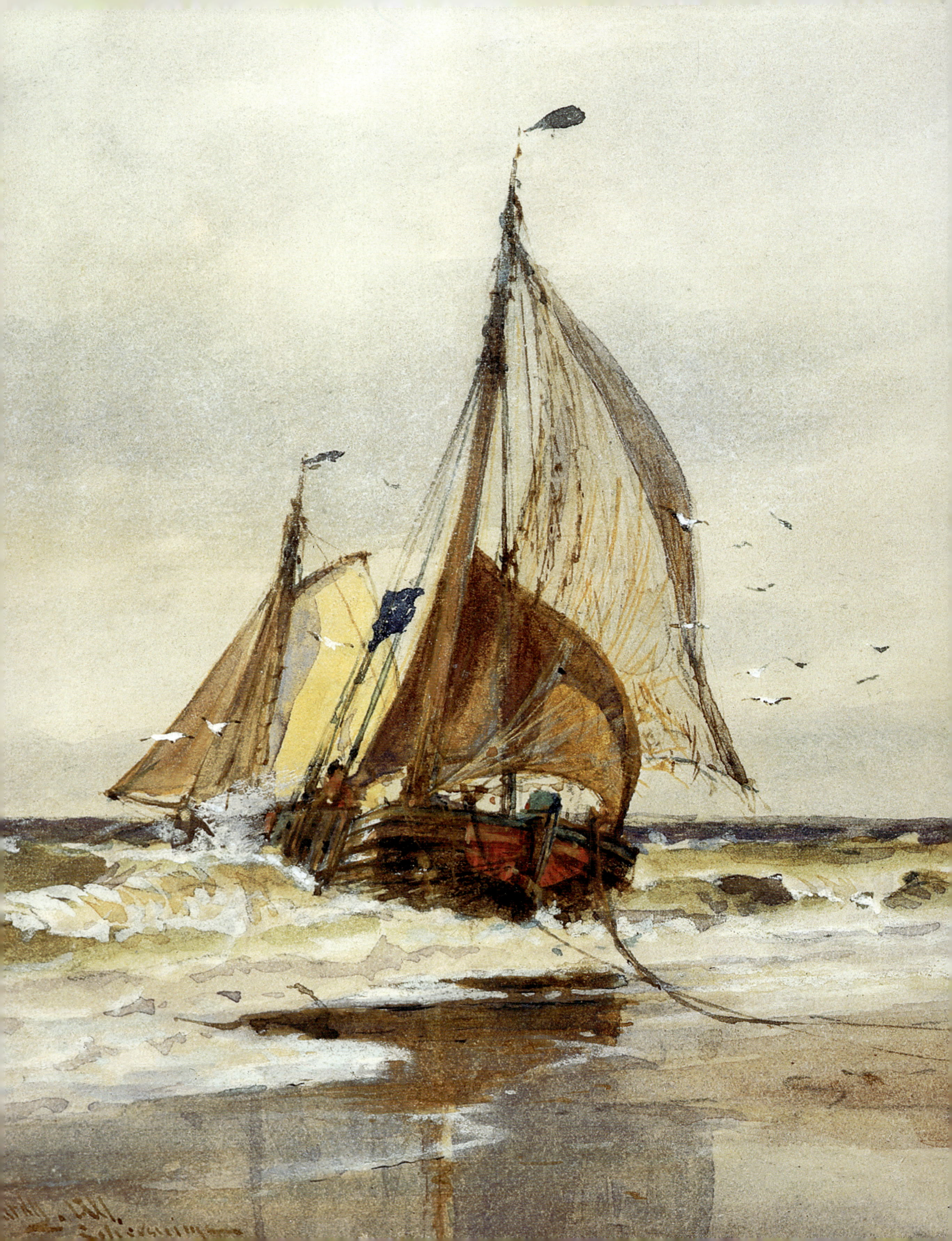

THOMAS BUSH HARDY RBA
1842-1897

A Master Painter of Marine and Coastal Watercolours

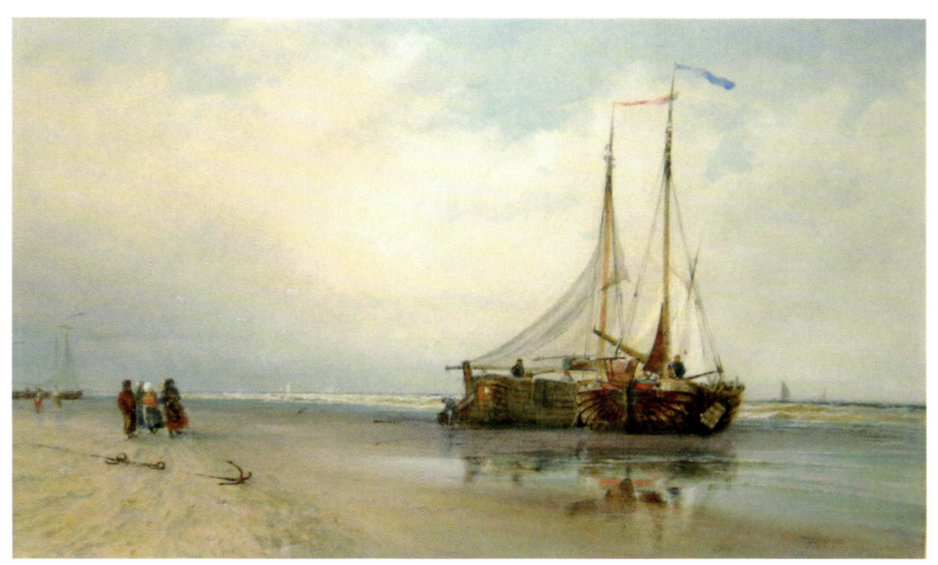

David H. Kirby-Welch

John Morton Lee

ANTIQUE COLLECTORS' CLUB

For Margaret and Paddy,
our respective and long-suffering wives,
who have lived with the piles of paperwork
and, in Margaret's case, the typing!

©2009 David H. Kirby-Welch and John Morton Lee
World copyright reserved

ISBN 978-1-85149-597-9

The right of David H. Kirby-Welch and John Morton Lee to be identified
as authors of this work has been asserted by them in accordance with
the Copyright, Designs and Patents Act 1988

All rights reserved. No part of this publication may be reproduced, stored
in a retrieval system, or transmitted in any form or by any means
electronic, mechanical, photocopying, recording or otherwise, without the
prior permission of the publishers.

British Library Cataloguing-in-Publication Data
A catalogue record for this book is available from the British Library

Frontispiece. *Scheveningen* (detail from Plate 4.19).
Title-page. *An April Day, Scheveningen* (see Plate 4.7).

Printed in China
for the Antique Collectors' Club Ltd, Woodbridge, Suffolk

Foreword

I bought my first watercolour – an endearing composition by William McTaggart (1835-1910) – when I was just eleven years old. Was I precocious? No, I do not think so, just passionate about art. Soon after, I added to my burgeoning collection by acquiring an unsigned, postcard size watercolour of a Venetian scene. Despite being a teenager, I was awestruck by its fresh washes and simple, loose, *plein air* execution. Bursting with verve and unobtrusive beauty, it reminded me of a Turner sketch. It was over a decade before I discovered that the creator of my 'little gem' was Thomas Bush Hardy.

There can be very few collectors of maritime art who are not familiar with Hardy's distinctive watercolours and occasional oil paintings (for example, *Towing Boats out of Calais*, a canvas of 1878, the Laing Art Gallery, Newcastle upon Tyne, and *Off the Dutch Coast*, an oil on board, the collection of Calderdale Metropolitan Borough Council, West Yorkshire). He was after all perhaps the most productive of all the late nineteenth century marine painters, of which there are many. However, for somebody whose work was well known in his day – he exhibited quite extensively, including major mixed shows in London, Brighton, Dublin, Glasgow, Liverpool, Manchester and York – and who *The Times* described as 'the most rapid and facile watercolour painter of his generation', surprisingly little biographical information is recorded about him.

This dearth of information motivated me in the 1990s to take up the challenge to uncover more details about the inscrutable Mr Hardy. It proved a formidable assignment. I spent hours searching through late Victorian newspapers and art magazines. Numerous days were given over to perusing exhibition catalogues at the Victoria & Albert Museum Art Library. My endeavours did not reward me with a great deal of information but I was able to knit together sufficient to write an article on Hardy, which was duly published.

This led to many suggesting I write a book on Hardy, but the years ticked by and it just never happened. So I am elated that at long last two avid Hardy enthusiasts, John Morton Lee and David Kirby-Welch, have penned this handsome and extremely enlightening volume. I salute their enterprise, which will be very warmly welcomed by Hardy and marine devotees.

Anthony J Lester, AICA, FRSA
Art critic, writer and broadcaster

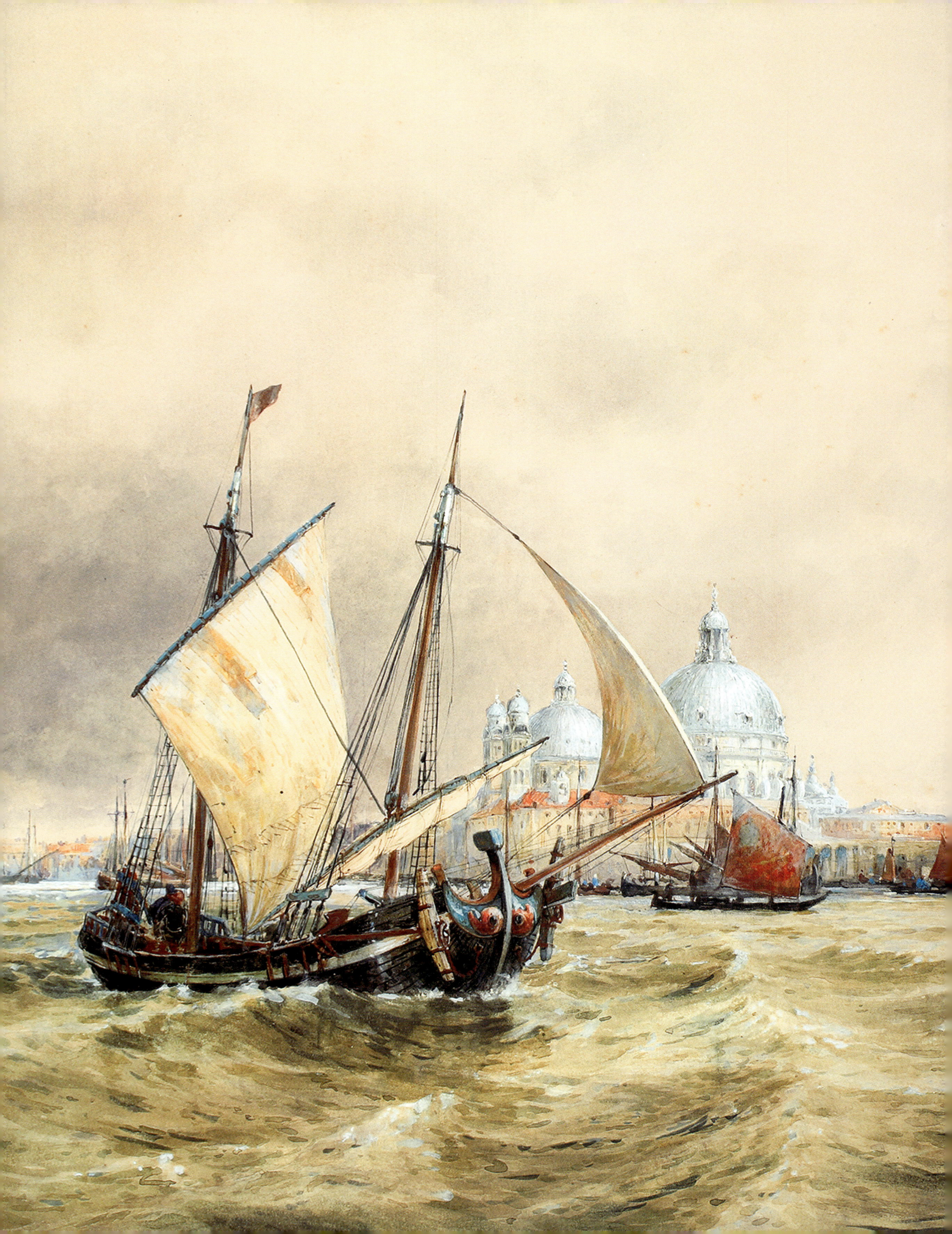

Contents

The Dogana and Santa Maria della Salute (detail from Plate 6.3).

Acknowledgements

The organisations and people mentioned below are in no particular order, but have all contributed immensely in the preparation of this work.

It was particularly exciting to meet Diana Davies (Thomas Bush Hardy's great-granddaughter) and Jean Dudley Hardy (widow of his first grandson) who racked their memories to provide some personal items about a relative they never met. Thank you.

The British institutions – the British Library at both St. Pancras and Boston Spa; the Victoria & Albert Museum; the British Museum; National Maritime Museum – are remarkable places for research and learning. They are all free and the dedicated staff gave us their time and help in a most professional and cheerful manner.

At Sheffield Galleries and Museums Trust Liz Haine, Visual Art Curator, successfully located forty-one of the forty-five paintings in their possession. Well done and thank you!

Our thanks also to all the private collectors who welcomed us into their homes to photograph their paintings; to the Naval Club for permitting use of the Gun Room where the book took shape on the boardroom table; to Diana Steel and her staff at the Antique Collectors' Club who guided and prodded us from start to finish; to our respective wives, Margaret and Paddy, for their encouragement, help and constructive criticism. Margaret must have typed a dozen drafts of the book when she had much better things to do.

And finally our thanks to T.B. Hardy, for giving us and the many hundreds of collectors the pleasure of his paintings. We hope you, the readers of this biography, gain as much pleasure from it as we have had in its preparation.

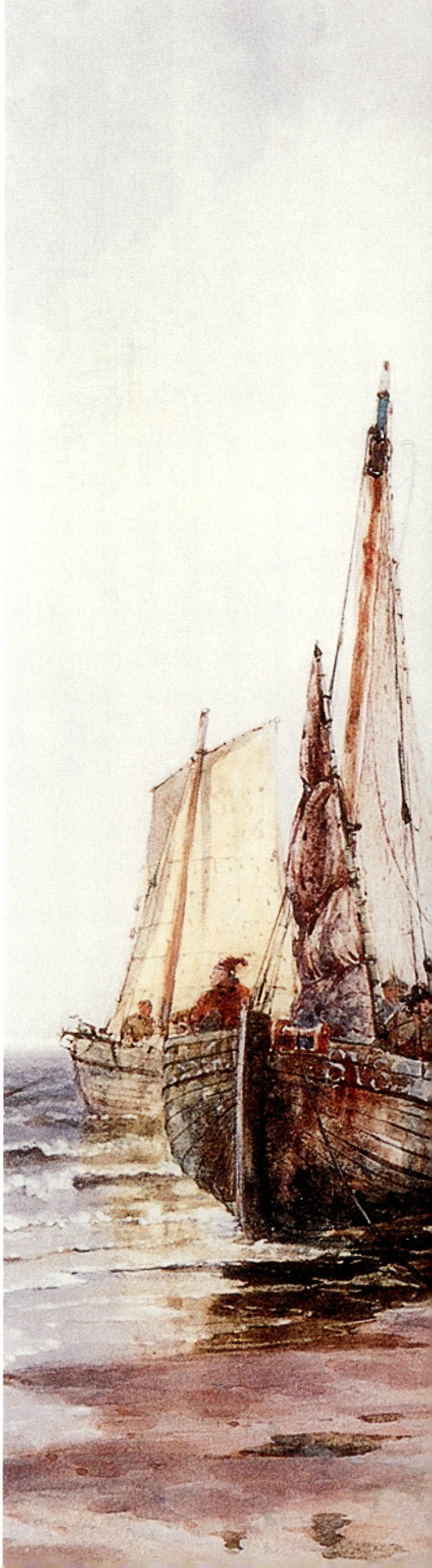

A Hazy Morning, Picardy (detail from Plate 5.17).

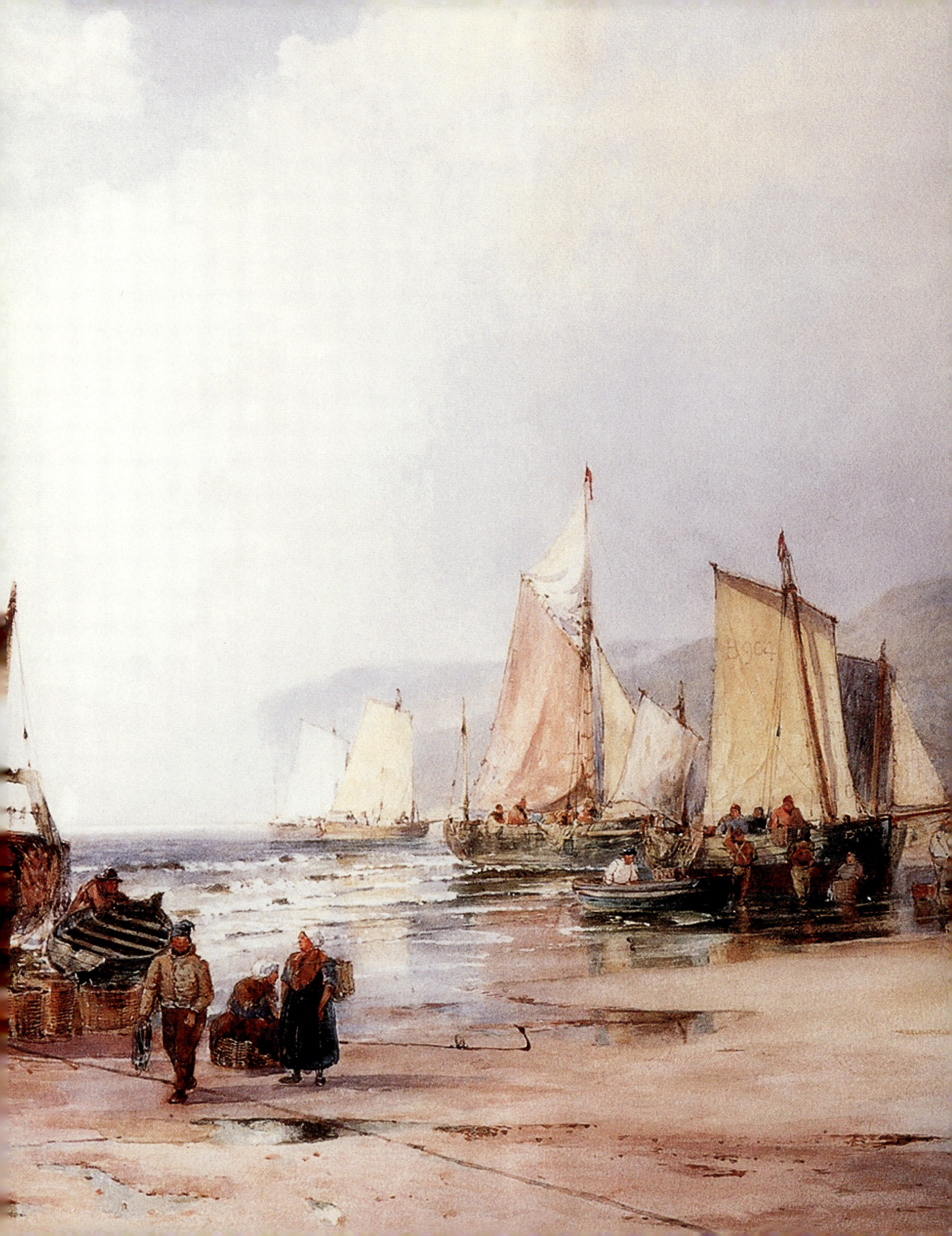

Introduction

Thomas Bush Hardy needs no introduction to those discerning collectors and fortunate inheritors who own one or more of his marine and coastal paintings, most of which are watercolours. Many more people have seen his pictures in art galleries, at auctions and in private collections up and down the country, for he was very prolific. Despite this, very little has ever been published about his life and works. To rectify this, a leading dealer in marine watercolours and an equally enthusiastic collector have collaborated with the Antique Collectors' Club to produce a book which they hope will not only satisfy those who have always held Hardy in high esteem, but will also bring much pleasure to those who may never have come across his fine work.

The book does not pretend to be a detailed biography, nor is it a 'catalogue raisonné' of his works. Research suggests he never kept a diary, no family correspondence.has emerged, and no record exists of the number and details of the oil paintings and watercolours he completed and sold during his thirty active years as a recognised artist. Fortunately, lists do exist of the paintings he exhibited at the Royal Academy and at the Royal Society of British Artists and of the many paintings currently in public collections. Also, of invaluable help to the researcher, catalogues from the major auction houses give details of the majority of Hardy's paintings that have passed through their hands. Finally, Hardy himselfar, mindful of posterity, kindly inscribed and dated a significant number of his paintings.

The book explores the development of sailing ships through the ages, the birth of British marine painting and the emergence of watercolours as arguably the best medium in which to portray the sea in all its moods. The Victorian awareness of the importance to the country of seaborne trade and the fishing industry, the advent of seaside holidays and leisure sailing and the increasing interest in art galleries and exhibitions gave marine artists a most welcome boost. Hardy took full advantage of this and, with his contemporaries, has left us a remarkable record of the maritime scene in the late nineteenth century.

Hardy's career as an artist covered a comparatively short thirty years – from the late 1860s after his return from the USA until his death in 1897. During that time he painted offshore, harbour and beach scenes in England, France, the Netherlands and Italy, Venice in particular. He was one of the few artists who took the trouble to study, understand and then reproduce all the elements of a successful marine painting. From the very start he developed an extraordinary bond with all the fishing communities he met,

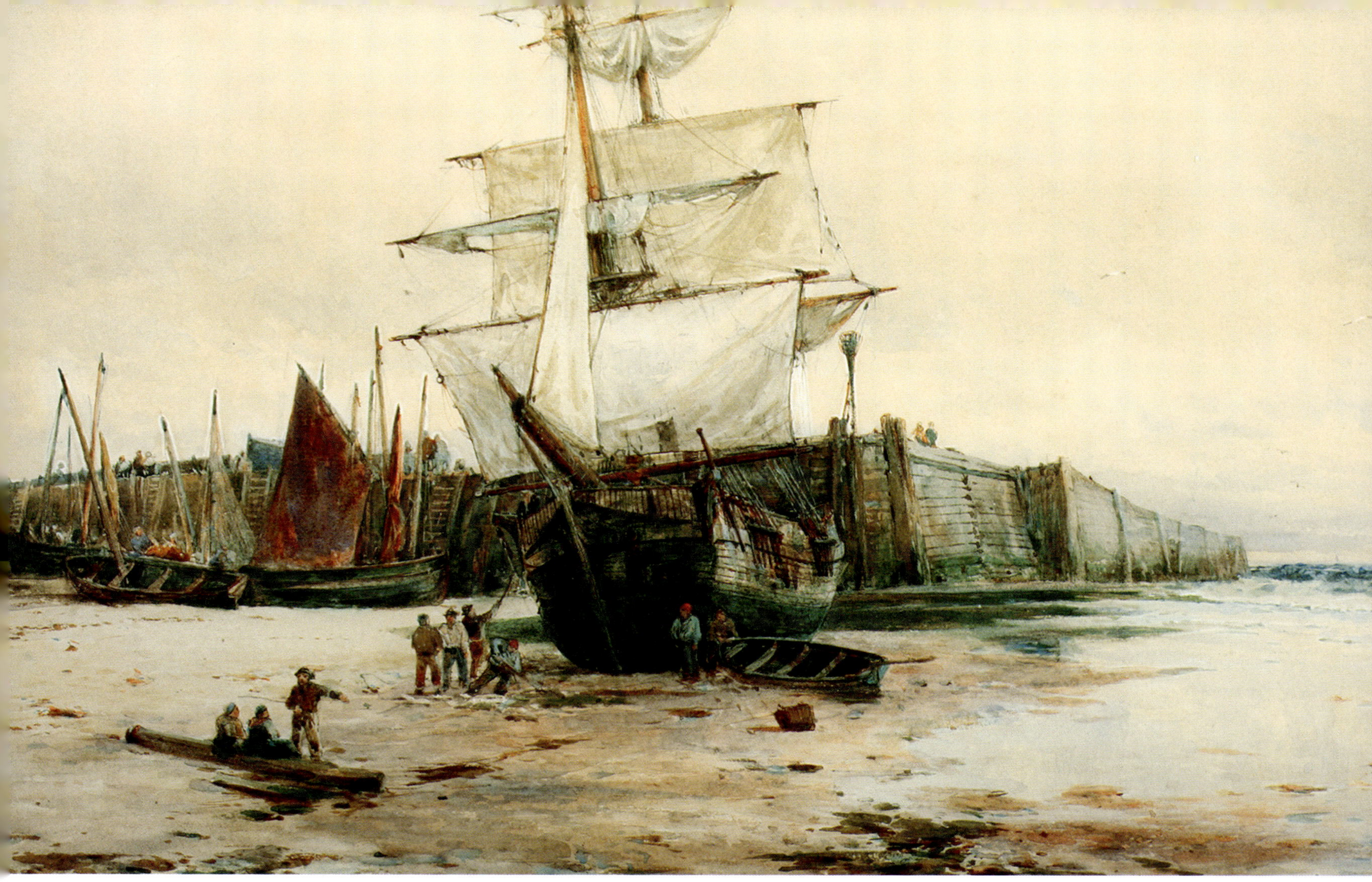

Broadstairs
(detail from Plate 3.29).

both in England and on the Continent. His high regard for these men and women and their way of life is evident in all his paintings. It is fascinating to compare one of his tranquil beach scenes of a Dutch fishing boat reflected in the shallows with one of a pair of trawlers in a rough North Sea, or with another of fishermen mending their nets on the Venetian Lagoon. As the many illustrations will show, Hardy had an enviable capability of capturing the atmosphere, calm or dramatic, whatever the occasion.

The book illustrates and describes a representative selection of oils and watercolours – the great, the good and the indifferent – that Hardy painted during his lifetime. There is no doubt that, just as he was capable of some truly wonderful watercolours, there were times in his later years when, troubled perhaps by family and financial problems, he produced some inferior work which, inevitably, damaged his reputation. Many of these paintings – not all – were by another hand; but the authors make no apology for including some obvious 'fakes' and some others optimistically 'attributed' to Hardy. His painting was normally of a high standard; indeed, in the authors' opinion, his better watercolours stand comparison with those of the finest marine artists of his and every other generation.

Introduction

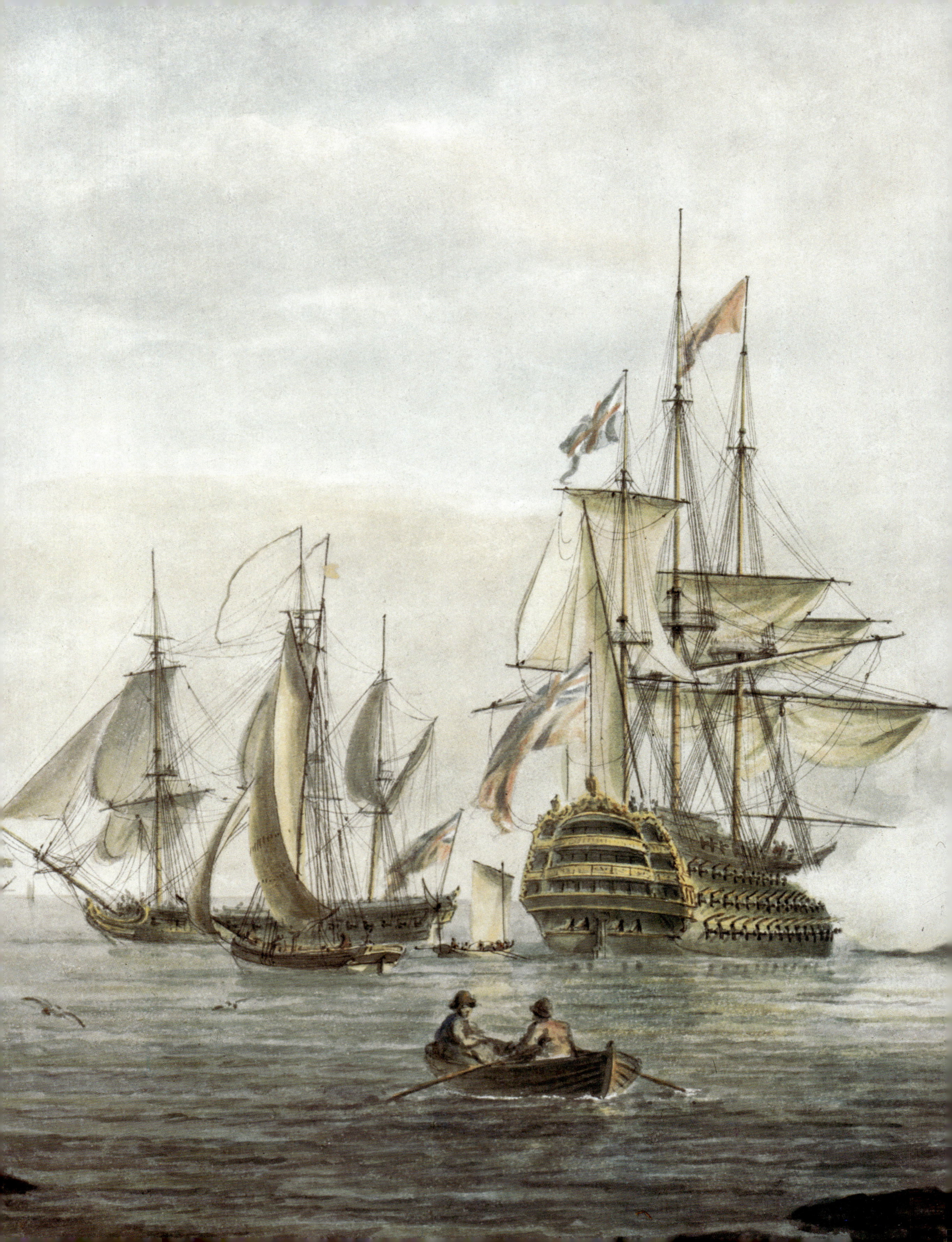

Chapter 1

A Brief History of Sailing Ships and British Marine Watercolours

Thomas Bush Hardy is universally accepted as one of the most prolific and energetic marine artists of his time, despite a relatively short painting career. As the following chapters will reveal, however, some of his work was so mass-produced that quality was sacrificed for quantity. Conversely, his better works are so delicately painted that the viewer could well be standing on the beach behind the artist and many are amongst the highest calibre of nineteenth century watercolours. Despite Hardy's contrary results, no biography exists. This book attempts to remedy the situation and bring his undoubted talents to the notice of an even wider public.

Perhaps the big conundrum about Hardy is how and why a boy born in Sheffield, which has no significant rivers or waterways and is seventy miles from the nearest coast, came to paint marine subjects almost exclusively. Unfortunately no personal diaries or records are available to answer this question. It is therefore pertinent to set the scene and trace the development of shipping leading up to the mid-nineteenth century, to explore the development of European marine painting – especially in watercolour – and examine the social and political circumstances that together set Hardy on a career as a successful marine artist.

It may be that Hardy had a particularly enthusiastic history teacher who romanticised man's achievements on the high seas. With Queen Victoria on the throne, expanding seaborne trade and a fast-growing Empire guarded by an all-powerful Royal Navy, it would be surprising if a young man did not grow up aware and proud of his maritime heritage. And, whenever he journeyed to the coast, there would have been communities of fishermen in their varied craft braving the elements to provide for their families and supplement their countrymen's diet. The seas around our coasts gave an artist all the movement, colour and drama he could wish for. But this is jumping ahead.

As long as man has been on this planet he has endeavoured to construct a vessel to cross a river or lake and venture beyond the horizon of the sea. Thanks to the Egyptians' remarkable preservation of artefacts

Detail from Plate 1.1. **Nicholas Pocock, OWS**. *Flagship of an Admiral of the Red firing a Salute. c.1790. 33.5 x 49.5cm (13¼ x 19½in.)*

within their tombs, we have a pretty clear picture of their cargo boats in 3000 BC. Amongst their earliest recognisable boats were the reed boats – typically 54ft. (16.5m) in length and made of papyrus reeds – which plied the Nile delta. This simple craft had a very short shelf life and it was not until the Egyptians began importing cedar wood that the first substantial timber-built boats appeared. A wide range of vessels have been preserved including a 54ft. Nile river boat and a 70ft. (21.3m) warship.

Moving forward to 500 BC we find that the Greeks had developed the then state-of-the-art warship – the trireme. This vessel, whose basic design lasted for nearly two thousand years, was over 100ft. (30m) in length, displaced 50 tons and carried 170 oarsmen on three decks. It was capable of attaining a ramming speed of over eleven knots.

For the next thousand years the Mediterranean countries developed and refined timber-built ships for both trade and warfare. The Northern European nations adopted very similar designs and were quick to exploit their potential for exploration and world-wide trade. In the fifteenth century the building of larger three-masted vessels with better stability and seaworthiness permitted extended sea voyages. Gradually, advances in scientific instruments such as the compass, quadrant and chronometer, together with more accurate mapmaking and charting, enabled mariners to navigate with increasing confidence.

In England, in 1510, the *Mary Rose* was launched. Named after Henry VIII's sister, she was 105ft. (32m) in length, had a beam of 38ft. (11.5m) and displaced 600 tons. Originally armed with seventy-eight guns, a further thirteen pieces of ordnance were added during a refit in 1536. She was widely admired for her appearance and one of her captains, later Admiral Sir John Edward, was full of praise for her manoeuvrability. Sadly, in 1545, to the horror of the King and many thousands of spectators near Southsea Castle, the *Mary Rose*, turning to engage a French squadron of warships off the Isle of Wight, heeled over and, with the sea pouring through her open gun ports, capsized and sank. Over four hundred years later much of the Tudor ship and most of her fascinating Tudor artefacts have been recovered and are now preserved for posterity in Portsmouth's historical dockyard.

The next date of importance in English marine history was the launch, probably in Portsmouth, of the 70ft. (21.3m) *Golden Hind*. Commanded by Francis Drake, she left London in 1577 with orders to navigate the West Coast of South America, attack the Spanish ports with her armament of eighteen guns and return via the famous North West Passage. Although she failed to find the Passage, on her return to Portsmouth in 1580 she became the first vessel to circumnavigate the globe – an awesome achievement for such a small ship with a complement of less than eighty men.

There were, of course, many remarkable voyages of exploration and enterprise made by other European nations during the late fifteenth and sixteenth centuries. The Spanish, Portuguese, Dutch and French companies, and individuals, all at one time or another competed with each other and the British, settling in the Americas and South Africa and opening up trade routes in the Indian Ocean and Far East.

Special mention must be made of the *Mayflower*. She was approximately 90ft. (27.5m) long, displaced 180 tons and, with a small crew of twenty, could carry one hundred passengers. The Pilgrim Fathers embarked from Plymouth on 6 September 1620 for Virginia. In fact the ship made a landfall at Truro, Cape Cod, before finally returning to England in 1621 and resuming the cross-Channel trade for which she was originally built.

Some other ship names are justly famous. In 1764 the little *Endeavour* was built and launched in Whitby. She was a three-masted barque, 98ft. (30m) in length with a beam of 29ft. (8.8m), drew just over 11ft. (3.4m) and displaced 366 tons. With a crew of eighty-five and under the command of Captain James Cook, she was ordered to establish whether a southern continent existed. Cook left Plymouth in 1768 and circumnavigated New Zealand, mapping and charting both islands and the eastern coast of Antarctica before returning to England in July 1771. In 1772 he returned to the South Seas and continued his outstanding hydrographic and other scientific work. Cook's leadership throughout was exemplary; one of his greatest contributions to the success of both voyages and to maritime affairs in general was the way he looked after his ship's company – scurvy was eradicated thanks to regular issues of fresh fruit and vegetables. William Hodges RA, appointed official draughtsman, produced some fine watercolours and, later, engravings of the second of the two epic voyages which ended on the ship's return to England in 1775. Subsequently she visited the Falkland Islands three times before being sold by the Admiralty, finally being used as a whaler under French ownership off Newport, Rhode Island. The thousands of miles covered by that little ship remind us of man's maritime fortitude.

Built at much the same period as the *Endeavour*, but for a very different purpose, was the famous *Victory*, flagship of Vice-Admiral Sir Horatio Nelson at the decisive battle of Trafalgar in October 1805. One of the largest three-masted ships of her time, she was 186ft. (56.7m) in length, had a beam of 52ft. (15.8m), a draught of 21ft. (6.4m) and displaced an impressive 2,162 tons. In fighting trim she carried one hundred guns on three gun decks. She was a masterpiece of design by the then principal English naval architect, Sir Thomas Slade, Surveyor of the Royal Navy. The illustrious life of the *Victory* is already well documented; she is still very much alive as flagship of the Second Sea Lord and Commander-in-Chief, Naval Home Command and, in her final resting place in dry dock in Portsmouth, she remains an icon for hundreds of thousands of visitors every year.

By contrast, the largest ever eighteenth century warship was the Spanish *Santissima Trinidad*. Built in Savanna in 1769, she was 200ft. (61m) long with a beam of 63ft. (19.2m) and displaced a massive 4,572 tons. She carried 130 guns and had a complement of nearly a thousand officers and men. Despite her size, she was no match for the better-trained and healthier British crews she was up against at Trafalgar.

In addition to the need for effective warships, sailing ships were being built to ever increasing demands for speed to expand overseas trade. Among the most beautiful sailing ships ever to grace the oceans, the clipper *Cutty Sark*, built in Dumbarton in 1869, designed to capture the Far East trade in consumables, was a stunning ship. 212ft. (64.6m) in length, she had a gross displacement of 963 tons and achieved remarkable speeds, completing the passage from Shanghai, via the Cape, to London in 110 days.

Just as the age of sail reached its pinnacle, in 1869 the Suez Canal was opened to steamships and cut the distance to the Far East by a third. The end of the era of sailing ships as cargo vessels was fast approaching and most of the handsome tea clippers were forced out of business by the much more economical steamships. Even so, a well-crewed clipper could outrun a coal-fired freighter on the busy cross-Atlantic route for a few more years and, compared with steam, most marine artists of the late nineteenth and later centuries found sail a much more attractive and commercial subject.

With the exception of some of the larger trawlers and supply ships, most fishermen would still be under sail for many decades. Furthermore, the Port of London and many other centres of maritime trade would be making use of barges and other shallow draught boats for the local collection and distribution of cargoes for more than a century. The Thames barge and similar craft on the Continent were a common sight and have featured in hundreds of marine paintings. Hardy himself would have seen and painted barges running up the Thames from the Essex fields with great loads of hay to keep the capital's half million horses at work, returning the following day with holds laden with manure for the next crop. With their brown canvas mainsails and orange spritsails they not only made a fine picture but were an enviable example of an eco-system that worked, reducing both waste and pollution at minimal cost.

Having briefly summarised the history of sail, it is appropriate to explore the origins and development of British marine art and the stage it had reached by 1850. Thomas Bush Hardy's first exhibited painting was dated 1869 and this, like the majority of his artistic output, was a watercolour. It

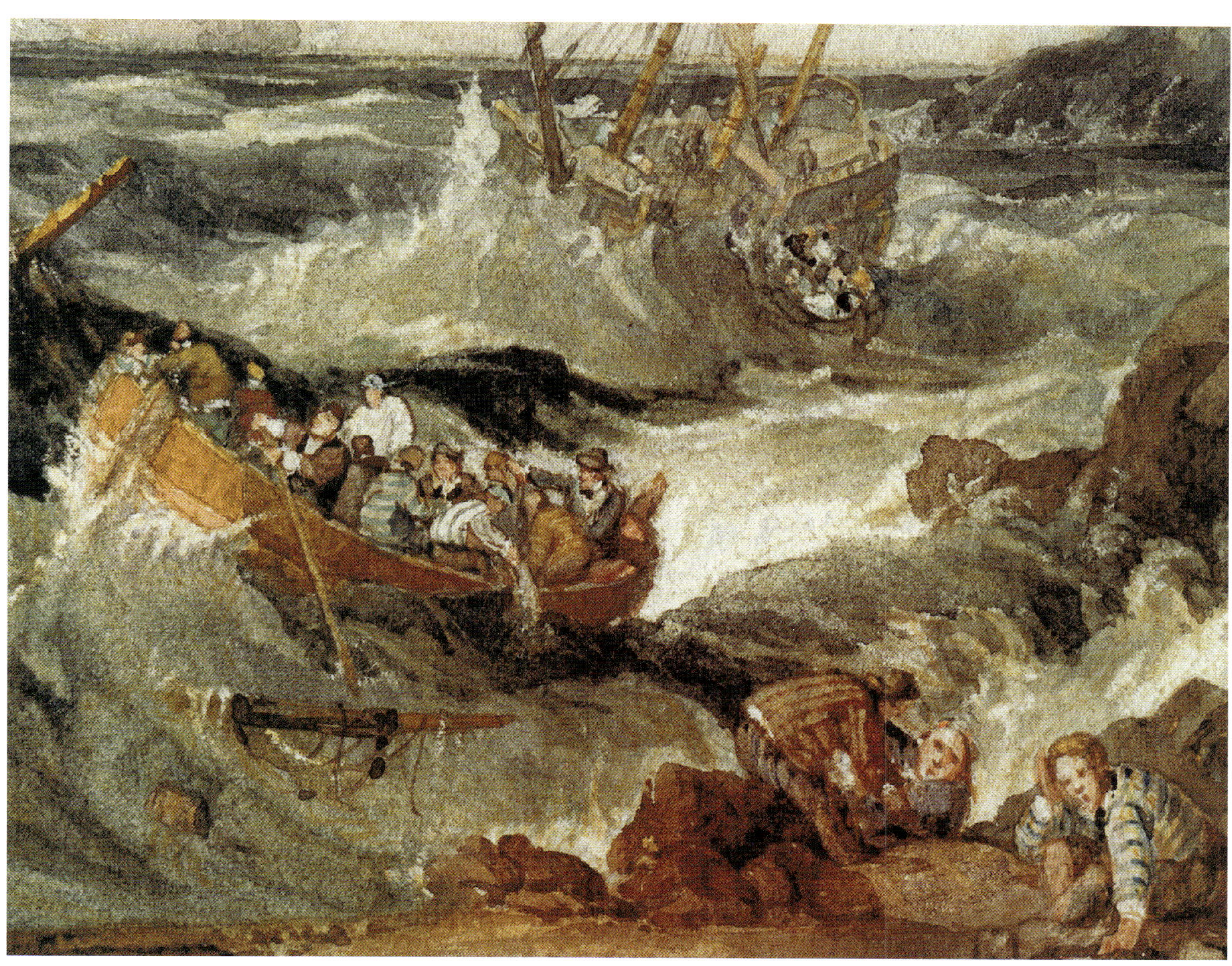

Detail from Plate 1.3.
Samuel Owen. *The Rescue.*
c.1810. 18.5 x 14cm
(7¼ x 5½in.)

is therefore necessary to examine the development of watercolour as a medium which, from the late eighteenth century onwards, provided both the artist and his patron with an alternative to oil paintings. The social climate in Victorian England is also relevant, particularly the increasing popularity of summer holidays by the seaside.

The Egyptians not only preserved their early Nile craft in tombs but also recorded in their mural paintings images of their sailing ships and beach scenes. Although such paintings can be traced back about four millennium, marine art developed very slowly until the sixteenth century when artists from the Netherlands, in tandem with their country's maritime aspirations, tended to dominate the scene. To some extent this was at odds with the earlier development of shipping and the greater artistic talent in the Mediterranean countries. There, however, where wealth and patronage were concentrated in the Catholic Church, artists were more concerned with religious subjects, leading on to their mastery of portrait painting.

Hendrik Cornelisz Vroom (1566-1640) is generally accepted as the founding father of marine painting, but his work was stylised and often criticised for its artificiality and unnatural colouring. It was his followers, particularly William Van de Velde the Elder (1611-1693) and Younger (1633-1707), who pioneered realistic studies of shipping, beautifully harmonised with the natural colours of sea and sky. Whilst there are a plethora of famous and successful Dutch maritime artists of the seventeenth century, it was undoubtedly the Van de Veldes' arrival in England in about 1672 that provided the inspiration for the first English marine painters.

Hendrik Vroom and his pupils and followers had created an important market for their work in Holland and at first glance it seems odd that the Van de Veldes should move to England, especially given the antagonism between the two countries during the Anglo-Dutch Wars, fought to establish the right to trade in the East Indies. For personal reasons, however, Charles II's invitation for Dutch artists to settle in England suited Van de Velde Senior very well and father and son soon settled down at Greenwich, where they were given studio space in the Queen's House, now part of the National Maritime Museum.

The Van de Veldes' arrival in London and their wide patronage undoubtedly gave birth and impetus to British marine painting. Their style may have lacked atmosphere but established a successful formula for accurately recording the sailing vessels of the day. Their attention to detail will be contrasted later with that of J.M.W. Turner and his followers who were more concerned with atmosphere and the play of light on sea and sky than with correct and precise portrayal of hulls, masts, sails and rigging.

Rightly, the Van de Veldes' legacy was the awakening of interest in marine art, especially in their pen, pencil and wash drawings, but it was Peter Monamy (1681-1749) who was responsible for launching native British marine painting. Although he probably executed many drawings, few remain; first and foremost he is celebrated for his spectacular oil paintings. Monamy was born in 1681 in the Minories, a street in the City of London. Following his release from apprenticeship in 1704 from William Clarke of the Painter-Stainers' Company, Monamy painted professionally for the next forty-five years until his death in 1749. His life and work are superbly researched and documented in Frank Cockett's biography.

Two other eminent artists added further impetus to the development of British marine art – Charles Brooking (1723-1759) and Dominic Serres (1719-1793). Charles Brooking was born to impoverished parents; his father, also called Charles, had only just paid off his creditors following bankruptcy proceedings four years earlier. Brooking spent his early years in East Greenwich where the close proximity of the Thames with its vibrant and colourful river traffic would have been a constant source of interest and inspiration. As his father was a painter and decorator, Brooking would have been encouraged to paint the subject matter on his doorstep. He would certainly have been familiar with Peter Monamy's work and may even have been taught by him.

Brooking's early works were clearly influenced by, and were often copies of, Van de Velde's paintings. Soon, however, he was to develop his own style and, breaking away from the 'painting to order' tradition followed by his predecessors, used his talents in observing and recording natural effects to create a marine work of art. Brooking died aged thirty-six; had he lived longer he would surely have become one of the greatest marine painters. An excellent example of his atmospheric paintings, *A Royal Yacht in a gale,* can be seen on page 32 of Charles Brooking's biography by David Joel.

Dominic Serres was born near Auch in Germany of a good family and was brought up in his father's country mansion at Beauperre, attending the English Benedictine School at Douai. Refusing to enter the priesthood as his family intended, he ran away, first to Spain and from there to sea, where he gained quick promotion and a command. He came to England after his capture in 1748 or thereabouts and, well educated and evidently well liked, quickly made his mark on the social scene. He met Charles Brooking and was certainly influenced by him when he began to earn his living as an artist. He remained an avid follower of the Van de Veldes, however, and on his death owned almost two hundred of their pictures and sketch books.

Serres was a prolific painter and through his good friend Paul Sandby had access to an influential and affluent clientele, all of whom gave him commissions. His early works were aimed at the commercial market – romantic pictures rather than the more realistic paintings of later years such as the naval actions of the Seven Years War and the War of American Independence, many of which were of historical importance. It was well known that naval officers demanded accuracy of detail, uninhibited by any artistic impression, so for many years Serres' own style would have to be held in check; the pay was too good to ignore the flow of profitable commissions. Such was his success that in 1768 he became a founder member of the Royal Academy and, before he died, was appointed Marine Painter in Ordinary to George III. Two of his sons, Dominique (1761-1804) and John Thomas (1759-1825), were also successful artists, both accepted into the Royal Academy.

By the end of the eighteenth century, England, from a slow start, had moved to the forefront of marine painting. Many artists were self-taught, others were apprenticed to recognised successful artists while a growing number came from the Navy itself. Drawing had been taught at the Naval Academy,

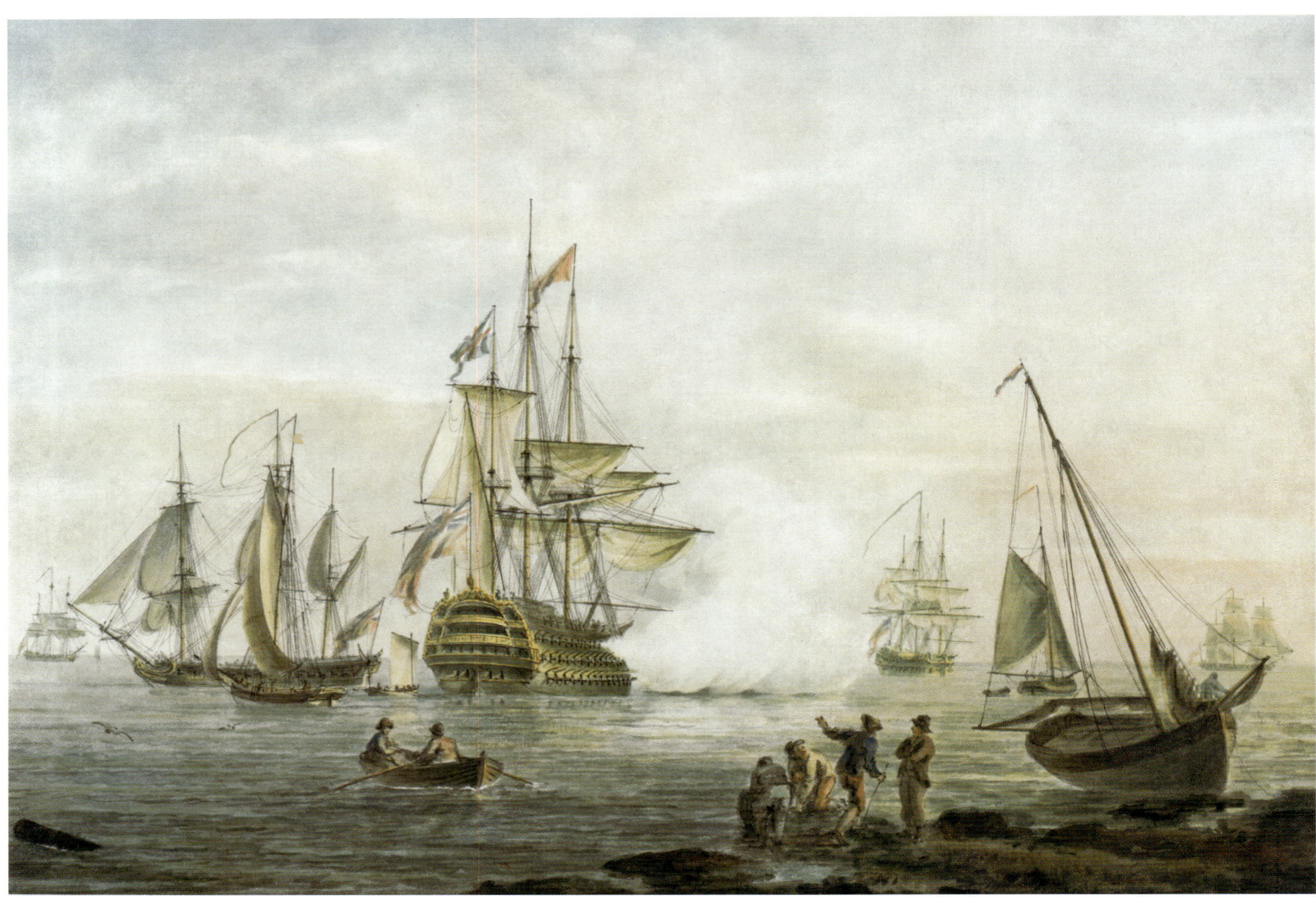

naval colleges and to midshipmen at sea since the early eighteenth century for very sound reasons: to encourage observation and identification and, in the days before photography, to assist in cartography and pilotage. John Christian Schetky (1778-1874), who had served as a midshipman in a frigate until he was sixteen, took up teaching drawing, first at a military college followed by twenty-five years at the Royal Naval Academy at Portsmouth. Many captains were acutely aware of the opportunity to record their endeavours themselves. One such mariner, Nicholas Pocock (1740-1821), who was widely travelled in the Americas and West Indies, provided numerous fine watercolour drawings of naval actions and harbour scenes for the *Naval Chronicle* (***Plate 1.1***). His son, William Innes Pocock (1783-1836), who, like his father, served at sea in merchantmen before being commissioned lieutenant in the Royal Navy, was also an accomplished watercolourist of marine subjects.

Other artists, such as the members of the Cleveley family – father John (c.1712-1777) and his twin sons Robert (1747-1809) and John (1747-1786) – all talented artists with considerable experience of working in the dockyards

Plate 1.1. **Nicholas Pocock, OWS.** *Flagship of an Admiral of the Red firing a Salute. c.1790. 33.5 x 49.5cm (13¼ x 19½in.)*

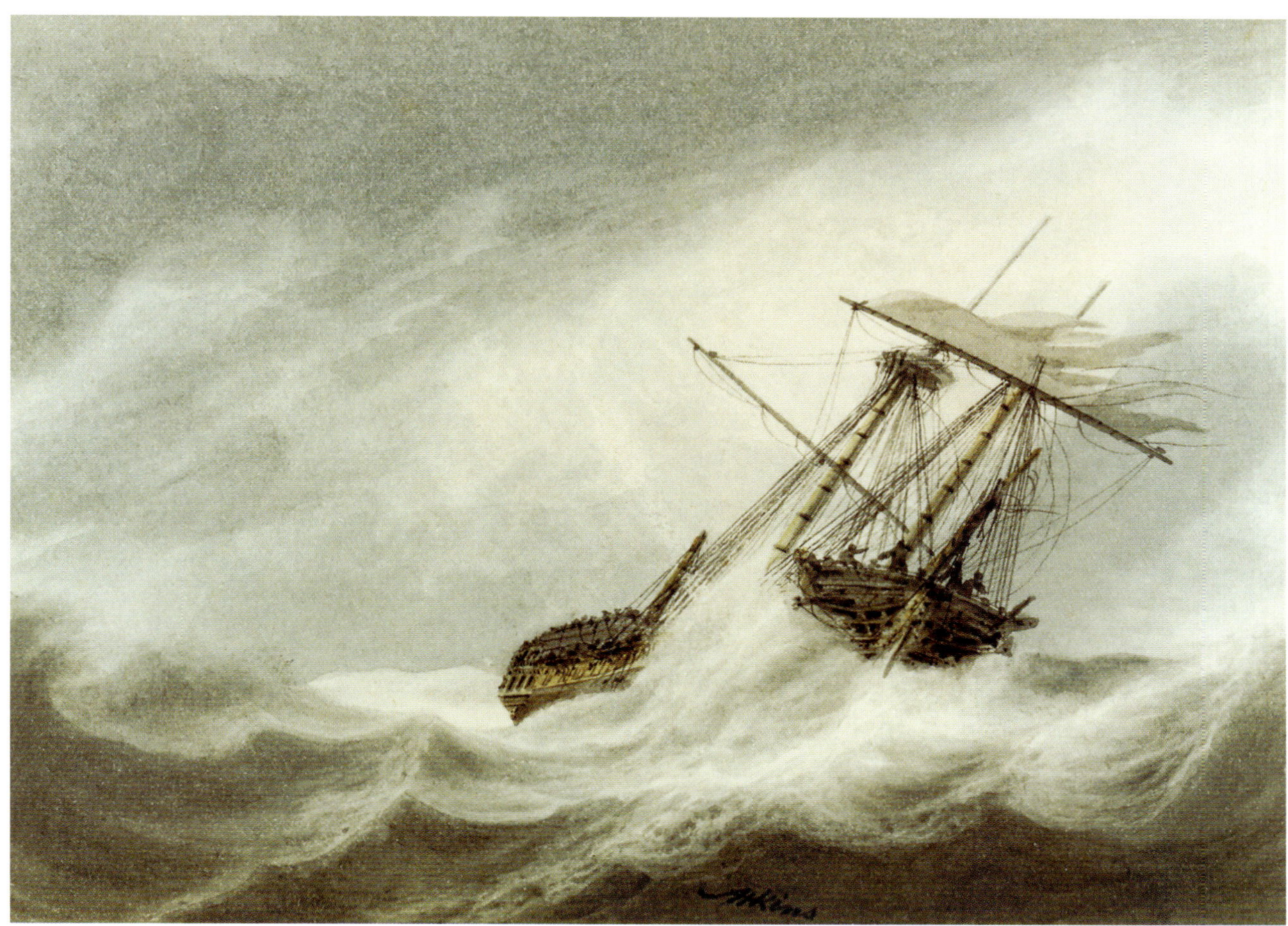

Plate 1.2. **Samuel Atkins.**
East Indiaman hit by a
Typhoon in the South China
Sea. c.1798. 13 x 17cm
(5½ x 6¾in.)

of the day, produced finely drawn warships and lesser craft in harbour and coastal scenes. Sadly, their attempts at drawing the sea in all its moods were considerably less successful – calms were no problem but any hint of a breaking wave was beyond them. The results were very stylised and unrealistic. William Anderson (1757-1837), also a shipwright in his younger days, became a very accomplished artist in both oils and watercolours but, again, he was far more adept at painting a calm anchorage than a rough sea.

Like the Pococks, there were two other artists, both painting at the turn of the eighteenth/nineteenth centuries and both painting in watercolour, who could paint any sea condition from a flat calm to a raging storm (***Plate 1.2***). Unsurprisingly, both had considerable sea experience. Samuel Atkins (fl.1787-1808) exhibited shipping scenes at the Royal Academy from 1787 until 1796 before joining an East Indiaman and spending two or more years in the Indian Ocean and Far East. During that time he not only sailed up past the Yangtze forts but experienced at least one terrifying typhoon which he later painted with chilling veracity and effect.

Samuel Owen (1768-1857) produced a significant number of extremely well-executed marine and coastal watercolours, many of which were based on the Thames estuary and Kentish coast. He clearly had a close knowledge of warships, merchantmen and fishing boats of the period and drew them and their crews in sympathetic detail. Above all, he was able to paint rough, sometimes ferociously rough, seas (**Plate 1.3**). At the very start of the nineteenth century only Atkins was his equal in this respect and Turner himself, once he turned to painting coastal scenes, was clearly inspired by Owen's swelling seas and curling waves.

Although British watercolourists were now appearing on the scene in increasing numbers, the Dutch School had been the driving force for nearly two centuries. Its objective was to reproduce marine scenes and naval encounters accurately in well-balanced pictures with increasing dramatisation of light and shade, calm and storm. Marine artists in general have followed this basic concept to the present day, but two artists were about to launch an entirely different style from the accepted 'genre'.

De Loutherbourg (1740-1812) was born in Strasbourg but settled in London in 1771. By then he was already an established painter and had been accepted as a founder member of the French Academy. His marine drawings and paintings were uninhibited by the painstaking demands for accuracy from the Dutch School, but instead revealed a passion for dramatic sea scenes and wild coastal subjects. There is little doubt that De Loutherbourg's theatrical style impressed a number of later artists, none more illustrious than Joseph Mallord William Turner RA (1775-1851). Turner needs no further introduction, having gained lasting fame for his truly atmospheric and often impressionistic paintings. He, more than anyone previously or since, pushed the boundaries of light, movement and atmosphere to new levels. Even in his lifetime controversy surrounded this exciting new style – it was, and still is, a 'love or hate' relationship with the viewer. Turner was also one of the first marine artists to experiment with watercolours and, before the second decade of the nineteenth century was over, he not only dominated the market but set a standard to which, in most respects, few of his contemporaries could aspire.

One very good reason why artists were slow to adopt painting in watercolours was the comparative difficulty in mixing and applying the colour pigments. It was not until 1832 that two friends, William Winsor and Henry Newton, by adding glycerine to the pigment with gum arabic, produced 'moist' watercolours. These could be pre-mixed and supplied in small porcelain cups and, by applying a wet brush, could be used immediately on paper. A greatly increased range of colours were made available and painting outdoors became a popular option. The introduction

Plate 1.3. **Samuel Owen.**
The Rescue. c.1810.
18.5 x 14cm (7¼ x 5½in.)

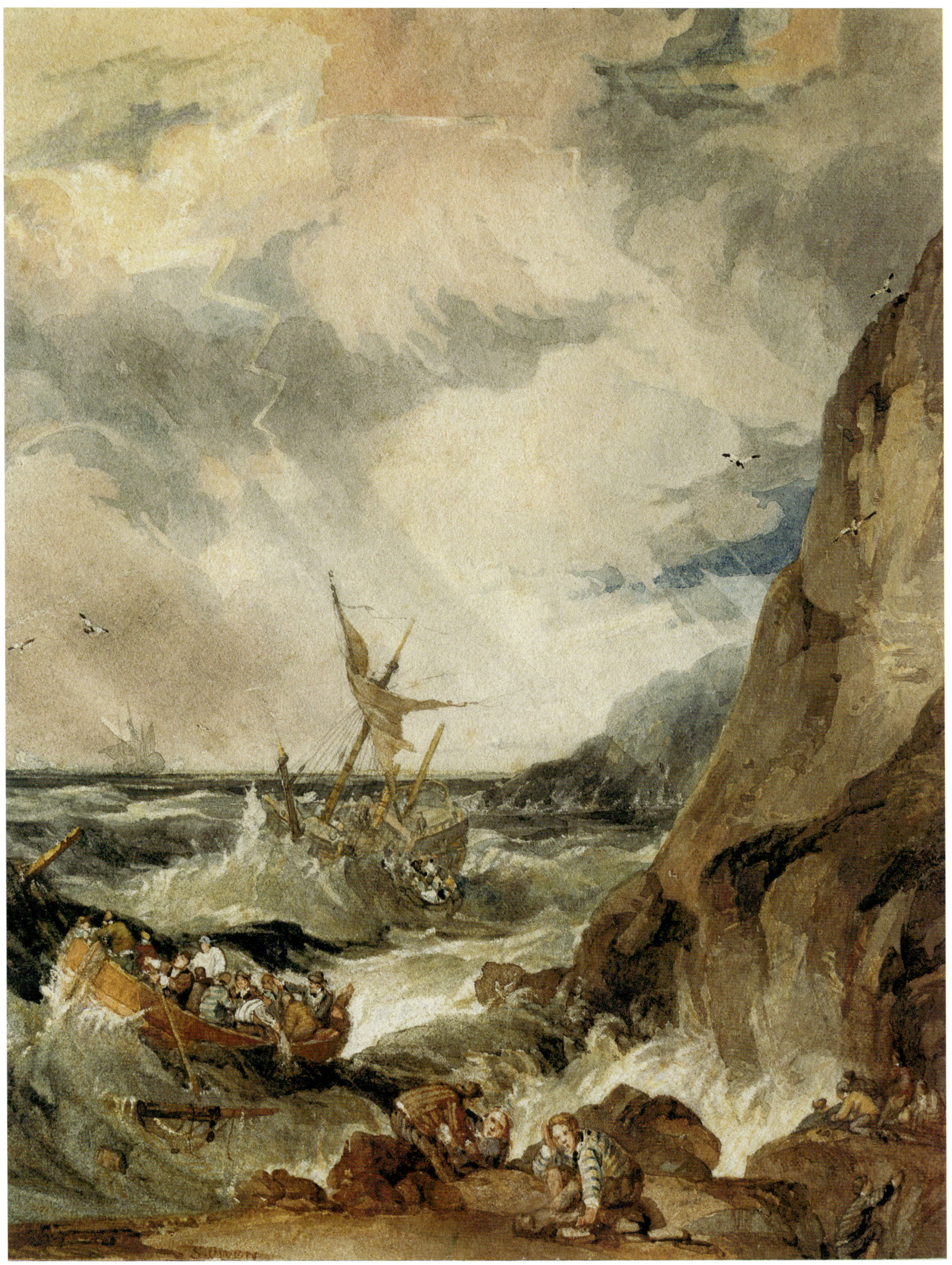

of zinc-based Chinese White overcame the discoloration observed when using the previous lead-based white product. Watercolourists were also helped by the technical advances made in paper manufacture. Wood pulp paper, such as that produced by the renowned Whatman mills, ensured a consistent and long-lasting surface which in turn helped to preserve the transparency and brilliancy of watercolours.

Many purists would argue that a painting completed with watercolours only is more professional than one where the artist has used 'bodycolour' or 'gouache', which is Chinese White on its own or mixed with other pigments. It is fairly obvious that transparency can be achieved only with a very light wash or washes over a white paper. Cumulus clouds, waves, surf and spray are common ingredients of most maritime scenes which artists have dealt with in many ways – leaving the paper untouched (perhaps by use of a water-resistant substance), Chinese White, scratching out, rubbing out, slicing and lifting the paper etc. Turner used everything in the book and why not? Hardy also experimented – with mixed results!

While watercolour manufacturers strived to enhance the range and durability of colours, artists and their patrons were beginning to understand some of the other factors affecting watercolour paintings on paper. Damp was and remains a problem. A framed watercolour hanging on an outside wall or exposed to humidity of any kind will quickly develop staining due to fungal and chemical reactions. Discoloration and brown spots known as 'foxing' will spread. More serious is over-exposure to the ultra-violet component of light – especially direct sunlight – which quickly breaks down pigments, causing colour distortion and severe fading overall. Inappropriate cleaning can also destroy the brilliance and subtlety of a watercolour: what may well have been a fine painting by a good artist may, after so-called 'restoration', bear little resemblance to its original state. Condition – and value – have always been of the utmost importance. The Victorians were well aware of the comparative fragility of watercolours, of colour deterioration in particular, and often protected their framed pictures behind a cloth or curtain by day. This and the practice of keeping the smaller watercolours in albums and folios have conserved many works of art in pristine condition. Today, the advent of 'Conservation' and 'Museum' glass, both guaranteed to block the most damaging UV light rays, have revolutionised watercolour collecting, but direct sunlight, fluorescent light, high heat and humidity should always be avoided.

The eighteenth century is widely recognised as the great age of British watercolours – names like Paul Sandby (1725-1809), Francis Towne (1740-1816), John Robert Cozens (1752-1797), Thomas Rowlandson (1756-1827), John White Abbott (1763-1851) and Thomas Girtin (1775-1802). Cozens deserves special mention as he is generally credited with being the first English watercolourist to recognise the importance of 'atmosphere' by concentrating on light and cloud formation. Girtin and Turner were both employed in their late teens to make copies of Cozens' work and Girtin's talent was demonstrated in his further development of 'atmosphere' achieved in his fine watercolours of Yorkshire and the North-east. But, inspirational, innovative artists that they were, they showed little interest in ships and the sea.

The eve of the nineteenth century heralded the arrival on the scene of some fine marine artists in watercolour, many of whom, like Turner, were to progress from painting purely topographical and landscape subjects to marines. Mention has already been made of Serres, Pocock, Atkins and Owen who, at the turn of the century, were all painting exclusively marine and coastal subjects with a new-found realism – all five possessed a 'seaman's eye'. Very soon, well-established and highly respected artists like John Sell Cotman (1782-1842), John Constable RA (1776-1837), David Cox OWS (1783-1859), Samuel Prout OWS (1783-1852), Copley Fielding POWS (1787-1855) and Clarkson Stanfield RA (1793-1867) began to make important contributions to the marine scene. Constable's enduring legacy was his ability to paint the sky in all its moods, a skill emanating from long hours of studying and sketching different cloud formations and their effects of light on the landscape.

Between 1800 and 1820 major British military successes at sea and on land, including Trafalgar and Waterloo, and the expansion of Empire were to presage a century of comparative peace – Pax Britannica. In the art world, after an understandable flurry of paintings glorifying these achievements, a growing public began to seek a wider choice of subjects. The Royal Academy, established in 1768, had largely ignored watercolours, deeming them 'unprofessional', but, with the founding of the Old Watercolour Society in 1804, watercolour artists at last had a recognised body championing their cause. Throughout the nineteenth century an increasing number of local authorities opened up art schools, museums and art galleries for the benefit of a public keen to view and participate, but, for the moment, few with the resources to buy.

Two early and successful artists who contributed greatly to marine painting were Richard Parkes Bonington (1802-1828) and George Chambers OWS (1803-1840). Both died young, tragically so in Bonington's case for all his contemporaries recognised his exceptional talent and ability. The family had moved from Nottingham to Calais when Bonington was fifteen and already an aspiring young artist. He soon came to the notice of François Louis Thomas Francia (1772-1839), a French-born artist who had spent the previous twenty-seven years based in London, teaching and completing a number of sketching tours of the British Isles. Francia, recognising the young man's precocious talent, was ideally placed to introduce him to wealthy patrons. Later, in Paris, while studying in the Louvre, he met Delacroix with whom he was to share a studio, but throughout his short life he kept closely in touch with Francia and most of his translucent and immensely atmospheric marine watercolours were painted *en plein air* on the Picardy and Normandy coast.

George Chambers came from a very different background. Son of an impoverished Whitby seaman, he first went to sea himself at the age of ten. He may have had a humble background but George Chambers was a born artist – he spent all his infrequent leisure hours with pencil and paper drawing little sketches. Arriving in London in 1825, lodging with his sister, he met up with another Whitby man, now running a riverside pub at Wapping. This led to a number of commissions with other seafarers, culminating in a visit arranged by an illustrious client, Lord Mark Kerr, to Windsor Castle. There, King William IV, the Sailor King, and Queen Adelaide gave him further commissions which remain to this day in the Royal Collection.

Chambers had great talent and was capable of painting a diversity of subjects in both oil and watercolour (**Plate 1.4**). He could paint detailed topographical studies of Greenwich and Portsmouth with the same confidence and conviction as a dramatic seascape. He had an inbuilt understanding of wild seas and awesome skies. In Alan Russett's brilliant biography subtitled *The Sailor's Eye and the Artist's Hand* he quotes Lord Mark Kerr's letter to Chambers accrediting him with 'the hand of a master and the eye of a seaman'.

Other major marine artists painting in both oil and watercolour who were nearing the end of illustrious careers when Hardy was a young man were Clarkson Stanfield (1795-1867) and John Wilson Carmichael (1799-1868). Both nautical and dramatic blood flowed in the Stanfield family. His father, originally a merchant seaman, was so horrified by his experiences in a Liverpool-based slave ship in 1776 that he became a confirmed abolitionist. By 1782 he was a provincial actor, marrying Mary Hoad, an actress and amateur artist, and settling at Sunderland where they brought up five children, the youngest being christened Clarkson Frederick in honour of the abolitionist Reverend Thomas Clarkson. When he was eleven, Clarkson was apprenticed to an heraldic painter but after two years he persuaded his father to let him go to sea in the brig *Alexander* working out of North Shields. Taken over as a 'military transport', the brig's crew were press-ganged and drafted to the *Namur,* the port guardship at Sheerness. Here his ability to paint scenery was noticed, but, possibly due to over-exposure to lead paint, he became ill and in 1814 was discharged from the service. A long and successful career, first as a theatrical scene painter, was followed by recognition as a major landscape talent and, after the death of Turner, as the finest marine artist of his time. Once again, a background at sea coupled with an inherited and encouraged ability to paint, produced an artist who was an example to later generations.

Like Stanfield, Carmichael, also from the North East, went to sea at an early age, spending three years on a merchantman trading between Spain and Portugal. It seems that, before the war with France ended in 1815, he may have been press-ganged and served for a time as a cabin boy in a powder vessel whose captain encouraged his talent for drawing. Much later, Carmichael wrote of his experiences 'not only in big ships but also in the cobles and herring boats of the north, the dainty yachts of the south and indeed every variety of craft'. Based on that intimate knowledge of sailing vessels and his experiences at sea in all kinds of weather conditions, his oil paintings and watercolours were an outstanding con-

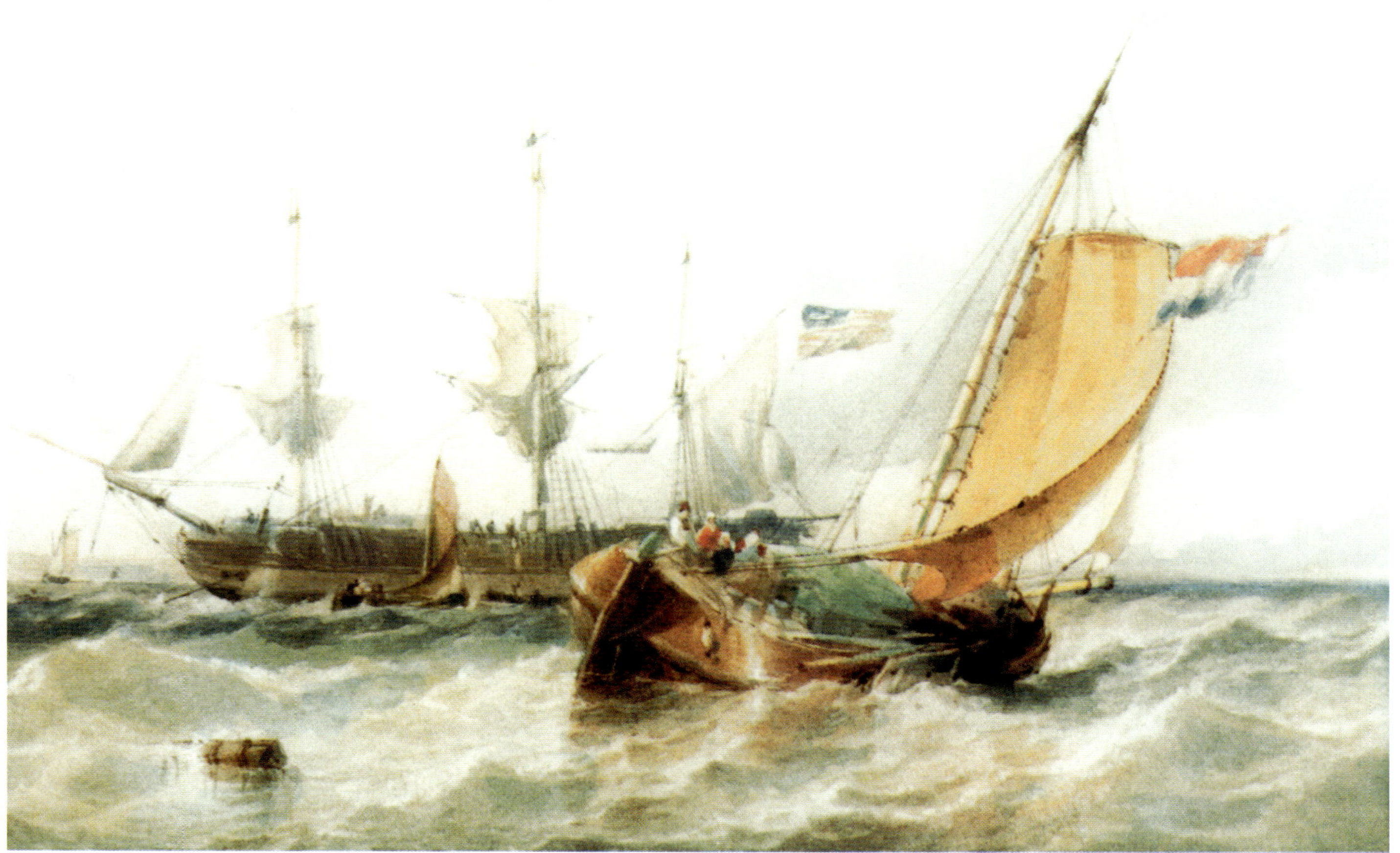

tribution to marine art (***Plate 1.5***). Diana Villar's fascinating biography of her great-great-grandfather pays tribute to a fine artist whose exceptional skills may not have been fully appreciated during his lifetime.

Henry Barlow Carter (1803-1867), born in Scarborough, served in the Navy and lived in various coastal towns before settling down in Scarborough as a drawing master for the next thirty years. He and his son, Joseph Newington Carter, to whom he passed on his style and expertise, became well known for storm-lashed coasts and dramatic wrecks (***Plate 1.6***). He seldom painted a calm scene but occasionally the sight of Scarborough Bay on a fine day subdued his more passionate nature. He then painted a blue sea and sky as well as any man. In failing health, he spent the last few years of his life in Torquay, sometimes visiting the wild Cornish coast to sketch and bring back memories of the sights and sounds of the sea pounding against the cliffs of North Yorkshire.

William Joy (1803-1867) and his younger brother, John Cantiloe Joy (1806-1866), were both born in Yarmouth, Norfolk and, as artists, were

Wren's magnificent Hospital at Greenwich has been a favourite subject for generations of artists. Carmichael painted this watercolour in 1848, the year the decision was made to 'hide' the unsightly and generally rather unsavoury industry and dwellings on the Isle of Dogs by building an embankment and garden facing the Hospital. The merchantmen alongside the wooden pier in the foreground would probably be unloading materials for this purpose, aided by a hand-operated light railway. There are many more skiffs and sailing cutters on the river than one would expect; recreational rowing and sailing on the tidal Thames was clearly gaining popularity. A painting full of interest from a viewpoint Hardy, thirty years later, seldom if ever attempted.

Plate 1.5. **John Wilson Carmichael** (1799-1868). *The River Thames at Greenwich. Signed with monogram and dated 1848. 31 x 46cm (12½ x 18 in.)*

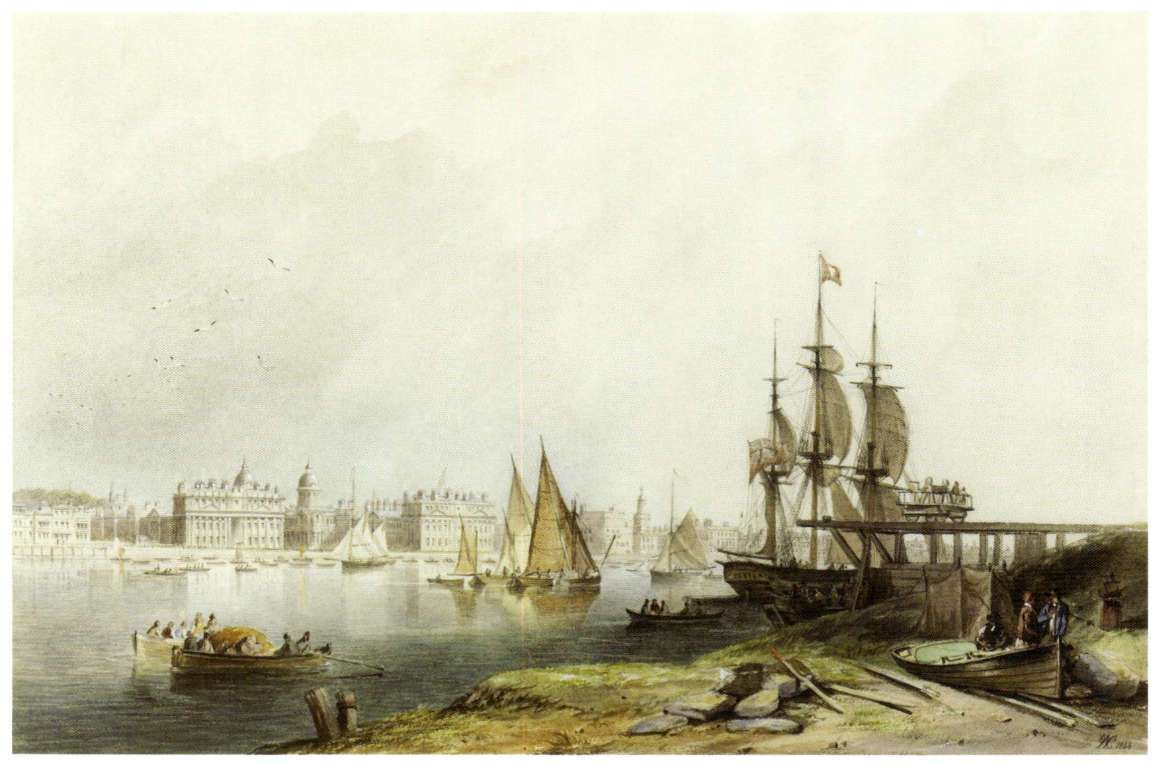

largely self-taught. In 1832 they moved to Portsmouth where they were employed as naval draughtsmen and where, in due course, they accepted commissions to paint portraits of the warships in which naval officers were serving. As far as is known, neither brother married, they lived together all their lives and collaborated in most of their marine watercolours (***Plates 1.7 and 1.8***). Where they collaborated the watercolour would be signed JOY or left unsigned. Where the work, oil or watercolour, was by William it was normally signed W.JOY. The ship portraits were correct down to the last detail, painting equivalents of a top French prisoner-of-war model and, where necessary, the ships' companies and boats' crews were shown all drawn to scale. Warships at Spithead were normally drawn at anchor in a calm or slight breeze – those under way would be battling against a rough and often luridly coloured sea. The Joy brothers are mentioned in this chapter for their historical importance as ship portraitists and their photographic accuracy in everything they painted. In effect, they had little influence on the mainstream of marine artists and even less on T.B. Hardy.

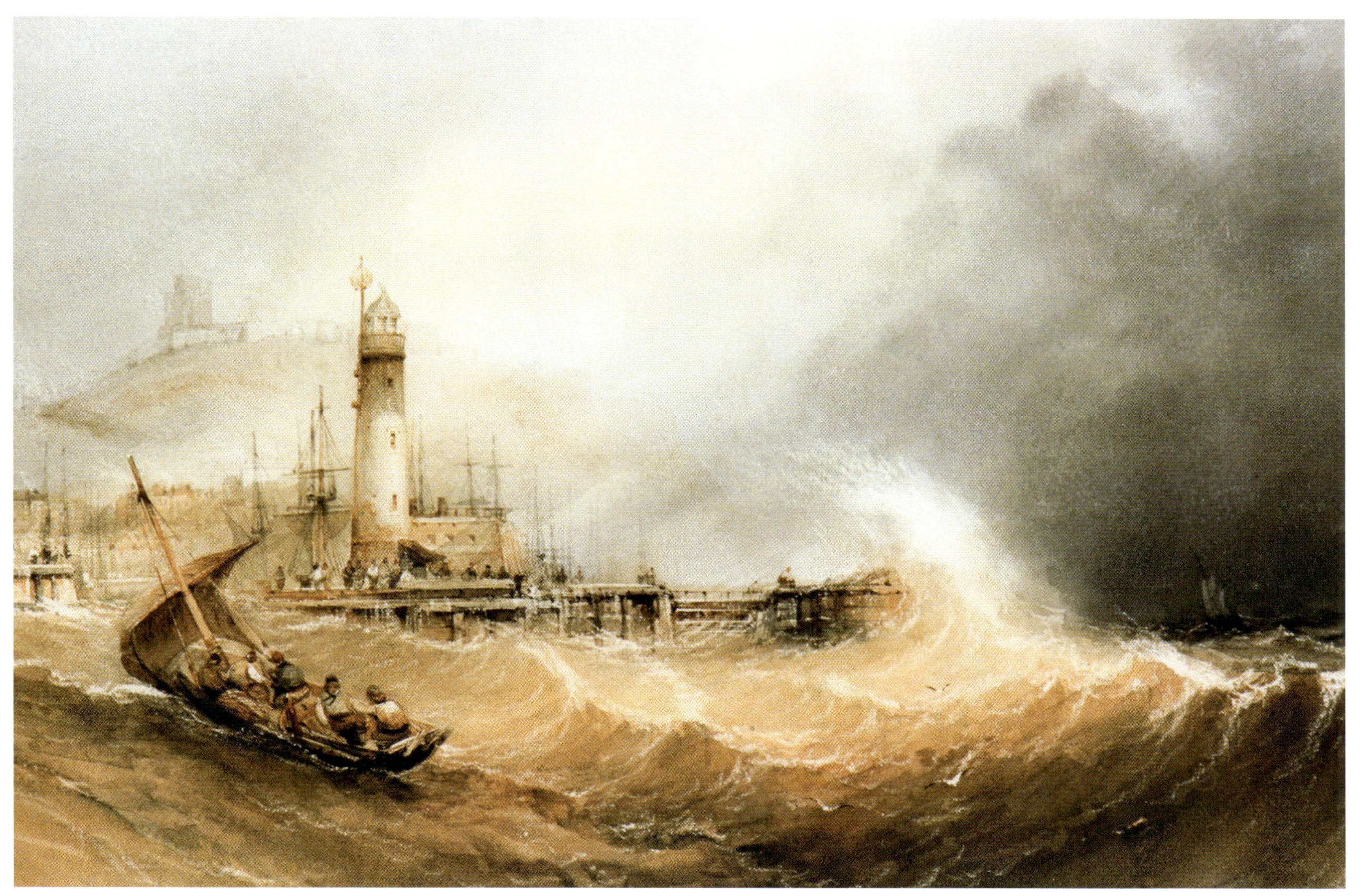

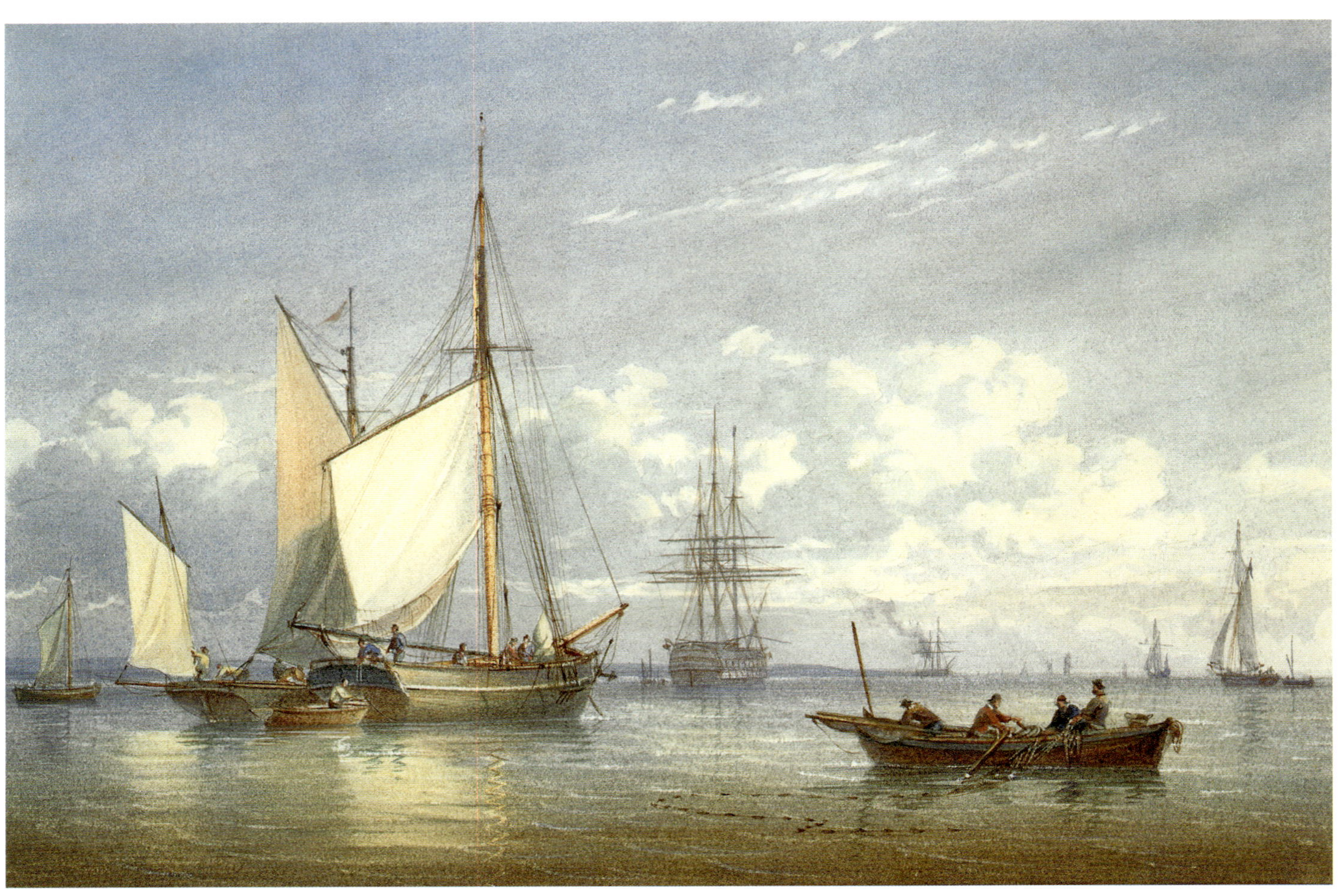

Before closing the window on the turn of the eighteenth century, which saw the birth of so many exceptional marine artists in watercolour, there is one, Charles Bentley OWS (1806-1854), who deserves more than a passing mention. Like so many embryo artists of distinction, Bentley was apprenticed to an engraver, in this case Theodore Fielding, elder brother of the more famous Copley Fielding. His work connections with Bonington and, more intimately, with William Callow inspired his progress as a painter in marine watercolours. His paintings covered most of the English coastline, including the Channel Islands, and he visited France in the late 1830s and early 1840s with William Callow. His sea paintings, primarily of fishermen and their boats, have a rawness and vitality that few other artists could match (Plate 1.9).

One of the most successful nineteenth century marine artists was Edward William Cooke (1811-1880). His oils, watercolours and many hundreds of drawings are instantly recognisable for their almost photographic clarity (***Plate 1.10***). The attention to detail in his rendering of background buildings is reminiscent of Canaletto at his best and few marine artists have ever achieved his masterly drawing of a sailing ship's rigging. Cooke travelled widely through Europe and seems to have been

Plate 1.7. **William and John Cantiloe Joy.** *Fishermen hauling in their Nets, Shipping beyond.*

Plate 1.8. **William and John Cantiloe Joy.** *Brigantines hit by a Storm and in Trouble. c.1850. 14 x 20.5cm (5½ x 8in.)* This was probably one of the best seascapes that the brothers painted, the colouring of both sea and sky being particularly well done, unlike some of their more garish efforts.

particularly captivated by Dutch beach scenes which he visited frequently from 1837 onwards. He also made ten trips to Venice between 1850 and 1877. These were later T.B. Hardy's favourite sketching grounds and it is inconceivable that he would not have been familiar with, and strongly influenced by, Cooke's widely exhibited and acclaimed paintings.

Despite his long painting career from his first works in 1828 to his last in 1879, the quality remained completely consistent. He also kept a remarkable record of his output in diaries, letters and sketchbooks enabling John Munday, after years of painstaking research, to produce the ultimate in comprehensive biographies, affectionately known as the 'cookbook'.

There were, of course, many other successful artists born in the early nineteenth century who contributed to an astonishing flowering of marine art in Europe and on both sides of the Atlantic, but especially in the British Isles. There are far too many to name here, but a list of recommended reading would certainly include Denys Brook-Hart's *British Nineteenth Century Marine Painting.* A list of other suggestions can be found in the Bibliography.

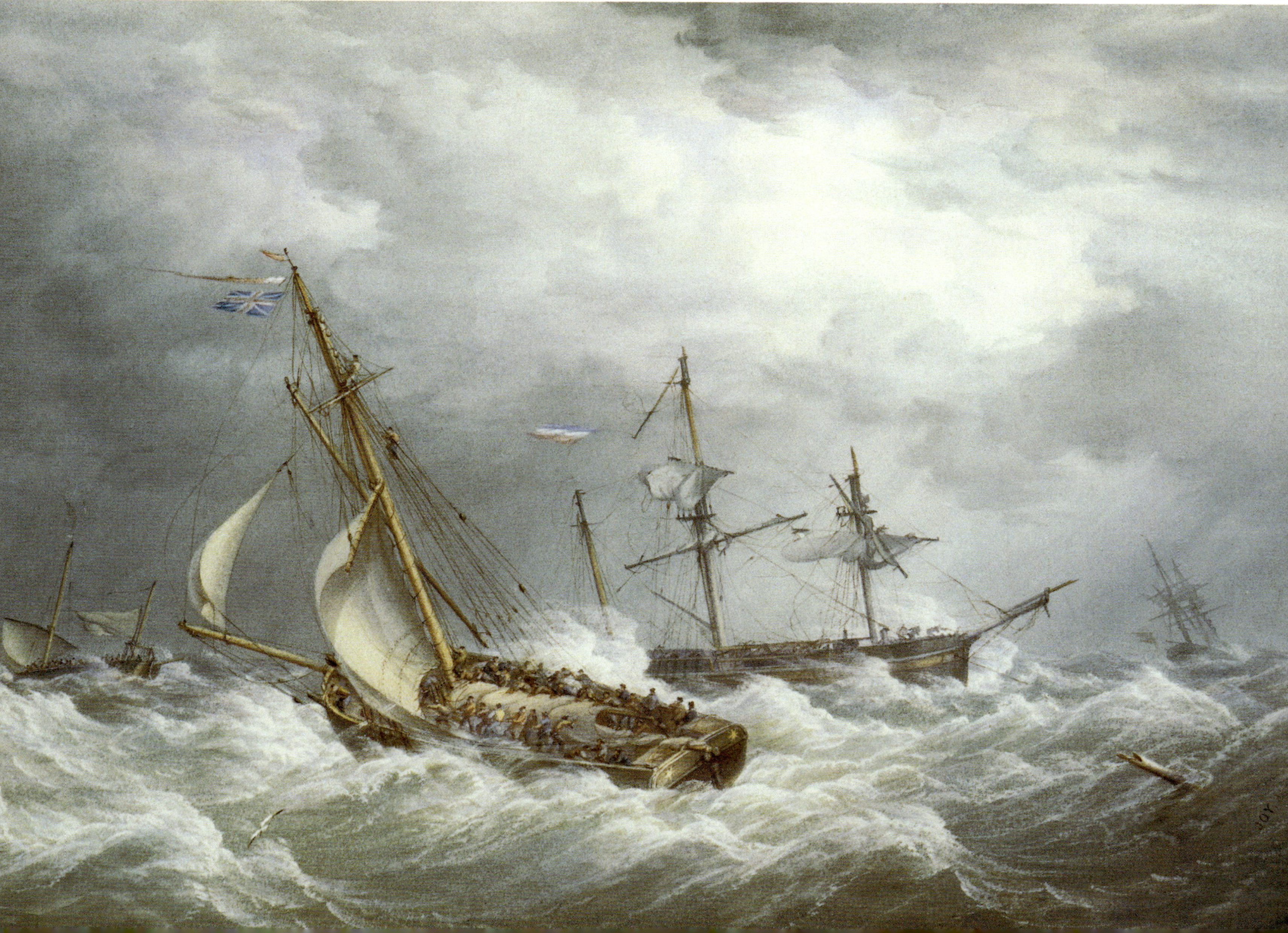

By the mid-1850s Victorian middle class families, following royal example, had started to visit the seaside in earnest. After a visit to Brighton on 30 July 1847, Queen Victoria wrote in her diary:

Drove down to the beach with my maid and went into a bathing machine, where I undressed and bathed in the sea for the first time in my life, a very nice bathing woman attending me. I thought it delightful until I put my head under the water, when I thought I would be stifled.

Brighton was obviously one of the more fashionable resorts, given its proximity to London, despite the one guinea stage trip which took six to seven hours. This all changed when Brighton station was opened in 1841, serviced by the yellow painted carriages of the 'London, Brighton and South Coast Railway', nicknamed the 'Sunshine Line'.

With the establishment of more and more rail links, seaside resorts became all the fashion. Scarborough was already popular, being dubbed 'The Queen of Watering Places' following the discovery of mineral springs which attracted visitors to the town. Its Grand Hotel, opened in 1867, for

Plate 1.9. **Charles Bentley, OWS.** *A Heaving Line Transfer between Fishermen in a Rough Sea. c.1840. 24 x 35cm (9½ x 13¾in.)*

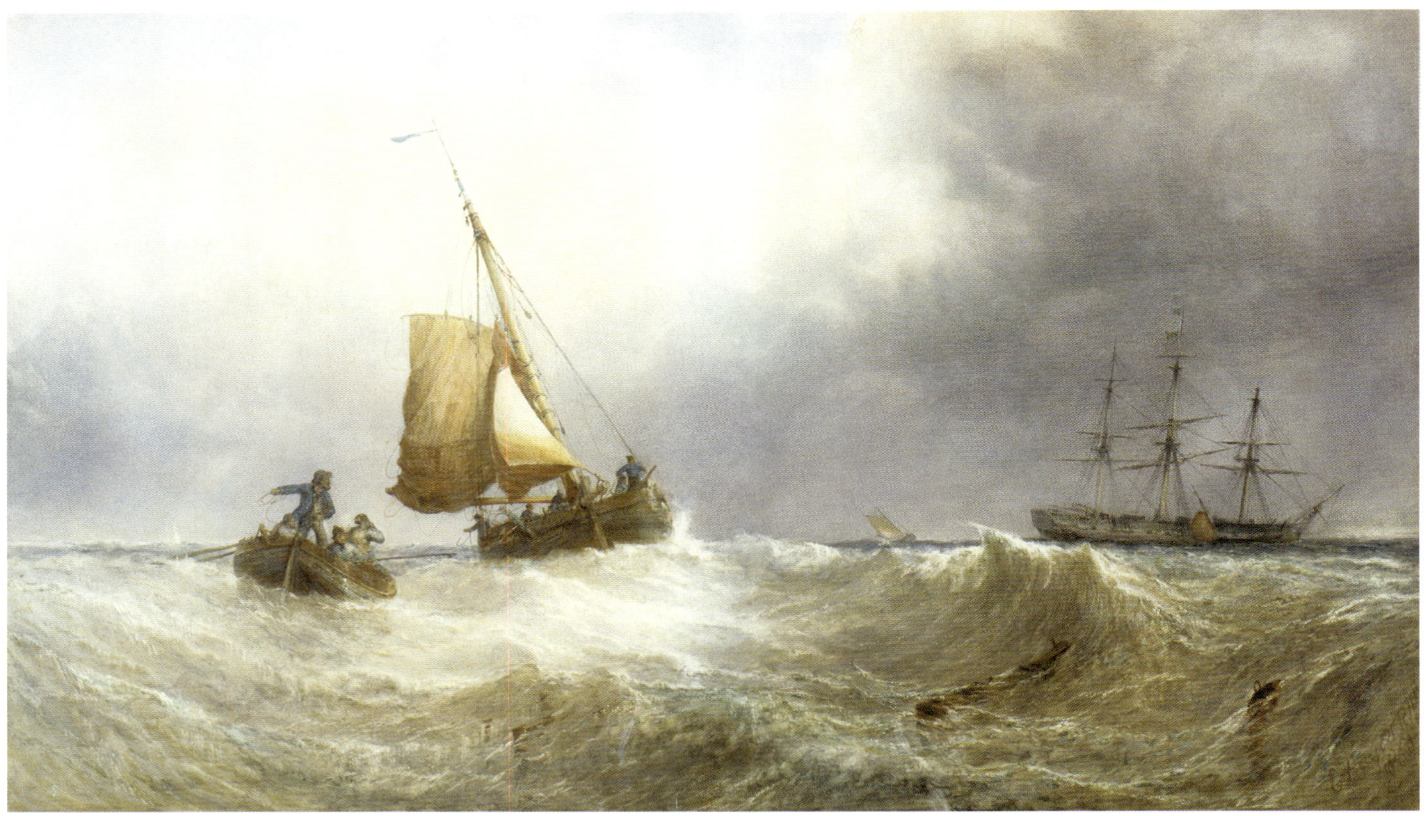

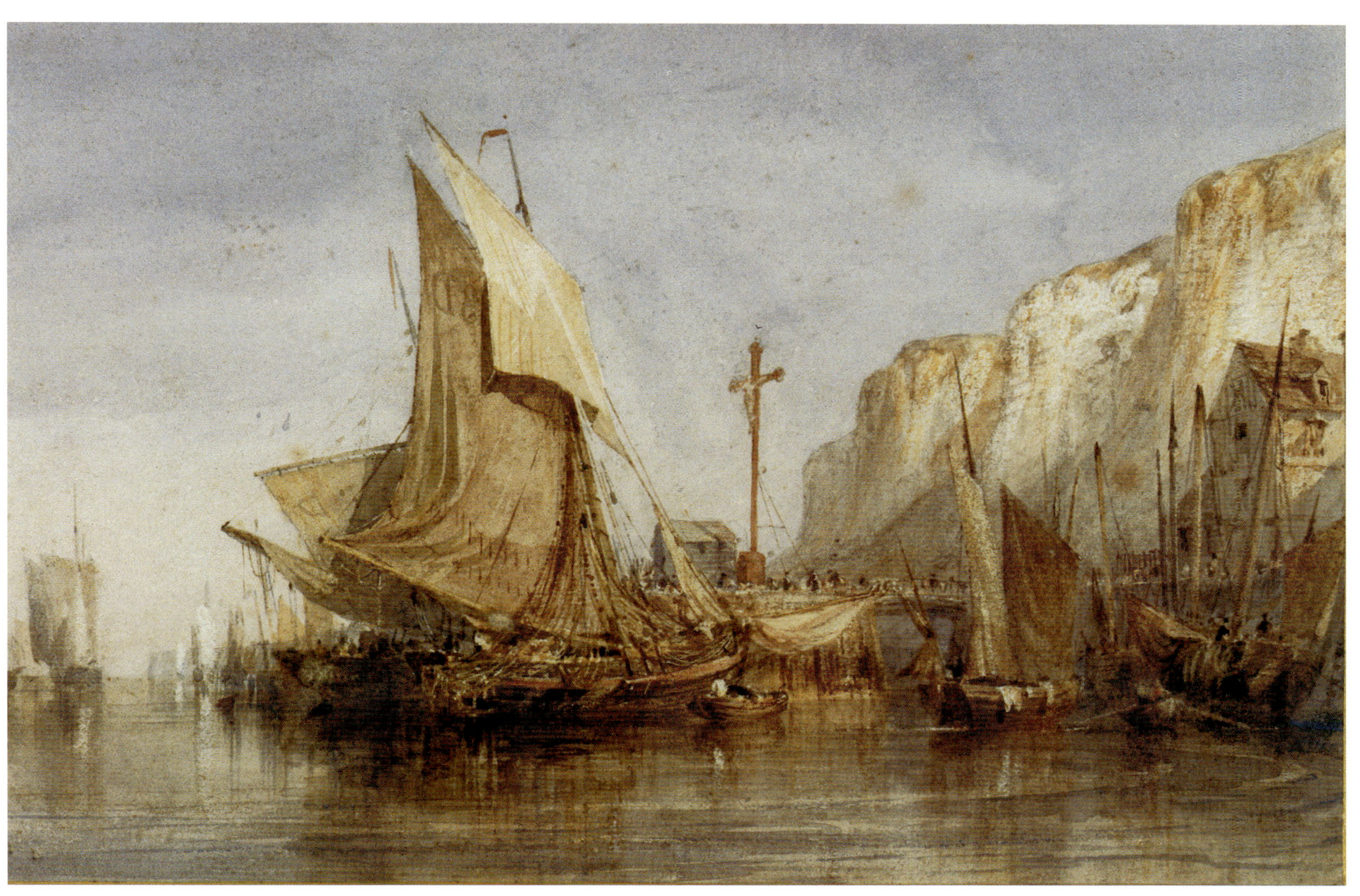

Plate 1.10. **Edward William Cooke, RA.** *Dieppe, Fishing Boats arrived. Signed, inscribed and dated verso 1833. 13 x 20cm (5¼ x 8in.)*

long the largest building of its kind in Europe, was the first of many luxury seaside hotels being built along the entire British coastline. Victorians visiting seaside towns and villages were struck with the beauty of coastal landscapes, the picturesque harbours and beaches and, above all, by colourful fishing vessels going about their business. There was a growing demand for well-executed watercolours of marine and coastal scenes to adorn the walls of Victorian villas. Painting in watercolours became an increasingly popular pastime.

This rapidly expanding domestic market and resultant increase in the number of art galleries brought marine art to a peak in the late nineteenth century. Watercolour artists now had a great tradition and plenty of material to draw upon. At last a capable artist could make a reasonable living out of his profession, and many did. T.B. Hardy was one of them.

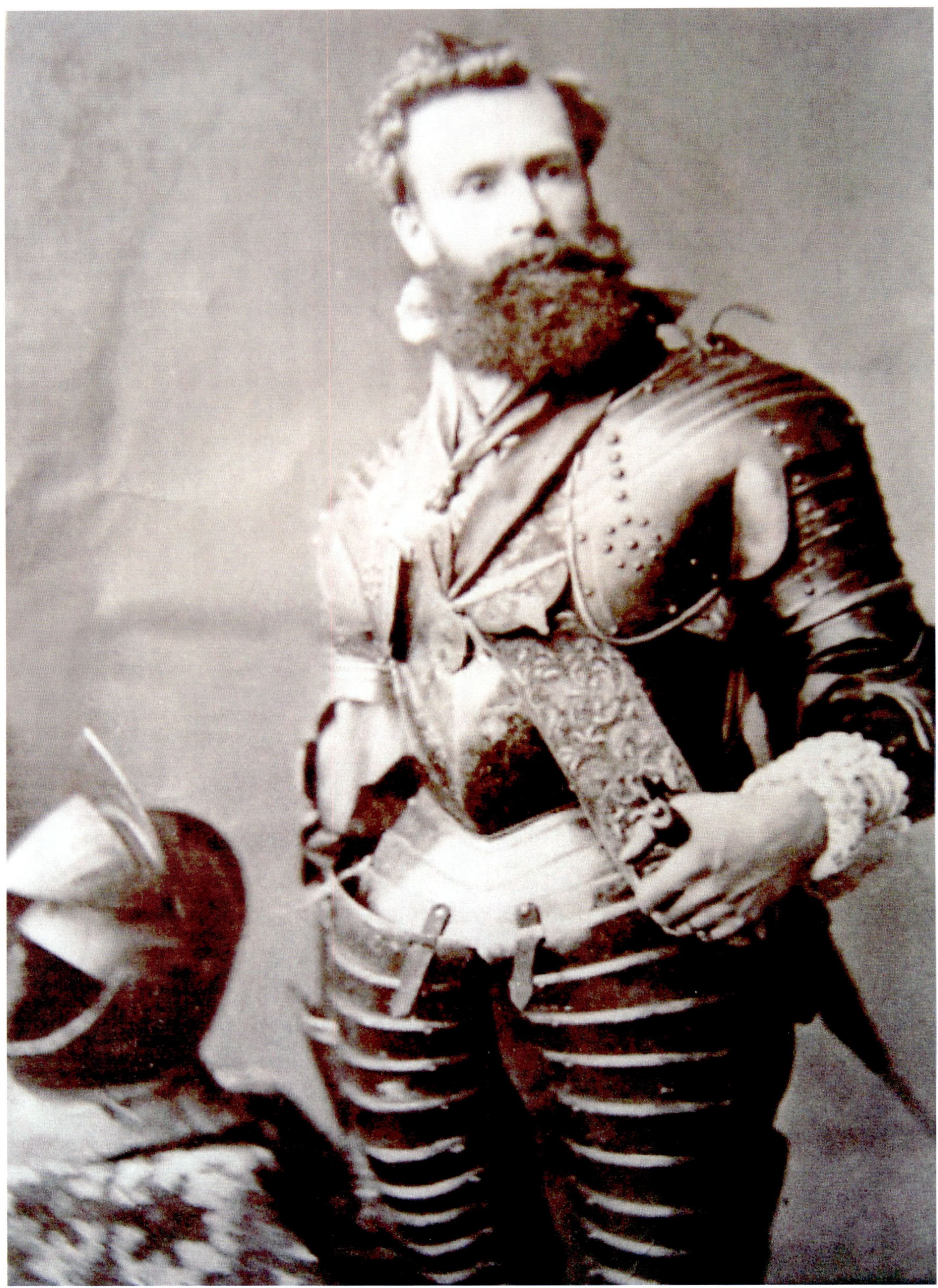

Thomas Bush Hardy and his Family – a Biography

Thomas Bush Hardy was born in Trafalgar Street, Sheffield, on 3 May 1842 to Thomas Hardy and his wife Amelia. Amelia was the eldest of five children born to William and Mary Bush and the 1851 Census finds them living together with their daughter and grandson at 115 Devonshire Street, Sheffield. There is no mention of Thomas Hardy, however, who perhaps had died in the intervening period. Why the young Thomas Bush Hardy was so named, to include his maternal grandfather's surname, is perhaps that his mother, Amelia, wished to preserve her maiden name of Bush.

Ten years on finds William and Mary with daughter Amelia and grandson Thomas Bush Hardy still together at 178 Upper Hanover Street. William was an optician and it appears the young Hardy was apprenticed to his grandfather for a while.

Sadly, few family documents or letters are available, but it is known that Thomas Bush Hardy enlisted in the North America Federal Army. Some time in the summer of 1861, when just nineteen, Hardy apparently had a quarrel with his fiancé, Mary Ann Lovne. He decided to go to America and worked his passage and joined General Handcock's North Brigade. Following injury, he was invalided out and returned to Sheffield where he found a job in the local Silver Assay Office. He obviously made up with Mary Ann as they were married in Sheffield in the summer of 1862. Both were twenty. The first of seven daughters, Edith Kate, was born in Sheffield in 1864. Two other children, a son, Dudley, born in 1867 and a daughter, Florence, born in 1868, were the only others to be born in Sheffield, although six further children were born after the move from Sheffield. By 1870 the young family had moved to London and in 1871 were living at 84 Regina Road, Upper Holloway in Finsbury.

Hardy initially worked as a clerk with the Inland Revenue at Somerset House until he felt he could earn sufficient income from full-time painting to support his young and increasing family. Jessie was born in 1870, his second son, Francis Chaplin, in 1872 and Winifred in 1873. As Hardy's family grew and as he flourished as an artist, so he seems to have moved fairly regularly during the

Plate 2.1.
Thomas Bush Hardy

early years in London. Whether all the following addresses are different homes or accommodation addresses for exhibition purposes one cannot be sure.

By 1873 the family are listed at 42 Gordon Square, but later in the same year they moved to 38 St Julian's Road in St John's Wood – quite upmarket.

Between 1877 and 1880 Hardy moved the family to France and lived at Villa de Wicardene in Boulogne. Hardy's fifth daughter and seventh child, Jacqueline, was born there. Dorothy, the next daughter was conceived in Boulogne, but was born back in London. The family moved to 50 Gower Street in 1881 and the following year to Damesmire, Lambolle Road.

In 1886, when Dorothy was only six years old, Mary Ann died at the age of forty-four, having given birth to eight children in sixteen years. Thomas Bush Hardy then moved the family into a substantial property in Barnes. 32 Castlenau Villas was described as *'substantially as well as ornamentally built … with a two horse-drawn carriage drive up to the door'*. This move seems at odds with his financial position since in April 1886 it appears that he was broke as he wrote to his friend and physician, Dr Watson: *'… I must tell you that, as a measure of protection against any further calls or further worry on the part of demons who have put me in this hole, Miss Hardy, my daughter, will take the house in her name and the furniture in her name and will infect* [sic] *be mistress of it all'*. The daughter was his eldest, Edith, by then twenty-two, who no doubt had her hands full taking over her late mother's role as the four youngest children were then aged fourteen, thirteen, nine and six. Despite this letter, Hardy's finances must have improved quickly to afford not only this property, but the four staff he engaged.

In March 1890, Thomas Bush Hardy married Muriel, who was only twenty (twenty-eight years younger than her new husband), and in the same year he made what was to be his final move when the family took up residence at 88 Portsdown Road in Maida Vale. Here he also employed four staff – a live-in cook, two housemaids and a nursemaid. He and Muriel had one daughter, Barbara, who was born in 1891, but who sadly died at the age of two.

Thomas Bush Hardy must have been a great family man to have persevered in producing two sons and seven daughters with an age range of twenty-seven years. Indeed, his eldest four children (Edith, Dudley, Florence and Jessie) were older than his second wife, Muriel. He was obviously a gregarious fellow who certainly enjoyed his drink! He was an active member of the male-only Savage Club, which was founded on 12 October 1857, its original purpose being to provide a convivial meeting forum for artistic, literary and other like-minded people. Apart from his artistic prowess, Hardy was a self-taught musician who had the wonderful ability to hear a piece of music once and then be able to replay it almost note perfect on the piano.

It was a major part of life in nineteenth century London for gentlemen to frequent their club to catch up on news, exchange views over supper and no doubt partake of copious amounts of alcohol. Art historians frequently refer to Hardy's less successful paintings as being the result of working with a pounding headache from the after effects of too much gin the night before. Perhaps he needed adult male company as a refuge from his ever increasing family. The Savage Club was not large and on its twenty-fifth anniversary had only 272 members of which 206 attended a special birthday dinner on 11 February 1882 held in the presence of H.R.H. The Prince of Wales – later King Edward VII – who was welcomed as a member. The dinner was held in Lancaster House, behind the Savoy Hotel, and one can image that it was a grand and alcoholic evening.

Hardy was also a member of the Langham Sketch Club which was founded in 1838. Members, who were elected by their peers, met every Friday afternoon during the winter months, defined as October to May. Each member made a two hour sketch from one or two given subjects. These were then hung on the walls and a general critique followed which in turn led to supper and an evening of talk and entertainment. Hardy often sold these works, which are inscribed 'The Langham Club'.

Hardy clearly enjoyed entertaining at home and often invited friends for supper. They apparently arrived in some trepidation, never quite knowing how their host would be attired – either sporting the latest Savile Row suit or casual clothes or in a suit of armour as the picture on page 34 testifies. Hardy was a great collector of antique armour and at one time was reputed to have the largest private collection in England. His collection, which included eighteen pieces from the famous Meyrick Collection, was later sold at Christie's.

His first exhibited work is recorded at the Royal Society of British Artists in 1871 when he showed his painting *Robin Hood's Bay, Yorkshire*. He exhibited frequently at the RBA between 1871 and 1893 and was elected a member in 1884. This will have appeased his disappointment at being turned down on several occasions for membership of the Royal Institute of Painters in Water Colours. He exhibited thirty-five works at the Royal Academy between 1872 and 1897, eleven works at the Royal Institute of Painters in Water Colours between 1883 and 1890 and over ninety-five at Suffolk Street between 1871 and 1893. The given prices ranged from six guineas to £262.10s. in 1892 for *Her Majesty's Tower*.

Hardy's sudden death at the relatively early age of fifty-five robbed his family of its breadwinner and undoubtedly deprived the art world of many more years of marine watercolours. *The Times* obituary noted:

Mr T B Hardy who died suddenly last week, was remarkable as the most rapid and facile water-colour painter of his generation. His genuine artistic gifts, which he transmitted to his son Mr Dudley Hardy, and to more than one of his daughters, would have led him far if he had cared to submit to discipline of study and labour. He painted chiefly in marine subjects and these he treated with unusual freshness and force, only failing in the qualities that give permanence, thought and subtle observations. His sketches, which are numbered by the thousands, have unmistakable vigour and no little beauty. He was a very frequent exhibitor at the Royal Academy and other Exhibitions.

This was a rather mixed obituary and, although certainly praising his obvious talent, clearly acknowledged his ability to produce poor quality works on an off day or as a result of a hangover. Where all the 'thousands' of sketches' referred to are remains a mystery. There is a volume of some ninety-five sketches dated from 1871 to 1893 in the Victorian and Albert Museum and a handful of other sketch books remain.

His local paper offers a further insight into his life through its obituary:

Another distinguished local resident has just passed away in the person of Mr. Thomas Bush Hardy, the well known artist, and the father of Mr. Dudley Hardy. Death occurred early on Sunday morning at his house in Maida-vale, and came as a great surprise to his friends, for he was in the best of health. Mr Hardy had crowded into his six and fifty years [sic] many thrilling adventures. Born in Sheffield he went to America as a mere boy, and served with the Northern Army in the war. When he returned to this country he got a position in Somerset House. All the time he was cultivating art assiduously, though he never had a lesson in his life. At last he gave up all his time to painting, and during the later quarter of a century he has turned out an enormous amount of work, frequently exhibiting at the Academy and the other galleries. At the time of his death (due to an apoplectic stroke) he was engaged on a huge 18 ft. [5.5m] panel representing the destruction of the Armada, which he had been commissioned to do (after competition) for the Army and Navy Club. Mr. Hardy was an extraordinarily quick worker and his lightning sketches became famous at the Savage Club, of which he was a devoted member. One of the best of these rapid chalk drawings belongs to Mr. Penley, and hangs in the Globe Theatre with an inscription on it, detailing how many minutes it took to do. In such feats Mr. Hardy had simply no rival whatever. He was twice married. By his first wife he leaves seven daughters, several of whom are artists, and Mr. Dudley Hardy, in whose studio he was working on his Armada panel.

The *Young Sheffield*, a then recently launched publication, produced its obituary of Hardy in the January 1899 issue. It read:

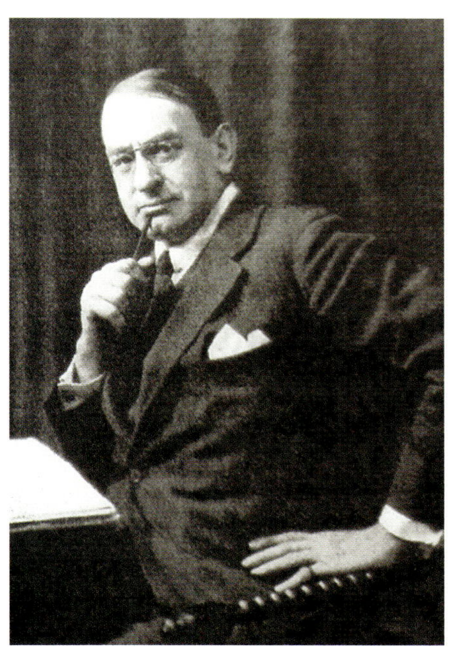

T. B. Hardy, Artist. *It is with real regret we note the recent death of a distinguished Sheffield-born artist, in the decease of Mr. Thomas Bush Hardy, of London. Though practically self-taught, Mr. Hardy attained to the highest prominence as a Marine painter, and his rapidity of execution gained for him the well deserved title of the "King of Sketchers". The late President of the Sketching Club, Mr. George Haite, sent a wreath on the occasion of Mr. Hardy's interment, bearing a motto to that effect. In his younger days Hardy was engaged in a Sheffield writing school, but being of an adventuring nature he endeavoured to enlist during the Crimean War. Failing in this he went to America, joined a regiment, and served in the ranks of the North in the great civil war. Being bought out he returned to England and obtained an appointment in Somerset House. Possessed however with a born aptitude for painting, he exercised his natural talent in that direction, and his pictures were quickly appreciated, being exhibited in due time on the walls of the Royal Academy and other Art Exhibitions. Travelling through Scotland, Germany, France, and Italy, he found artistic material in each country, but perhaps the "Queen of the Adriatic," Venice, inspired him with subjects for his finest efforts; and the splendid chromo-lithographic reproductions of some of these pictures attest the popularity of his numerous marine and architectural performances. At the time of his death Mr. Hardy was engaged on a large canvas representing "The Armada" and intended as a companion to Mr. Wyllie's "Battle of Trafalgar" at the Junior United Service Club. Our Mappin Gallery displays several of Mr. Hardy's works, though not of his most important productions, and it may be noted that the artistic faculty of the father is strongly developed in his son, Mr. Dudley Hardy, whose magazine illustrations and wall posters are well-known and of the finest excellence. In the death of Mr. T.B. Hardy, Sheffield adds another to the long record of notable worthies she is proud to own as her sons.*

On Hardy's death it was noted that Mr. George Haite, the then President of the 'Sketching Club', sent a wreath with the greeting 'King of Sketchers'. It seems likely that this was the Langham Sketch Club which Hardy was elected to in 1879 (the same year that he was elected to the Savage Club) because it was not until 1898 that the London Sketch Club was formed (see below).

Thomas Bush Hardy's legacy lives on, as evidenced by the strong demand for his better paintings whenever they come on to the market, some 110 years after his death.

Dudley Hardy inherited his father's artistic talents, and perhaps character as well. In A.E. Johnson's biography of Dudley, first published in 1909, the author wrote *'… Dudley Hardy, one is tempted to declare, has not one personality but half a dozen'*. His diversity was quite remarkable, ranging from rich and glowing oriental scenes, subdued studies of peasant life in Brittany, humorous and satirical black and white sketches which were often published in *Punch* and not least his fame as a poster painter. Indeed his work for the Savoy Theatre and D'Oyly Carte's Opera Company ensured his name is remembered as the public dubbed him the *'Poster King'* **(Plate 2.4).**

He spent his boyhood in his father's studio and, showing natural talent, he was packed off to study under Crola and Lowenstein in Düsseldorf at the age of fifteen. However, the discipline required in class did not sit well with a teenager after the relaxed style of his father's studio and he was dismissed, with the suggestion that he abandon any thought of a career in art. He was later re-admitted, when he studied assiduously for three months before returning to London. The Academy praised his landscape painting but advised him that figures were beyond his powers! A lesser person might have heeded their advice, yet Dudley achieved immediate fame for his countless black and white sketches of attractive young milliners and beauteous 'coryphées' in gay and frisky insouciance.

Another side was more serious and an early oil, 'Sans Asile', completed in 1888 was exhibited in Munich, Düsseldorf, Berlin, Paris and the Royal Academy in 1893. This painting **(Plate 2.5)**, dark and gloomy, depicts a group of unemployed men sleeping out rough by the base of a lion in Trafalgar Square. Dudley Hardy first exhibited in 1885 at the age of eighteen at the Royal Academy and continued throughout his life. He was a member of the Royal Institute of Painters in Water Colours, the Royal Miniature Society and the Pastel Society.

Dudley first married Elizabeth who died in 1906 and they had a son, Cameron, who it is believed went off to America. Dudley subsequently married Ann Morrison, known as 'Billy', in 1907. They had two children, Ian (born 1910) and Peggy (born 1914). He was so busy painting that fate was to lend a watchful hand as Dudley had booked Ann, himself and baby son, Ian, on to the *Titanic*. All was prepared; Ann had bought her new wardrobe and awaited the day of departure. At the last moment, Dudley received a commission he could not refuse so the family cancelled their booking!

Ian Dudley Hardy, T.B. Hardy's second grandson, was born in 1910 and, after completing his education in the Merchant Navy, decided on an acting career. He made his West End debut at the London Pavilion when

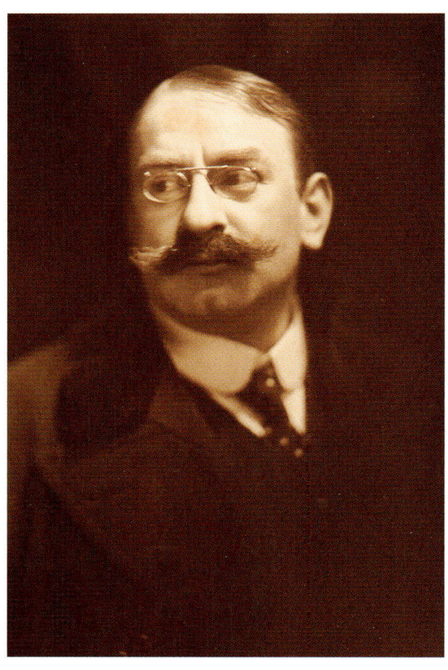

Plate 2.3. **Dudley Hardy.**

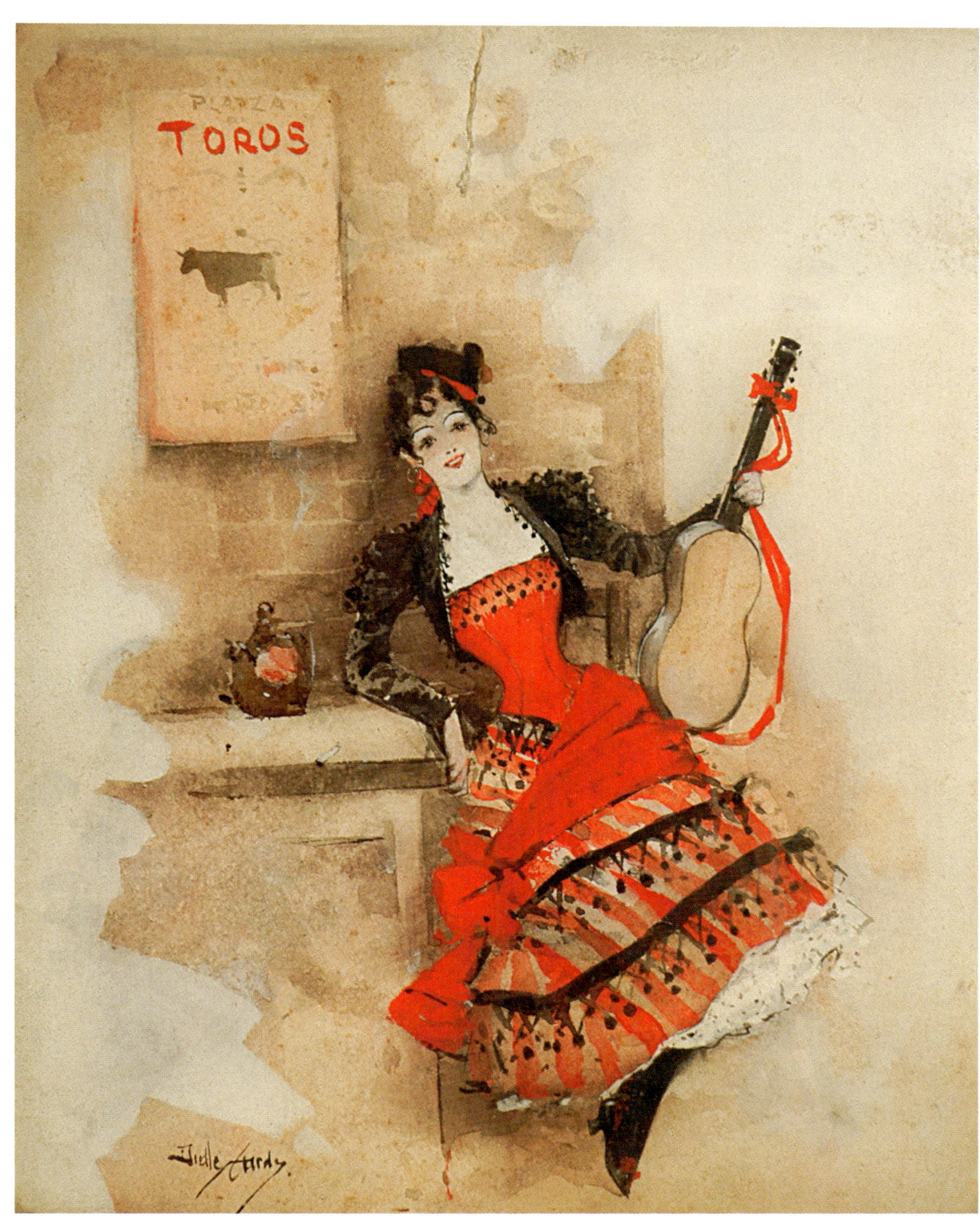

Plate 2.4. **Dudley Hardy.**
Lady in Red.

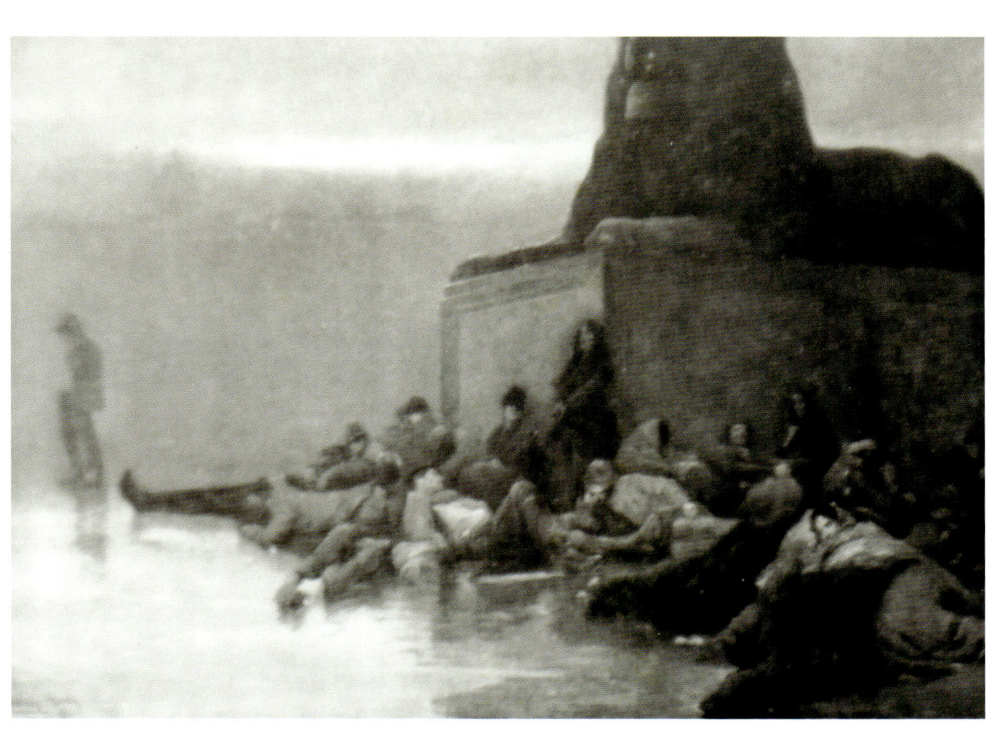

Plate 2.5. **Dudley Hardy.**
'Sans Asile'. 1888

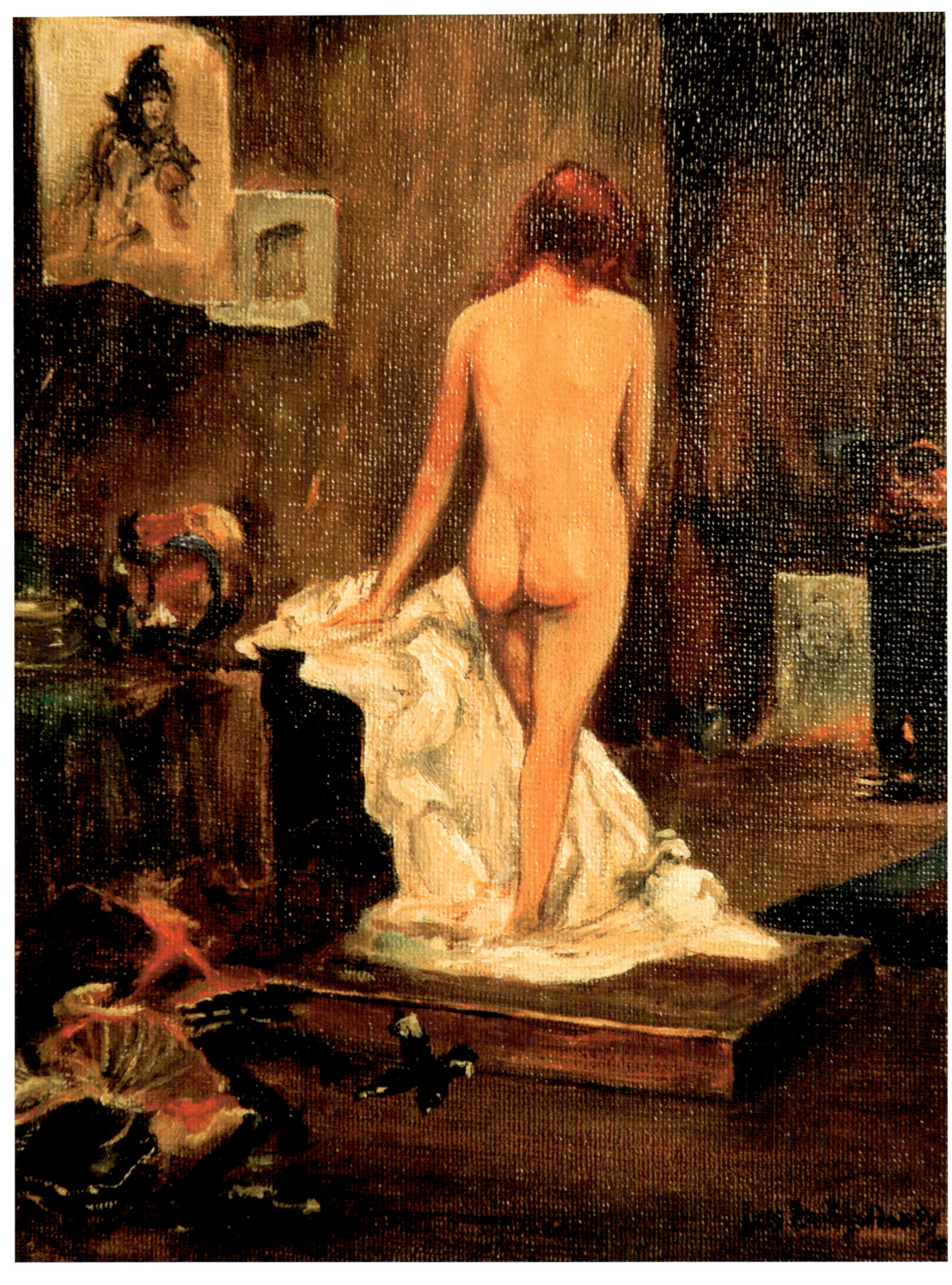

Chapter 2 – Thomas Bush Hardy and his Family – a Biography

only sixteen. From then on he appeared in cabaret, the West End and films, including *Meet the Duke* in 1948 and *Never Say Die* in 1950. Ian was also a talented painter in both watercolour and oil *(Plates 2.6 and 2.7)*, but perhaps unsurprisingly never pursued his talent professionally, feeling in the shadow of his father's and grandfather's reputation. He painted seascapes in watercolour as well as landscapes in oil. Ian married Jean Higgis in 1960; she was a stage dancer with the Tiller Girls troupe. Ian was killed, aged seventy-nine, when a two hundred year old cedar tree fell on to the car in which Jean and he were travelling. Jean survives.

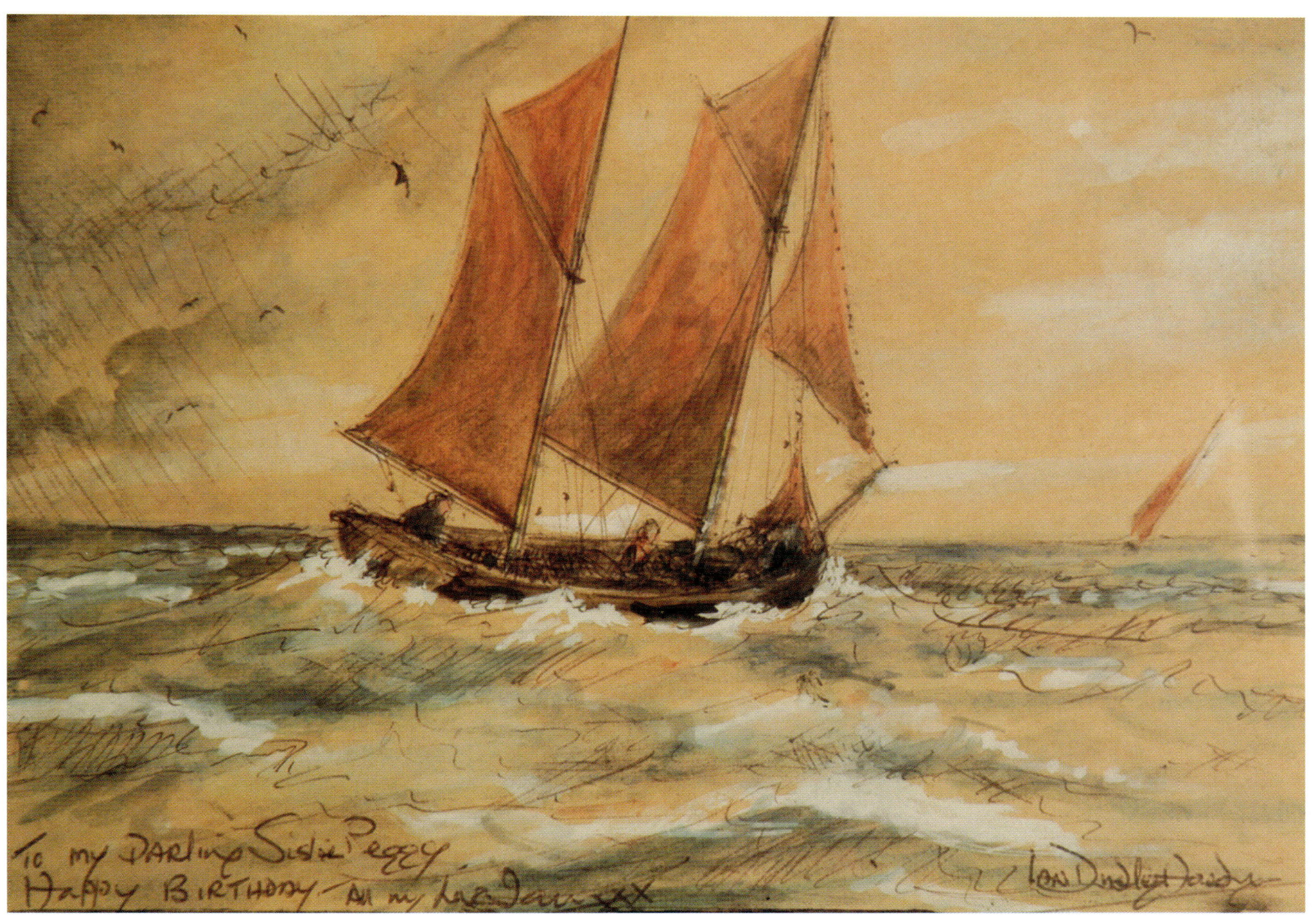

Of T.B. Hardy's seven daughters, only Jessie was to marry. She married Frank Richards *(Plate 2.8)*, who was also to become a renowned and successful artist. Frank Richards was born in Sutton Coldfield on 18 September 1863 to Samuel Wall Richards (1836-1908) who was active in business and local government, with a particular passion for attempting to improve the welfare of the then oppressed workforces. One of his particular successes was the question of postal deliveries. In 1867 the last postal delivery commenced at 7.30pm, which the postmen felt to be a hardship – a view shared by Richards. Accordingly he wrote to the Postmaster General showing how deliveries could be re-arranged and his scheme was adopted. He went on to form the Postmen's Benevolent Association and acted as its Secretary.

Plate 2.8. **Frank Richards.**

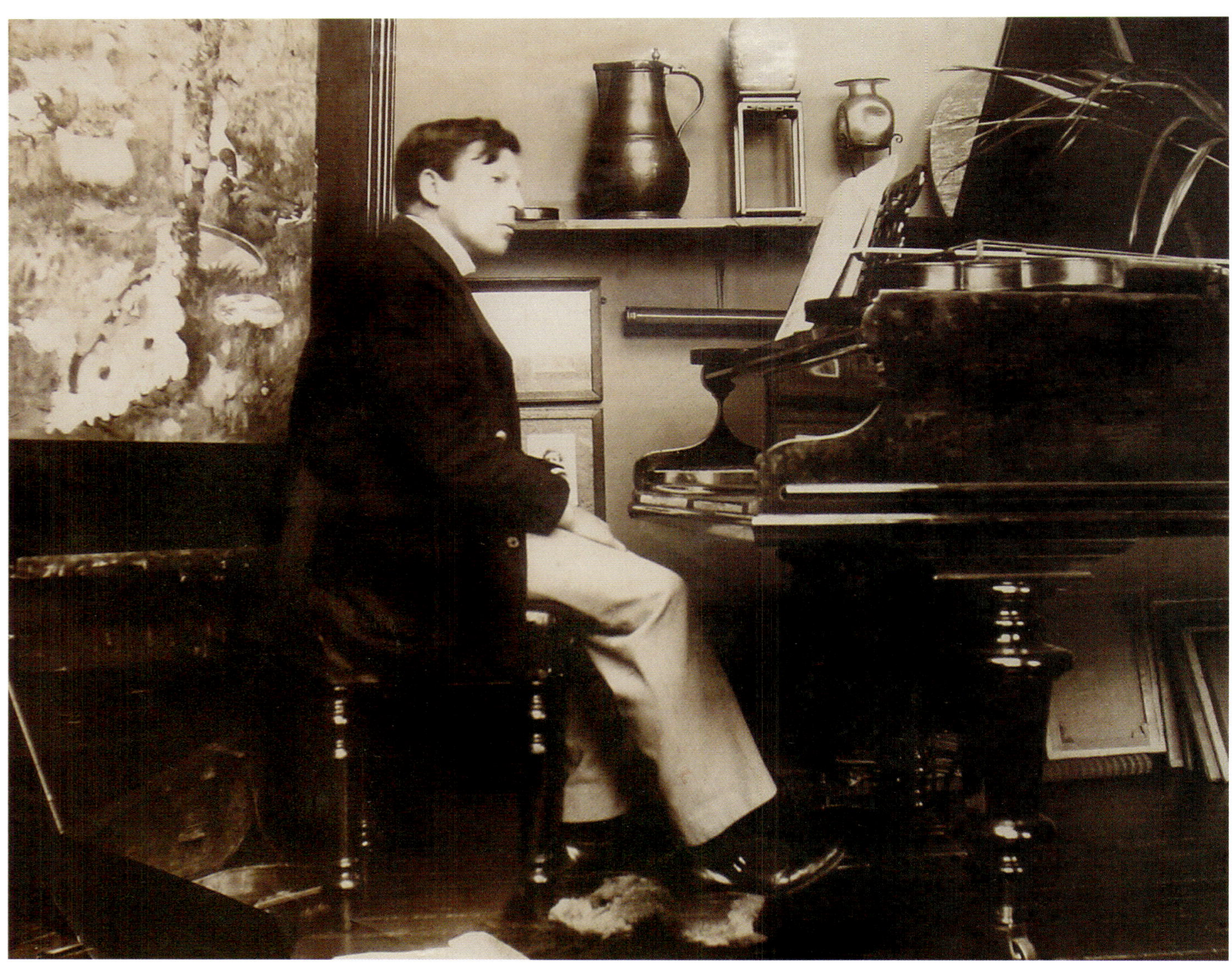

Frank Richards studied sculpture and painting at both the Birmingham School of Art and in London and later painted at Newlyn, where he was initially influenced by the Newlyn School. He travelled extensively throughout Italy, Holland *(Plate 2.9)* and Egypt, often in the company of his brother-in-law, Dudley Hardy. In 1898 the more boisterous behaviour of the younger members of the Langham Sketch Club caused them to break away and form the London Sketch Club. It appears Dudley Hardy, Walter Fowler, Frank Jackson, Lance Thackery, Robert Sanber and Tom Browne were the founding members, along with Frank Richards. The new club followed the style of the Langham and met every Friday afternoon to draw, have supper and talk into the night. Dudley and Frank, who were similar ages (thirty-one

Plate 2.9. **Frank Richards.**
Dutch River Scene. 1903.

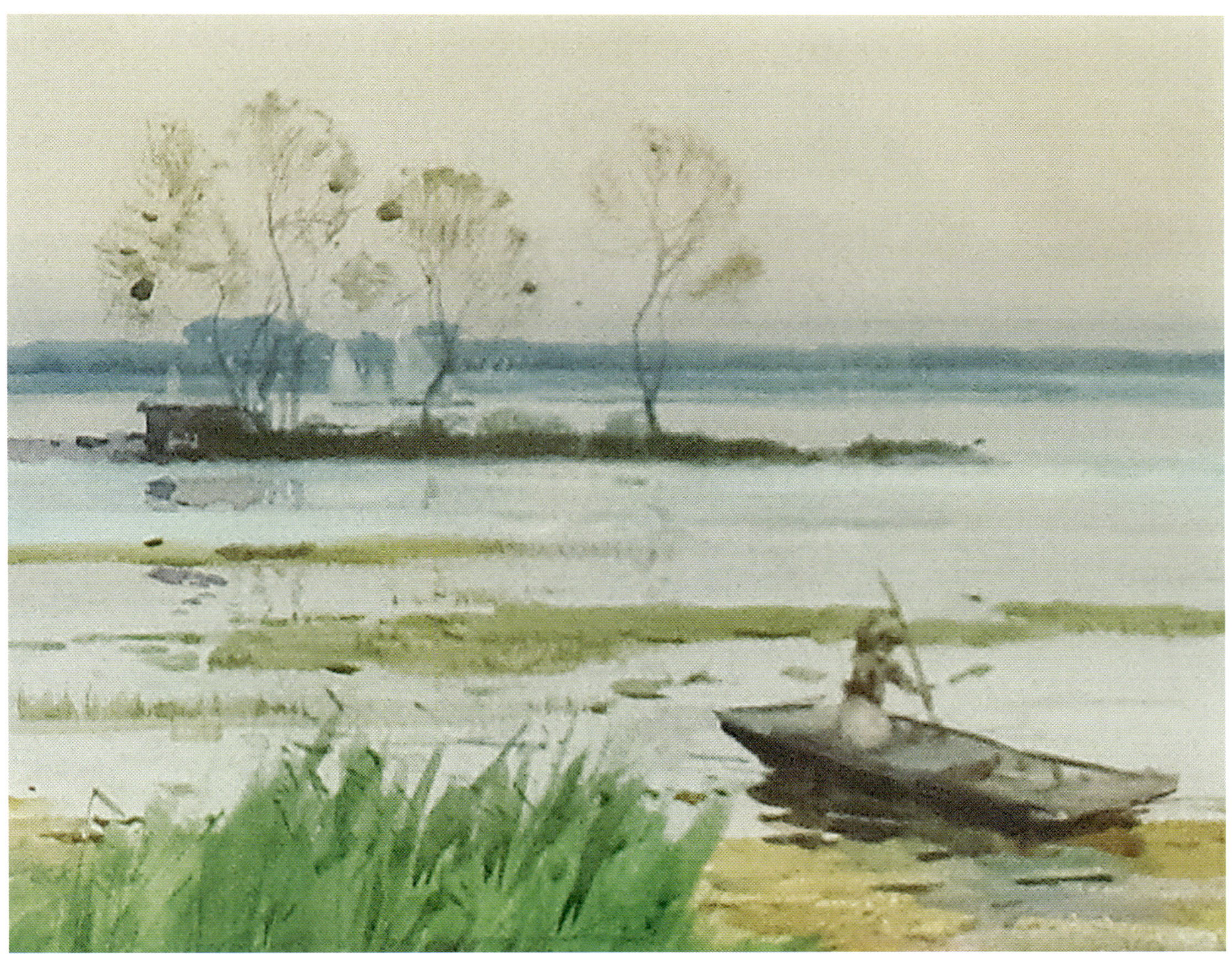

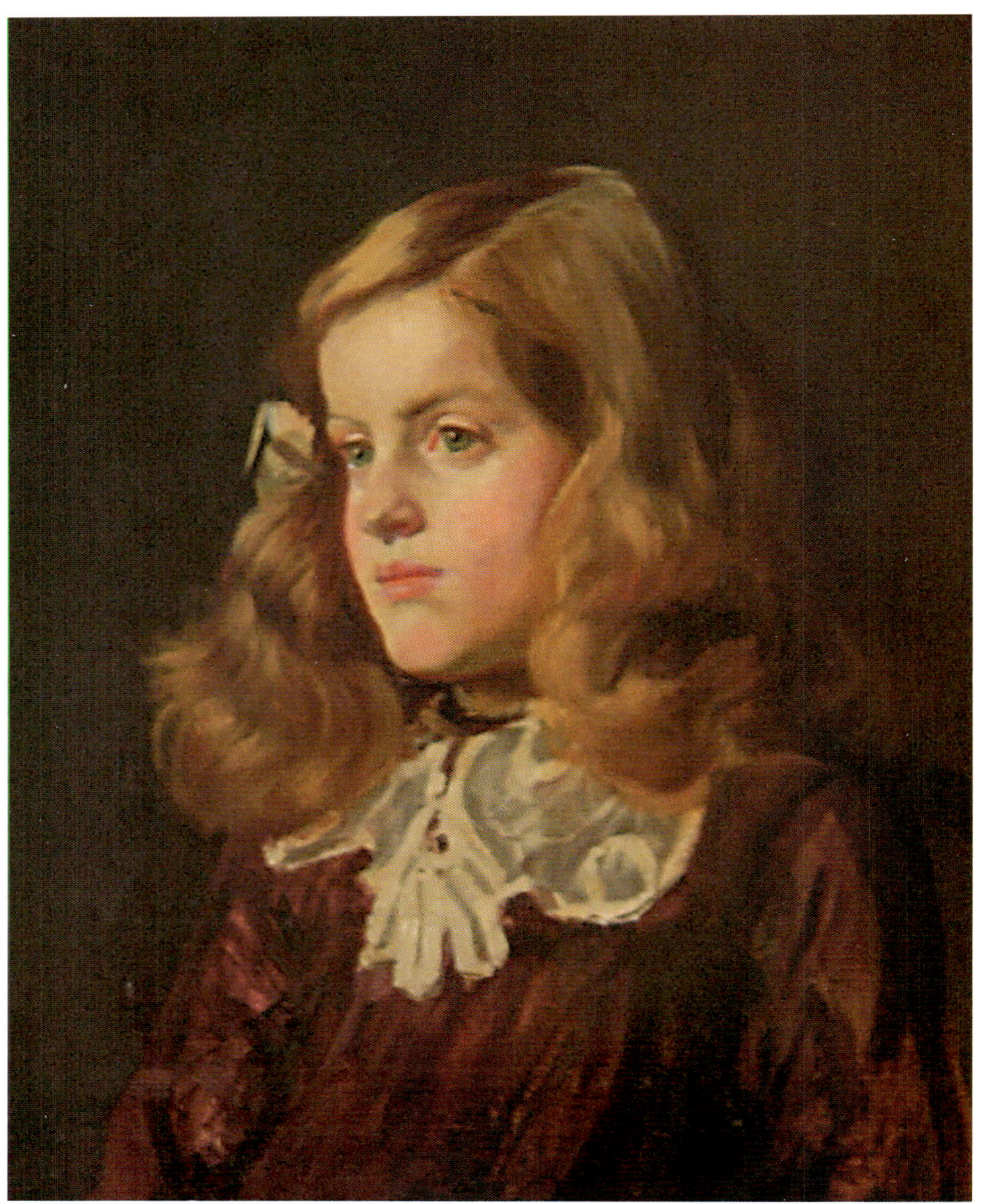

Plate 2.10. **Frank Richards.** *Lamorna (Bonnie) Richards. Signed, inscribed and dated 1904 (oil)*

and thirty-five respectively), were obviously good friends in 1898.

Frank Richards was a versatile artist in oil and watercolour and painted land and seascapes, but his principal interest was portraits. He was commissioned to paint various Royals and, by Royal Command, a number of miniature watercolour pictures or 'folios' for the Queen's Doll's House. He initially lived and had a studio in South Kensington, London, before moving to Bournemouth in about 1903, where he subsequently died in 1935. He first exhibited at the Royal Academy in 1893 and was elected to the Royal Society of British Artists (RBA) in 1919. The various obituaries and reports of exhibitions held during his lifetime all attest to his great artistic talent, best in watercolour, with his ability to create well-constructed landscapes with a real understanding for colour.

Chapter 2 – Thomas Bush Hardy and his Family – a Biography

Frank and Jessie had three children (***Plates 2.10-212***) – Lamorna (always known as Bonnie), a son Alfred Coombe Walls (known as Coombe) and a second daughter, Elaine (known as Paddy). Paddy also inherited the family's artistic gene and studied at the Bournemouth School of Art and thereafter painted all her life, both professionally and for her own pleasure.

The eldest daughter, Bonnie, was obviously a stunningly attractive little girl as there are family portraits of her at all ages painted by her portrait painter aunt, Florence, and her father, Frank Richards. Bonnie eloped with Gerald Fitzgerald, a wealthy Irish landowner, and they lived in Ireland. In due course she became his fourth wife and stepmother to six or seven children, most of whom were older than her – thus repeating family history. They had one son, Patrick, who was killed in action on 1 June 1943 whilst serving as a pilot on board HMS *Indomitable.*

Coombe Richards inherited his artistic talent from both parents, but his own early life was largely in the services. Along with a school friend two

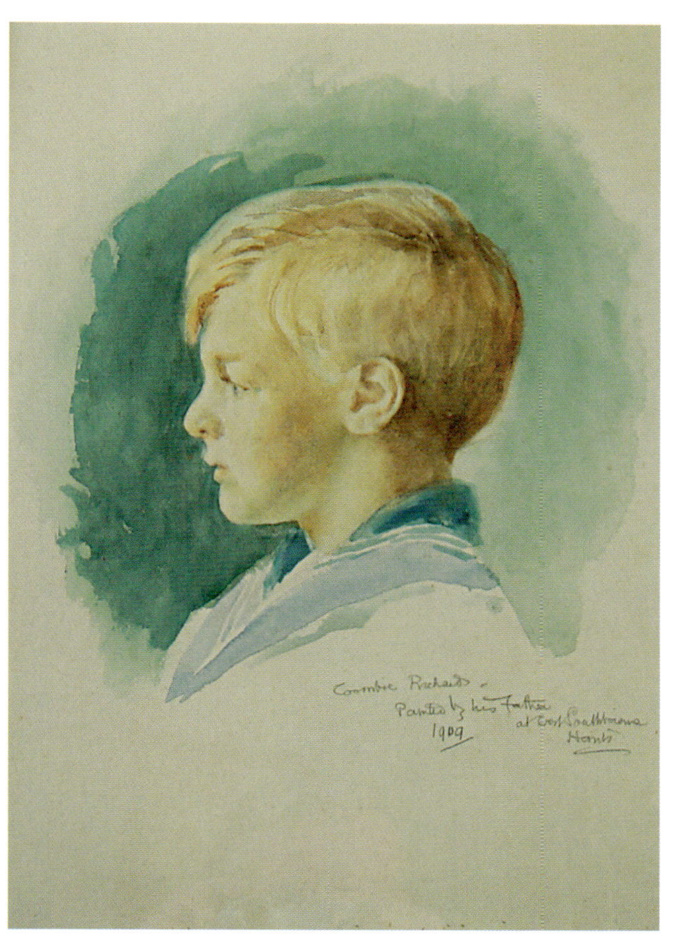

Plate 2.11. **Frank Richards.** *Alfred Coombe Walls (Coombe) Richards, aged nine. Signed, inscribed and dated 1909*

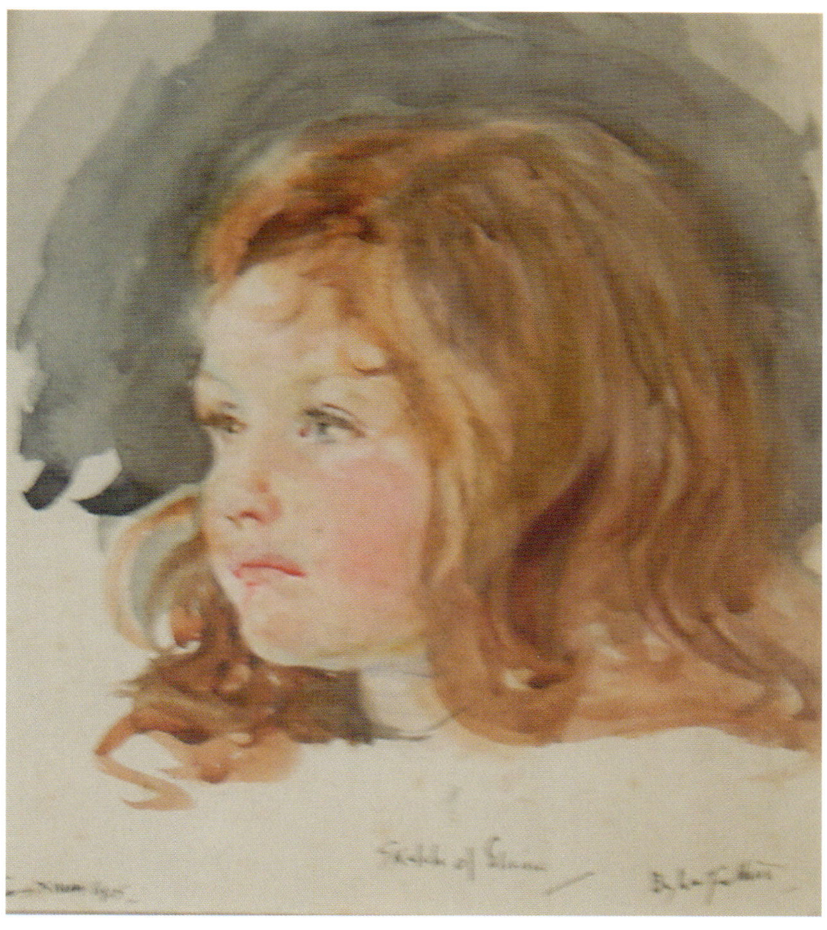

Plate 2.12. **Frank Richards.** *Elaine (Paddy) Richards. Signed, inscribed and dated 1925*

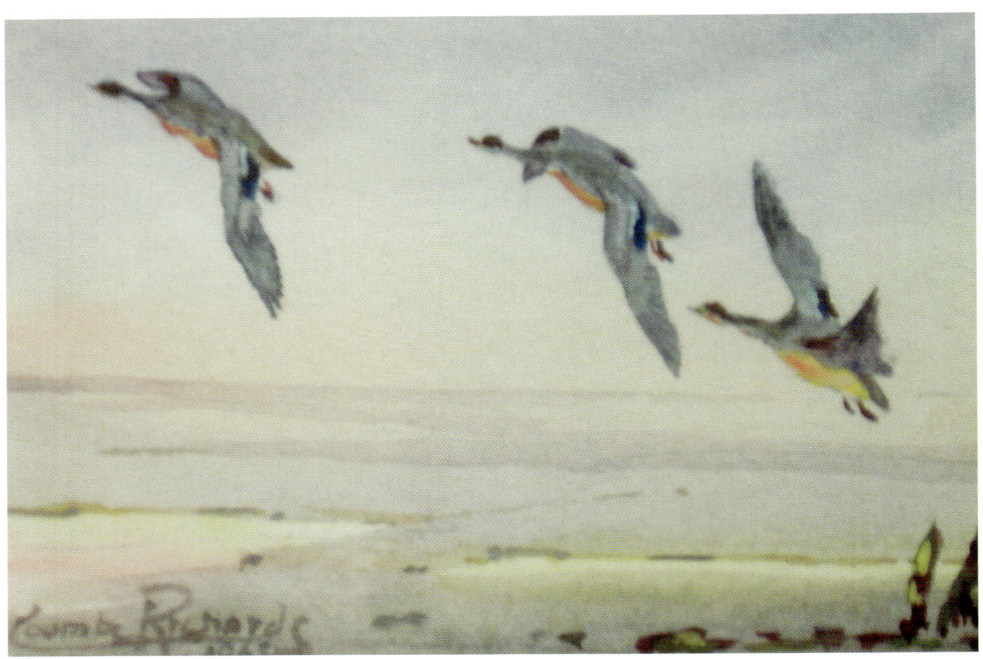

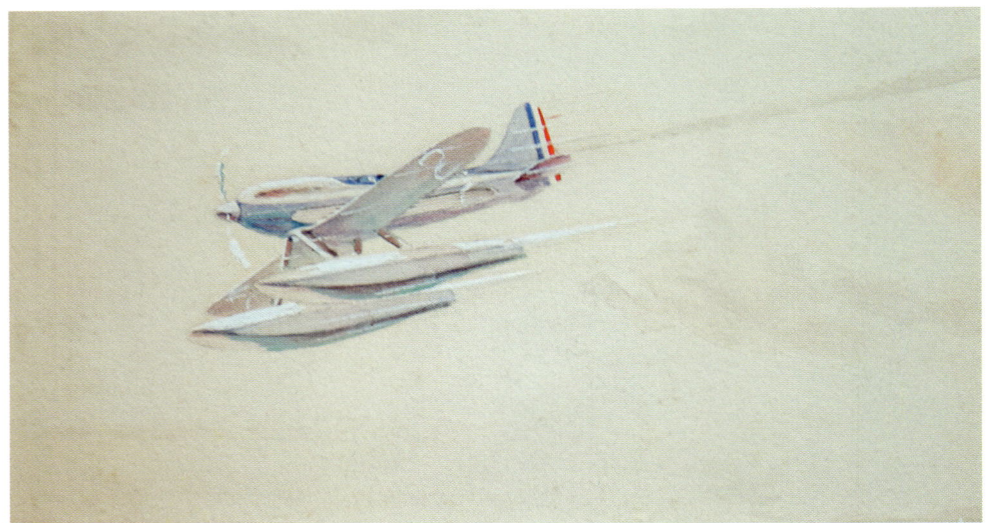

years his senior, he joined the Army as a despatch rider at the age of fourteen. Not surprisingly, his true age was discovered after a few weeks and he was sent home. He then joined the training ship *Worcester* from which he passed out into the Royal Navy as a junior officer. He remained in the Navy until 1921 when he transferred to the RAF, stationed at Calshot. Promoted to Flight Lieutenant, he subsequently resigned in 1926 in order to get married in June of that year. In 1928 he joined the Prison Service, retiring as a Senior Prison Governor in 1957 due to ill-health.

Coombe's hobbies included salmon fishing and he was a proficient angler, retiring to the Wye Valley. His love of the outdoors enabled him to study and paint wildfowl, which he executed with no mean skill (***Plate 2.13***). In 1929 he was the official artist to the Schneider Trophy Contest on 6 and

Plate 2.13. **Coombe Richards.** *Wild Geese. Signed and dated 1963*

Plate 2.14. **Coombe Richards.** *British Supermarine S66. 1929*

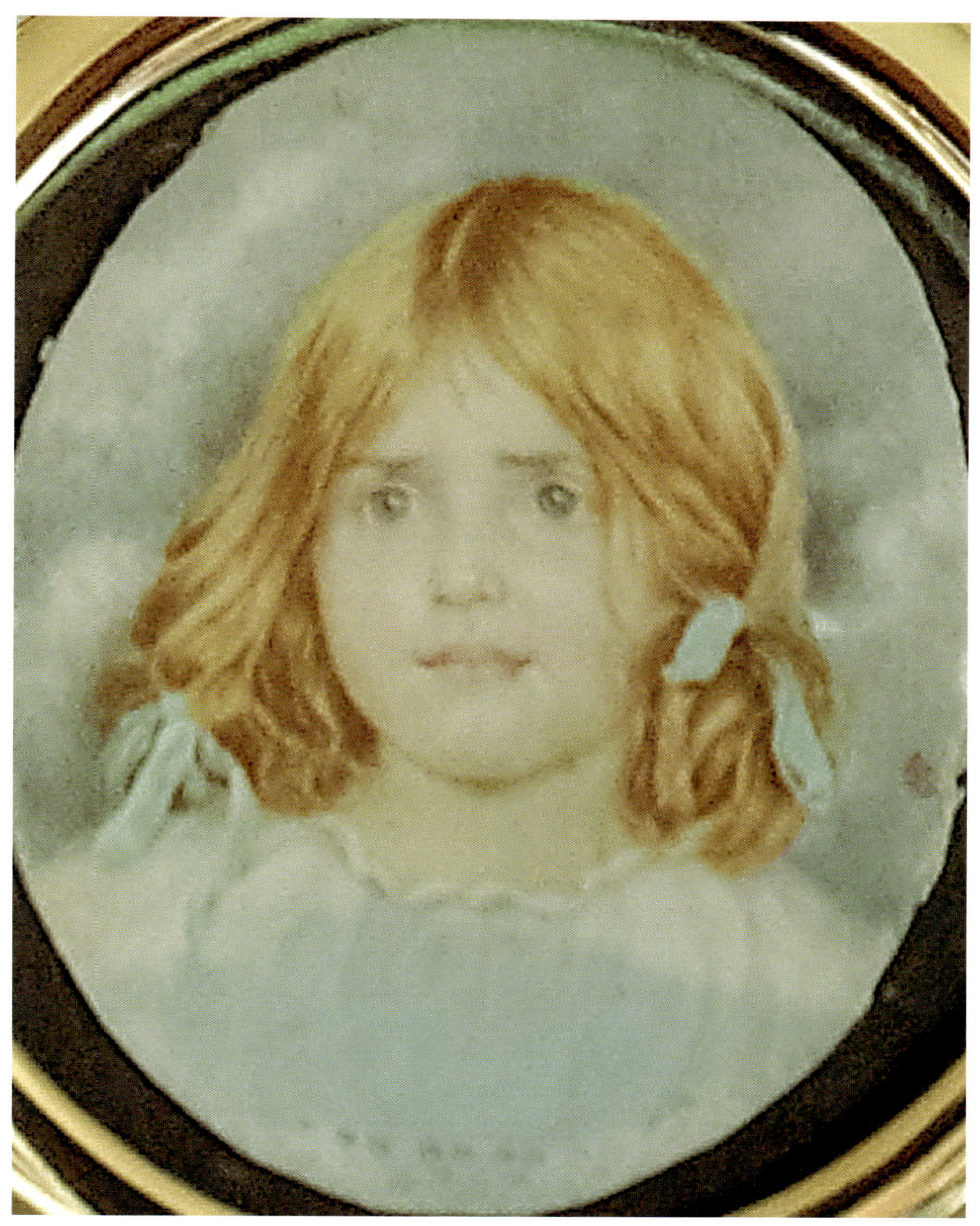

7 September 1929 off the Isle of Wight. This competition, begun in 1913 in Monaco, saw the industrial nations of Europe and America strive to develop faster and faster seaplanes. In 1913 the average speed was about 45 mph and by 1929 speeds in excess of 300 mph were achieved. Coombe was responsible for painting the commemorative postcards of the entrants' machines, including the winning British Supermarine S66 (*Plate 2.14*).

Coombe was married to Esther Mary Woodin and they had one daughter, Diana, who is T.B. Hardy's sole great-granddaughter. She, too, inherited the Hardy artistic gene and, despite no formal training, performed for many years on the local amateur stage in addition to painting pantomime scenery. Diana married Captain Malcolm Davies, RE, in December 1949.

Of T.B. Hardy's seven daughters, Florence and Jessie both received

Plate 2.15. **Florence Hardy.**
Lamorna Richards.

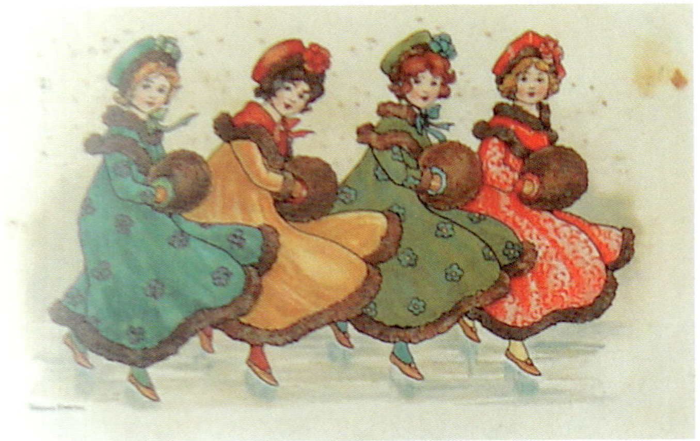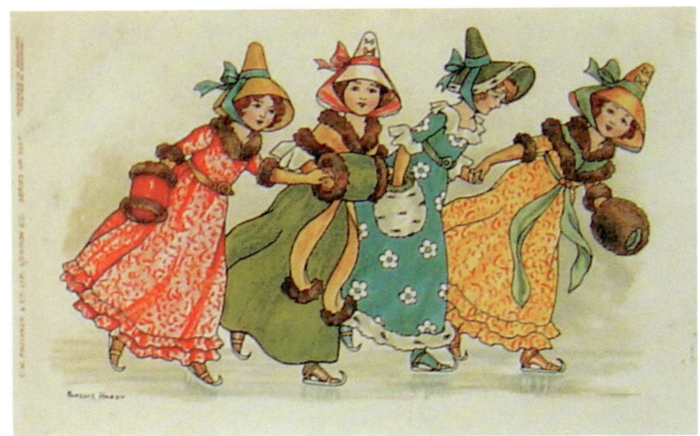

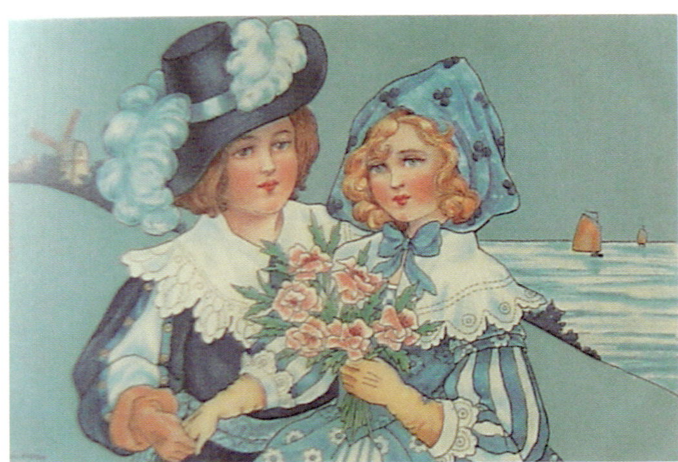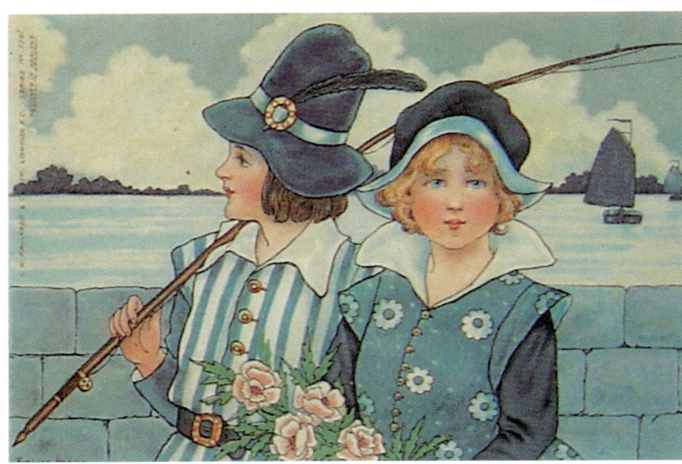

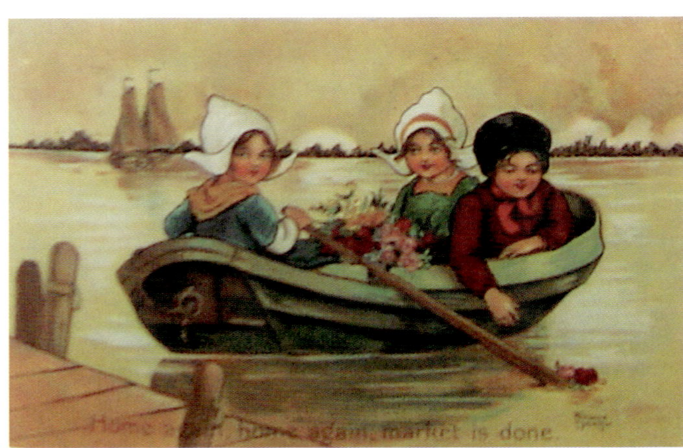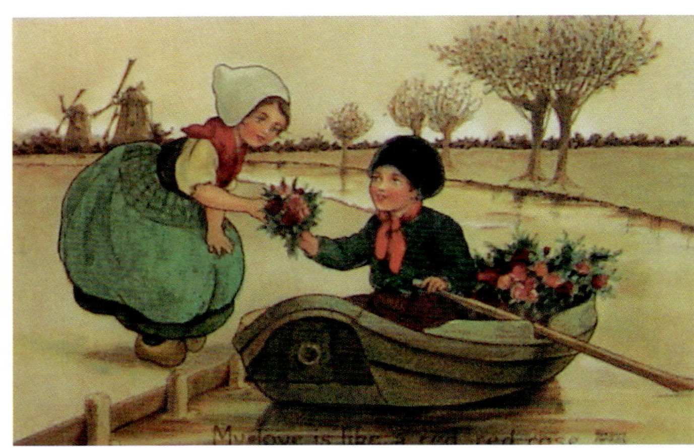

formal training, attending the Sorbonne in Paris in their teens. Jessie was an able drawer and also very skilful at embroidery. Florence was a painstaking and meticulous draughtswomen and became a successful miniaturist, exhibiting regularly between 1887 and 1897 at the Royal Academy, the Royal Society and the Society of Women Artists. Her father's premature death, when she was only twenty-nine, curtailed her portrait work (as did the arrival of the camera) as she had to support the young

Plate 2.16. **Florence Hardy.**
Postcards

Chapter 2 – Thomas Bush Hardy and his Family – a Biography

family. Luckily a new craze had begun – the demand for picture postcards – which soon filled the gap. She had an innate sense of composition and colour and, with her portrait training, became a renowned postcard artist. Many scenes and Christmas cards depicted Dutch and French children reliving childhood memories of summer holidays spent across the Channel, including the three years the family lived in Boulogne when she was aged nine to twelve. In the 1920s she lived in Maida Vale and appears to have been close to her other sisters (***Plates 2.15 and 2.16***).

At some stage Florence and her sisters Edith, Winifred and Dorothy all moved to Bournemouth to be closer to their sister Jessie and her husband, Frank. Diana, the great-niece of the four sisters, recalls visiting them in Bournemouth where she nearly electrocuted herself by dismantling an electric bell! Around 1935 the four sisters moved into a small house in Ditchling in Sussex where they were joined in the next door house by Jessie, following her husband's death. Jacqueline or Jack as she was known, joined them on her retirement from her position as a hospital matron (***Plate 2.17***).

* * * * *

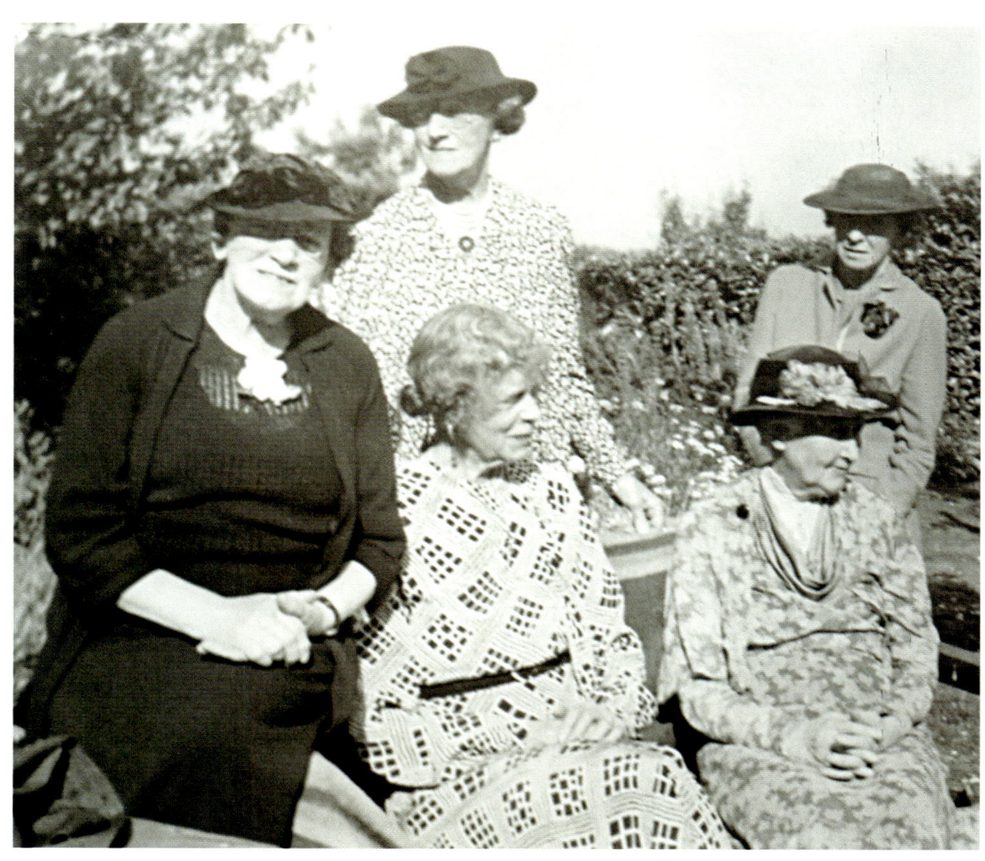

Plate 2.17. **Florence, Jessie and Jacqueline (Jack) Hardy at Ditchling,** *1936*

Nineteenth century marine painters have earned their place in shipping history by recording so accurately the many types of early coastal sailing vessels plying the North Sea as cargo boats and fishing vessels. With the development of the marine engine, sailing vessels quickly disappeared. This was highlighted by Lord Stanhope, who on 18 July 1834, in the House of Lords, moved the Second Reading of the National Maritime Museum Bill, the purpose of which was to restore and maintain a collection of all types of coastal sailing vessels before they were replaced by motor driven vessels. Marine artists, and particularly watercolour painters, sitting on beaches or harbour walls, accurately recorded the different coastal craft of the era.

Thomas Bush Hardy's paintings are therefore important in recording the coastal craft he painted down the East and South coasts of England and in Dutch and French beach scenes. The different craft, their construction and purpose, will be further highlighted in examining the pictures reproduced in the following chapters.

Opposite. Thomas Bush Hardy family tree.

Chapter 2 – Thomas Bush Hardy and his Family – a Biography

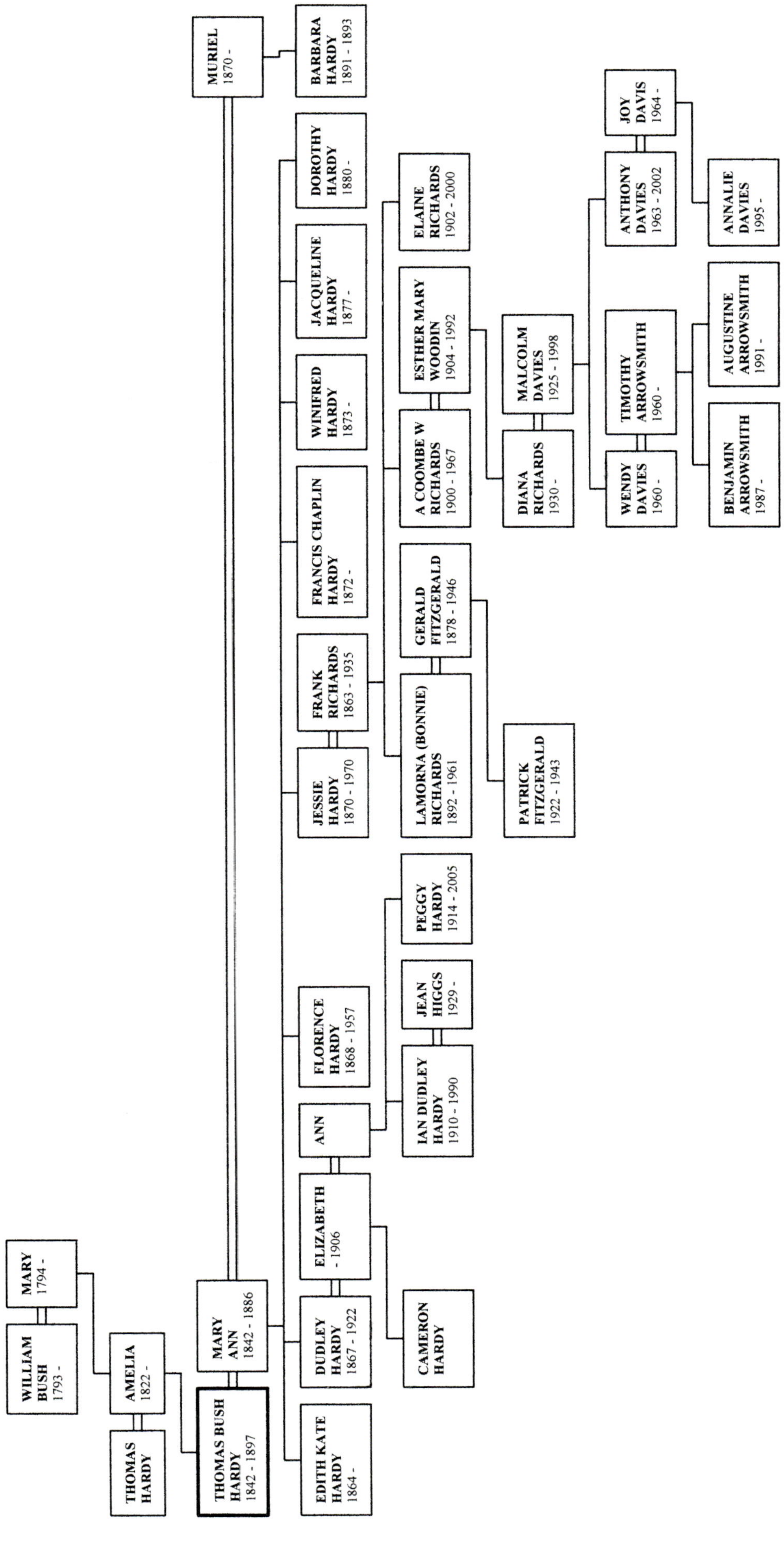

Chapter 2 – Thomas Bush Hardy and his Family – a Biography

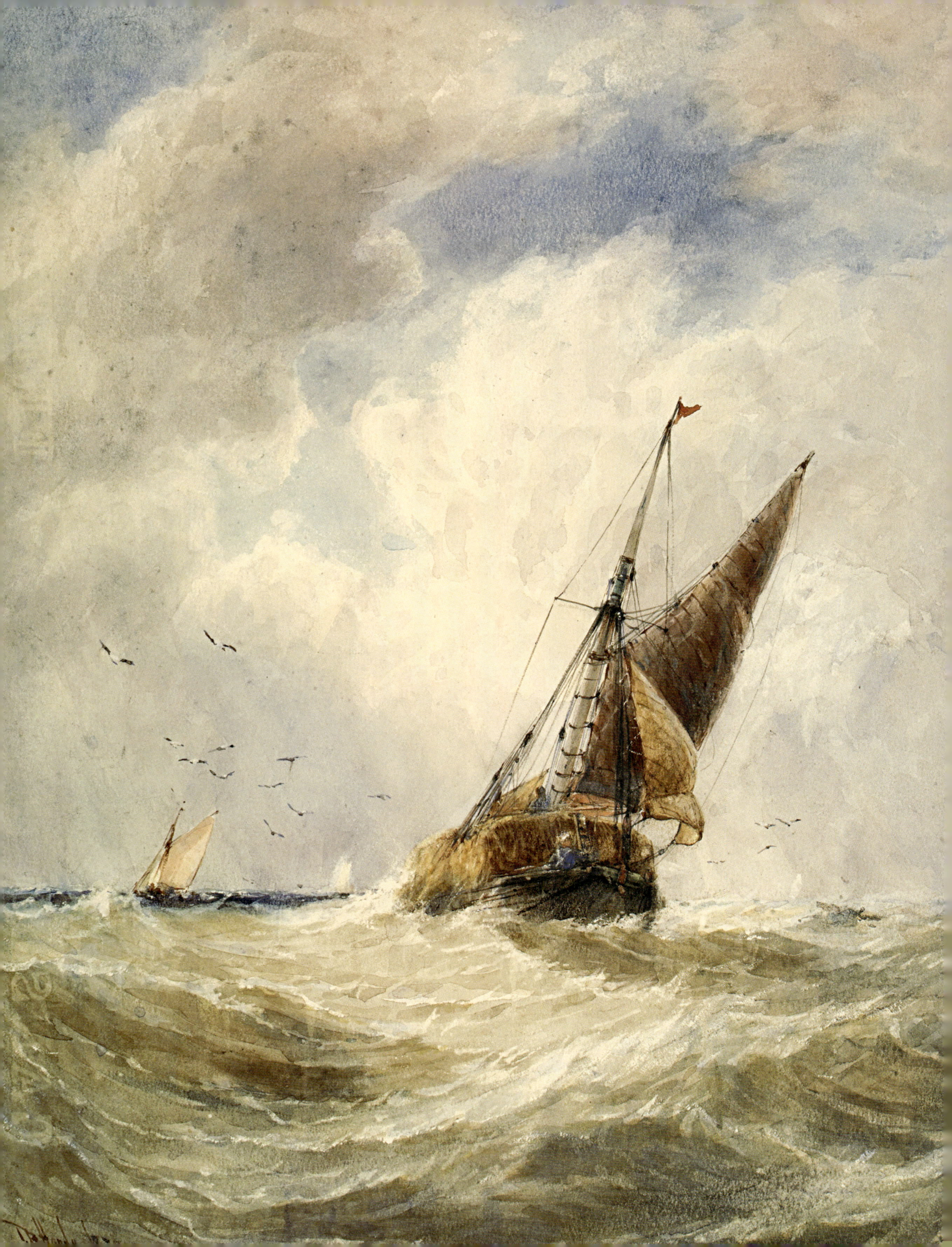

The English Coast

Unlike William Callow and E.W. Cooke, both well-established marine artists before Thomas Bush Hardy was born, Hardy never kept a diary and was clearly not a prolific correspondent. This would have proved a major obstacle for any biographer but, fortunately, he not only signed but also inscribed and dated a large proportion of his paintings. This allows us to trace his movements around England, the Netherlands, France and Italy with some accuracy and, more importantly, to see when, why and how his artistic style and technique developed over the years. It also helps to separate the good from the indifferent, for an inscribed title in his spidery handwriting is a reliable indication that the work is a genuine Hardy and one of which he personally approved.

In common with many other marine artists, Hardy covered most of the East Coast, the Rivers Thames and Medway and the South Coast as far as Cornwall. Bamburgh Castle, a scene he was to visit and paint many times, appears as early as 1871, followed by the Tyne, Whitby, Scarborough, Caister, Lowestoft and Yarmouth. Greenwich Hospital would become one of his favourite subjects; the Pool of London, Lower Thames, Medway and Essex Coast also featured regularly. The Kent Coast including Margate, Broadstairs, Ramsgate, Deal, Dover and Folkestone were often visited in the 1880s and 1890s. Further along the South Coast, Hardy painted scenes at Hastings, Pevensey, Eastbourne, Newhaven, Shoreham, Portsmouth, Bridport, Torquay, Dartmouth, Plymouth and Fowey, most of these in the period 1885-1895. He also paid at least one visit to Wales to paint the

Plate 3.1. **Hay Barge in a Rough Sea.** *Signed and dated 1878. 33.5 x 24.5cm (13¼ x 9⅝in.)*

This portrait-shaped watercolour of a hay barge making fine progress with a blustery wind and heavy sea on her starboard quarter is an example of Hardy at his brilliant best. Here he has painted the kind of short, steep waves that can be whipped up off the Essex and Kent coasts by a combination of wind against tide. Hardy's waves here have an extraordinary realism – cold, wet, moving masses of continually changing colour and density, spume and spray. Later on in his career, in painting the sea Hardy experimented by using more Chinese White and by rubbing, cutting and slicing the paper, but he never again attained or even approached the standard he himself had set in the late 1870s.

Mumbles outcrop of rocks off the Gower Peninsula, the scene of many ship-wrecks over the centuries. He may also have spent a day or two in the Channel Islands, but a watercolour of Guernsey currently attributed to Hardy may have been painted by one of his students.

A selection of Hardy's paintings of the English Coast is reproduced in the following pages in approximate chronological order, by location, accompanied by a text commenting on each picture and any subsequent painting of the same subject.

Only a few works by Hardy have been found that genuinely date from the 1860s. Very recently a private collector, Mr Paul Petrou, acquired a fine drawing in brown washes of a marine subject clearly signed (in capital letters) and dated 1867 (see Plate 3.2). The concentration of shipping in the picture, including a number of square-rigged merchantmen and at least one East Indiaman, suggest that the subject could be Liverpool, to which port Hardy had returned from the United States in 1862. For an amateur, not known to have had any previous instruction in painting, he has already begun to show a good grasp of essentials – composition and, for a budding marine artist, the ability to paint boats and every other type of vessel actually floating in the water: 'seaborne' best describes it.

Plate 3.2. **Liverpool.** *Signed and dated 1867. 12 x 10cm (4¾ x 4in.)*

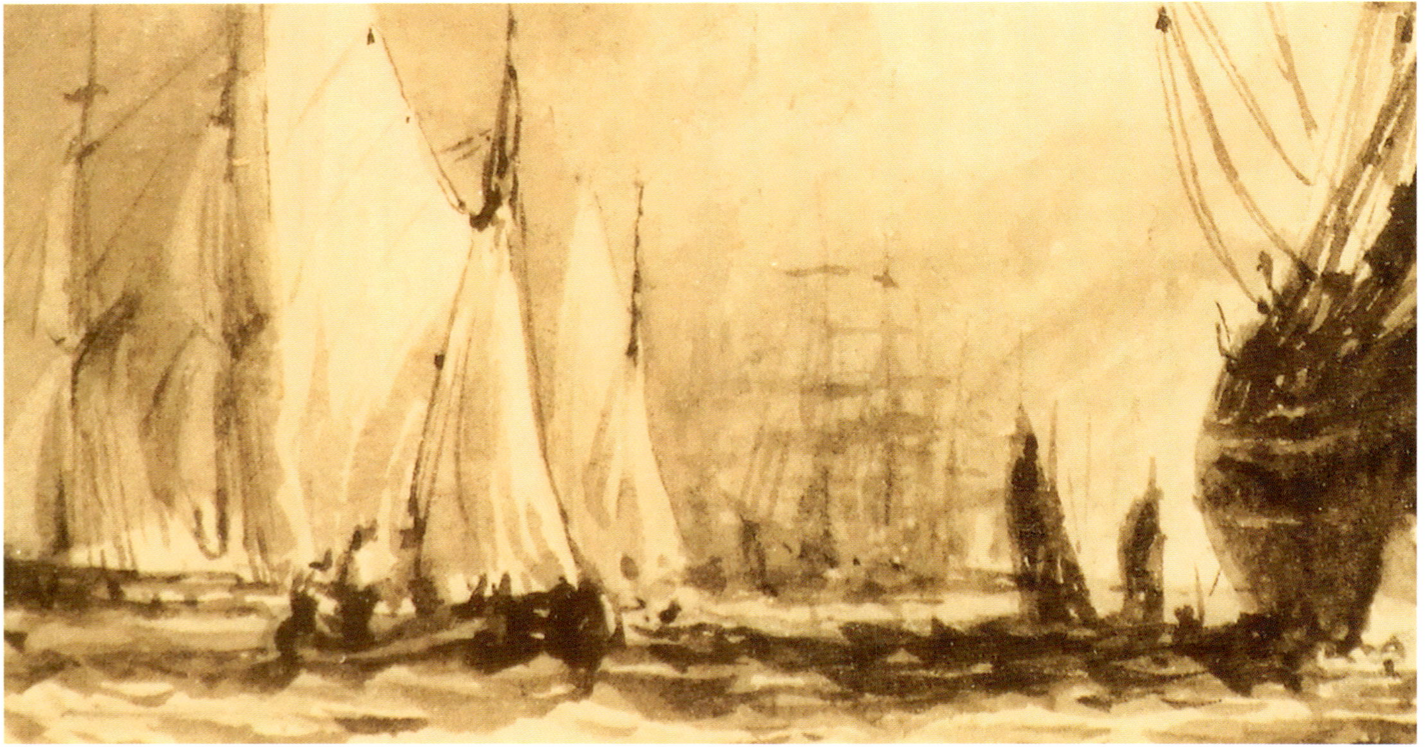

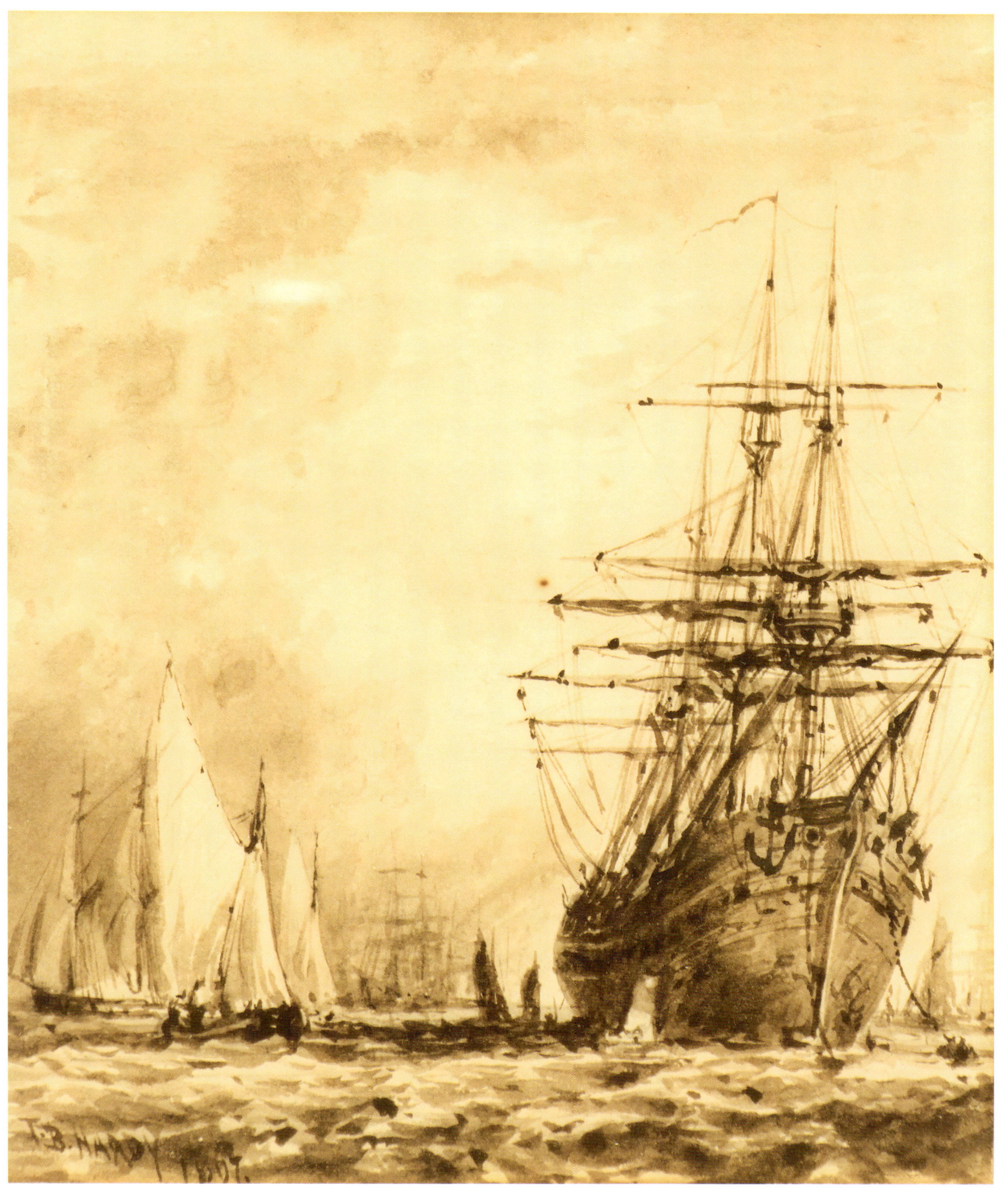

One of his earliest known dated watercolours to reach the market in recent years was a delightful study of a river ferry dated 1869 (see Plate 3.3). The only other known watercolours with a date prior to the 1870s were both of Scarborough. This would imply that, before the family moved from Sheffield to London in 1870, Hardy restricted his subjects to local Yorkshire scenes and the opportunities provided by the occasional summer holiday on the East Coast.

The earliest of Hardy's dated watercolours, this delightful rural scene shows a shallow draught wooden ferry about to transport two ponies and a number of foot passengers across a tree-lined river. Waiting on the other bank, about eighty yards away, is a small group of people, while upstream two anglers in waders are fly-fishing for brown trout. The stone cottages on the country road leading down to the ferry are probably in Yorkshire, not far from Sheffield.

This watercolour shows that Hardy, now in his early twenties, was already a very competent artist and was probably beginning to exhibit some of his work in a local gallery. The subject is interesting, the composition and colouring are good, the figure and animal drawing is of a high standard and the reflections in the water are excellent. Altogether a most attractive painting.

Plate 3.3. **The River Ferry.** *Signed and dated 1869. 26.5 x 21cm (10⅜ x 8¼ in.)*

It could well have been Scarborough with its crowded harbour, beaches and colourful fishing boats that inspired Hardy to concentrate on painting more and more marine and coastal scenes. Thanks to the rapidly growing railway network, improved roads and steam packet ferry services from London and other ports, artists were able to travel extensively and provide their patrons, art galleries and publishers with what are now historic images of nineteenth century England.

Chapter 3 – The English Coast

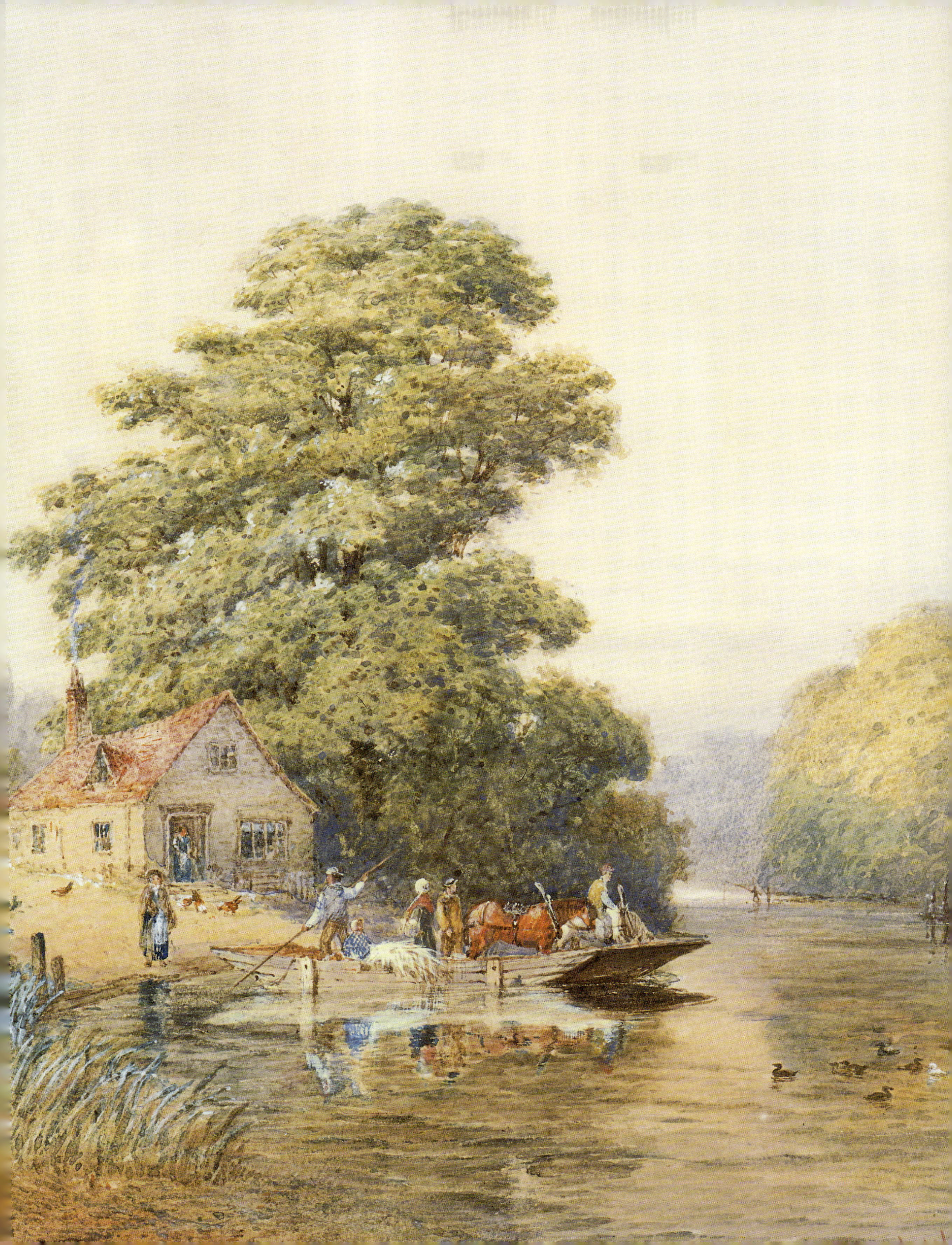

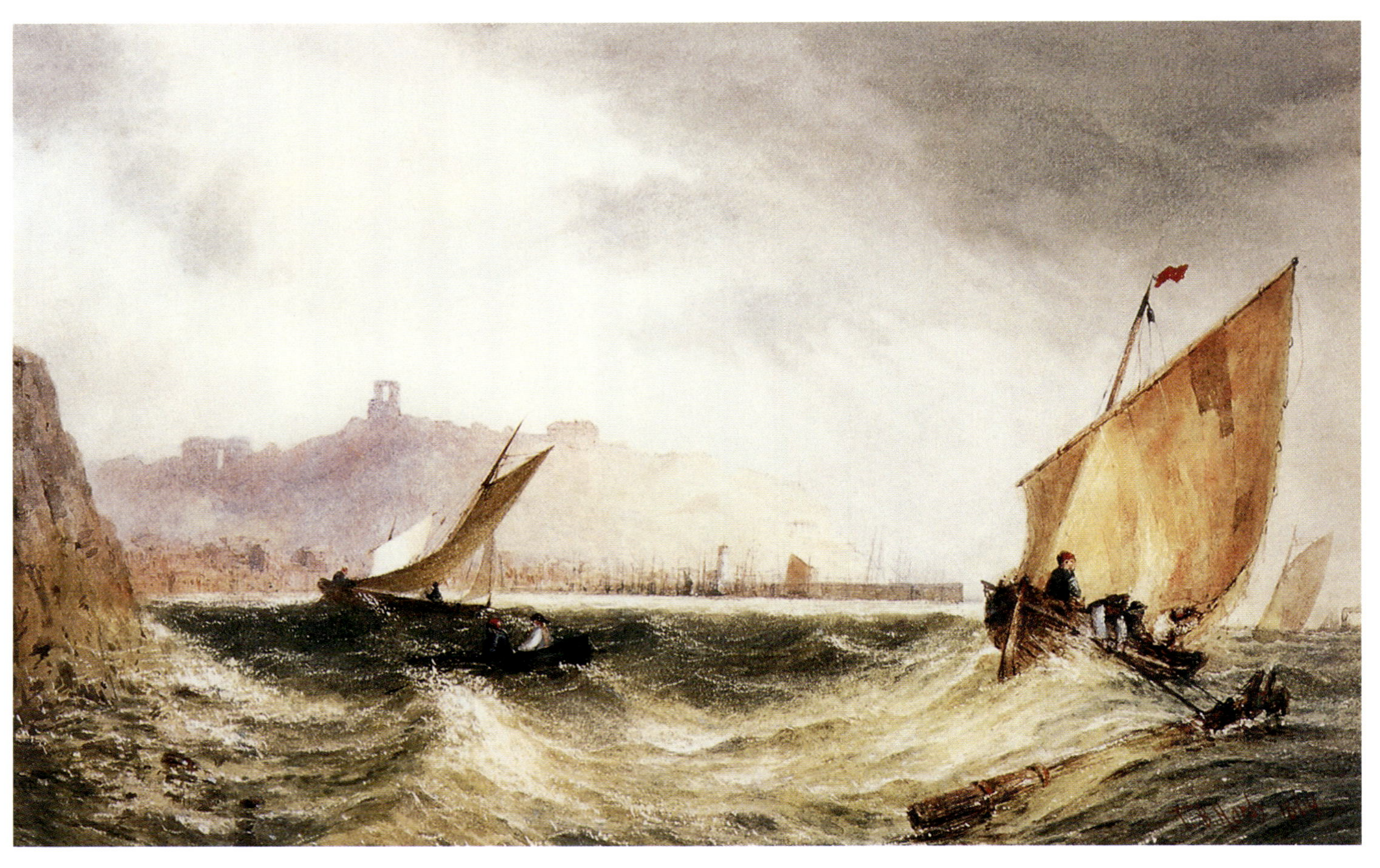

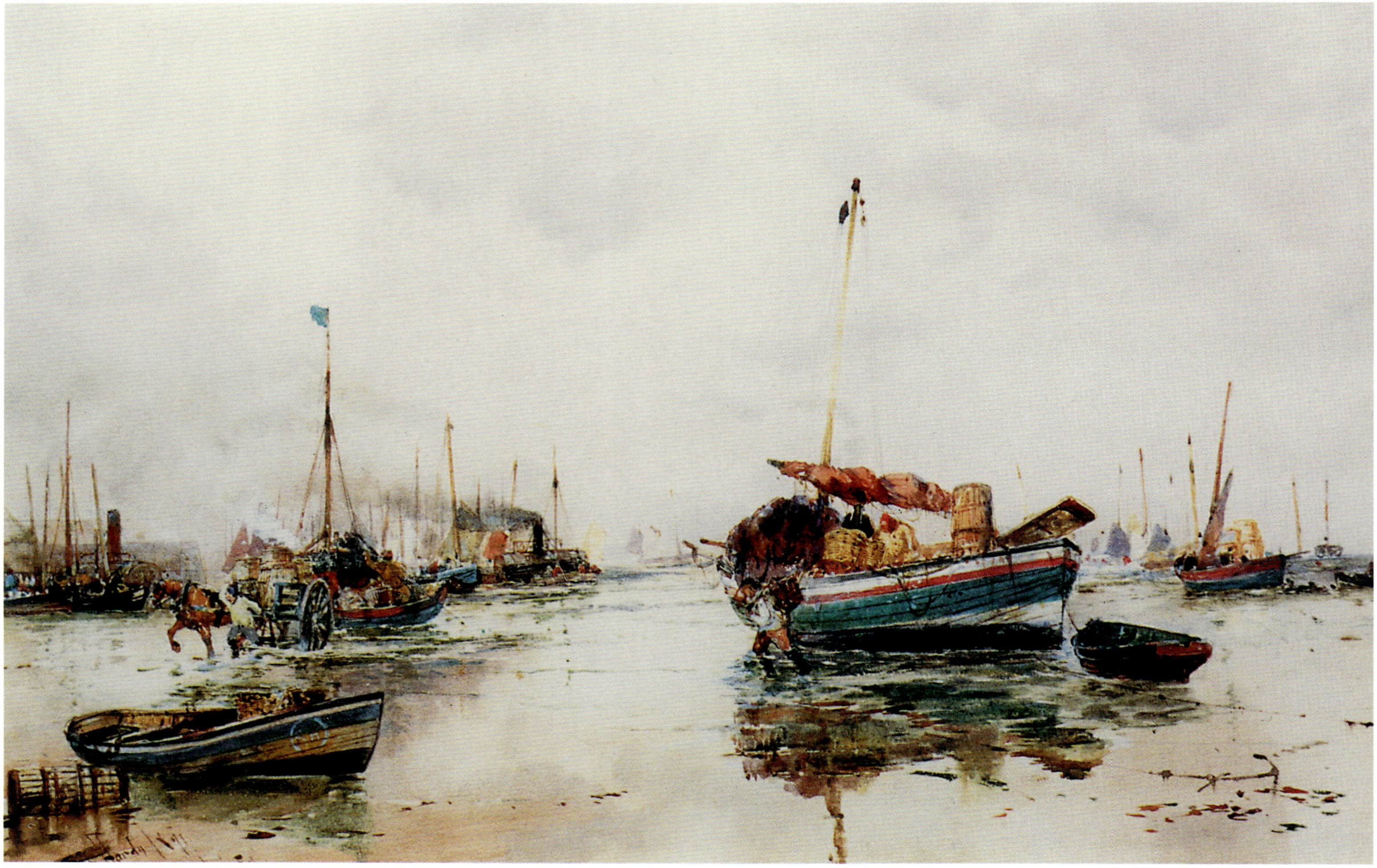

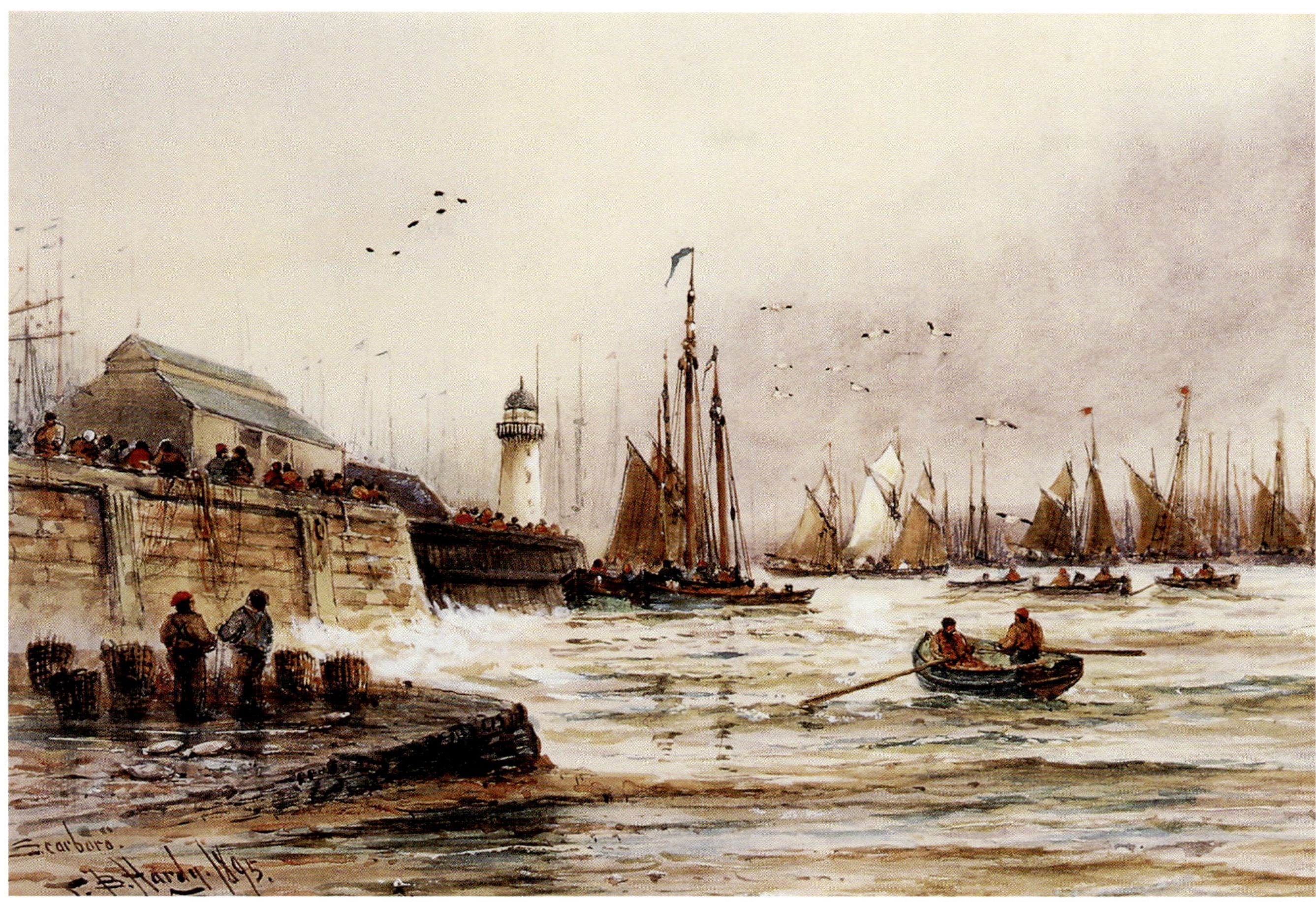

Plate 3.6. **Scarborough.**
*Signed, inscribed and dated
1895. 31 x 48.5cm (12¼ x
19⅛in.)*

Opposite above. Plate 3.4.
Shipping off Scarborough.
*Signed and dated 1869.
21 x 33cm (8¼ x 13in.)*

Opposite below. Plate 3.5.
**South Bay, Scarborough,
Landing Fish.** *Signed,
inscribed and dated 1891.
35.6 x 50.8cm (14 x 20in.)*

This is undoubtedly one of Hardy's better paintings of the mid-1890s when, sadly, much of his output was of very indifferent quality. Here, however, he was very much on home ground, in an environment he knew well and among people whose company he enjoyed. A calm evening with the sea lapping gently against the harbour wall, scores of fishing vessels arriving to unload their catches, many small boats ferrying to and from the anchorage and an expectant crowd awaiting their fishermen's return. This was a scene he had witnessed so often in the past, but now so seldom. One gets the feeling that, away from London and all his actual or imagined problems, here, back in Yorkshire, he was probably at his happiest and most contented.

This is a very interesting early watercolour as it pre-dates every other marine watercolour Hardy painted (and dated) by at least a year. The scene is certainly Scarborough and the fishing boats very close inshore near the Nab Rocks are experiencing a strong offshore breeze. In the authors' opinion it is a perfectly genuine and correctly dated watercolour by Hardy, probably painted during a summer holiday at Yorkshire's developing spa resort. It is not the best of compositions, but Hardy has painted the turbulence where waves meet a rocky shore with some panache.

This colourful and busy picture shows two crabbing cobles being unloaded at low tide with an array of small craft in the background. Hardy draws on his experience and makes full use of his ability to create stunningly realistic reflections in the water, full of colour and movement. The hazy blue sky forecasts a pleasantly warm summer's day and the prospect of some good catches.

Chapter 3 – The English Coast

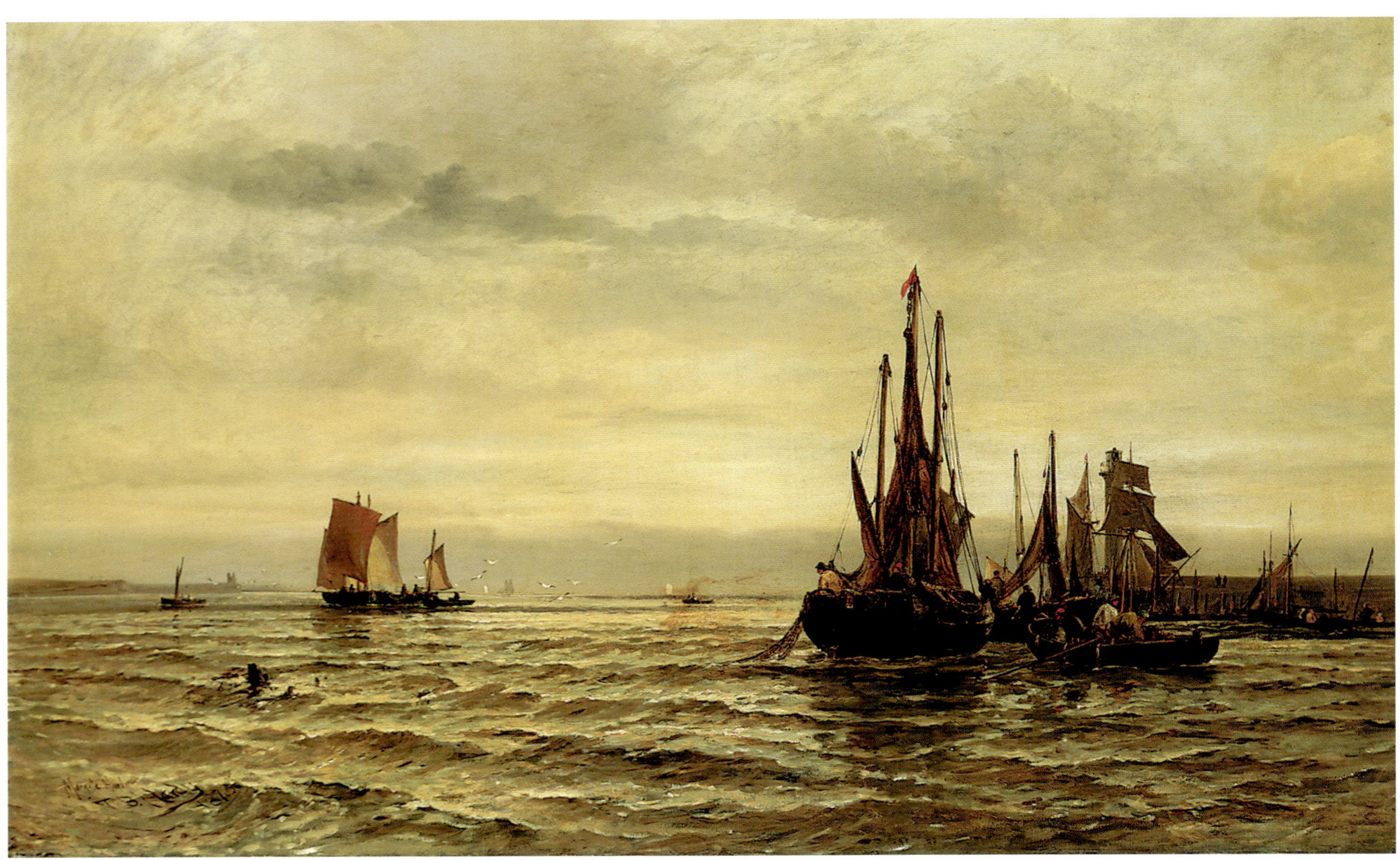

An early painting and one of Hardy's few oils. A comparatively large work showing Margate harbour in an evening light not long before dusk. A moderate breeze is filling the sails of two fishing boats leaving harbour, while inside, obscuring the lighthouse on the end of the breakwater, a cluster of fishing boats complete their day's work, washing and drying their nets and sails. Hardy has drawn the incoming tide and wavelets with convincing observation.

Plate 3.7. **Margate Harbour.** *Signed, inscribed and dated 1873. 77 x 127cm (30¼ x 50in.)*

Another early work in watercolour, recording a cloudy, calm day at low water. Running from the right towards the centre is a wooden groyne built of sturdy timbers. In the foreground and to the left, two women discuss the catch of the day while behind them two men prepare their small boat for fishing – one is preparing his line while the other digs for sandworms as bait. Beyond, a Thames spritsail barge is about to pass the tall lighthouse to join other sailing craft already secured alongside. The reflection of the clouds in the flat harbour waters adds further tranquillity to an essentially peaceful scene.

Opposite above. Plate 3.8. **Margate Harbour.** *Signed, inscribed and dated 1874. 23.8 x 36.5cm (9⅜ x 14⅜in.)*

A rare landscape by Hardy, a stunning downland view over the woods above Arundel Castle and the winding river Arun to the sea. It is an autumnal scene, the harvest has been gathered and the trees are beginning to turn. Two figures are seen resting in the foreground after an exhausting climb up from the town, now a very elegant and fashionable place to live – and a famous Roman Catholic Cathedral about to be completed. Hardy was known to have painted the nearby village of Rustington, much closer to the sea, and the lobster fishermen still active in the area.

Opposite below. Plate 3.9. **Arundel Castle to the Sea.** *Signed, inscribed and dated 1875. 32 x 50cm (12⅝ x 19⅝in.)*

Chapter 3 – The English Coast

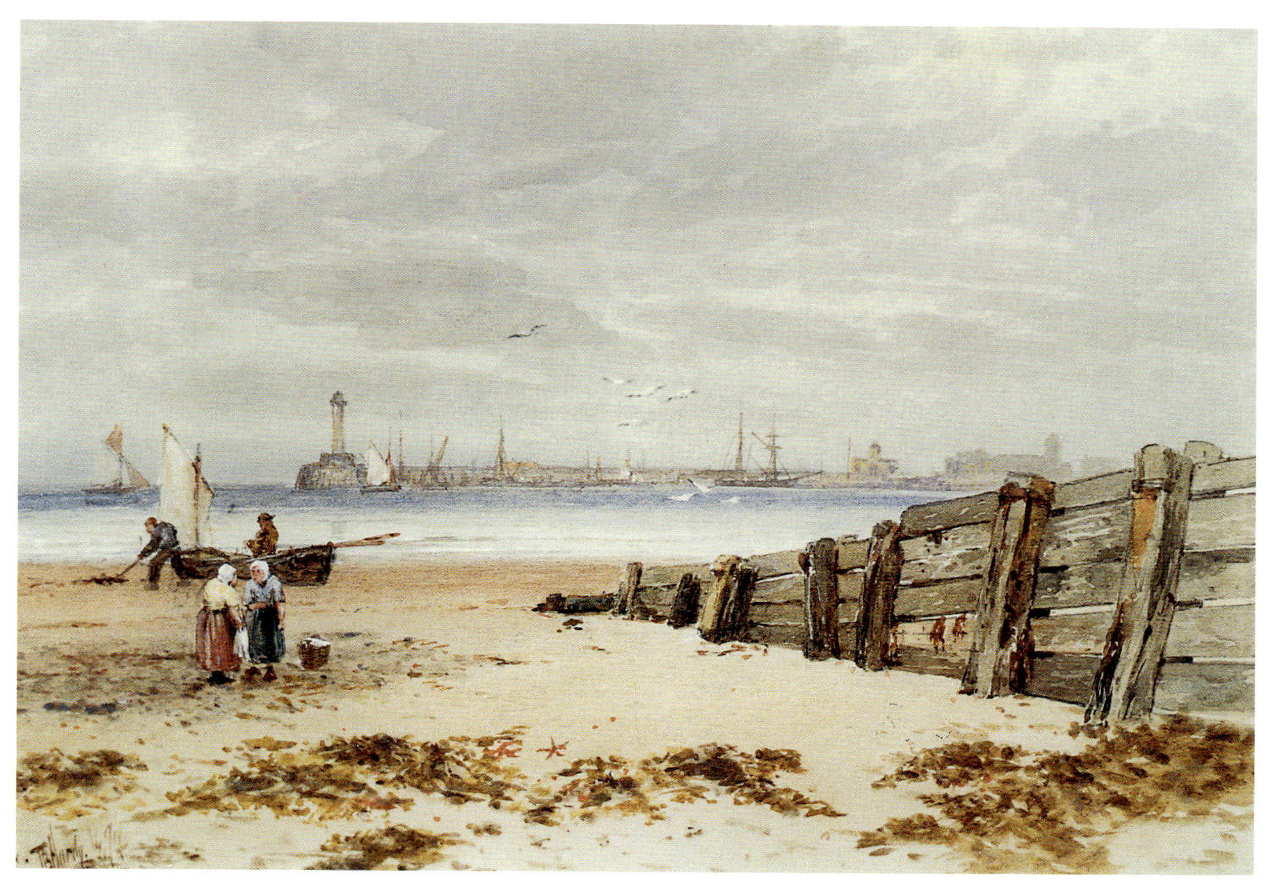

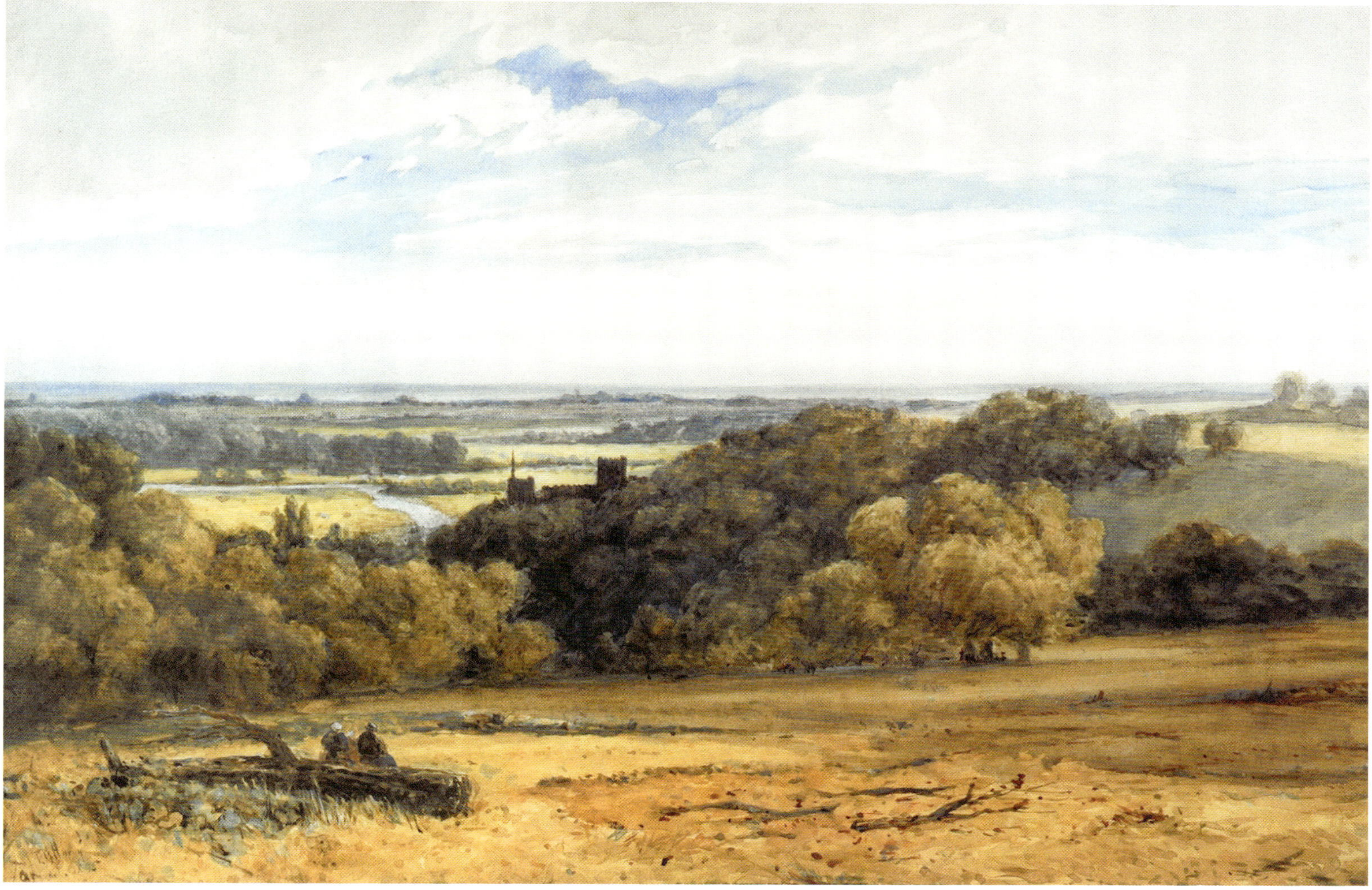

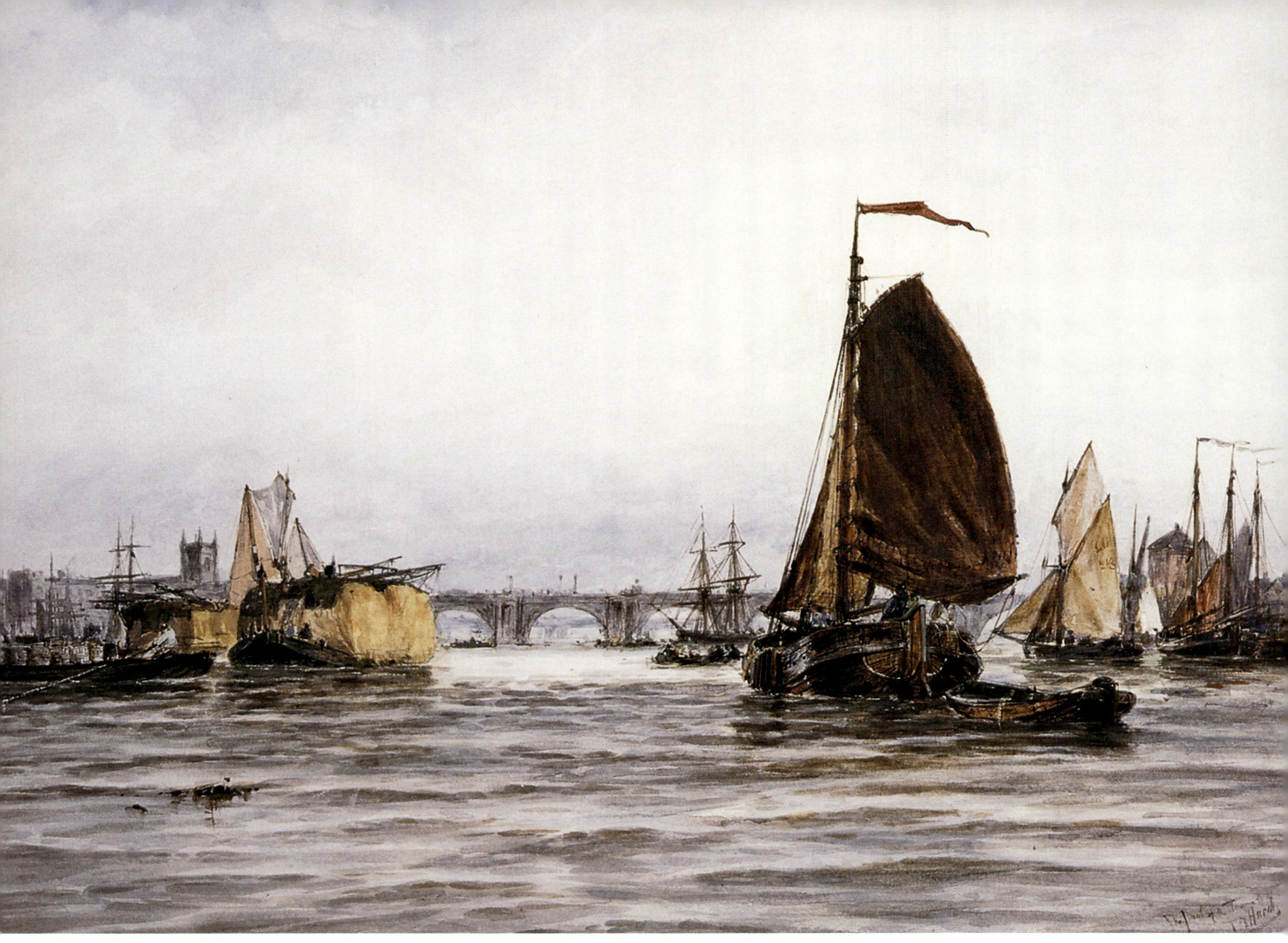

An early, highly finished watercolour showing Hardy's already well-developed ability at painting rippling water beneath a rather colourless, cloudy sky. The subject itself is one Hardy must have seen many times and he has done it justice. Note particularly the way the barges and smaller craft are floating correctly in the water, a displacement problem proving too difficult for many artists. Hardy has shown us a busy Thames but one still, for the time being, relatively empty of coal-fired steam tugs and freighters. We can be sure that the Thames itself was pretty filthy – the population was increasing rapidly and, despite Greater London having the finest sewage system of any European city, two tides a day left a lot not to be desired. But the smoke, grime, coal dust and oil had not yet arrived in force – other artists were to portray that era before the end of the century. Meanwhile, for most of the year, the air was reasonably clean, the visibility clear and the atmosphere probably sweeter on the river than on the streets.

Plate 3.10. **The Pool of the Thames.** *Signed, inscribed and dated 1875. 33 x 47cm (13 x 18½in.)*

Chapter 3 – The English Coast

Until the completion of Tower Bridge in 1894, London Bridge remained the only link for road traffic and pedestrians from the south serving a busy and fast-growing commercial port. Long delays were inevitable and for years the situation in this area was pretty chaotic. Notwithstanding, Hardy has managed to give the impression of some calm and control amid the confusion. At least it is dry and warm, the central arches of the bridge gleaming in the sunlight. It is also very windy, the ensign on the Dutch barge and the flapping foresail on the adjacent freighter bear witness to that. On the left, the skipper of the hay barge unloading his cargo into a dumb lighter is having difficulty preventing the hay from blowing away. Many other barges can be seen up river from the bridge transporting coal and newly arrived goods from abroad to the suburbs up to and beyond Teddington Lock. The Thames, its tributaries and canals were vital arteries in the country's transport system in those days. Hardy is telling us that the heart still beat well in the Pool of London.

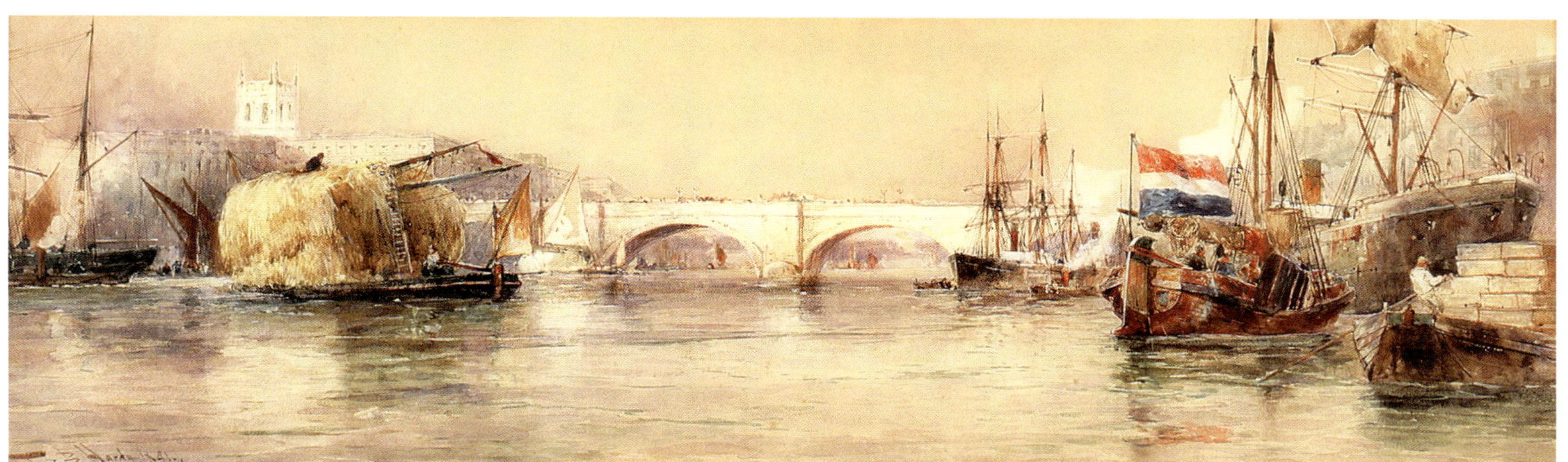

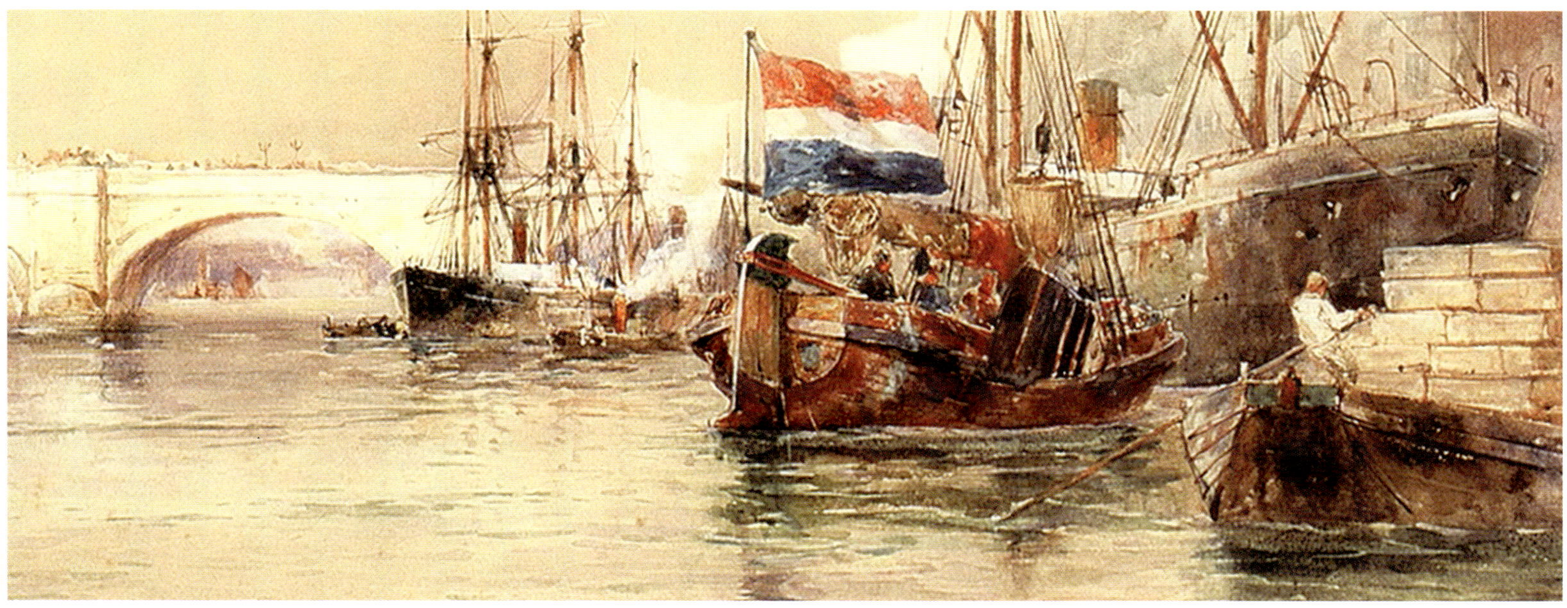

Chapter 3 – The English Coast

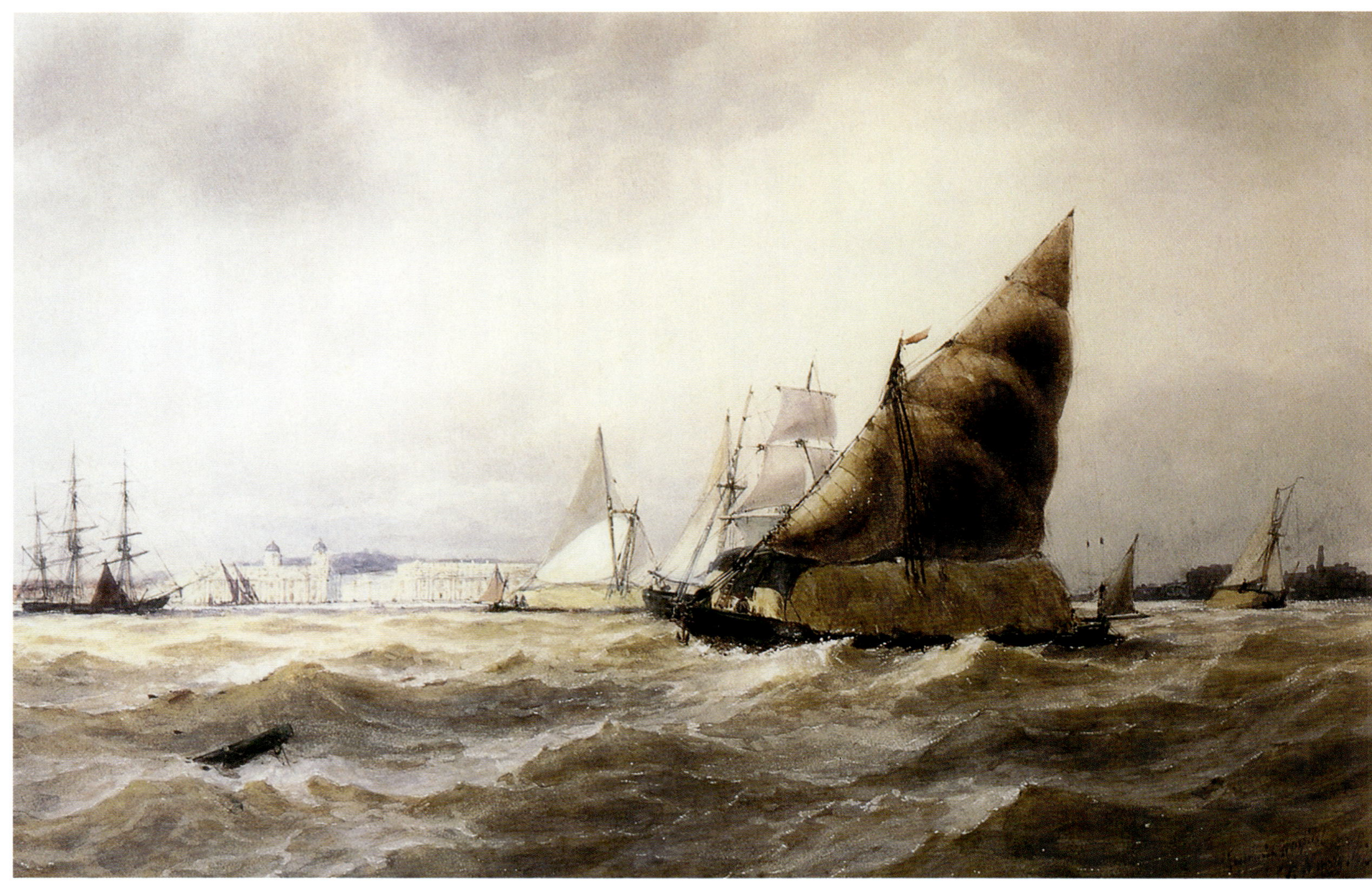

For an artist living in or near London, the Thames at Greenwich, with its wonderful backdrop of Sir Christopher Wren's Hospital, the Queen's House and the Observatory, was a compelling subject. Hardy's first recorded watercolour sketch of the scene is dated 1871 – four years later the above painting shows him approaching his most productive and artistically successful period. As with many of his Thames views, the ubiquitous hay barge dominates the foreground, but it is the totality of the composition that makes this a fine painting. It is a cold, rather colourless day, but not lacking in interest and beauty for that. And there is plenty of movement in London's ebbing river. Note the Royal Hospital School's training ship moored just down river from the Hospital on the far left.

Plate 3.12. **Off Greenwich Hospital.** *Signed, inscribed and dated 1875. 30 x 46cm (11¾ x 18⅛in.)*

A small pair of watercolours of Greenwich, each showing a view of the Hospital from a different angle. Unlike the earlier painting, Hardy has this time remembered to crown Wren's magnificent buildings with their superb domes. In both watercolours a gaff-rigged barge is the central subject but, in contrast to earlier images, a stiff westerly breeze is creating sizeable waves in a muddy River Thames, testing the seamanship of the barge skippers and their traditional one boy crew. Hardy has captured the low scudding clouds, and you can almost hear the slapping of heavy brown canvas as the lumbering barge forces its way through the choppy waters. All this on a piece of paper not much larger than a small envelope.

Opposite. Plate 3.13. **Off Greenwich.** *A pair, both signed, inscribed and dated 1883. 12 x 17cm (4¾ x 6¾in.)*

Chapter 3 – The English Coast

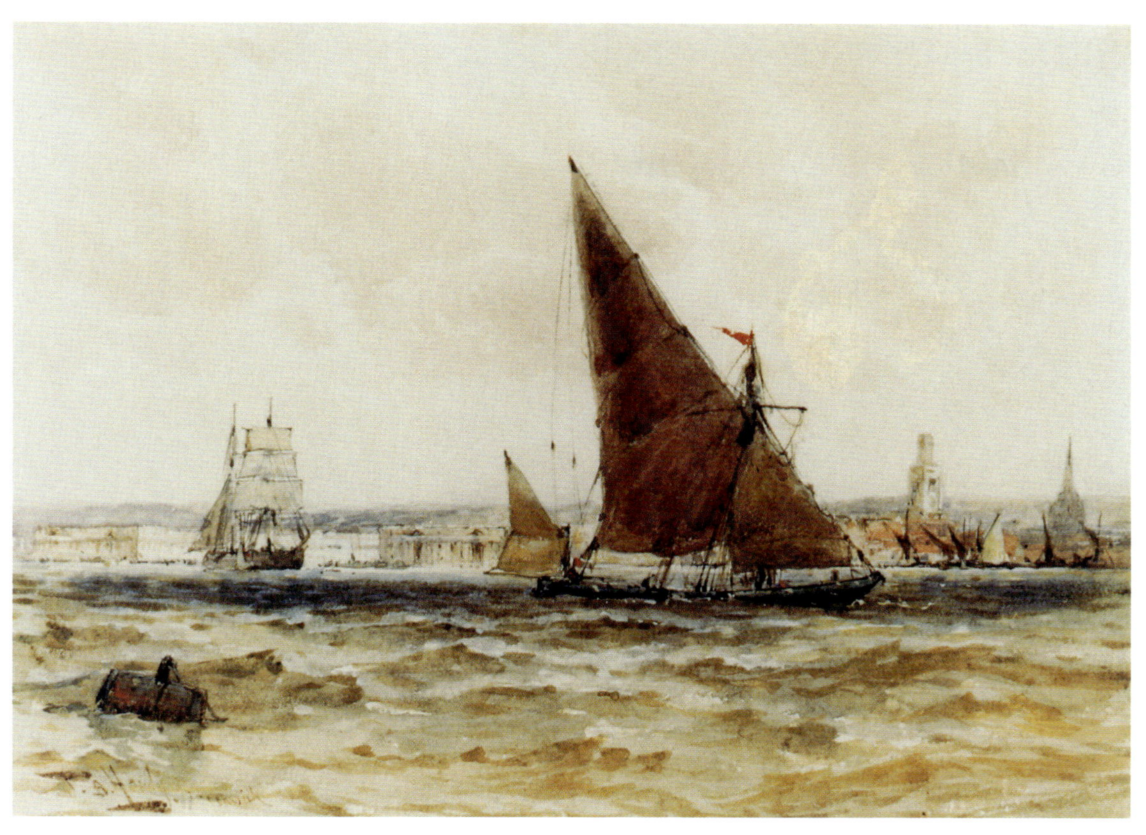

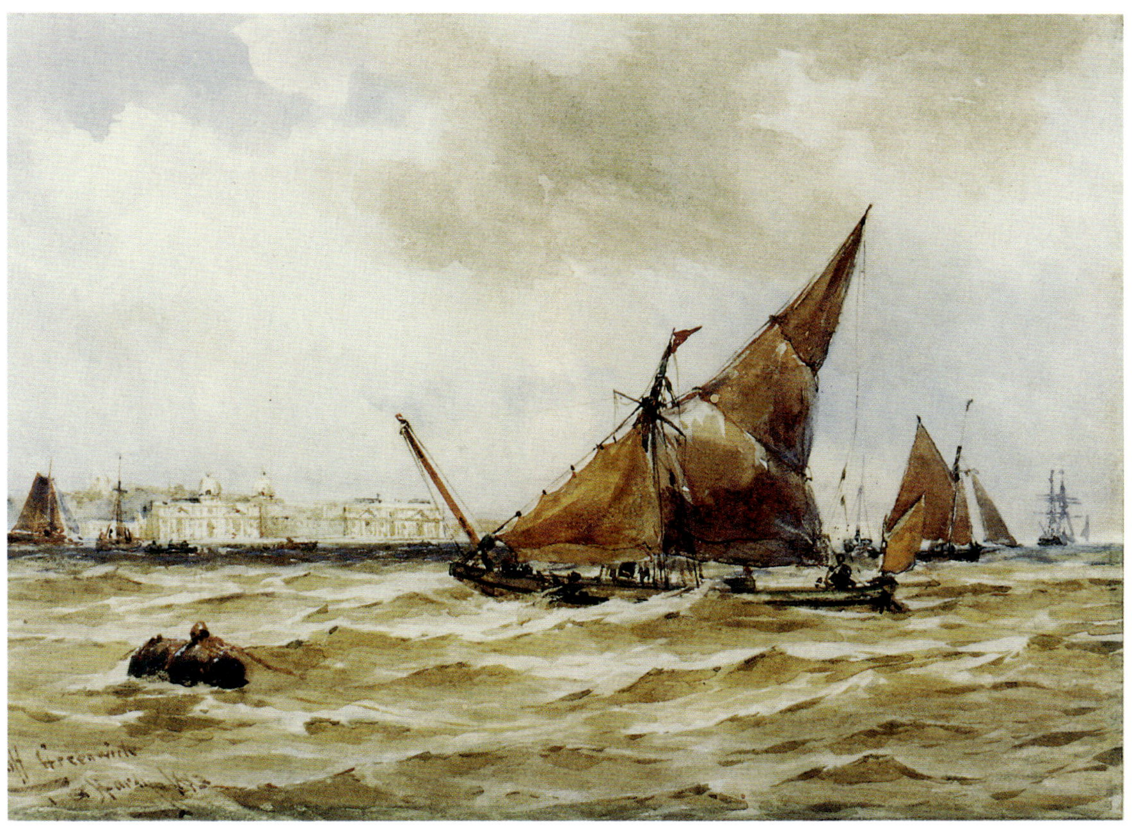

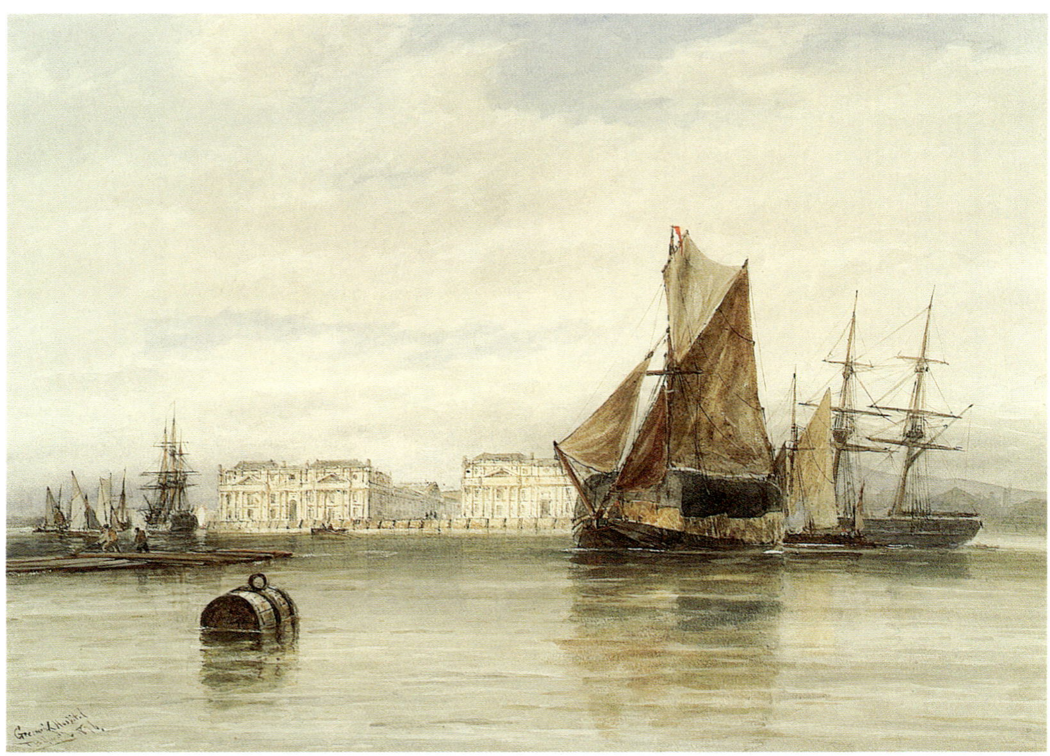

This is the earlier of two watercolours of Greenwich Hospital in the collection of the National Maritime Museum and is noteworthy for the fact that Hardy has omitted Christopher Wren's twin domes! Apart from that artistic 'howler', the painting has much to recommend it. It is probably just before high water and, in very light airs, the ketch-rigged hay barge is making slow progress upstream, reflected quite beautifully in the calm eddies of the Thames. Behind is another hay barge on its way downstream with a load of horse manure for the Essex fields. On the left, moored to a buoy down river from the Hospital, lies the Naval College training ship and some more barges.

This is a particularly fine example of Hardy's many versions of 'The Thames at Greenwich', none of which can be regarded in any way as 'copies'. In this watercolour the artist has painted the scene from a viewpoint many hundreds of yards downstream of the Hospital on a cold, wet and windy day. The tide is flooding against the strong south westerly wind, creating a very choppy Thames which Hardy has drawn with great skill, scraping and rubbing the washed paper to simulate spray and breaking waves. Grey clouds race across the sky and reflect in the dull brown river below. In the foreground a barge laden with manure from the streets and stables of London passes a barge fresh from the hayfields of Essex. To the right, the Royal Hospital School's training frigate strains at her buoy in the tidal stream. Beyond, the wonderful façade and domes of Wren's Hospital shine out of the gloom, arguably better portrayed by Hardy here than on any other occasion.

A bright and breezy sunlit scene that has inspired Hardy to use more colour than usual. It is mid-morning on a summer's day, the barge in the foreground is returning on the ebb tide to its mooring on the Essex coast and there is plenty of other activity on the river on the Deptford side. Greenwich Hospital and adjacent buildings are bathed in sunlight, but the Observatory is in the shadow of a passing cloud. The river itself looks a bit muddier than usual but, on the whole, this scene has much beauty, drawn by an artist who obviously enjoyed painting it and has done so freely with an unerring sureness of touch.

Plate 3.14. **Greenwich Hospital.** *Signed, inscribed and dated 1876. 35.1 x 50cm (13¾ x 19⅝ in.)*

Opposite above. Plate 3.15. **Off Greenwich.** *Signed, inscribed and dated 1876. 19.5 x 30cm (7⅝ x 11¾in.)*

Opposite below. Plate 3.16. **Off Greenwich.** *Signed and inscribed c.1884. 28 x 40.7cm (11 x 16 in.)*

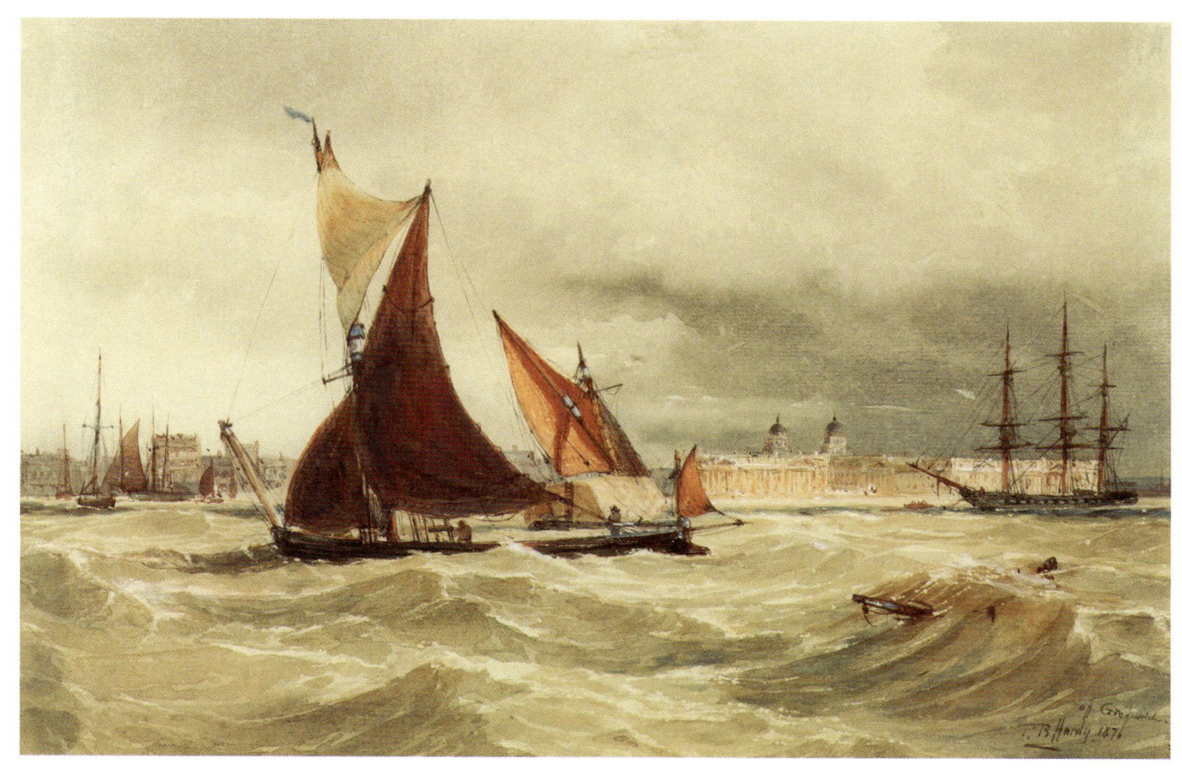

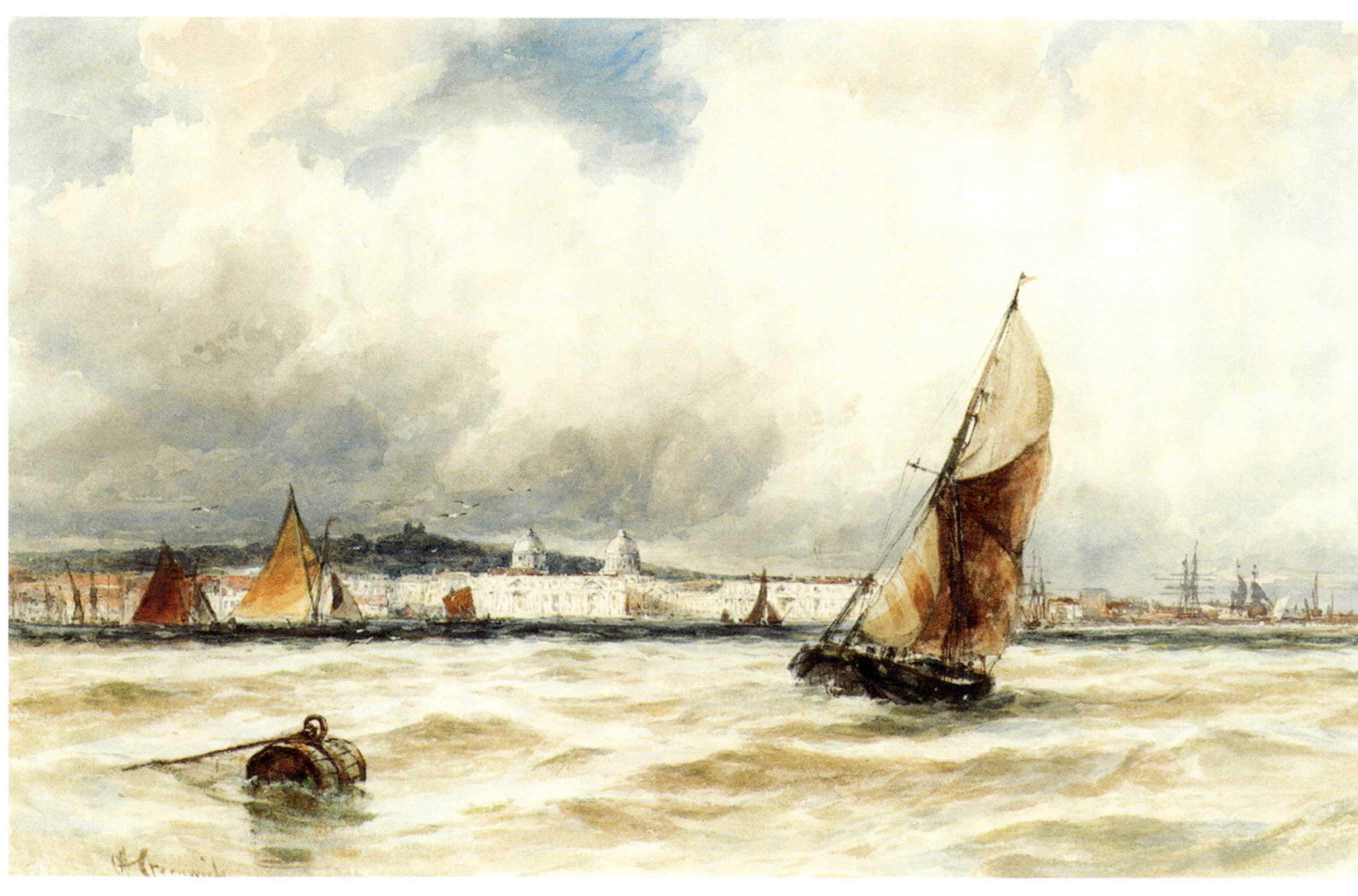

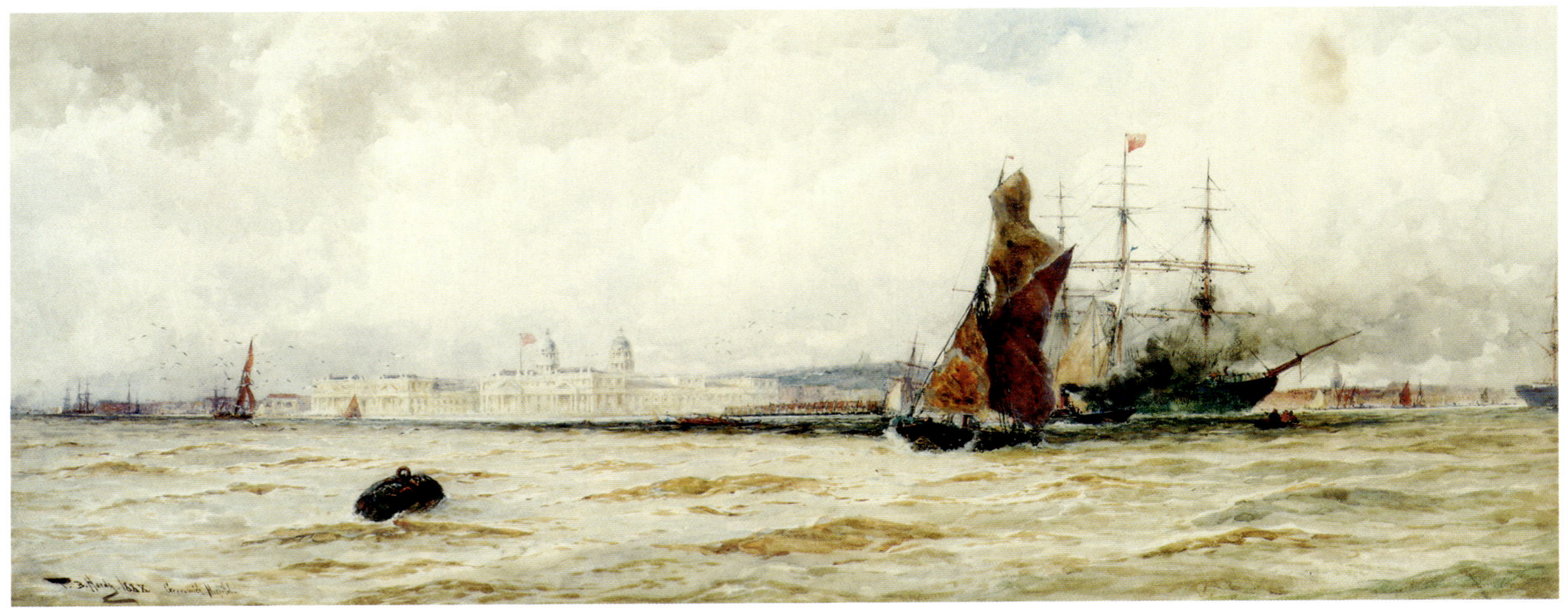

An example of one of Hardy's larger, longer watercolours in which he was able to exploit longitudinal space to great advantage in portraying seascapes, river and beach scenes. Here he has painted an unobstructed and more prominent view of Greenwich Hospital in the background without reducing the importance of the river and its perpetual flow of shipping. Conditions are quite calm with a gentle swell, possibly caused by a fast running ebb tide.

Plate 3.17. **Greenwich Hospital.** *Signed, inscribed and dated 1888. 39.5 x 99cm (15½ x 39in.)*

Another long, narrow watercolour, again of Greenwich from much the same viewpoint as the previous example. The only major difference is that Hardy has placed the Hospital in the background to the right of centre, allowing more space for the shipping moored and under way downstream of the main buildings. An excellent subject which Hardy must have painted many, many times, but this must be numbered among the best. This time he has made full use of Wren's superbly designed buildings as the finest backdrop to be found on London's river.

Opposite above. Plate 3.18. **Off Greenwich.** *Signed and dated 1888. 17 x 50cm (6¾ x 19⅝ in.)*

A very late example of Hardy's watercolours of the Thames at Greenwich if, indeed, it is by Hardy. The one major difference between this and previous examples is the preponderance of blue, grey and green washes he has used in painting the Thames itself in contrast to the muddy browns and yellows in earlier examples. Perhaps it was a much sunnier day, but one suspects that the artist was not painting *en plein air* but used previous sketches and some imagination in trying to produce a different, but still visually attractive image. And, as noted before, the artist has again failed to do justice to Wren's superlative domes. But examine more closely the actual drawing technique. It lacks substance, style and conviction. Look at the hay barge in the foreground, the two men in the boat and the schooner beyond. Hardy was incapable of such weak drawing and would never have signed the finished painting even if it had emanated from his studio. In our opinion this is a very poor copy which should never have come on to the market as being attributed to Hardy.

Opposite centre. Plate 3.19. **Shipping of the Thames off Greenwich.** *Signed and dated 1896. 24 x 59cm (9½ x 23¼ in.)*

Chapter 3 – The English Coast

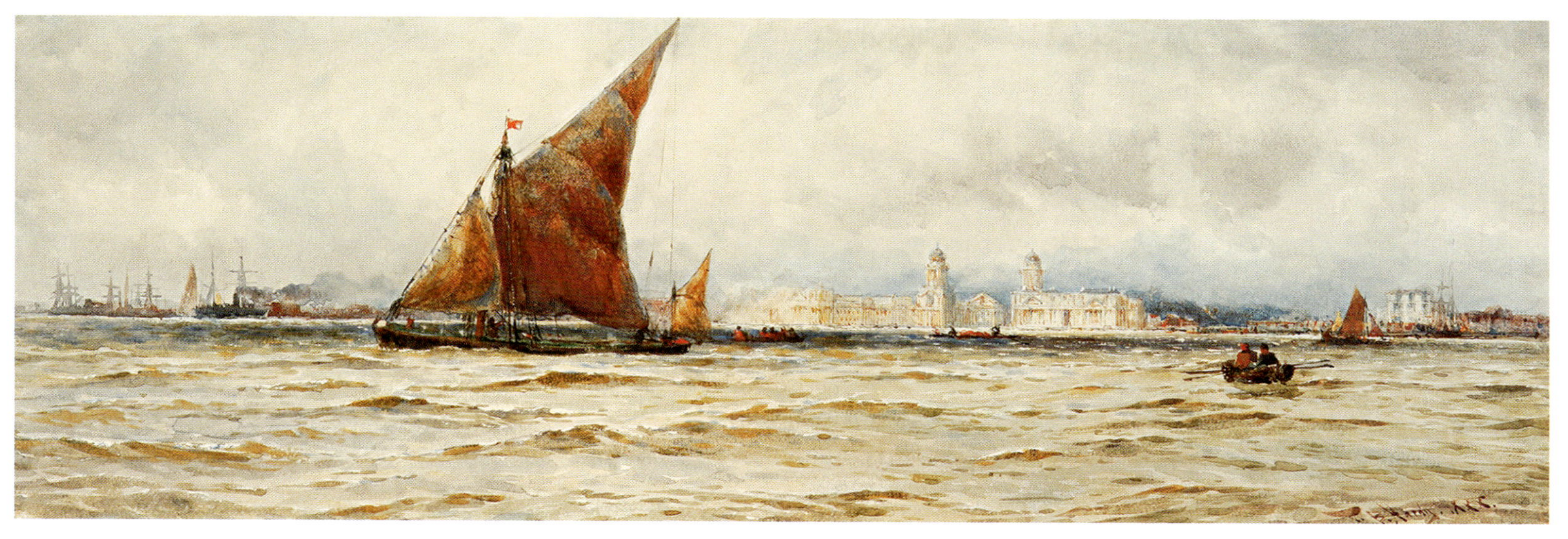

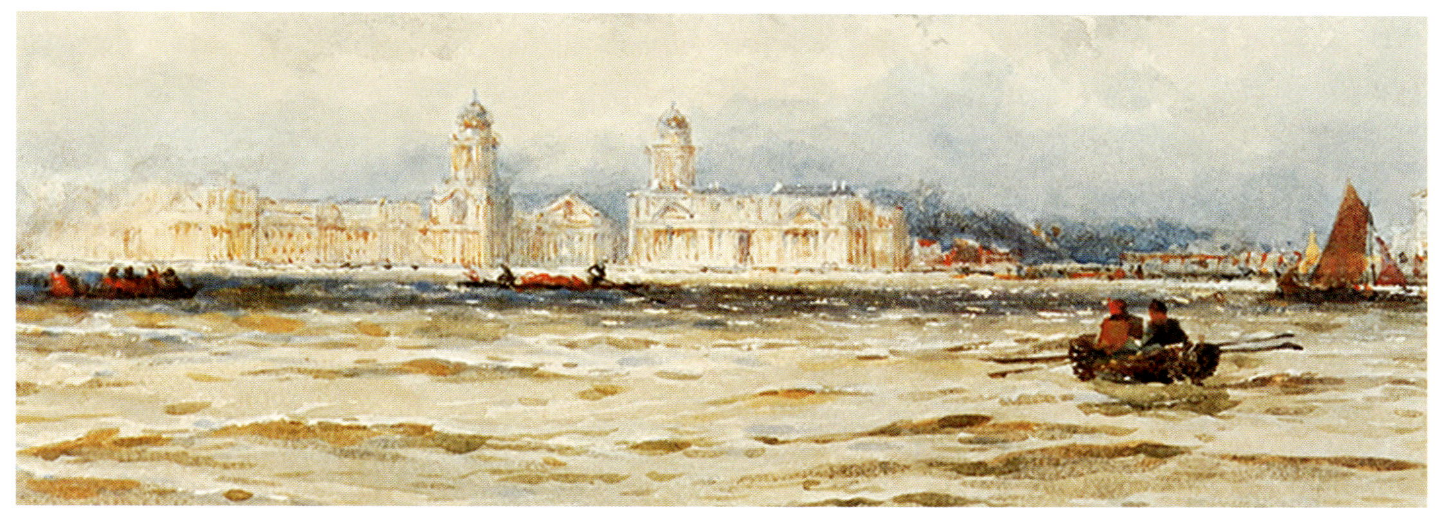

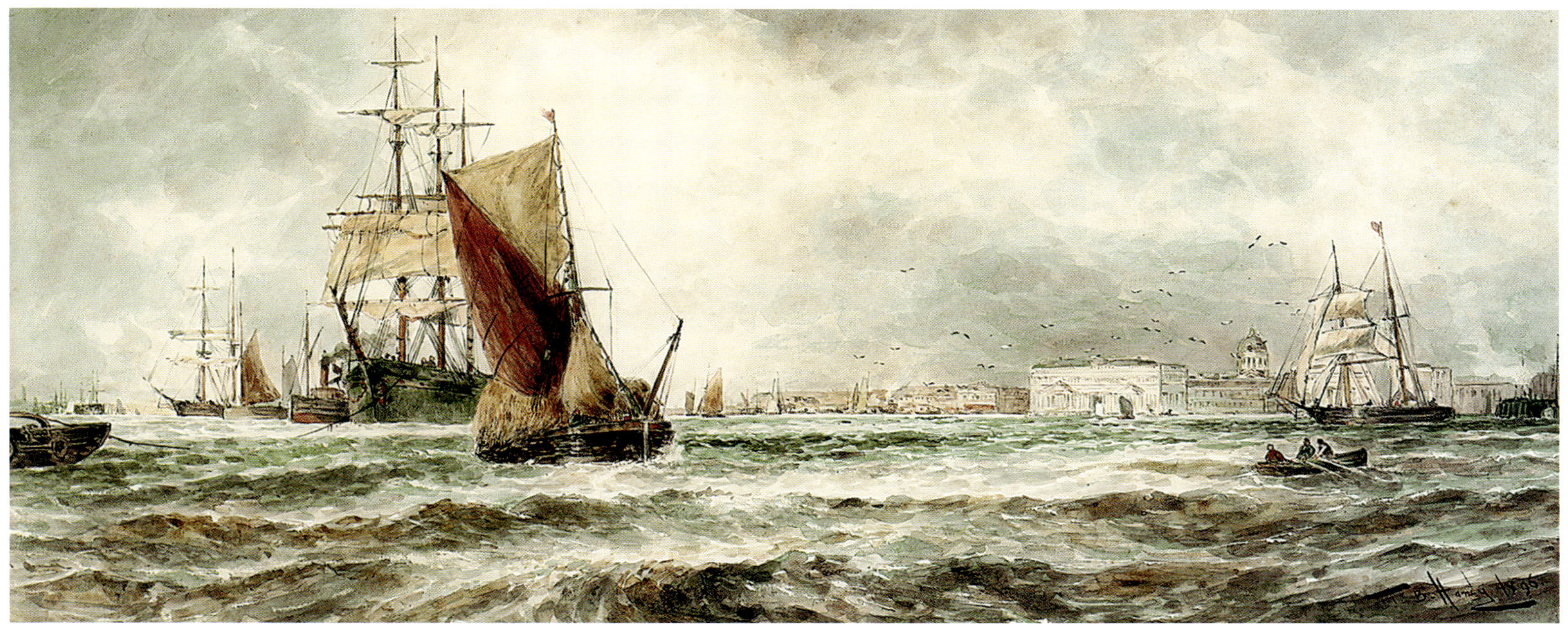

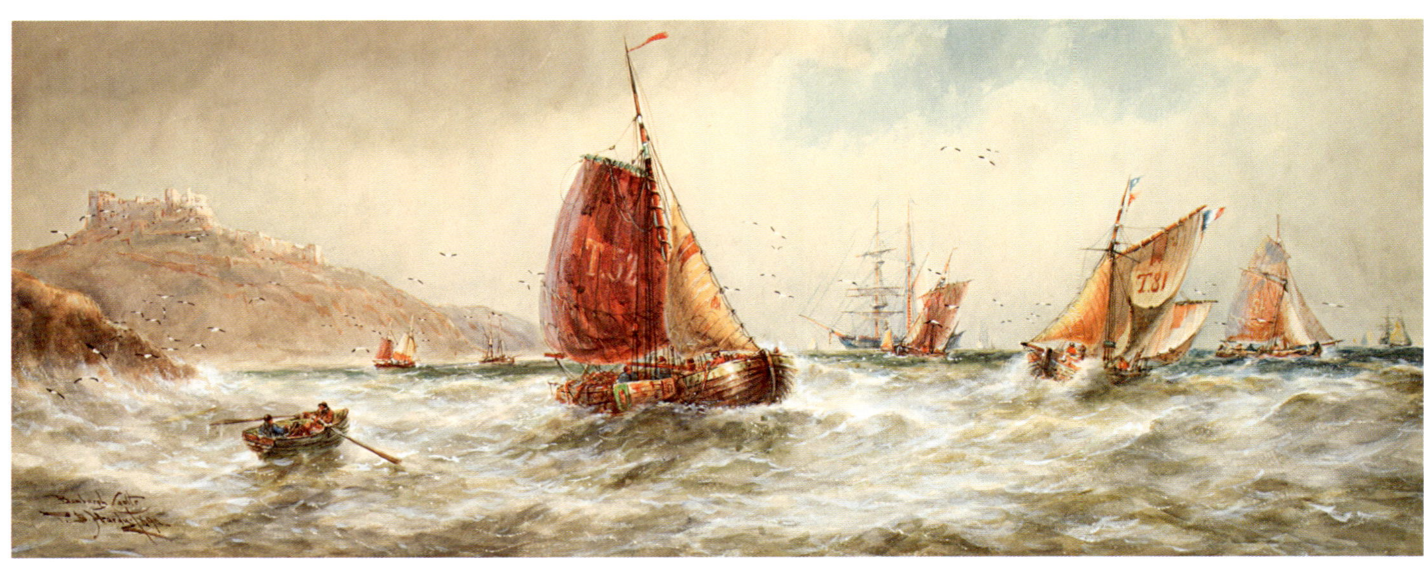

This quite large watercolour evidently portrays a number of Tynemouth cobles and other fishing vessels close inshore in the vicinity of Bamburgh Castle. A strong north-easterly wind and a moderately rough sea seem to be creating some confusion among the craft, which are sailing in all directions dangerously close to the rocky sea shore. In particular, a small dinghy, manned by a single oarsman with an anxious passenger, is unlikely to avoid being swept ashore. Except for the sea, which is well drawn, the entire scene is unconvincing. The composition is clumsy and the colouring pedestrian. The boats themselves, especially the sails, must surely be the work of a student. It is a pity that Hardy signed this work – if indeed he did!

Plate 3.20. **Bamburgh Castle.**
Signed, inscribed and dated 1894. 28.5 x 75.5cm (11¼in. x 29¾in.)

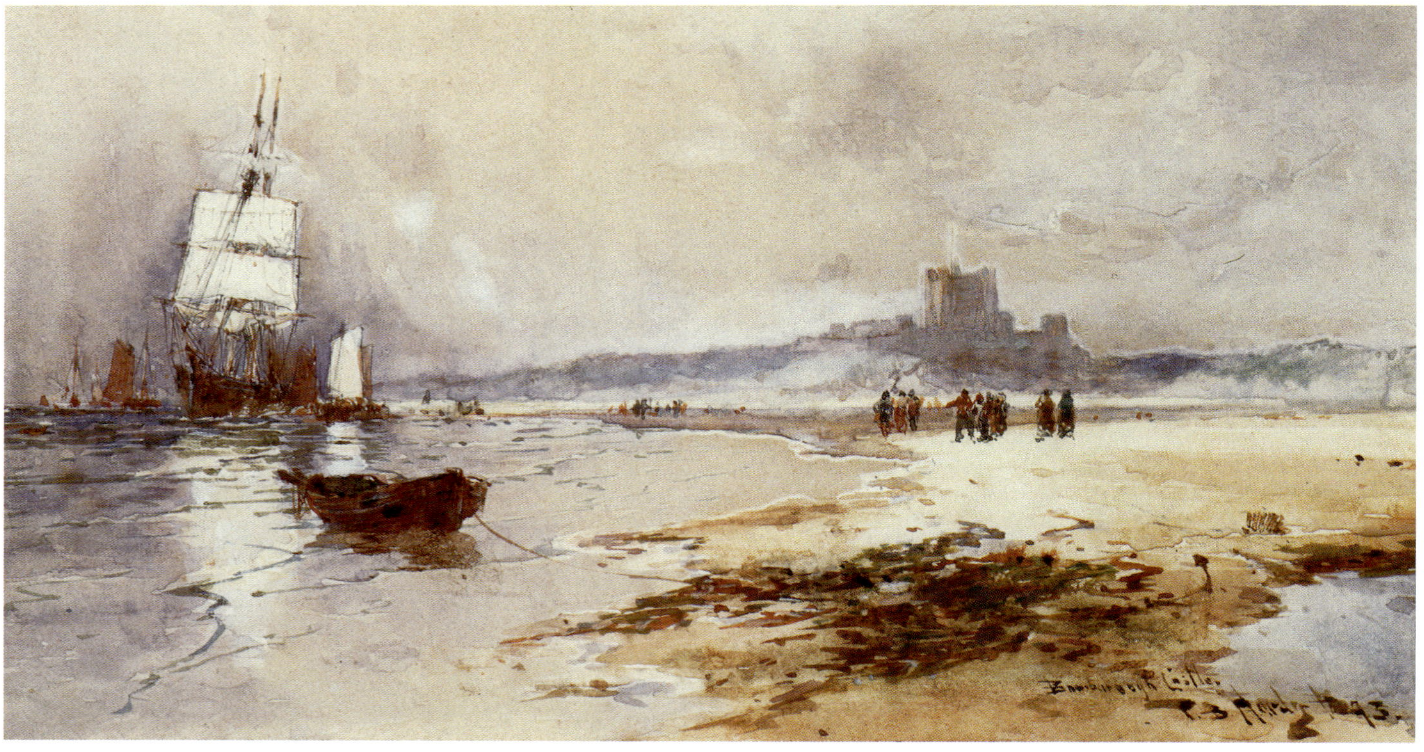

Chapter 3 – The English Coast

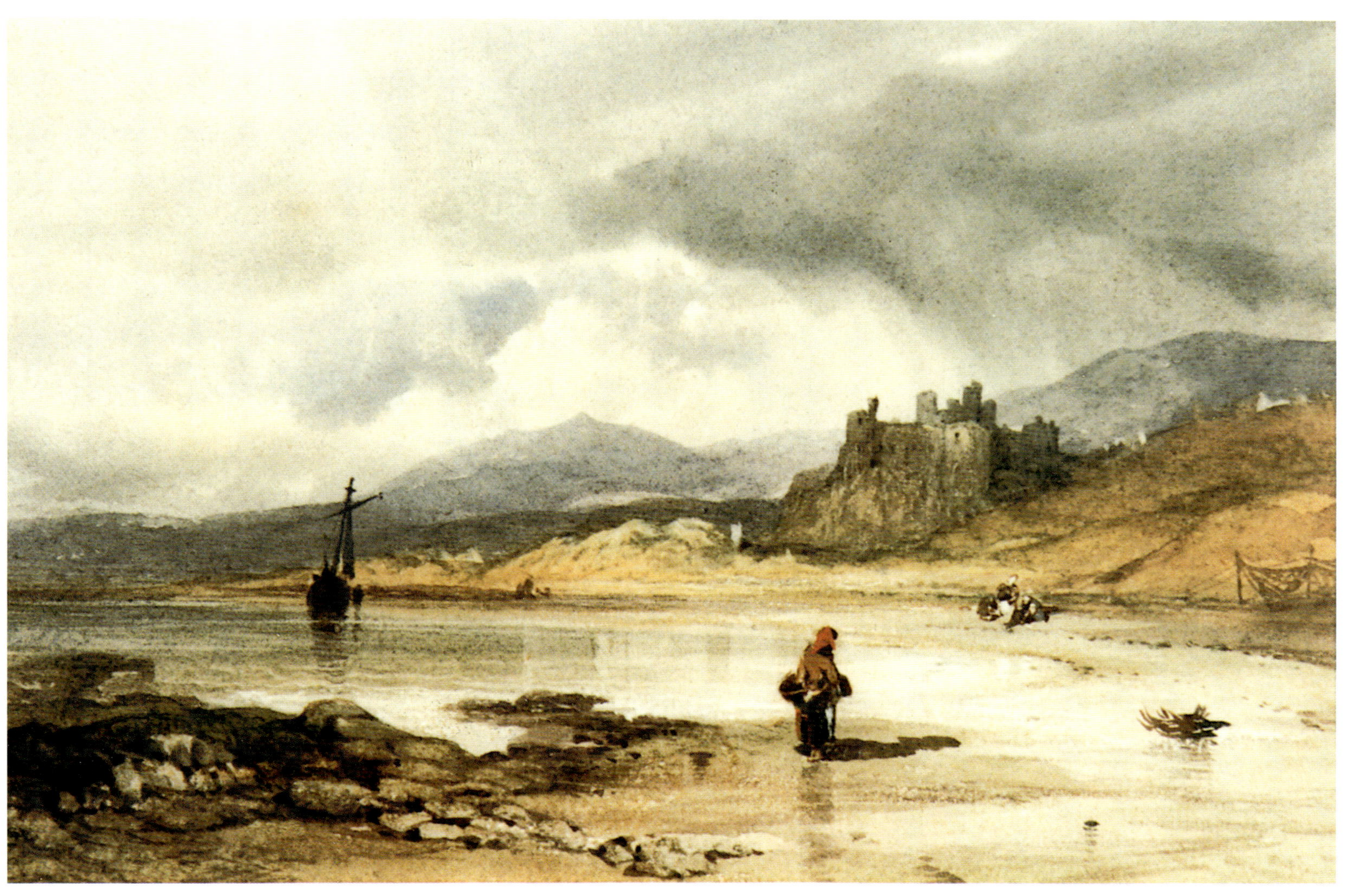

Plate 3.22. **Bamburgh Castle.**
Signed, inscribed and dated
1876. 24 x 47cm (9½ x 18½in.)

Opposite below. Plate 3.21.
Bamburgh Castle. *Signed,*
inscribed and dated 1893.
10.5 x 20cm (4⅛ x 7⅞in.)

Hardy is known to have visited and painted Bamburgh in the early '70s, a scene on the Northumbrian coast which many regard as one of the outstanding views in the British Isles. In this unusually calm painting a beached fishing boat is reflected in the mirror-like sea, but he has hinted at the kind of weather that the local people have been experiencing – ominous clouds and a rain squall just clearing the grim outline of the castle. The sun has just appeared and momentarily lights up the rather forlorn figure in the foreground, beachcombing perhaps before the fishermen return. This is a wild part of the coast and life is hard – Hardy has expressed this supremely well.

A later painting looking south towards the Castle on a more benign day with many groups of people on the strand. Wisps of mist are still hanging around the foreshore and it is calm enough for a two-masted schooner to run on to the beach at low water prior to kedging herself off as the tide rises. Meanwhile she is drying two of her foresails, both reflected strongly in the wavelets lapping the wet sand. Here is an excellent example of Hardy tending to use too much Chinese White. This may have looked realistic when the watercolour was painted, but as some fading is almost inevitable over the years, any Chinese White stands out like a sore thumb. The advantage of allowing the whiteness of the paper to show through a coloured wash rather than the use of bodycolour is obvious.

Chapter 3 – The English Coast

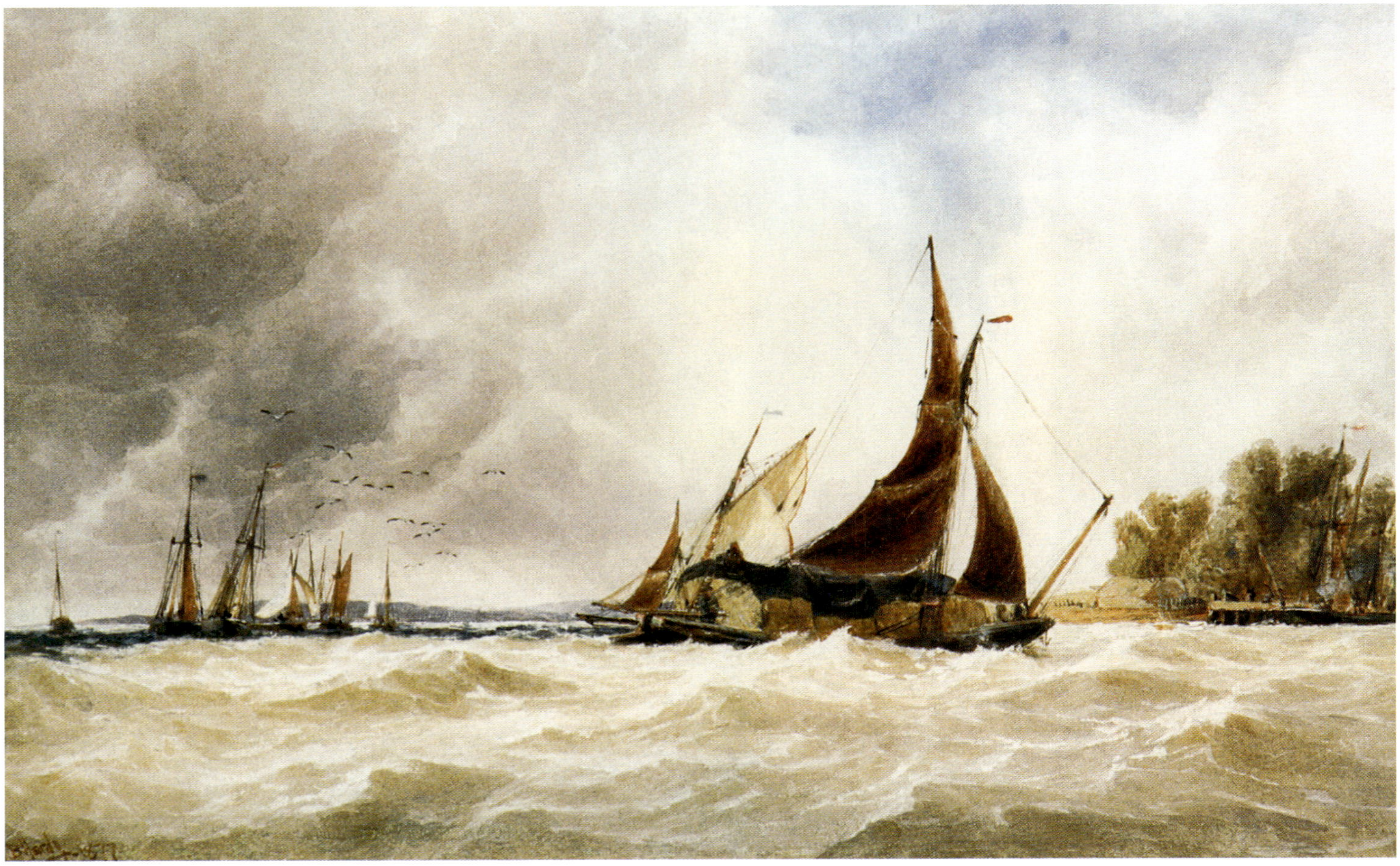

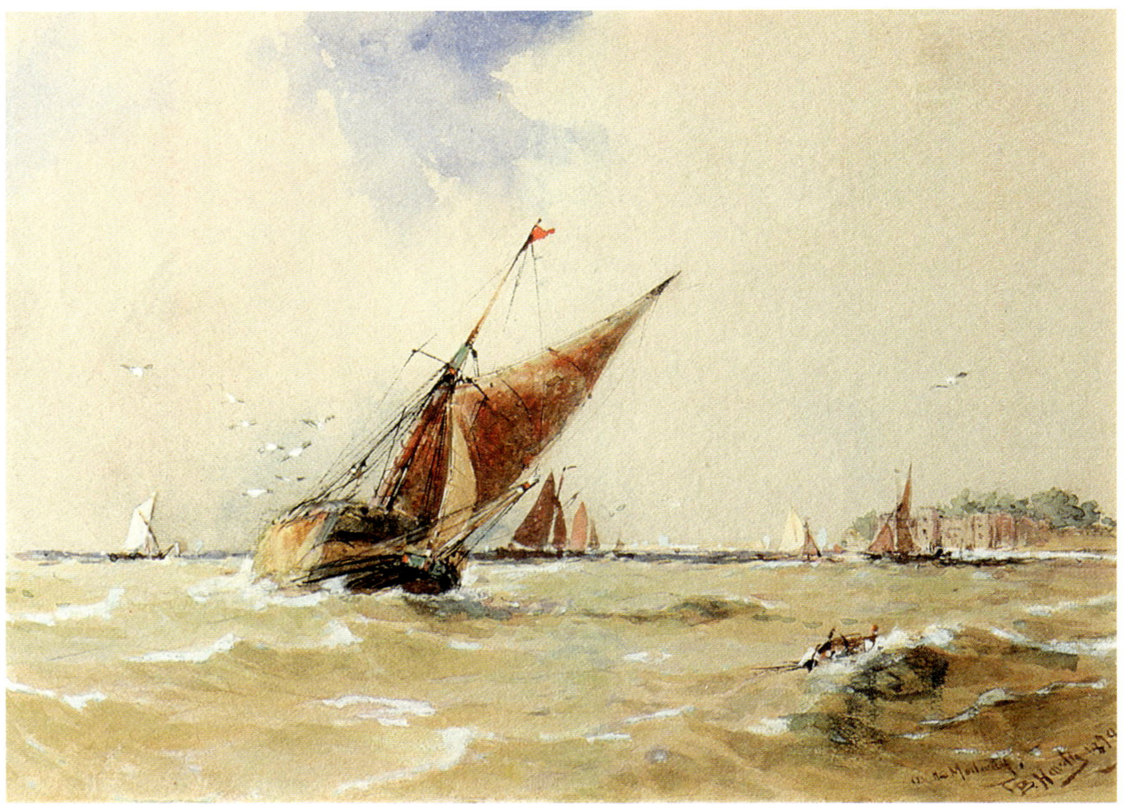

Chapter 3 – The English Coast

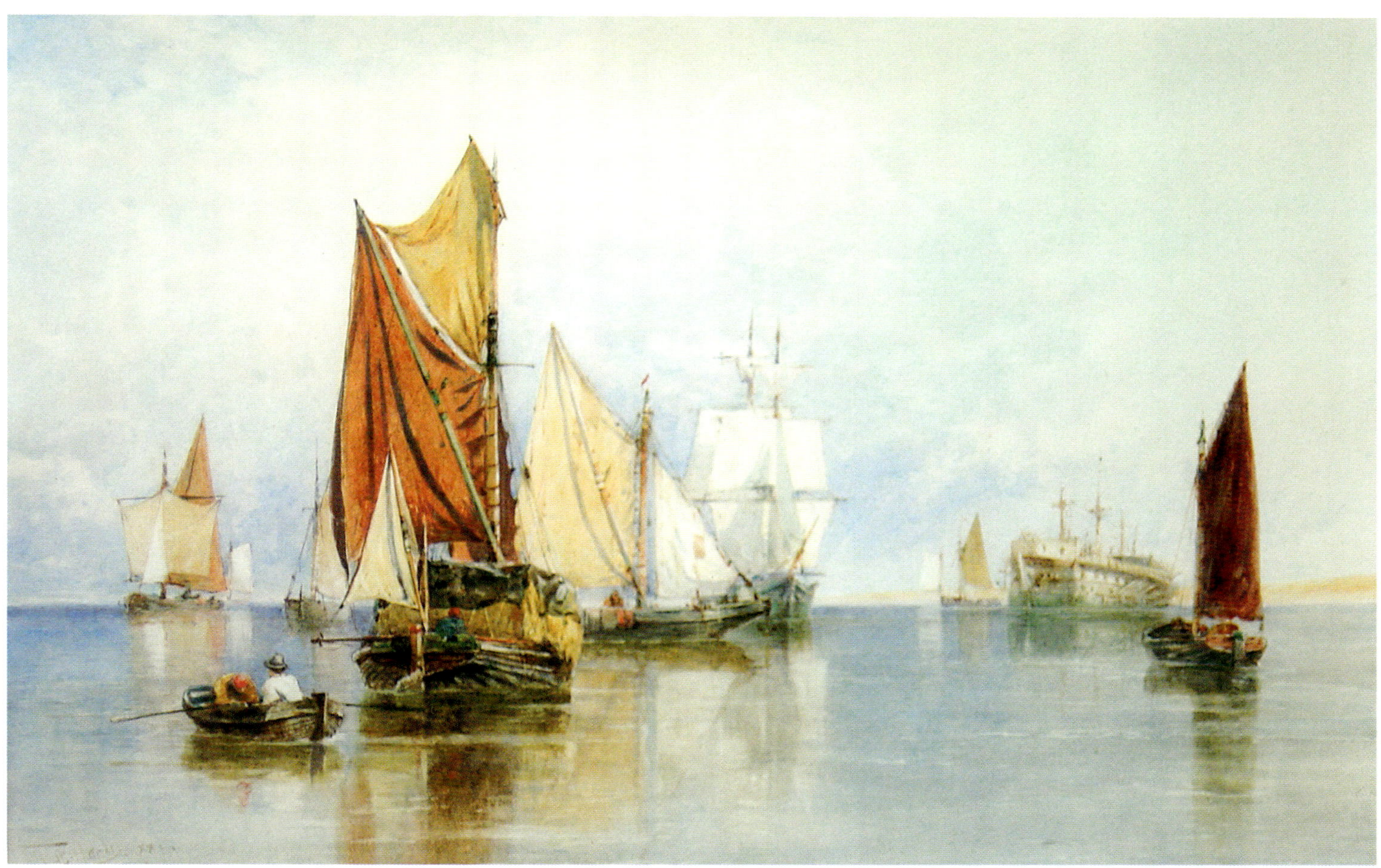

Plate 3.25. **On the Medway.**
*Signed, inscribed and dated
1881. 31 x 48.5cm
(12¼ x 19⅛ in.)*

Opposite above. Plate 3.23.
**Hay Barges off the Essex
Coast.** *Signed and dated
1877. 29 x 47cm (11⅜ x 18½ in.)*

Opposite below. Plate 3.24.
The Medway. *Signed and
dated 1879. 12 x 17cm
(4¾ x 6¾ in.)*

A very fine watercolour of various ships becalmed in the Medway on a glorious summer's day. In the foreground to the left a laden hay barge tries to capture the light airs. In the centre an empty barge crosses in front of a two-masted schooner whose white sails hang limply from their yards. To the right a single-masted lugger makes slow progress across the bay. Beyond, at anchor, is a hulk, probably still being used as a prison ship. The mirror-like surface of the river reflecting the hazy blue sky and the many-coloured vessels is beautifully drawn. This is Hardy in a spectacularly cheerful mood.

Perhaps painted on the shore of the River Blackwater, this painting witnesses a strong east wind blowing off the North Sea, churning up the relatively shallow waters. The principal hay barge with its cargo well covered against rain and spray is running before the wind on a broad reach. Beyond, another barge is tacking into the wind towards a group of fishing boats and other craft at anchor. The darkening sky and turbulent inshore waters capture the prevailing conditions and are well harmonised.

This is a very early example of Hardy experimenting with marine subjects on a small scale. His choice of subject – a hay barge in a fresh breeze with no recognisable background – is hardly ambitious. Nevertheless it is a competent, well-composed little picture and the colouring has remained fresh and unfaded. Many of his later watercolours of similar size remain in very good condition, probably due to being preserved in folios and albums.

Chapter 3 – The English Coast

Unlike the previous example, Hardy has captured quite a dramatic scene – a moment of decision for the skipper of the hay barge closing rapidly on the three-masted merchantman at anchor. Will he have to give way and pass under his stern? These barges are unable to sail very close to the wind and, if he maintains his present course, collision seems inevitable. It is a snapshot full of suspense, colour and movement, action in the foreground, interest in the background and a finely painted wind-blown sea and sky.

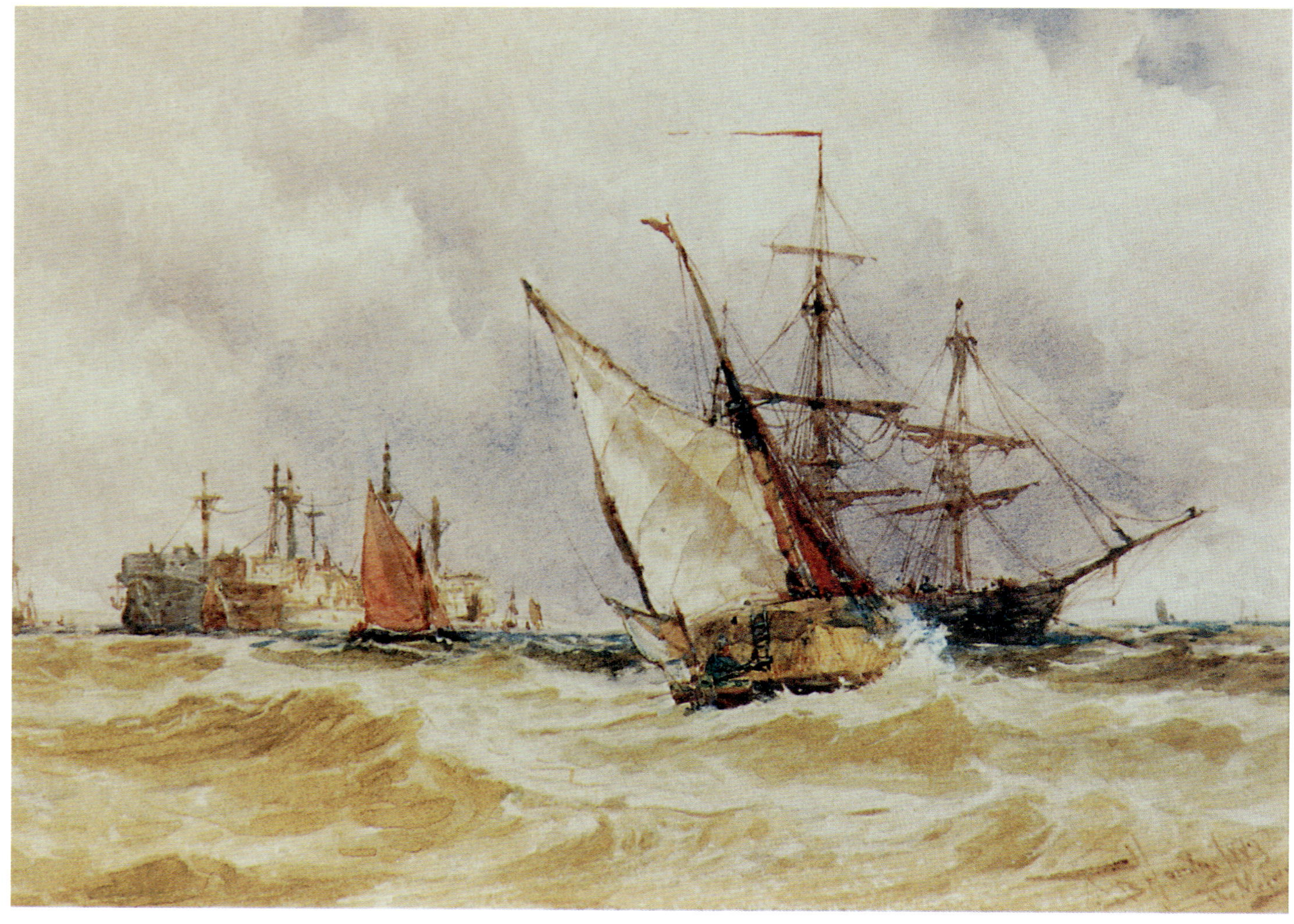

Plate 3.26. **Hay Barge on the Medway.** *Signed, inscribed and dated 1883. 12 x 17cm (4¾ x 6¾in.)*

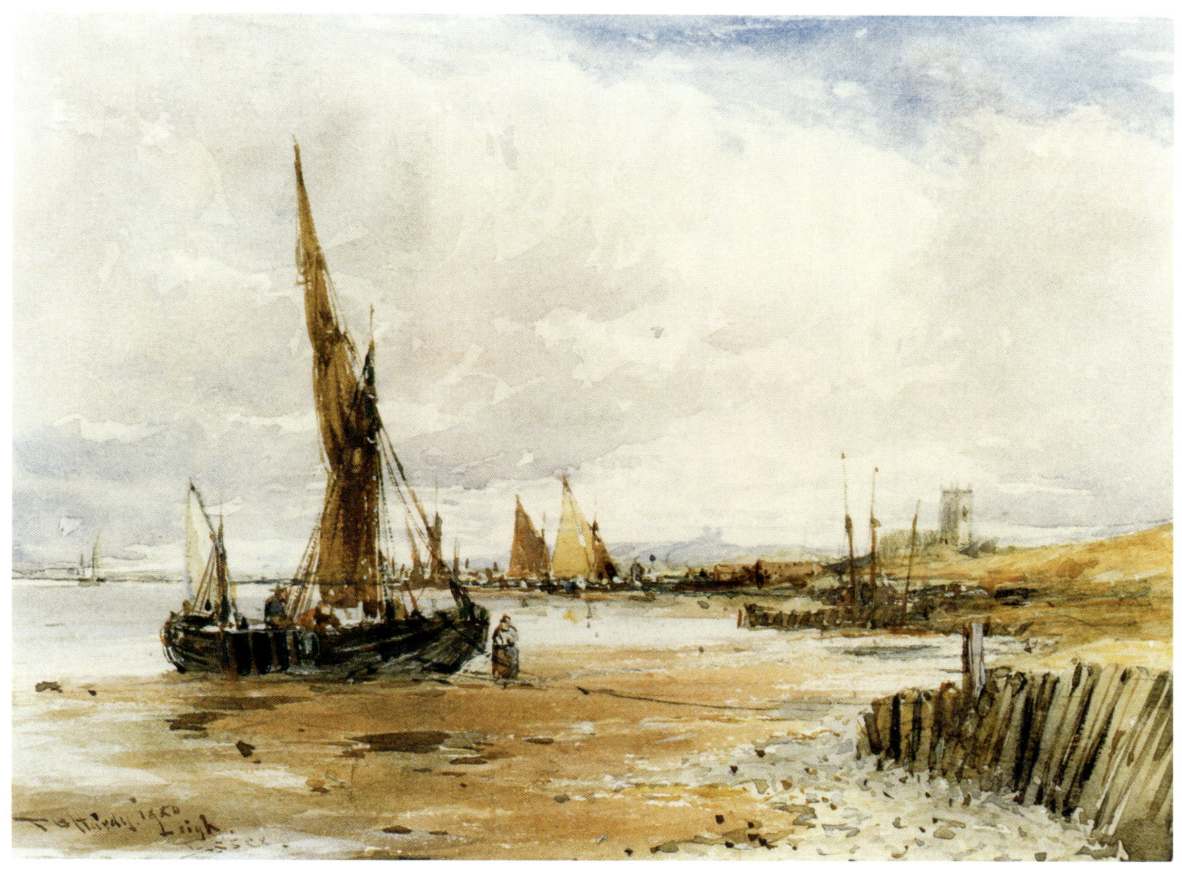

Plate 3.27. **Leigh-on-Sea, Essex.** *Signed, inscribed and dated 1880. 12 x 17cm (4¾ x 6¾ in.)*

This little watercolour is a good example of some of Hardy's best work. He was now beginning to paint watercolours of this size with a sure touch. Some, like this one, are looser than others, but nothing important has been omitted. The more one examines the painting the more becomes visible, yet there is no unnecessary obtrusive detail. The composition and colouring are superb, but it is Hardy's ability to convey the atmosphere that day on the Essex coast with its hard-working fishing community that is so remarkable.

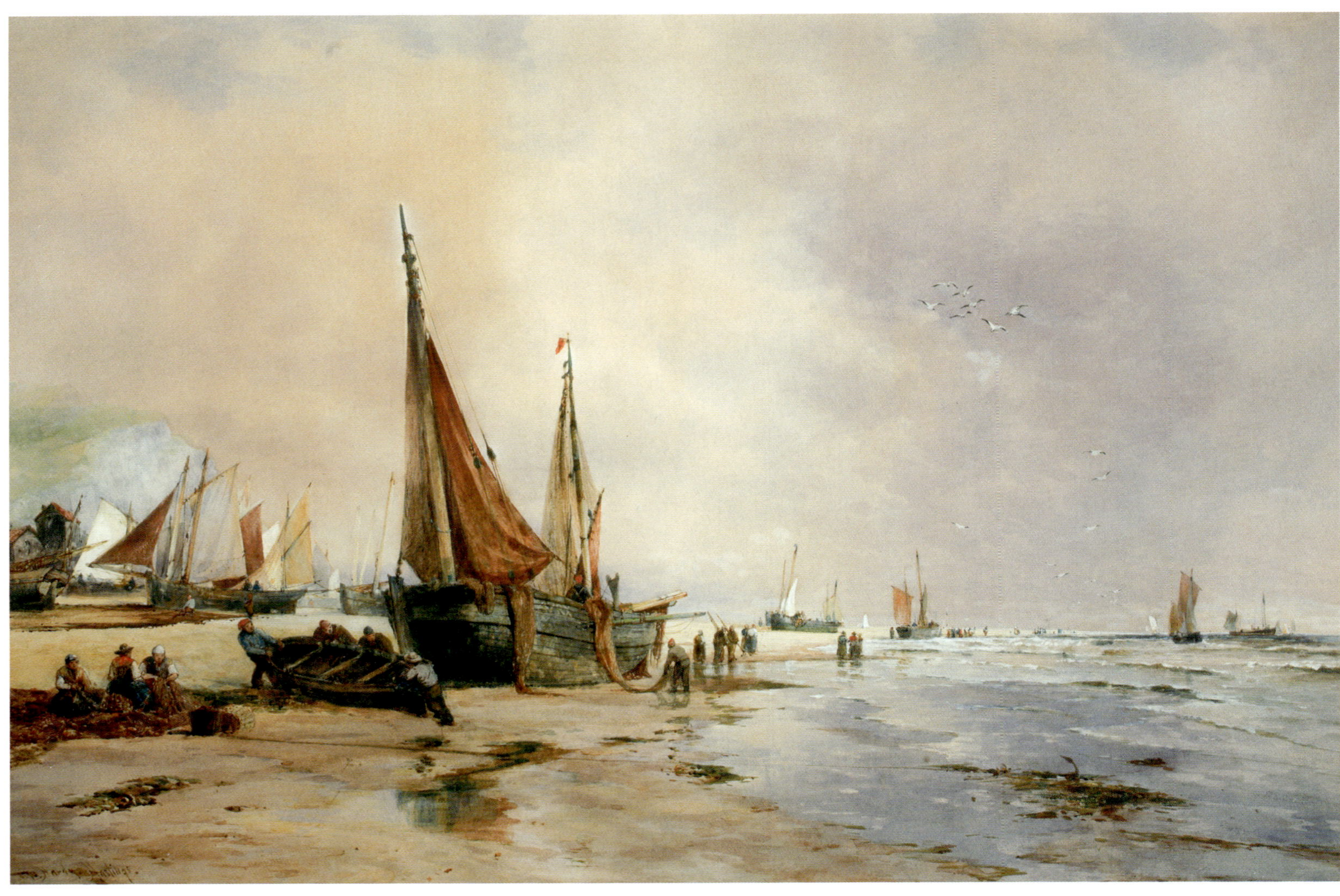

A large and finely painted scene, similar to many of his Dutch beach watercolours and probably painted in the early 1880s. Hastings had not yet been fully exploited as a tourist centre and fishing remained an important part of the town's economy for many more years. Shortly after Hardy painted this watercolour, a project to build a sheltered harbour was shelved for lack of money (a truncated 'harbour arm' remains to this day). The town still has the largest beach-based fishing fleet in the country.

Hardy has made the most of the artistic potential of the scene – the number and variety of boats on the beach, the men and women who work them and the beauty of the sea advancing and retreating on the sand and shingle. This was a world that Hardy knew well and greatly admired.

Plate 3.28. **Hastings Beach.**
Signed and inscribed. c.1880.
47 x 71cm (18½ x 28in.)

Chapter 3 – The English Coast

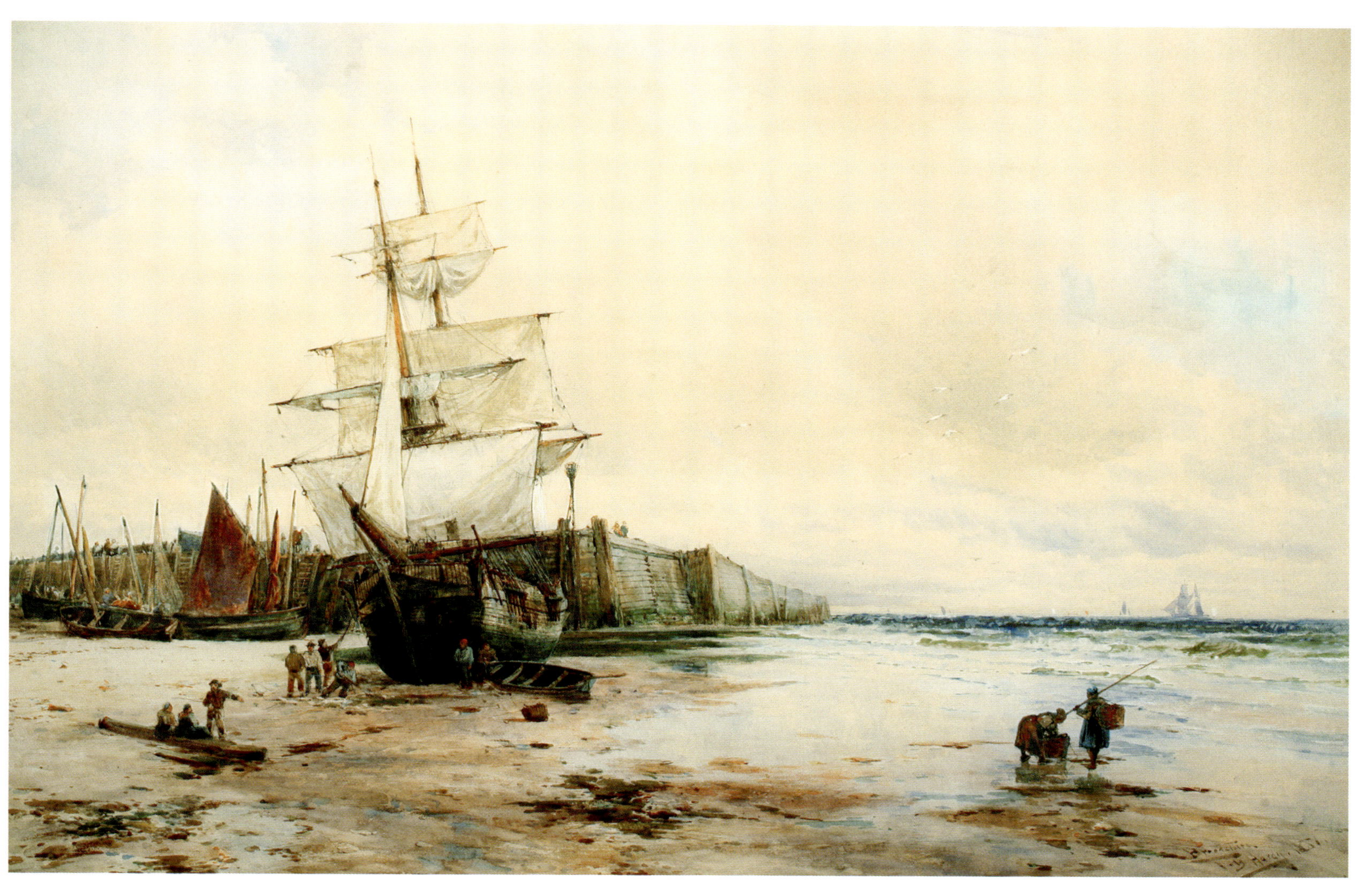

Plate 3.29. **Broadstairs.**
*Signed, inscribed and dated
1881. 45 x 75cm
(17¾ x 29½in.)*

The beached two-masted brig drying sails in the left foreground dominates the painting, surrounded by crew members scrubbing down the exposed hull. In the left foreground, three children are playing in the sand. To the right two fishermen dig for sandworms. Behind the brig a number of fishing vessels can be seen alongside the harbour wall, the extension to which is a substantial stone breakwater. The hazy sky is reflected in the mirror-like waters as the tide turns and flows over the sands. Broadstairs, like its neighbouring towns of Ramsgate and Margate, was beginning to expand rapidly due to the development of rail and steamship services. Before the close of the nineteenth century not only did the professional classes move in but, due to the fresh sea air, many convalescent homes for both children and the aged were opened up. As in many of his English coastal subjects, Hardy, perhaps unknowingly, is painting history – the end of an era. This painting was probably exhibited at the Royal Academy in 1881, no 766.

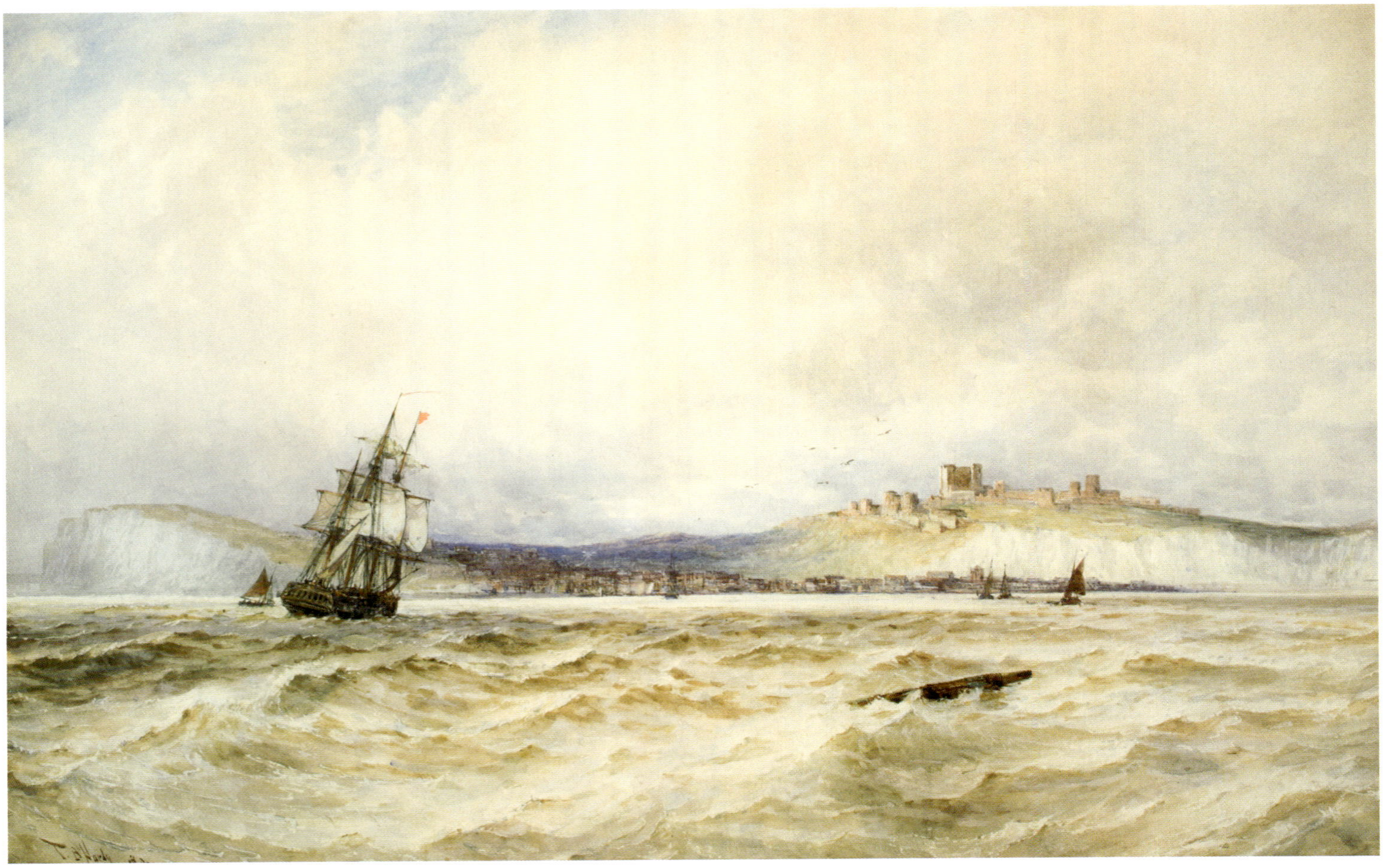

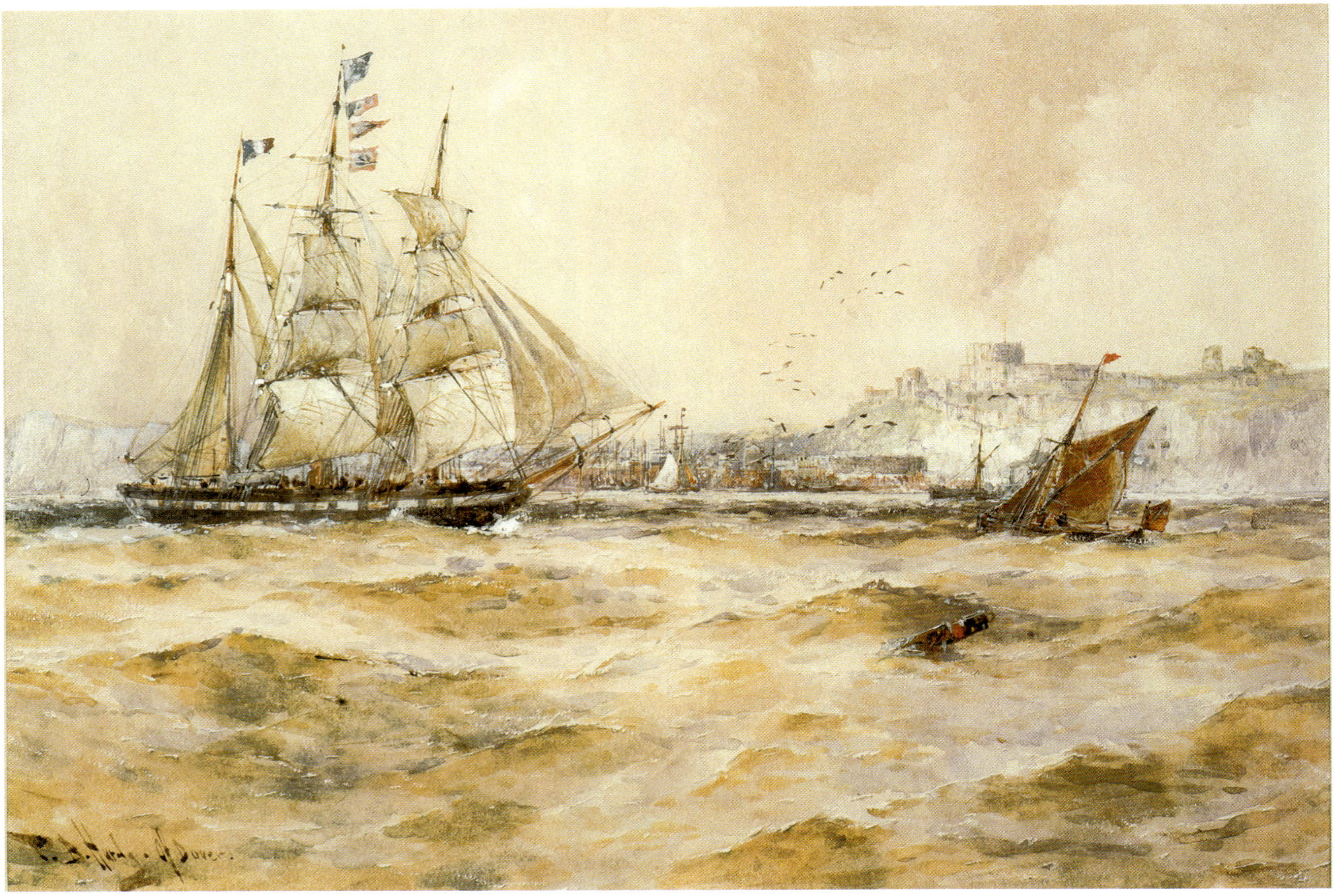

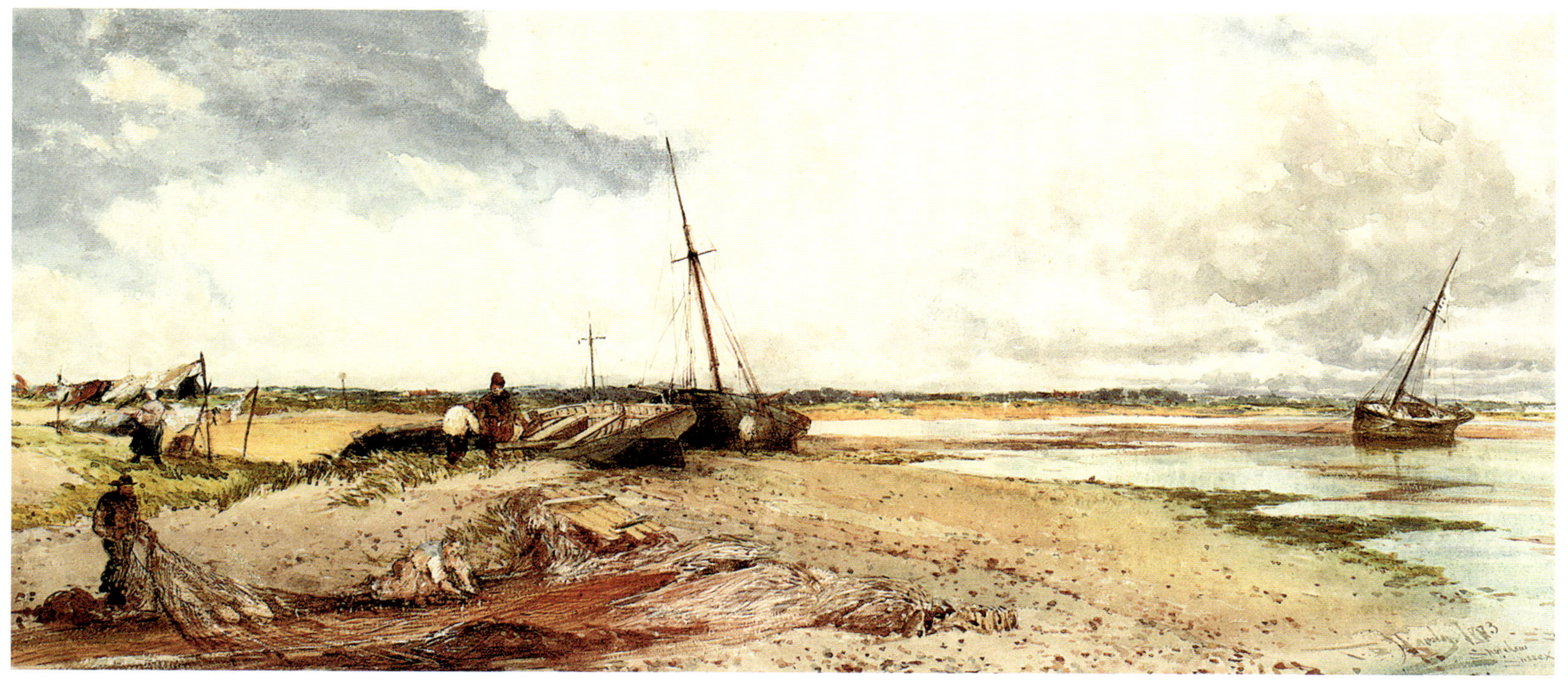

Plate 3.32. **Shoreham.**
*Signed, inscribed and dated
1883. 22.8 x 50.2cm
(9in. x 19¾in.)*

Opposite above. Plate 3.30.
Off Dover. *Signed, inscribed
and dated 1887. 43.2 x 68.6cm
(17 x 27in.)*

Opposite below. Plate 3.31.
Off Dover. *Signed and
inscribed. 23 x 33cm (9 x 13in.)*

A summery day on the beach at Shoreham where fishermen beached their boats before the harbour was developed. Of interest is the intensely blue patch dominating the otherwise rather colourless sky – Hardy seldom used this technique which other artists used including the great Richard Parkes Bonington. In the left foreground a fisherman and his wife are inspecting and mending nets while the rest of the crew attend to the boat. Beyond to the right a recently beached boat awaits the next flood tide. As always, Hardy makes good use of reflections in the pools left by the receding tide. Most noteworthy is the way he has used the narrow paper profile to give the impression of a wide, almost deserted beach that was to become a distinctive feature of his work.

A substantial work painted when Hardy was at or near his peak. In the centre background lies the port of Dover, dominated by Dover Castle and flanked on both sides by white chalk cliffs. The cliffs appear to be in bright sunlight, the town itself in shadow. Heeling over in a fresh westerly breeze, a three-masted brig approaches the harbour. A swell is building up in the Channel and Hardy has painted a moderately rough sea, noting the change in colour caused by sand in shallow water and the reflection of darkening skies to the west. A fine panoramic view of a nationally revered coastline, uncluttered by nothing more than a floating spar to balance the composition.

A much smaller watercolour than the previous example and, although undated, it was probably painted the same year. On the face of it Hardy has painted a very brown, churned-up sea, surprisingly so as there is comparatively deep water this far off Dover. It is not a pleasant day and there is a lot of smoke in the vicinity, but there are signs of some fading – not serious yet, but blues and greens as always are the first to suffer from over-exposure to any ultra-violet radiation. Here Hardy has painted a fine French frigate, probably a sail training ship from Cherbourg, in a fresh westerly breeze off Dover. She is flying an unidentified flag at the main which may indicate a senior naval officer on board, below which the flag hoist is probably requesting a pilot. Relations between the two countries and their respective navies were better after the Franco-Prussian War than they had been for many years.

Chapter 3 – The English Coast

Besides having all the credentials of a good picture – subject, composition, colour and movement – this unusual little watercolour tells one a great deal about the windswept north-east coast and the people who live there. Hardy's inscription is very helpful – this is a small fishing community living and working in a sandy cove on the north shore at the very mouth of the Tyne. Several colourful boats, known as cobles in this part of Northumbria, are drawn up on the beach clear of the incoming tide. Normally protected to some extent from the northerly winds by the spit of land on which stand the ruins of Tynemouth Castle and Priory, these fishermen have wisely decided not to go to sea in their small boats in the prevailing conditions. The men are using the time examining and mending their nets while the women collect the washing before it blows away. In the distance many larger vessels, having shortened sail, are returning to shelter in the Tyne. Hardy's painting of the waves sweeping into the cove is masterly, but more impressive is how he has captured something of the way of life and spirit of an isolated community.

Plate 3.33. **The Mouth of the Tyne.** *Signed, inscribed and dated 1883. 12 x 17cm (4¾ x 6¾in.)*

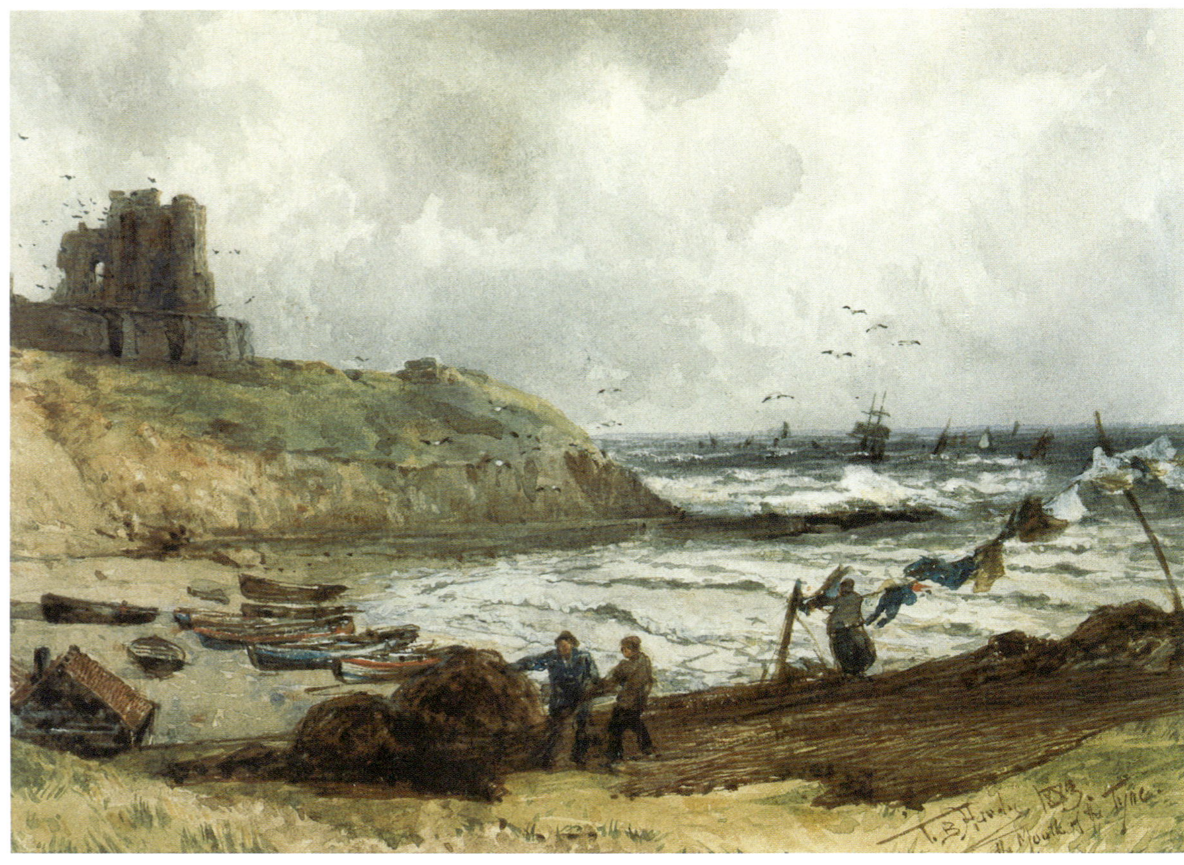

The next two paintings turned up in a recently discovered trunkload of unframed watercolours from the studio of the Sheffield artist, George Hamilton Constantine (1875-1967). Over two hundred and fifty of these were by the artist himself, but the others comprised examples or copies of earlier nineteenth century artists including these two beach scenes signed by Hardy. Could they possibly have been copies, including a false signature and a false date? We know that Constantine was close to his uncle, Frederick William Hattersley (b.1859), also a Sheffield artist specialising in beach scenes, and it is almost certain that he and Hardy were at some time in close contact. Perhaps Hardy gave the young artist some examples from his studio to help him improve his technique. If so, are these the Constantine copies or the Hardy originals? There is a greater use of bodycolour and a slightly less convincing feel about both these paintings which must create some doubt about their attribution. Whatever the truth, they provide confirmation that Hardy had considerable influence on the up-and-coming artists of the next generation. The subject here is probably Scarborough beach on a wintry afternoon and, like all the other watercolours in this unique find, it is remarkable for its totally unfaded, original condition.

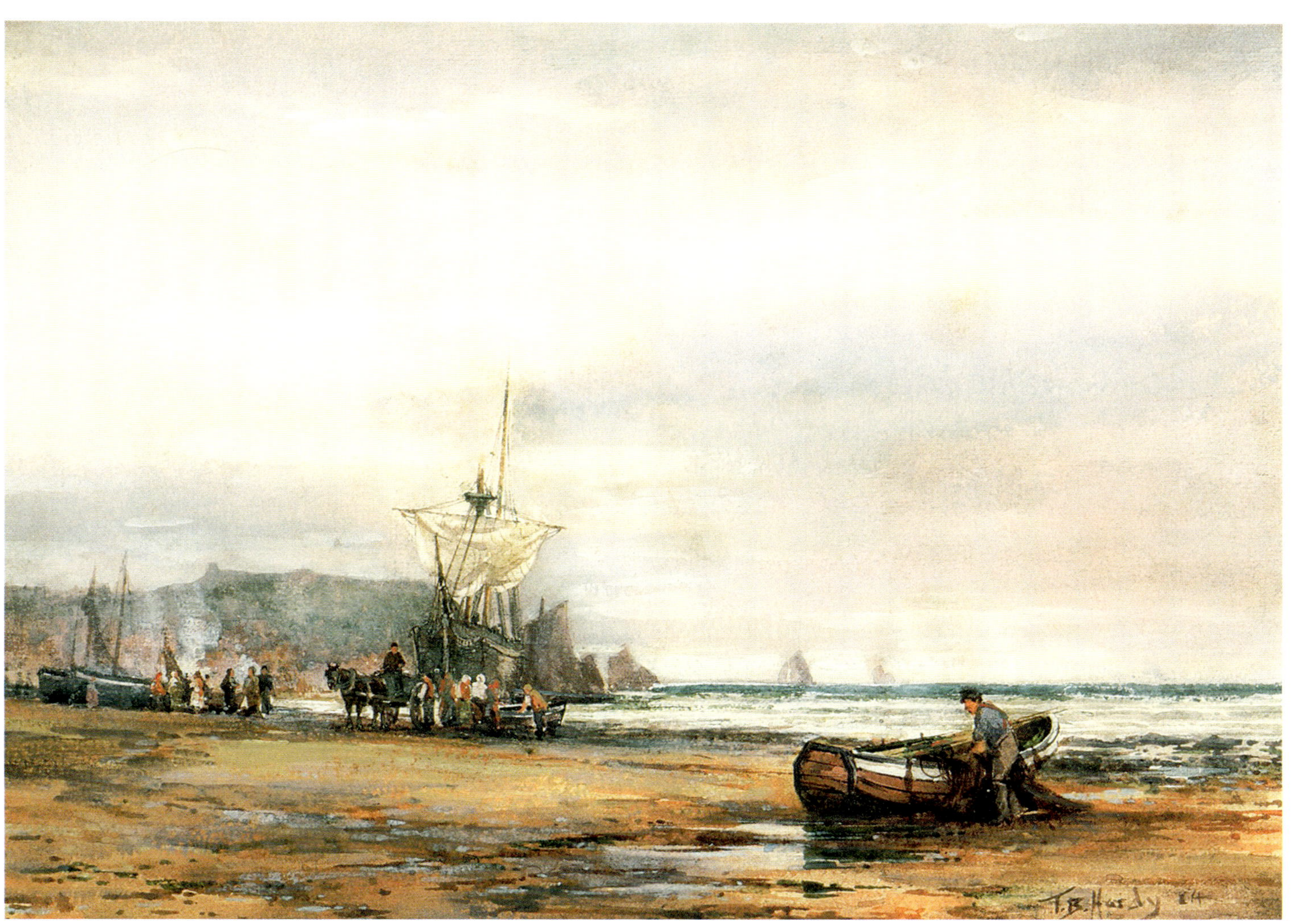

The second of the watercolours, apparently signed by Hardy, hiding in a trunk for nigh on a century. The subject could well be Scarborough again but might be a scene south of the Thames estuary where Hardy painted frequently in the late 1880s. It is low water and late in the day and the smacks are obliged to ferry their catch to the beach in smaller boats. The fisherwoman in the foreground is carrying away what appears to be a fine cod or halibut, probably for family consumption. The brooding sky threatens rain and a steady breeze but the odds are that the little fishing fleet will rest and wait for the morning flood tide. A well-composed watercolour based on careful observation. Young Constantine was eleven years old when this was painted and one wonders whether he might have been given this by an indulgent 'uncle'. Like the earlier example, the provenance and attribution of this competent and interesting painting is unclear.

Opposite above. Plate 3.35. **Fisherwomen collecting the Catch.** *Signed and dated 1889. 20 x 40cm (7⅞ x 15¾in.)*

This may not be one of Hardy's best compositions, but it is an excellent example of his now mature ability to paint a realistic rough sea. The central subject, a two-masted schooner, appears to have just avoided running down a hay barge and another smaller vessel. Whatever has happened or is about to happen, it is not normally advisable to pose a question like this in a painting, unless the artist wants to disturb and/or irritate the viewer. A wider separation between the vessels would have produced a much better artistic composition. But back to the sea itself; the relationship between the colouring of sea and sky is very well done and the implied movement of spray-topped waves is particularly good.

Opposite below. Plate 3.36. **A Rough Sea.** Indistinctly signed, inscribed and dated 1885. *33.5 x 53.5cm (13¼ x 21in.)*

Chapter 3 – The English Coast

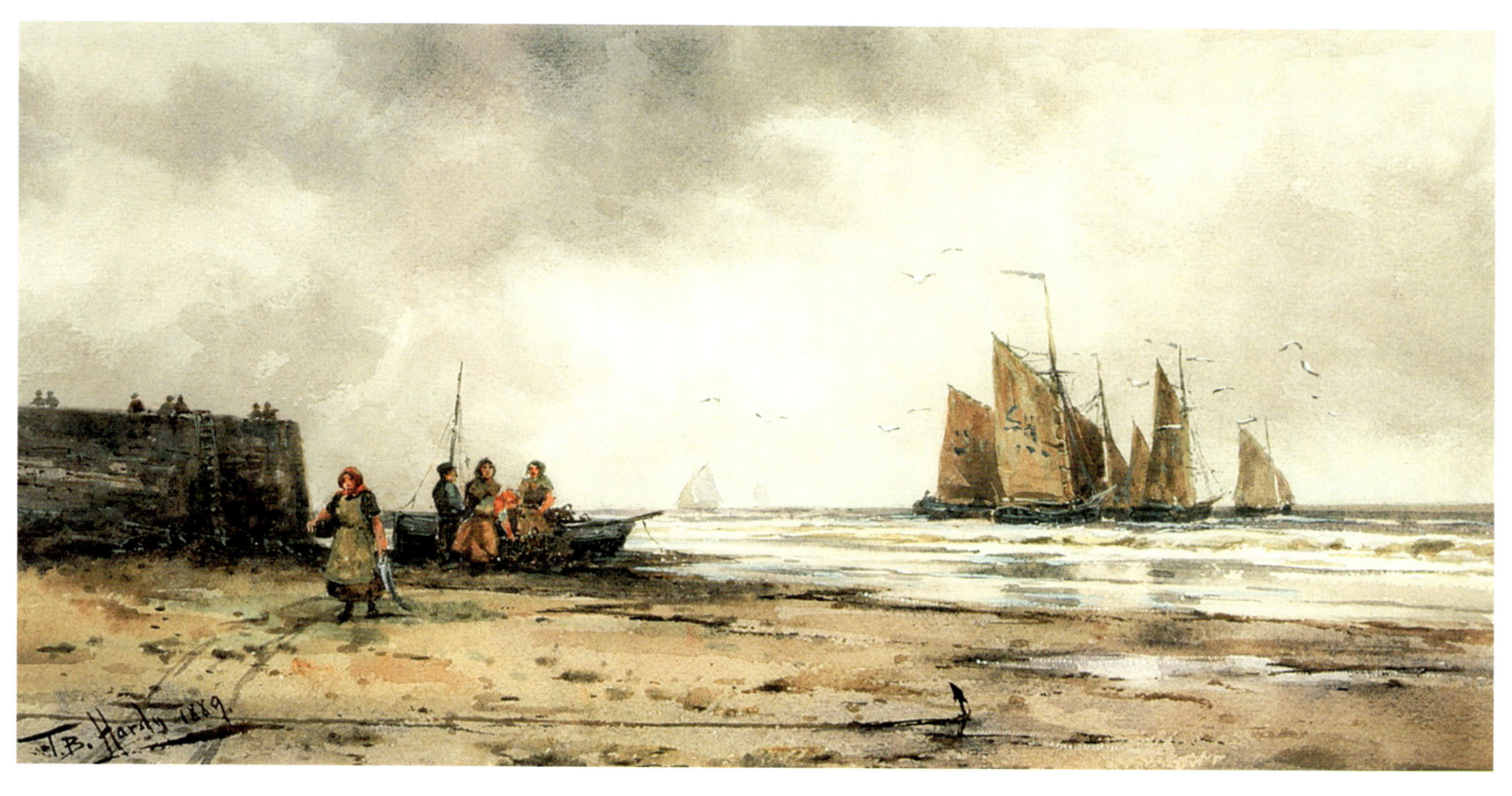

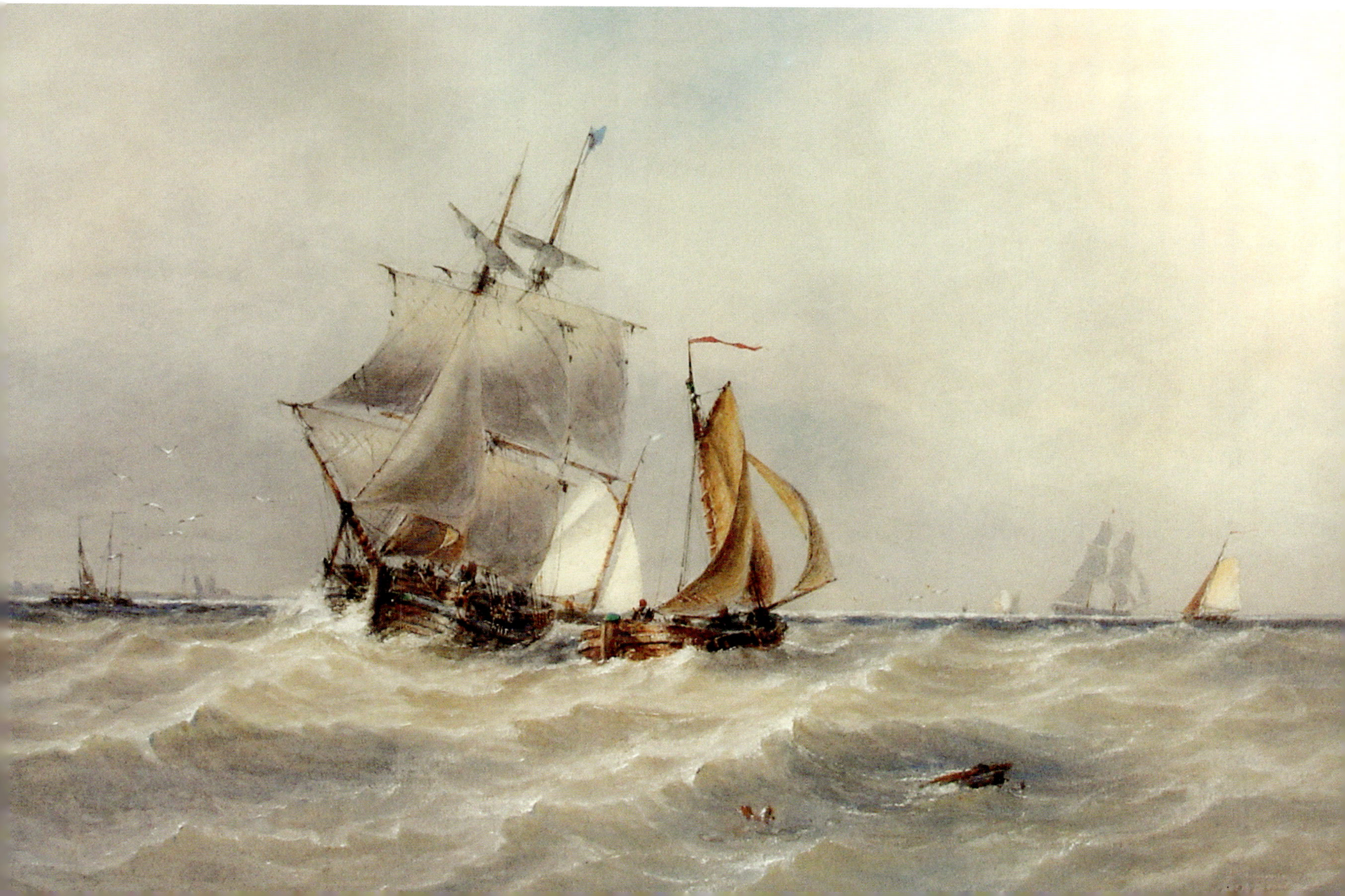

This is one of Hardy's earlier and more successful attempts at painting Britain's premier naval port. Surprisingly, perhaps, he has chosen the view of the very narrow entrance, guarded by the fifteenth century Round Tower to the East and the much later Battery to the West, both clearly visible. Not a sign of the Royal Navy's rebuilding and re-arming programme as Their Lordships recognised, somewhat reluctantly, the need to change from sail to steam and from oak to steel. Indeed the only visible warships are HMS *Victory*, flagship of the Commander-in-Chief, Portsmouth, and another wooden wall, now a hulk, moored further up harbour. Hardy seems far more interested in the working brig leaving harbour and other smaller sailing vessels going about their business. From an artistic point of view, there is a notoriously swift ebb through the entrance which, in conjunction with a spring tide and southwesterly wind, creates an unusually rough sea. Hardy has painted this very convincingly.

Plate 3.37.
Entrance to Portsmouth Harbour. *Signed, inscribed and dated 1885. 24 x 34cm (9½ x 13⅜in.)*

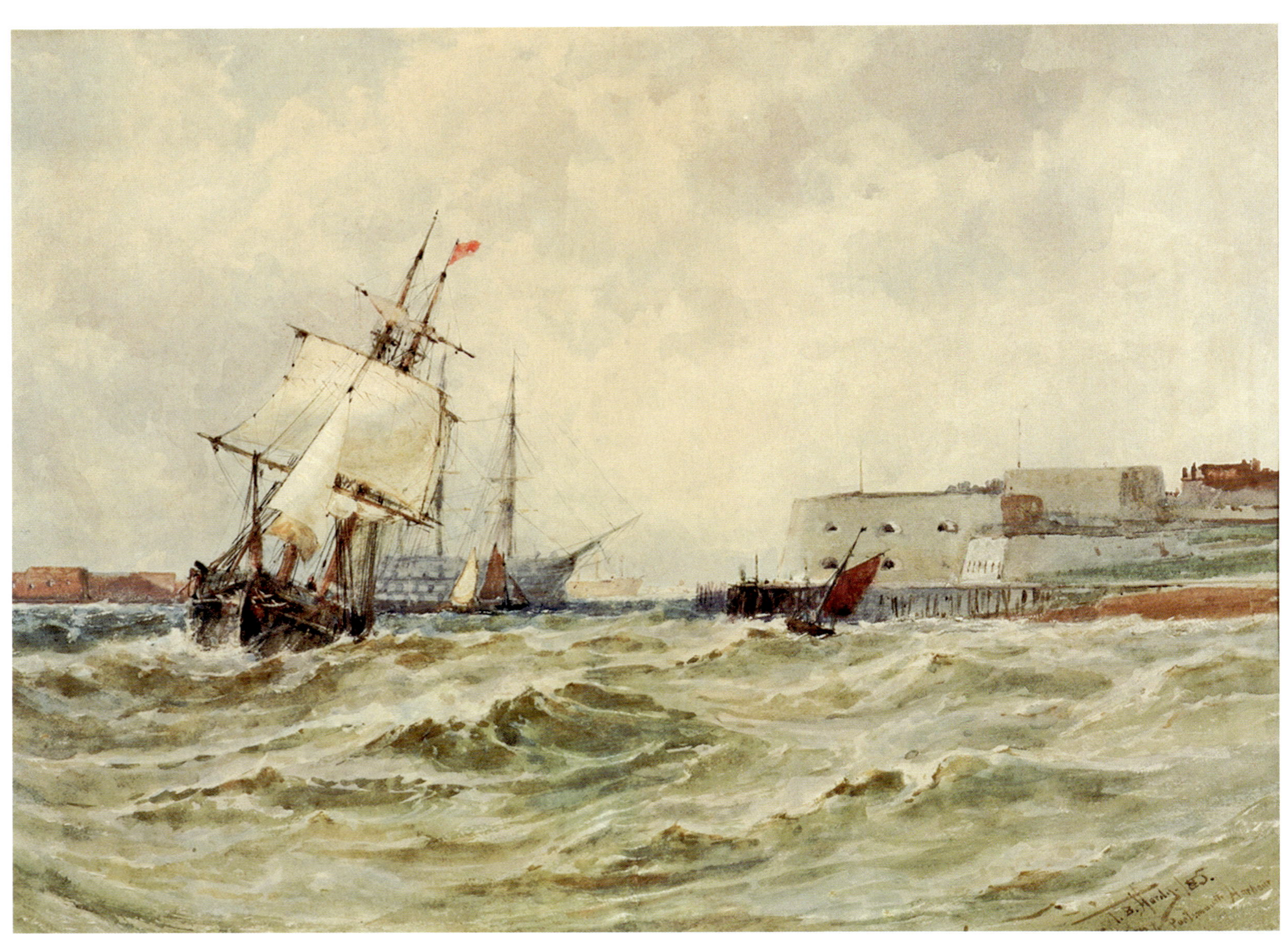

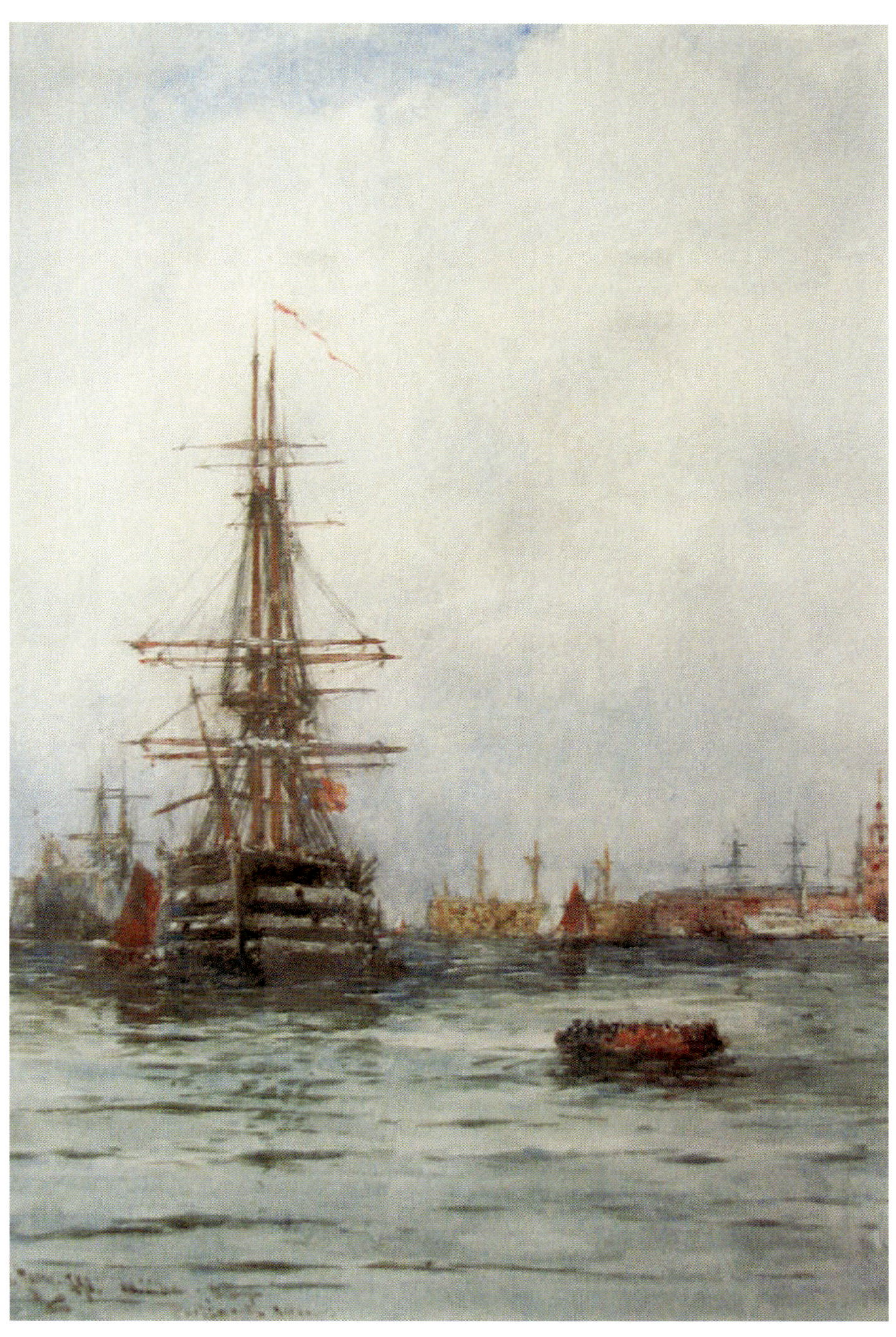

Plate 3.38. **HMS Duke of Wellington, Portsmouth Harbour.** *Signed, inscribed and dated 1890. 25.5 x 17cm. (10 x 6¾in.)*

It was probably in 1890 that Hardy first set up his easel and may have rented a studio in Portsmouth. And it was probably from the Camber, where fishermen moored their craft, that Hardy painted this splendid old wooden wall. Built at Pembroke Dock as the *Windsor Castle* and launched on 14 September 1852, the day of the Duke of Wellington's death, this fine First Rate, mounting 131 guns, was renamed in the old Duke's honour two weeks later. After a distinguished career as flagship in the Baltic during the war with Russia in 1854-55, she was relegated to harbour service and remained a familiar sight in Portsmouth Harbour until finally broken up in 1904. Beyond, on the right, can be seen the Semaphore Tower and at least one rather more modern warship alongside. Interestingly, it seems that HMS *Victory*, still flying the flag of the Commander-in-Chief, Portsmouth, is undergoing one of her periodic visits to the famous old dry dock which, thirty odd years later, was to become her permanent home.

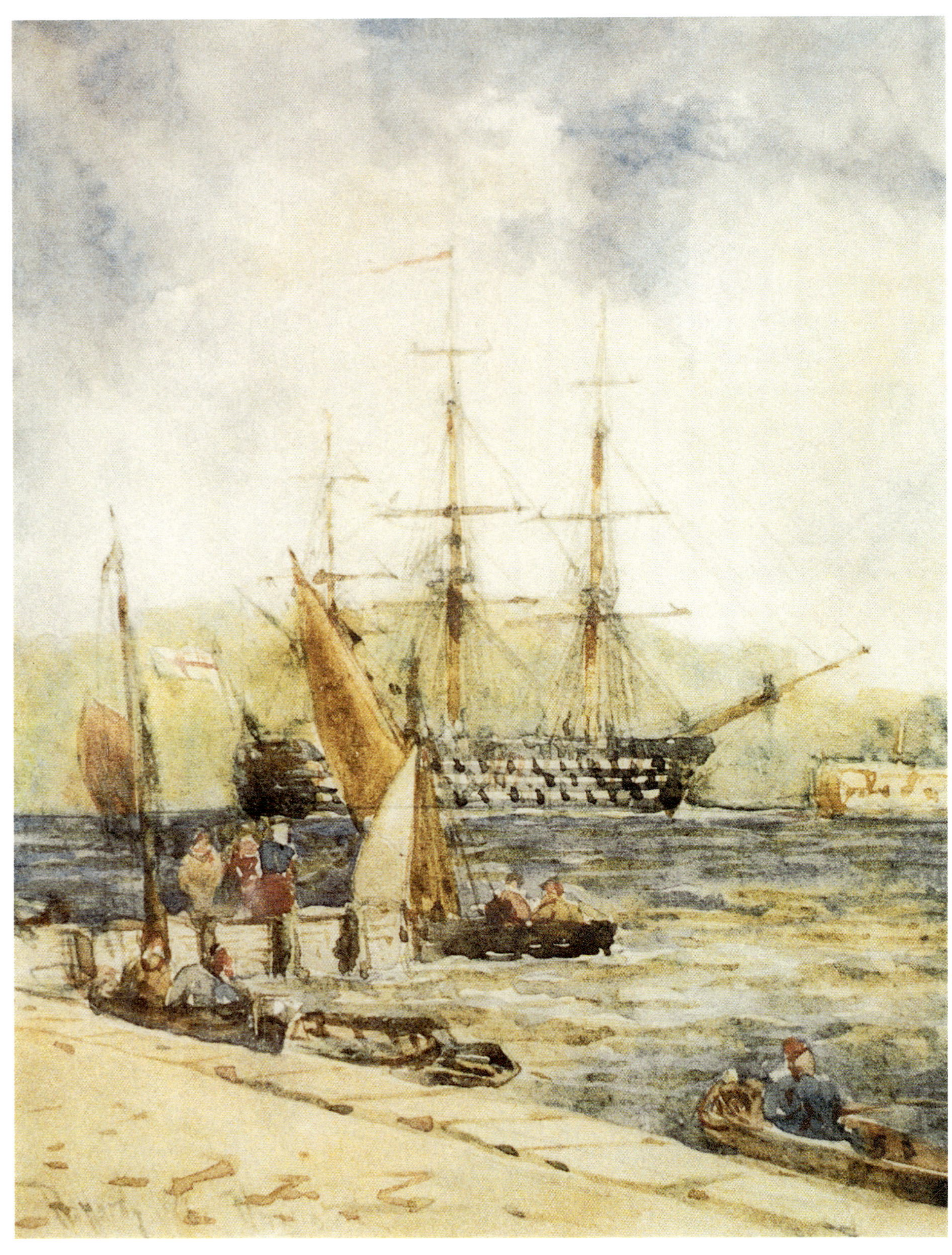

One of the smallest watercolours that Hardy ever painted, but none the worse for that. Hardy himself must have been satisfied or he would never have signed it. Plymouth was just about the westernmost limit of his travels in England and no doubt he was happy to renew his acquaintance with the Royal Navy. Here he depicts a three-decker moored in the Hamoaze off Devonport dockyard, probably HMS *Defiance*, one of two old 'wooden walls' which continued in commission as training and accommodation ships until after the Second World War. Hardy would probably have travelled down to Plymouth by courtesy of the Great Western Railway and may later have crossed the river Tamar into Cornwall via Brunel's great railway viaduct, the Royal Albert Bridge at Saltash, a mile or two upstream from where he painted this view. An interesting little 'on the spot' sketch which Hardy may well have presented to his host for the day.

Unfortunately, Hardy has not given any indication as to the whereabouts of this offshore scene. A reasonable suggestion is that the three-masted merchantman is anchored in the Downs awaiting a favourable wind and tide before proceeding on the next leg of her journey. Meanwhile, a red-sailed barge and other vessels are making good progress in what may well be a freshening breeze, judging by the breaking waves in the foreground. Hardy has painted a somewhat enigmatic, dappled blue and grey sky and one cannot be too certain what is going to happen next. What is beyond doubt is the proximity of shallow water.

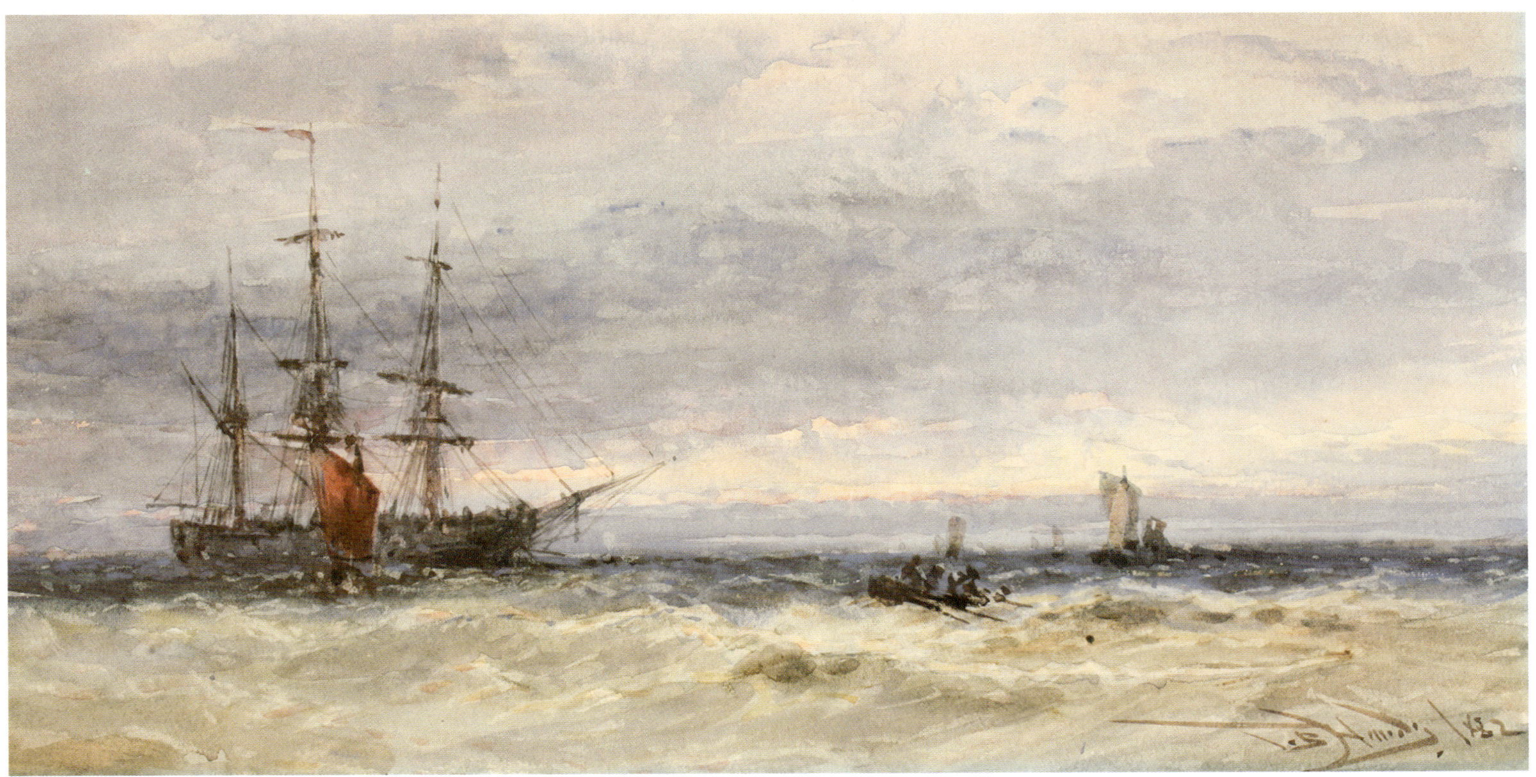

Although not inscribed, this oil painting is probably either of Pevensey or Seaford beach and would have been painted in the early 1880s. It is shortly after sunset and the figures ashore are hauling the fishing boat on to the beach stern first to avoid the risk of it being swamped in the surf. The evening sky, not always one of Hardy's strongest points, is beautifully painted, as are the colourful reflections in the not so calm sea. A fine, perfectly balanced composition.

A most dramatic oil painting of a three-masted merchantman, her sails in tatters, driven on to a cliff-lined coast in a violent storm. Beyond, to the right, the crew, for the present safe in their lifeboat, watch and hear their ship break up on the rocks. Hardy, possibly influenced by some of Henry Barlow Carter's watercolours of the storm-lashed Yorkshire coast, has used a fierce and threatening range of dark colours for the cliffs and clouds to contrast with the white spray and spume thrown up by the angry sea. It is a depressing, doom-laden picture, a subject which Hardy seldom attempted (his wrecks were normally stranded vessels on beaches surrounded by happy beachcombers!). But it is also convincing evidence of his artistic prowess in oils as well as watercolours.

Plate 3.41.
On the Rocks. *(Oil.) Signed
and dated 1880. 49.5 x 75cm
(19½ x 29½in.)*

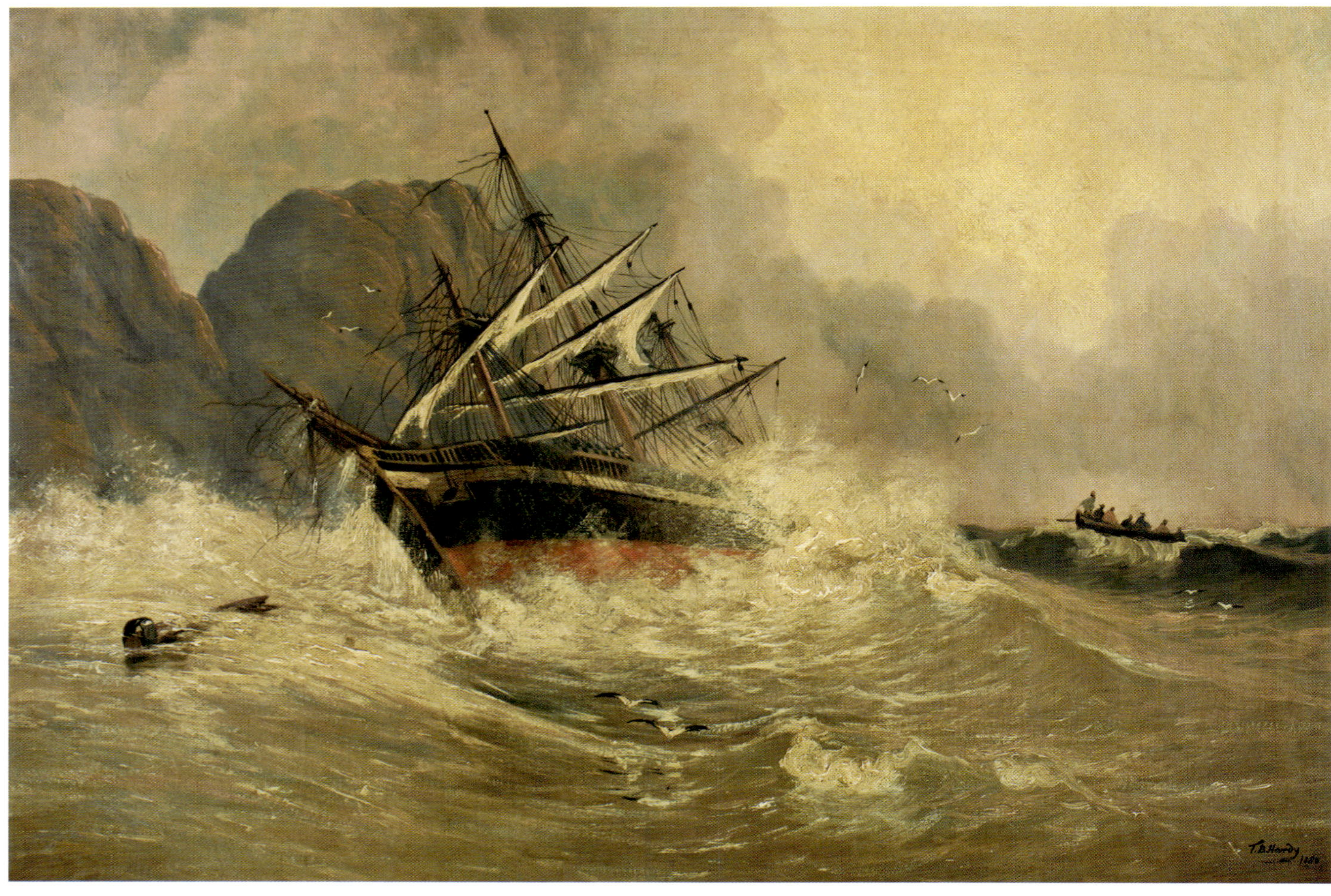

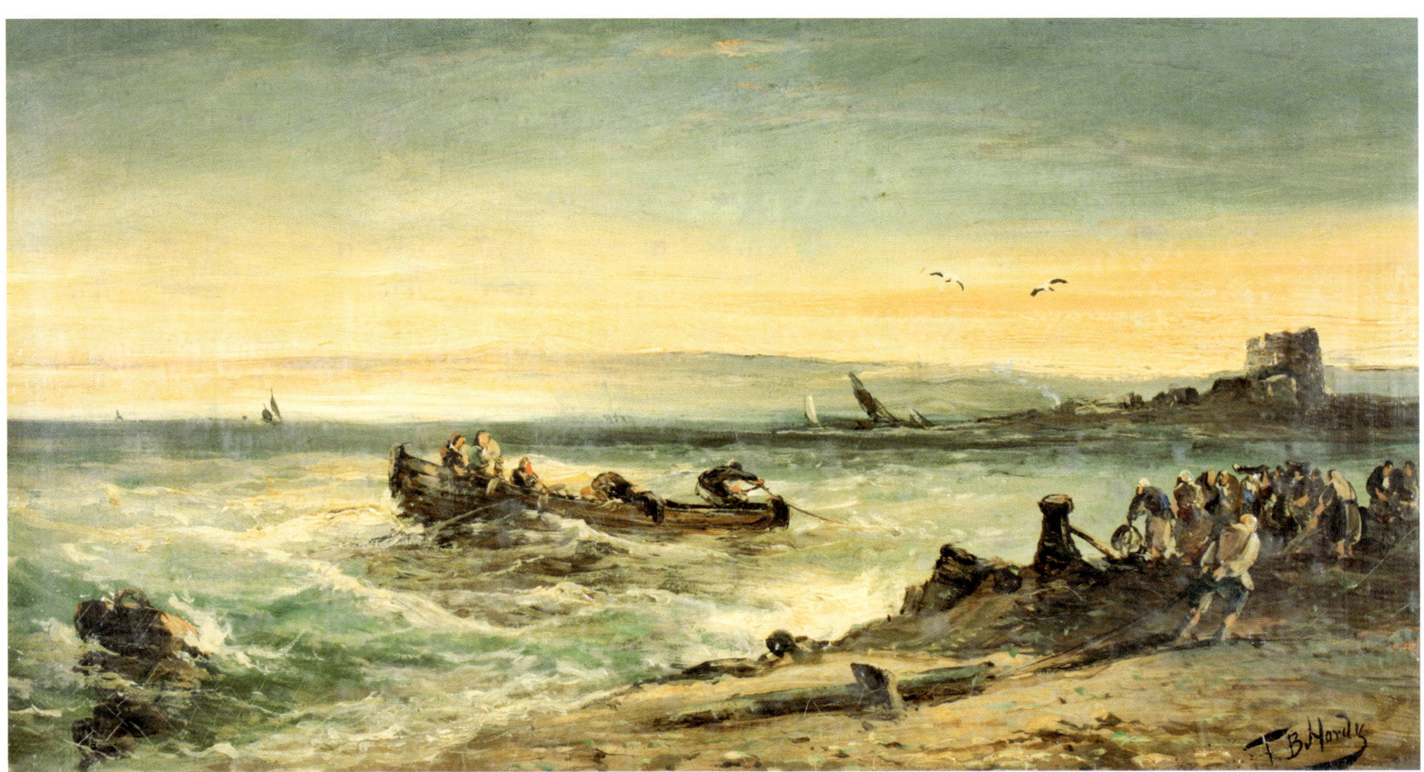

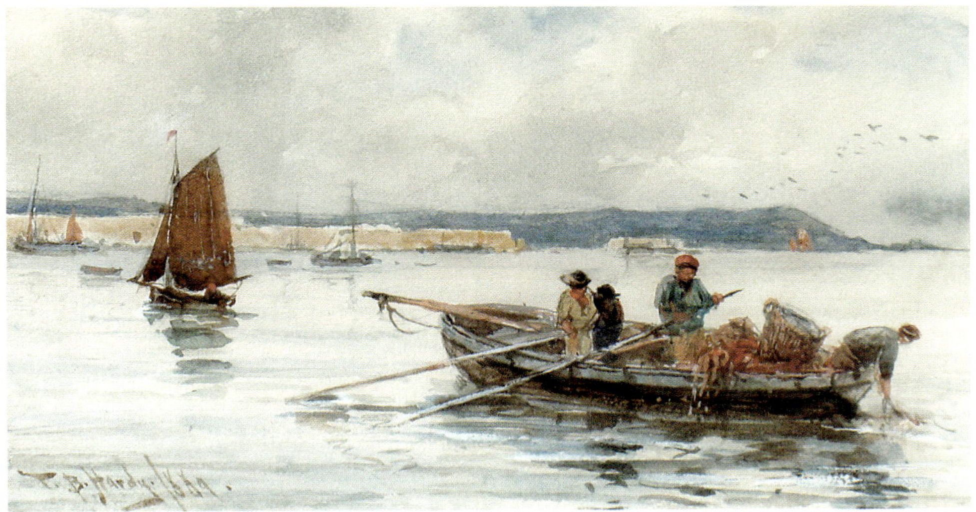

One of the smallest watercolours by Hardy, this little study of fishermen gathering in their nets and wicker lobster and crab pots on a calm sunny day could be almost anywhere on the south coast. The background of what appears to be a line of white stuccoed terraces suggests it might be Hastings, Eastbourne, Weymouth, Torquay or Plymouth – all of which had long established fishing communities but were rapidly becoming desirable places in which to live for both work and leisure. Here is an example of Hardy's ability to draw figures. Most of his paintings have an appropriate number of people, all actively employed or waiting for something to happen. Like Turner, he was not particularly interested in close-ups of features, but the correct dress, attitudes, body language and sense of movement were all there. In this painting all four fishermen are working, all four know exactly what they are doing and so does Hardy. Again a very well-balanced composition.

Chapter 3 – The English Coast

One of Hardy's wide, narrow beachscapes which allow the artist to explore horizontal space to advantage. Leading down from the sand dunes to the sea, many acres of deserted beach provided a perfect place for meditation – in the nineteenth century. Only a few miles north of Yarmouth, the small town of Caister had little to recommend it – remains of a Roman settlement and a fifteenth century castle whose hundred foot tower can be seen in the painting, but not much else. Today it is a popular family holiday resort and would not provide Hardy with the 'space' most artists need from time to time (especially those with large families!). Interestingly, the only other known image of Caister by Hardy was a quite beautiful small watercolour painted shortly before he died in 1897, a year when he was not well and when most of his output was way below his usual standard. One theory is that he produced this exceptional painting, and maybe others, during a short convalescence with an old friend.

Opposite above. Plate 3.44.
Caister near Yarmouth.
Signed, inscribed and dated 1889. 21 x 68cm (8¼ x 26¾in.)

A totally different scene from the view below London Bridge that Hardy had painted fifteen years earlier, and not all that convincing. The Tower of London has been reduced to an insignificant building block. By contrast, the Portland stone Customs House shines out like a white marble Taj Mahal. St Paul's cathedral is only just visible in the distance. On the river a Thames barge and lighter are under way in the foreground, behind which a coal-fired freighter seems to be moored alongside. However, work on Tower Bridge had started in 1886 and for the next eight years river traffic and alongside berths must have been severely affected. Of this new and important construction there is no sign. Some of Hardy's talent shows through – the reflection of the barge's sails in the rippling Thames is good – but the overall impression is of a lack of both care and inspiration.

Opposite centre. Plate 3.45.
The Thames at the Tower of London. *Signed and dated 1890. 23 x 71.5cm (9 x 28⅛in.)*

This is not one of Hardy's best watercolours but it shows he was still visiting that part of the English Coast in the 1890s. There was nothing particularly attractive about Newhaven – the most interesting feature was the long beach at Seaford with the most westerly Martello tower on the South Coast. Coincidentally, another fine nineteenth century artist, Thomas Goldsworth Dutton, perhaps better known for his lithographs than his watercolours, painted a very fine view of Seaford Beach in the same year, 1890. Newhaven itself, nestling under the protective chalk cliffs leading to Beachy Head, was no more than a minor fishing port until the arrival of the railway in 1847 and the development of a dedicated ferry service to Dieppe (the shortest geographical route between London and Paris). It is a little surprising that Hardy made no reference to this in his painting – a fine schooner can be seen at anchor, but little sign of any steam packets.

Opposite below. Plate 3.46.
Shipping off Newhaven.
Signed and dated 1890. 25.5 x 51.5 (10 x 20¼in.)

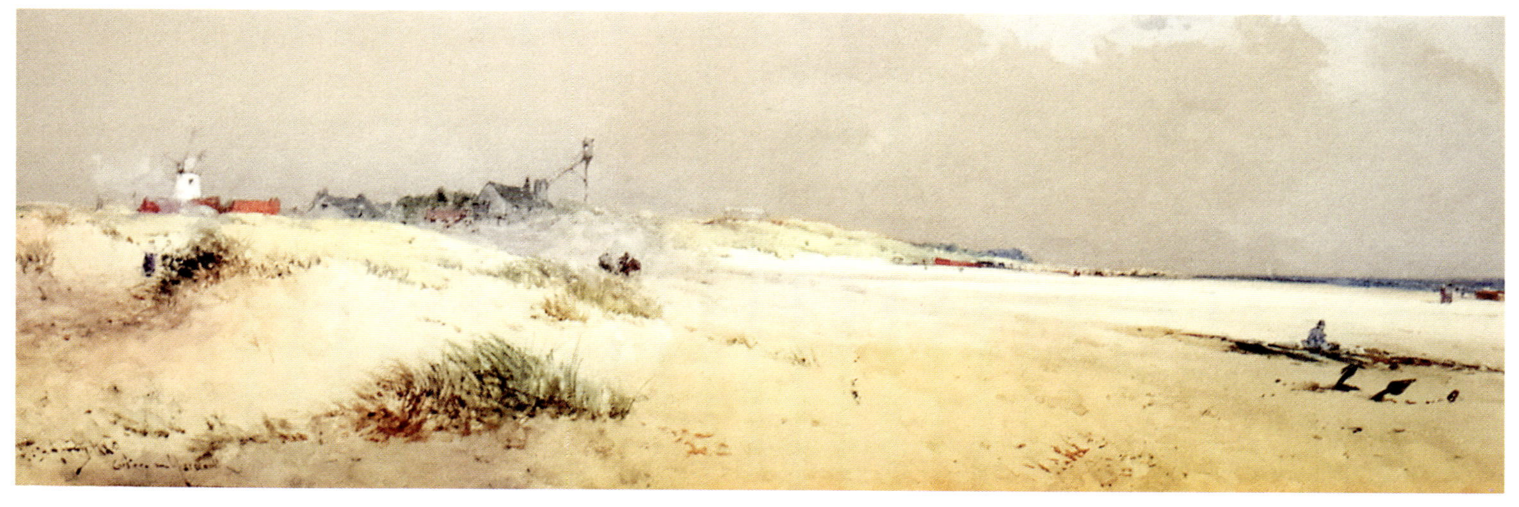

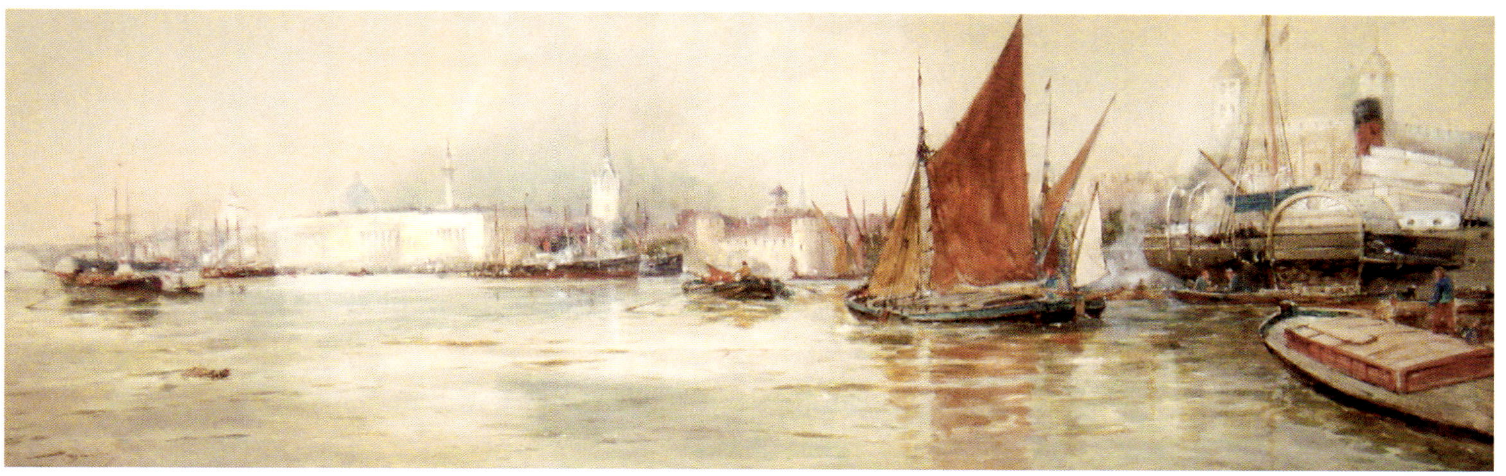

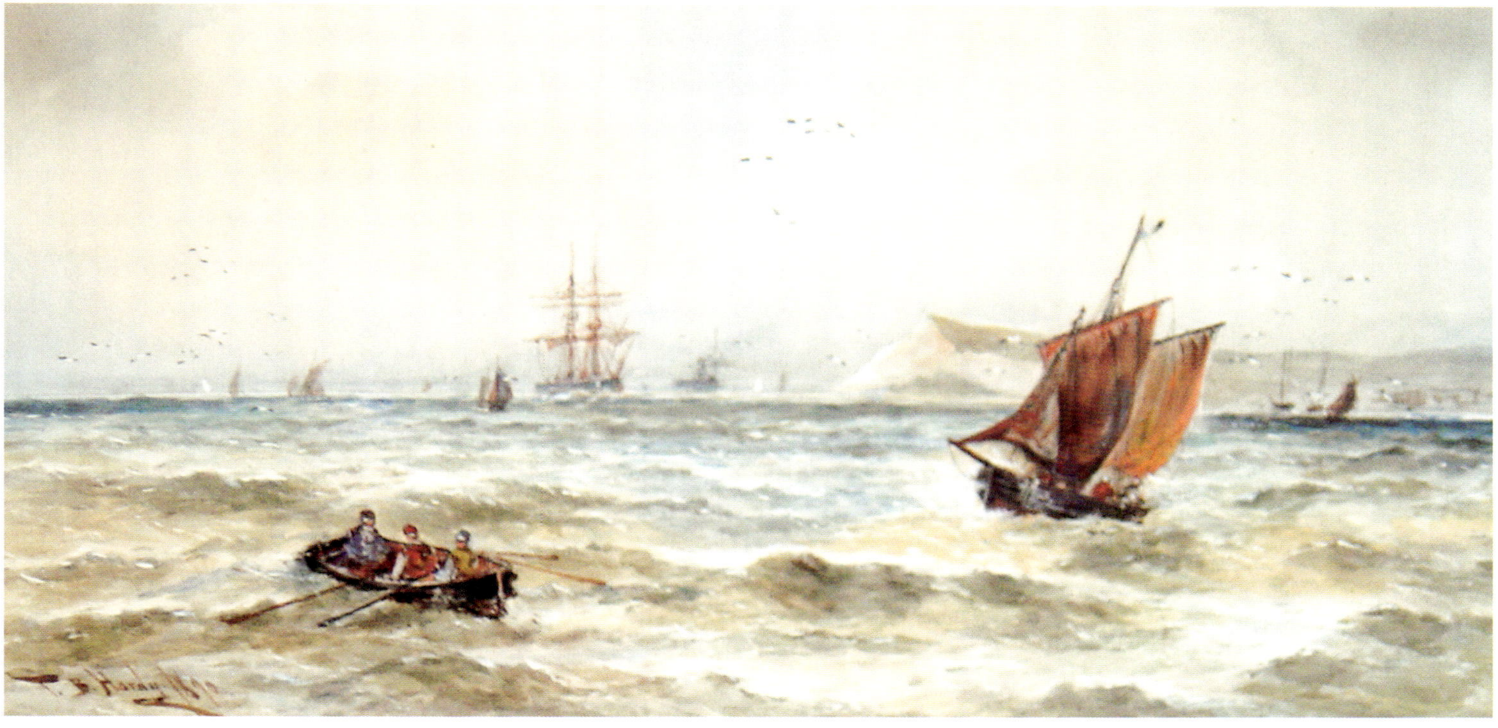

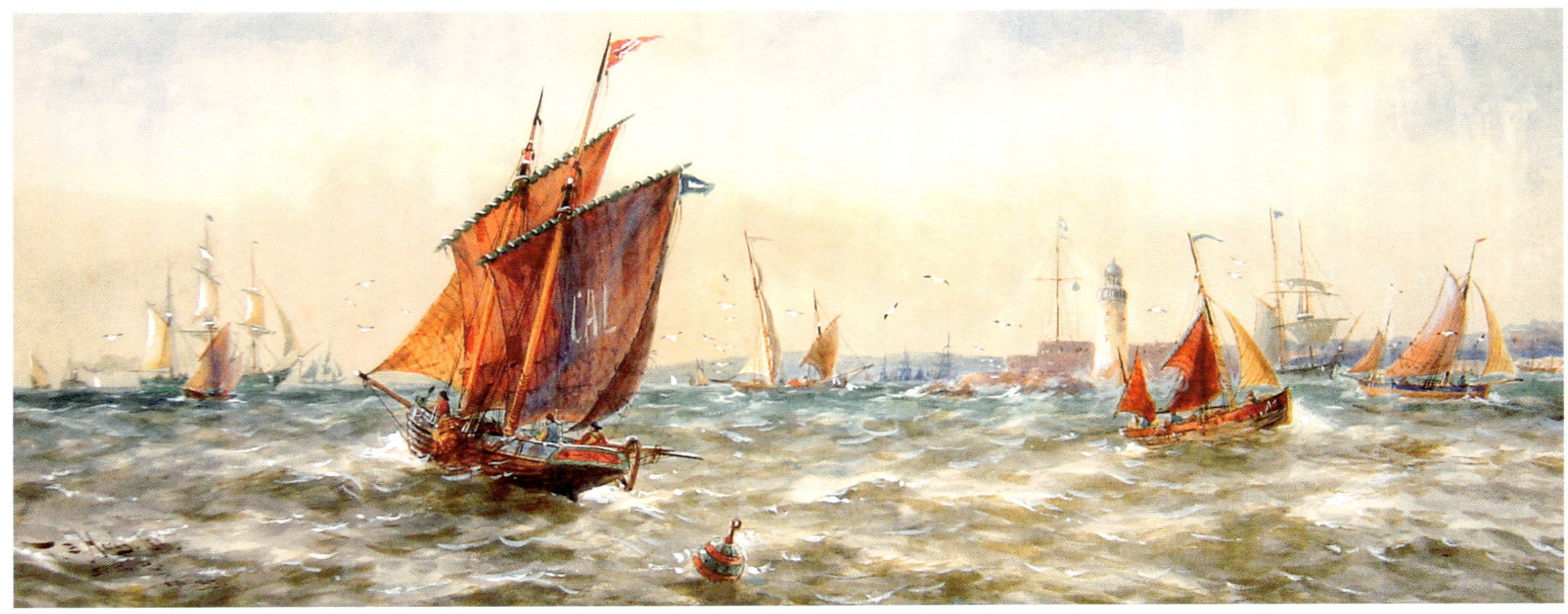

Everything about this large watercolour screams 'This is *not* me, Thomas Bush Hardy'. Not only is the composition and drawing poor but, for the first (but not the last) time, the palette is completely wrong. This artist is using a different mix of colours and has achieved an unrealistic and very unsatisfactory result. Anything that looks even vaguely 'chocolate boxy' should be treated with the utmost suspicion. As for the signature – regrettably signatures can be copied. Hardy's signature changed over the years from a modest simple script to a bold, somewhat flamboyant and often heavily underlined scrawl. Little reliance should be placed on a late Hardy signature, much more on his spidery inscriptions where they exist.

Above. Plate 3.47. **St Pierre Point, Guernsey.** *Signed, inscribed and dated 1891. 26 x 69cm (10¼ x 27⅛ in.)*

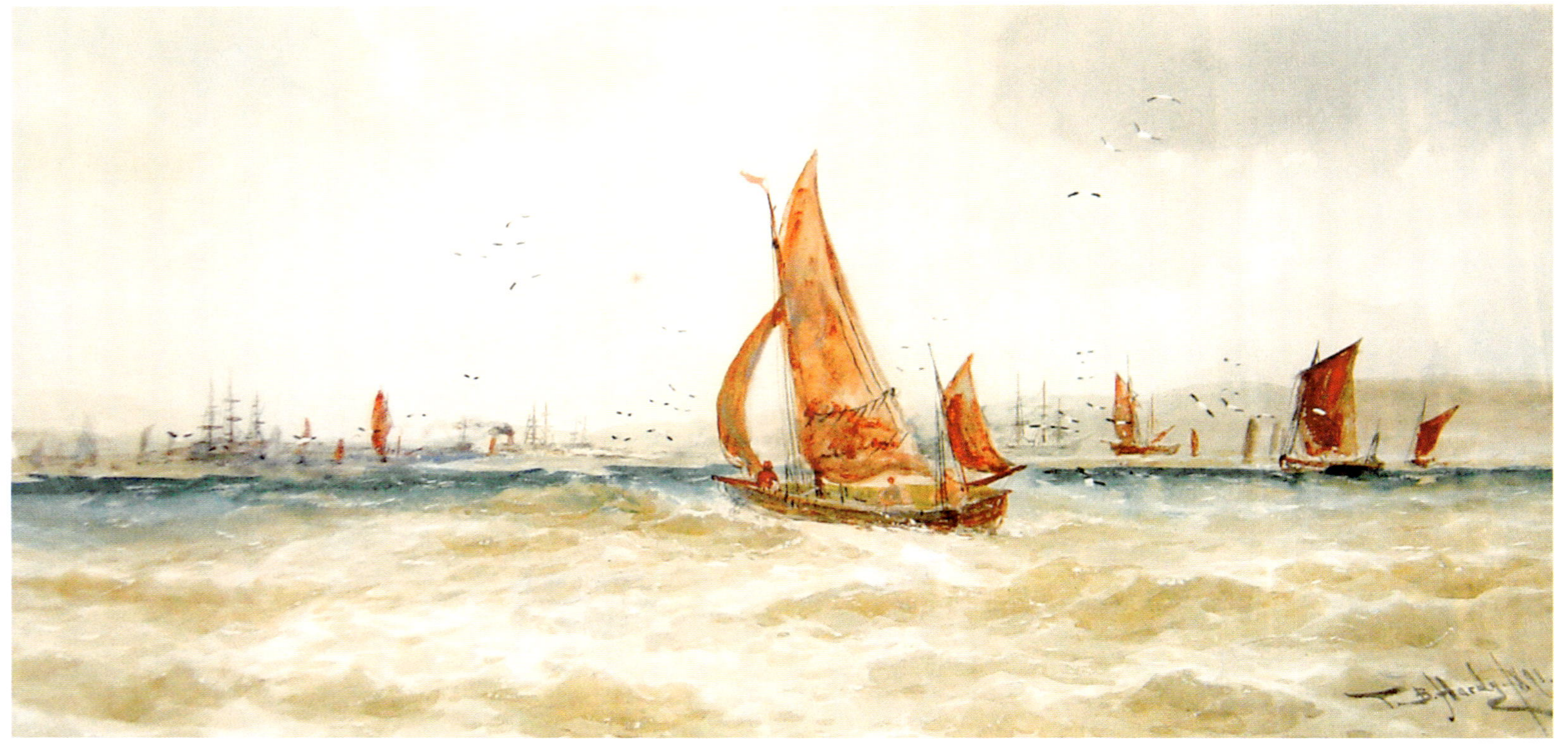

Chapter 3 – The English Coast

There must be some doubt as to whether Hardy himself painted this poorly composed picture and whether he was responsible for its sale. At some time during the early 1890s Hardy, like many other successful artists, began to take on students. This was one way of augmenting his income and also allowed the artist more time for the social and promotional aspects of his career. Unfortunately, besides bringing additional responsibilities, all students bring potential problems. There are indications that most of this watercolour has been painted by one or more of his students and even the signature looks a little shaky. A good auctioneer (and an honest dealer), unless he is certain a work is by the artist, would never catalogue an item above 'Attributed to …'. In this case, where experience suggests much of the work is by a student, possibly under Hardy's supervision, a valid description would be 'Studio of …'.

Although of a different size and shape, this watercolour is clearly based on Hardy's 'Entrance to Portsmouth Harbour' (Plate 3.37) painted six years earlier. By this time Hardy had acquired a number of students and painting this view would have been a tough test of their ability. It had all the ingredients: a fine breezy day, a choppy sea, some fine 'wooden walls', a smack leaving harbour, some interesting historic buildings and an 'atmosphere'. Portsmouth, Britain's premier naval base and dockyard, was a very commercial subject, and many similar views would be sold in the years to come, not necessarily to naval men who, by this time, were more interested in supporting local artists producing accurately detailed portraits of the ships in which they served. That was not Hardy's forte; there is a notable absence of contemporary warships in this painting. It can also be criticised for some sketchy, rather slipshod work and unusually bold colouring, very different from his more delicate and subtle palette of earlier years. One suspects that this painting is not necessarily all of Hardy's hand.

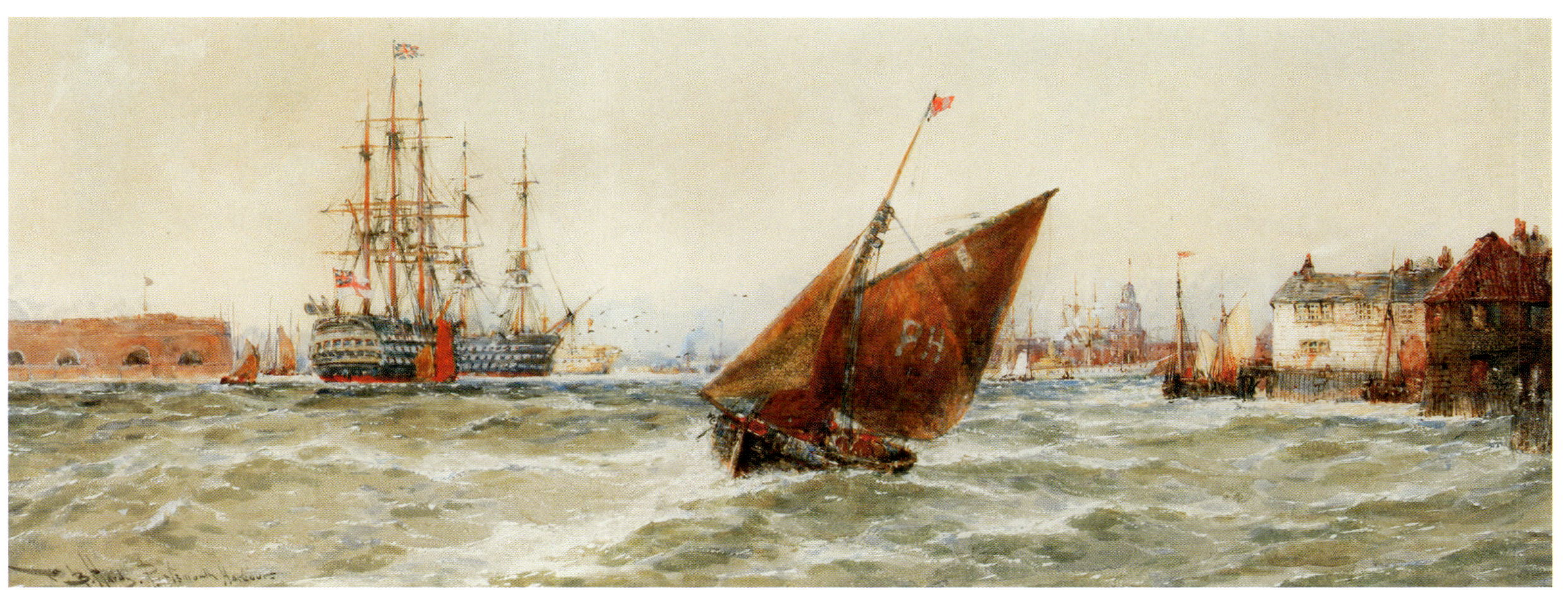

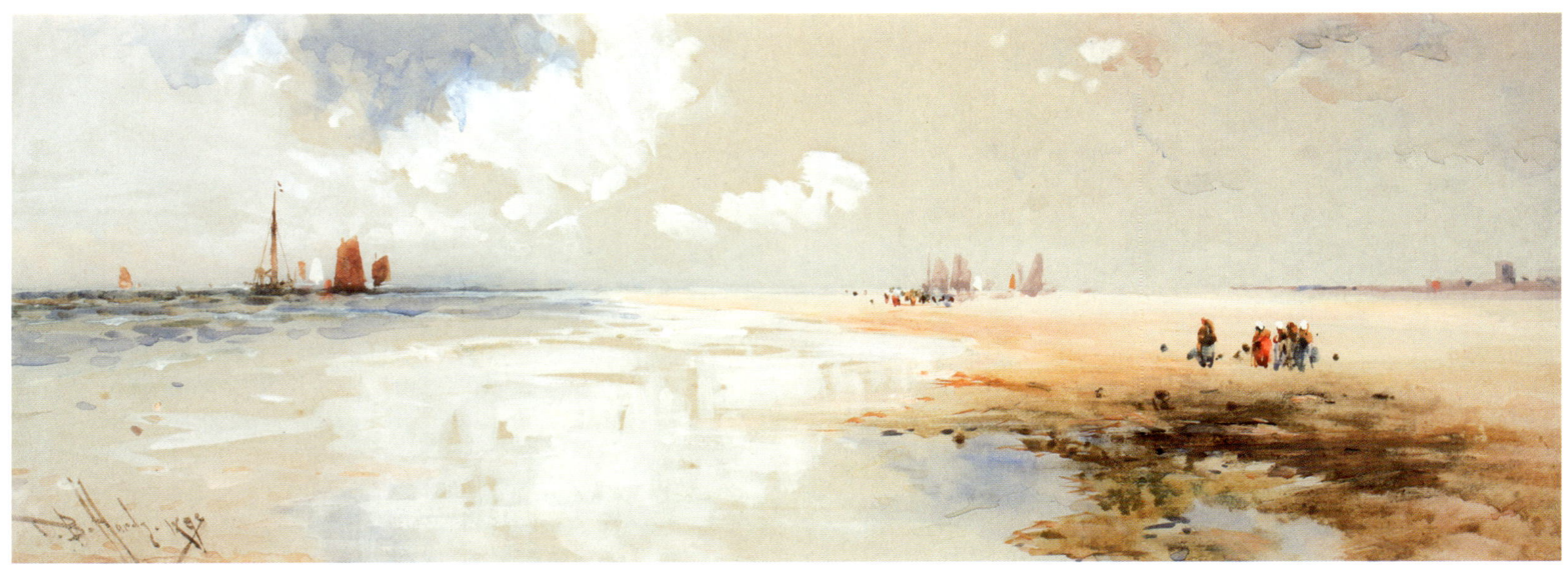

In our opinion, this painting, quite apart from being in an unfortunate condition, is not nearly good enough to be by Hardy. Hardy seldom used Chinese White in painting clouds, and then only sparingly. The composition is poor, the drawing of all the elements – sea, sky, boats, beach and figures – shows little artistic talent. Finally – the least important consideration but another indication – the signature and date are singularly unconvincing!

Plate 3.50. **A Sandy Shore.** *Signed and dated indistinctly. Size 16 x 44cm (6¼ x 17⅜in.)*

This remarkably fine drawing was completed by Hardy in sixteen minutes in front of admiring members of the Savage Club on 16 December 1893. No wonder he was later awarded the distinction 'King of Sketchers'! Evidently the sketch was purchased by W.S. Penley Esq. for the then considerable sum of twenty guineas and was later presented to the Trustees of the British Museum. There may still be a number of such lightning sketches in existence, for the Savage Club, of which Hardy was a distinguished member, met regularly.

Opposite above. Plate 3.51. **The Port of London.** *(Charcoal sketch.) Signed, inscribed and dated Dec 16 1893. 38 x 72 (15 x 28⅜in.)*

This very large charcoal drawing was a birthday gift from Hardy and his wife Muriel to Mrs Alex Bruce Payne 'With the artist's sincere regards April 28th 1894…Many Happy Returns of the Day'. Quite clearly this is all in Hardy's handwriting but, for no good reason, the bold signature and date lower left have almost certainly been added by another hand. The drawing itself is certainly by Hardy and a very fine one at that. The scene, probably imaginary, but based on an east coast port or the Thames estuary, shows a steam trawler and a number of sailing vessels in a strong following wind. A break in the clouds is reflected in the roughening sea, lighting up a flurry of seagulls and a listing lightship marking a shoal. In the foreground some flotsam and jetsam posing a threat to mariners gets carried along by wind and tide. A very handsome present – but a dark and disturbing subject which might not have been to Mrs Payne's taste!

Opposite below. Plate 3.52. **Entering Harbour.** *(Charcoal drawing.) Signed, inscribed and dated Apr 28 1894. 61 x 102.5cm (24 x 40⅜in.)*

Chapter 3 – The English Coast

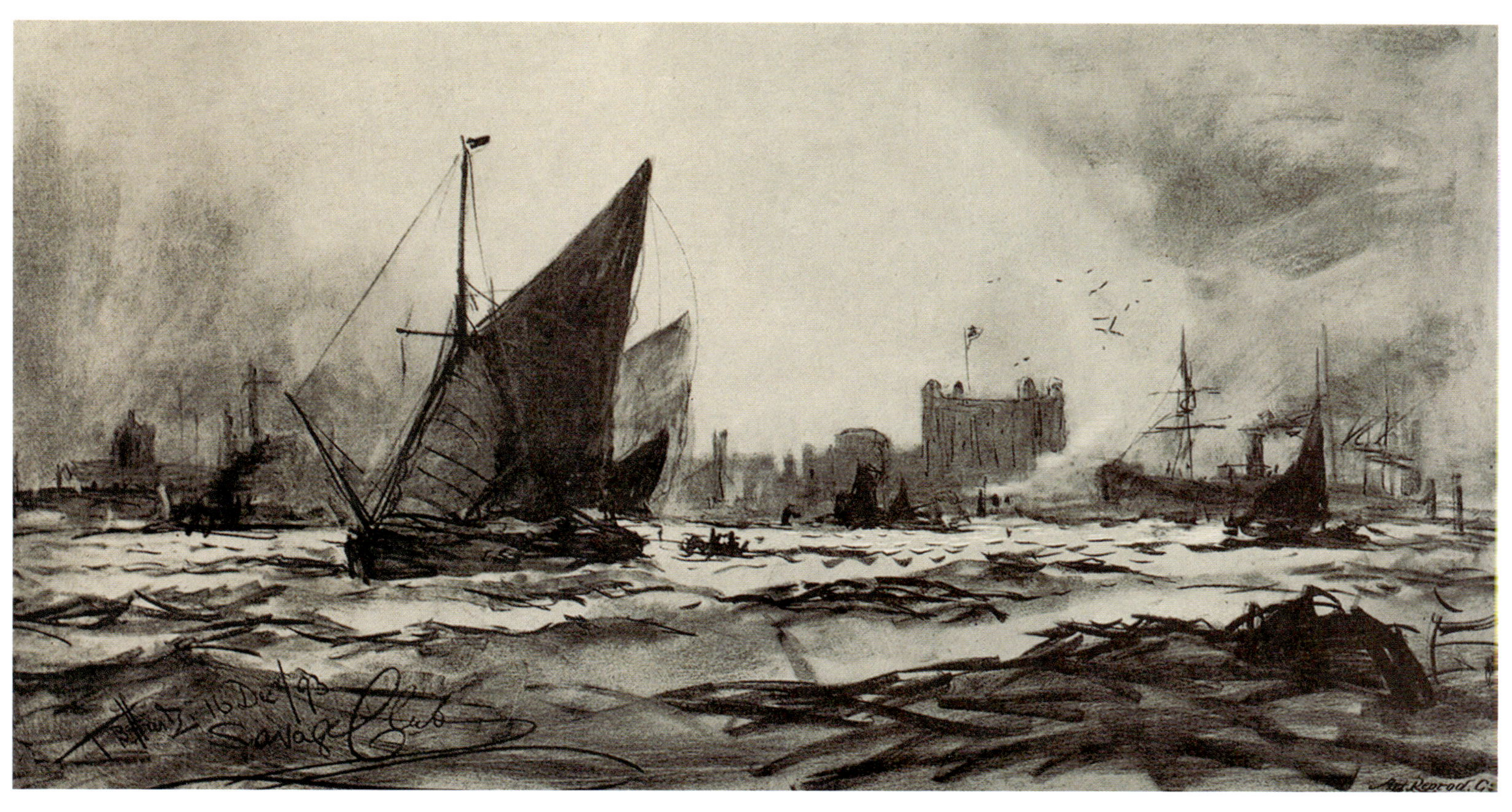

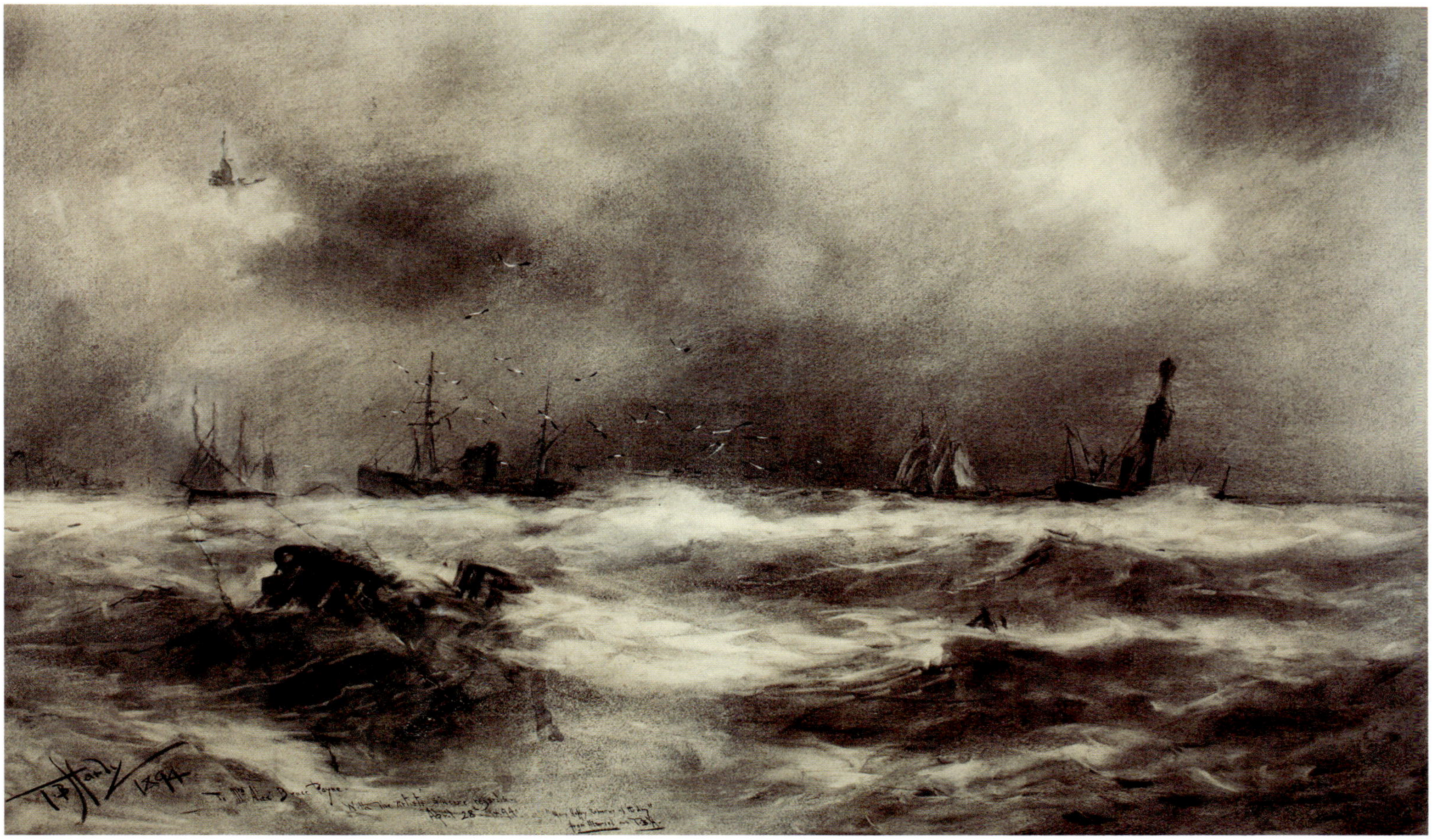

This may have been Hardy's first visit to Wales and he could not have chosen a more appropriate scene than the Gower Coast and the dreaded Mumbles. It was here that James Harris (1810-1887) and Edward Duncan (1803-1882) painted most of their seascapes, including many dramatic rescues at sea. In this watercolour the day is fine, there is just a moderate breeze and the visibility is excellent. The light marking the Mumbles rocks can be seen in the distance; a small steamship and a variety of sailing vessels are making their way round the Gower Peninsula. In the foreground a fishing vessel with a crew of four is heading back to Swansea. It was unlikely that there would be any dramas that day.

Plate 3.53. **Off the Mumbles, near Swansea.** *Signed, inscribed and dated 1894. 45 x 77.5cm (17¾ x 30½in.)*

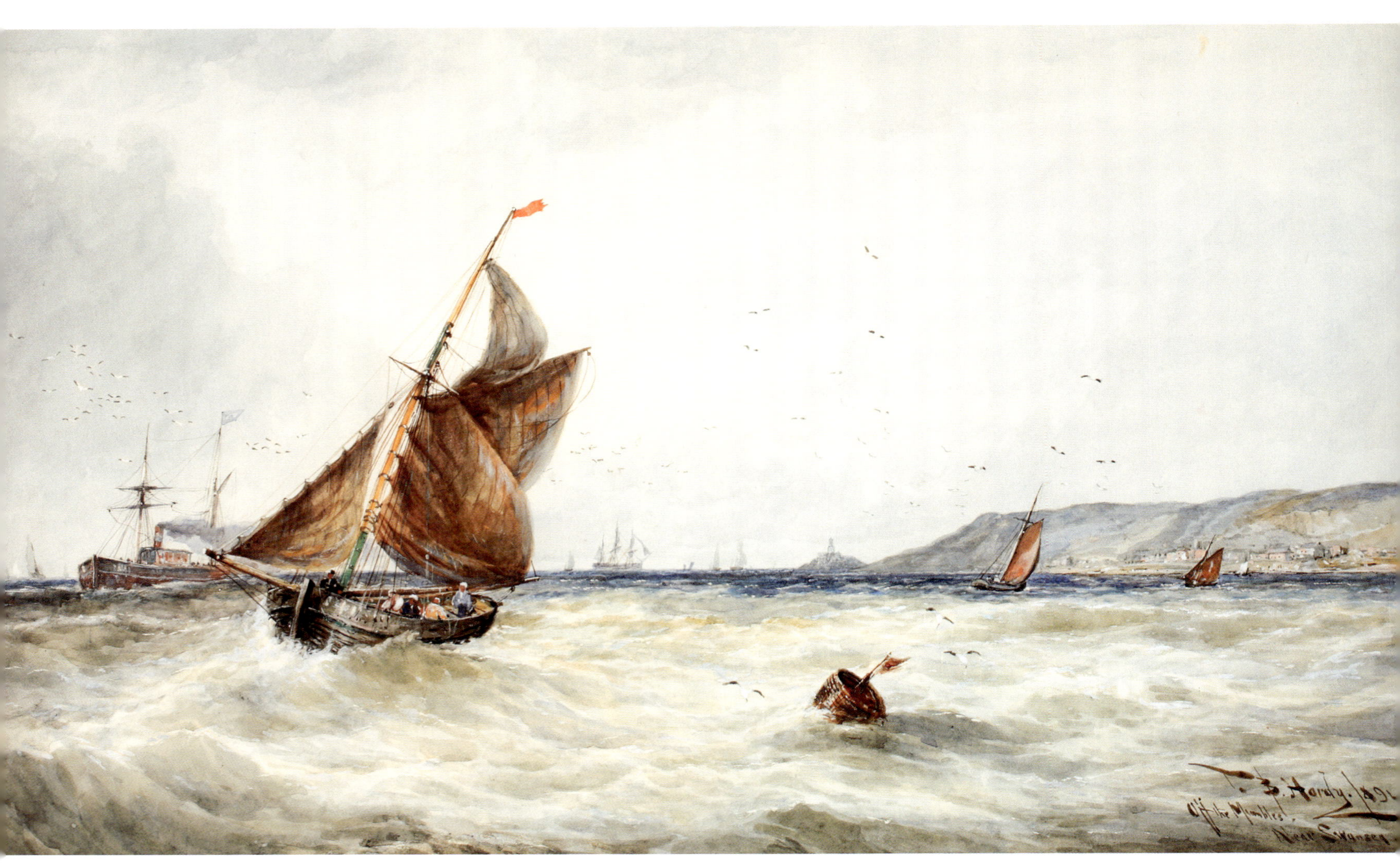

Chapter 3 – The English Coast

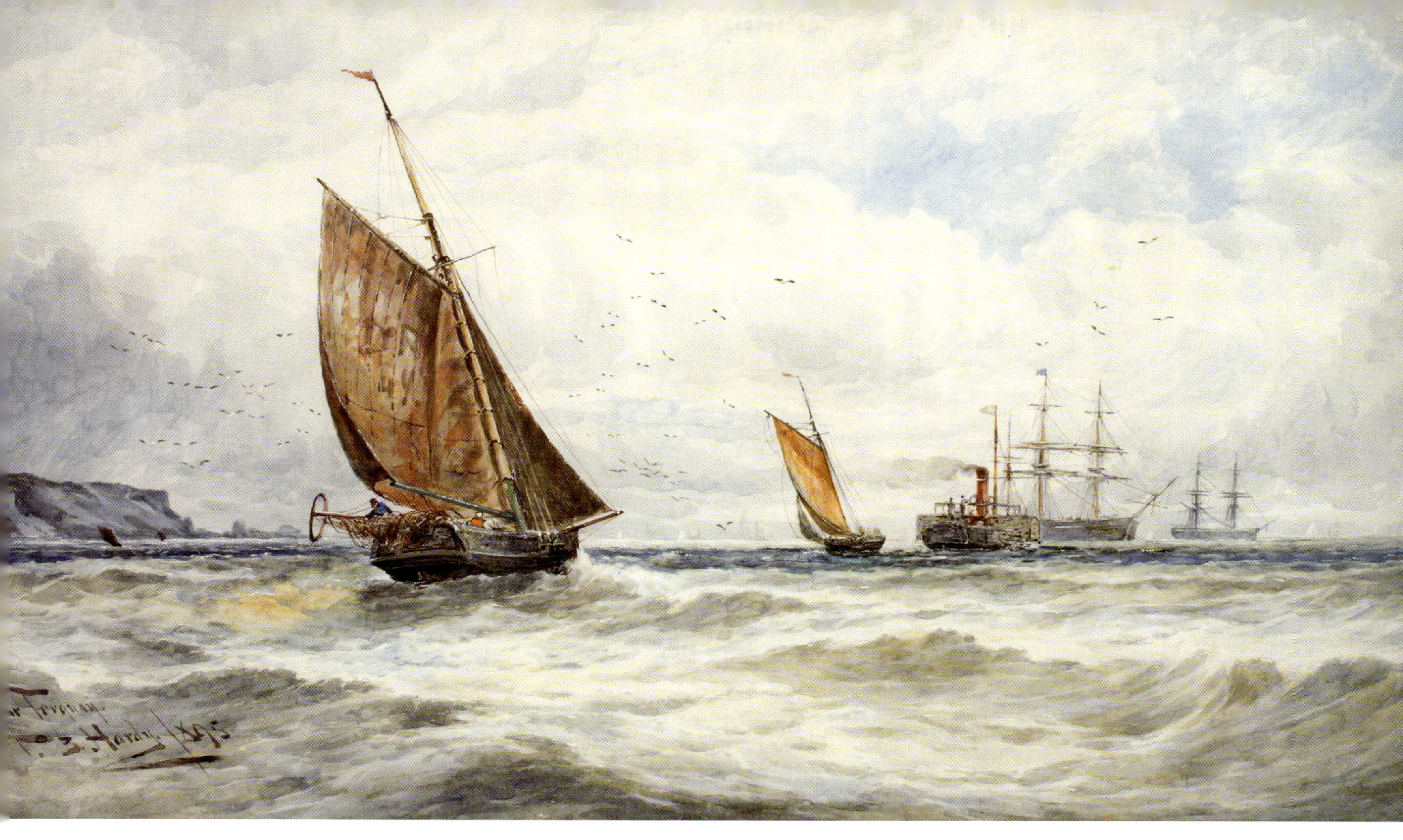

Plate 3.54. **Near Torquay.**
Signed, inscribed and dated 1895. 44 x 77cm (17⅜ x 30¼ in.)

Another late work, but again well composed and executed. Here, on another fine day with a light to moderate south-westerly breeze, two fishing boats out of Brixham are crossing Torbay to their favourite fishing grounds north and east of Hope's Nose. Further offshore a paddle steamer is making towards two brigantines lying at anchor. The hazy summer sky and gently breaking waves create a very peaceful atmosphere. It is a finely painted picture by a man who, perhaps briefly, was enjoying a spell away from the stresses of life in London.

This is a particularly interesting picture from one point of view – precisely where was this pleasant tree-lined quay? This was a quay providing temporary berths for vessels rather than a wharf where ships load and unload their cargoes. Several brigs and other tall-masted sailing vessels are secured alongside at what must be high water. As none of these vessels would be capable of striking their masts to pass under any of London's bridges upstream from the recently opened Tower Bridge, the quay must be well downstream, possibly as far down as Greenwich. Wherever it was, Hardy has painted the scene with much panache. The river, as always, is the dominant feature, the ebb beginning to speed the barges on their downwind journey back to the Essex fields. As with many of Hardy's paintings of this period, his overall colouring showed an increasing use of brown and yellow pigments, often unsuitable in a marine subject. This is not by any means an extreme example but, sadly, in the late 1890s there were too many occasions when Hardy did not live up to his normally high standards.

Plate 3.55. **The Quayside, River Thames.** *Signed, inscribed and dated 1895. 32 x 48cm (12⅝ x 18⅞in.)*

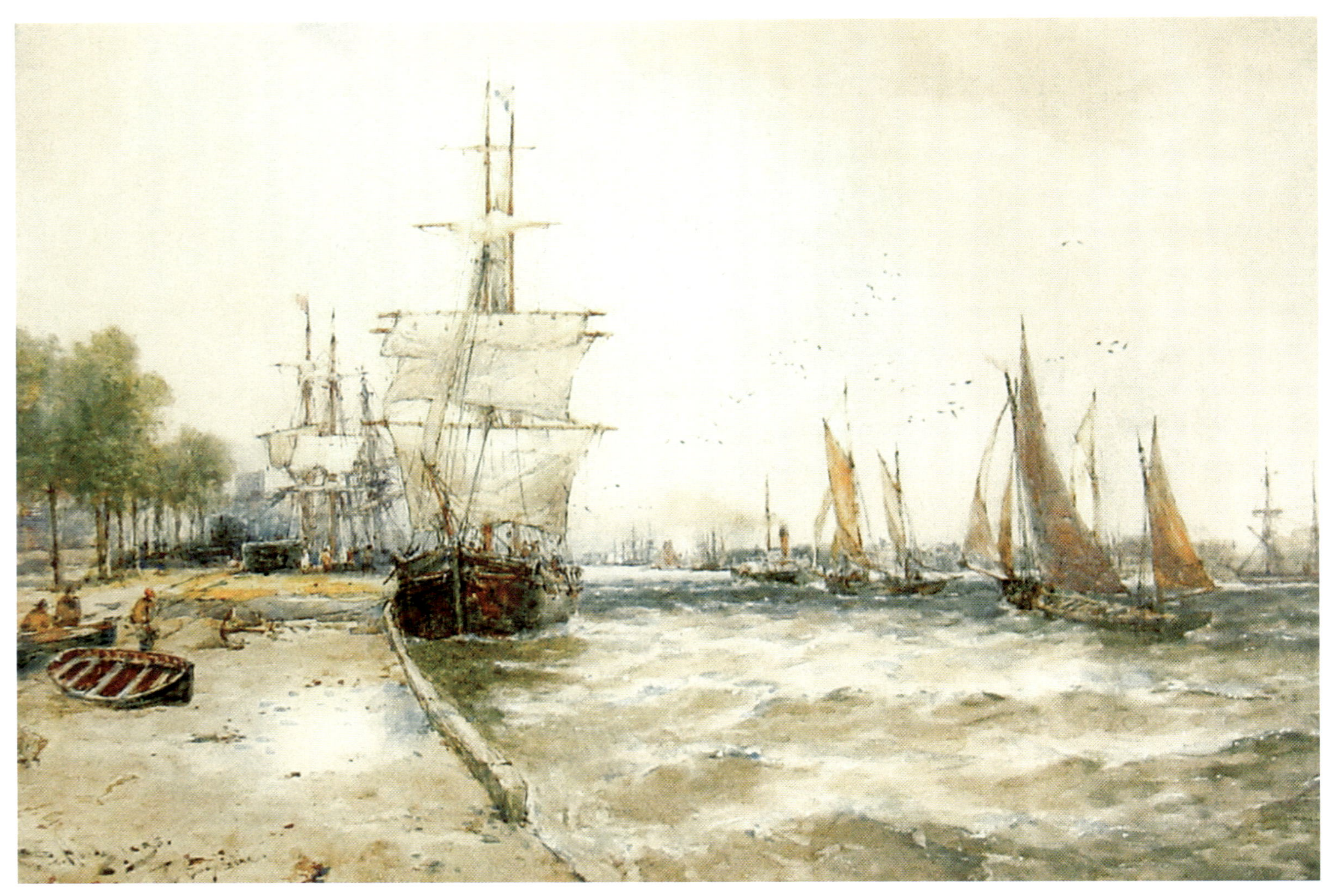

This is a fine oil painting of a cluster of fishing vessels and their crews resting in a quiet anchorage on the coast, probably in Torbay. Hardy was not well known for his oils – he did not paint very many – and the majority were probably his Dutch beach scenes. This is a notable exception. There is one conundrum: the signature appears to be a replica of the signature common to his watercolours in the 1870s – it bears little resemblance to the one he used in the late 1890s and has clearly been added at some later date. This should not detract from the excellence of the painting but it would be interesting to know a little more about its provenance – as with so many others!

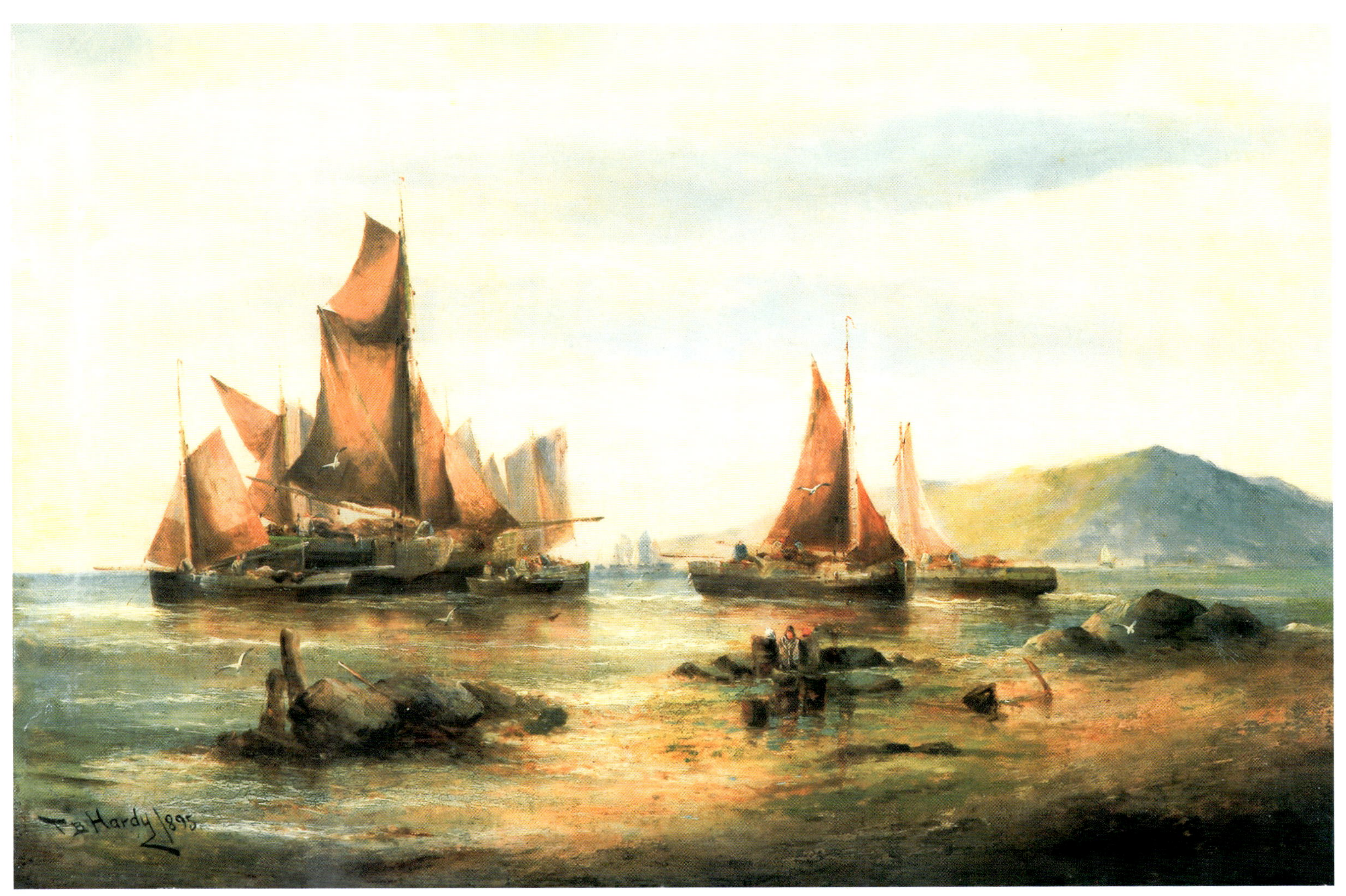

A good example of Hardy's later work at its best – a splendid subject which Hardy has exploited well. Here he has painted a troopship, a converted old ironclad still with her full set of sails but many fewer guns, leaving Portsmouth Harbour on her way to the Far East, maybe to relieve the garrison at Hong Kong or re-commission some Yangtze gunboats. Behind her, moored off Haslar Creek, lies the naval training ship HMS *St Vincent* and to the right the old Customs House. Hardy has painted the choppy, discoloured water with practised skill as it begins to ebb rapidly through the narrow entrance. The troopship's international code flags and white ensign are straining at their halyards in the strong south-westerly, forecasting a rough day or two in the Channel and Bay of Biscay. But they will soon be in the Mediterranean, passing through the Suez Canal and on into the Indian Ocean, where the traditional warship's white hull will reflect the sun and keep the heat bearable on the crowded troop decks. Before the year was out, many more troops would be shipped out to South Africa and elsewhere to protect the Empire's interests, and so it would continue – but not, sadly, for Thomas Bush Hardy, whose health was failing fast.

A very good example of Hardy's colour, style and technique in his later years. This watercolour is 100% Hardy but very different from his earlier work and perhaps a less desirable purchase for the galleries and clients who supported him in the past. This one is not a 'pot-boiler' and no part of it has been siphoned off to a student as might have happened from time to time. This is a very accomplished painting of a fishing smack entering the river Arun on the flood tide. The topography is interesting, there is plenty of movement and even excitement as the onshore wind and sea sweep across the harbour entrance. This is a Hardy still experimenting with new, but not always successful, techniques and colours. Had he lived longer, who knows in what direction he might have sailed and what his reputation might be today?

Opposite. Plate 3.58. **Troops for the East.** *Signed, inscribed and dated 1896. 59.5 x 36.5cm (23⅜ x 14⅜in.)*

Plate 3.57. **Littlehampton.** *Signed, inscribed and dated 1896. 25.5 x 51cm (10 x 20in.)*

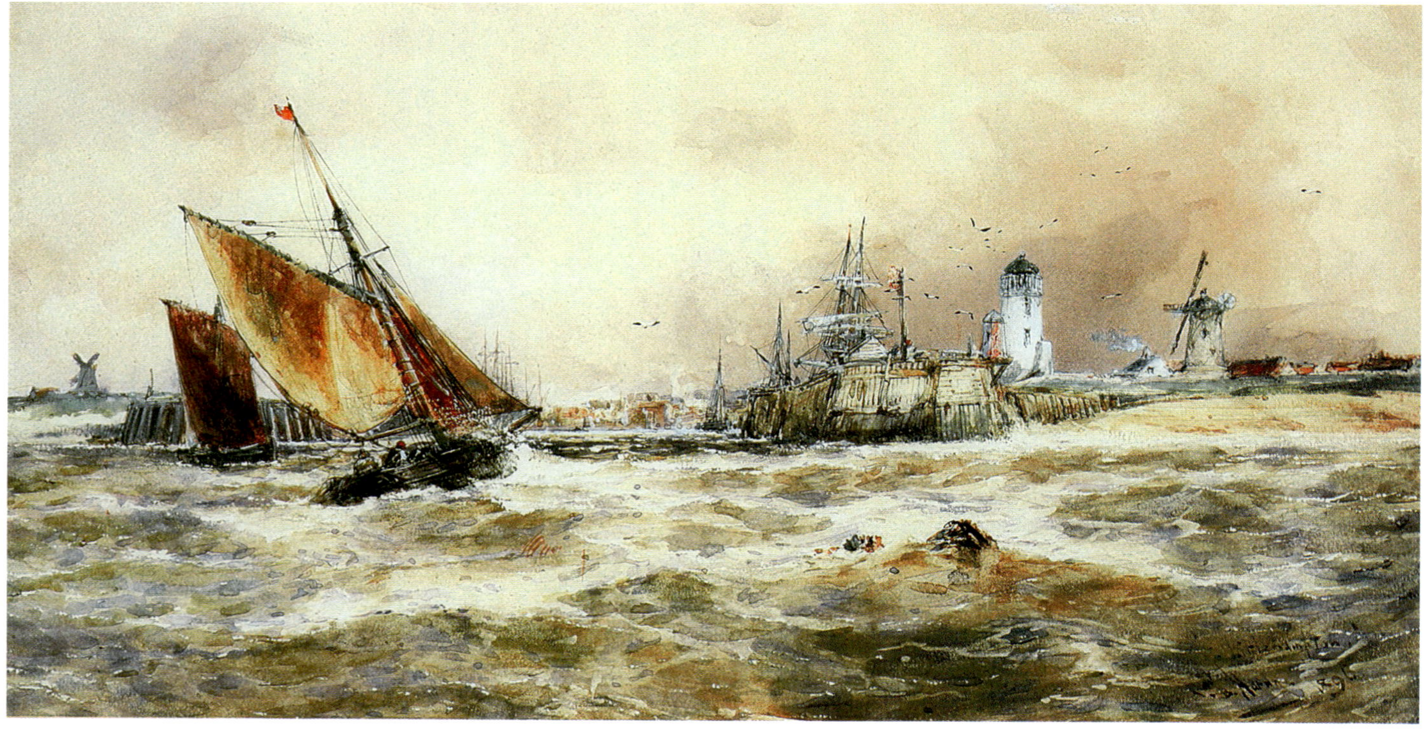

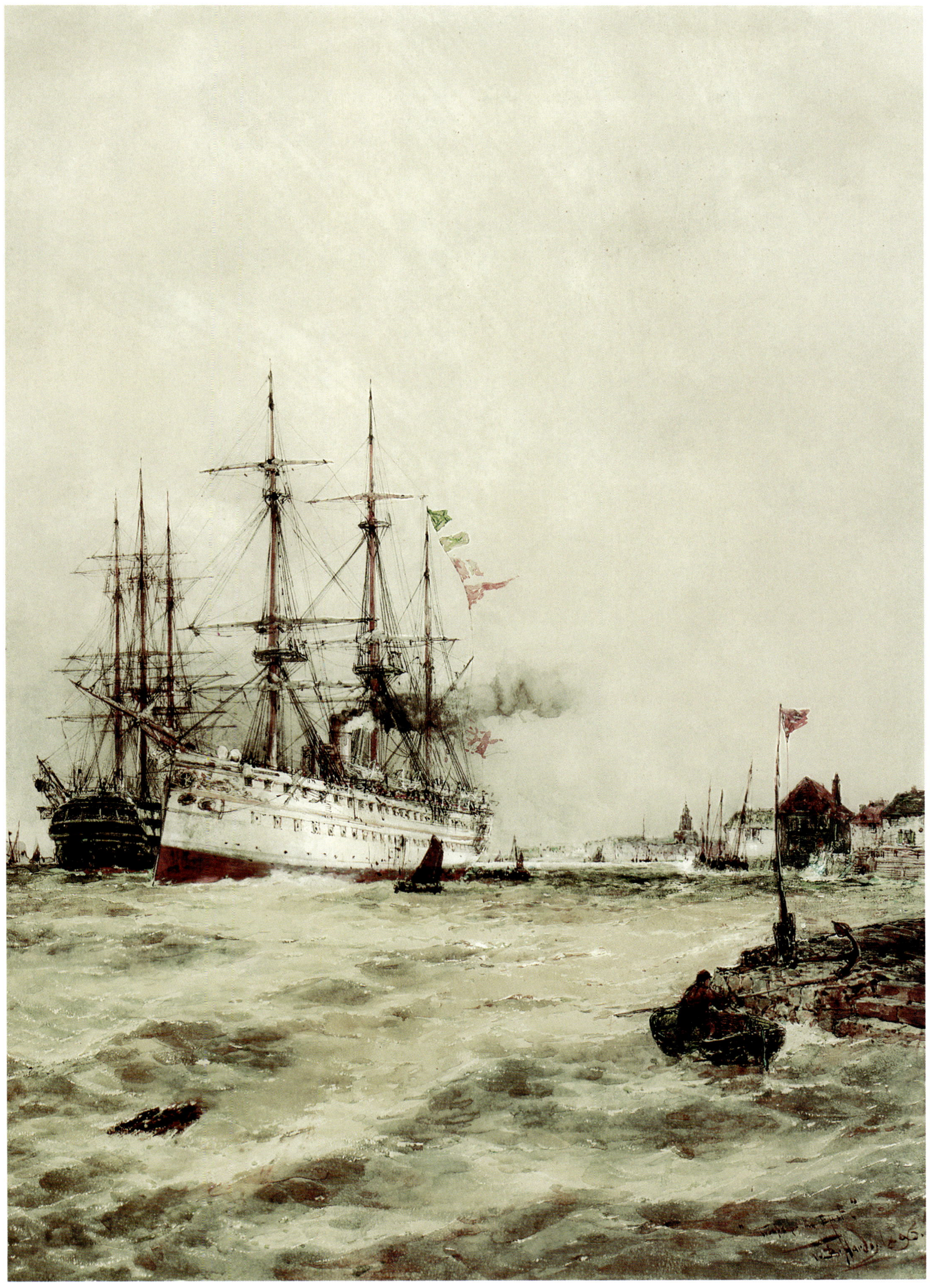

We may never know for certain why, with a few notable exceptions, the standard of Hardy's work gradually deteriorated from the early 1890s until his death in 1897. There is evidence that he began to face quite serious financial problems – not unusual in the artistic fraternity, and especially so for a middle-aged man with a second wife and eight daughters to be married off! Maintaining a suitable lifestyle in Barnes was doubtless very expensive.

The problems that may arise from taking students have already been discussed. We know that Hardy enjoyed the social side of the clubs and societies of which he was a member. It seems likely that he also enjoyed the company of the aspiring artists he was tutoring – young men who, after a day's work, may have encouraged him to join them for one drink too many rather than go home early to a female-dominated environment.

Poor Hardy. Once his patrons detected or suspected a lowering of his normal standard his reputation suffered – and still does. But what evidence is there that his ability to paint a fine watercolour was affected by over-indulgence? There is some – much of it apocryphal (the image of Hardy setting up several easels at the Portsmouth pub 'The Still and West' before a liquid lunch comes to mind). There is little doubt that in the 1890s much of his work was hurried and careless. Anxiety about finances has led many artists to sacrifice quality for quantity.

There is one other important factor. While Hardy himself was maturing as an artist, reaching his peak in the 1880s, a whole new generation of artists was beginning to make their presence felt. Perhaps unwillingly, he began developing new techniques, not always with a favourable reaction from his clientele. Even so, in the last two years of his life, when much of his output was way below his normal standard, he was still capable of some excellent traditional work. These watercolours must have been painted by a Hardy enjoying a few days' relaxation among fishermen well away from London and Portsmouth, centres now exhibiting the profound change from sail to steam that had occurred in Hardy's lifetime, a change he found hard to accept and difficult to portray.

Despite Hardy's latter era of sometimes second class works which, of course, may have been done by his students, this must not detract from his obvious enormous ability. From the paintings reproduced above, let us return to Hardy's consummate ability to paint the sea on calm and rough days. Plates 3.25 and Plate 3.26 epitomize his attributes and are shown again opposite.

Opposite above. Plate 3.25. **On the Medway.** *Signed, inscribed and dated 1881. 31 x 48.5cm (12¼ x 19⅛ in.)*

Opposite below. Plate 3.26. **Hay Barge on the Medway.** *Signed, inscribed and dated 1883. 12 x 17cm (4¾ x 6¾ in.)*

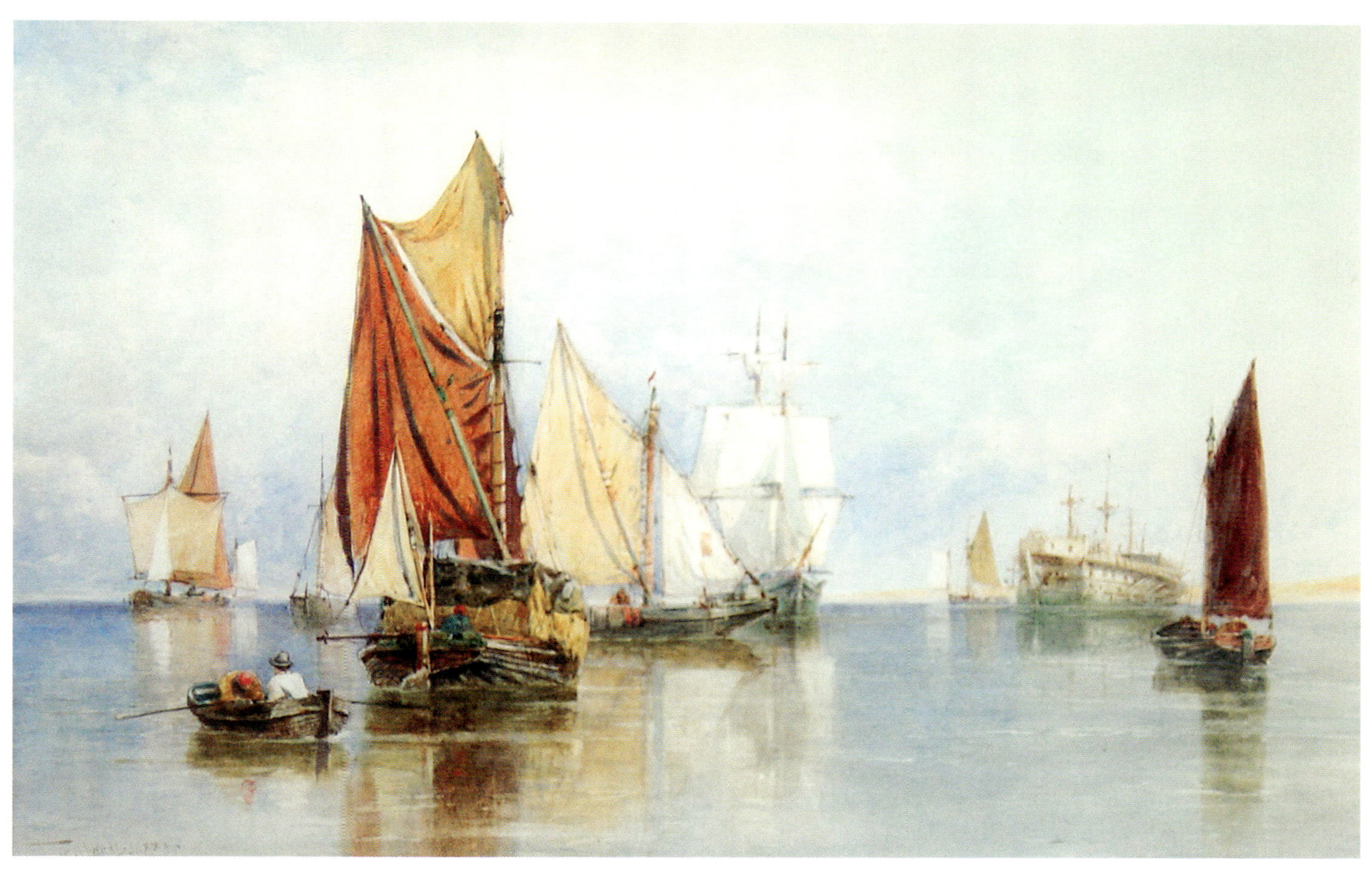

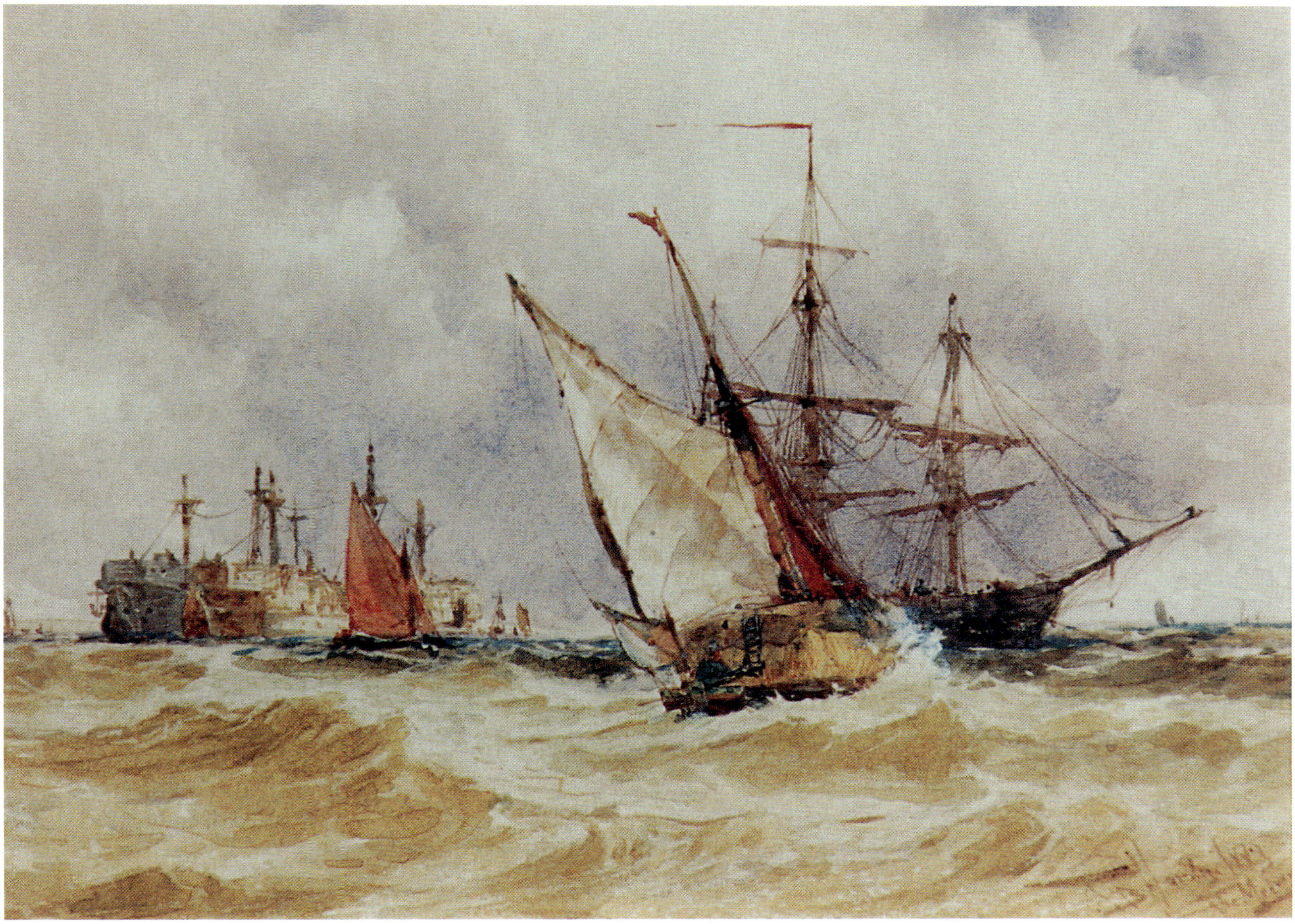

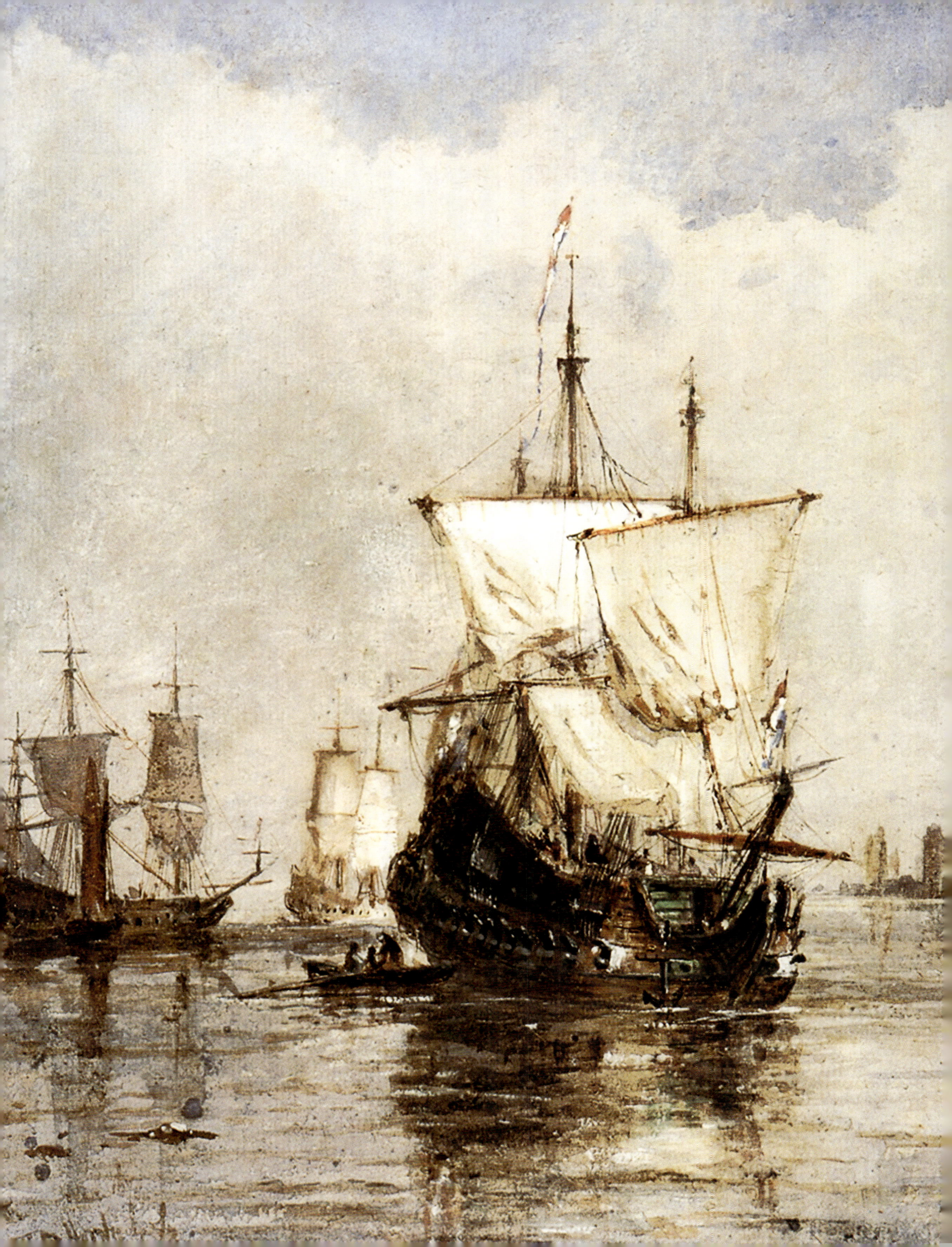

The Dutch Coast

Regrettably, there is no record of why and when Hardy decided to travel abroad in search, presumably, of experience and inspiration. The trans-Atlantic crossings in his teens and more recent contacts with fishing communities on the North East coast would have motivated him to concentrate on sea subjects. He had moved to London with his young and rapidly increasing family in the late 1860s, but the metropolis, despite the ever-present Thames, was short of scenic backgrounds and subjects for a budding marine artist. Visits to London's museums and art galleries with their fine collections of early Dutch and contemporary British marine paintings and watercolours (which were beginning to sell quite well) may well have provided the additional incentive, if any was required.

In 1870, the Hardy family were living in Finsbury, North London, reasonably close to the Great Eastern Railway terminus, then at Bishopsgate. It was now possible for travellers to the Continent to go by train from London to Harwich, changing at Colchester, before boarding a steam packet to Rotterdam (Hook of Holland). From there it was but a short journey by rail and road to the Hague and Scheveningen with its long sandy foreshore.

Now a modern seaside resort, Scheveningen had for centuries drawn the finest artists to a fishing village supporting a fleet of over a hundred flat-bottomed fishing boats hauled up on its gently shelving beach. The Van de Veldes, Simon de Vlieger and, in Hardy's time, Hendrik Willem Mesdag were some of the Dutch artists who succeeded in capturing on paper and

Plate 4.1. **Dutch Merchant Flutes at Anchor.** *Signed and dated 1873. 22 x 17cm (8⅝ x 6¾in.)*

This rare portrait-shaped watercolour of a group of seventeenth century Dutch merchant-men is an indication that, working close to the Hague, Hardy visited a number of museums and art galleries there and, understandably, was greatly impressed by examples of Dutch marine art of that period. The Dutch merchant fleet of those days comprised large numbers of these 'flutes', so-called due to the shape of their stern, and, like the British East Indiamen, they were often as well armed as a naval frigate. As can be seen, this is a fine sketch of three of these classic vessels, probably moored off Dordrecht. Unlike his carefully applied colour washes on the smooth paper of his calm beach scenes, Hardy has here used a less detailed technique on a paper with a much coarser texture. It worked very well.

canvas both the calms and storms of a fisherman's life. There was much beauty, despite the hardships, in this ever-changing maritime environment – a combination which will always appeal to an artist.

One of Hardy's earliest works is a typical watercolour of a Dutch pinck drawn up on Scheveningen Beach, painted in 1870, so it would seem that he had taken someone's advice to travel by one of the easier and cheaper routes to an 'artist's paradise' on the Continent. The indications are that he never regretted the decision: Scheveningen and, later, Katwijk, another village some ten miles to the north, were to remain his favourite sketching grounds for many years.

Other routes to the Continent included the shortest sea crossing from Dover to Calais and the neighbouring ferry service from Folkestone to Boulogne – both of which Hardy was to use in the early 1870s. But constant travelling could be expensive, tiring and may have caused problems at home. In 1877 he decided to move his entire family to Boulogne where they lived for three years before returning full-time to London. Hardy was taking full advantage of the opening up of the Continent by independent British railway and associated ferry companies. From now on he would be able to bring some of Europe's finest maritime scenes on the Dutch and French Coasts to British galleries and drawing rooms.

Of all the craft featured in Dutch paintings, the fishing *pinck* is the most common. Clinker built with heavy planking and a carvel bottom, they came with a curved, raked stem, very rounded bows and a raked sternpost with tiller – in essence, a flat-bottomed rectangular hull with rounded corners! The larger boats featured a low cabin aft and a small cabin under the foredeck. A distinctive feature common to craft of every size were the broad lee-boards. The larger vessels were gaff-rigged with a mainsail on a mainmast stepped amidships, a small forward-rated foremast, a staysail and jib to a long bowsprit. The length varied between 9 and 13 metres (30 and 42 feet) with a beam of 3 to 4 metres (10 to 13 feet) and a minimal draught for navigating and beaching in shallow waters. Over the years these versatile fishing boats accumulated various alternative names: *pinkje, pinkschip, pinque, scholschuitze, scholschuyt, scheveningen pink, zeeboot, zeepink* and *bomschuiten*.

A larger version of the pinck, the *smalschip* or *wijdschip*, featured a carvel-built hull with a length varying between 14 and 22 metres (46 and 72 feet), a beam of 4.5 metres (14 feet 9 inches) and drew a maximum of 2 metres (6 feet 6 inches). These boats carried a large spritsail, a foresail and a small square topsail. Still larger vessels were the *galliott* and *koff*, both featuring a substantial mainmast set two-thirds forward and an additional smaller mizzen mast stepped behind the after deck cabin. These seaworthy.vessels were often used as mother ships for groups of smaller, more vulnerable fishing boats in the event of worsening weather conditions. The North Sea could be rough!

From the very beginning of his time on the Dutch Coast, Hardy was clearly entranced by the beauty of his surroundings and the fisherfolk he met. It is almost impossible to find fault with any of the watercolours he painted during his many excursions to this part of the Netherlands He may be accused of being repetitive but each beach scene has its own originality and atmosphere. The many days and weeks he spent sitting on the sand, watching the sea, the sky, the tide and the wind, gave him a clear understanding of the relationship between those elements and the main subject of his paintings – the coastal fishermen of Holland.

Hardy was not the only artist to be dubbed repetitive. A catalogue of E.W. Cooke's Dutch paintings would reveal canvas after canvas and drawing after drawing of pincks landing or beached at Scheveningen. But no one painting is exactly like the next. From time to time an artist may be asked to paint a 'copy' of one of his own works. If he agrees, you can be certain that he will quite deliberately ensure that it will not be an exact copy. Original art is one thing – an exact copy, whether it be a print, an engraving or etching, a photograph or something produced by the very latest technological process will always be a copy, of intrinsically less interest and value than an original.

Over the centuries Dutch and British artists have recognised the sales potential of these marine and coastal paintings and demand was greater in the 1870s than it had ever been. Hardy had the talent, the ability and the belief in himself to make the most of the opportunities offered on the Continent. Most importantly, he was able to identify himself with the local people and the elemental factors on which their livelihood depended. He quickly mastered the art of reproducing atmospheric works recording, without embellishment, the everyday life of the fisherfolk. The daily task of beaching the boats and unloading the catch was an operation which, depending on the weather, often involved the whole village. In his Dutch paintings Hardy was able to convey the especially strong bonds which distinguish most fishing communities.

As will be seen in many of the illustrations, Hardy's ability to paint the shallow pools of water on the hard sand, mirroring translucent images of the beached pincks, was quite remarkable. His paintings on a sunny day exude warmth and tranquillity – unlike those on a grey day which convey all too chillingly the effects of the cold east wind.

Every painting is as different as the changing conditions of sea and sky, of temperature, humidity, wind force and direction. In calm or stormy weather, his artistic grouping of women on the beach anxiously awaiting the return of the fishing fleet was masterly. His watercolours of pincks beaching through heavy surf, often with the help of a horse and rider to gather the warps, were outstanding. No wonder he quickly gained a reputation in the galleries and drawing rooms of Victorian London.

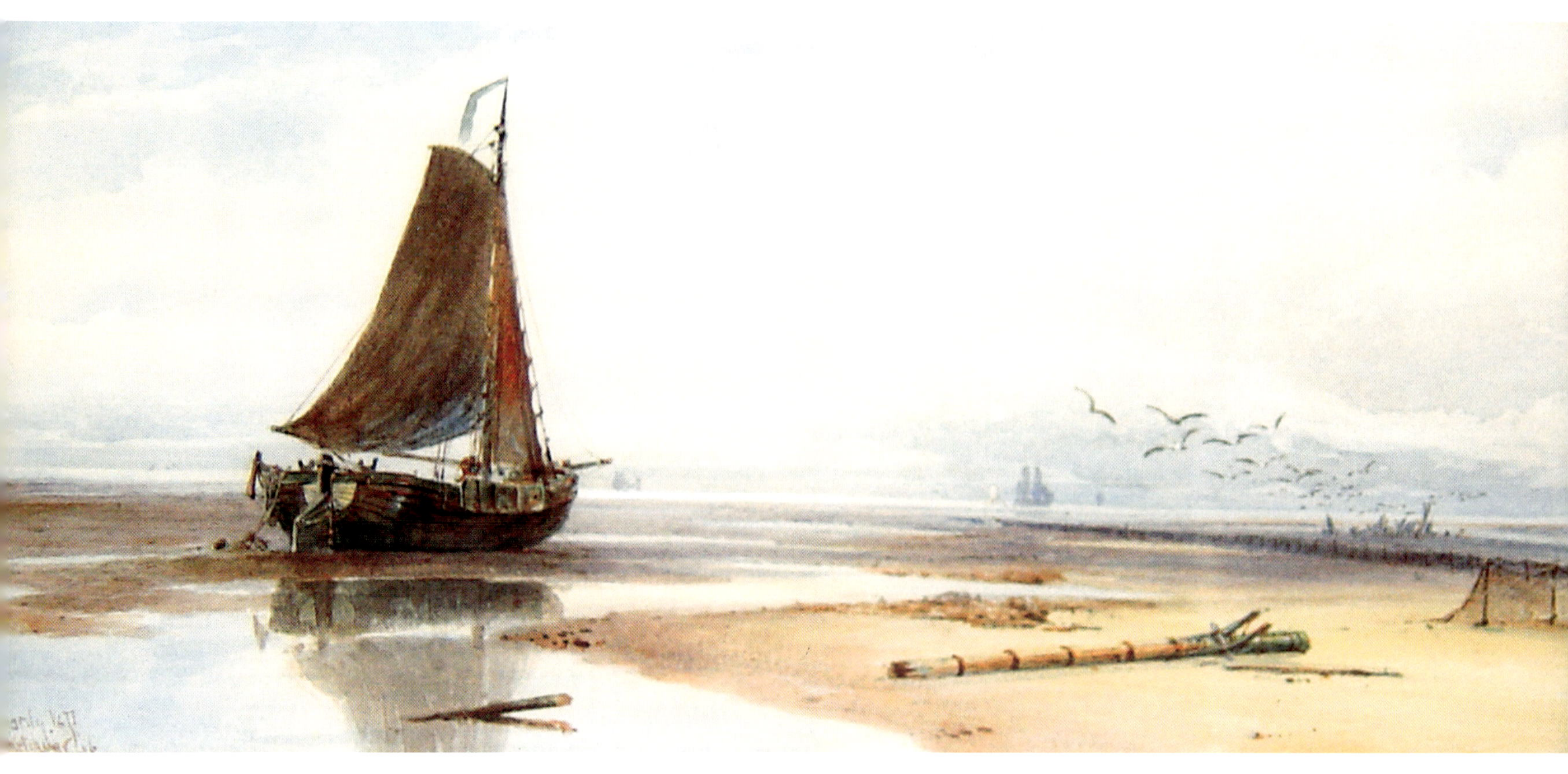

It is very unusual to find any Hardy watercolour of a Dutch coastal scene dated earlier than 1872. Here is one of the few known to have survived, and a very fine example it is. The title 'Silence' perfectly describes this stunning watercolour. The pinck on the left sits on the sand at low water, her sails drying in the gentlest of breezes, the crew resting inside the hull. Possibly for the first time, Hardy has shown how well he could paint a reflected image in a pool left by the receding tide. This would become a feature of many, if not most, of his beach scenes, adding tranquillity and much beauty to his compositions. Apart from the the wheeling gulls, nothing moves. Simply executed, this is a lovely work showing great potential.

This must have been one of the first wrecks seen by Hardy on a European beach but it would not be the last. In those days, a merchantman of this size driven ashore in a westerly gale would remain there for many months until finally broken up. The French and Dutch fishermen never had a reputation as 'wreckers' (unlike some of their counterparts on the other side of the Channel!) but they lost no time in salvaging anything movable – stores, rigging, spars and masts were all fair game.

An early Scheveningen beach scene, the inspiration for most of his Dutch paintings over the next twenty-five years. Unlike the previous example, this painting is full of colour and movement. Hardy here shows his growing skill at harmonising the prevailing conditions – scudding grey clouds, sand-filled waves breaking against the beach and a huddle of wind-swept figures awaiting the return of the fishermen still at sea. The main focus of attention is the well-built pinck resting at the water's edge with a crew member hurrying to secure an anchor warp to the stern. On the horizon, left and right, ships in full sail go about their business.

Plate 4.2. **Silence.** *Signed and dated 1871. 21.5 x 45.5cm (8½ x 17⅞in.)*

Opposite above. Plate 4.3. **Her Last Anchorage.** *Signed, inscribed and dated 1872. 23 x 39cm (9 x 15⅜in.)*

Opposite below. Plate 4.4. **Scheveningen.** *Signed and dated 1872. 33 x 50cm (13 x 19⅝in.)*

Chapter 4 – The Dutch Coast

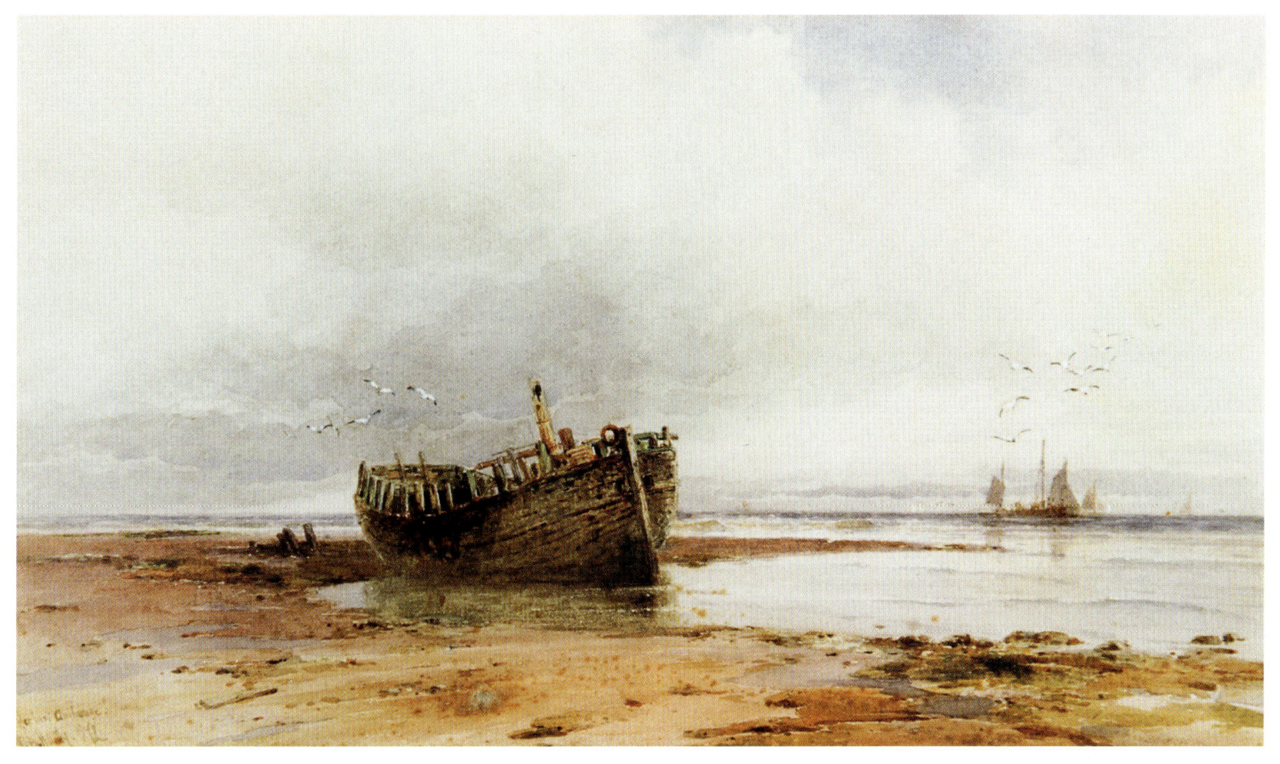

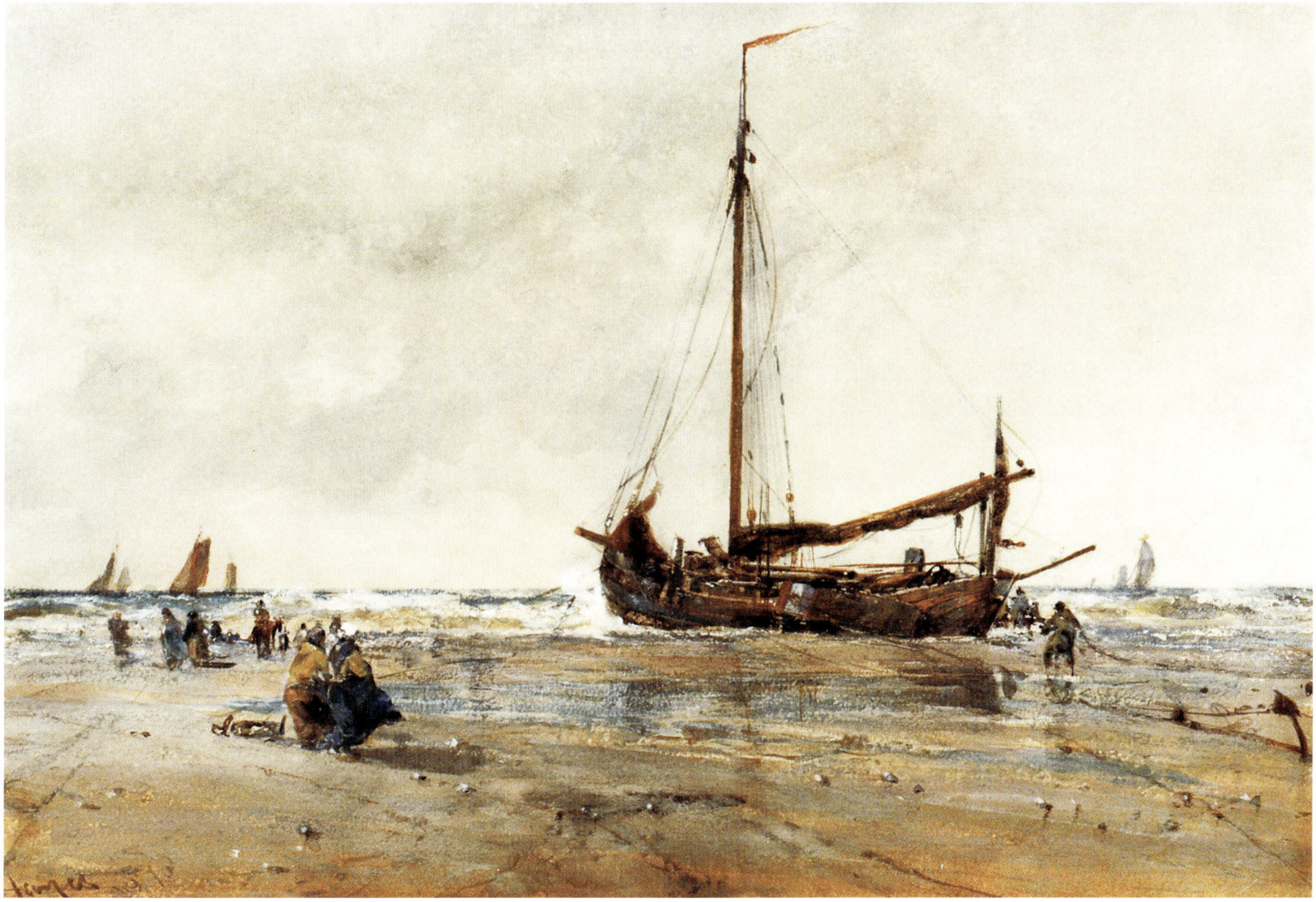

Chapter 4 – The Dutch Coast

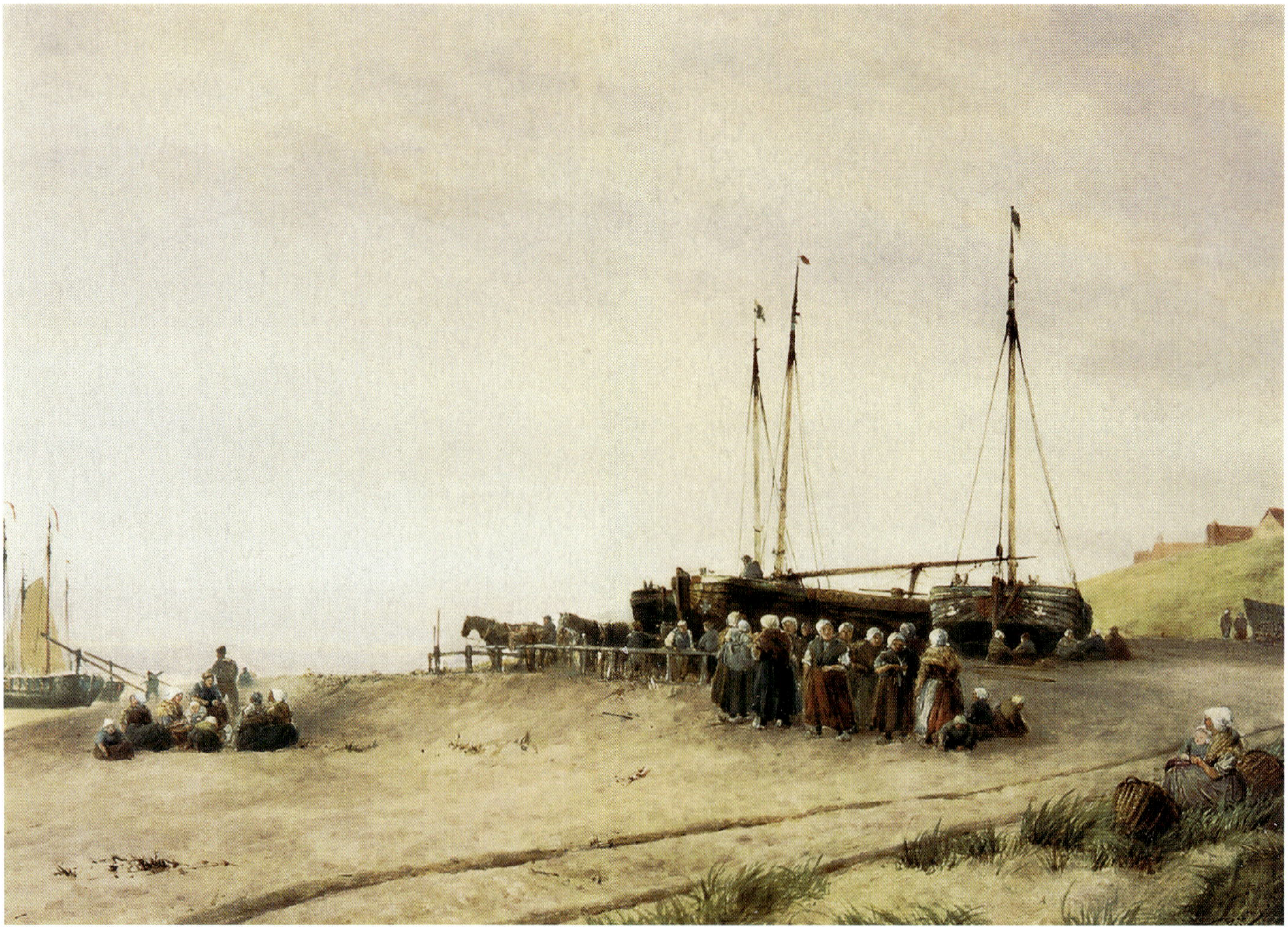

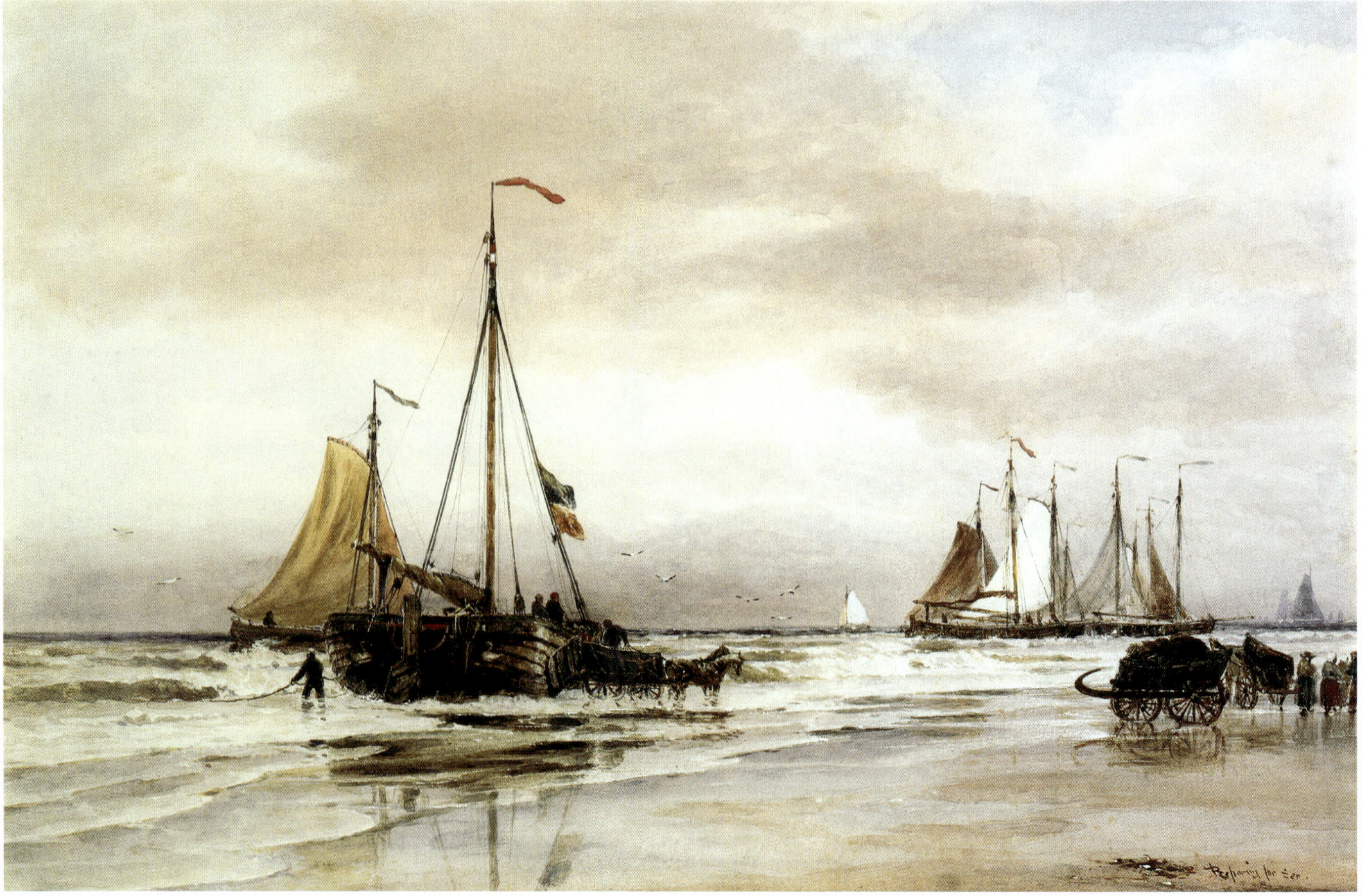

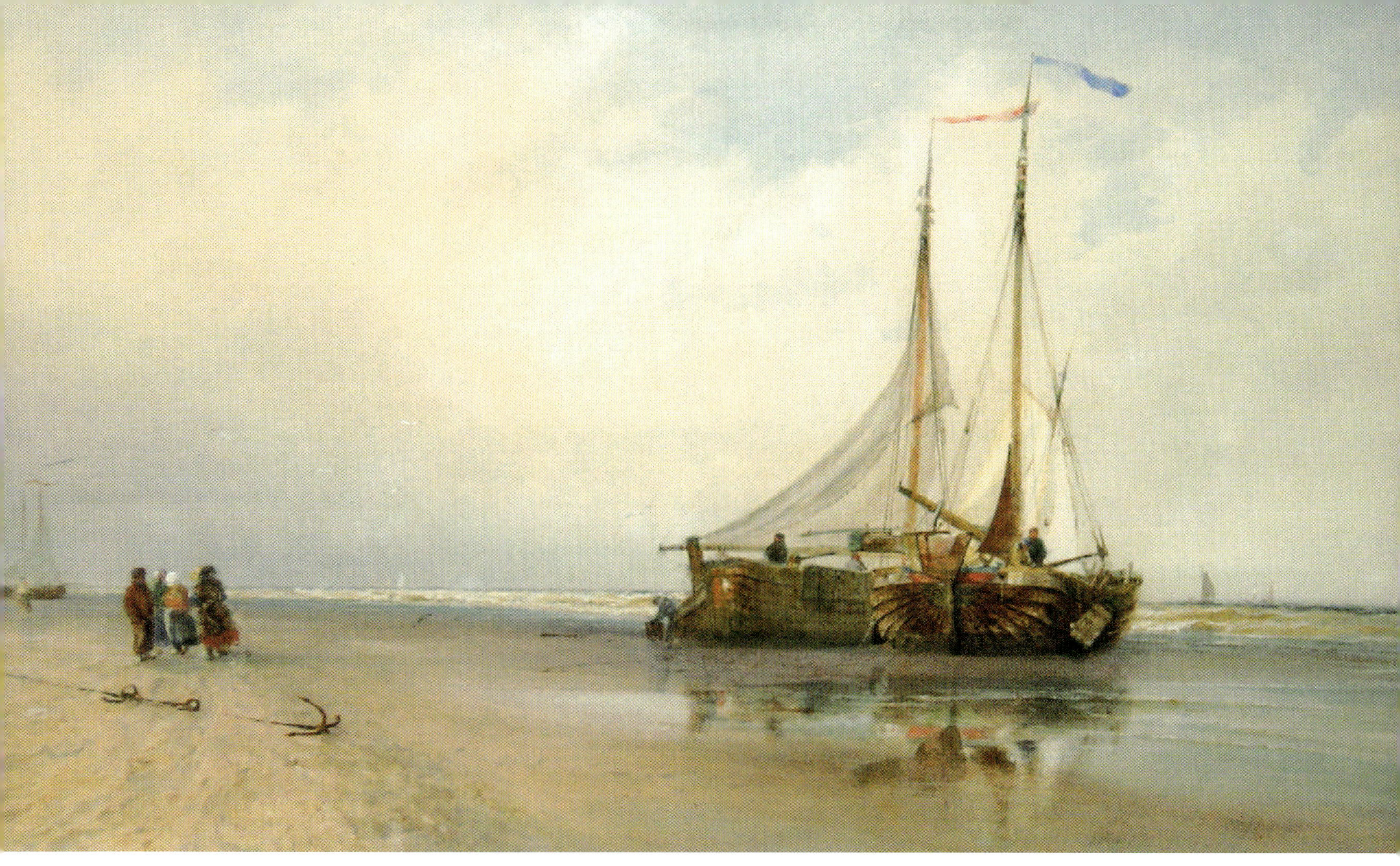

Another early painting of a calm spring morning, bringing out Hardy at his best. Two pincks beached firmly on the sand are catching just enough sun and breeze to dry their nets. Watched by their womenfolk on their left, the crews are completing their preparations for sea. Their boats, mirrored in the patch of wet sand and the pool created by the incoming tide, should soon be afloat. In the right hands, watercolour is the ideal medium for portraying these wonderful natural reflections. They help to create a remarkably peaceful scene but, sadly, not one which will always guarantee these hard-working families a good day's fishing.

Opposite above. Plate 4.5. **Evening Hour, Scheveningen.** *Signed, inscribed and dated 1872. 43.5 x 60cm (17⅛ x 23⅝ in.)*

An unusual early work where Hardy has concentrated on a beach scene in the early evening. Interestingly, he has shown us the slope of the beach from two boats at the water's edge to a low sand dune probably a hundred yards away and, beyond, the shapes of two village houses. In between, he has positioned three fishing pincks at the high water mark together with their crews and a brace of horse and carts. Finally, in the foreground, two groups of women, one sitting, the other standing, complete the composition – an extraordinarily calm, warm and peaceful summer evening scene.

Opposite below. Plate 4.6. **Preparing for Sea.** *Signed, inscribed and dated 1874. 38 x 57cm (15 x 22½in.)*

Another early, well-composed and executed beach scene capturing the morning ritual of preparing the fleet for a day's fishing. Horse-drawn carts convey the nets and lobster pots to the boats whilst a crew member recovers the beach anchor warp. The boats' pennants are fluttering in a gentle breeze and the mainly overcast sky is reflected in the shallow pools. It should be a good day.

Chapter 4 – The Dutch Coast

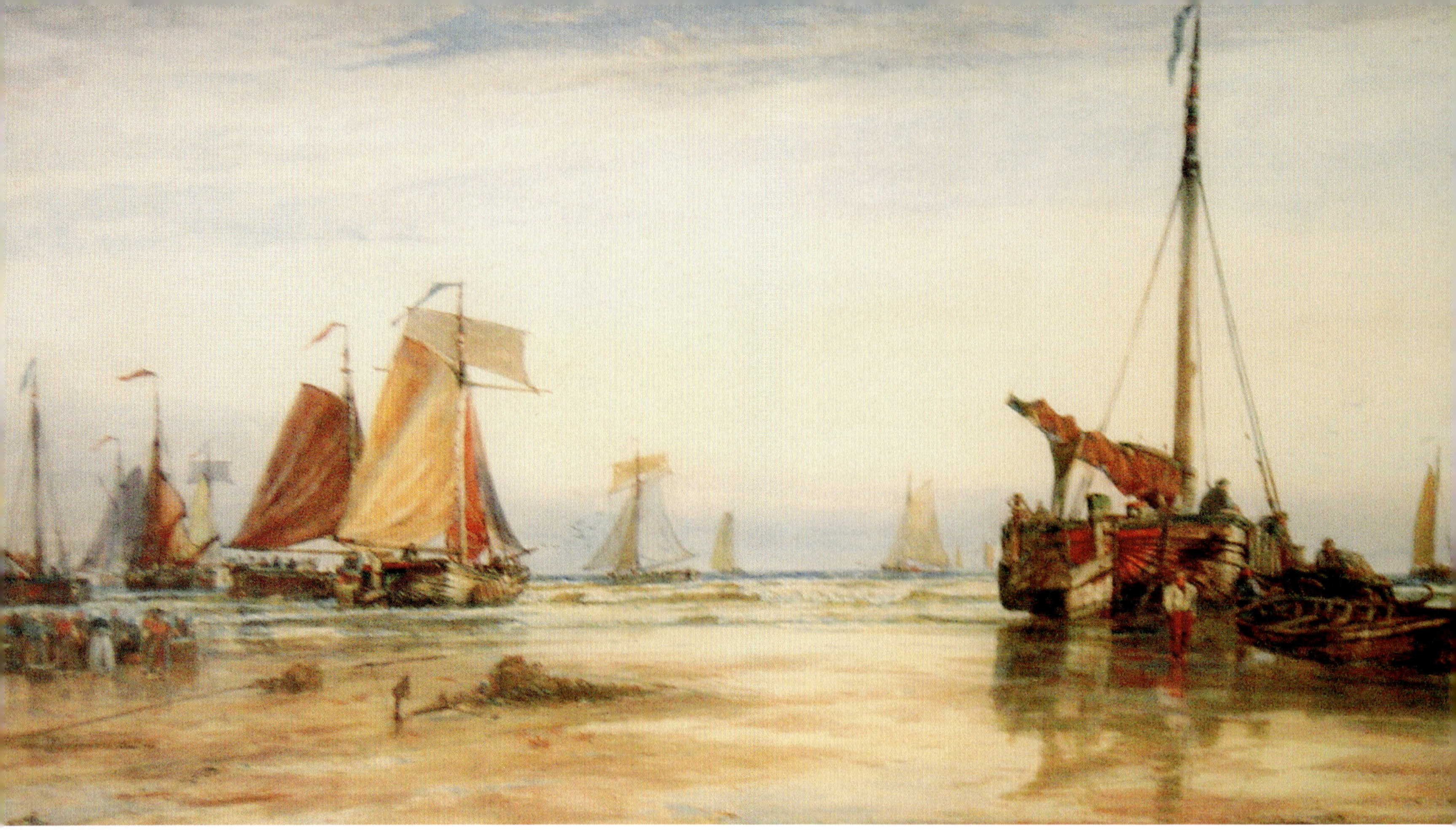

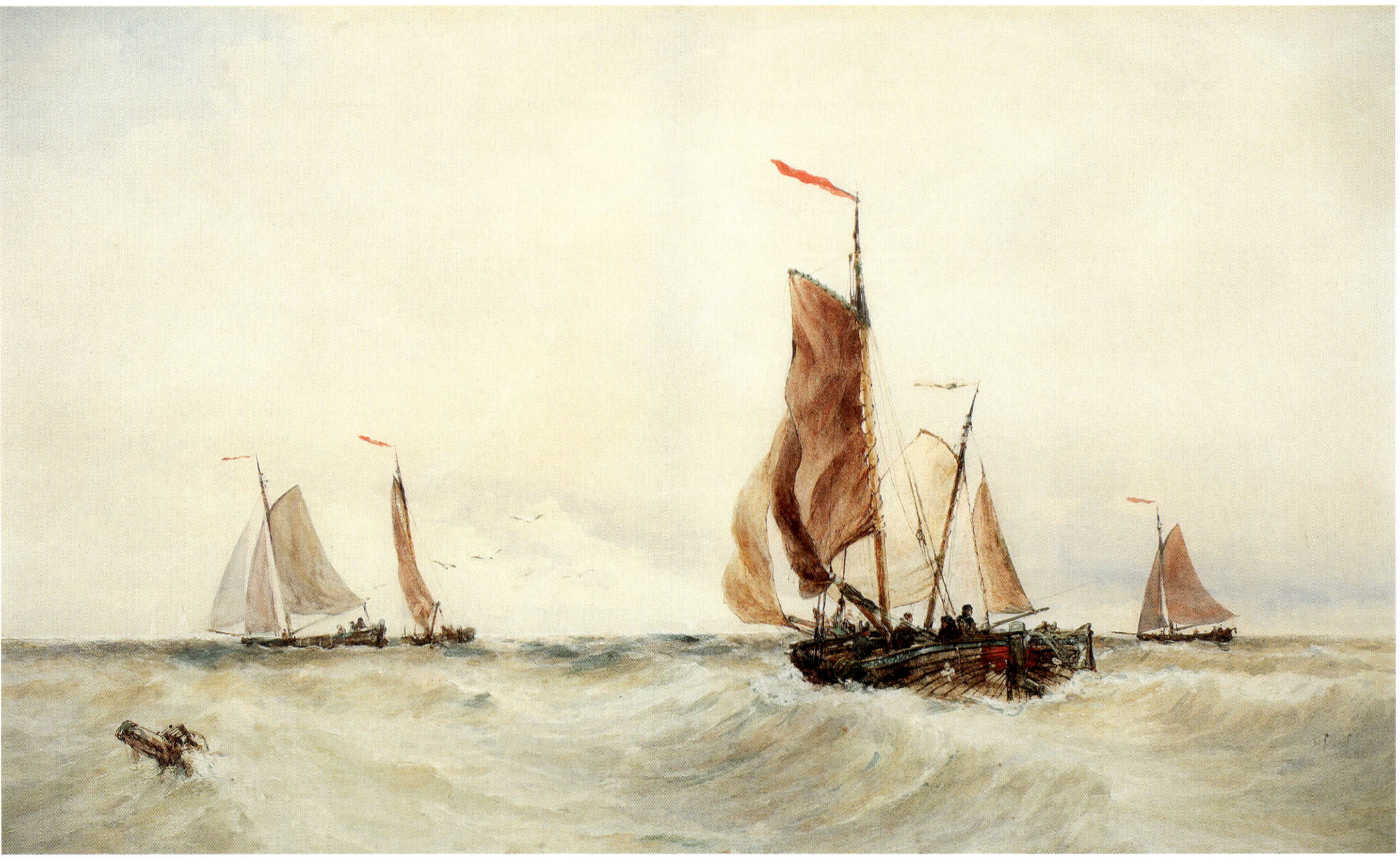

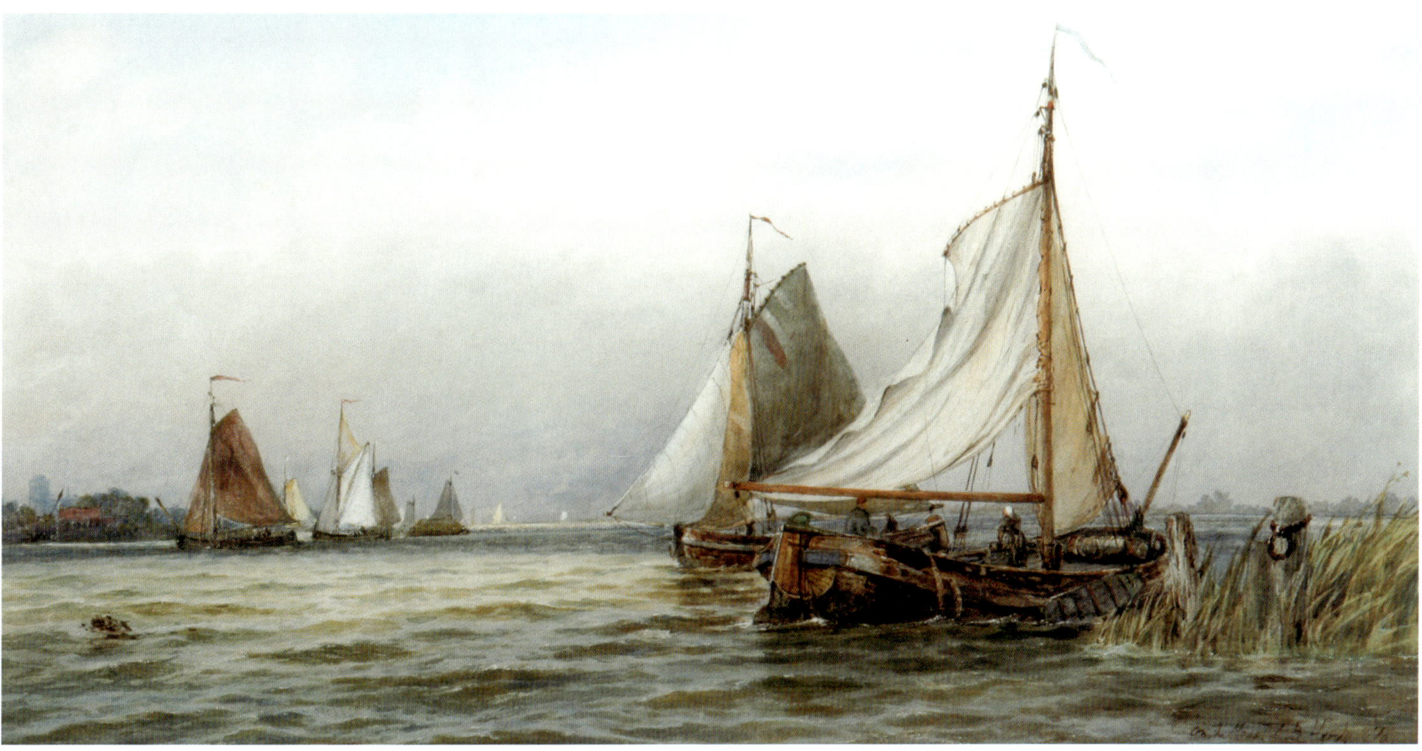

A fine large watercolour of a typical scene on the river Maas, a location Hardy was to visit several times in the next twenty years. Painting here must have been a totally different experience – and perhaps a refreshing change – from the wide sandy beaches stretching north from Scheveningen to Katwijk. On the right of the picture a pinck, which might have been resting secured to the mooring post in the reeds, is getting under way, its sails flapping in a light breeze. In the distance are several other fishing boats probably en route to and from various destinations on the river. Hardy has painted every aspect of the scene quite beautifully, especially the lopping wavelets on the river itself. The colouring too is remarkably fresh and natural. This painting must rate among Hardy's very best.

This is one of Hardy's largest paintings of Scheveningen. The sea is calm and a gentle breeze just moves the boats' pennants. To the right the pinck's crew are unloading their nets at the end of a long summer's day. To the left four other pincks are lowering their sails and unloading their fishing gear. A group of figures on the beach are examining the baskets full of fish, probably herrings, the predominant fish in the area at that time. In the distance a number of other pincks are making their way home. A well-composed picture with soft colours reflecting the light of the evening sun. As in so many of his Dutch watercolours, Hardy again demonstrates his ability to create a pellucid beach scene.

So far as is known, this is the earliest of Hardy's watercolours showing the Scheveningen-based pincks at sea with no land in sight. Apart from the fact that it has faded quite badly, it gives the impression of being unfinished. It is a comparatively large painting but, after sketching in the main components, the artist seems to have given up, perhaps after painting the two pincks in the right foreground which appear to be locked together. Neither the sea nor the sky have any definition and it may be that, after this experience, Hardy gave up going to sea with the fishermen and restricted his painting to the beach scenes he knew would sell.

Opposite above. Plate 4.8.
**A Summer's Eve,
Scheveningen.** *Signed,
inscribed and dated 1874.
52 x 94cm (20½ x 37 in.)*

Opposite below. Plate 4.9.
Dutch Fishing Boats at Sea.
*Signed and dated (?) 1874.
45.5 x 71cm (17⅛ in. x 28in.)*

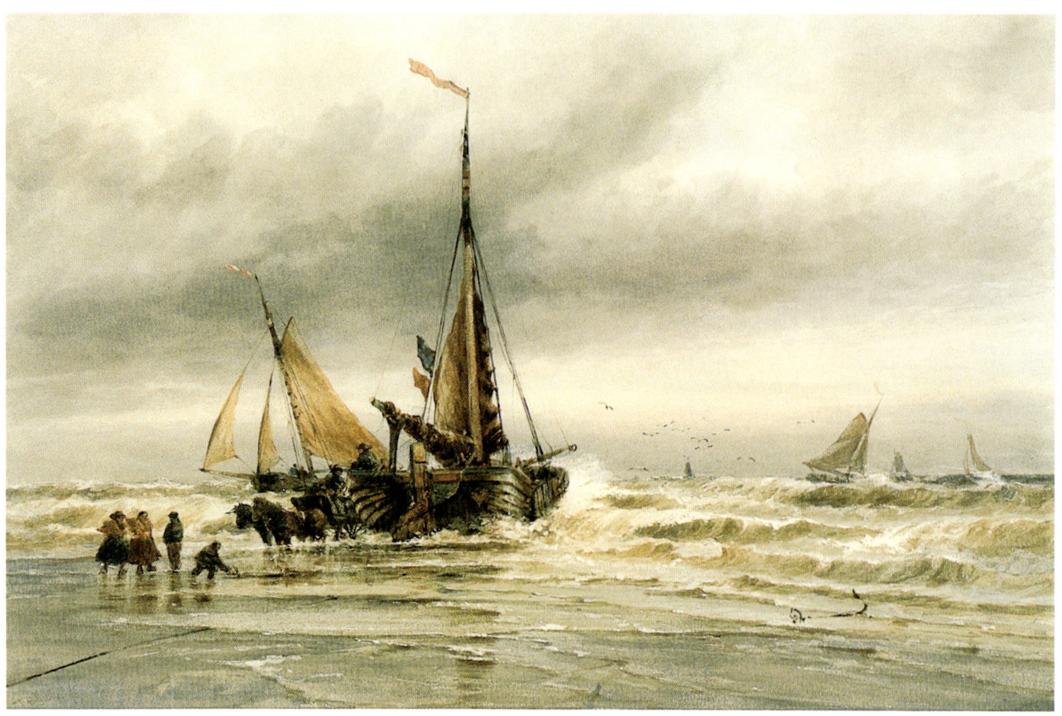

This watercolour is a fine example of how adept Hardy became at painting a really unpleasant day at the seaside! Here are a number of pincks waiting their turn to be beached safely in what appears to be a strong northerly wind. Substantial waves are running in to the gently shelving beach, driving spray over the blunt bow of the pinck. On her more sheltered leeward side a team of men and a horse and cart are unloading the catch, but conditions are difficult, and some wives and an older child are waiting anxiously to provide help if needed. Hardy here has captured the cold, wet, windy and often dangerous sea conditions that many fishermen have to face the world over, particularly in Northern Europe.

Above. Plate 4.11. **Collecting the Catch on a Stormy Day.** *Signed and dated 1875. 33 x 50cm (13 x 19⅝in.)*

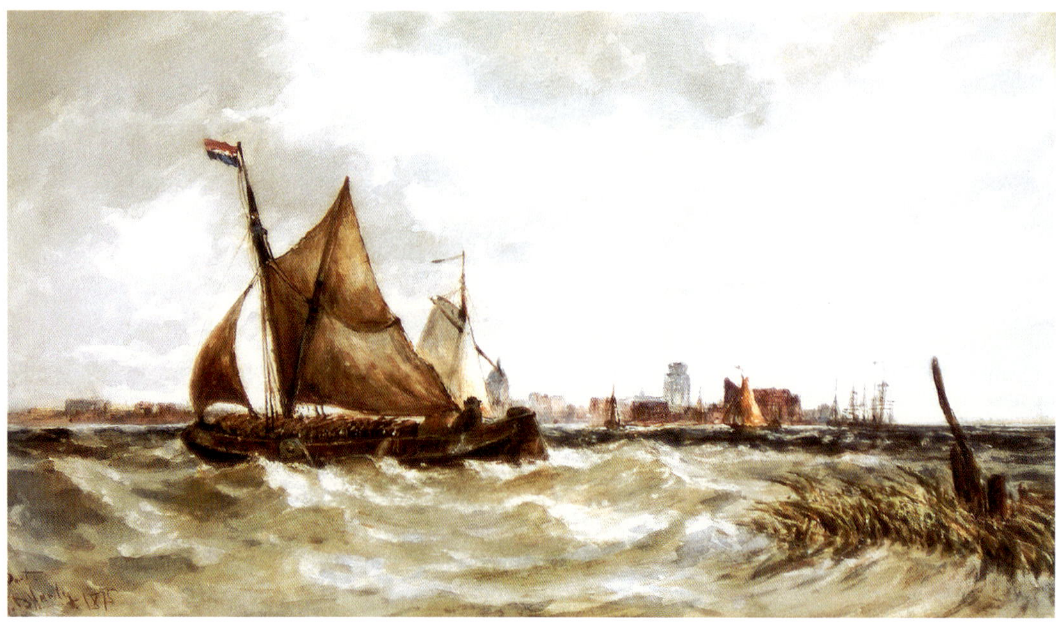

Chapter 4 – The Dutch Coast

This is probably a sketch which Hardy may have intended to use towards a larger, more elaborate watercolour and then decided to abandon the project. As a sketch it indicates that the artist knew what he was doing so far as the subject, the composition and the suggestion of movement were concerned. But there are many other factors to be considered in a finished watercolour. There is just no comparison between this, to be kind, 'unfinished' painting and Plate 4.10 above which has the colouring, the necessary detail, the 'space' and the 'atmosphere' to succeed.

This is a fine view of two barges on the Scheldt, both carrying cargoes of relatively light material. Hardy has left it to the viewer to decide precisely where they are and where they are going. One clue is the beacon painted in Dutch colours which probably marks the entrance to a canal. The barge flying the Dutch flag appears to be heading for a town on the far bank where Hardy has drawn, in some detail, a domed building of some stature. It should be recognisable but this is a part of the world where both political and physical changes have occurred regularly over the centuries. What has not changed is the importance to a seafaring nation's defence and prosperity of a broad-based maritime capability including, of course, coastal transports and fishing fleets.

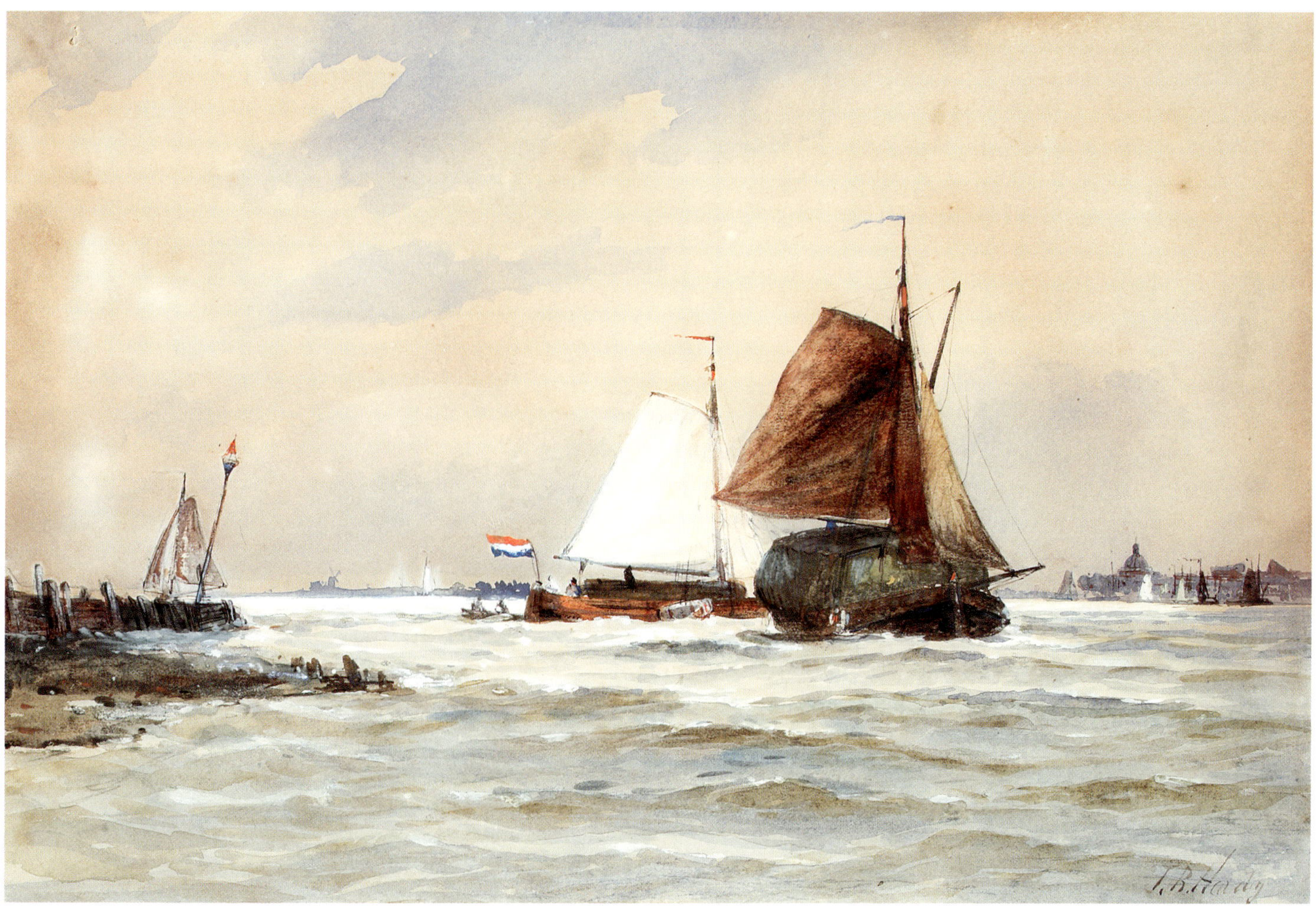

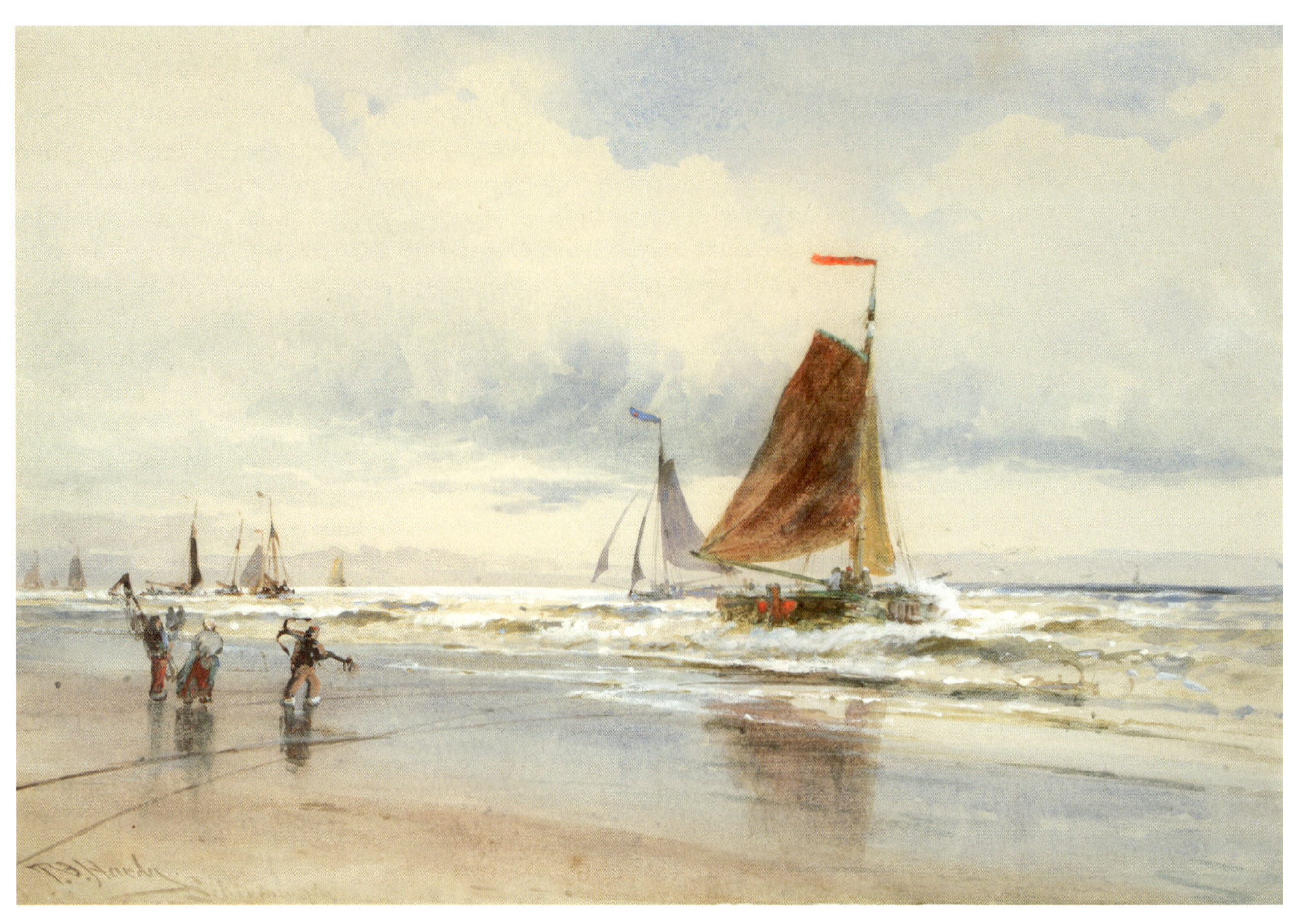

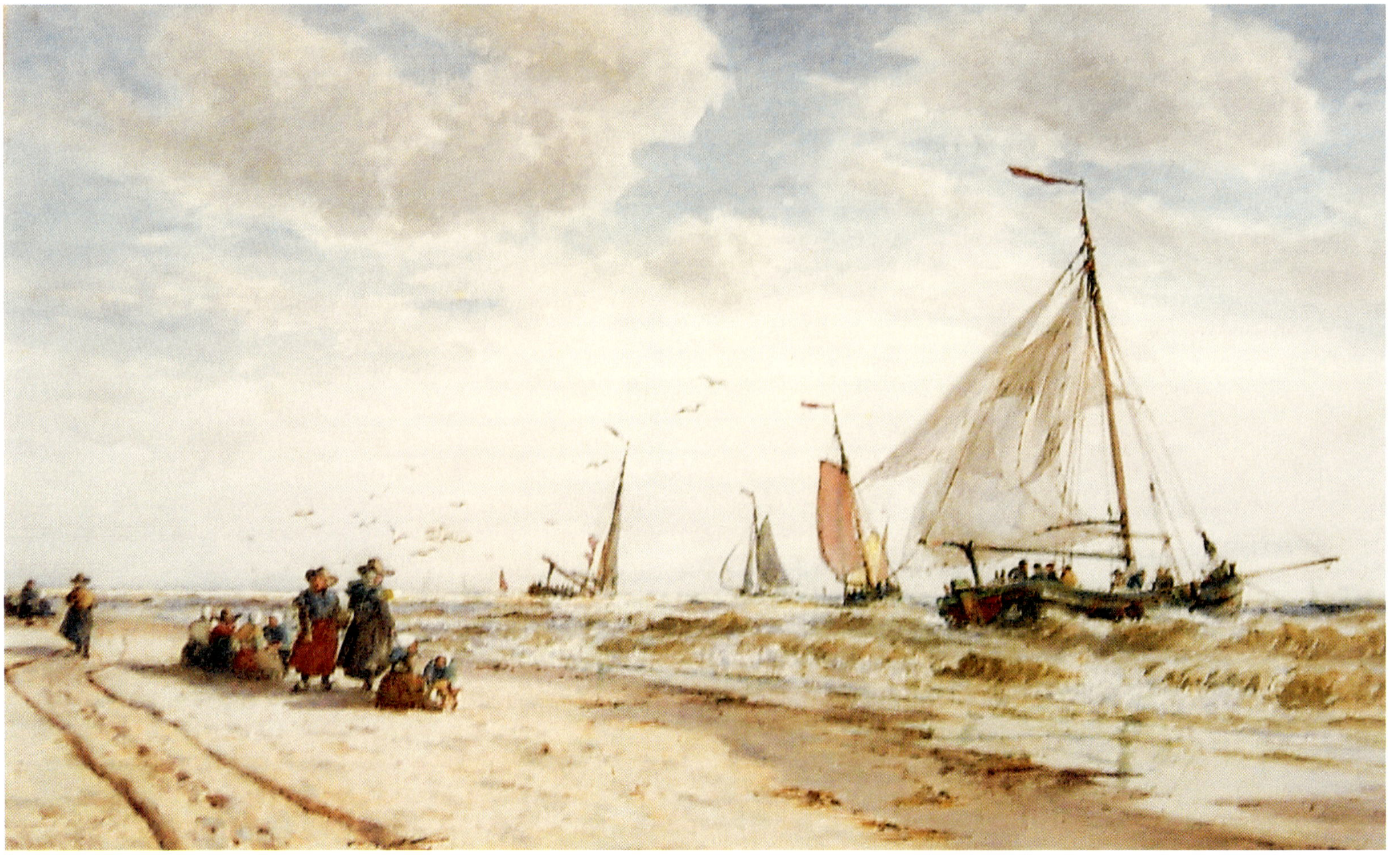

Not a very large watercolour but one which exemplifies the importance of creating 'space' in a picture. In this summertime painting Hardy has given the viewer a remarkable panorama of Scheveningen's famous beach, the sea stretching to the horizon and the fishing boats that give the scene its depth of field and, of course, its main subject matter. Due to the onshore breeze the pinck at the water's edge may be having some difficulty getting seaborne. Hardy would have known exactly what was going on, but we can only surmise. Is the anchor being taken to the crew for use as a kedge now or on their return? Or for some other reason? A good artist will often pose similar questions – Hardy was no exception.

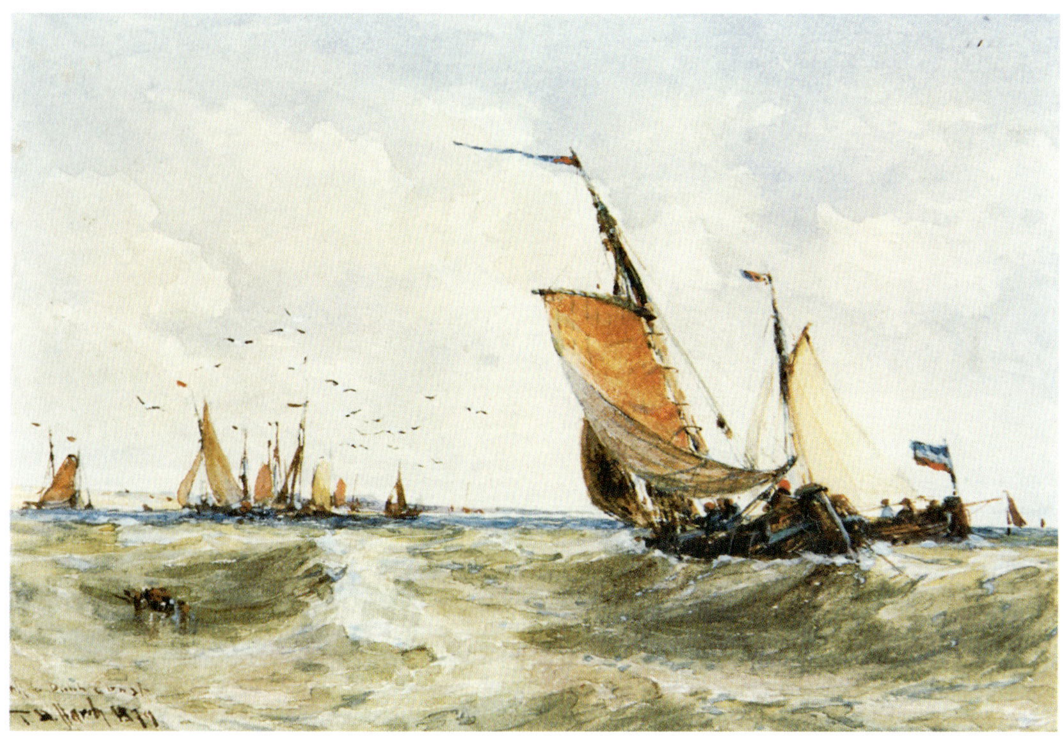

Loosely painted on a breezy day at sea off the coast between Scheveningen and Katwijk, this seascape works well. Judging from the large group of fishing boats in the distance, watched by hundreds of gulls, the two pincks in the foreground are making for a known fishing ground as quickly as they can. This watercolour would have been based on sketches Hardy made *en plein air* although it is unlikely that he went to sea very often in the pincks – there was very little room for a passenger. The best thing about this painting is the harmonious relationship the artist has achieved between the fishermen and the elements.

Painted on a bright, sunny summer's day, with high clouds and a fresh westerly breeze that brings choppy waves to the beach from which the pincks are leaving for a day's fishing. On the right a pinck has just got underway and has successfully breached the surf. Nearby, the crew's womenfolk watch the boat head out to sea. In the centre of the scene three other pincks are kedging themselves off the sand and will soon be sailing towards the fishing grounds. A colourful and well-executed painting.

Opposite above. Plate 4.14. **Scheveningen.** *Signed and inscribed. 24.2 x 34.3cm (9½ x 13½in.)*

Plate 4.16. **Off the Dutch Coast.** *Signed, inscribed and dated 1879. 25.4 x 40.2cm (10 x 16in.)*

Opposite below. Plate 4.15. **Scheveningen – Getting underway.** *Signed, inscribed and dated 1879. 31.7 x 49.5cm (12½ x 19½in.)*

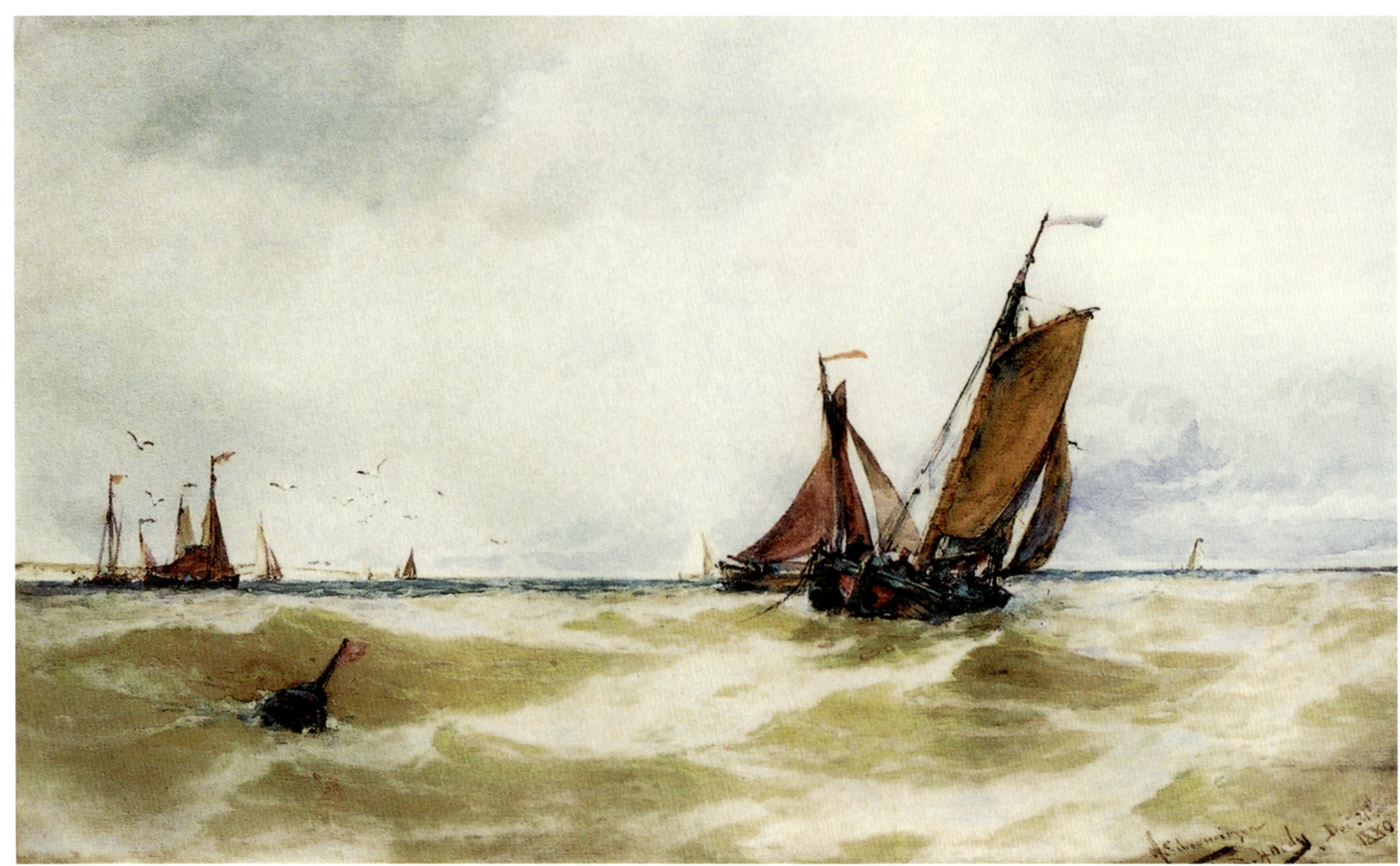

Painted on what would normally be one of the coldest days of the year when, in the Netherlands, the harbours and canals would be frozen to a depth of a metre or more. One wonders whether Hardy was sitting on the beach sketching this scene or, even less likely, embarked in one of the pincks. Wherever he was, he produced a delightful little watercolour, the strongly coloured fishing boats etched against a fine, cold sky, a favourable wind and a persistent low swell. The pinck in the foreground appears to be trawling very close inshore, possibly for shrimps with a fine mesh net. The rest of the fleet are after bigger game.

Plate 4.17. **Off Scheveningen**. *Signed, dated and inscribed 31/12/1880. 21 x 33cm 8¼ x 13in.)*

A finely-detailed action-packed scene, showing Scheveningen beach a hive of activity. Nearing the end of a long blustery day, the pincks are returning home where teams of men are standing by to help them beach and unload their catch into the waiting cart. As can be seen, on a day like this the entire community is involved. Hardy, by clever positioning of figures, all of whom are contributing in one way or another, tells the whole story. This is one of his very best watercolours.

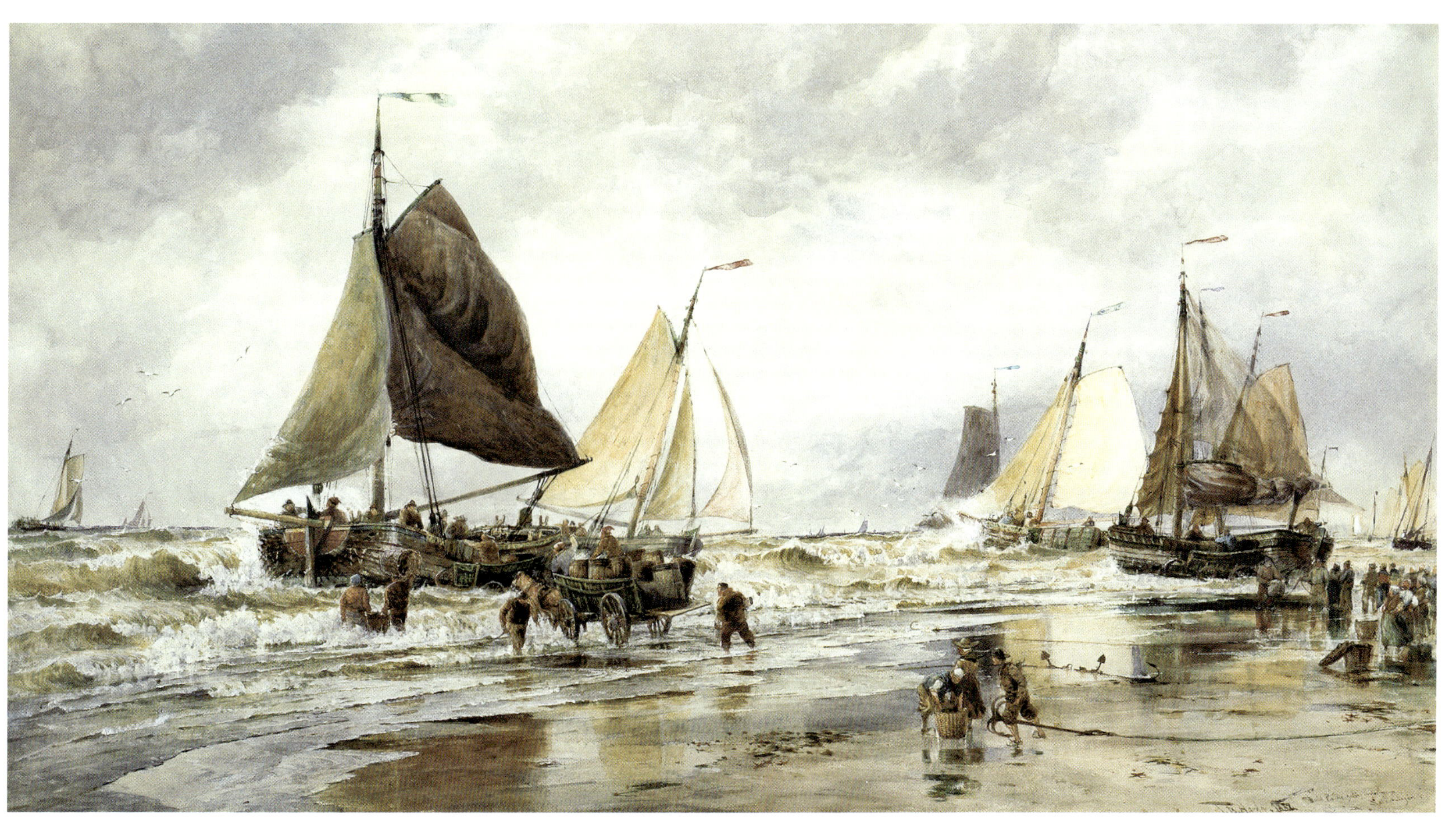

Chapter 4 – The Dutch Coast

A beautifully executed small watercolour of a size which Hardy had been painting since the mid-1870s. Everything about this little painting is good – composition, colour, detail – all the artistic components are there on a small scale. Judging from the shadows, it is early afternoon on a sunny spring day. A brisk breeze is blowing from the south-west. Later than the rest of the fishing fleet, the pinck in the foreground is hauling in on her kedge anchor and setting her sails to clear the surf. Here, on a piece of paper no larger than a postcard, Hardy has encapsulated ten years of experience with the fisherfolk of Scheveningen.

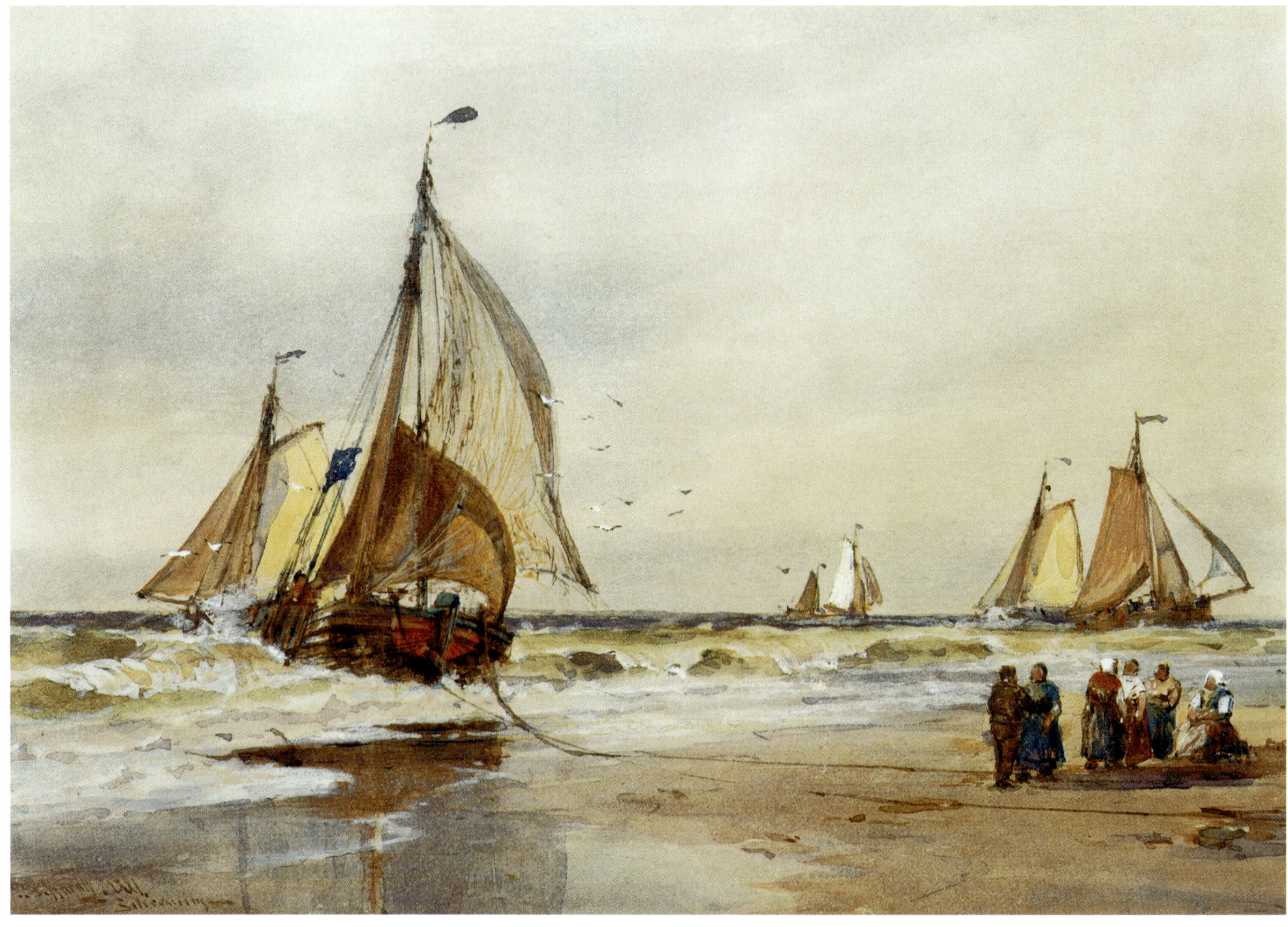

Plate 4.19. **Scheveningen.**
Signed and dated 1881. 12 x 17cm (4¾ x 6¾ in.)

The small town of Katwijk to the north of Scheveningen was the other fishing community which Hardy began to visit rather more often in the 1880s. Having developed over the centuries independently from the Hague, improved communication links now gave it a number of advantages over Scheveningen, not only as a fishing port but also, for Hardy, a more convenient and perhaps more comfortable pied-à-terre. This watercolour shows one of the larger smalschips with a topsail awaiting the tide at the water's edge, while the crew go back and forward loading their gear. To the left, on the sand, a group of people are discussing the day's events. Behind and beyond them, several other pincks appear to be becalmed offshore. A pleasantly warm day, a flat sea and hazy sky combine to make quivering reflections in the sand.

Plate 4.20. **Katwijk on Sea.**
*Signed, inscribed and dated
1881. 23 x 33cm (9 x 13in.)*

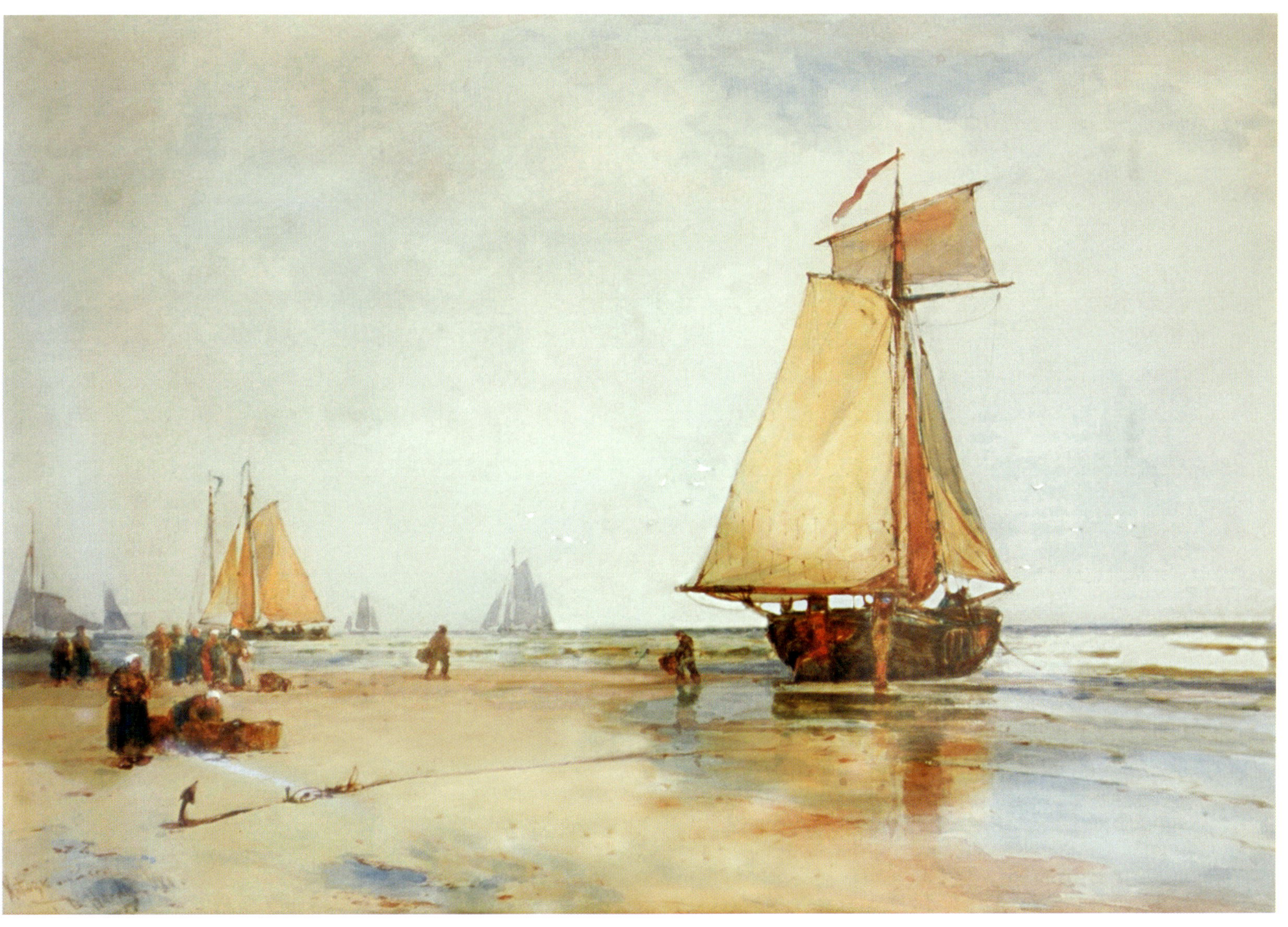

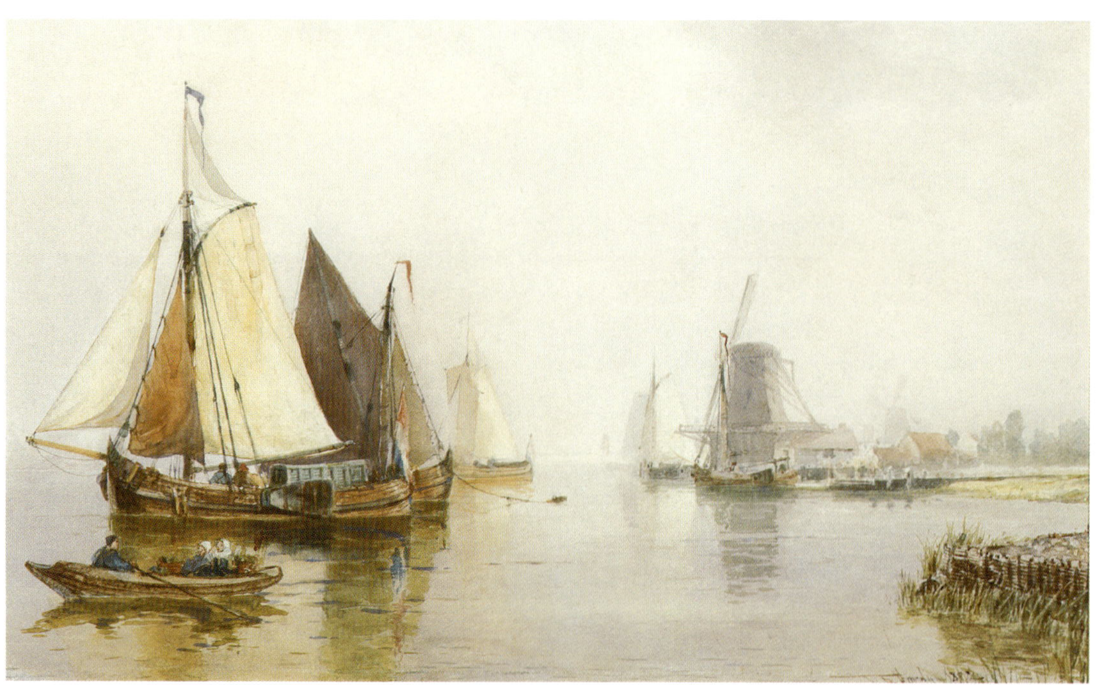

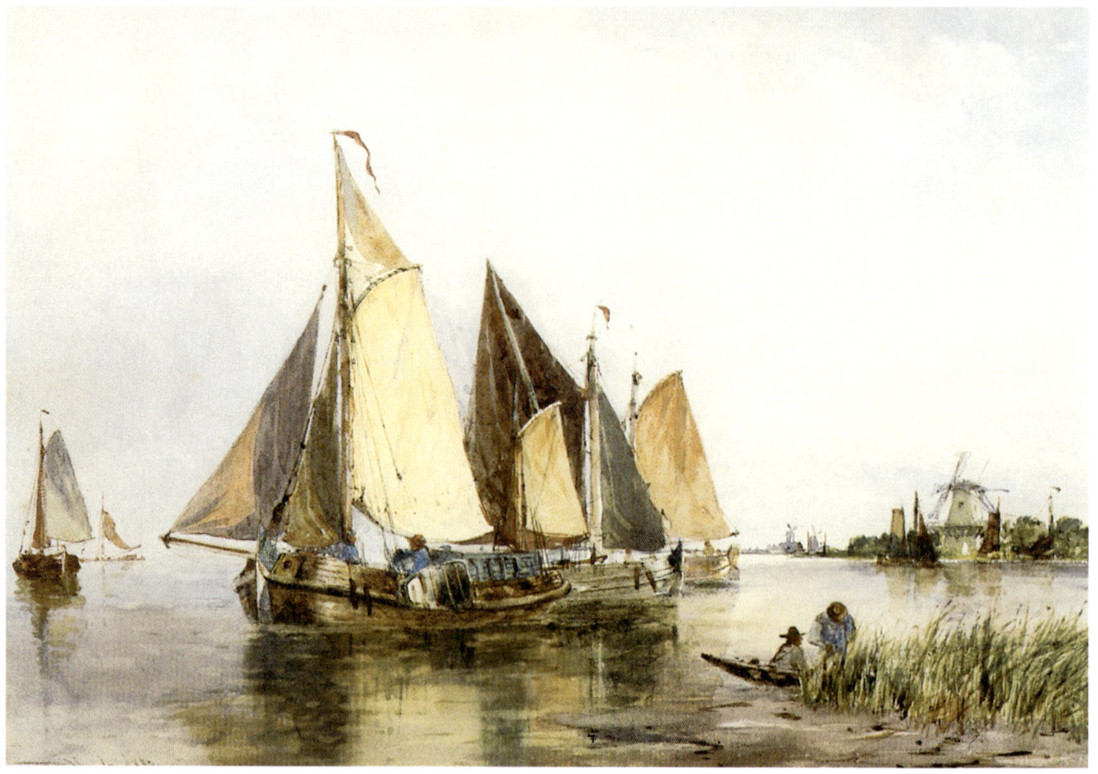

A particularly beautiful watercolour for two main reasons: its colouring and its tranquillity. Hardy is back on the River Maas and, due perhaps to the soft light filtering through the clouds that day, the sails and hulls – and their reflections on the water – are painted in muted, almost pastel shades of their primary colours. The artist's use of these, combined with his more obvious portrayal of a misty calm, give the watercolour a rare serenity. Regrettably, these conditions were an anathema to fishermen in the days of sail. Perhaps the ladies in the skiff are going ashore to replenish their stocks of aquavit.

Above. Plate 4.21. **Calm off the Dutch Coast.** *Signed, inscribed and dated 1882. 27 x 44cm (10⅝ x 17⅜in.)*

This is almost a copy of Plate 4.21 above in respect of the two closest pincks to the viewer, but has two major differences. First, and most importantly, it is a fine day and Hardy has made the most of it. The visibility is excellent and the colours brilliant. The second observation is that the ladies have stayed ashore. Two men in a skiff are either examining the nearby reeds for birds' nests or answering the call of nature. In the middle distance, two pincks have moored alongside a windmill, its sails stilled. On the far shore two more windmills can be seen but little sign yet of any wind or, indeed, any unusual activity anywhere. But great care has been taken in recording the light from the right and the shadows of the fishing boats on the still waters. A very well-executed and appealing painting.

Although research has not yet revealed the identity of the ship, nor exactly where she went aground, there is every chance that this was a three-masted merchantman grounded on the sands between Scheveningen and Katwijk and that Hardy had the good fortune to be there at the time. The two fishing communities were ideally placed to help in any rescue attempt and, later, to profit from salvaging some of the cargo. The watercolour depicts the calm after the storm with the fisherfolk gathering early in the morning on the beach to save and carry away anything of value. Already there are two horse and carts alongside and plenty of men and women around to assist in unloading – and keeping an eye open for the customs and excise officers. The barrel washed ashore to the high water mark probably contains salted fish – but you never know! An interesting scene, very well painted.

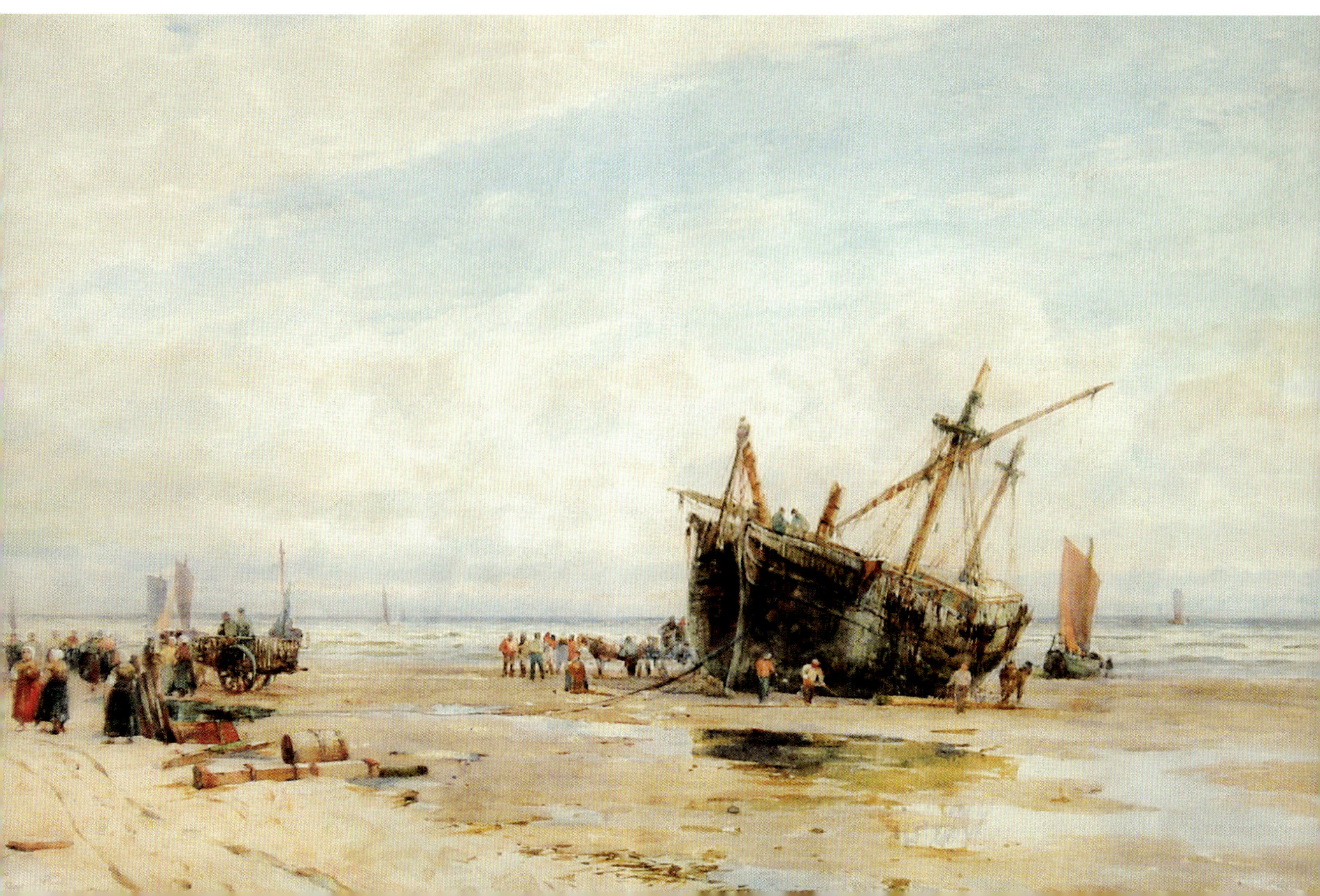

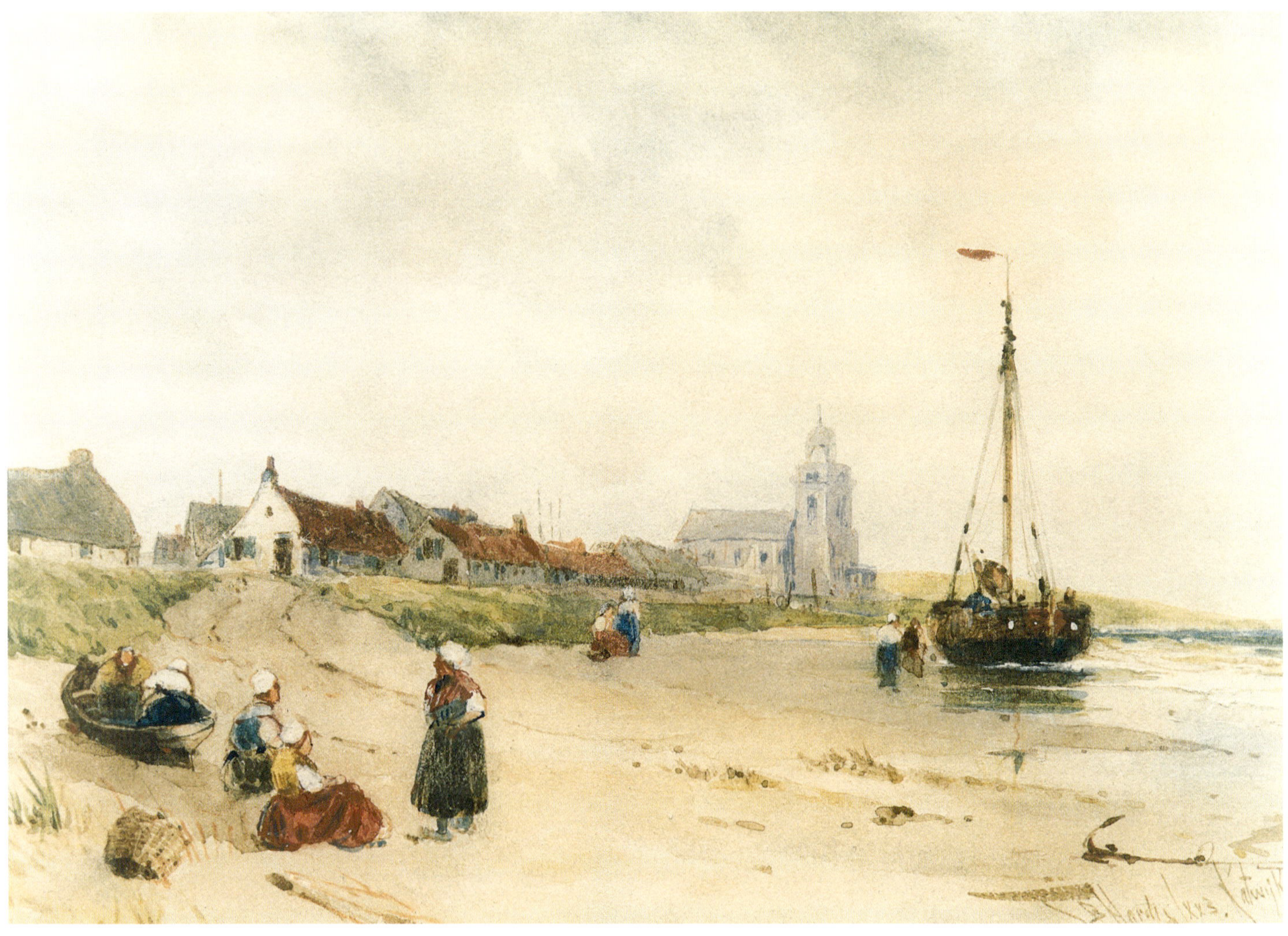

In such a small painting it is remarkable how successfully Hardy has contrived to tell a complete story. In the left foreground a group of six women await the return of their men who no doubt are still fishing offshore. To the right a pinck has just landed and the crew are unloading the catch. Above the beach a line of fishermen's cottages lead towards the church. A calm summer evening, painted in quite strong colours. A lovely little work.

In stark contrast to the bright summer's day depicted in Plate 4.24, one can only suppose one morning that the inclement weather, not unheard of in these parts, drove Hardy and his sketchbook inside the church. A fascinating scene awaited him. Sitting in the pews and standing in the dark shadows of the aisle is an all-female congregation, no doubt praying that their husbands return from their fishing with full holds. In the pulpit an energetic priest is either haranguing or blessing the women or, more likely, a bit of both. But the magic of this watercolour lies in the light cast by the stained glass windows and, to a lesser extent, by the white bonnets and coloured shawls of the fisherwomen. What could have been a rather sombre painting comes brilliantly alive.

Plate 4.24. **Katwijk Church.**
Signed, inscribed and dated 1883. 12.5 x 17.5cm (4⅞ x 6⅞ in.)

Opposite. Plate 4.25. **Inside Katwijk Church.** *Signed and dated 1883. 31.8 x 49.5cm (12½ x 19½ in.)*

Chapter 4 – The Dutch Coast

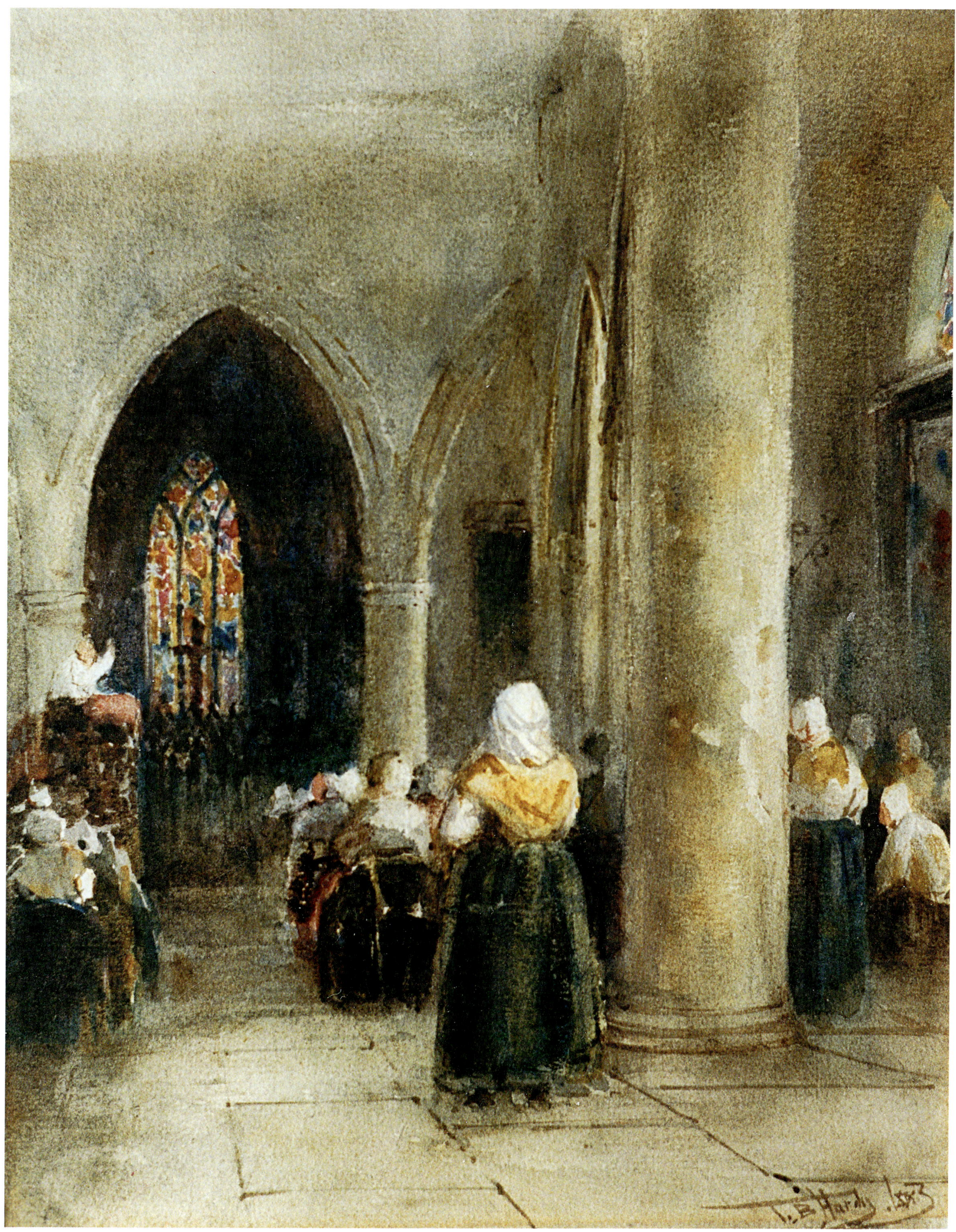

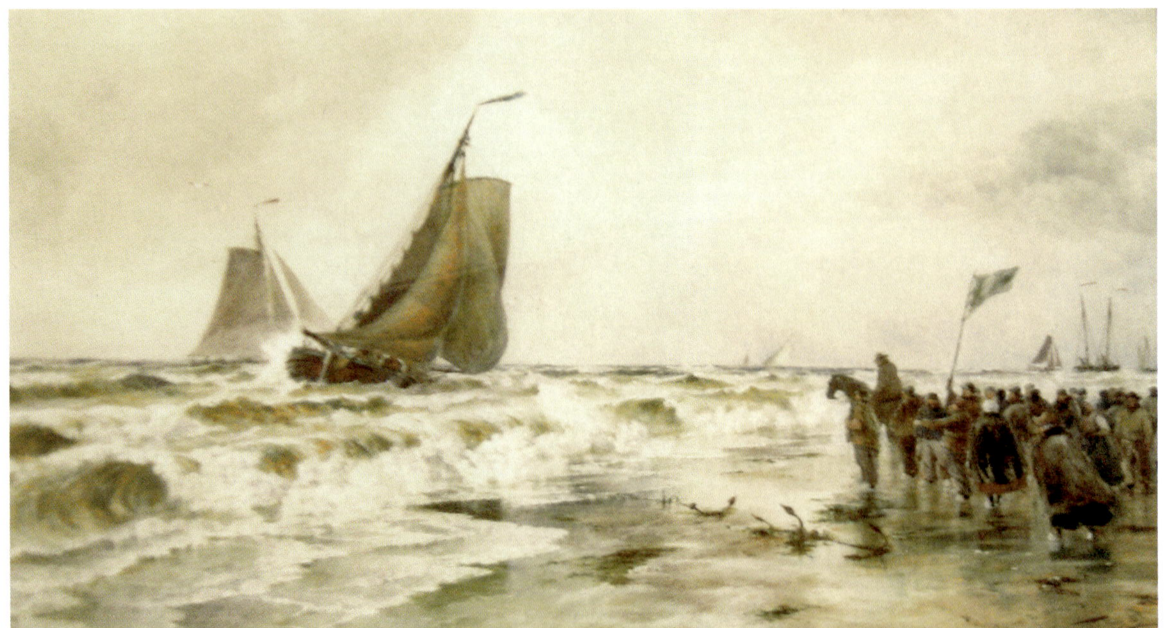

An immediate reaction to this large and well-painted watercolour is that the colours have faded. It is emphatically not a monochrome drawing but, sadly, the original blues, greens and, to a lesser extent, the reds have all been affected, usually by the ultra-violet rays present in daylight, especially so in direct sunlight. Unfortunately, there is very little that even the best restorers can do about fading once it has occurred. Prevention is the only answer; this can be virtually guaranteed by avoiding exposure to sunlight and by framing all watercolours and drawings in one of the types of anti u/v conservation glass currently available.

Although fading can reduce the value of a painting very considerably, this particular watercolour has much merit and no little interest. In the prevailing conditions of a rough sea, a strong westerly wind and an outgoing tide, the pincks at sea are struggling to position themselves prior to beaching. On the right a substantial crowd of helpers are watching and waiting, including a man holding a marker flag and a horse and rider ready to brave the surf to collect the pinck's warps. In rough weather this would be a well-practised procedure.

Above. Plate 4.26. **Wind against Tide, Scheveningen.** *Signed, inscribed and dated 1883. 54 x 94.5cm (21¼ x 37¼ in.)*

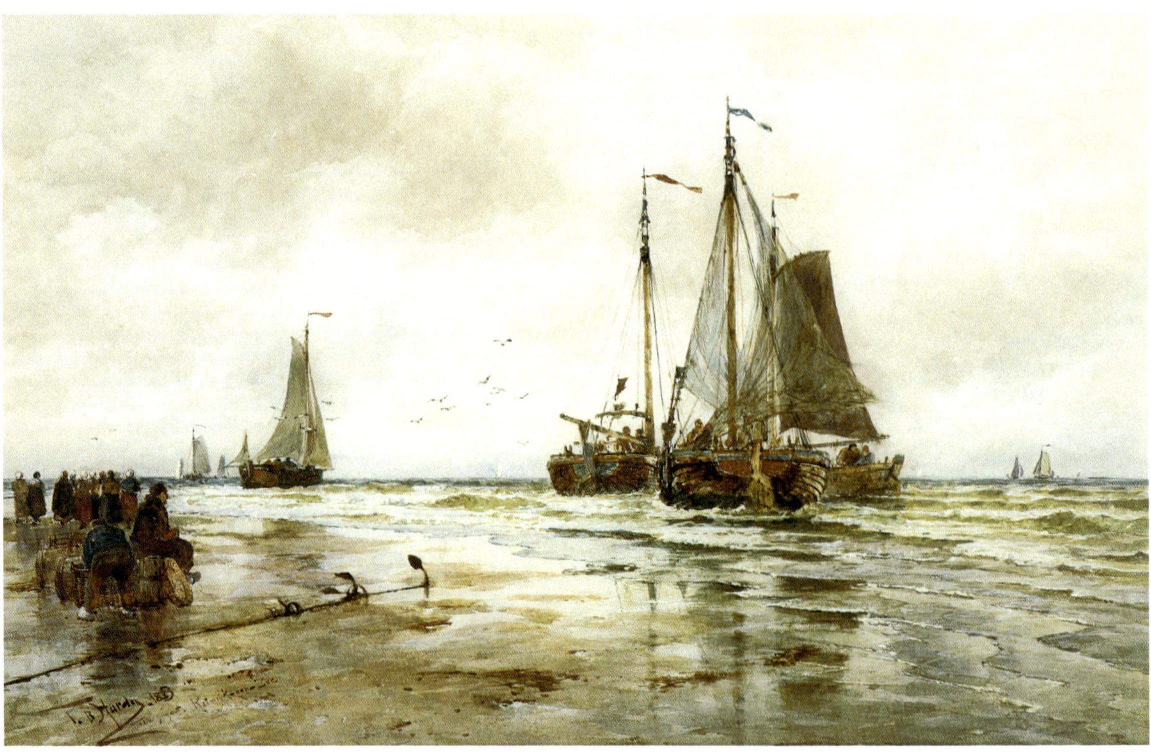

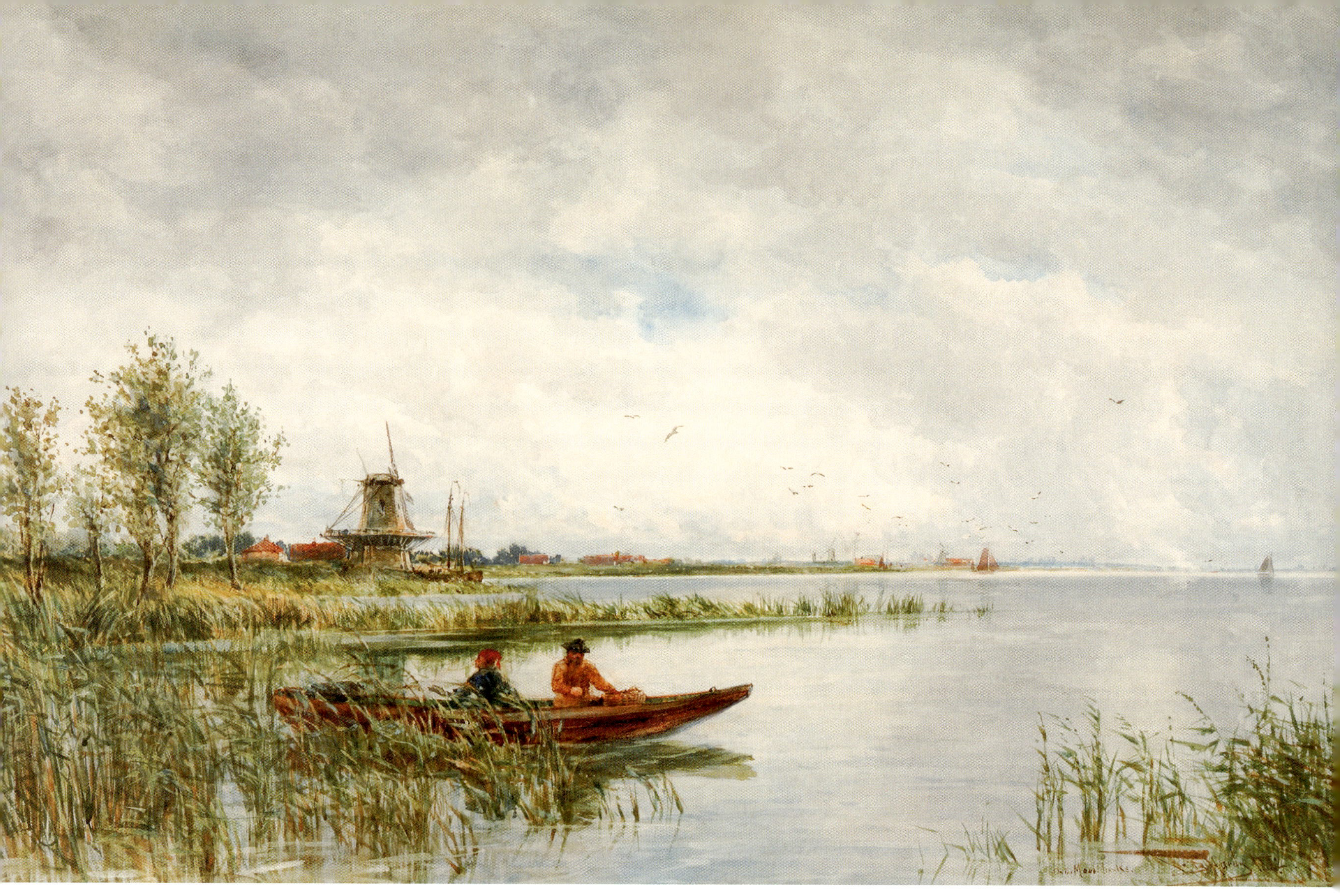

A relatively large and colourful example of Hardy's Dutch river scenes. He seemed to favour the River Maas which probably provided him with a greater choice of subject and, like his seascapes, with a less restrictive field of view than the other rivers and canals in Holland. Here he has shown two people in a skiff drift fishing close to the reeds with a hand-held line, probably for eels. In the adjoining bay is a fine windmill with two boats alongside loading flour. There is an almost complete lack of wind and, as one would expect, few sailing craft on the river. Nor does the sky, well reflected in the calm river, hold out much hope of a breeze springing up. This is a picture one could live with very happily, and it answers any criticism that might arise about a marine artist's ability to paint anything green!

Looking south on what appears to be a cold day with an east wind blowing off the land. To the right of centre a pinck, not long back from the fishing grounds, has her nets raised and drying in the breeze. To the left, further along the beach, another pinck is settling down on the sands. On the extreme left a group of women huddle in the wind with two crewmen examining the contents of some wicker lobster pots. Judging from the number of similar watercolours that have survived between 1882 and 1884, Hardy may have spent more time than usual with the Scheveningen fishing community during those years They are all of a uniformly high standard.

Plate 4.28. **On the Maas Banks.** *Signed, inscribed and dated 1884. 45 x 70cm (17¾ x 27½in.)*

Opposite below. Plate 4.27. **Scheveningen.** *Signed and dated 1883. 31.5 x 46cm (12½ x 18in.)*

Chapter 4 – The Dutch Coast

Probably painted within a few days of Plate 4.28 with similarities to a very much earlier painting of the River Maas (Plate 4.10). The colouring and clarity of this watercolour, as in many of Hardy's inland river and canal scenes, is quite outstanding. The windmill dominating the skyline rises above the neighbouring cottages on the banks of the canal. The two men in the skiff may be gathering reeds for roof thatching. A beautifully composed work.

Plate 4.29. **Dutch Canal Scene.** *Signed and dated 1886. 25.4 x 35.5cm (10 x 14in.)*

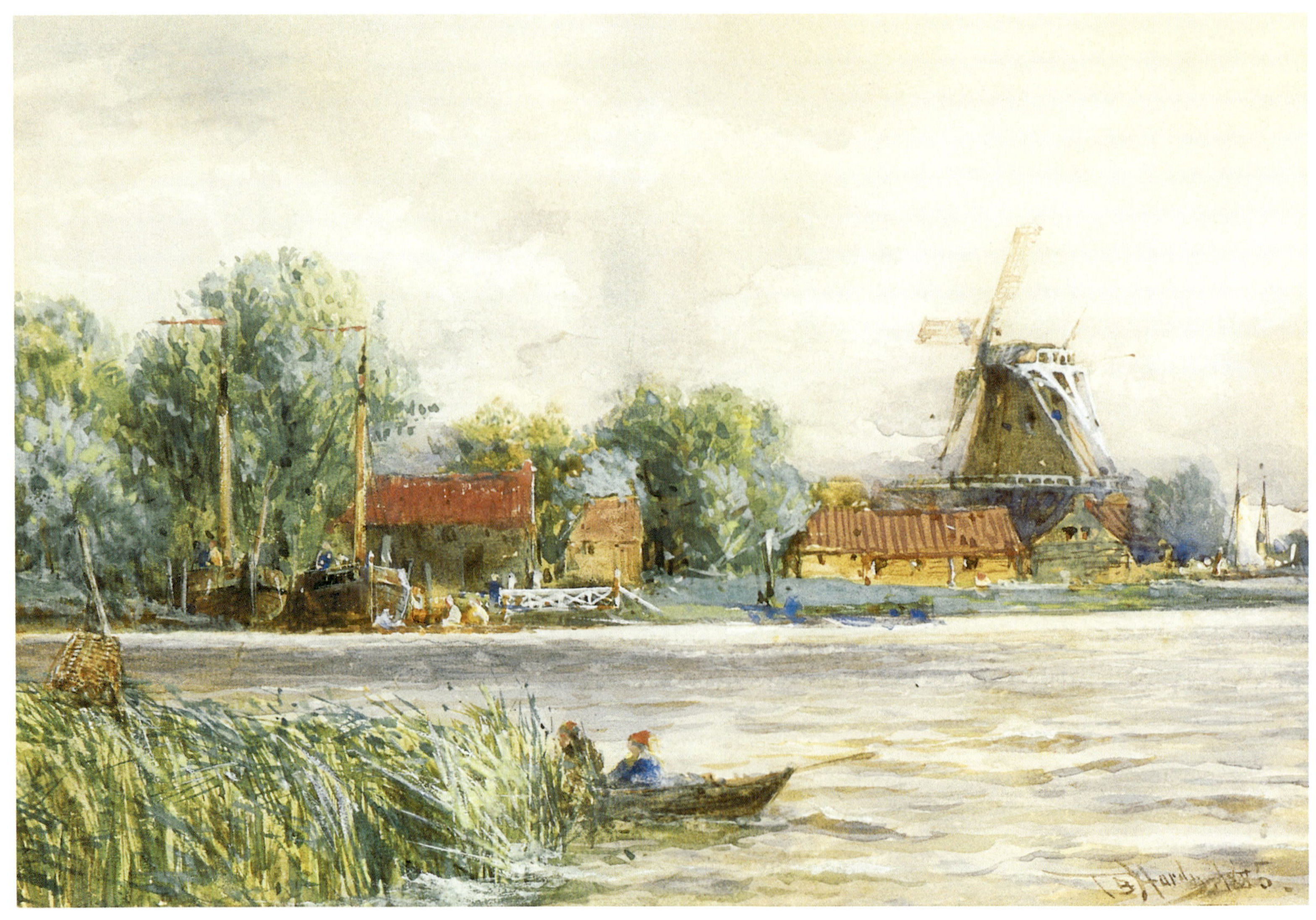

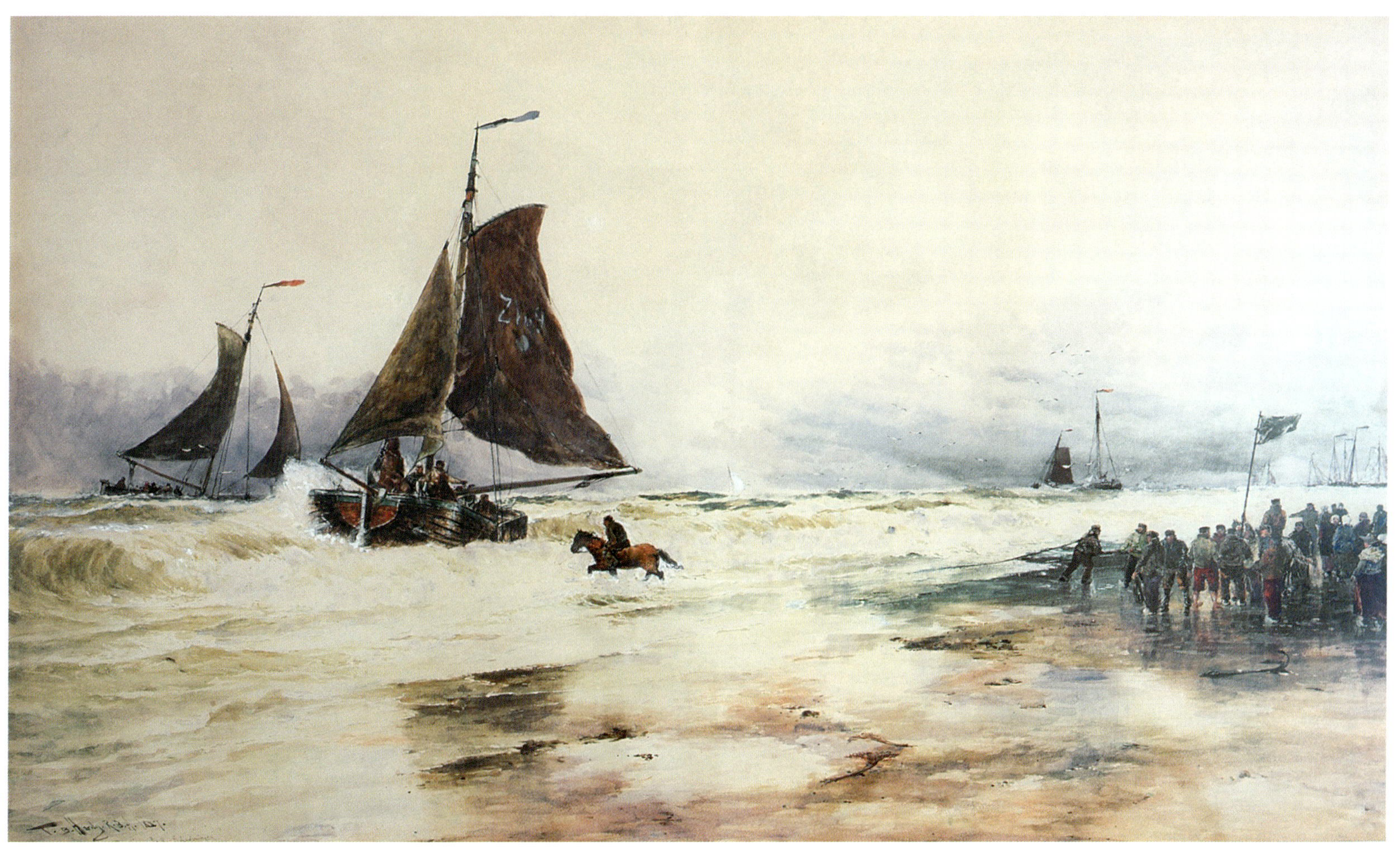

Plate 4.30. **Beaching a Pinck at Scheveningen.** *Signed, inscribed and dated 1887. 55 x 85cm (21⅝ x 33½in.)*

This is one of Hardy's largest and most dramatic paintings of the Scheveningen scene. In Plate 4.26 he painted the predicament of a pinck battling against wind and tide to position herself so that the party ashore could assist in beaching her safely. Here is the same situation a few moments later. The pinck has reached the point where they must turn into the wind and sea and drop the bower anchor. For the boat to negotiate the heavy surf without capsizing they must keep her pointing to seaward. This can only be done by getting warps ashore from the stern to the handling parties on the beach. In these rough conditions the horseman is the invaluable link – charging into the surf, collecting the warps and passing them to the men who will have to haul the pinck steadily as far up the beach as they can. Hardy has used rather sinister contrasting colours to depict the angry sea and sky, the foaming surf and the dark brown sails of the fishing boats fighting the elements. It is an authentic piece of history. Hardy's evidence does the fishermen proud.

Of interest is that, on this occasion – but on very few others – Hardy had appended 'RBA' to his signature. He had had watercolours accepted for exhibition at the Society of British Artists since 1871 and the first of his Dutch watercolours the following year. In 1884 he was elected to the Society which was finally granted 'Royal' status by Queen Victoria in 1987, her Golden Jubilee year. This accolade, engineered by Whistler, gave a tremendous boost to the Society and for a short time Hardy, among others, may have profited from the prestigious letters after his name.

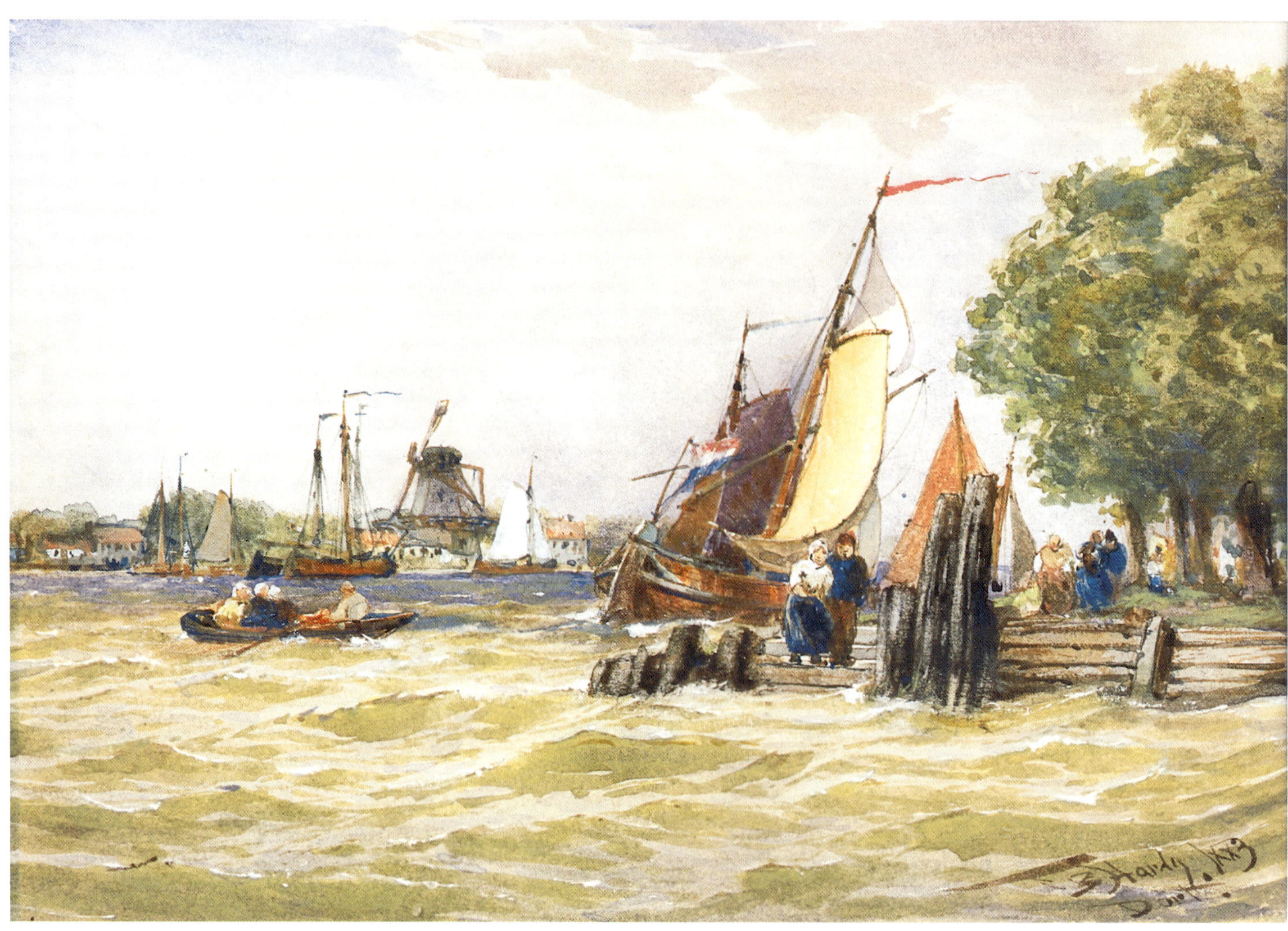

This is an unusual view of Katwijk, if indeed it is that town, as it is more likely to be a village on the canal system in the vicinity. Hardy has shown that, winter and summer, the wind can be very strong inshore. He may have decided not to venture on to the sands that day. The scene he chose was a busy waterway running between tree-lined banks with a smalschip berthed alongside a windmill on the far shore. Several sailing craft are making the most of the brisk wind, but a rowing boat with three women in the sternsheets is finding the choppy waters decidedly uncomfortable. Small groups of people on the near bank and a passing pinck are watching their progress with interest.

There is no record of Hardy having spent any time over the Saint Nicholas or Christmas period in Holland in 1892 and it is reasonable to assume that he painted this charming little watercolour in his studio, based on sketches from a previous visit. The artist has assumed the following day is a rare holiday and, thanks to his skill, we can imagine the fishermen's delight at returning back early for a short break from routine. Nearly all the pincks are home and hauled high up on the beach, drying nets and sails in the dying rays of the sun. The weather is bitterly cold; already there is a dusting of snow on the dry sand and flakes of ice sparkle in the shallows. The screaming seagulls attest to the fact that the catch has been good and the fisherfolk, wending their way home well wrapped up against the wind, will be looking forward to a festive evening.

Plate 4.31. **Near Katwijk.**
Signed, initialled and dated 1889. 20.3 x 28cm. (8 x 11in.)

Opposite above. Plate 4.32.
Back from the Fishing Grounds, Scheveningen.
Signed and dated and inscribed 'To Mr T.F.Ferriman with the artist's best wishes, Xmas 1892.' 14 x 22cm (5½ x 8⅝in.)

Chapter 4 – The Dutch Coast

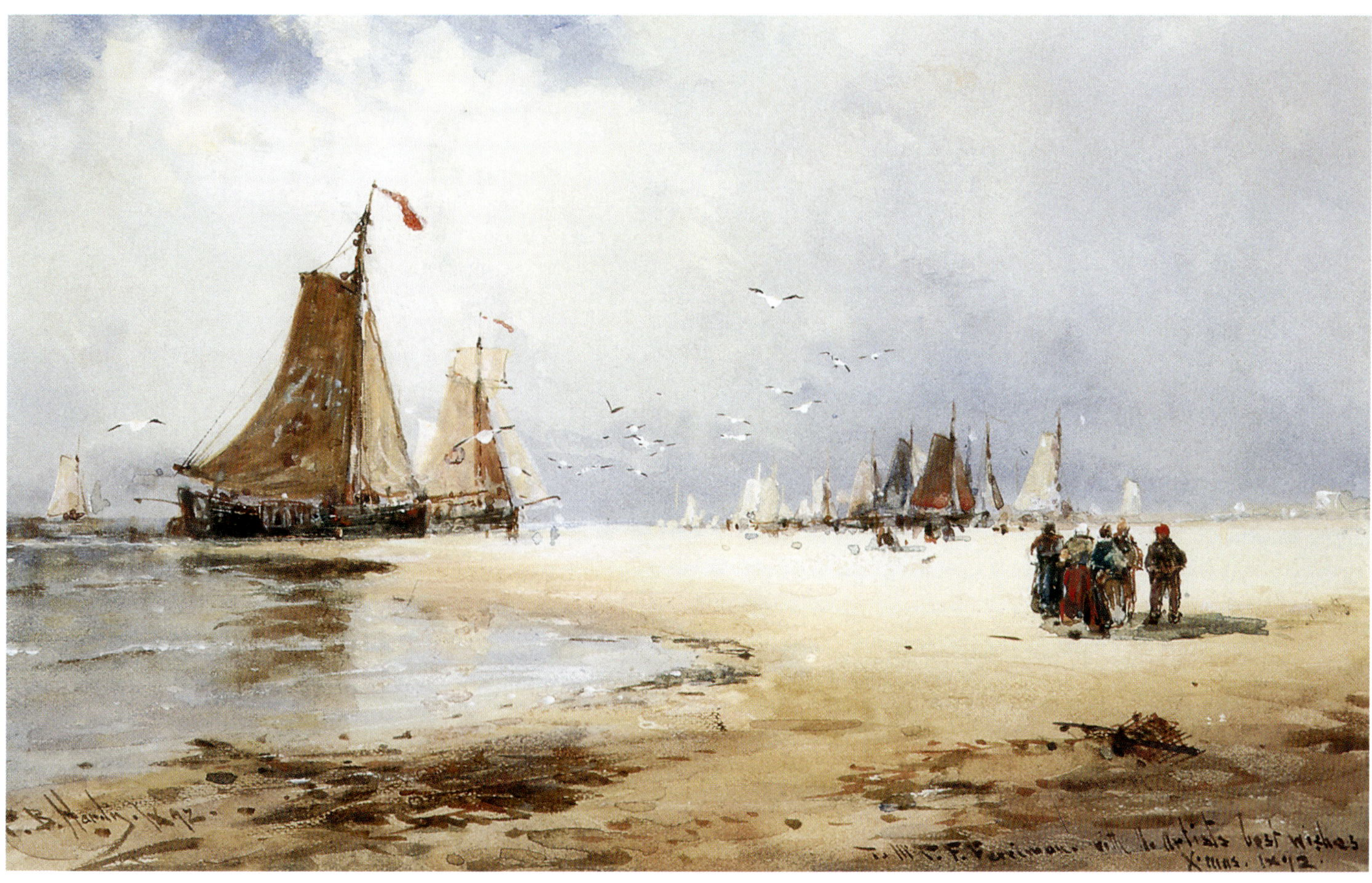

A long narrow watercolour which serves Hardy's purpose ideally. Here, by showing us a long scattered procession of women walking towards a small fleet of pincks clustered on the sands, he is able to emphasise the extraordinary extent and beauty of the beach itself. The women are very well drawn and the painting also shows his mastery of proportion and perspective. This late work also features a steamer offshore heading north – now becoming a more common sight, but heralding the eventual demise of these fine communities. To balance the composition, Hardy has introduced three men wading ashore from a small boat at the water's edge – quite what they are up to is unclear, but what looks like a small mast and furled sail lying further up on the beach may provide the answer.

Below. Plate 4.33.
Katwijk Shore. *Signed, inscribed and dated 1892. 22 x 70.5cm (8⅝ x 27¾in.)*

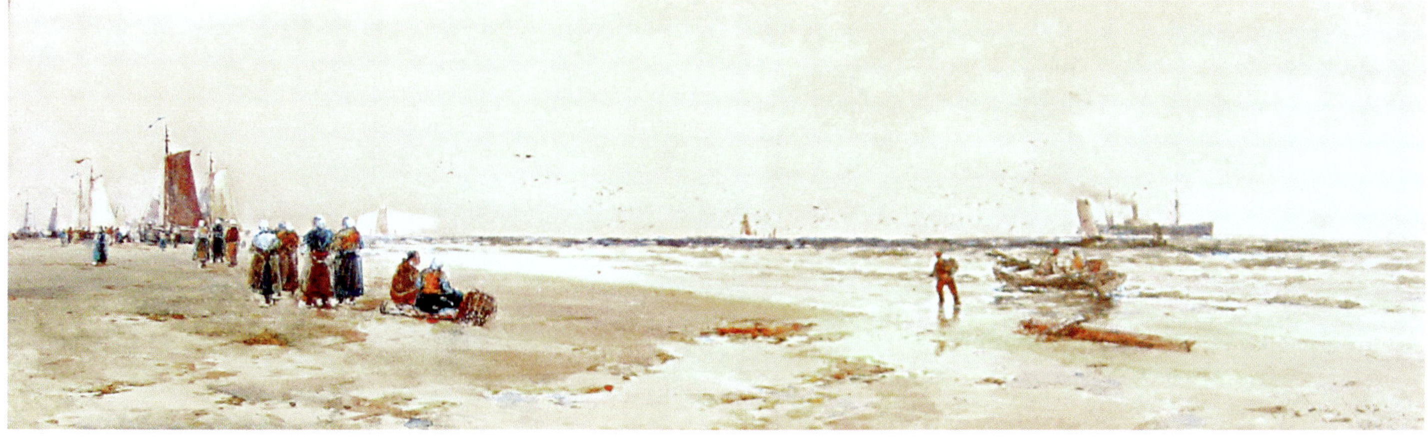

Slicing the paper to represent the initial breaking of a wave or spindrift was a technique introduced by Hardy in his later years (and followed by some of his students). Comparing the sea in this example with almost any previous work, it can be appreciated why the method was not universally admired and, wisely, seldom adopted by other marine artists. Rubbing, scraping and many other methods of using the whiteness of the paper as a pigment have all been used with greater success. This watercolour gives the impression it has been poorly conceived and hastily sketched. It is a genuine Hardy but not up to the normally high standard of his finished watercolours.

This is quite a small watercolour and, like the previous example painted in 1894, cannot be regarded as anything more than a loosely painted sketch. As such it has something to commend it. There is a lot going on and Hardy has succeeded in describing it all for us – the presently calm conditions, practically no wind, a near flat sea, flapping sails, but in the sky a squall approaching. Meanwhile a number of pincks are shown slowly drifting towards the shoreline where their teams are waiting to help beach them and carry away the catch. But the actual drawing and colouring throughout is poor. It is more than possible that Hardy did the outline sketch in pencil before turning it over to a student. The signature and date are authentic.

It is unfortunate that, by introducing Hardy's Dutch watercolours in chronological order, the two most recent examples are the least impressive. Before continuing with the review of his other European paintings, the authors feel it is worth reminding readers that, taken as a whole, in their opinion they represent some of the finest watercolours of coastal scenes that have ever been painted. Fortunately, a great many have so far survived in good condition, but we would urge all museum and art gallery curators and private collectors to preserve most carefully this irreplaceable national heritage.

Chapter 4 – The Dutch Coast

Opposite above. Plate 4.34.
Off the Dutch Coast. *Signed, inscribed and dated 1894. 23 x 32cm (9 x 12⅝in.)*

Opposite below. Plate 4.35.
On the Maas. *Signed, inscribed and dated 1894. 15.5 x 34.5cm (6⅛ x 13⅝in.)*

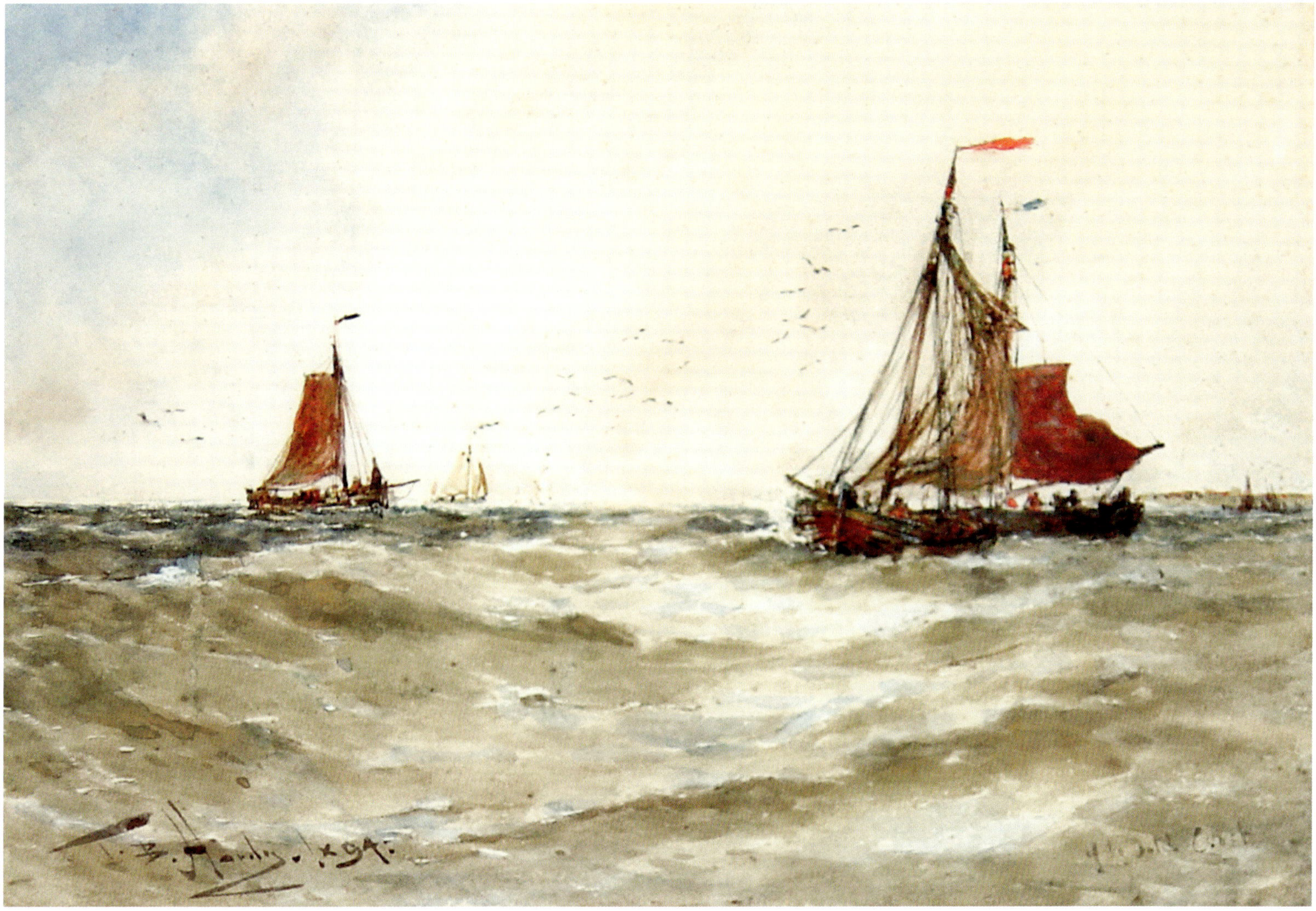

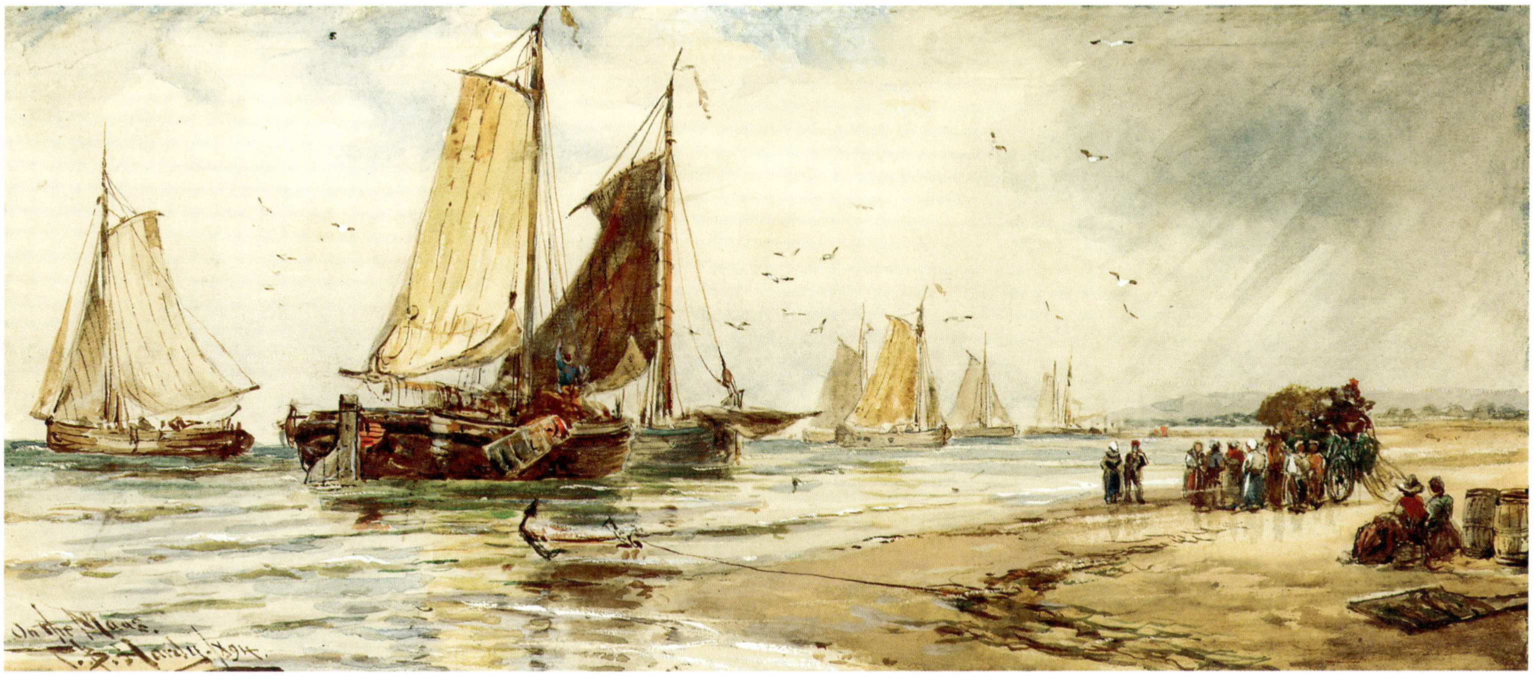

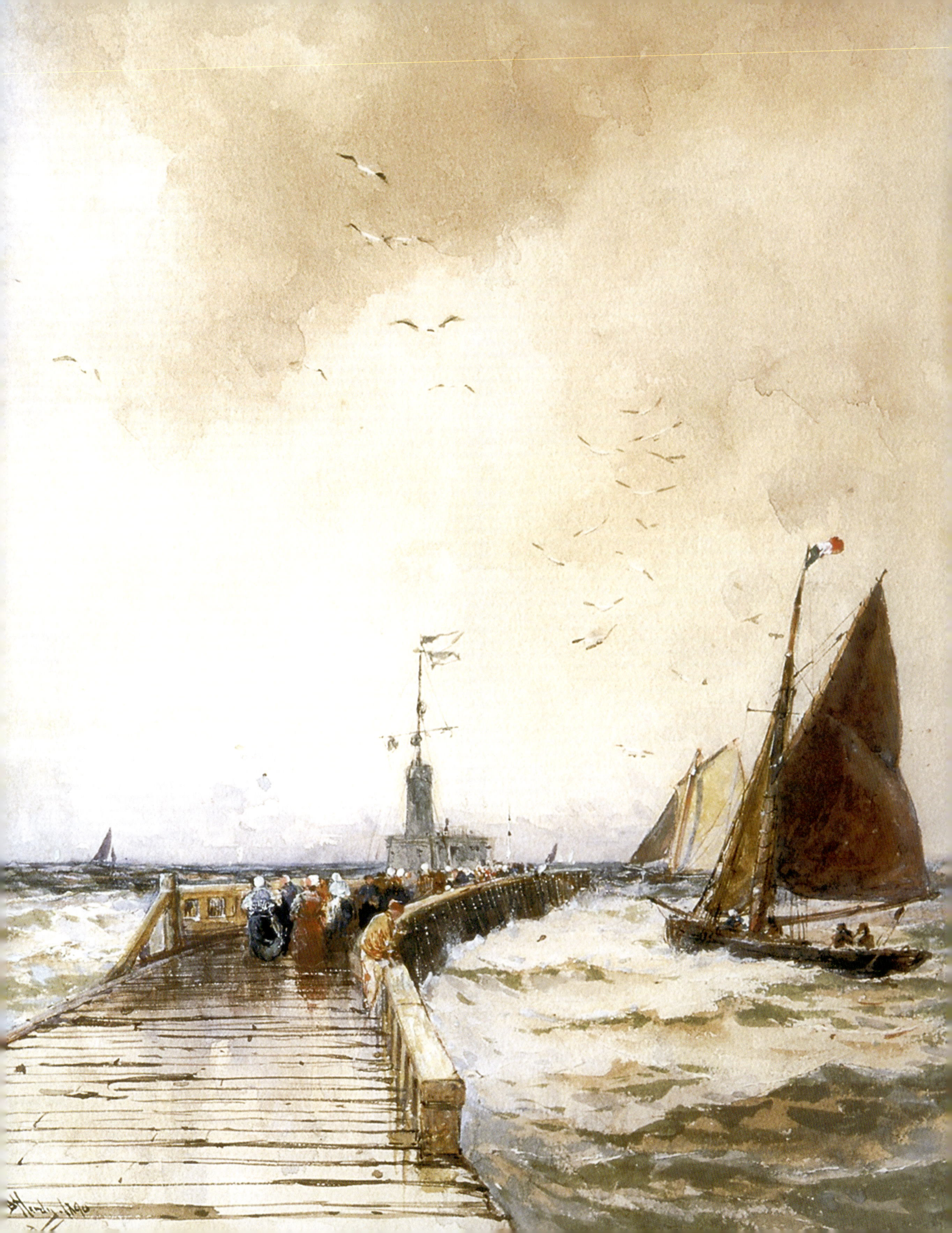

The French Coast

We believe that Hardy may not have used the Dover/Calais or Folkestone/ Boulogne routes to the Continent until 1874 but from then on probably used one or other of them regularly. His first large watercolour of Calais appeared that year, followed by increasing numbers of Pas de Calais subjects over the next two decades. The family move to Boulogne for three years in 1876 led to more paintings of Normandy fishermen and may have reduced travelling expenses for a time, but, although he would have sold a few paintings there to visiting Victorian tourists, his main market was in London. There was also the problem of educating seven daughters and launching them into society. Boulogne in those days was a good base for a marine artist but not necessarily the answer to a maiden's prayer!

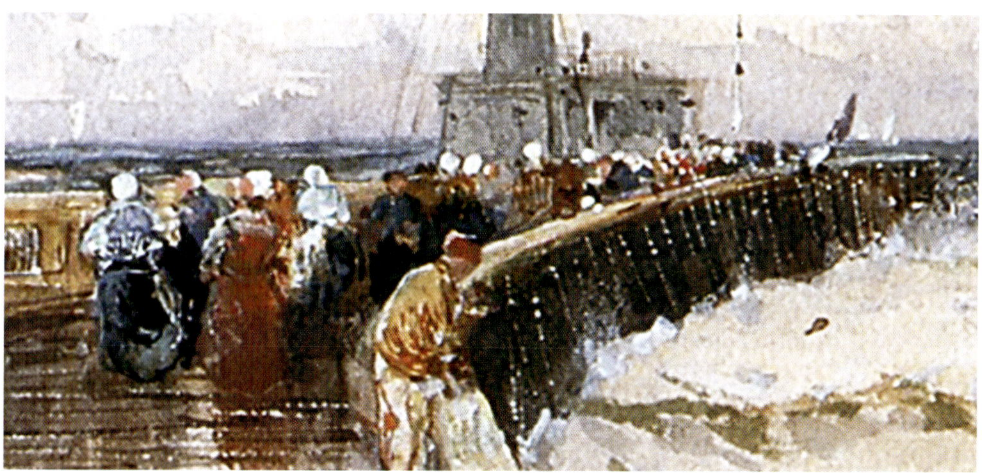

Opposite. Plate 5.1. **Boulogne Pier.** *Signed, inscribed and dated 1890. 26 x 21cm (10¼ x 8¼in.)*

A rare portrait-shaped view of the pier at high water. A fresh to strong sou'westerly wind prevails and a number of spectators have braved the wet and windy weather to watch the local fishing boats go about their business. This is a well composed and coloured watercolour – no frills, but a good, honest snapshot of life at the sharp end of the premier fishing port in Northern France.

This large and impressive watercolour is one of Hardy's earliest paintings of the French Channel ports, showing two Calais-registered gaff-rigged fishing boats alarmingly close to the pier in a strong sou'westerly and lively sea. Hardy was to spend a great many hours on, or in the vicinity of, Calais and Boulogne piers and jetties watching and sketching the local fishermen handle their boats. The two boats featured here each have a crew of three, the least number required to tend the sailing rig on three masts. Hardy is clearly admiring the skippers' skill in manoeuvring their craft in such a confined space, as are the many spectators on the pier. Beyond the fishermen is what appears to be the mainmast of a topsail schooner at anchor, awaiting an alongside berth. The greys of the clouds and the breaking waves harmonise well with the browns of the sails, the clinker-built hulls and the wooden pier. Cleverly, the artist has been very sparing with other colours; they would be superfluous to the impression he had already created.

Plate 5.2. **Calais Pier.** *Signed, inscribed and dated 1874. 39.5 x 70cm (15½ x 27½in.)*

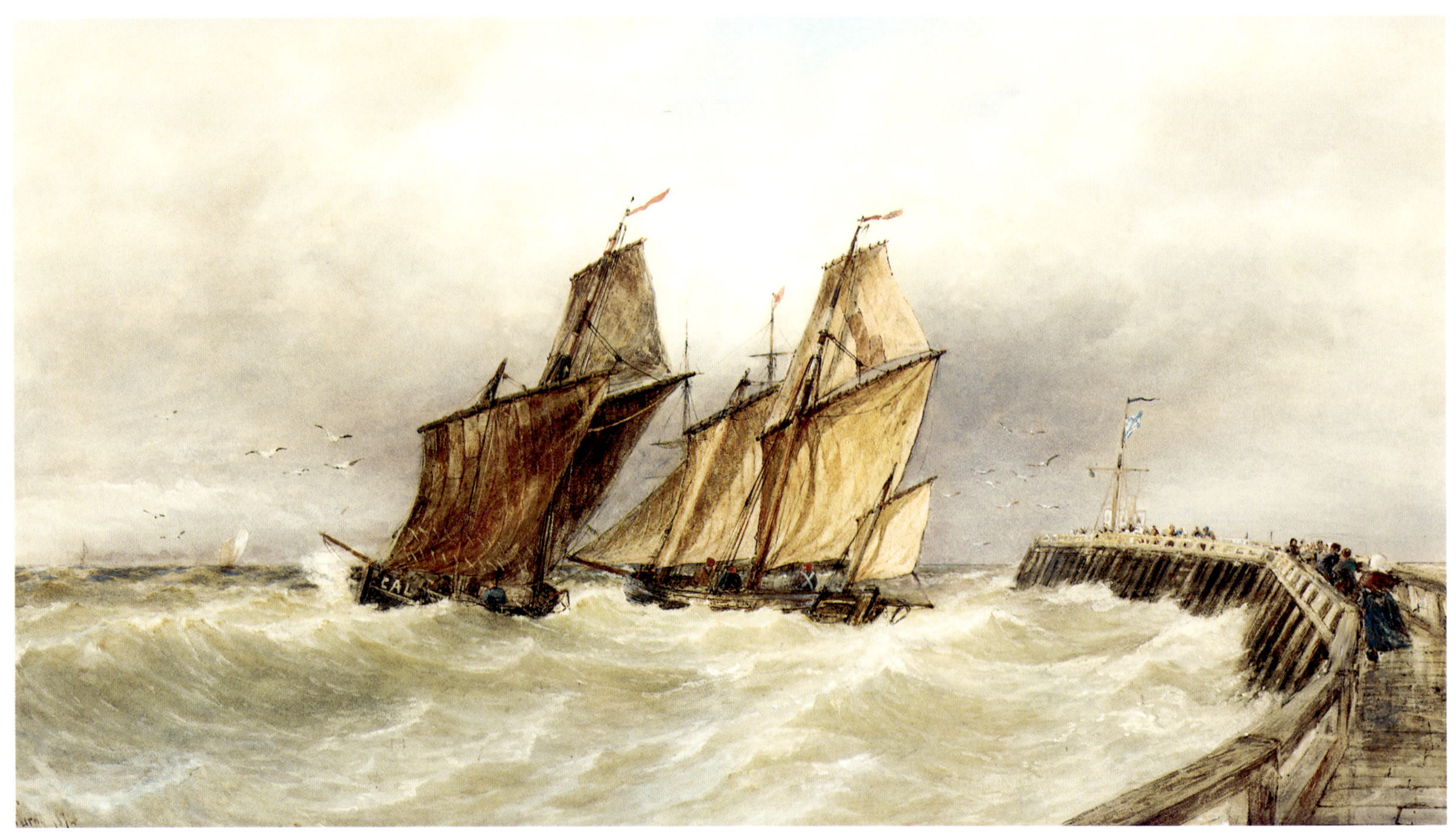

138

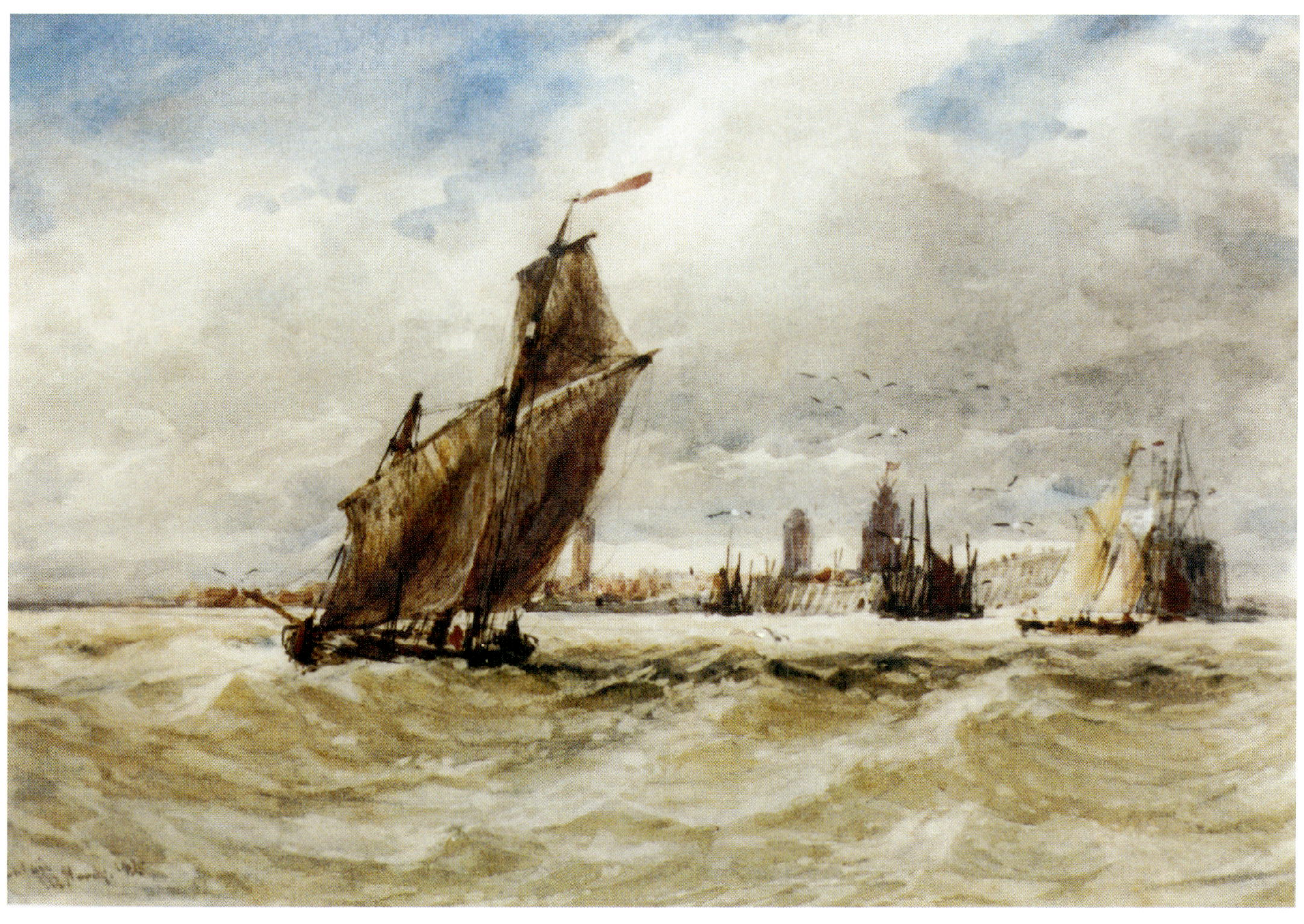

Plate 5.3. **Off Calais.** *Signed, inscribed and dated 1875. 12 x 17cm (4¾ x 6¾ in.)*

This is one of Hardy's earliest postcard-sized watercolours to survive, and a very good example too. Here the artist is looking from the sea back towards Calais with, in the foreground, one of the locally-registered boats off to a favourite fishing ground. It is a bright, breezy day, the sun shining spasmodically through a cloudy blue sky. The English Channel (La Manche to the fishermen) is being churned up by the northerly wind and a north-going tidal stream. The distant view of Calais shows a tall building finishing construction beyond the harbour. Calais, being only twenty-one miles from Dover, with which it was now linked by a frequent ferry service, had become the Victorian tourists' favourite gateway to Europe. The town and its fishing fleet was expanding fast, providing many suitable subjects for a marine artist.

Hardy had been painting Dutch beach scenes for at least four years when he turned his attention to the opportunities offered in the Pas de Calais region, equally famous for their fishing communities and equally dependent on being able to launch their boats off beaches with very shallow gradients. In this watercolour the three fishing boats in view are Calais-based luggers which would normally fish in deeper water. It seems that the smaller craft or 'flobarts' may have decided against going out on what must have been a pretty unpleasant day. Hardy may have been visiting the beach hoping to see some fishermen unloading their catch, but instead he has been able to give us a memorable painting of a thoroughly miserable, wet and windy afternoon – the rotting ribs of the wreck, the women braced against the squalls and a cart drawn by a horse clearly suffering from extreme depression. But on the western horizon there is a brightening of the sky which augers well for the morrow.

Plate 5.4. **Calais Beach.**
Signed, inscribed and dated 1875. 32 x 50cm (12⅝ x 19⅝in.)

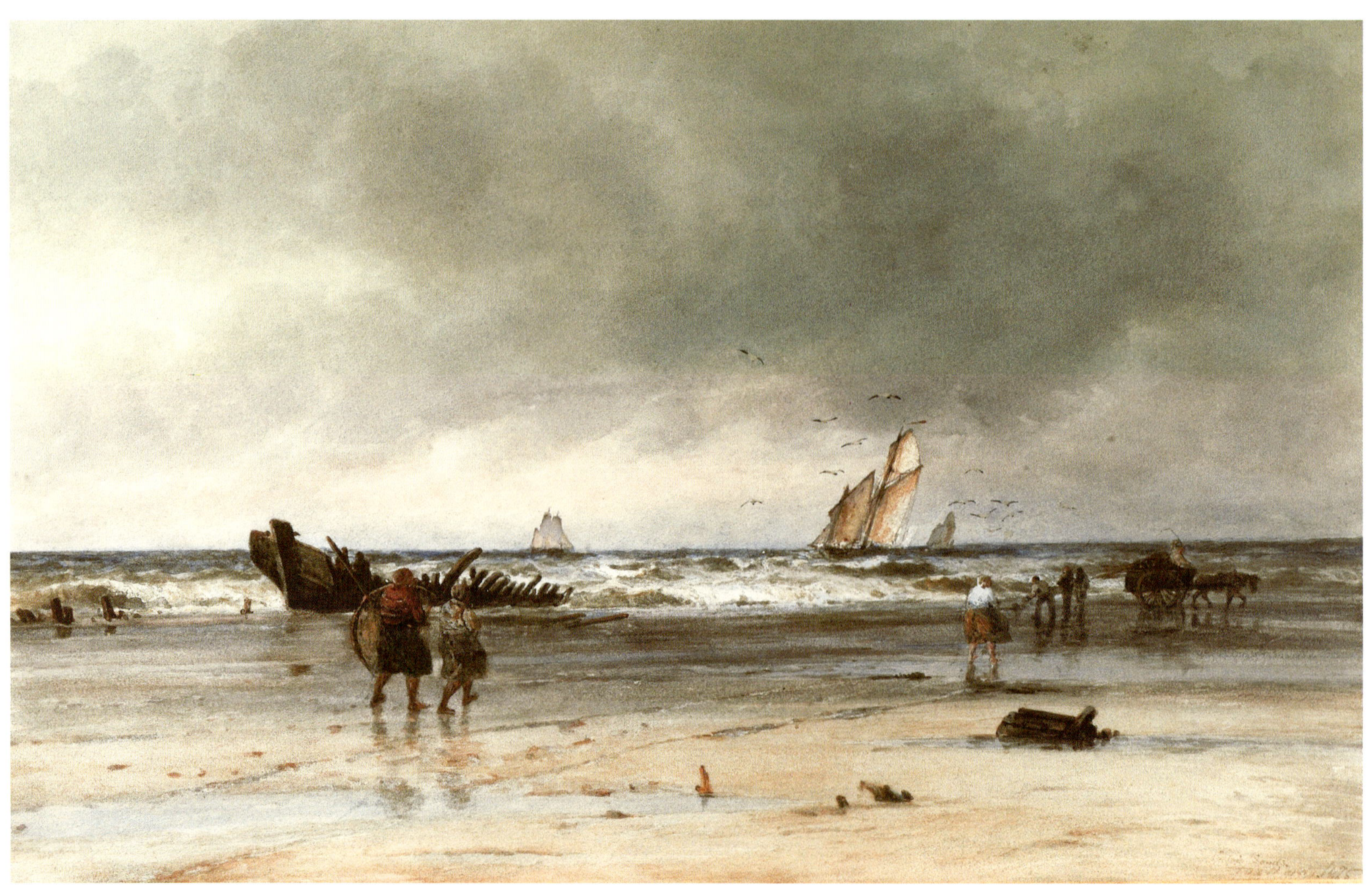

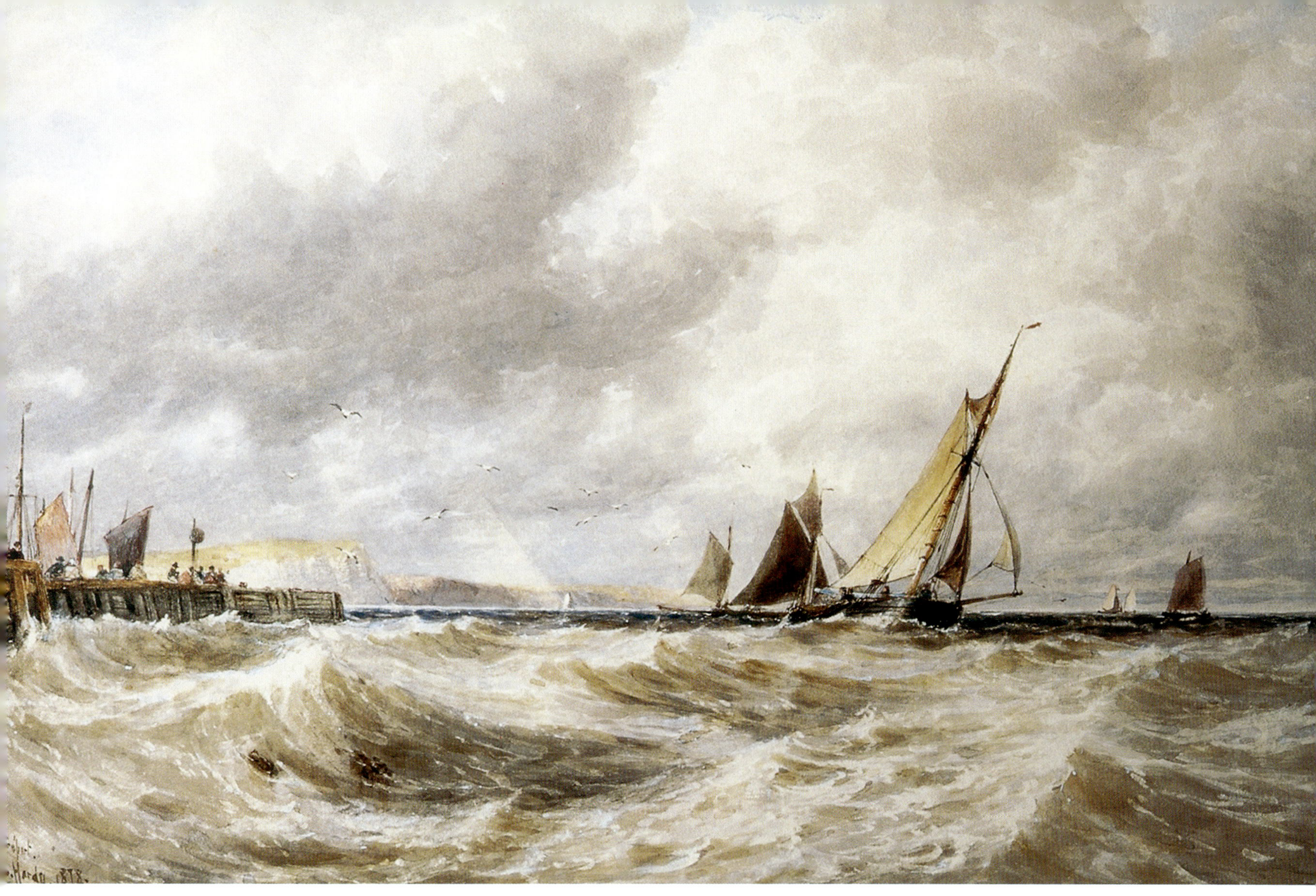

This is a particularly fine watercolour of fishing vessels off Tréport, one of Hardy's favourite French harbours. Le Tréport was where Queen Victoria met Louis Philippe on two occasions, in 1843 and 1855, meetings which many historians believe led fifty years later to the Entente Cordiale. There seems little doubt that Hardy developed a similar close relationship with the fishing community there which, in the 1870s, was still the town's main industry. With the arrival of the railway in 1873, Le Tréport soon became a favourite watering place for Parisiens, 'the prettiest beach in Europe, just three hours from Paris', and fishing declined in importance. Now, over a century later, the seaside town has lost most of its Victorian and Edwardian glamour but the stone quays, wooden piers, boats and fishermen are still there.

Returning to the painting, it is clearly based on sketches that he made *en plein air,* embarked in one of the fishing vessels, and then worked up ashore. It is a windy, squally day, with the sun occasionally breaking through the clouds to light up the distant cliffs and hills. Two fishing boats have just left the shelter of the harbour and are making good progress into a strong north-easterly. The sea, reflecting the grey, unsettled sky, swells and surges towards the wooden structure of the pier before retreating in foaming disarray. To put this on paper is great art.

Plate 5.5. **Off Tréport.** *Signed, inscribed and dated 1876. 33 x 49.5cm (13 x 19½in.)*

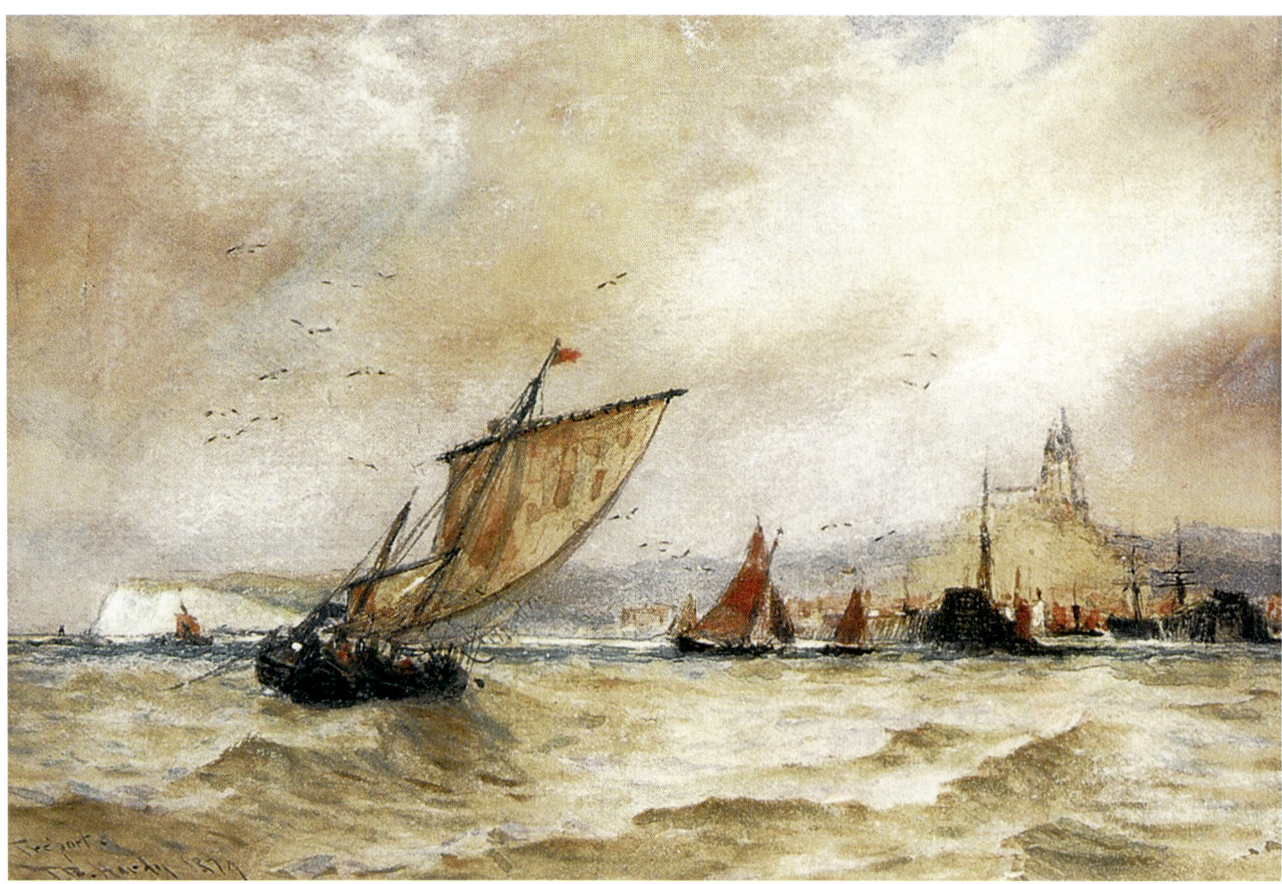

Very much a sketch, but capturing the essence of a fine, windy day, the local fishermen out in force, trawling close inshore. Tréport, its church dominating the scene, seems to be welcoming allcomers back to the shelter of its harbour. This is an example of Hardy at his most economic: restrained coloured washes over delicately etched images, a technique he seldom adopted, but which in this case works very well.

A small watercolour marine scene with an autumnal feel about it. Hardy has used an interesting mix of matching brown pigments and, in the sea and on the seagulls, quite a lot of Chinese White – perhaps too much. The problem with Chinese White is that, in some cases, as other colours fade the white becomes aggressively dominant. The focus here is on three luggers in a stiff westerly wind, tacking up and down off the harbour entrance watched by a few onlookers. In the interests of composition, the artist has intentionally reduced the distance between the fishing boats and the pier, overlooking the fact that the nearest boat still has her nets out! But the result can still be very pleasing, even to a seaman's eye.

This may be one of the few postcard-sized finished watercolours of Boulogne to have survived which, as he lived there and spent a lot of time sketching on the pier, is puzzling. Here Hardy has painted two very different types of sailing vessel passing Boulogne Pier – a square-sailed lugger followed by a ketch, both on a broad reach and giving the spectators something to talk about. It is high water, a strong breeze is blowing, and the short, steep seas, filled with sand, are beating against the pier's weather-worn timbers. A professional little picture.

Plate 5.6. **Tréport.** *Signed, inscribed and dated 1879. 11.5 x 16.5cm (4½ x 6½in.)*

Opposite above. Plate 5.7. **Off Tréport.** *Signed, inscribed and dated 1879. 12 x 17cm (4¾ x 6¾in.)*

Opposite below. Plate 5.8. **Vessels in the Channel off Boulogne.** *Signed and dated 1879. 12.5 x 18cm (4⅞ x 7in.)*

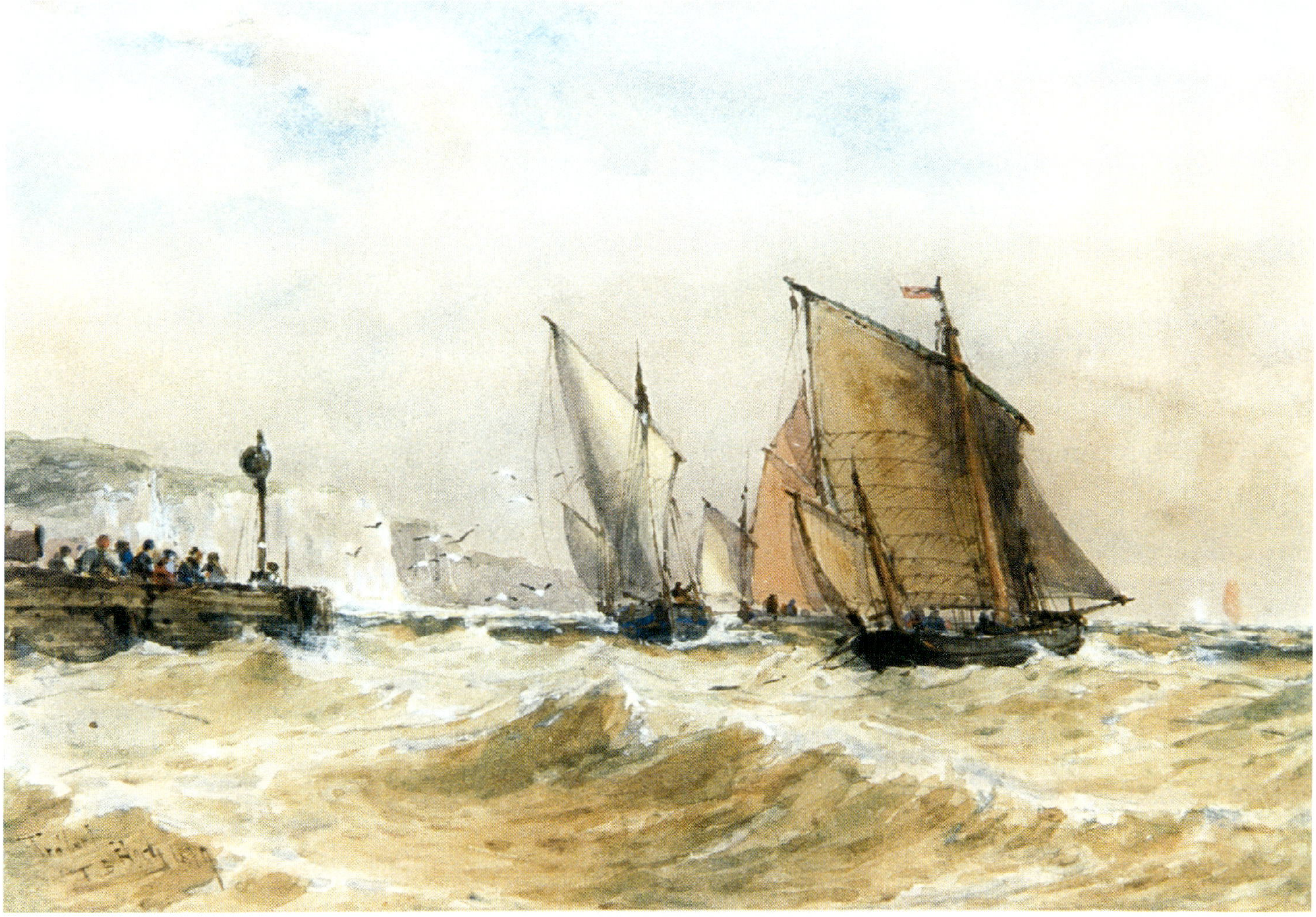

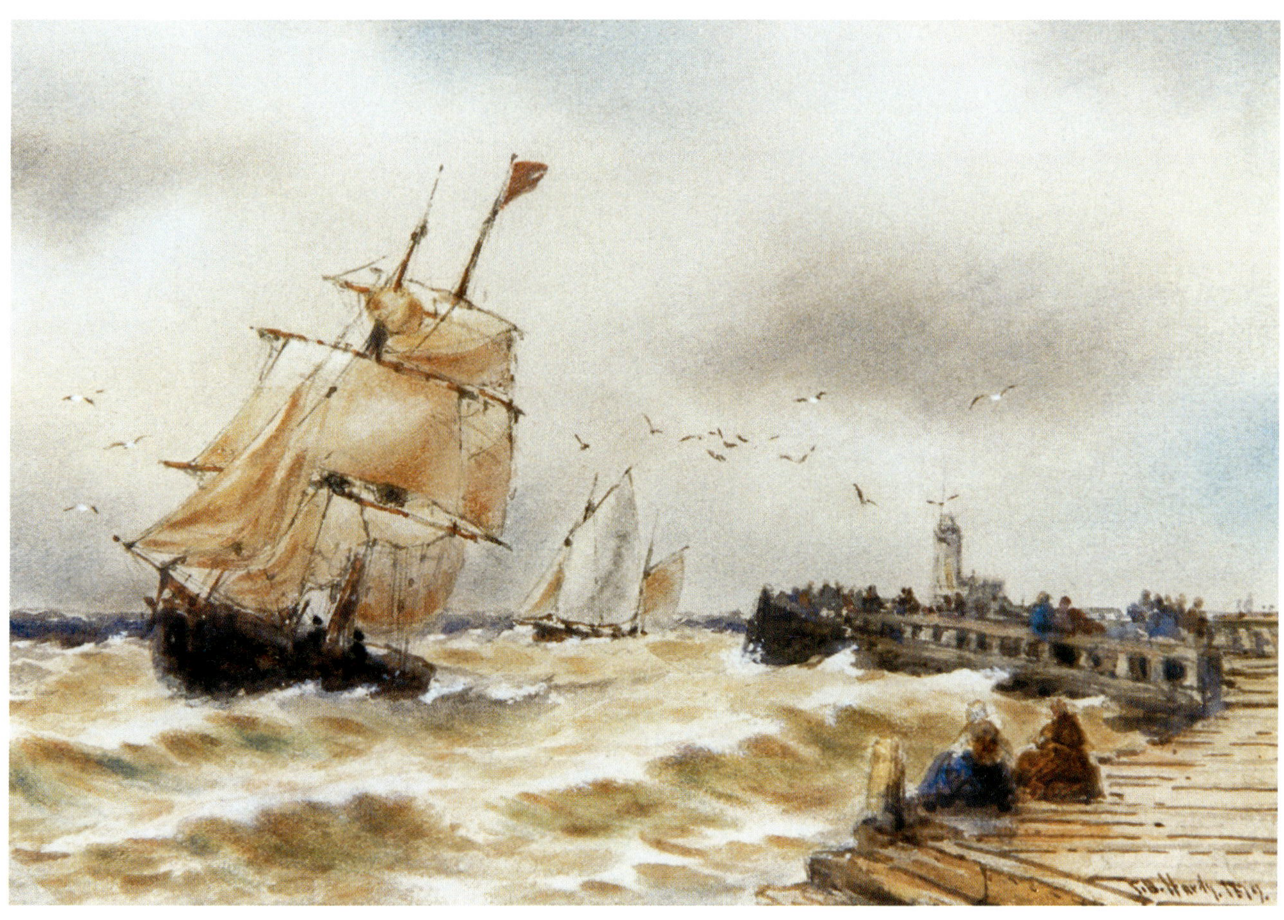

These three pages from one of Hardy's sketchbooks give us some idea of how he worked from day to day in Boulogne. They are very rough, impulsive pencil sketches, most of them covered with brief notes, Lear style, on colour, composition and prevailing conditions. Most of them featured the different types of fishing craft operating from the pier, the jetties and the beaches. However, it must be stressed that Hardy, unlike E.W. Cooke, eschewed detail and, apart from occasionally noting the date, as in two of the illustrations, never kept precise records of his work. How many of these scribbles and sketches contributed to finished watercolours is pure conjecture, but it is a strange fact that markedly few Boulogne subjects reached the market when the family was domiciled there from 1876-79.

Plate 5.9. **Boulogne Sketch Books 1875-76**

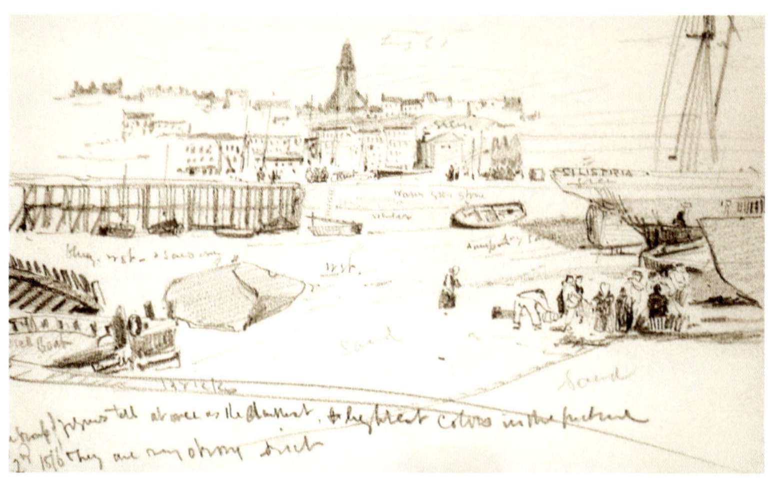

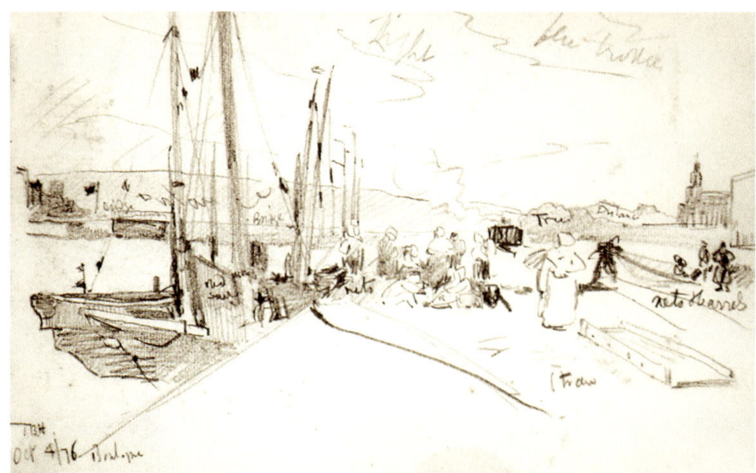

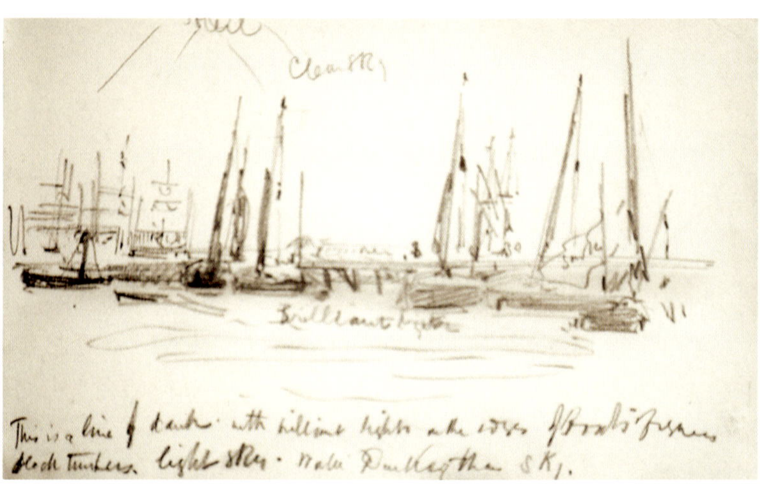

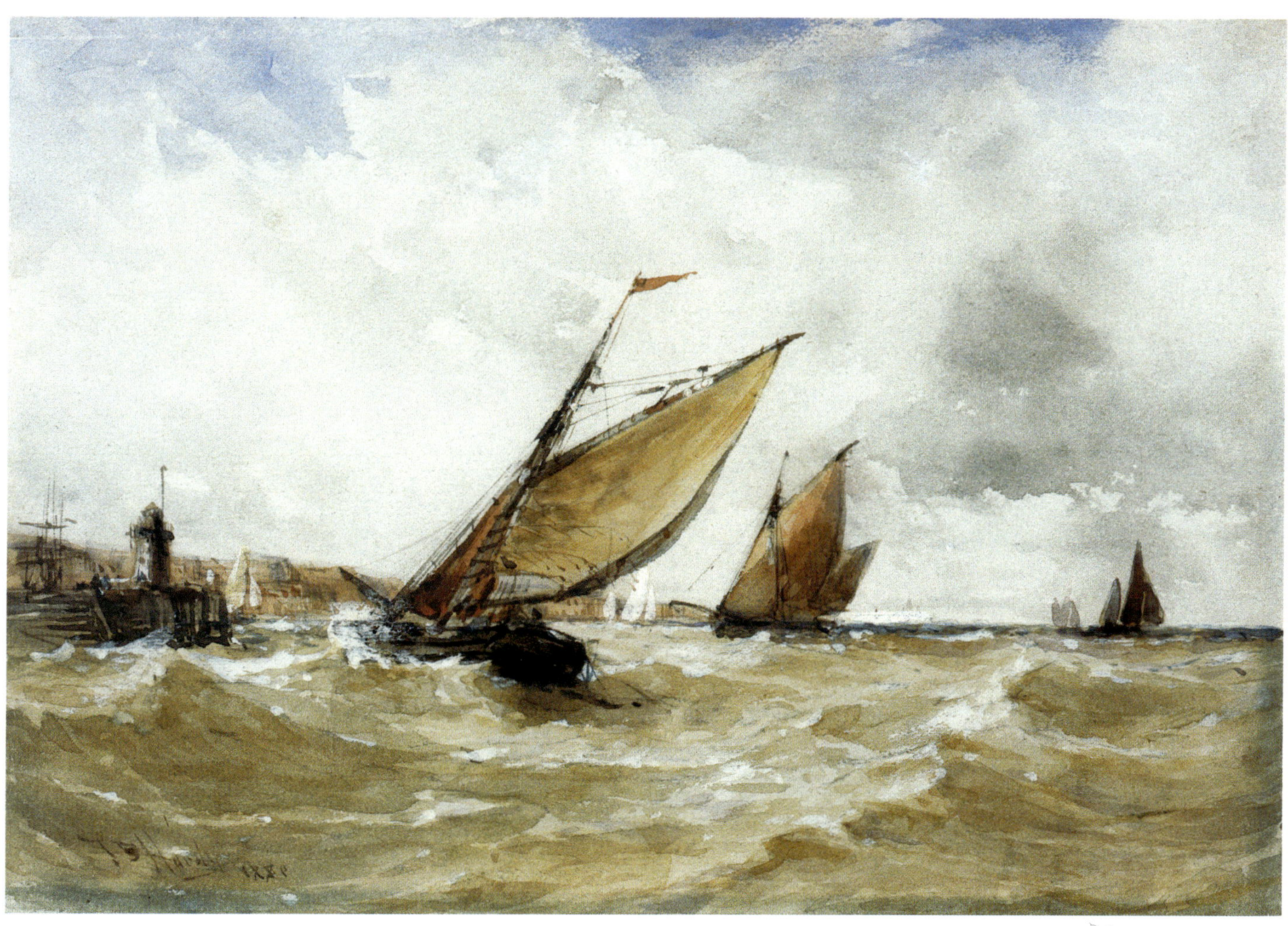

Plate 5.10. **Fishing vessels off Boulogne.** *Signed and dated 1880. 12 x 17cm (4¾ x 6¾ in.)*

Another fine postcard-size study of fishing vessels returning to Boulogne in a spanking breeze. The artist has achieved a nice balance between the elements – a largely cloudy wind-threatening sky and an increasingly rough sea yellow with sand, with waves smashing over the bows of the fishing boats making for the harbour entrance. The central theme of the two boats approaching each other on opposite tacks, enclosed on the left by the pier and on the right by a distant vessel, is well composed. As with most of these small watercolours, which have probably spent much of their lives in folders or albums, the colours are well preserved and strikingly realistic. An excellent example of its kind.

Chapter 5 – The French Coast

A still, grey day giving an unusual view of the town, but one that allows Hardy to show off his artistry in these conditions. A two-masted yawl with several people on board dominates the scene, her limp brown sails obscuring part of the town beyond. Alongside her a dinghy is about to cast off to take some of the crew ashore. A second dinghy in the left foreground may be bringing the remainder of the relief crew on board. Apart from the dipping of her oars in the water there is no noise and little movement. The fishing boats lying quietly on the town's jetties drying their sails would suggest this might be a Sunday afternoon. For the moment there is nothing to disturb the yawl's reflection. A very peaceful scene, beautifully drawn.

Plate 5.11. **Boulogne.** *Signed, inscribed and dated 1880. 31.5 x 49.5cm (12⅜ x 19½in.)*

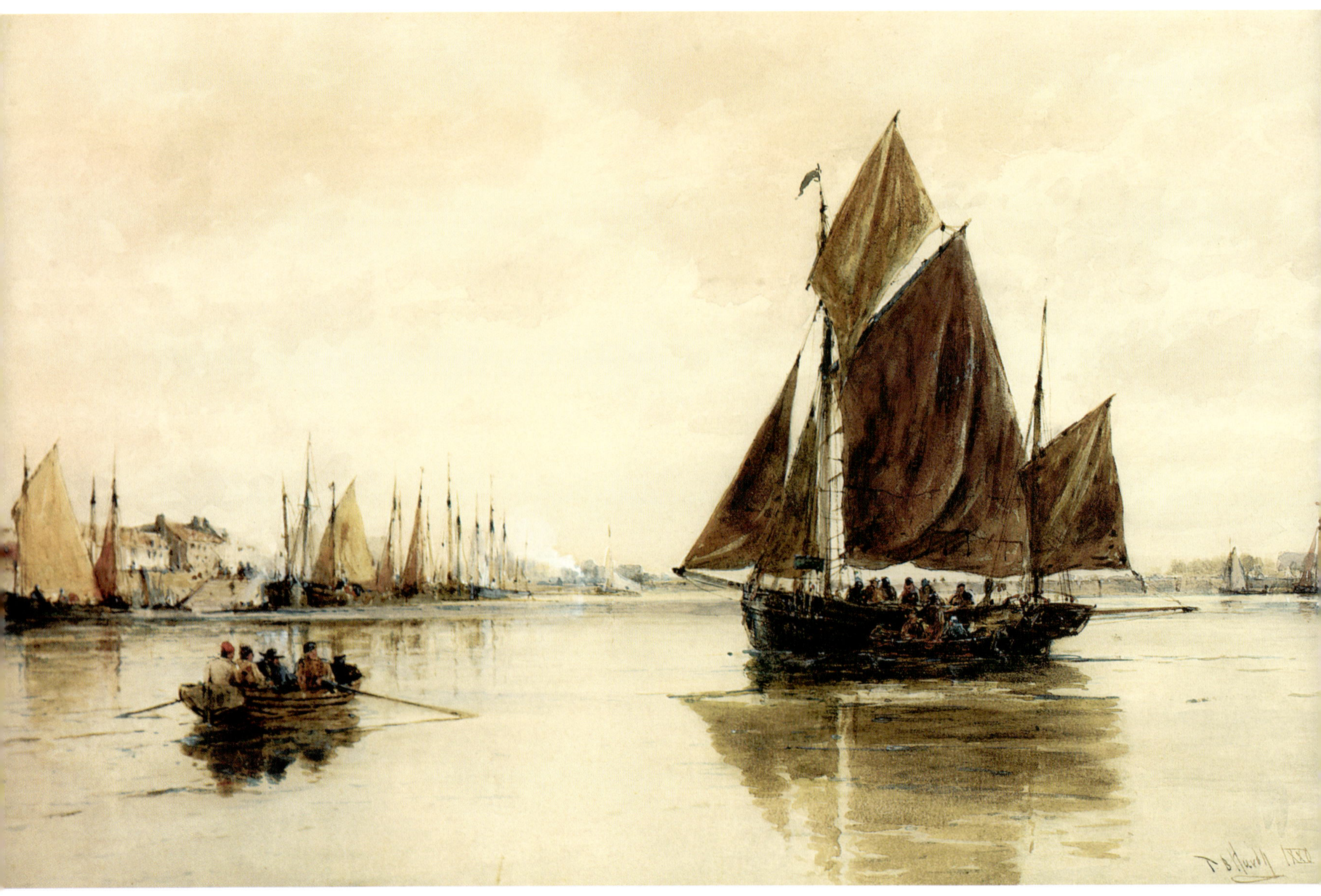

Chapter 5 – The French Coast

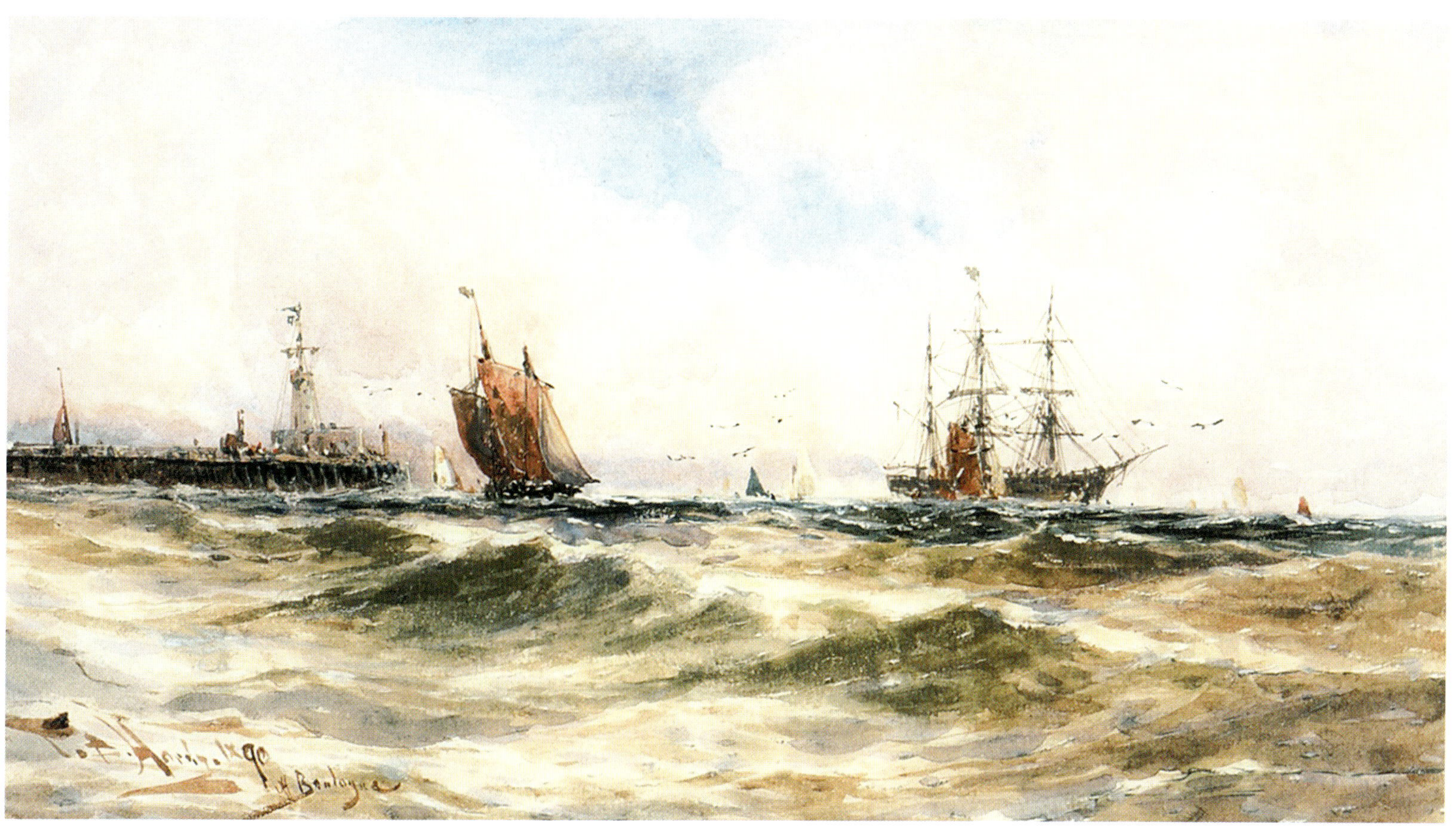

Plate 5.12. **Off Boulogne.**
Signed, inscribed and dated 1890. 13 x 25cm (5⅛ x 9¾in.)

This is Boulogne in a bracing northerly wind and, from the signals flying from the pierhead flagstaff, more to come. A locally-based lugger with all sails set has just passed the eastern breakwater, clawing her way off the shore towards Calais, while beyond a three-masted merchantman lies at anchor with all sails furled. In this relatively small watercolour, Hardy has used strong colours to emphasise the rough sea state and the likelihood of worsening conditions. The relationship between the sea, the ships, the pier and the people is well drawn in sharp detail, providing a convincing snapshot of a working day in Northern France's busiest port.

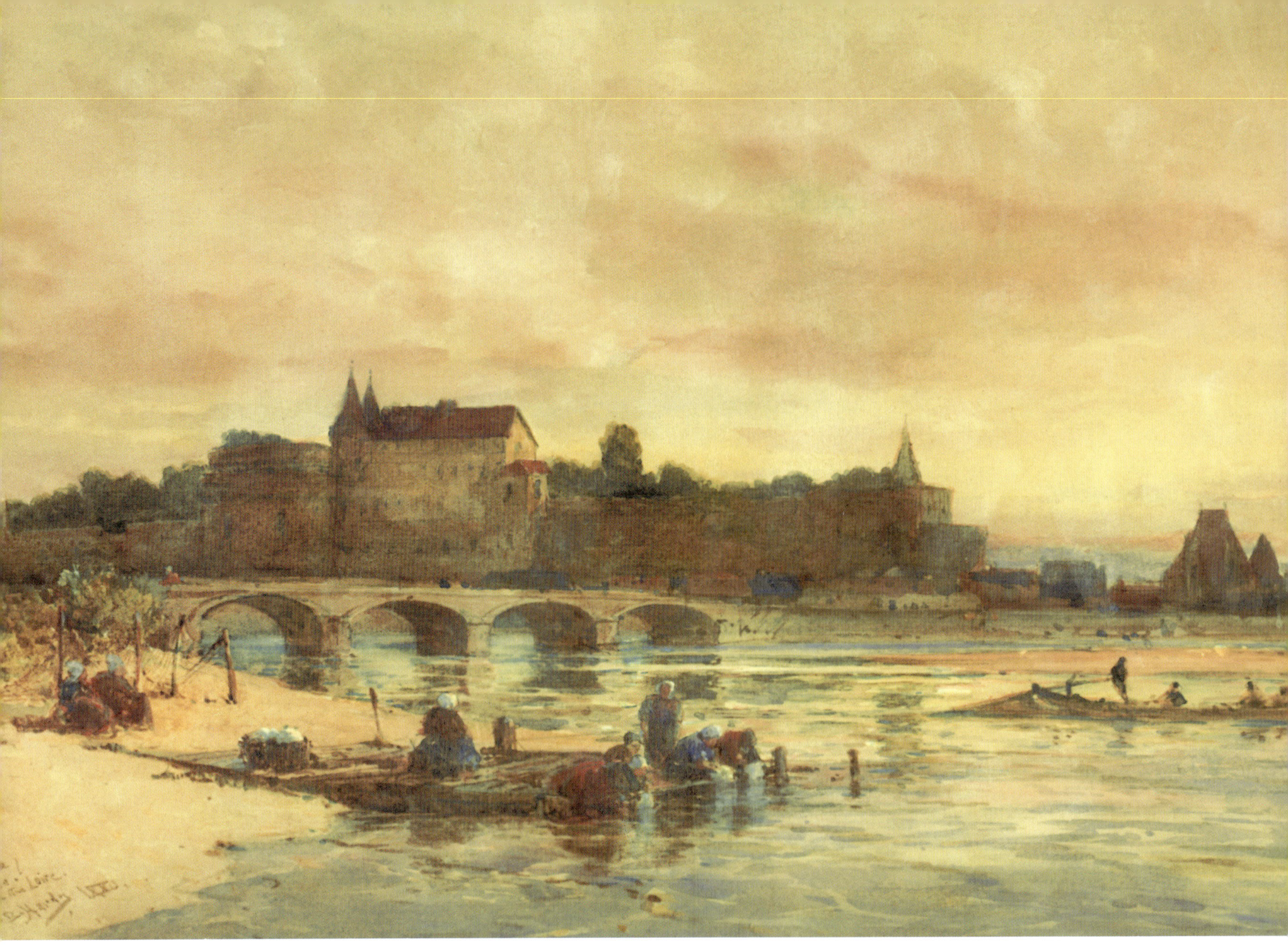

Plate 5.13. **Château d'Amboise.** *Signed, inscribed and dated 1880. 25.5 x 34.5cm (10 x 13⅝ in.)*

During his many months on the Continent, Hardy found time to visit and paint a number of outstanding river scenes. In France he visited both the Seine and the Loire where, at the Château d'Amboise, he was understandably inspired, not only by the beauty of the scene , but also by Leonardo da Vinci's historic links with the Castle where he spent his last years and where his remains still lie. Hardy has painted this watercolour on a late summer morning just after sunrise. The clouds are still tinged with pink lending a warm glow to the Castle walls, the old bridge and reflections in the river. It is a view well known to today's tourists but, sadly, they will not see what Hardy observed – the washerwomen up early to grab a place on the landing stage and the unusual craft being sculled down river. An interesting and well-drawn painting.

Chapter 5 – The French Coast

Equihen-plage is now one of the better-known beaches for kite-surfing on the Picardy coast. A hundred and thirty years earlier, this was the view that met Hardy when he started exploring the coastline a mere four miles south of the centre of Boulogne. After his experiences in Holland he would have been very much at home with the flourishing fishing community here. Most of the boats are smaller than the Scheveningen pincks and without lee-boards but, like them and their English counterparts on the Kent coasts, are hauled up on the beach when not fishing. In the left foreground of the watercolour three of the crew are unloading one of the tough clinker-built boats of the day's catch. To the north along the beach several boats have beached and are already drying their nets and sails, surrounded by a small crowd. Behind them a footpath leads up to a calvary and the hamlet housing most of the community.

Plate 5.14. **Equihen.** *Signed and inscribed. 21.5 x 34cm (8½ x 13⅜in.)*

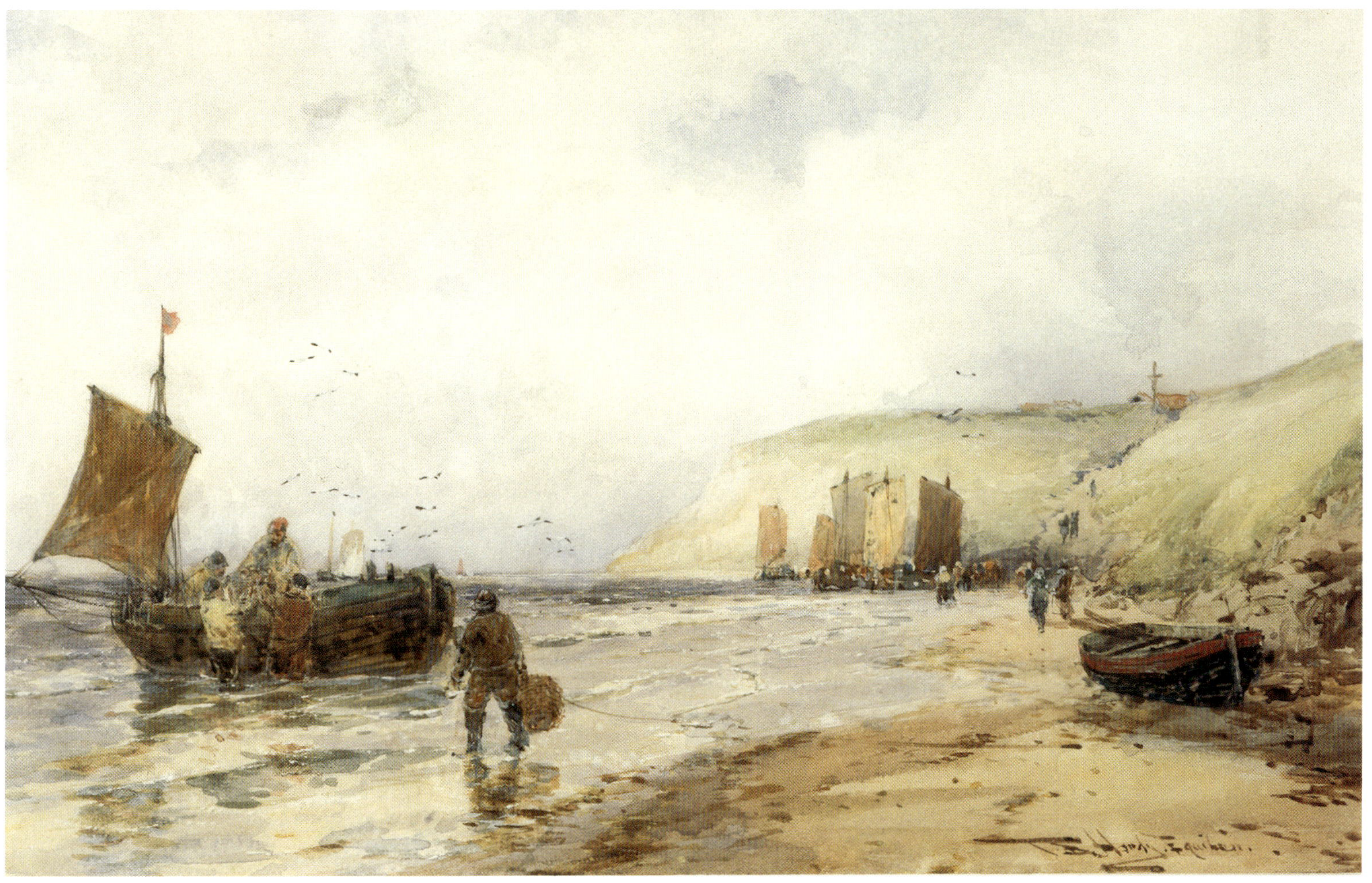

Full of interest, this fascinating watercolour is proof, if any doubts existed, that Hardy could not only draw figures but was extremely adept at their disposition in a scene such as this, where perspective is of singular importance. The viewer's eye follows the dispersed groups of fisherwomen from the sand dunes down to the wreck, the mast of which hovers like a calvary admonishing the assembled crowd. It is low water on a fine summer's morning, the sand stretches out westward to the Channel, now relatively calm, and to the lighthouse on Cap Gris-Nez. Nowadays, windswept Wissant, a village halfway between Calais and Boulogne, is a holiday resort for all kinds of surfers, but it has always been home to an important fishing community and, to this day, the fishermen beach their boats (called *flobarts)* before selling their fish directly to local people and tourists. In this regard, the only change is that tractors have taken the place of horses hauling the boats to and from the sea.

Plate 5.15. **Clearing a Wreck, Wissant, Picardy.** *Signed, inscribed and dated 1881. 31 x 48cm (12¼ x 18⅞in.)*

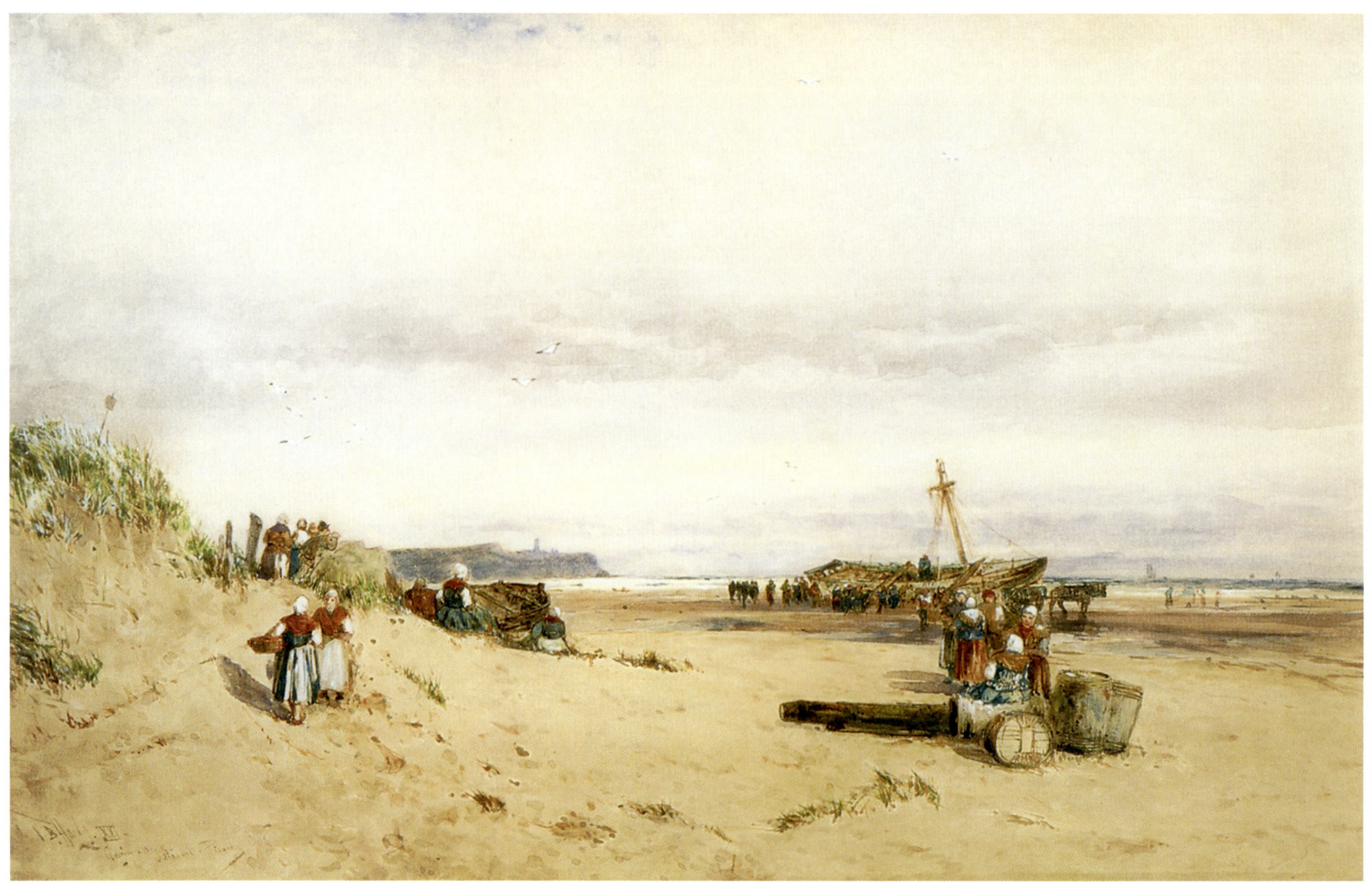

Plate 5.16. **The Wreck.**
Signed and dated 1882.
16.8 x 24.3cm (6⅝ x 9½in.)

This is almost certainly the wreck that Hardy painted earlier in the year but, covered in snow and icicles, she now presents a very different picture. Although there are still a few people satisfying their curiosity in the vicinity of the stricken vessel, she is now lying in shallow water on what is left of her port side and seems to have been totally abandoned. Hardy, deliberately ignoring any warm colours, has used a great deal of pale blue, grey and white to indicate a miserably cold day. The beach itself, normally an expanse of fine yellow sand, has succumbed to the unusually wintry conditions, the crisp snow and icy pools reflecting what colour there is in the sky. An atmospheric painting which Hardy was unlikely to repeat.

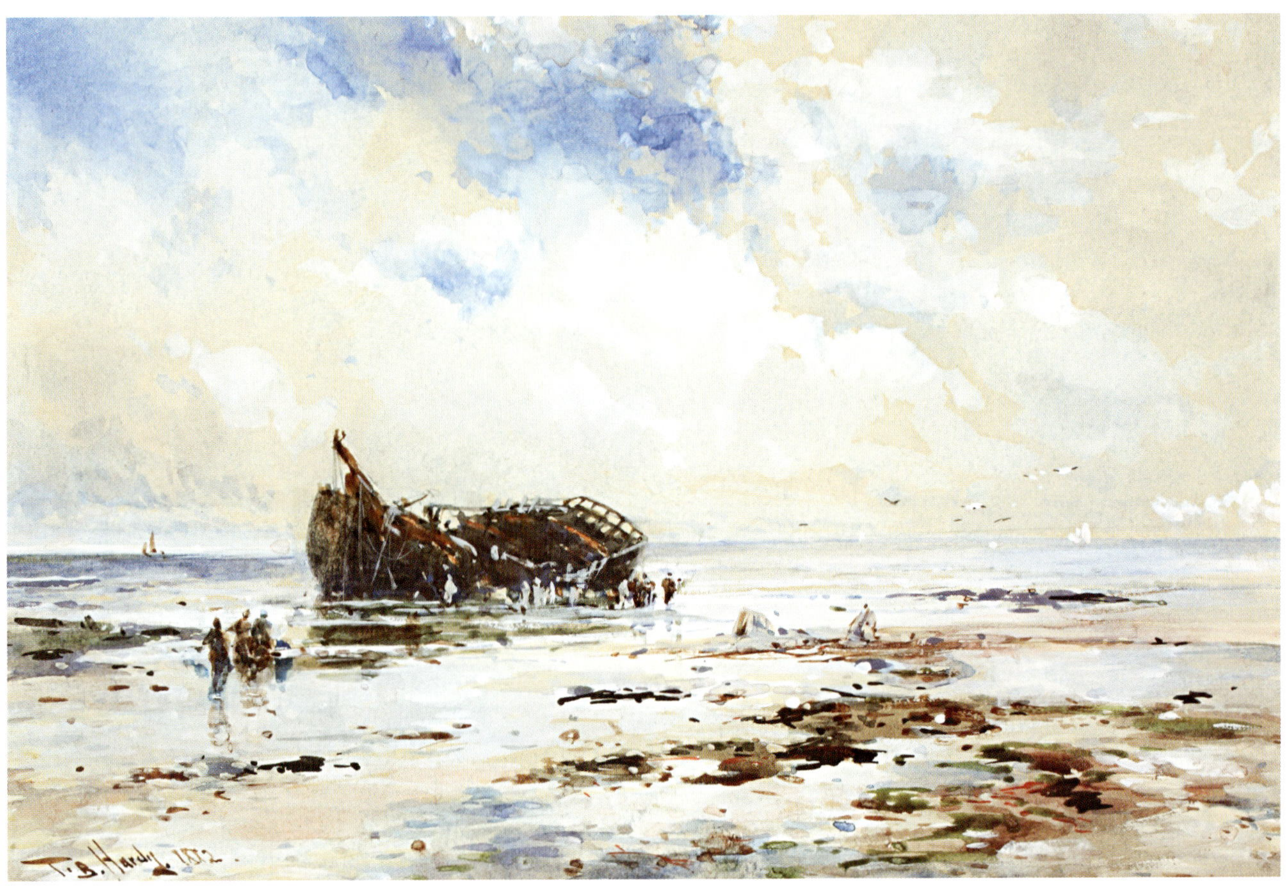

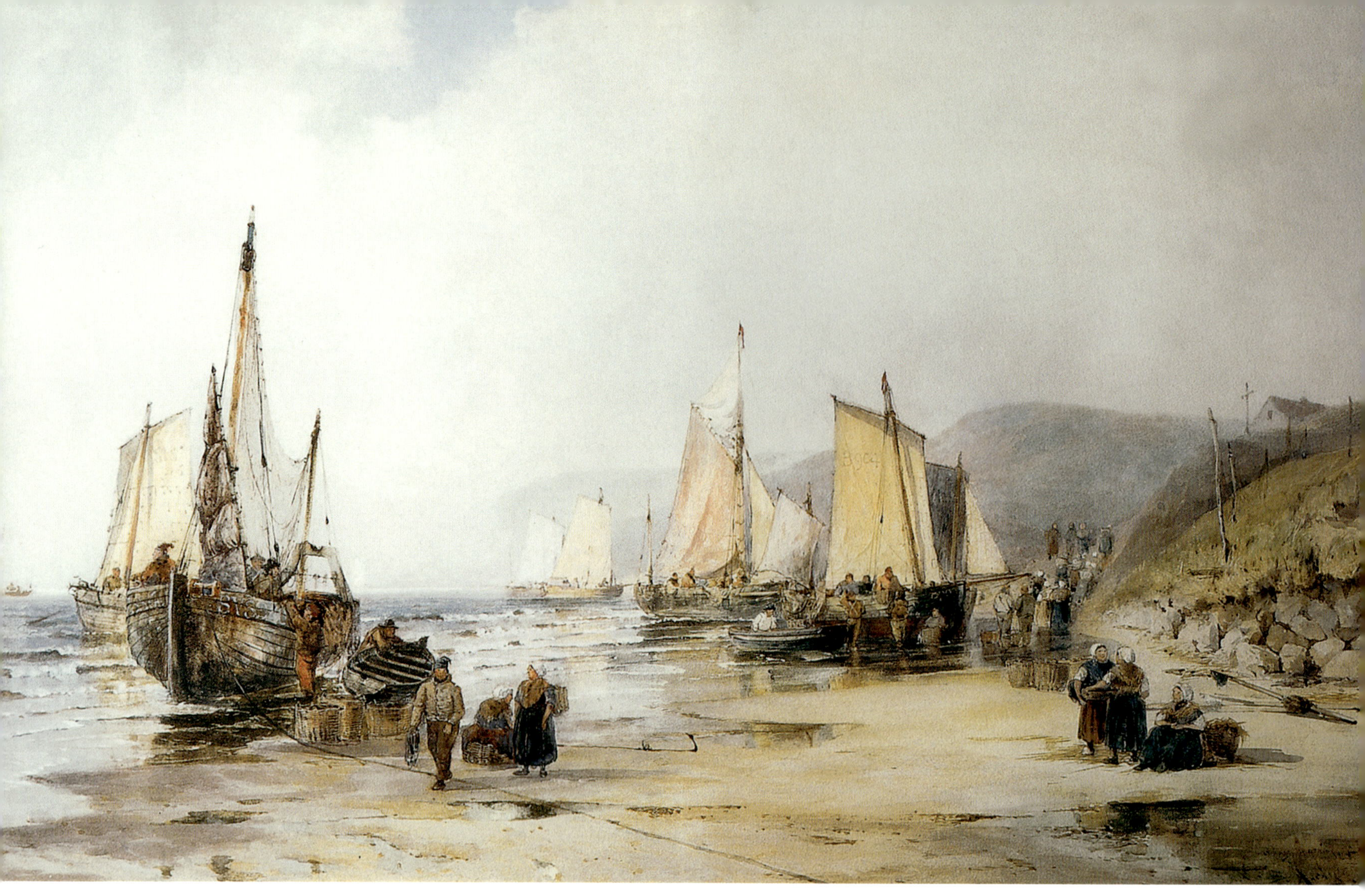

This is unquestionably one of the very best watercolours Hardy painted on the French Coast – a bustling scene involving most of the fishing community of one of the Picardy beach villages, probably Wissant. It is a fine summer morning and the last of the boats can be seen returning from a longish spell on the fishing grounds. Most of them have already unloaded their catch; many women can be seen carrying the traditional wicker baskets away from the boats and up the steep path that leads to the village, others are waiting patiently for the latecomers. There is still much to be done – the boats to be dragged higher up the beach and anchored securely, the sails and nets to be dried and repaired where necessary. Hardy has seldom painted figures with greater realism as they go about their tasks. In essence, this is a remarkably accurate and colourful picture of life as it was on the Picardy beaches over a hundred years ago, drawn with great feeling and understanding.

Plate 5.17. **A Hazy Morning, Picardy.** *Signed, inscribed and dated 1882. 45 x 69cm (17¾ x 27⅛in.)*

A subject Hardy was to paint frequently, possibly with the cross-Channel tourists in mind. Two or three Calais-registered fishing vessels are leaving harbour in a strong sou'-westerly, en route for the herring fishing grounds in the North Sea. From March onwards the bigger vessels from Boulogne and Calais would be fishing as far north as Iceland. Here, close to Calais Pier, the confluence of wind, tide and shallow water creates the kind of sea that Hardy depicts so well. The colour of the sea from the artist's low viewpoint is a steely grey tinged with blue, faithfully reflecting the generally cloudy sky. A rash tourist on the pier, looking down through the spray on the departing fishermen, would see a totally different mix of colours.

Plate 5.18. **Off the Pier.**
Signed and dated 1883.
19.5 x 30.5cm (7¾ x 12in.)

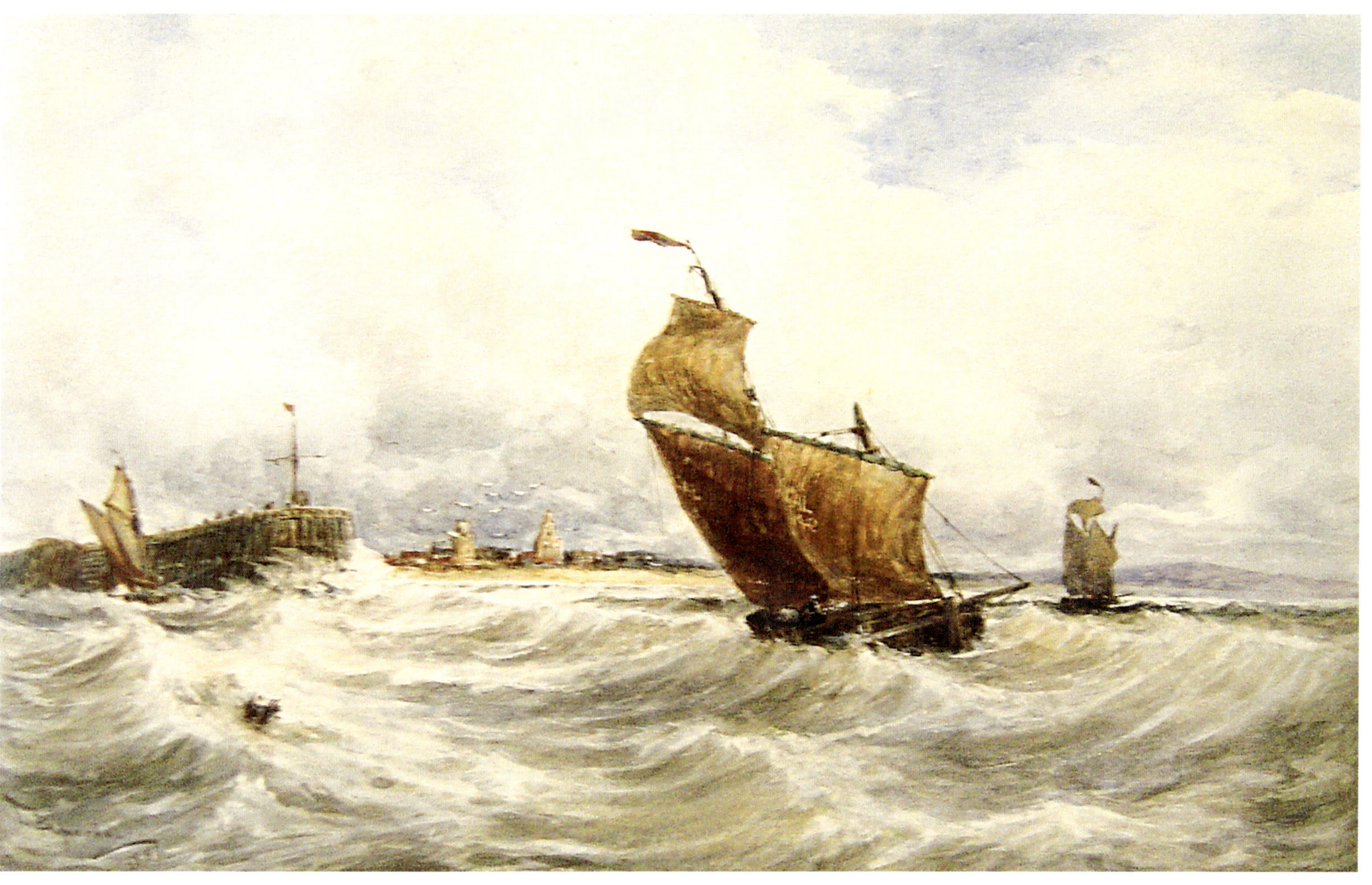

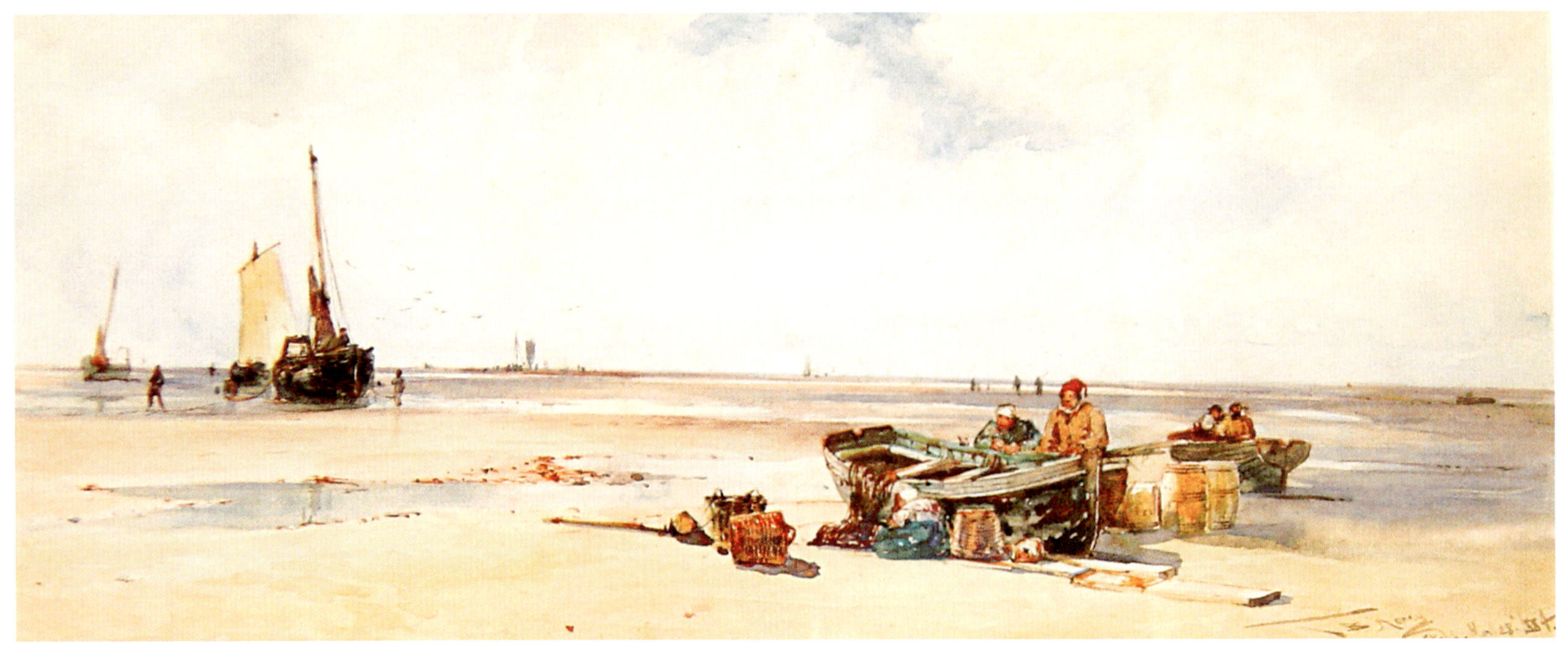

A watercolour showing the extent of the beach at Boulogne and the sense of distance and space created by Hardy's use of the long, thin format. Two of the local *flobarts* and their crews are prominent in the right foreground, together with their barrels, baskets and an assortment of fishing gear. Nearer the sea, three beached luggers are also clearing decks before the next high water and, still further to seaward, more vessels and their crews are watching the tide beginning to turn. Other very scattered groups of boats and figures lead the eye to the far horizon – a perspective tour de force.

Plate 5.19. **Boulogne Sands.**
*Signed, inscribed and dated
1884. 20.5 x 46cm (8 x 18⅛in.)*

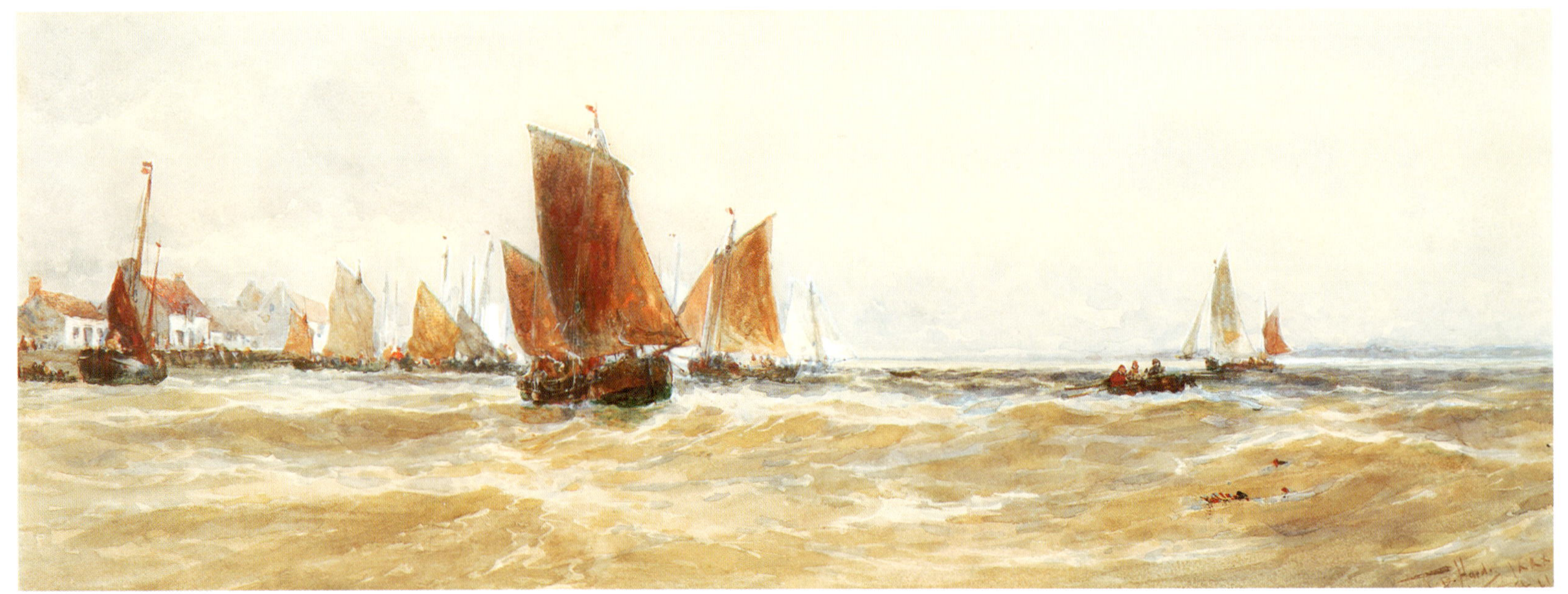

Chapter 5 – The French Coast

Only twenty odd miles from Boulogne and joined by rail since 1848, Etaples, at the mouth of the Canche, was bound to attract Hardy sooner or later. The area, known as the Côte d'Opale, was famed for the special quality of its light. Turner had painted there, Manet more recently and, in 1886, Eugène Boudin exhibited 'La Canche à Etaples,' now at the Château Musée, Boulogne. Hardy would certainly have been familiar with the Etaples School of Artists, founded in 1880, and must have been anxious to try his hand there. This is the first of two examples of his work painted at Etaples. There is no question that the light in this watercolour, and in the following example, is quite different from almost every other watercolour that Hardy ever painted. Whether he succeeded in reproducing this apparently unique light is a matter of judgement but the impression he gives is one of unnatural warmth.

Opposite below. Plate 5.20. **Etaples.** *Signed, inscribed and dated 1888. 20.5 x 46cm (8 x 18⅛in.)*

This is not one of Hardy's better paintings, nor does it have much in its favour. Its strong colouring, which may have been the artist's interpretation of the area's special light, and the sea, in particular, lack conviction. The three fishing boats and the dinghy in the foreground are quite well drawn but the left-hand lugger's trawl is shown to be streaming to leeward – an unlikely if not impossible situation and a mistake Hardy would not normally make…but one of his students might?

Plate 5.21. **Etaples.** *Signed and inscribed. 21.5 x 55.5cm (8½ x 21¾in.)*

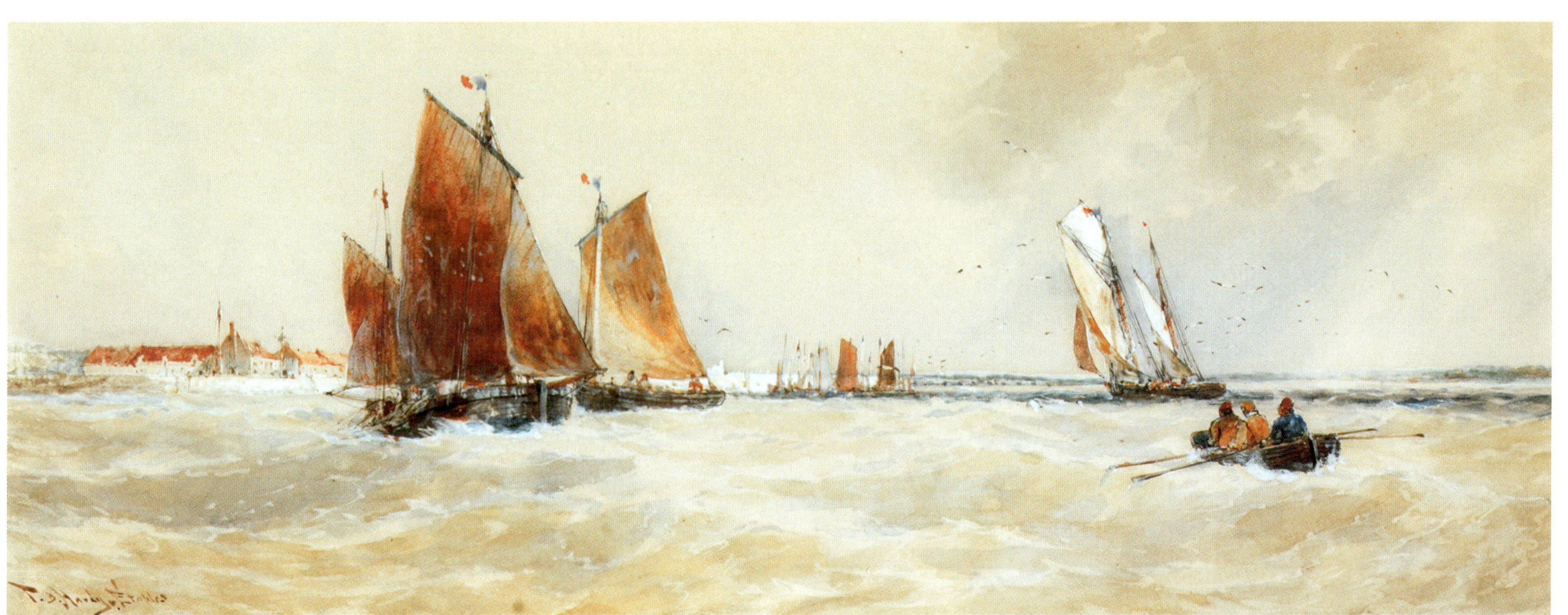

A vicious northerly wind is blowing and, according to the signal hoisted by the harbour-master, is likely to reach gale force. The local fishermen are wisely running for shelter and it is a fair bet that the passengers in the cross-Channel steam packets are having an horrendous time. Heavy, angry waves are breaking over the pier and threatening the survival of the nearest fishing boat. Ominous clouds race over the sky. It is a splendidly dramatic marine painting, a classic example of Hardy at the top of his form.

Plate 5.22. **Off the Pier, Weather Worsening.** *Signed and dated 1887. 19.5 x 30.5cm (7¾ x 12in.)*

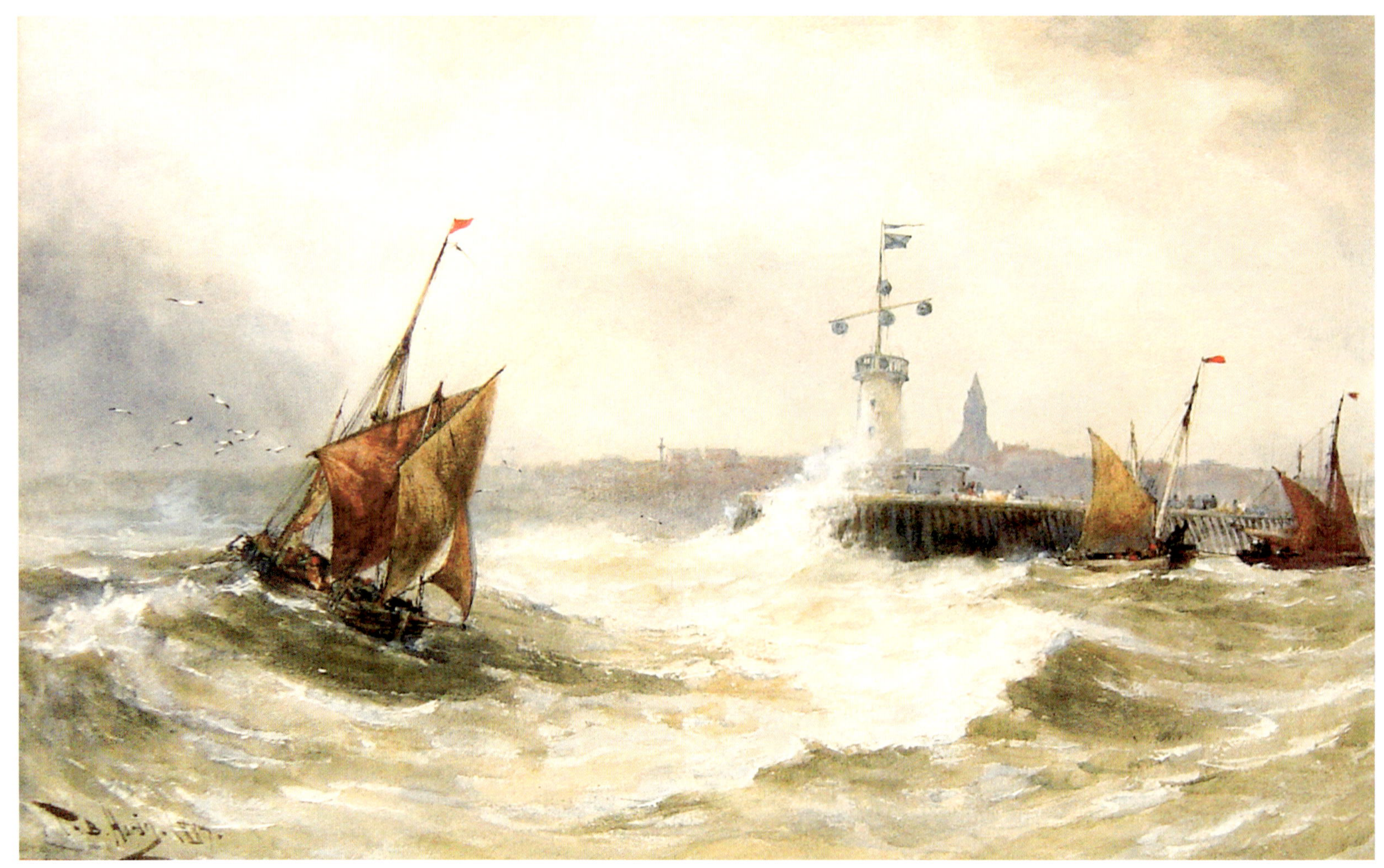

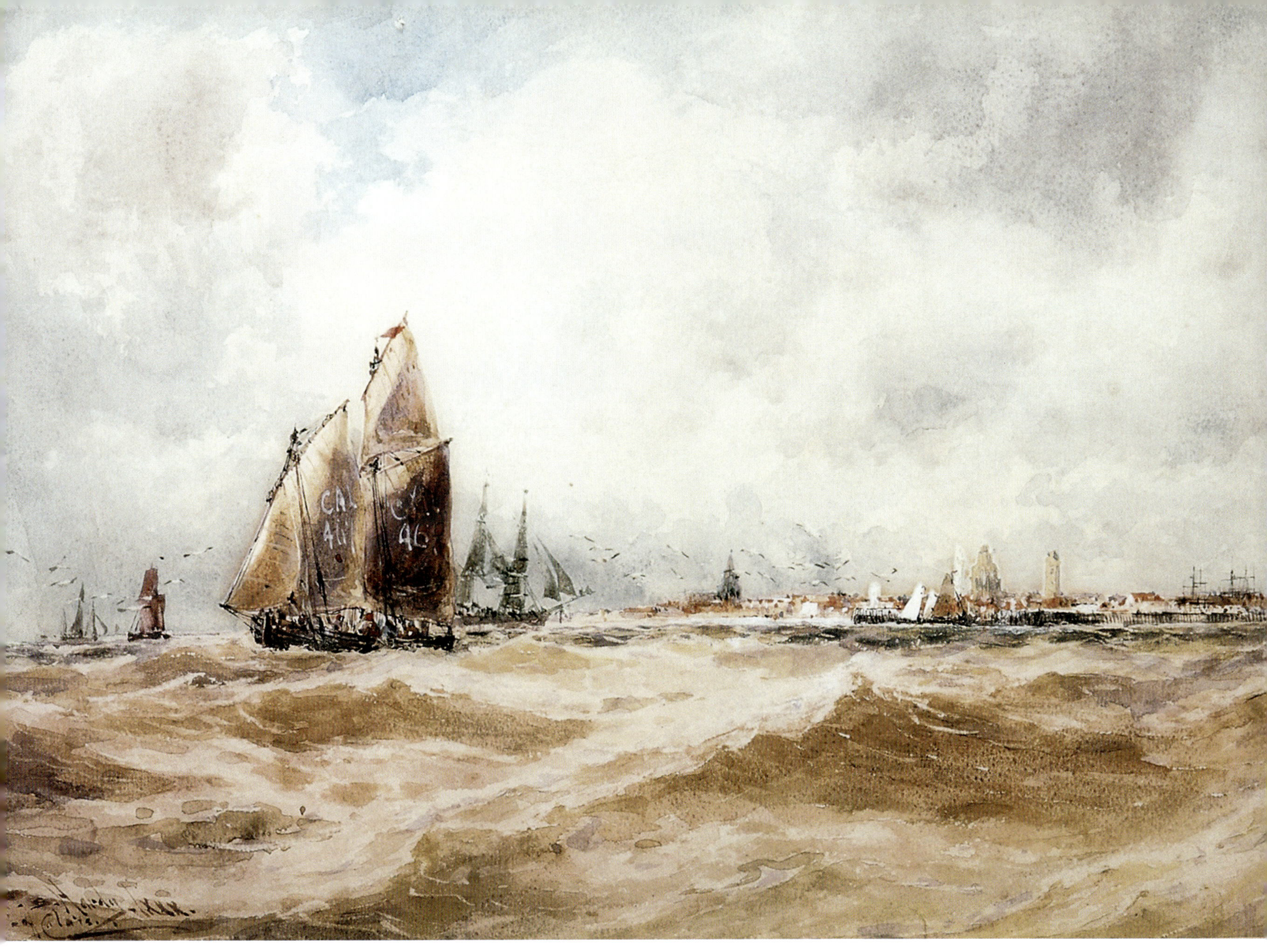

Plate 5.23. **Shipping off Calais Pier.** *Signed, inscribed and dated 1888. 23 x 32cm (9 x 12⅝in.)*

This medium-sized watercolour has much to recommend it. The scene is an everyday one, a Calais registered lugger leaving harbour for the fishing grounds to the north. A brisk northerly breeze is roughening up the relatively shallow sea and stirring up the sand. The weather is fine and the visibility excellent. Many other sailing ships and craft can be seen in the vicinity of the port and along the coast. In the distance the town of Calais, with its very recognisable landmarks, is painted in some detail. The two most striking features of the painting are its composition and colour, a combination giving the viewer a sense of pleasure and contentment.

Like most British tourists to France, Hardy was drawn to the valley of the Loire and the great chateaux that dominated the area. However, it was the river itself, the surrounding countryside and the people who lived there, that most appealed to him. Here he has drawn part of the amazing twenty-three arched bridge leading to the mediaeval fortified town, but gives the impression that he is rather more interested in the young fishermen on the shore and the women hanging up the washing in a drying breeze. The ducks seem unconcerned.

Plate 5.24. **Beauyonce sur Loire.** *Signed, inscribed and dated 1888. 43.5 x 69cm (17⅛ x 27⅛ in.)*

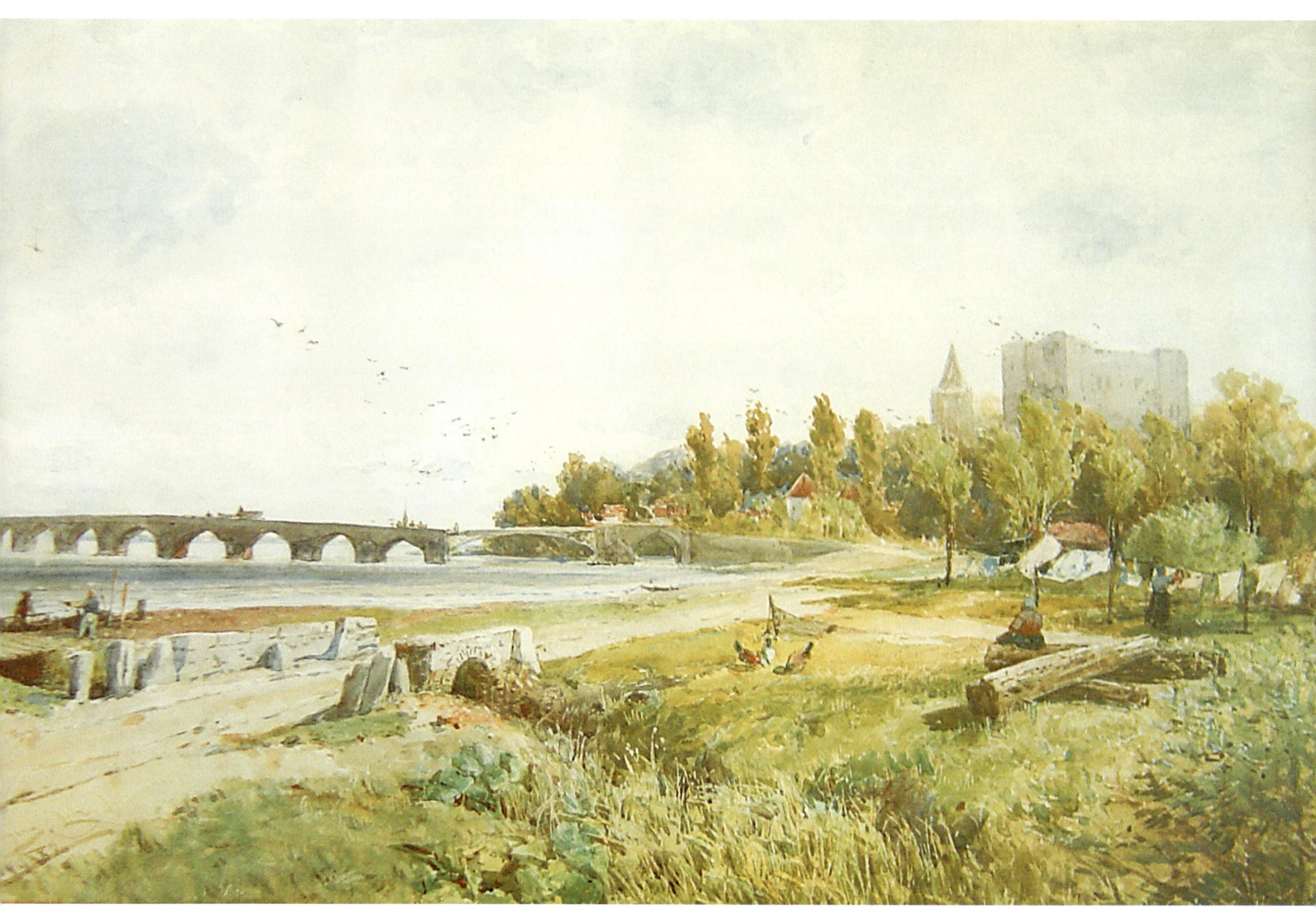

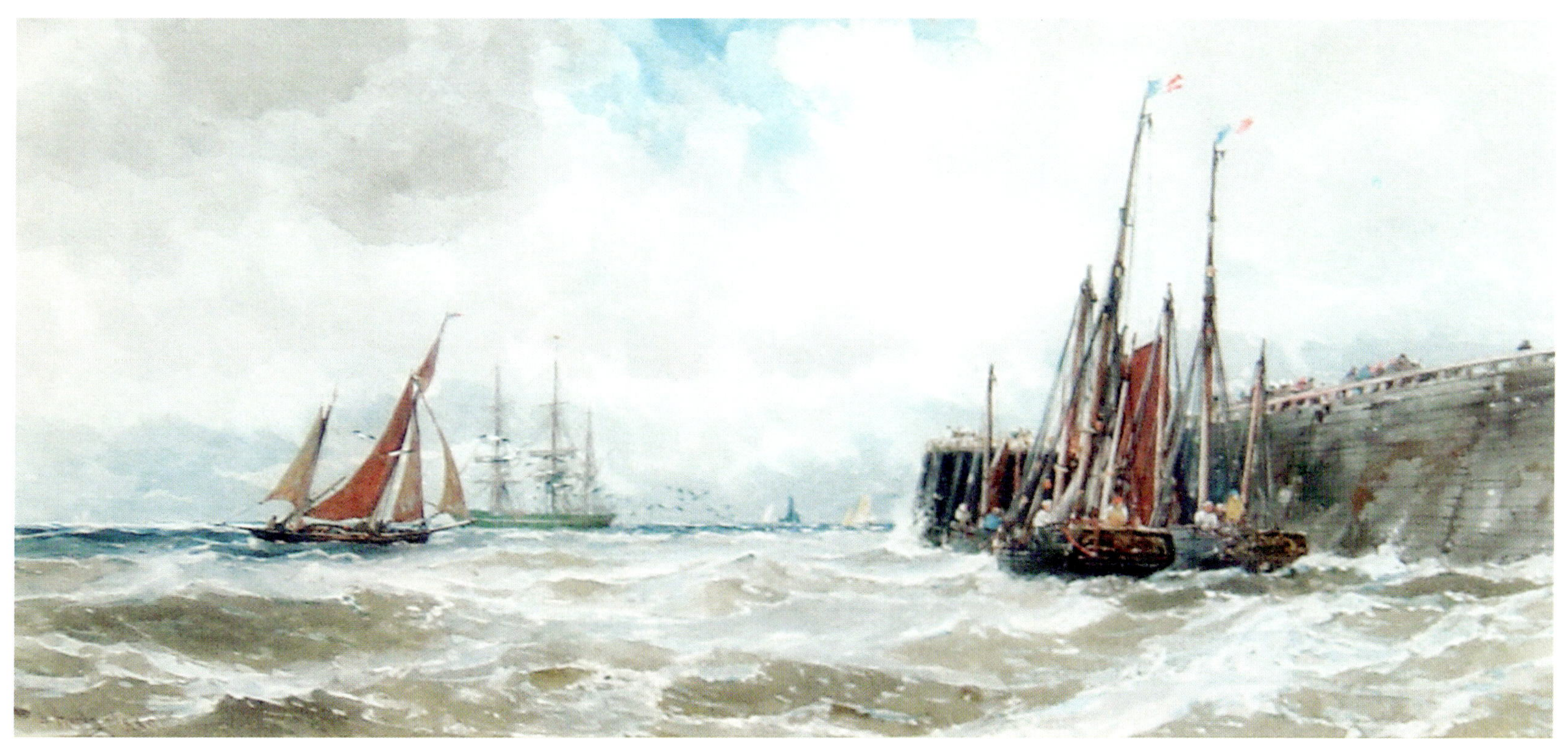

Painted at low tide in a freshening westerly wind, two fishing boats are preparing to leave for the open sea. Left of centre another similar boat heels over in the wind on a broad reach which should carry her well up into the North Sea and beyond. Further out, what could be a naval sail training ship is at anchor, perhaps awaiting high water before entering harbour. The sea is very well painted, especially where it meets the pier. Here Hardy has used a discreet amount of Chinese White to represent both spray and flecks of foam. It works very well.

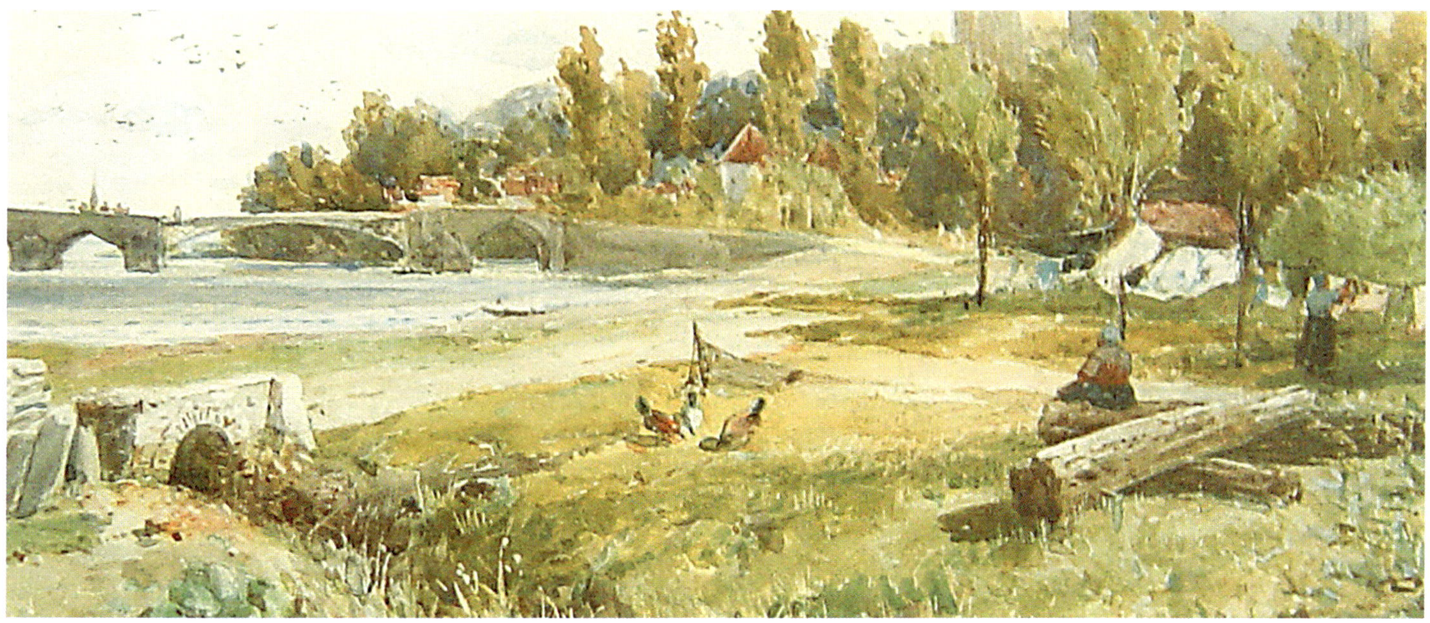

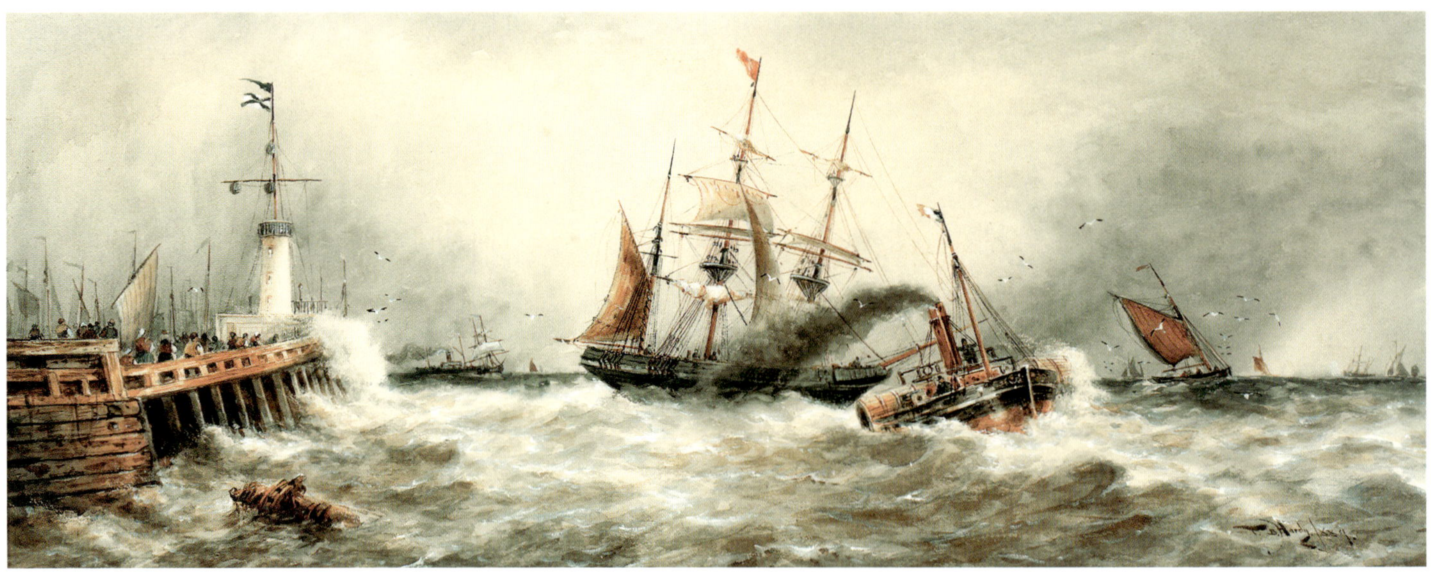

Apparently painted in 1889 *and* signed by Hardy, the work shows a paddle-driven tug towing a three-masted merchantman past the northern end of Boulogne Pier into the safety of the harbour. The weather is pretty horrible and there may be worse to come. It has to be said that this large and potentially important watercolour is in no way a typical Hardy and that there must be some doubts about its authenticity. Hardy's powers of observation were well developed and he seldom made fundamental mistakes in marine matters. In this painting, the barque being towed into harbour would not have had any sails set and the forest of masts beyond the pier could not have existed except in the artist's imagination. The use of finely etched detail and strong colours throughout, compromising spontaneity and movement, would have been eschewed by Hardy. Another criticism is the poor painting of the sea in the vicinity of the pier – streaks of Chinese White applied indiscriminately over the basic washes in an ineffective attempt to resemble breaking waves and spray. All in all, it is highly likely that the entire painting was an exercise for students based on an earlier work and that both the date and signature are false. Hardy himself obviously liked the subject and painted it at least three times, a small version in 1891 and two more in 1895, one being a preparatory work for the oil painting now in the National Maritime Museum.

Above. Plate 5.26.
Towing into Harbour.
Signed and dated 1889.
38 x 88.5cm (15 x 34⅞ in.)

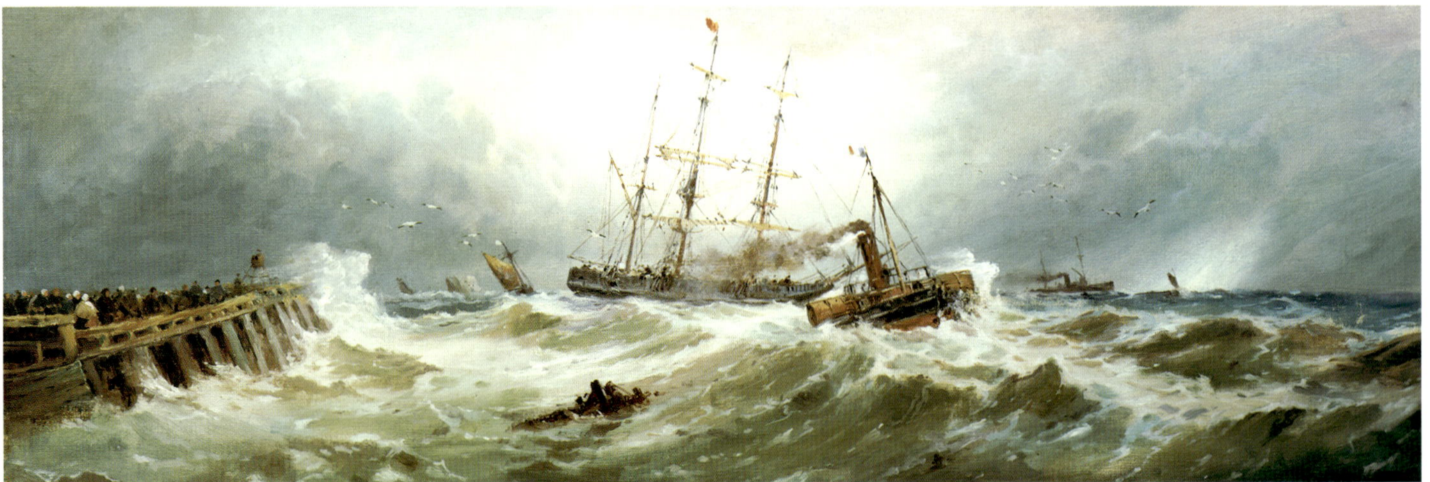

Chapter 5 – The French Coast

In this oil there are minor differences in the detail with Plate 5.26, the more important of which are the removal of the mast and signals on the end of the pier, indicating that this is Calais rather than Boulogne, and the fact that the barque now has all her sails furled. However, it is noticeable that both the sea and the sky now look much more realistic and, although Hardy still has a penchant for Chinese White, there can be no doubts about the authenticity of this entire painting.

An interesting view of the long beach north-east of Calais with three of the Calais-based luggers waiting to float off on the flood tide. To the right a trading barque appears to be anchored or, judging from the wind direction and proximity of shallow water, aground. Several other fishing boats can be seen, some beached, with the buildings of Calais in the background, others already at sea. It may be that the Calais fishermen are preparing to sail to Icelandic waters for the start of the herring season, normally March to October. Over the years, Hardy would have developed a very considerable respect for these men who, like the English and Scottish trawlermen, regularly faced difficult and dangerous weather and sea conditions in the North Sea and beyond.

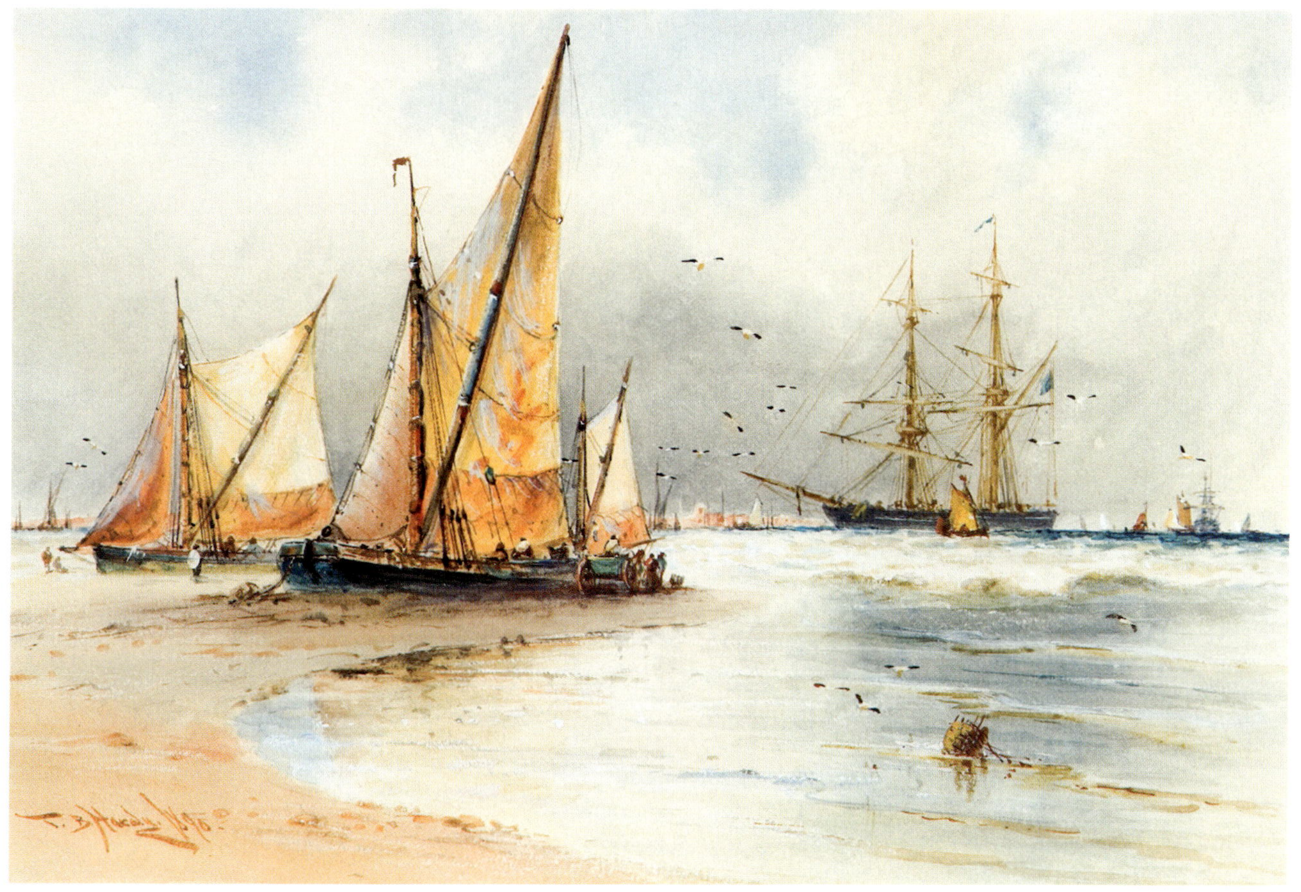

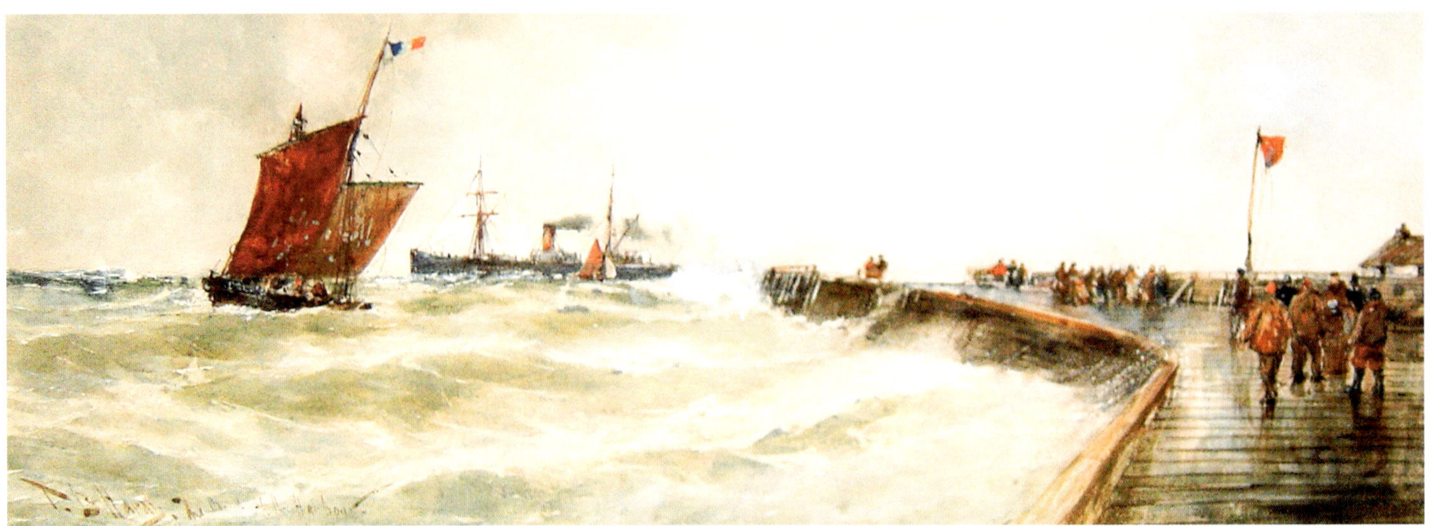

A view from inside Boulogne harbour looking along the length of the northern-most jetty. Maybe not the best of Hardy's Boulogne watercolours, but a distinct improvement on Plate 5.26 above. This is a very well composed picture with excellent perspective; the jetty, with small groups of onlookers braving the wind and rain, leads the eye to a coal-fired freighter steaming down the Channel. Sailing into harbour, after an exhausting spell of fishing for herring in the North Sea, is one of the Calais luggers – an historic design of boat to be replaced in less than fifty years by the steam trawler. Hardy could foresee the future and did not enjoy the prospect.

Although the signature and date bear some resemblance to Hardy's signature during the late 1890s, it is very doubtful indeed that he had anything to do with the painting of this watercolour unless he contributed to the sea, which shows some merit. Nor does the scene itself match any of the known piers and jetties on the French coast. Hardy knew these well and would never have signed a painting showing a harbour with such inaccurate details. Above all else the colouring points to the palette of Robert Thornton Wilding, one of his more prolific students. This may provide the clue to the painting's provenance: a preliminary, half-finished watercolour abandoned in the studio and completed by Wilding after Hardy's death.

Plate 5.29. **The Mouth of the Harbour.** *Signed and dated 1894. 22 x 56.5cm (8⅝ x 22¼ in.)*

Plate 5.30. **Off the Pier.** *Signed and dated 1894. 21 x 45cm (8¼ x 17¾ in.)*

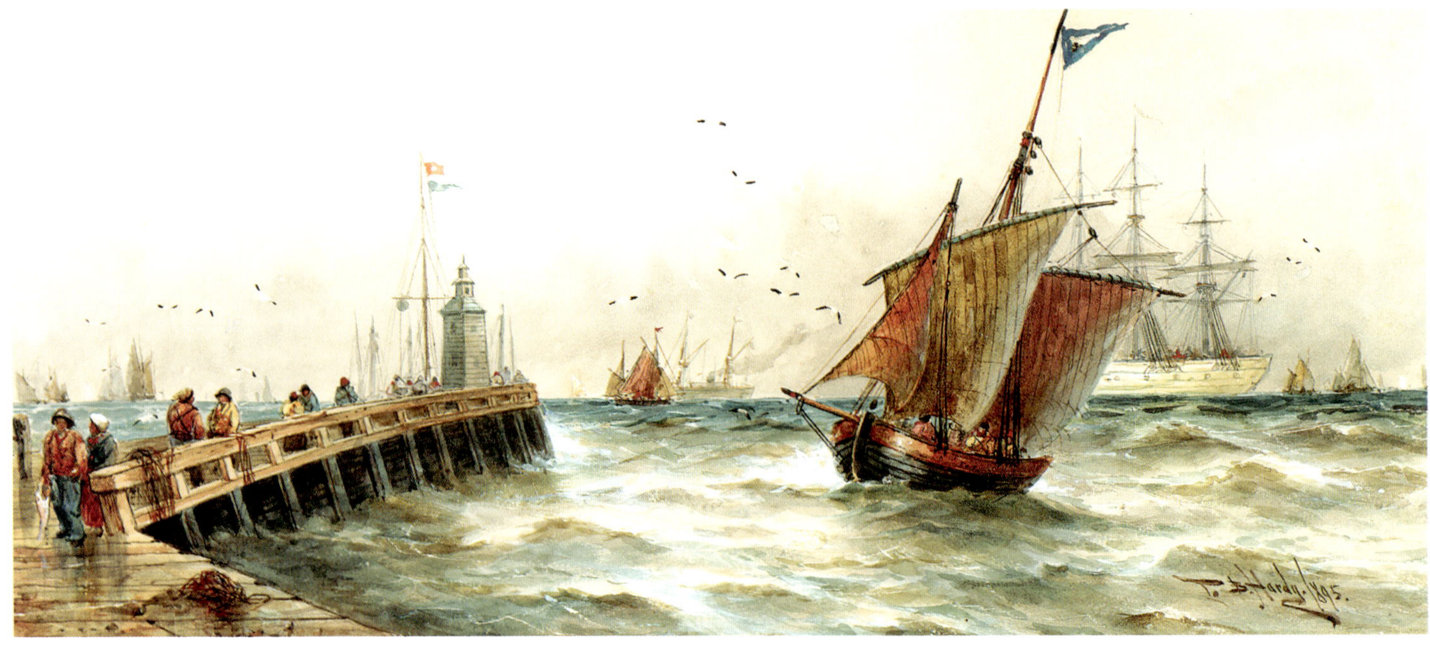

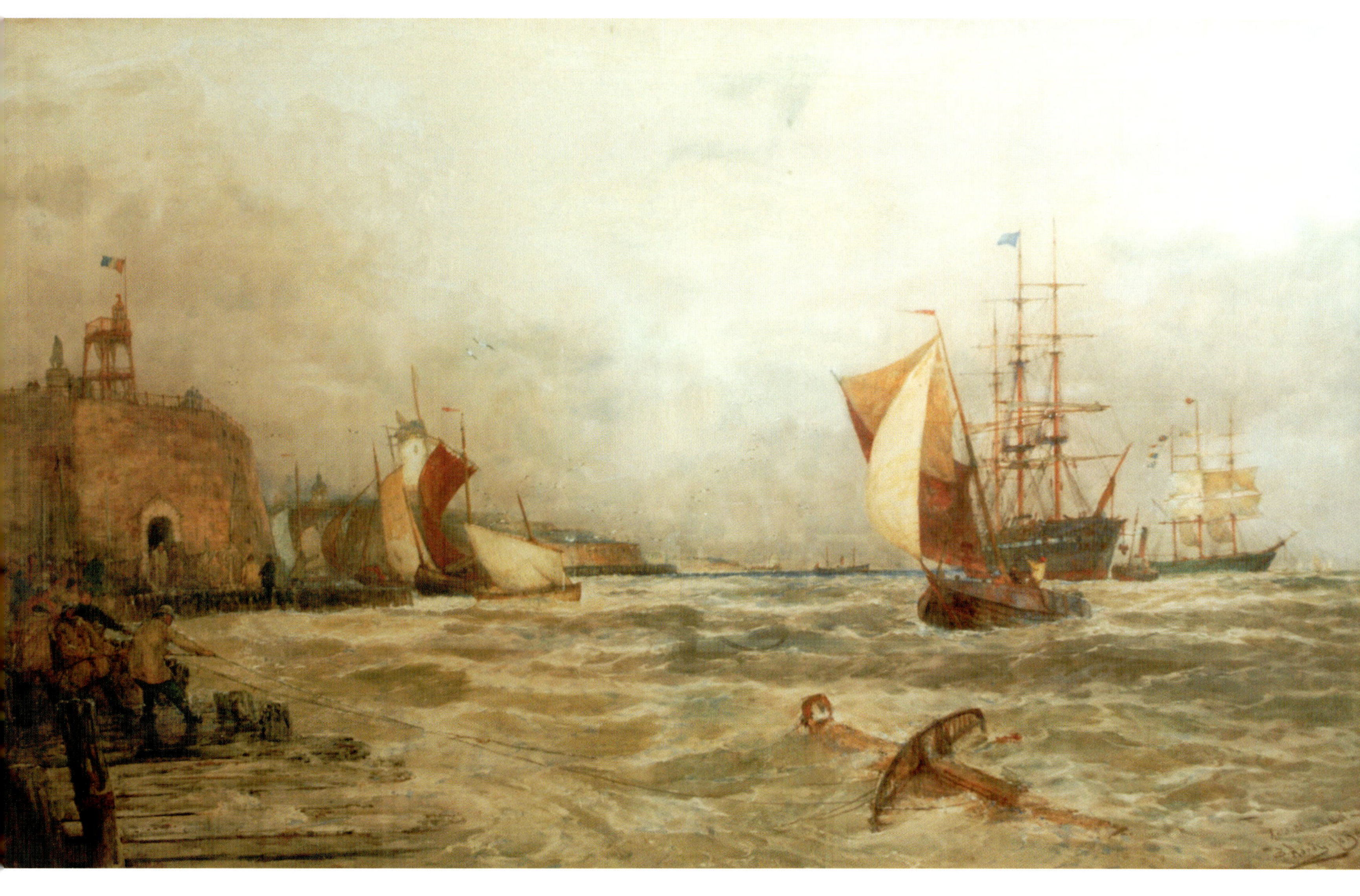

Plate 5.31. **Pilot Station in the North Sea.** *Signed, inscribed and dated 1896. 68 x 117cm (26¾ x 46in.)*

This very large, magnificent watercolour poses a very pertinent question – where is it? According to Hardy's inscription it is a pilot station in the North Sea. But where? A French tricolor is flying from the early stone building's mast, so surely it must be north of Calais. But look at the shoreline extending to the south and west – cliffs rather than sand dunes. And a windmill. The fishing boats entering and leaving a fairly narrow channel could be either French or Dutch or both. The nearer frigate or sail training ship or merchantman anchored offshore could be British, French or Dutch. The more distant three-master, flying her international call sign, may have just arrived or be on the point of departure. Perhaps the only clues we have are the remains of a topmast being hauled ashore after a severe gale – probably a sou'westerly – which might suggest somewhere in the region of Dunkirk. Whatever and wherever, it is a very remarkable watercolour, probably an important commission, painted at the end of a career when Hardy badly needed a boost to his self-confidence. This one might have done the trick.

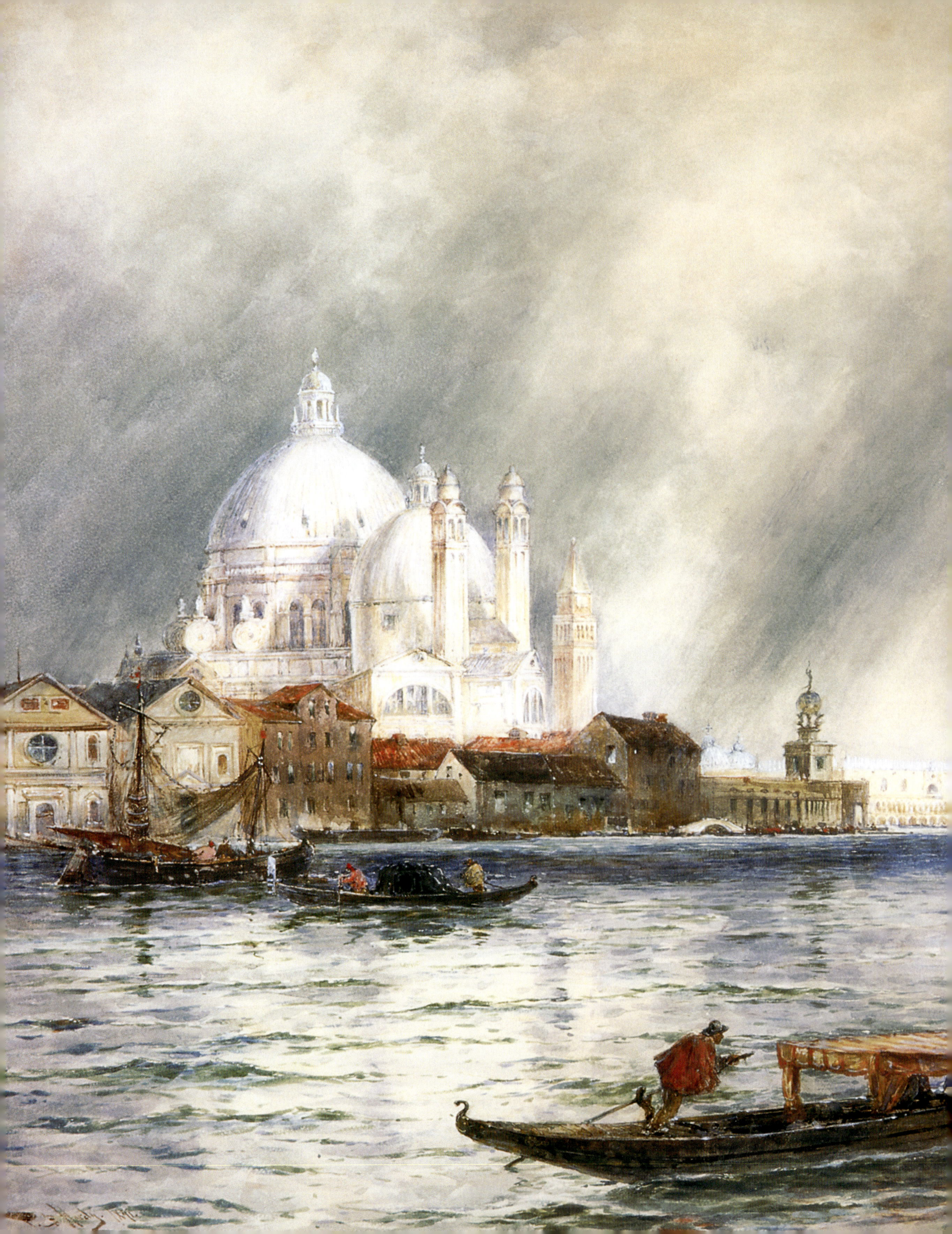

Venice

In 1581 Francesco Sansovino wrote the first tourist guide to Venice entitled *Venetia, citta nobilissima e singolare* (Venice, most noble and unique city). That title, coined over four hundred years ago, is as true today as it was then. An artist's paradise, featuring magnificent buildings, busy waterways, colourful sailing craft and the clear Adriatic light, Venice has inspired countless men and women to attempt to capture her soul on canvas and on paper. Little wonder that some of Turner's and Canaletto's most spectacular paintings are Venetian scenes.

Throughout the nineteenth century a steady stream of British artists journeyed to Venice, by sea or overland by coach and later rail. Following in the footsteps of Callow, Cooke, Holland and Clarkson Stanfield, it is known that Thomas Bush Hardy made several trips between 1879 and 1897, since paintings exist dated in all those years with the possible exception of 1887. He may well have been accompanied by some of his contemporaries who also fell under the Venetian spell – men like Frederick Aldridge, Oswald Brierly, Albert Goodwin, John Singer Sargent and Stanfield Walters. The turn of the century brought other watercolour artists such as Frank Mason and Hercules Brabazon Brabazon, both of whom contributed fine images of the magical city.

Plate 6.1. **Santa Maria della Salute.** *Signed and dated 1891. 53 x 43cm (20⅞in. x 17in.)*

Quite a late work in the chronology of Hardy's Venetian paintings but unquestionably one of his finest. Following in Turner's and Clarkson Stanfield's and many other watercolour artists' footsteps, Hardy has finally produced what might be described as a portrait of Santa Maria della Salute, the great baroque church standing at the entrance of the Grand Canal. Hardy is viewing the wonderful architecture from the Lagoon south of the island on which the church stands, an island consisting of over a million pine piles driven into the hard backbone of subsoil comprising Dorsoduro. Beyond the gondolas and fishermen on the Lagoon, the church's white marble domes and buttresses rise above what was then a comparatively modest environment. Emphasising the beauty of the domes, presently in sunlight, Hardy has given them a background of grey clouds and an imminent squall of rain. From the Dogana di Mare gusts of wind are beginning to sweep across the Lagoon, encouraging the gondolier in the foreground to redouble his efforts.

Unlike E.W. Cooke, Hardy did not keep meticulous records; the only records are the oils and watercolours that have survived in public and private collections to this day – fortunately in substantial numbers. Most of his watercolours were dated, but not necessarily painted in Venice – some would have been worked up at home from *plein air* sketches made during his previous visits. This would certainly apply to the larger works which would have been difficult to transport safely across Europe. With that in mind, Hardy concentrated normally on three basic sizes – a postcard size of approximately 12 x 17cm (4¾ x 6¾in.) and one twice and very occasionally one four times that size.

Before examining a selection of Hardy's highly acclaimed Venetian watercolours as well as examples of work by his contemporaries, it is worth looking at a few facts about the beautiful buildings and their setting that have inspired and enchanted artists and visitors alike. The Basilica of San Marco was begun in 1063 to replace the earlier building destroyed by fire in 976. Consecrated in 1094, the basic building was then complete, but decorations and adornments continued for many years. Even as late as the twelfth century the façade was transformed by rich marble carvings and gilded Byzantine mosaics. Later still in the thirteenth century five domes and the famous Greek horses were added to complete San Marco as we see it today.

A typical Venetian skyline is dominated by the Campanile, the great bell tower which stands in the Piazza San Marco – St Mark's Square. The first tower was built in the ninth century as a lighthouse and watchtower to protect the city against enemy fleets. The present design, completed in 1549, was the work of Bartolomo, whose golden angel weathervane still crowns the tower. The sixteenth century tower suddenly developed a very visible crack and, in front of the crowds who had ignored warnings to keep clear, collapsed in a pile of rubble on 14 July 1902. The present-day structure is an exact replica of the original design and was re-opened on St Mark's Day on 25 April 1912.

Perhaps the most frequently painted and photographed building in the City is the Palazzo Ducale or Doge's Palace, which faces both St Mark's Square and the Lagoon. Largely constructed between 1309 and 1424 it replaced a ninth century fortified castle and adjacent dwellings which had been destroyed by fire. The palace is a unique example of Venetian Gothic architecture at its most splendid. A ground floor arcade of seventeen white marble arches is surmounted by an open loggia of thirty-four pointed arches. On top of this airy base comes a similar number of cusped quatrefoil openings. The top half of the building is of pink and white marble arranged in lozenge designs interspersed, on the canal side, with six immense arched windows. In the centre is the spectacular balcony, designed and built between 1400 and 1404 by Jacobello and Pier Paulo Dalle Masegne, representing the 'Flamboyant Gothic' style.

This panorama of the Doge's Palace from the Dogana, with the Zecca on the left and the Ponte della Paglia and old Prisons to the right, is one of the best-known views in Venice. Painted in 1879, on his first visit to Venice, Hardy was clearly mesmerised by the stunning Gothic architecture and colour of the Palace and has faithfully reproduced every detail of its remarkable façade. Hardy has also shown the two granite columns of San Marco and San Teodoro which guard the entrance to the Piazetta and were said to have been erected by Nicolo Barattieri, the architect of the first Rialto Bridge. In the left foreground a large covered gondola is being worked down the Grand Canal on this hazy, sultry day. One of the *deojozzi* with its large emblazoned sail and some smaller boats lie alongside the Zecca and, away to the right, many fishing boats can be seen clustered around the Ponte della Paglia. Without painting many individual figures, Hardy has hinted at the hundreds of people thronging the promenades and piazzas. The reflections in the gently rippling waters of the canal add a marine artist's finishing touches to a fine painting.

Hardy completed many different views of the Doge's Palace during subsequent visits but few are on this scale. We know that three of his Venetian watercolours were exhibited at the Royal Society of British Artists in 1879. This could well have been one of them. The colours, composition and sheer technique exhibited in this watercolour surely justify his nomination as 'King of Sketchers'.

Plate 6.2. **Doge's Palace, Venice.** *Signed, inscribed and dated 1879. 31 x 48.5cm (12¼ x 19⅛in.)*

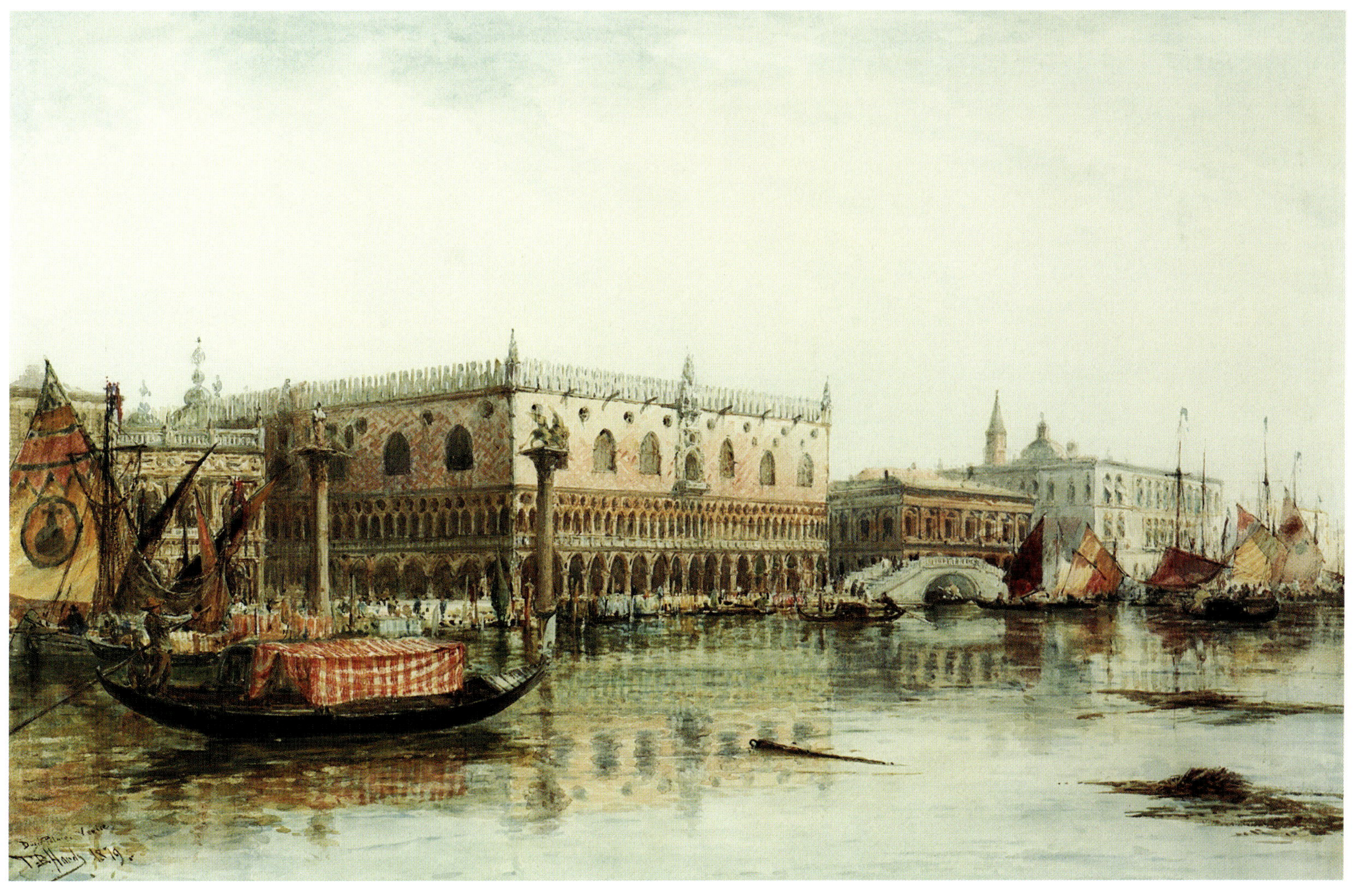

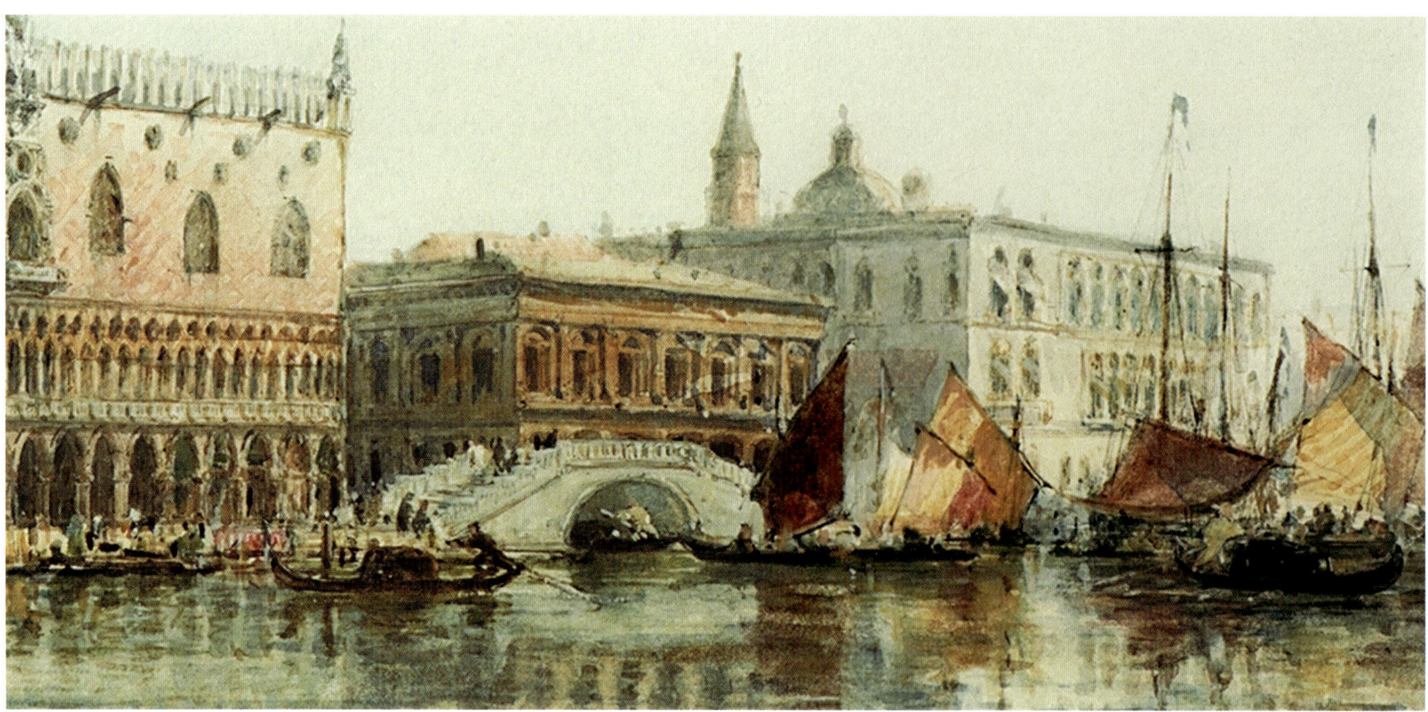

Running west, across the Piazetta, the next waterfront building is the Zecca. Designed with three floors of large windows by Jacopo Sansovino in 1537, this was the City's Mint until 1870. The 'Zeccino' or Venetian Ducat takes its name from this building. Moving east across the Ponte della Paglia leads to the Prison and down the renowned Riva degli Schiavoni. The Hotel Danieli, originally the fourteenth century Palazzo Dandalo, was turned into a hotel in 1822 and became the hostelry and meeting place for the literary and artistic set in the nineteenth century. Famous guests included Balzac, Dickens, Ruskin, Debussy, Wagner and Proust.

On the other side of the entrance to the Grand Canal from St Mark's Square is the Dogana perched on the eastern section of the Giudecca. The original Dogana di Mare or Customs House was built in the fifteenth century but the present building was not completed until the late 1600s . It was from the Dogana that so many artists chose to paint the view looking across the Grand Canal to the Zecca, Doge's Palace, Campanile and the golden domes of the Basilica San Marco.

One of the other most imposing and frequently painted churches, close to the Dogana at the southern entrance to the Grand Canal, is the great baroque church of Santa Maria della Salute. The church was built between 1631 and 1687 as a thanksgiving to the Virgin Mary for the end of the 1630 plague. Rising from an octagonal base is the immense hemispherical dome topped by the lantern with its statue of the Virgin.

Detail from Plate 6.2. **Doge's Palace, Venice.** *Signed, inscribed and dated 1879. 31 x 48.5cm (12¼ x 19⅛in.)*

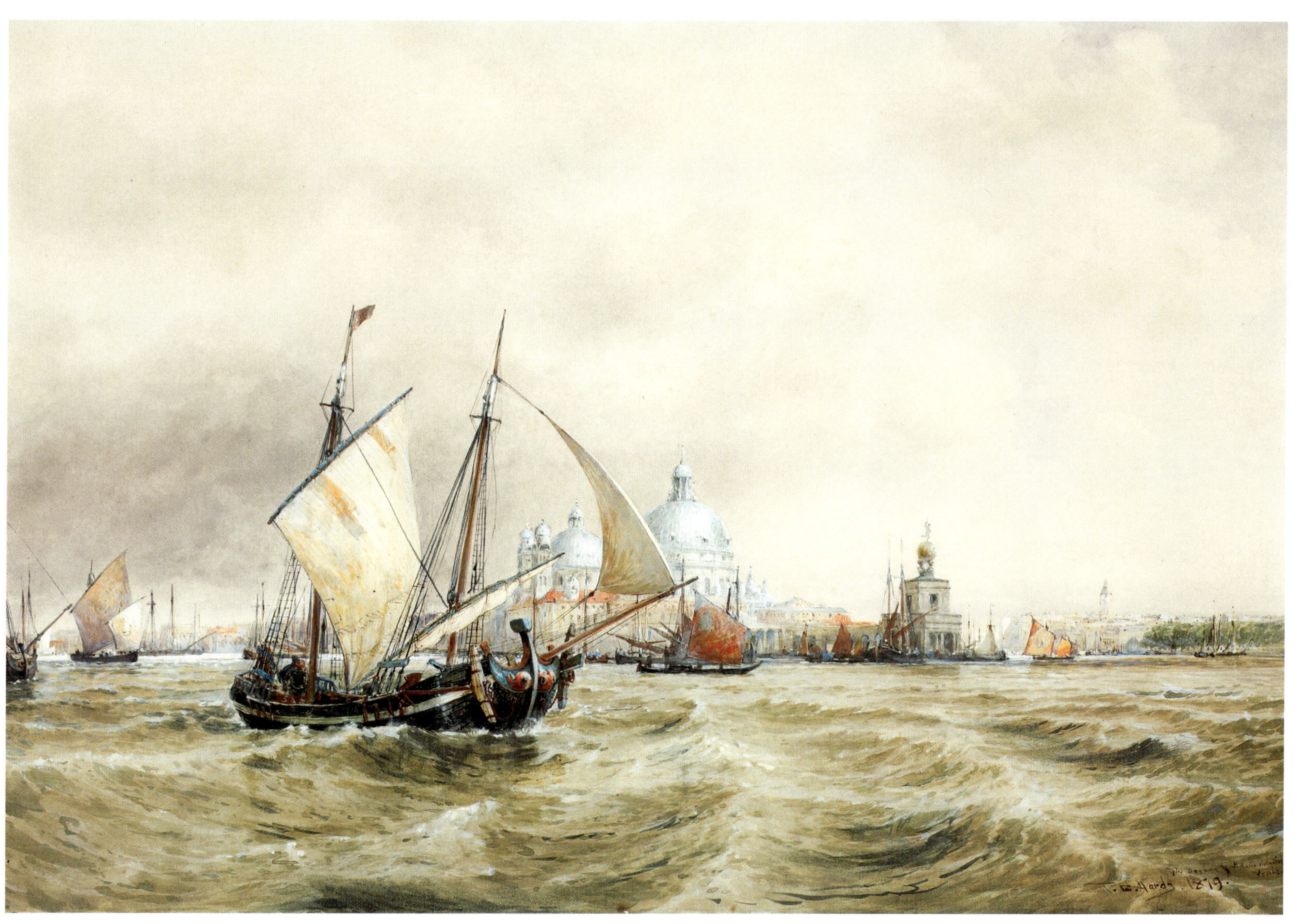

Plate 6.3. **The Dogana and Santa Maria della Salute.**
Signed, inscribed and dated 1879. 43.5 x 63cm (17⅛ x 24¾ in.)

Central to this watercolour is the very beautiful baroque church of Santa Maria della Salute with, on the right, the Dogana di Mare or Customs House. Hardy has done justice to both buildings. In the foreground a two-masted barge or *deojozza* is sailing through the Canale di San Giorgio towards the eastern side of the Grand Canal. A stiff southerly breeze is creating a choppy sea. A number of other barges can be seen going about their business. A dull, rather thundery looking sky is well reflected in the sandy coloured water that has been churned up by the wind. A well-composed painting with good detail bearing comparison with the style and topographical accuracy of E.W. Cooke.

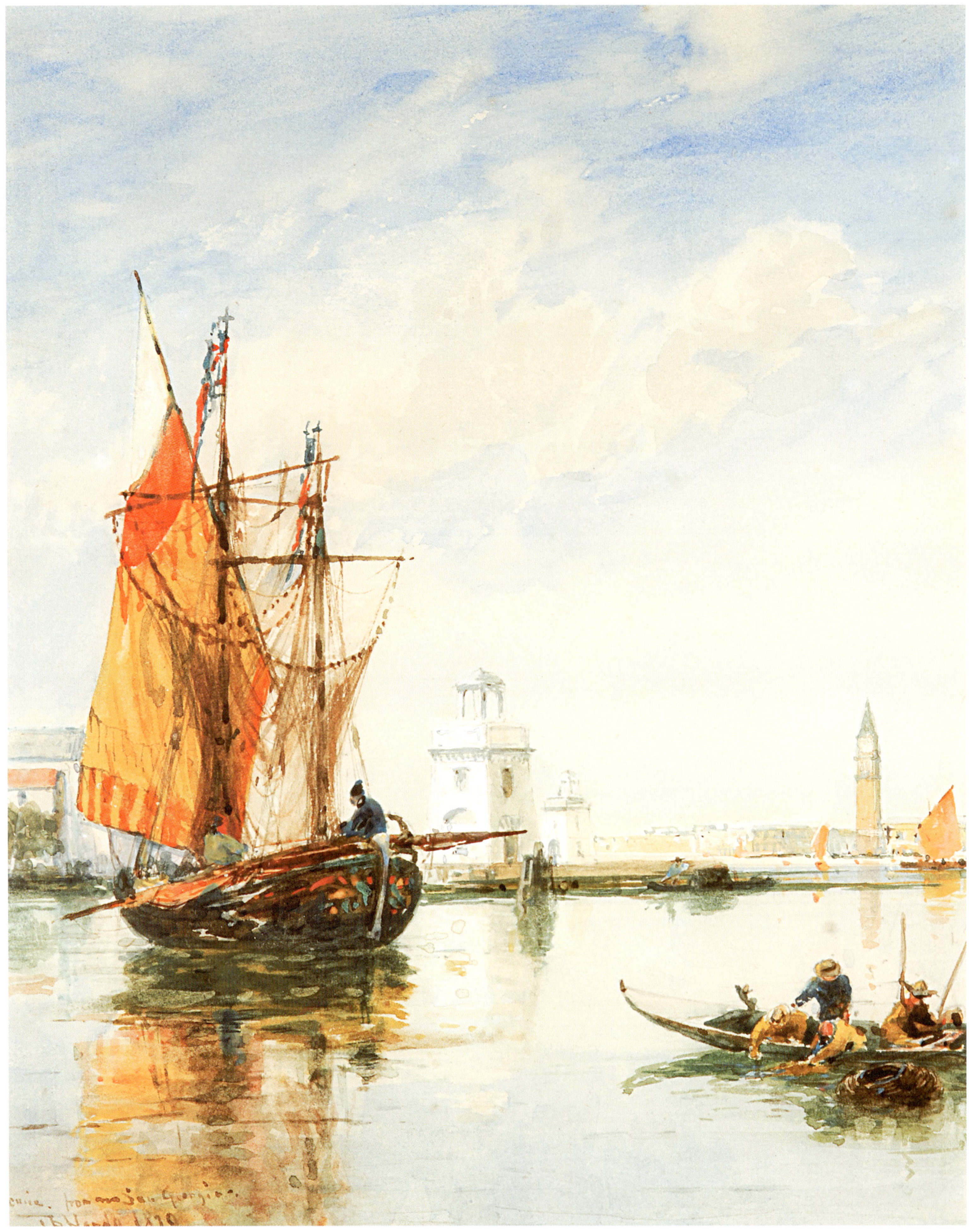

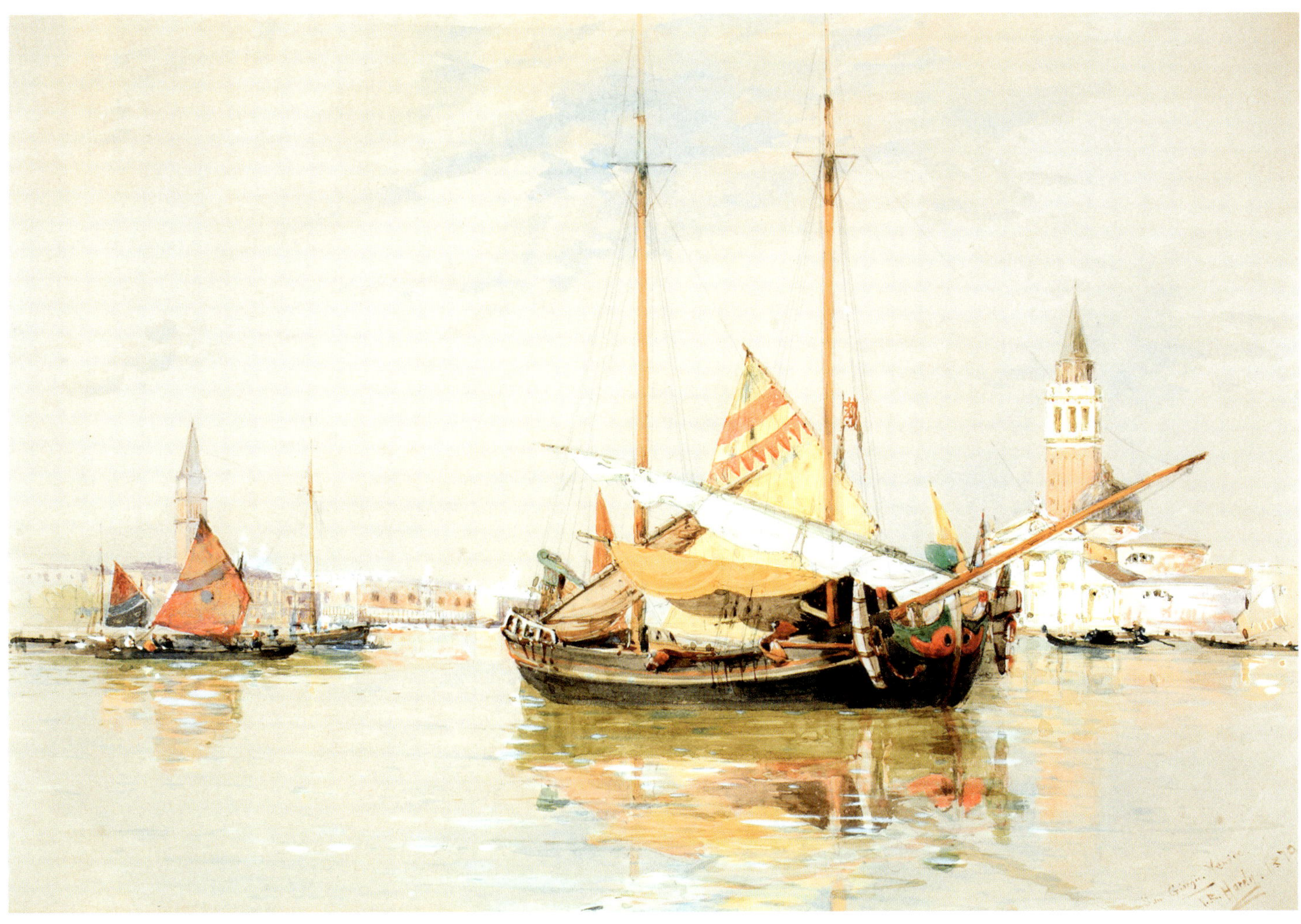

Unsurprisingly, Hardy has placed one of the grandest Venetian fishing boats as the centre of attraction of this watercolour. Behind and to the right is the church and monastery of San Giorgio Maggiore on the island of the same name. Both edifices, built between 1559 and 1580, are among Andrea Palladio's greatest architectural achievements. The temple front of the Church, based on ancient Rome, is a particularly fine example of the classic Palladian style. To the left, beyond the line of fishing boats, some under way, stand the Campanile and the Ducal Palace. A fine, warm day with interesting reflections on the calm waters of the Lagoon. There has been some fading, resulting in the Chinese White pigment, where it has been used, becoming too pronounced. This can be corrected by careful restoration but, sadly, some of the blues have gone for ever.

Plate 6.5. **San Giorgio.**
Signed, inscribed and dated
1879. 24 x 35cm (9½ x 13¾in.)

Painted on a typical calm summer's day, one of Hardy's first Venetian watercolours is a return to the scenes and the people he knows best – the fishermen and their way of life. Dominating the painting is a colourful fishing vessel drying her nets and mainsail from her two masts. In the foreground two men in a crowded gondola are mending their hand-thrown nets as they too prepare for the next day's fishing. The white tower of San Giorgio moves the focus of the painting to the background of the city and one of her major buildings, the Campanile.

Opposite. Plate 6.4.
Venice from San Giorgio.
Signed, inscribed and dated
1879. 17 x 12cm (6¾ x 4¾in.)

Chapter 6 – Venice

One of Hardy's rare portrait-shaped watercolours. Once again, bearing in mind that this was painted during his first visit to Venice, Hardy has turned his back on the more popular aspects of the city and sought the artistic potential of the nearby islands and their communities. This is a fine image of various types of fishing boats, mostly the two-masted *deojozzi*, off the island of Chioggia. Note not only the bright-hued distinguishing emblems on their sails but also the psychedelic colours of the flags at their mastheads. The sun is shining, a steady breeze is blowing; a good haul of fish is on the cards.

Another watercolour painted during Hardy's first visit to Venice, showing a pair of *deojozzi* transferring some gear in front of the Campanile and Ducal Palace. The entrance to the Grand Canal can be seen to the right of the tower on the isle of San Giorgio. Although an interesting and well-composed view, the painting lacks some clarity and definition and is slightly faded and discoloured. Like the previous example, Hardy has used far too much Chinese White, most notably in the sky where the effect of overall fading is particularly conspicuous. Ahh – if only artists had the self-belief that they were painting for posterity! And if collectors would only take precautions against ultra-violet light!

Opposite. Plate 6.7. **Off Chioggia.** *Signed, inscribed and dated 1879. 31 x 17cm (12¼ in. x 6¾ in.)*

Plate 6.6. **Fishing Boats on the Lagoon before the Dogana.** *Signed, inscribed 'Venice' and dated 1879. 21 x 31cm (8¼ x 12¼ in.)*

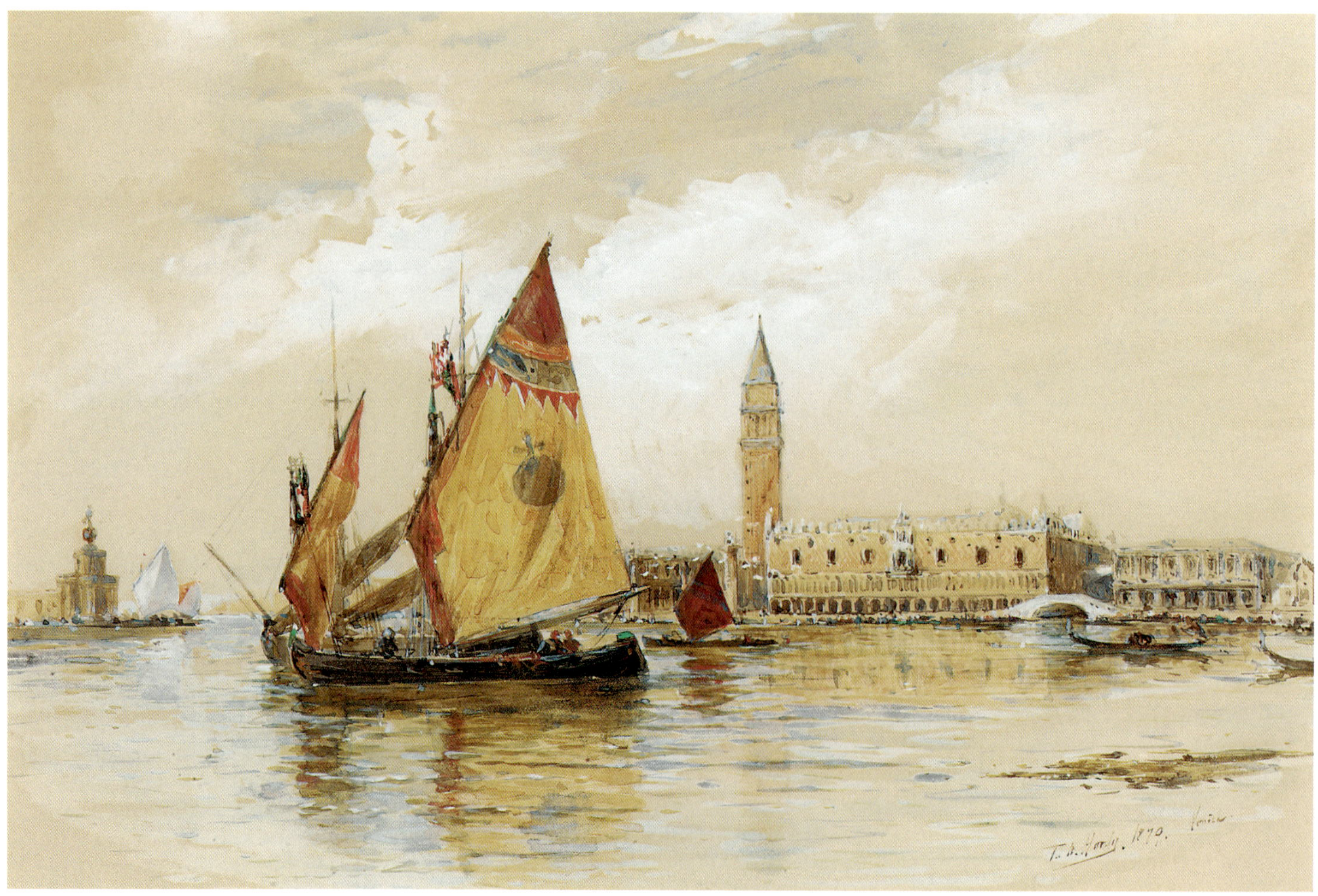

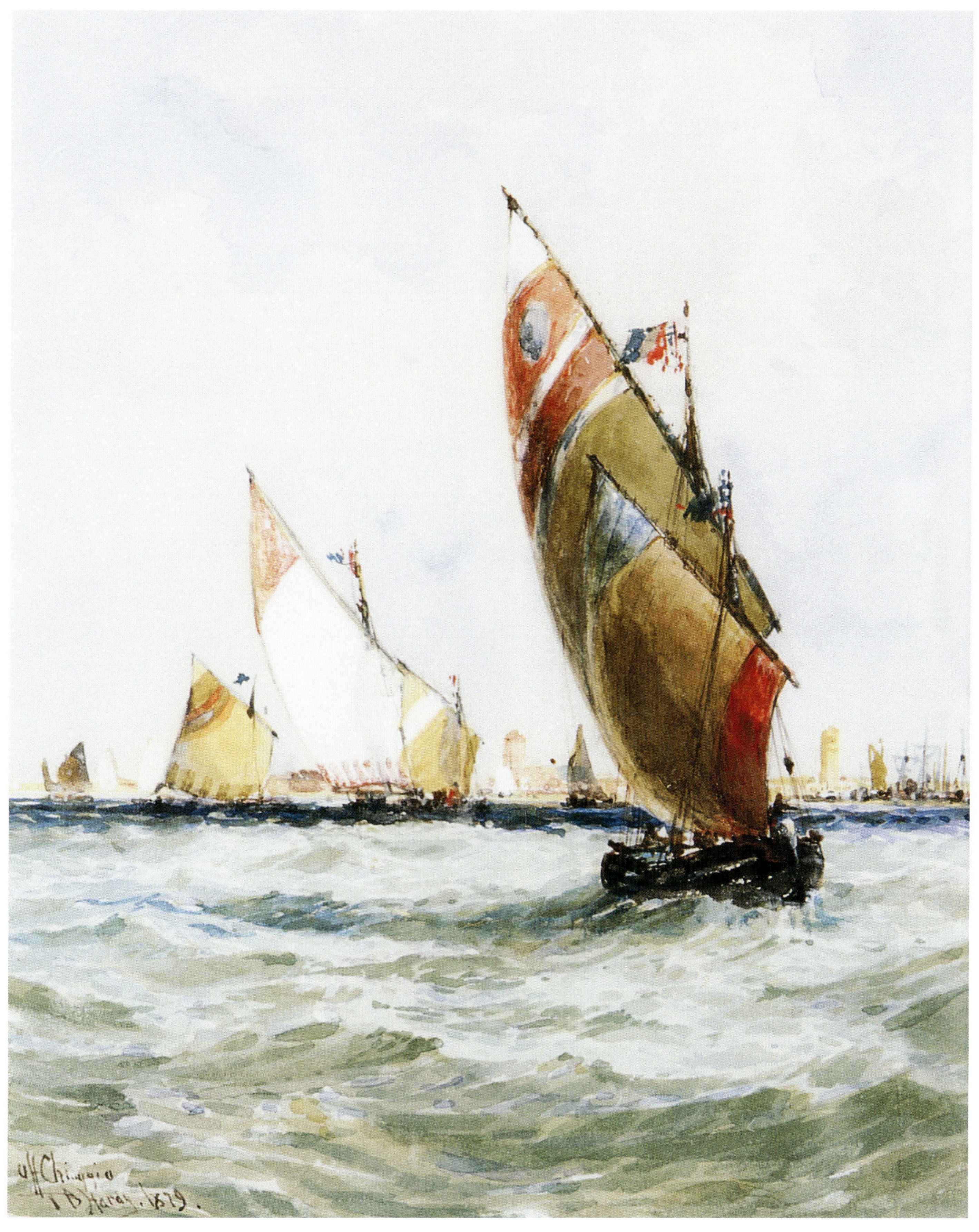

off Chioggia
B Hardy 1879.

Chioggia, situated on a small island at the southern entrance to the Lagoon, is a miniature version of Venice with canals, a colourful history and several medieval churches. Fishing has been the main livelihood of the island for centuries. Here is a two-masted fishing boat drying nets from the masthead on its way back to Chioggia harbour. Marked channels like the one in the painting have been a feature of the Venetian Lagoon for many centuries. A large and colourful watercolour, again spoiled by Hardy's use of Chinese White rather than using the whiteness of the paper itself and light washes to simulate clouds.

Plate 6.8. **Chioggia.** *Signed, inscribed and dated 1879. 35 x 52cm (13¾ x 20½in.)*

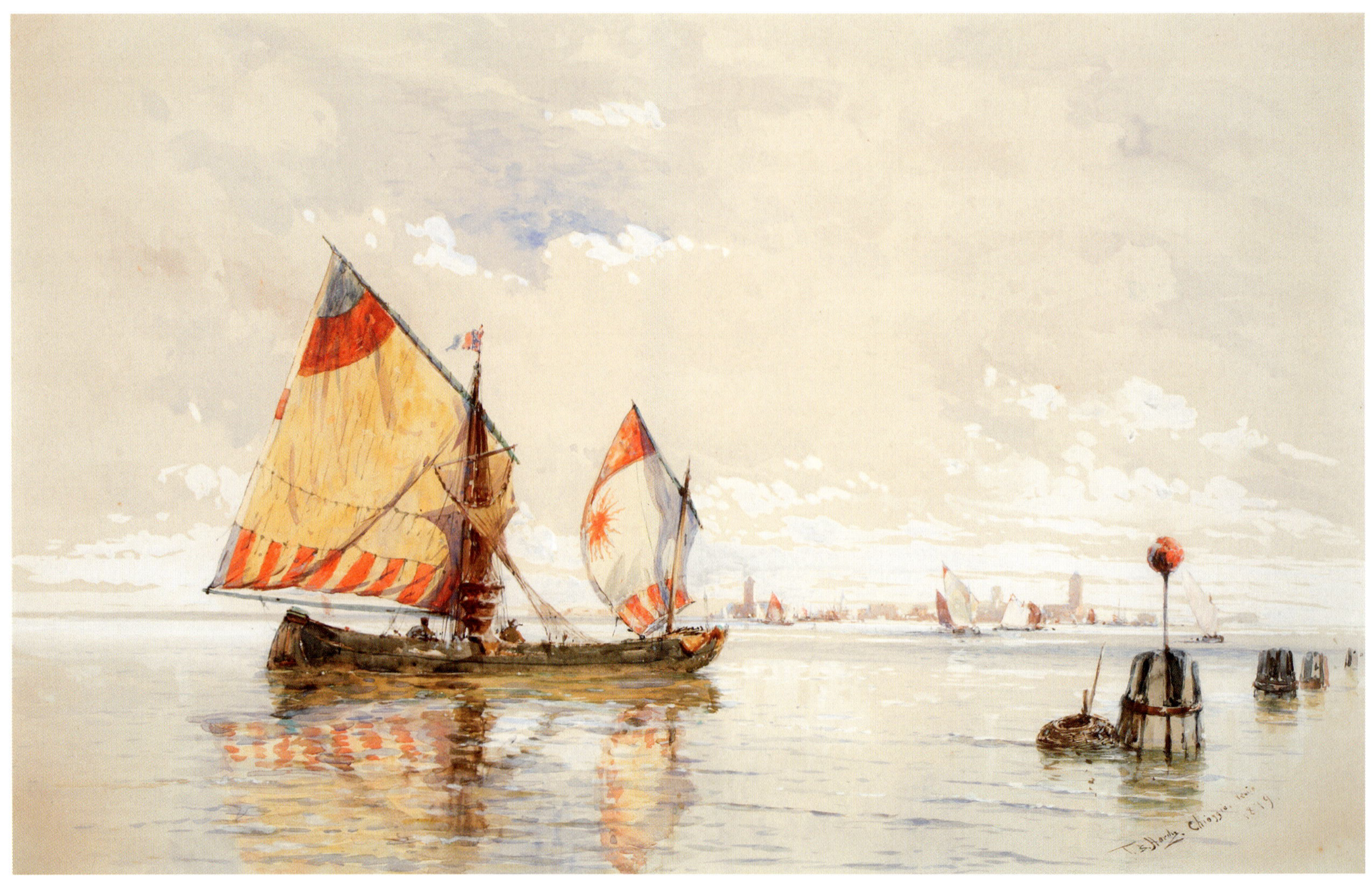

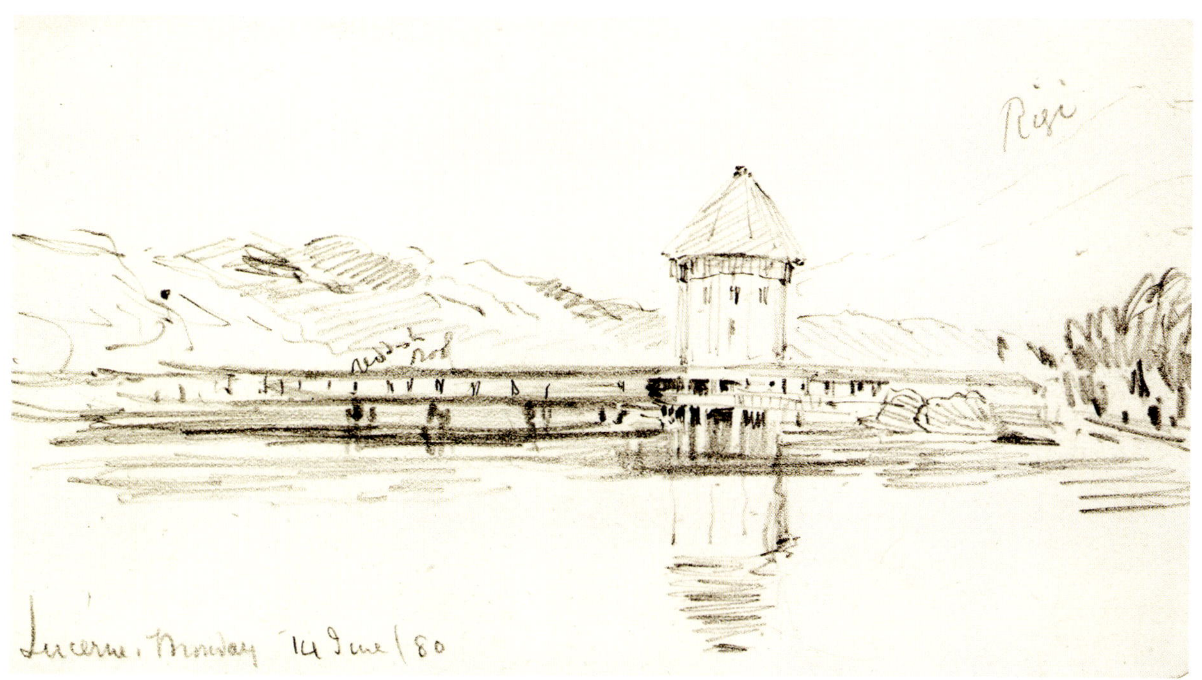

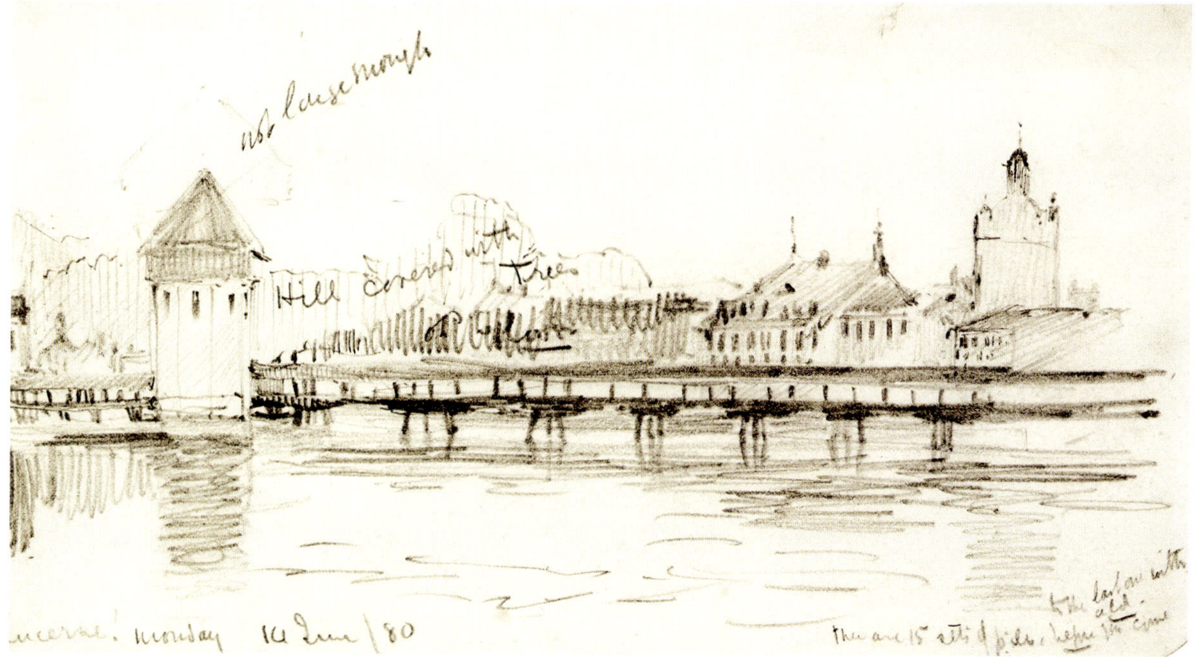

Plates 6.9 and 6.10. **Pencil drawings of Lake Lucerne.**
Both 14/06/1880.
Both 9 x 16cm (3½ x 6¼ in.)

Hardy found time to produce these two fine pencil sketches of Lake Lucerne en route to Venice for his second visit. With their scribbled memoranda on noteworthy features and colouring, they bear a striking resemblance to some of Edward Lear's preliminary drawings. Unlike Lear, Hardy showed no great interest in spectacular scenery unless it embodied a great deal of water; fortunately the Swiss and Italian lakes provided a combination which Hardy was able to exploit.

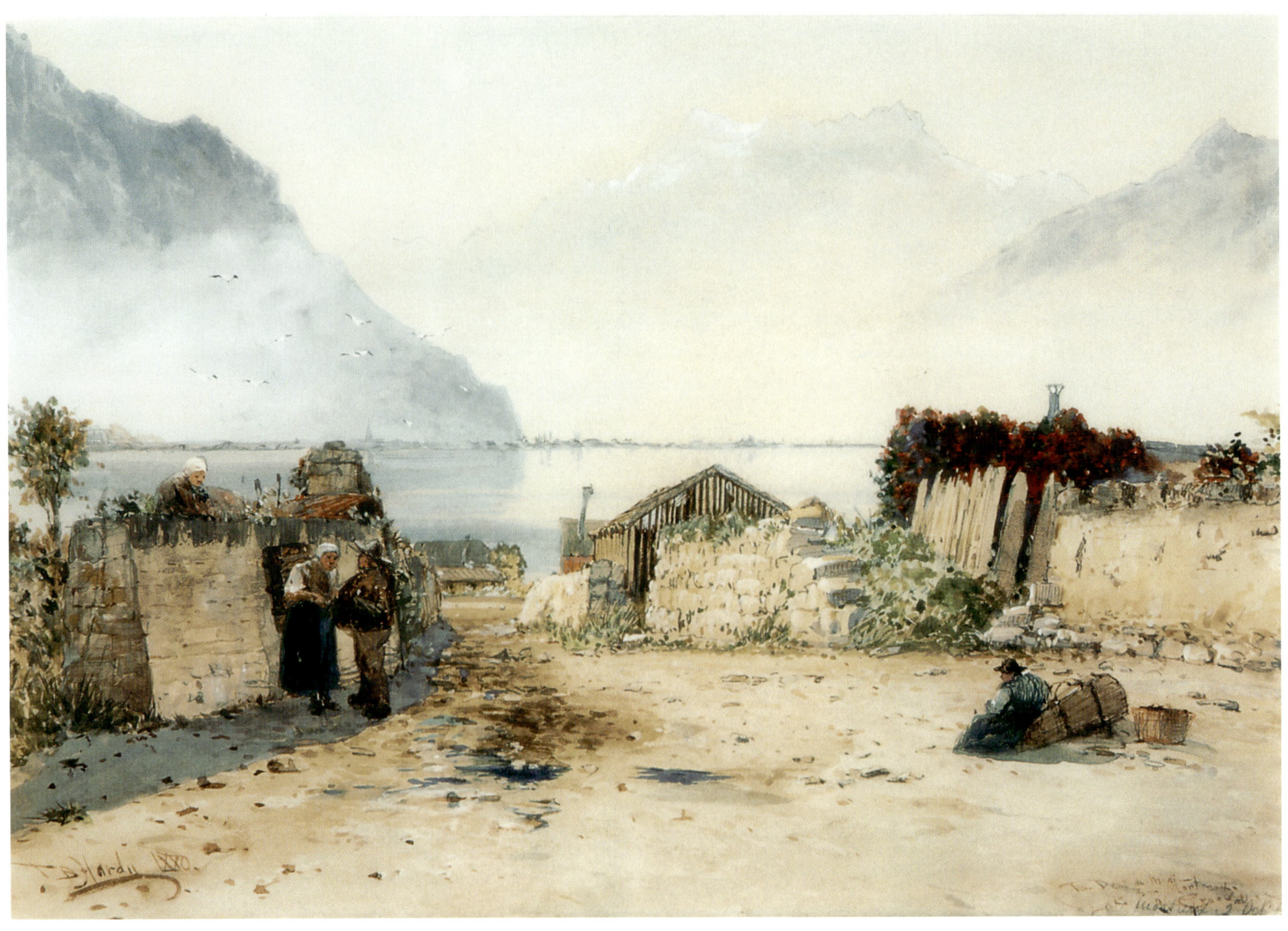

This watercolour is arguably the finest lake scene that Hardy ever painted. Although Hardy inscribed it 'le dent du midi', the full set of teeth are clearly visible in the distance, all seven peaks in the range being over 3,100m (10,000ft) high. The date in October would suggest Hardy painted this on his return from Venice in 1880. Here it is not so much the mountain scenery, nor even the placid lake, but the cottages and people in the foreground on which Hardy has concentrated. Local folk living a very simple life are subjects he would always select when he had the opportunity. The rest is background – of artistic but, to him, often of secondary importance. Hardy would usually tell a story if there was one to be told.

Plate 6.11. **Les Dents du Midi, Montreux, Geneva.** *Signed and dated 1880. Also inscribed dated 2 Oct. 24 x 34cm (9½ x 13⅜in.)*

Another view of Lake Geneva, this time from a village close to where the River Rhone flows into the Lake. Here Hardy has shown a number of the local fishing boats with their distinct lateen sails. Left of centre the two nearer boats, one abaft the other, make a remarkable pattern of masts, yard and sails pointing in every direction – a three-dimensional nightmare, but balancing the picture very nicely. Sadly, due to high levels of pollution throughout the Lake, the fishermen and the bathers have long gone, but the Swiss Alps and these very beautiful watercolours have survived.

Opposite above. Plate 6.12. **Le Bouveret, Lake Geneva.** *Signed, inscribed and dated 1880. 33 x 51cm (13 x 20in.)*

Chapter 6 – Venice

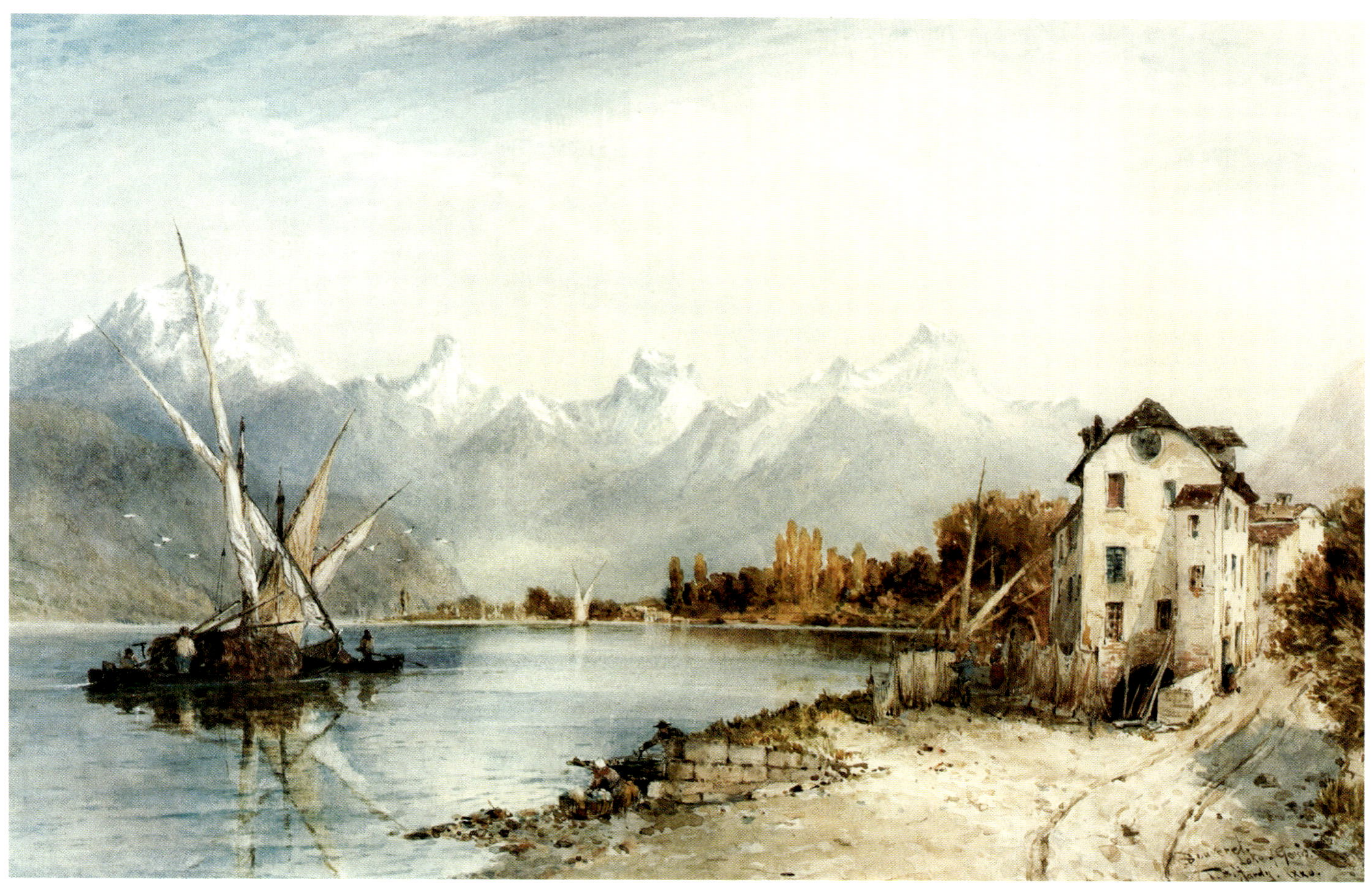

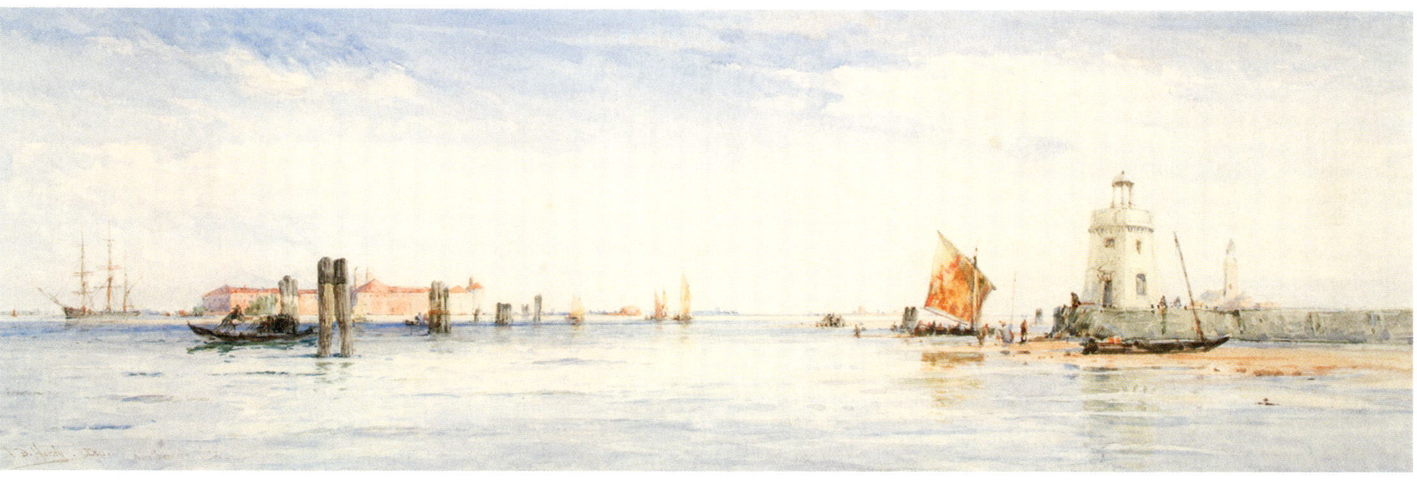

Plate 6.13. **Villa San Clemente.** *Signed and dated 1880. 17 x 50cm (6¾ x 19⅝ in.)*

An unusual but interesting view from San Giorgio Maggiore exploring the vista of the Lagoon to the south. To the centre and left is the island of San Clemente. Initially a hermitage and then a monastery, in 1630 it was taken over as a military depot. In the nineteenth century it became a lunatic asylum and the present building dates from that time. No longer a hospital, it is now a magnificent hotel away from the bustle of Venice. The painting shows the wooden piles marking one of the deeper water channels crossing the shallow Lagoon, with a three-masted merchant ship, possibly an East Indiaman, at anchor in the distance. Soft colours and mirror-like waters are unexceptional in this corner of the Adriatic.

Hardy must have spent some time exploring Venice on foot and by water. Here, at the junction of two canals, he has found the workshops which still survive where boatbuilders are working on upturned gondolas laid out in the square. On the left, a slim-hulled gondola is passing a substantial house, but this is clearly a district lived in by artisans and fishermen rather than by noble families and wealthy traders. Colourful though it is, the scene gives an impression of untidiness and decay – even the church and its bell tower look a little unsteady on their foundations. And the canal – Hardy has not over-burdened the viewer's imagination. Supporting some unappetising flotsam and jetsam, the waterways here are not reflecting a blue Venetian sky but are distinctly industrial. These are the unseen heart and arteries of Venice.

Plate 6.14. **Square of San Trovaso.** *Signed, inscribed and dated 1881. 43 x 69cm (17 x 27⅛ in.)*

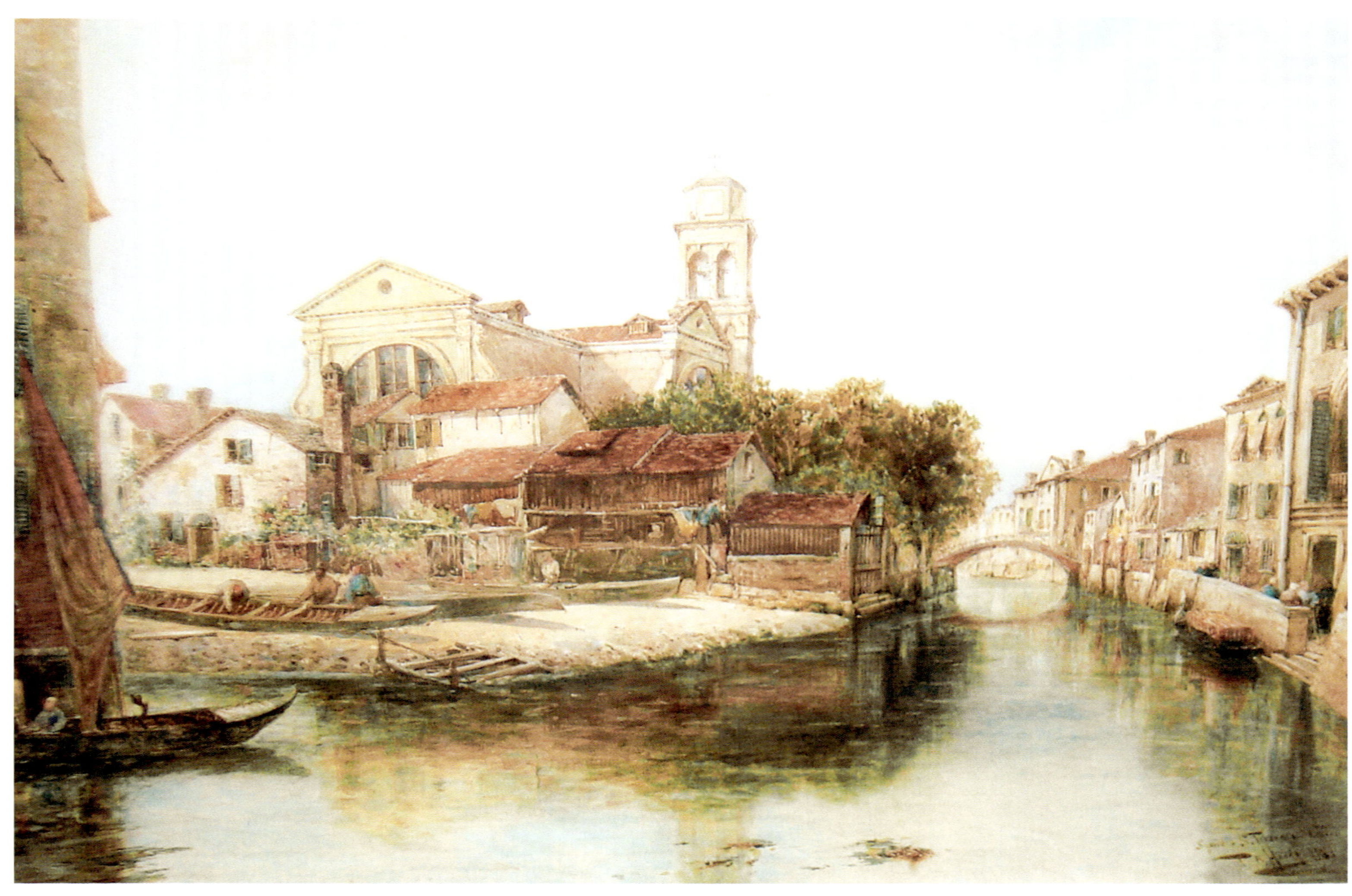

One of the very best scenes of fishermen in the Venetian Lagoon that Hardy painted. This is low water off the island of San Pietro, one of the Lagoon's earliest settlements. Two types of boats and their crews can be seen preparing for a day's fishing. On the left, three single-masted, carvel-built boats are drying their nets and sails while, closer to the artist, the crews of two working gondolas are dealing with several wicker pots, probably a type of keep net, placed at a previous low water. In the background many fishermen can be seen returning to harbour before dusk sets in. Hardy has drawn a brilliantly constructed cloudy evening sky above the remnants of the day's blue sky on the horizon. The reflections in the foreground are, as always, remarkable.

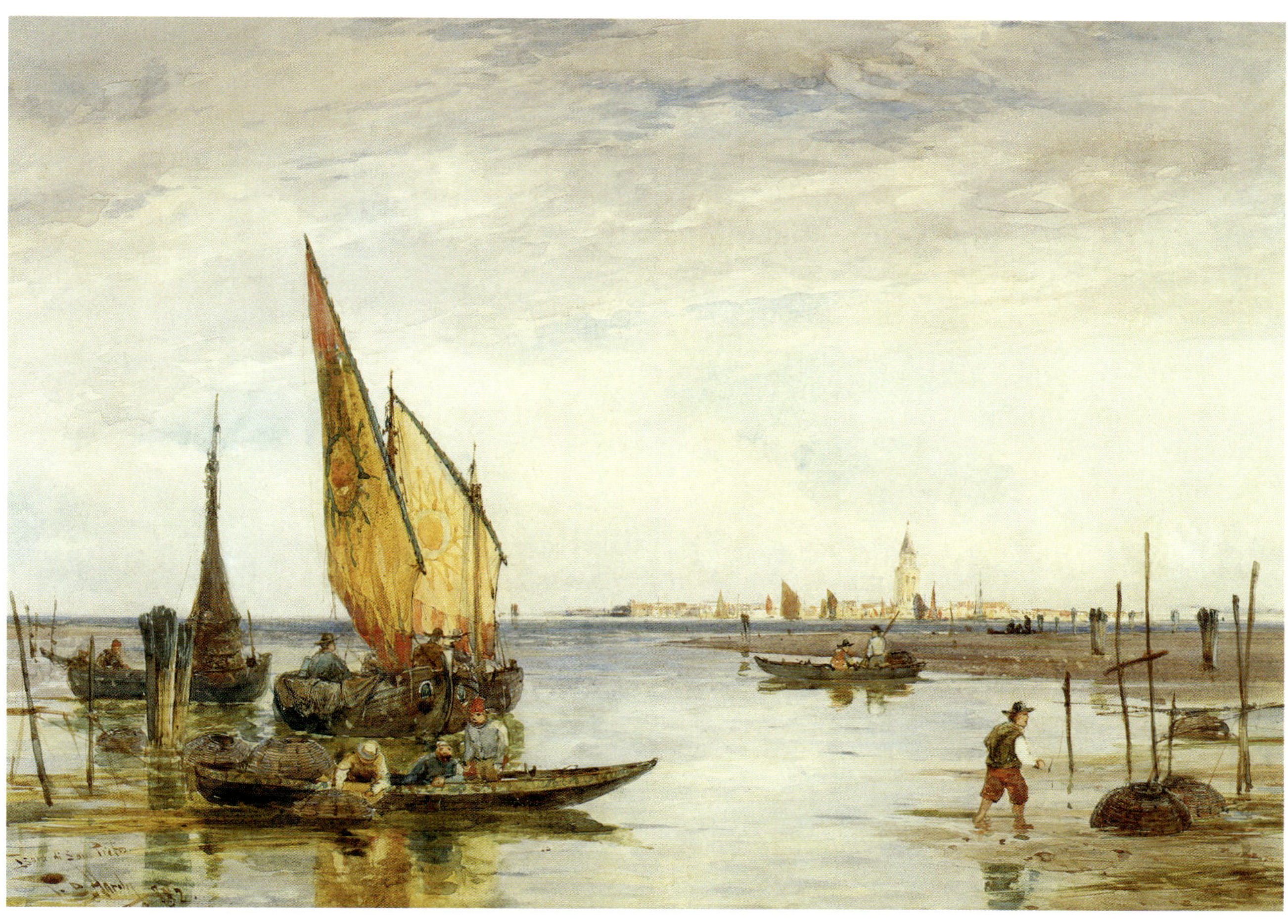

Plate 6.15. **Fishermen off Isola di San Pietro.** *Signed, inscribed and dated 1882. 22.5 x 33cm (8¾ x 13in.)*

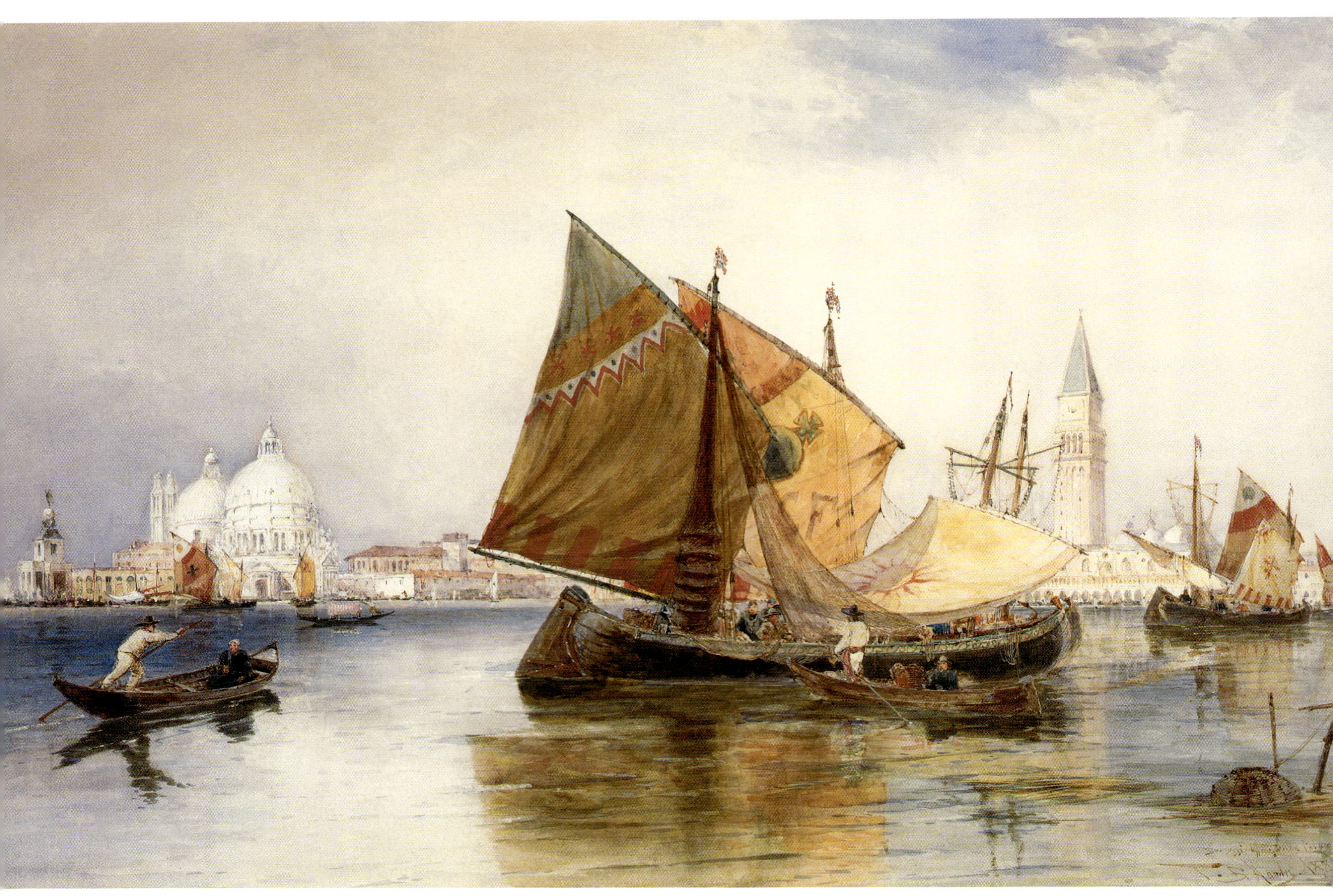

Plate 6.16. **Deojozzi off the Ducal Palace.** *Signed, inscribed and dated 1882. 43 x 85.5cm (17 x 33⅜in.)*

It is a perfect summer's day with hardly a whisper of wind, ideal weather for Hardy to paint a typical Venetian scene in all its wonderful colours. In the foreground are two *deojozzi* almost alongside each other making very slow progress across the Basin of St Mark's. They and some *deojozzi* ahead are returning from what was probably a disappointing day's fishing. Two types of nets can be seen hoisted to the masthead to dry while the foresail is being used as an awning, shading the crew and their catch from the fierce sun. A gondola is about to pass a line to a crew member, perhaps to transfer a few fish. Although the fishing boats are the main subject of the watercolour, the background here is of equal importance. Parts of the Campanile, the domes of St Mark's and some of the Ducal Palace can be seen behind the *deojozzi*. To the left Hardy has painted the church of Santa Maria della Salute in all its glory, glistening in the sun. Balancing this very strong composition a solitary gondola is being rowed towards the Square. A splendid painting.

This postcard-sized watercolour shows two of the smaller Venetian boats returning to one of the islands, probably Murano, at the end of a day's fishing. On their left, the snow-capped peaks of the Dolomites can be clearly seen – not always the case, but the visibility in this clean atmosphere is sometimes exceptional. When it is, the background to the fishermen working in this part of the Lagoon could not be more perfect. Hardy has put it all together supremely well.

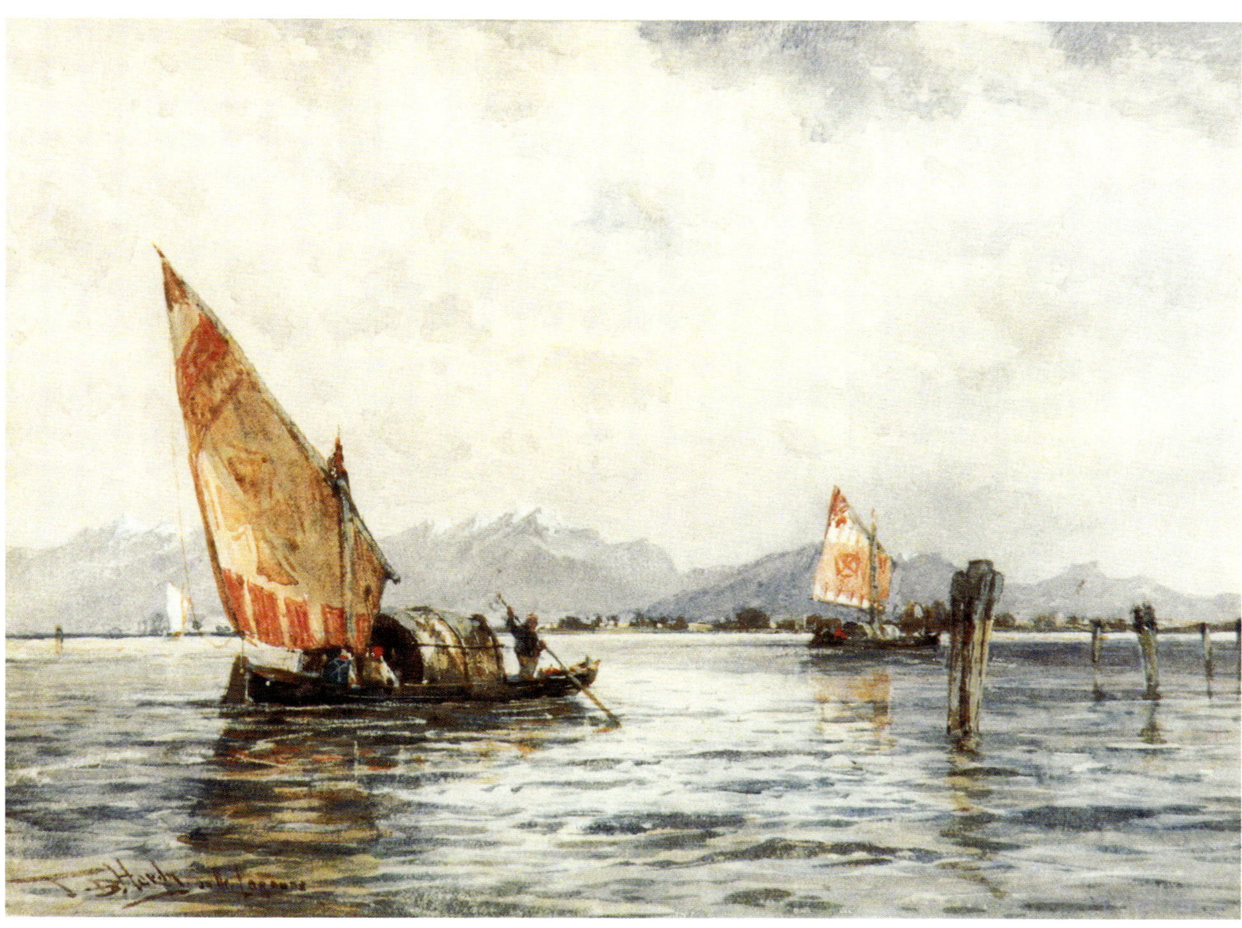

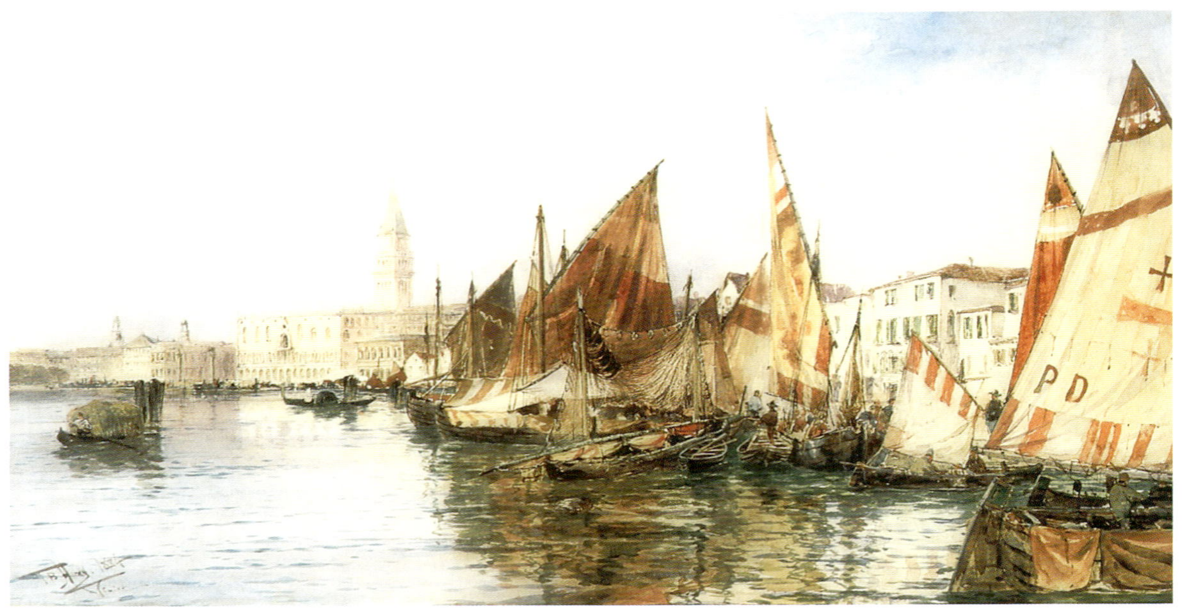

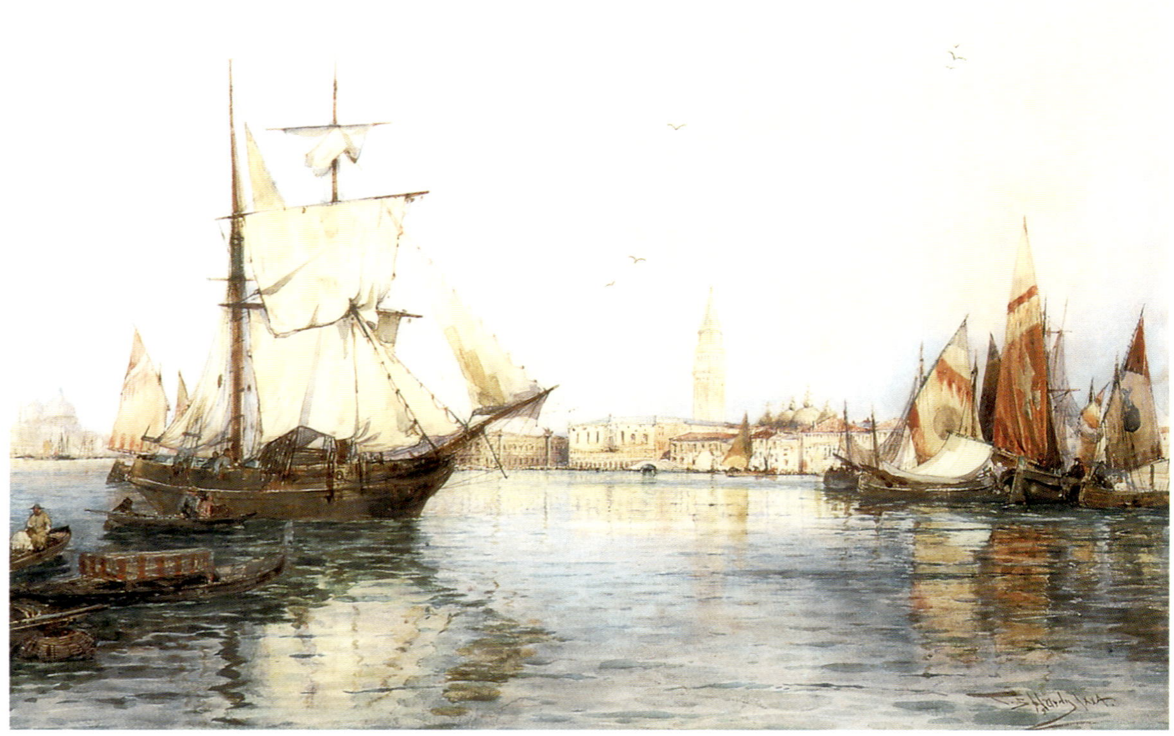

To the east of the Old Prison, but well within sight of the Ducal Palace, is this waterfront where many Venetian fishing families berthed their boats. Hardy was able to paint this colourful assembly of sailing craft, lighters and gondolas in great detail and still do justice to the central Venetian backdrop. It is a busy scene; most of the boats have just returned from a day's fishing in the Lagoon, the catch and some of the gear has already been landed. Now, sails and, in some cases, masts must be lowered and boats and the moorings squared off for the night. The women have gone home to prepare the evening meal. Hardy would also go back to his room with his sketchbooks and a sheaf of notes but would be unlikely to embark on a finished watercolour of this size until his return to London.

Above. Plate 6.18. **Off St Mark's Square.** *Signed, inscribed and dated 1884. 28.5 x 58cm (11¼ x 22¾in.)*

Painted from a very similar viewpoint to Plate 6.18, but fifty metres or so further out in the stream, Hardy has introduced a *deojozza* disembarking its catch before returning to a buoy or an alongside berth. Preliminary sketches for these two watercolours could well have been made on the same day in the same benign weather conditions. The background has been extended to include the church of Santa Maria della Salute, always a bonus, and the artist has cleverly planned for the *deojozza's* bowsprit to be pointing directly at the Campanile. Hardy's ability as a marine artist, his sensitive handling of the architectural beauty of Venice and his compositional skills are all represented in this admirable painting.

Excluding Venice and the Italian Lakes, this is one of the very few Italian scenes that Hardy painted, presumably when he made a detour on his way back from Venice. It has to be one of his very best coastal scenes, and perhaps his only painting of the Mediterranean. Here he met a somewhat different community of fishermen and their families. The climate is far more congenial in this part of the Mediterranean than that in the north Adriatic and the seas bordering Northern Europe. The sea itself is a very different colour most of the time. Hardy has achieved a near perfect Mediterranean blue in this watercolour – and it shows no sign of fading. There is little or no tide and usually early warning of strong winds, so the fishing boats with their lateen sails can be beached and left there quite safely. Finally, Hardy has observed and painted the Italian love and care for their children – lots of them and taken everywhere!

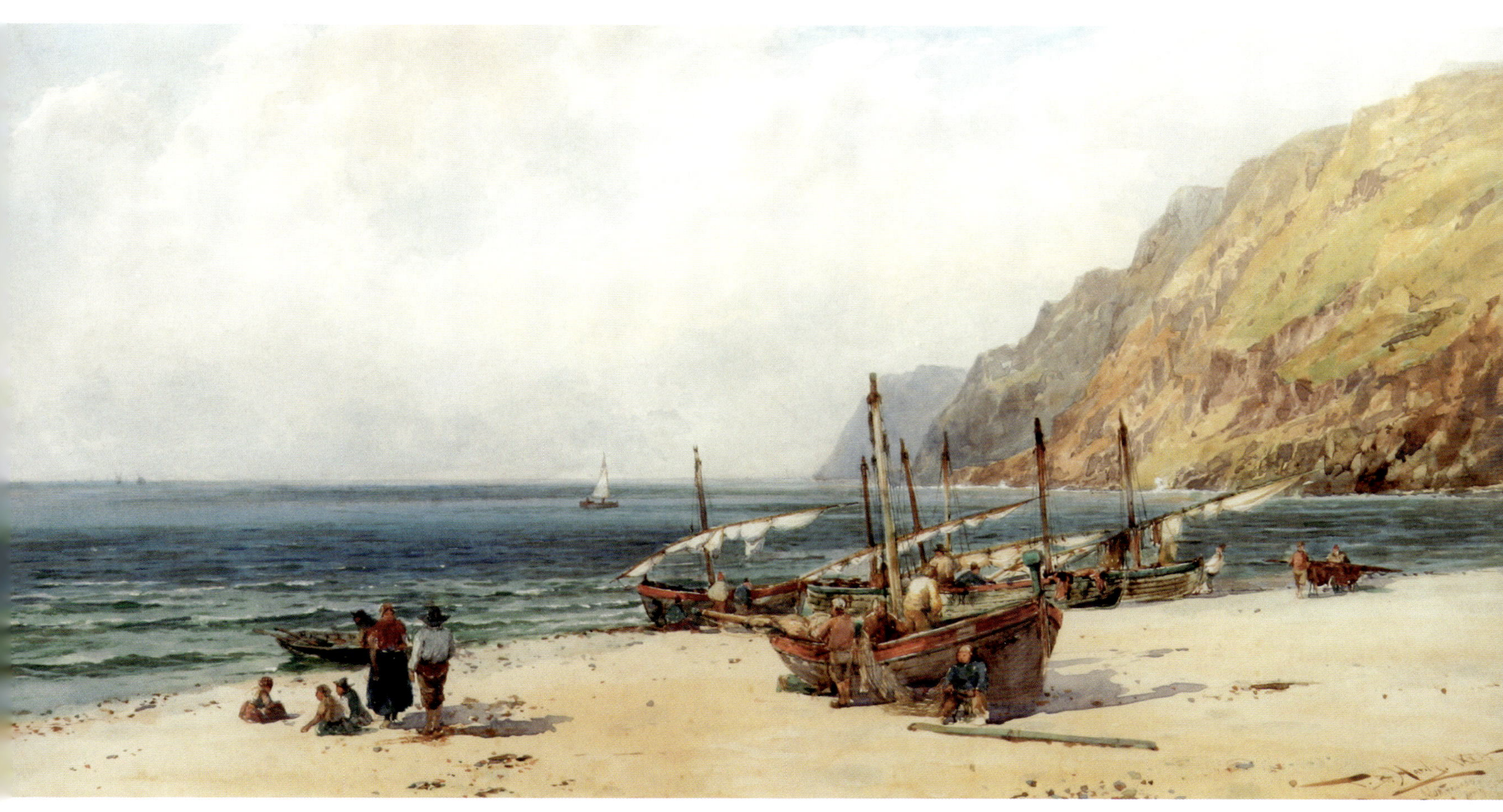

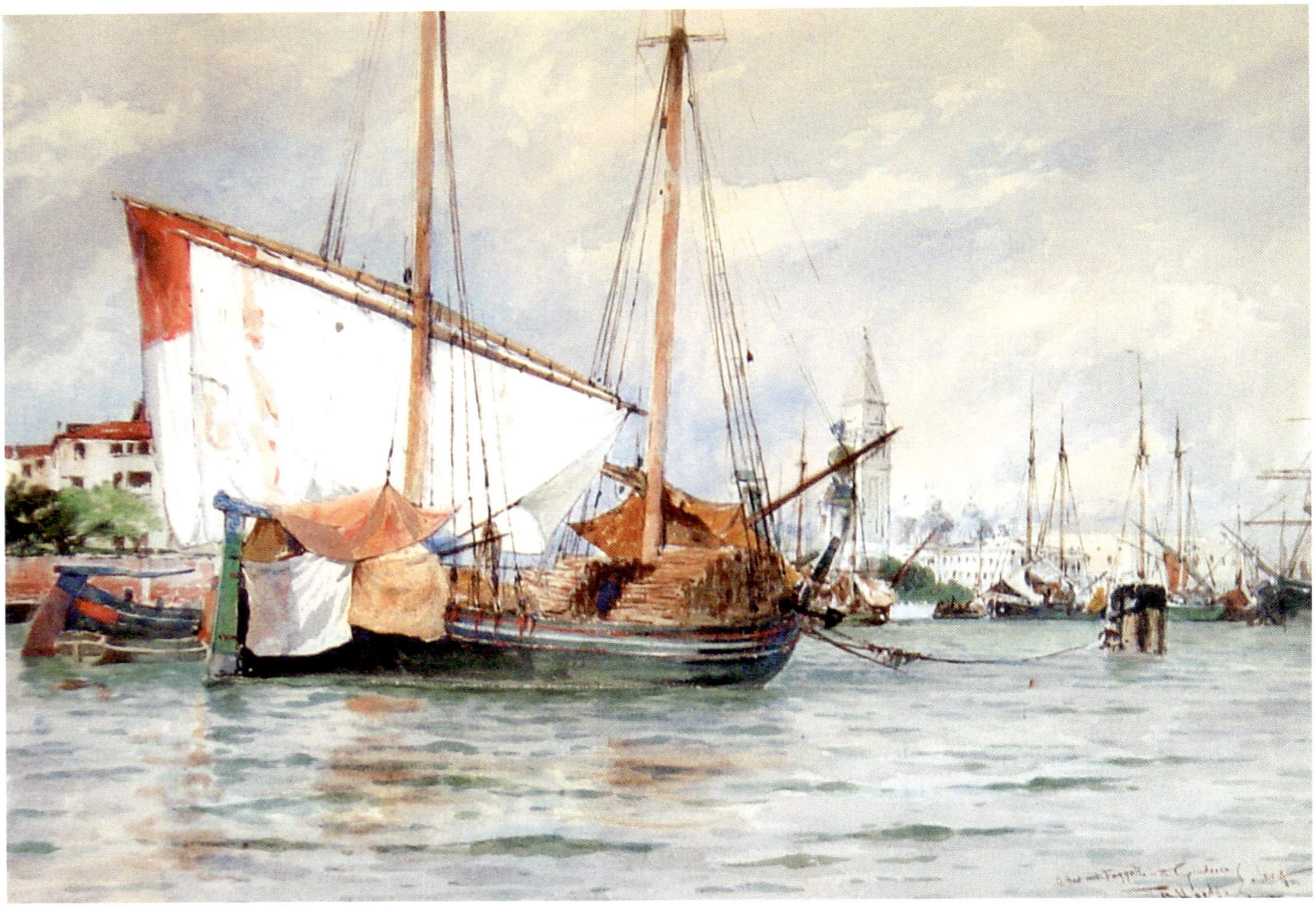

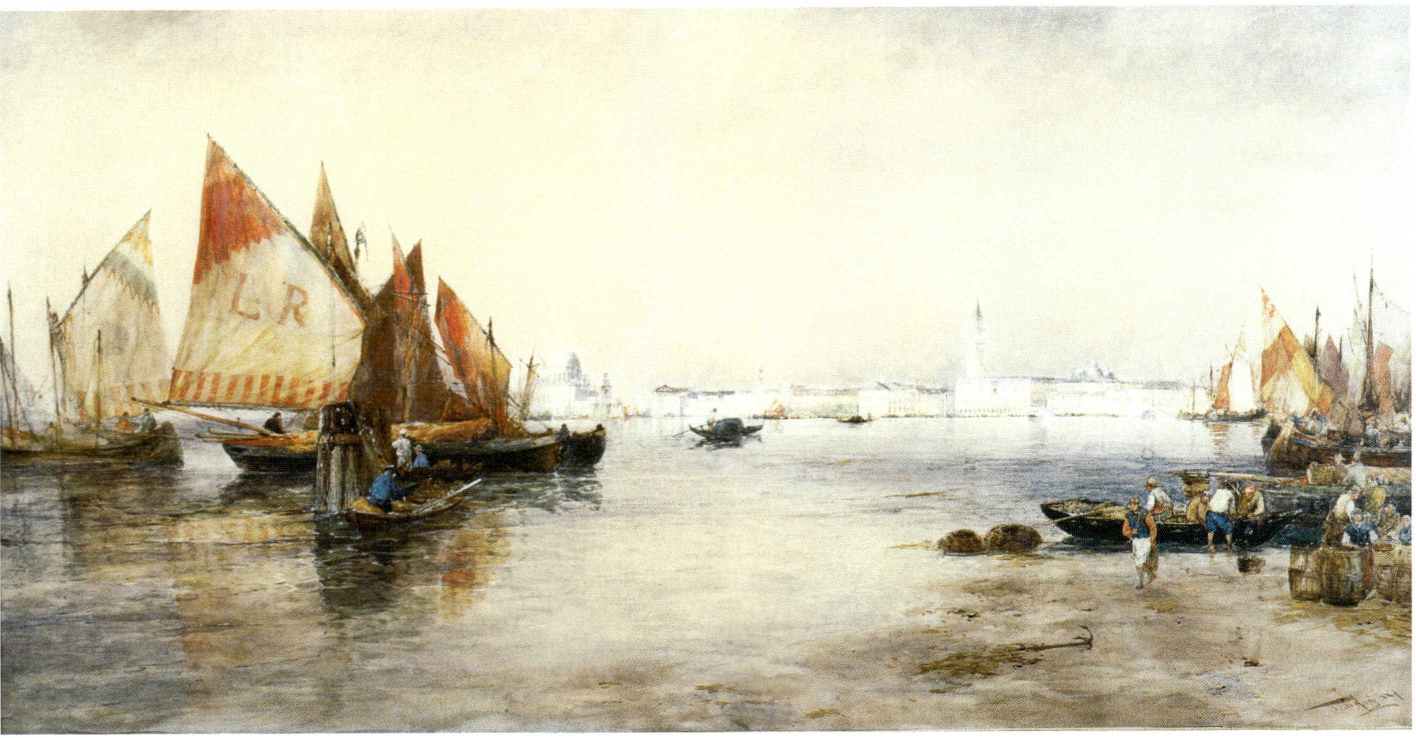

Chapter 6 – Venice

Most of this watercolour is taken up with a portrait of a two-masted barge laden with faggots, pinewood logs that had been used for centuries to build and repair the canal walls. Having secured the barge to a channel beacon in the Canale di Giudecca, the crew have either gone ashore or are taking a siesta. All their sails and tarpaulins are being used as awnings, providing some much-needed shade from the midday sun. Not far ahead there are numerous masts including those of a trading barque moored close to the Dogana di Mare, the Customs House of Venice. To the left and beyond, Hardy has given us a glimpse of the green Giardinetti Reali, the Campanile and St Mark's Square. Because the main subject of the painting, however true to life, is untidy and to some extent disorganised, this painting is bound to lack harmony. This may have been Hardy's intention.

Looking from the Arsenale towards San Marco, this fine watercolour enshrines the Venice of the 1880s from a marine artist's point of view. Here you see every type of fishing barge and boat from the two-masted *deojozzi* with their coloured emblazoned sails to a one-man gondola, all under way, moored, beached or alongside the jetties. Beyond, the wonderful backdrop of central Venice – Santa Maria della Salute, the entrance to the Grand Canal, the Campanile and Doge's Palace, all bathed in sunlight. Supporting and binding them together, the calm luminous Lagoon, its reflections duplicating the beauty of it all.

This is probably a view of one of the islands in the Lagoon with what should be a very recognisable church and bell tower. It is one of Hardy's narrow watercolours which allows the artist, in this case, to show a good deal of the surrounding Lagoon and other islands in the distance. A passenger-carrying gondola will soon reach shore, having just passed a *sandolo*, a slim lightweight boat perfectly suited to hunting and fishing in the shallow waters of the Lagoon. The composition is nicely balanced and, colourwise, the artist has achieved tonal harmony between the cloudy sky and the calm waters below.

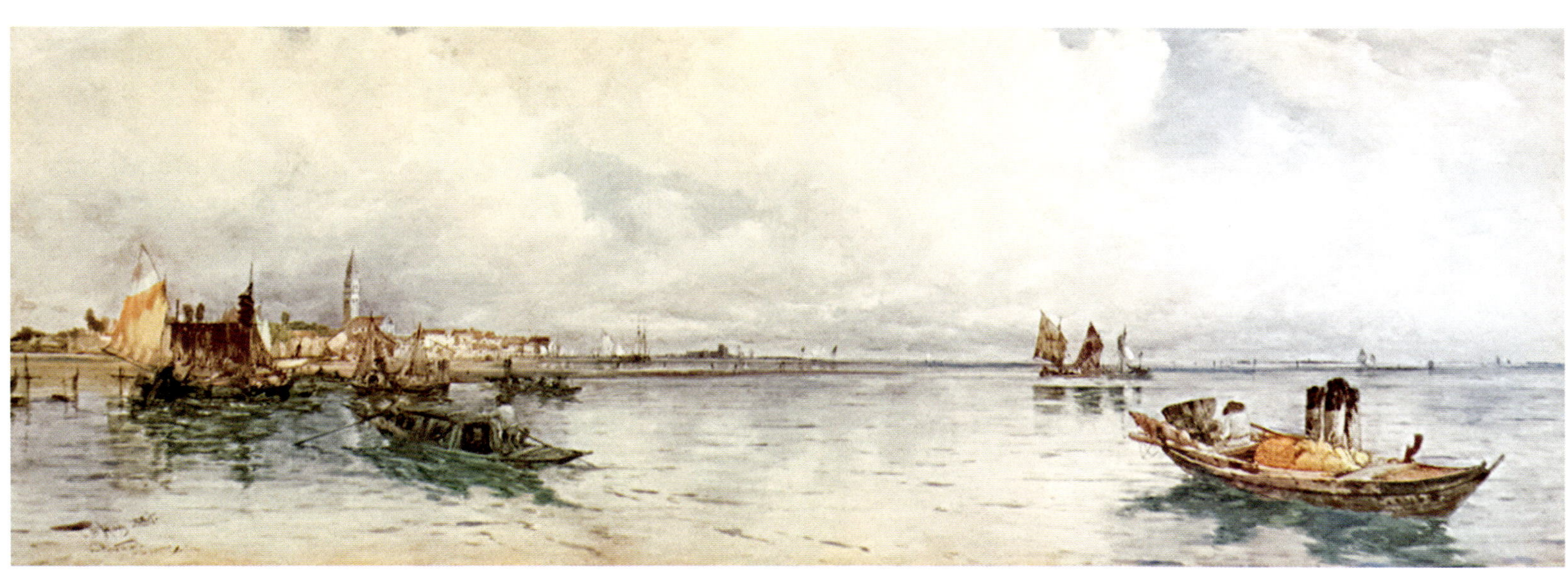

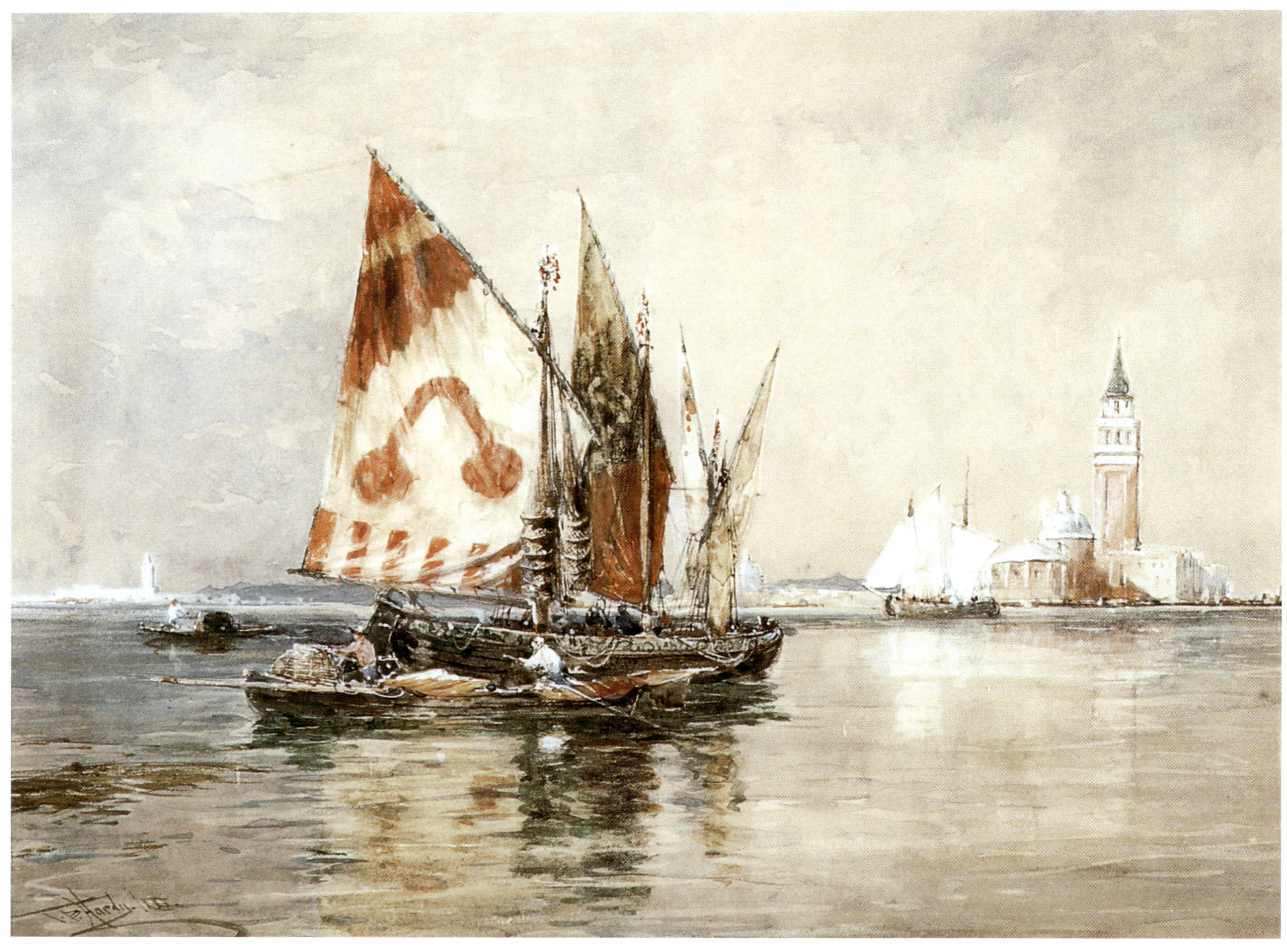

The overall pink tone of this work, possibly overdone, suggests it was painted in an evening light, which contrasts with a similar view in Plate 6.26, painted the following year. It also gives the impression of being completed in a hurry, paying little attention to detail – vigorous but sketchy. The composition is, as usual, good if Hardy can be forgiven for overlapping the drawing of two and often three boats. Seen from eye level, the mix of hulls, masts and sails can often be confusing. In a flat calm the craft may be deliberately communing together but, from an artistic point of view, some clear water might be more appropriate. In this case it is just possible that the gondola in the foreground is about to offer the nearer *deojozza* a tow.

Plate 6.24. **Off San Giorgio.**
Signed and dated 1888.
22 x 30cm (8⅝ x 11¾in.)

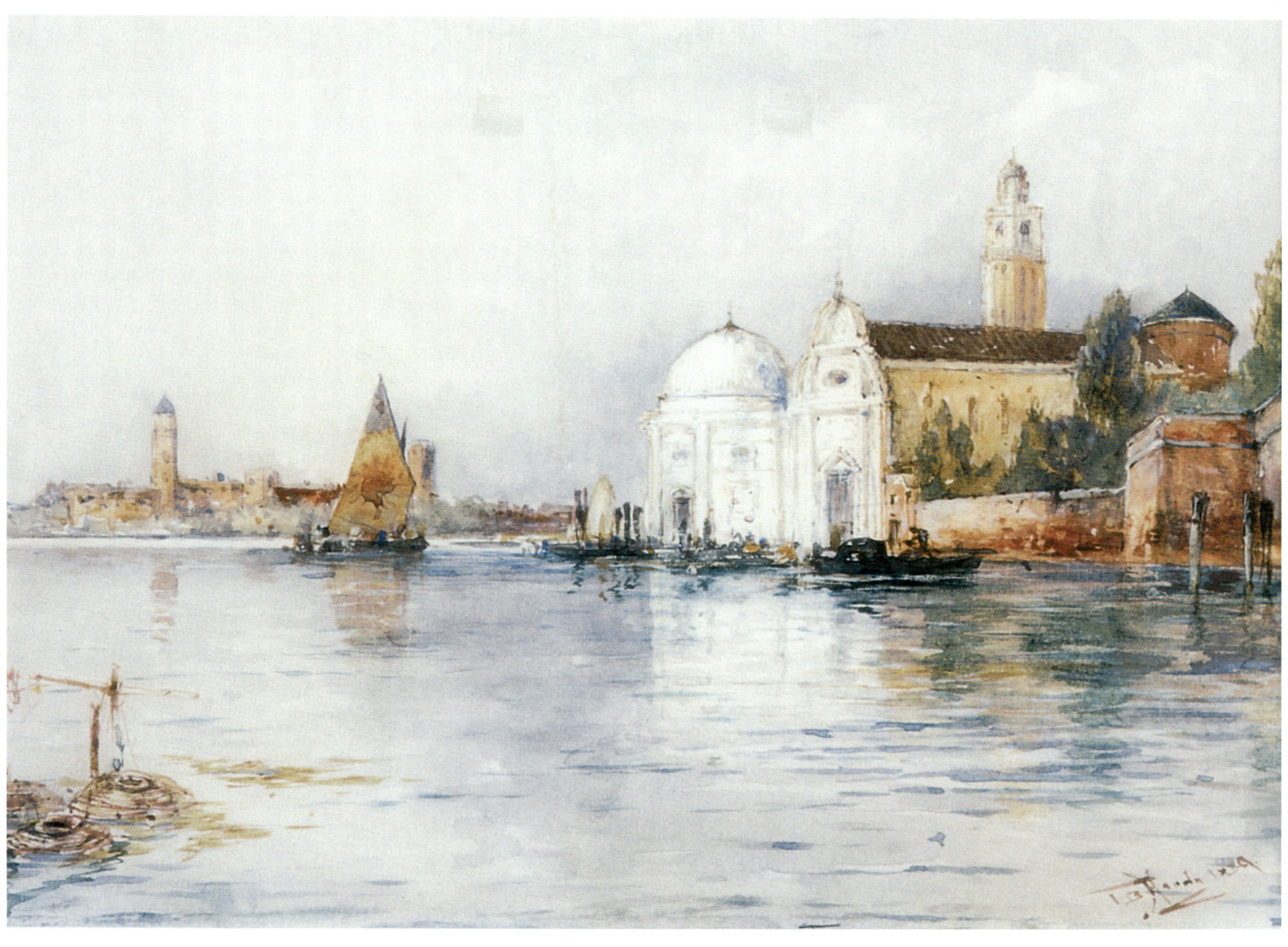

Plate 6.25. **By the Giudecca.**
Signed and dated 1889.
22 x 30cm (8⅝ x 11¾in.)

A late Venetian work, painted rather sketchily and unconvincingly but still retaining a charm that, with few exceptions, they all possess. It was a pity that Hardy did not inscribe this watercolour as, to date, research has failed to find the exact location. It is the kind of scene one would expect to find by the Giudecca but, from the Lagoon, circumventing the island, there are many similar views. The half-submerged round wicker pots in the left foreground have held their secret for over a century, but a reasonable assumption is that they are the Venetian equivalent of a keep net. Live fish and crustacea could be transferred to one of these and would remain cool and alive until sold or consumed. Not one of his better watercolours, but different.

There is some doubt about the date of this delightful watercolour, but in this case the date is irrelevant; this watercolour must rank among one of his best Venetian views. It is a fine, warm day: a hazy sky and a flat calm. A gondola, painted black in accordance with a 1562 decree forbidding vulgar displays of wealth, is approaching the nearer fishing boat that has hung nets to dry on its foremast. Neither of the fishing boats, now on opposite courses, is making much progress. Artistically, it matters not. The two boats with their colourful sails, static or not, are an important feature, but it is the wonderful scenery beyond that makes the picture.

Plate 6.26. **Venice.** *Signed, inscribed and dated indistinctly 1889. 31 x 45cm (12¼ x 17¾in.)*

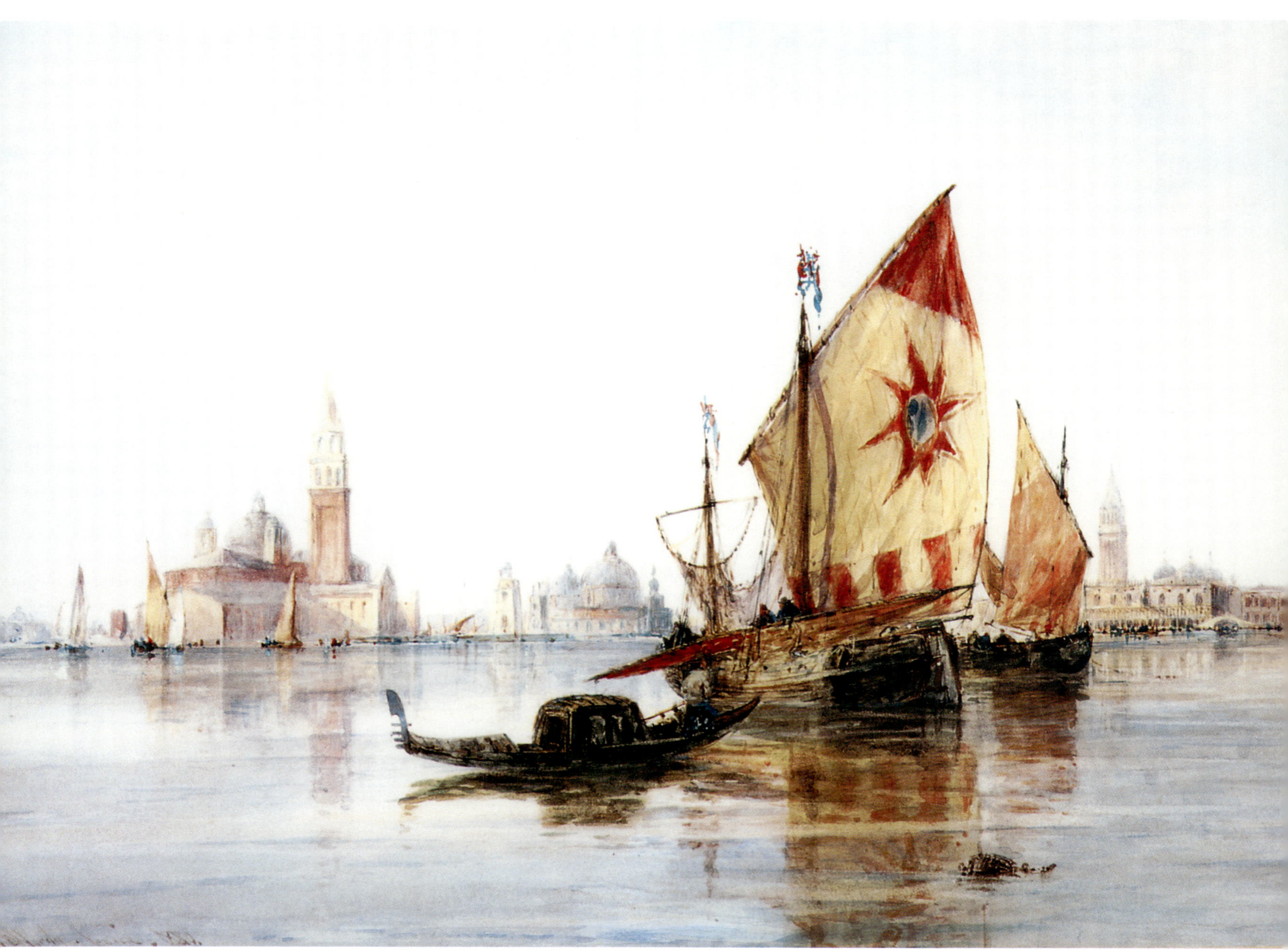

Chapter 6 – Venice

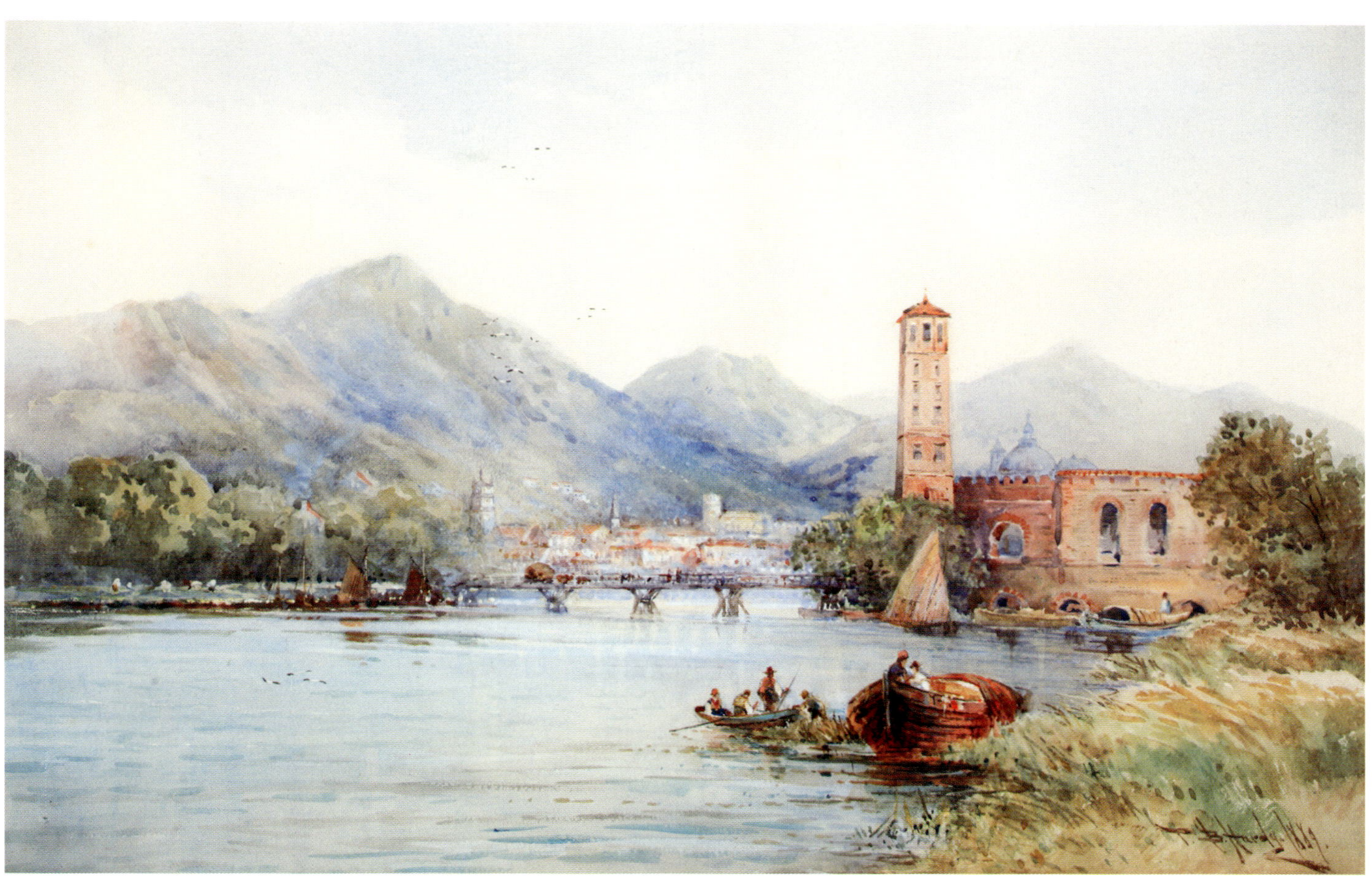

From this and the many watercolours of Venetian scenes dated 1889, it can be assumed that Hardy made the journey via this lake, probably Lake Garda, that year. Riva del Garda, at the very northern tip of the lake, guarded by a mediaeval castle and tower, would make a fine picture from the lake and would certainly have inspired Hardy. The two boats right of centre lead the eye to the nine storey tower and moated fortress. Beyond the wooden bridge lies a red-roofed town stretching back to the foothills of the Alto Adige. Unusually for Lake Garda there is no noticeable wind and the unruffled surface of the lake adds tranquillity to a strikingly beautiful scene.

Plate 6.27. **Italian Lake Scene.** *Signed and dated 1889. 37 x 60cm (14½ x 23⅜in.)*

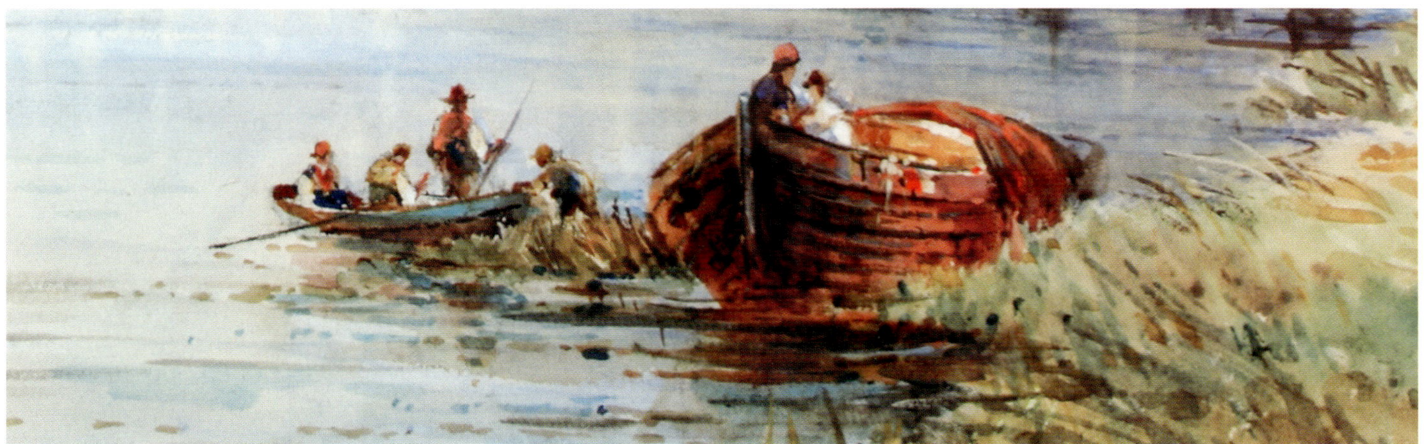

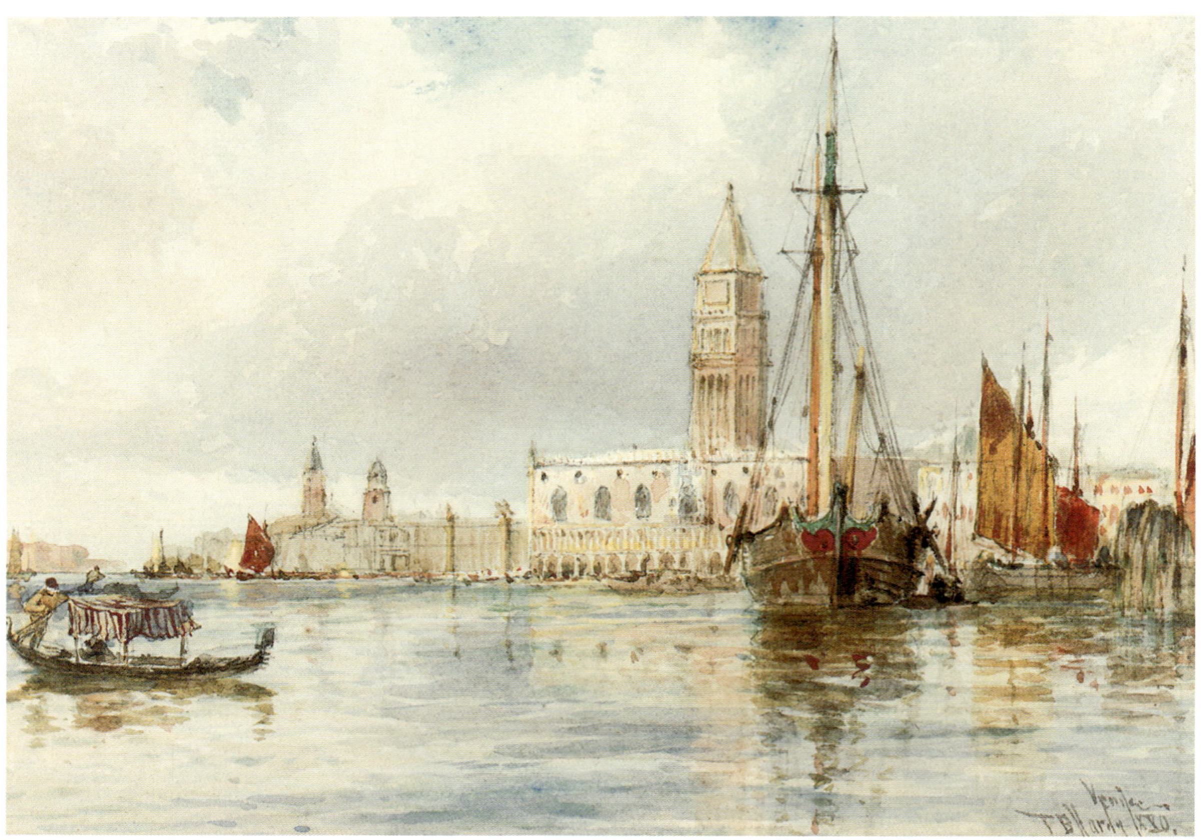

An early postcard-sized work with the Doge's Palace given prominence in the near background. A *deojozza* with its two tall masts, seen bow on, dominates the scene in clever juxtaposition with the Campanile. On the left, a loosely sketched gondola balances the picture. Beneath a grey sky, Hardy has drawn a very liquid Lagoon, welling up in the canals and around the low-lying city, threatening its survival. It could have been one of those autumn days when the floods come to St Mark's Square.

A rather loosely painted sketch of fishermen busy on their boats on a typically calm and hazy Venetian day, this time with the island of San Giorgio Maggiore in the background. Hardy seems to be fascinated by the large floating wicker baskets in the foreground – keeping fish alive ?

Another small sketch from one of Hardy's early visits to Venice showing a square-rigged trading brig furling sails with the Doge's Palace and Campanile in the background. A gondola and a group of *deojozzi* to the right of the Ponte della Paglia provide colour and balance to the picture. Hardy obviously based this watercolour on pencil sketches made while afloat *en plein air;* there is nothing contrived about this composition – he was there.

Unfortunately there is no record of how many of these small sketches Hardy produced during his visits to Venice; they probably numbered well into the hundreds and most of those that have survived are of fine quality and very collectable. Most of the examples that follow are from Mr Dudley Good's superb collection and give some idea of the range of Venetian subjects that Hardy covered over the years. They are also a further demonstration of his remarkable talent as a marine watercolourist.

Plate 6.28. **The Doge's Palace.** *Signed, inscribed and dated 1880. 12 x 17cm (4¾ x 6¾ in.)*

Opposite above. Plate 6.29. **On the Lagoon.** *Signed, inscribed and dated 1880. 12 x 17cm (4¾ x 6¾ in.)*

Opposite below. Plate 6.30. **The Doge's Palace.** *Signed, inscribed and dated 1881. 12 x 17cm (4¾ x 6¾ in.)*

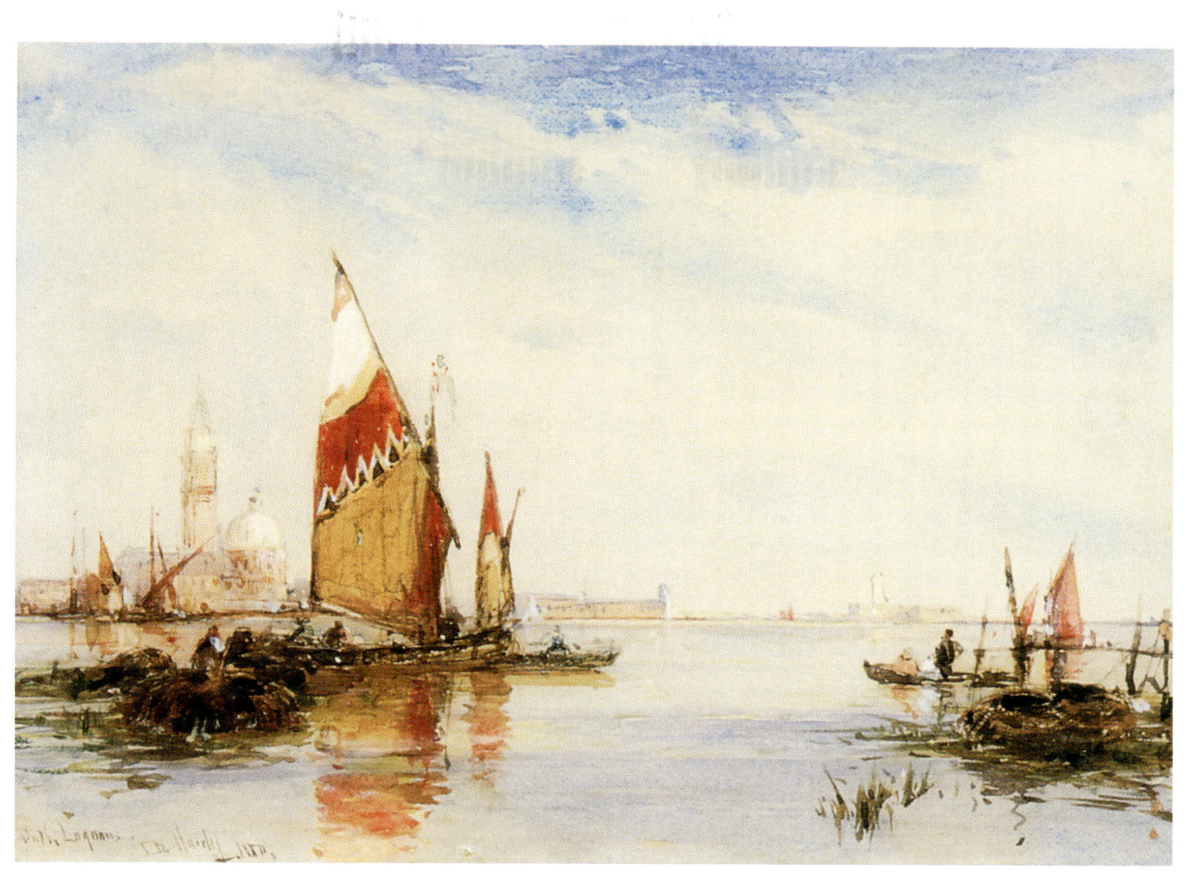

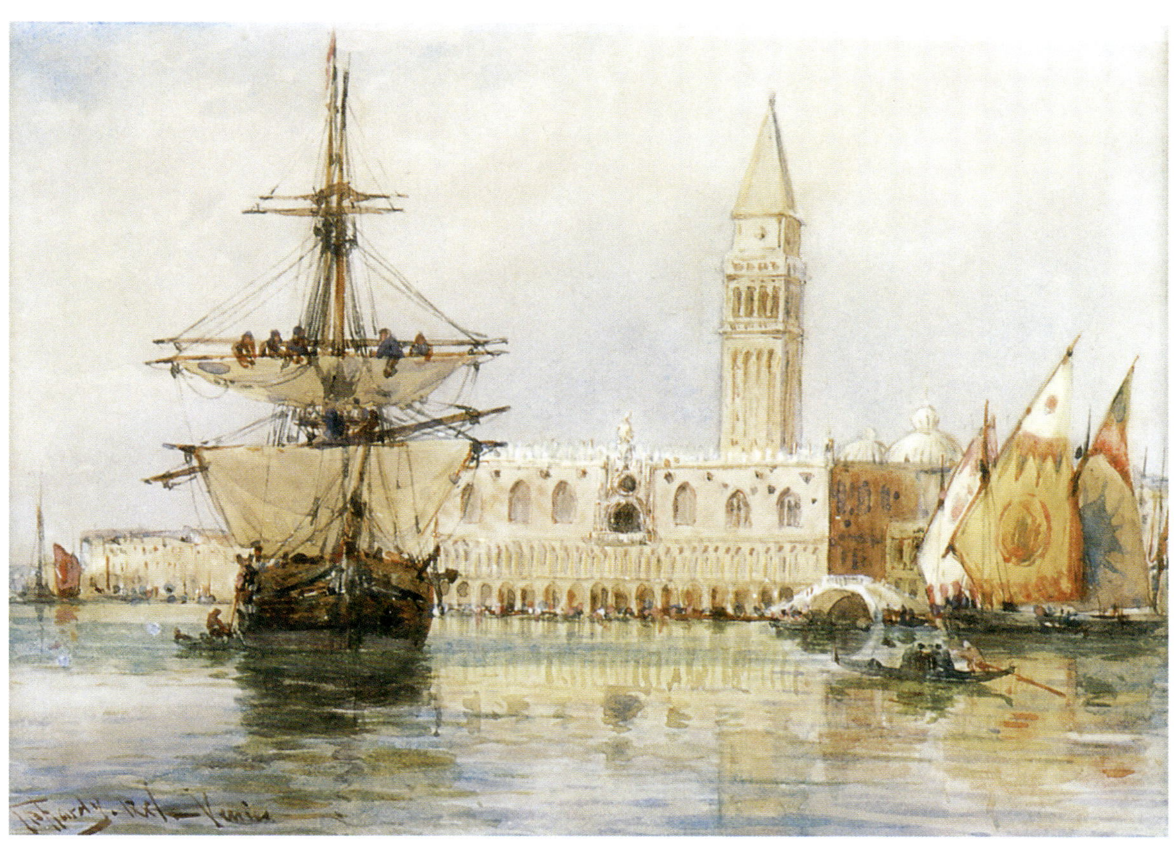

It is easy to imagine Hardy sitting on a collapsible stool on a quayside sketching this scene. This one is totally devoted to fishermen and gondoliers and their way of life. The viewer is only permitted a brief glimpse of what could be a church on one of the islands in the Lagoon. Far more important is the landing of the catch from the three *deojozzi* off the jetty and the subsequent bartering,

Plate 6.31. **Unloading the Deojozzi.** *Signed, inscribed and dated 1882. 12 x 17.5cm (4¾ x 6⅞in.)*

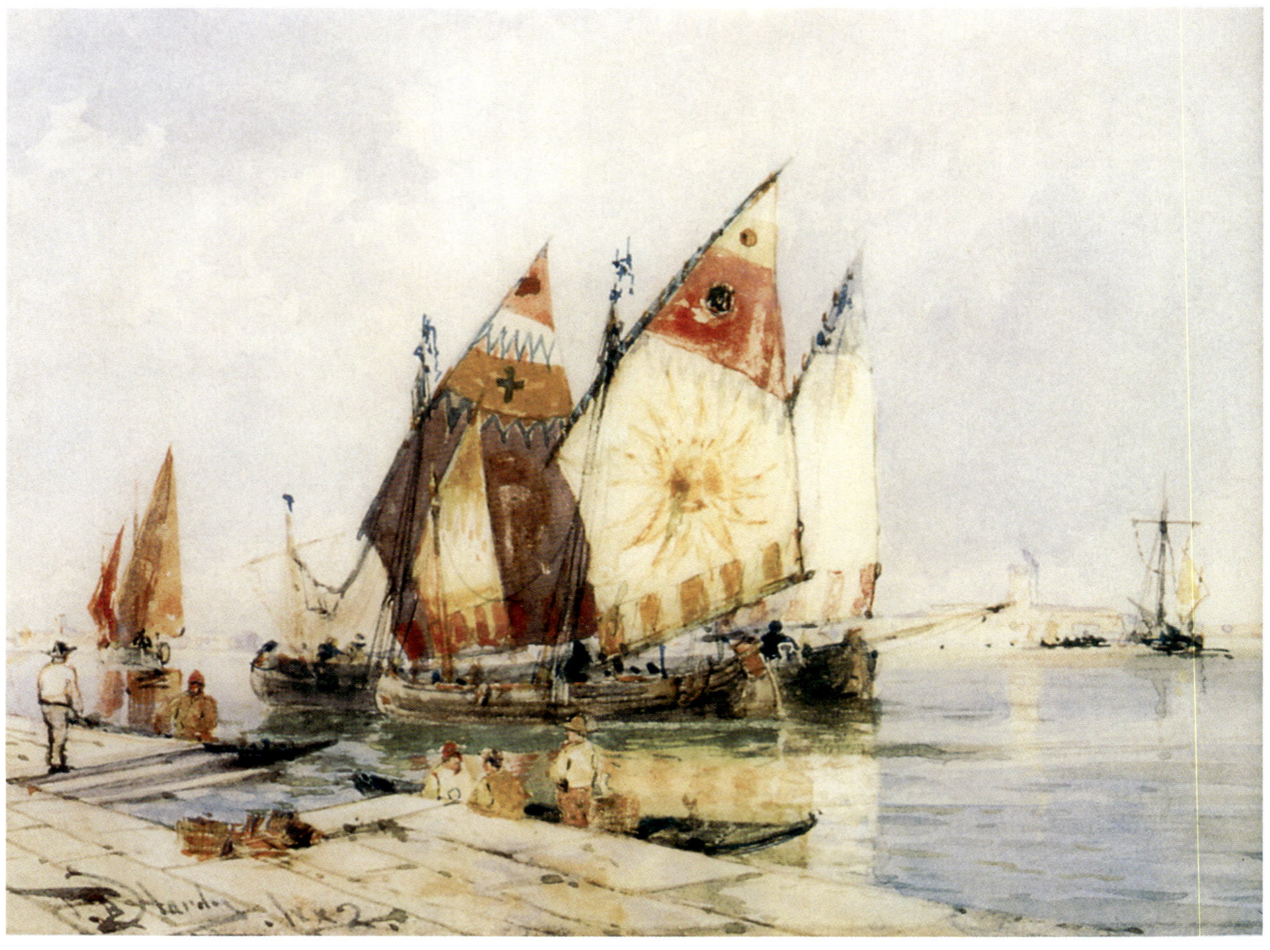

A warm, sunny afternoon with people out for a walk, pausing on a bend in the road to watch the local fishermen return alongside. Judging from the carved stone decoration this could be a private landing stage. The perspective and overall composition of this painting are quite superb. As with most of these small sketches, one suspects that many are unplanned; that Hardy comes across a scene that inspires him and out comes his sketchbook. It is often noticeable that, having completed a sketch to his satisfaction, he immediately used the same brush and colour to sign, inscribe and date the painting. Confident and impulsive, yes – when he knew it was good.

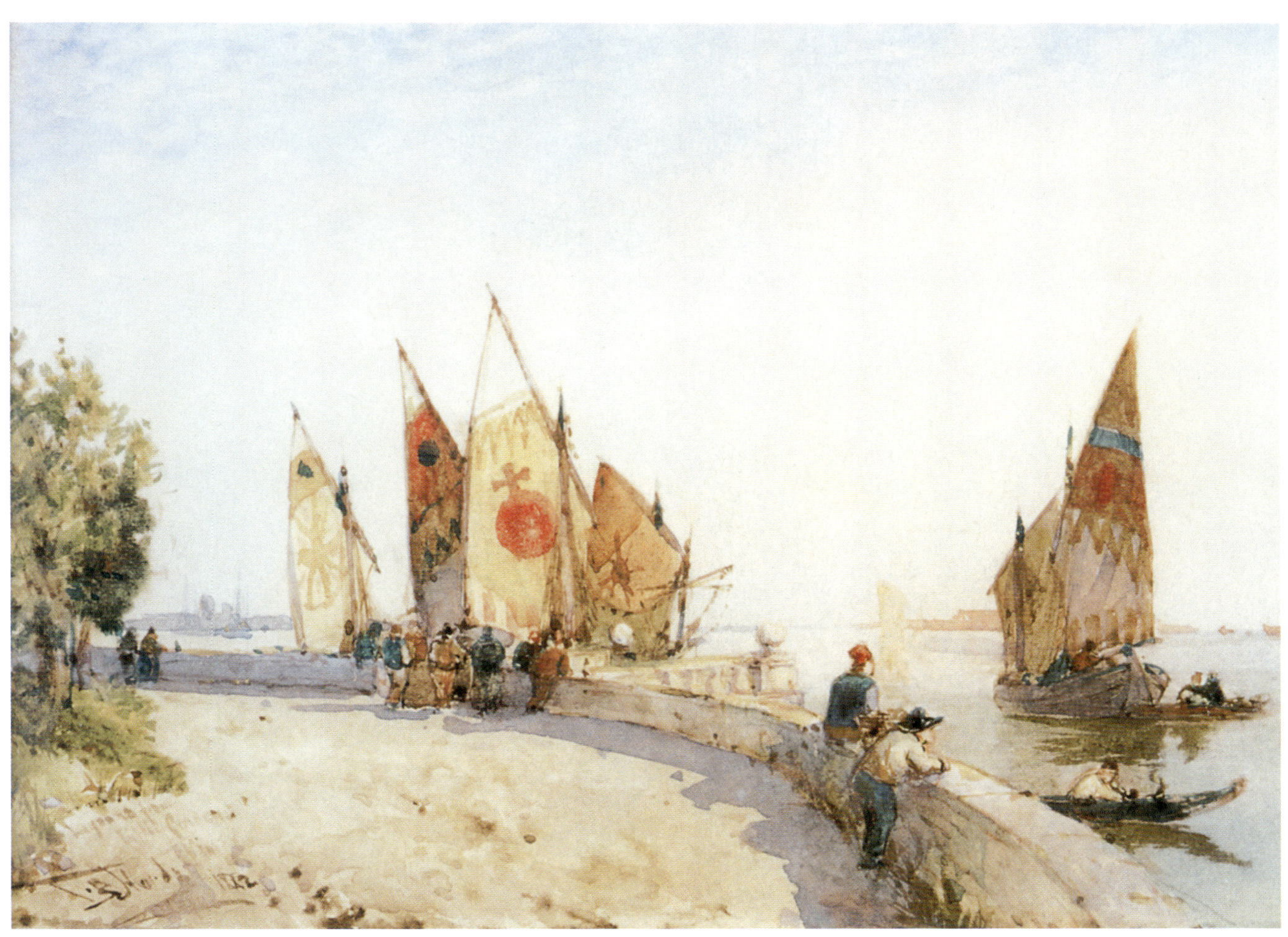

Another study of the everyday life of the Venetian boat people. There are well over a dozen men and women in this sketch and all of them, in one way or another, are involved in the daily tasks of a fishing community. Hardy has again concerned himself primarily with fishermen and their families and has ignored all the architectural gems normally associated with a Venetian landscape. But there is both interest and beauty to be found in this painting. The people, the old buildings, the boats and the shimmering Lagoon bathed in the Adriatic light all contribute to an image which is both colourful and authentic.

Plate 6.33. **By the Jetty.**
Signed and dated 1883.
12 x 17.5 cm (4¾ x 6⅞ in.)

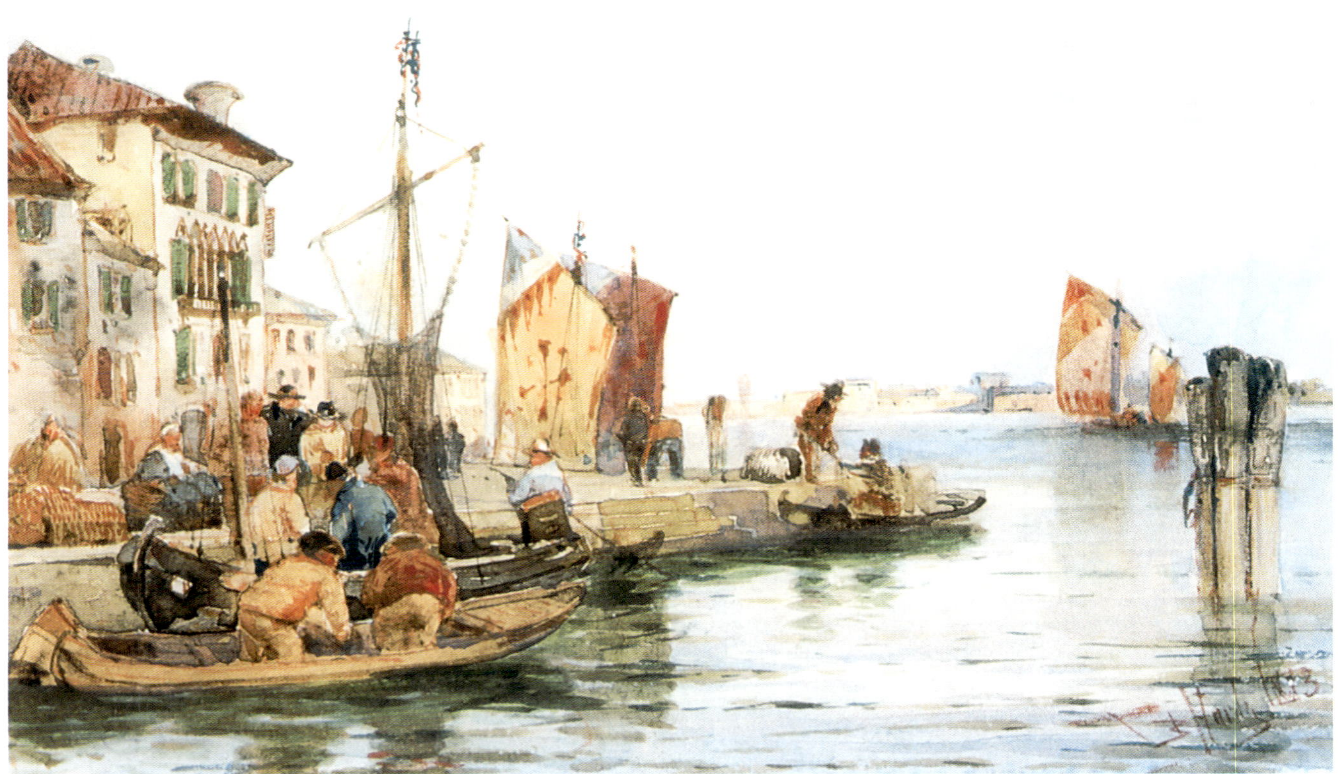

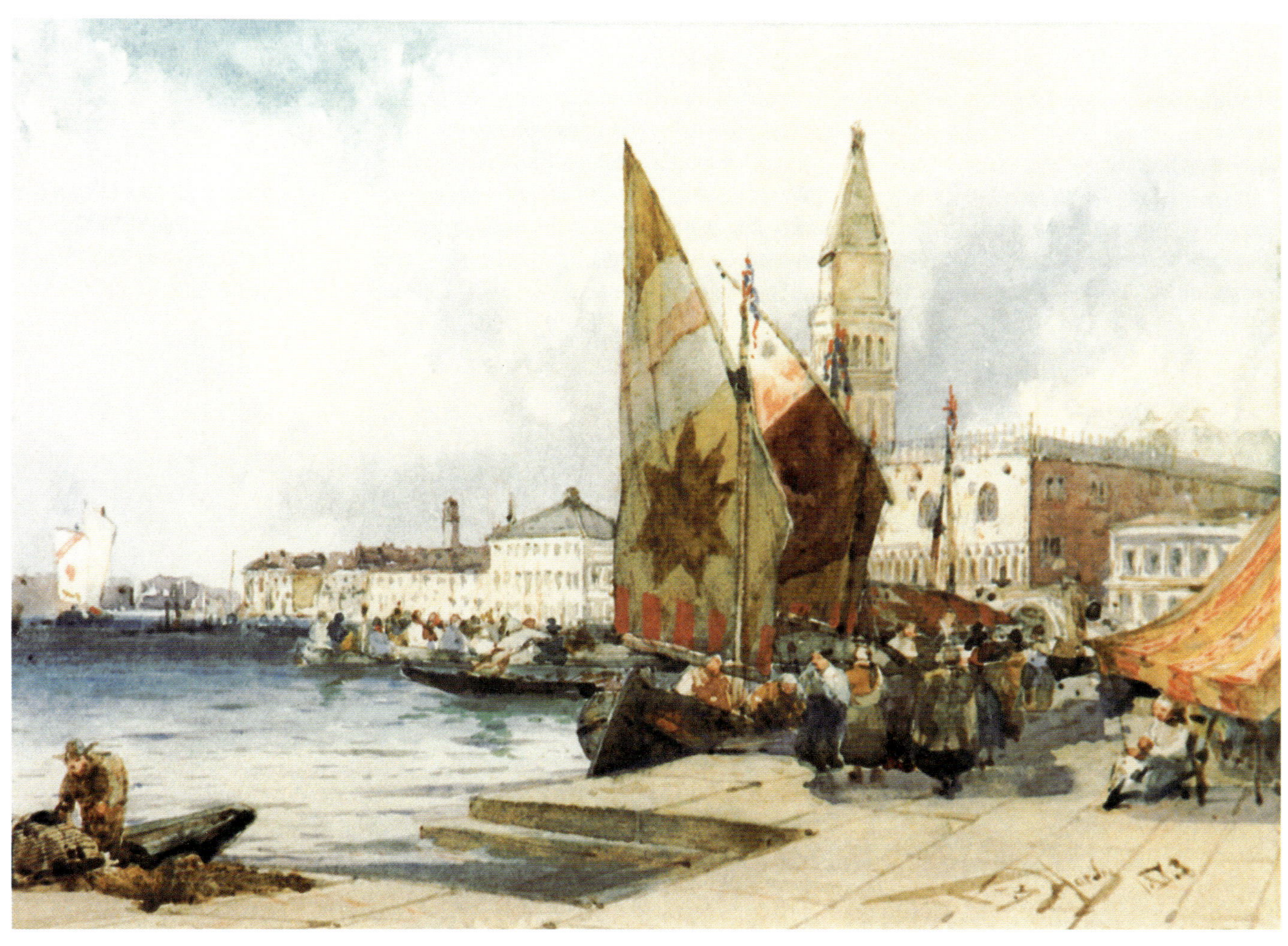

Plate 6.34. **Alongside the Riva degli Schiavoni.** *Signed and dated 1883. 13 x 18cm (5⅛ x 7in.)*

This is a wonderful little painting of the famous promenade close to the Ducal Palace named after the traders from Dalmatia (Schiavonia) who used to moor their boats and barges here. The Riva degli Schiavoni has always been busy with boats. Canaletto's drawings in the 1740s and 1750s show the Riva bustling with gondolas, sailing boats and barges. Little has changed. Hardy has captured the atmosphere quite beautifully. In the foreground the promenaders are pausing to inspect the the freshly caught fish on display in the covered market and haggle over the price of souvenirs. The sun is still high in the sky, gondolas are arriving and departing with visitors from other parts of Venice and *gelati* are selling well.

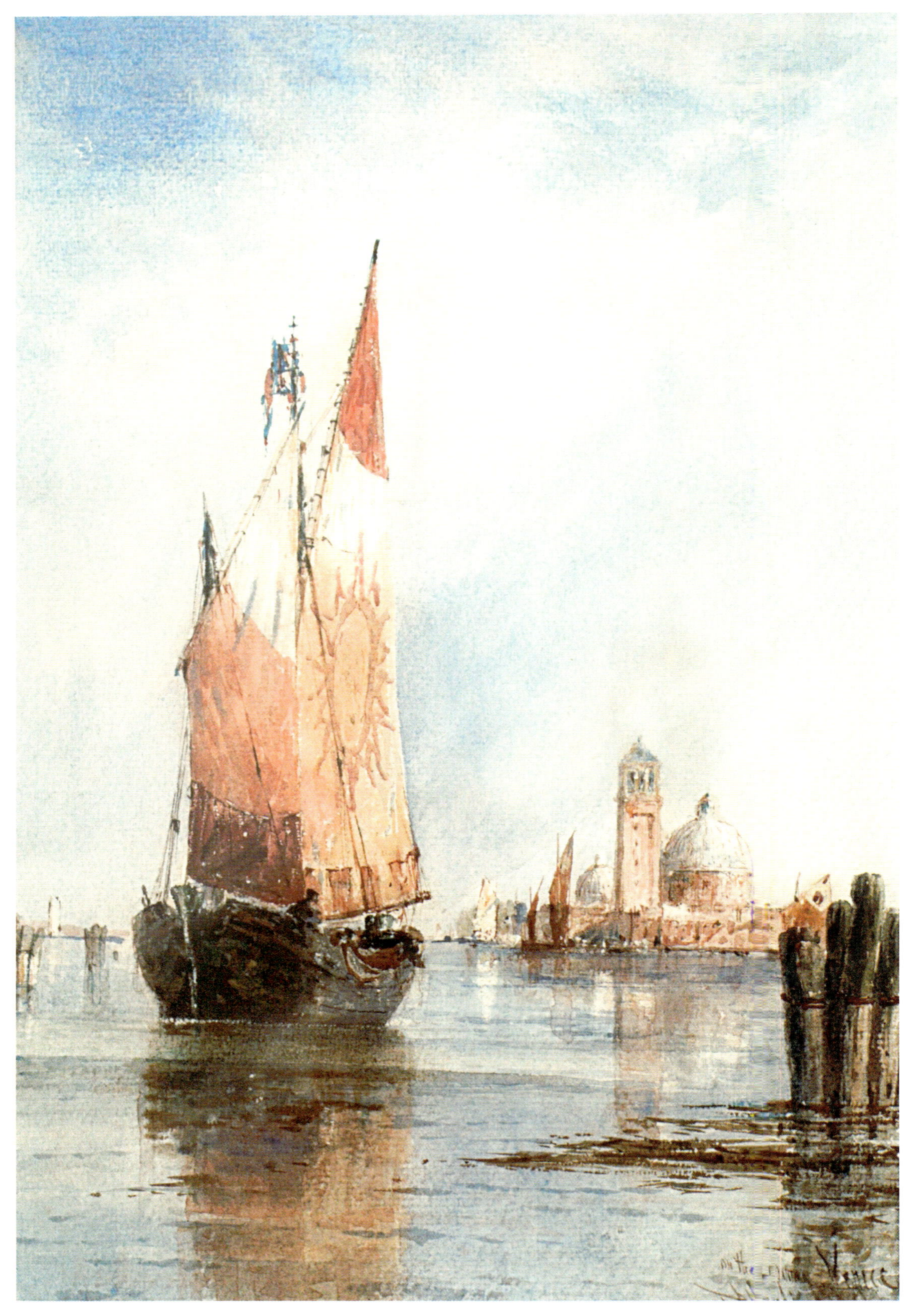

Chapter 6 – Venice

A rare portrait-shaped watercolour in the small format. As with nearly all watercolours of this size, the colours have survived extremely well. A *deojozza* is drifting, very slowly, towards the artist in a near flat calm. The reflections in the Lagoon of boat, sails, sky and the architectural beauties of Venice, real or imagined, are superbly painted – liquid luminescence at its best. The composition, balanced by weathered beacons marking the channel, is excellent. A lovely little picture.

Undated, but probably painted between 1882 and 1884 when Hardy seemed to be concentrating on fishermen operating in the less well-known areas of Venice and the Lagoon. This is a view that present-day travellers would not recognise due to the considerable expansion of the dockyard (Arsenale) to the north and east of the island, one of Venice's earliest settlements. The church, probably founded in the 7th century, became the city's cathedral and remained so until 1807 when San Marco took its place. Evidently the island has lost none of its sleepy charm, with fishing nets hung in the cloisters and brightly coloured boats moored in the waterways. In this watercolour the fisherman have had their siesta.

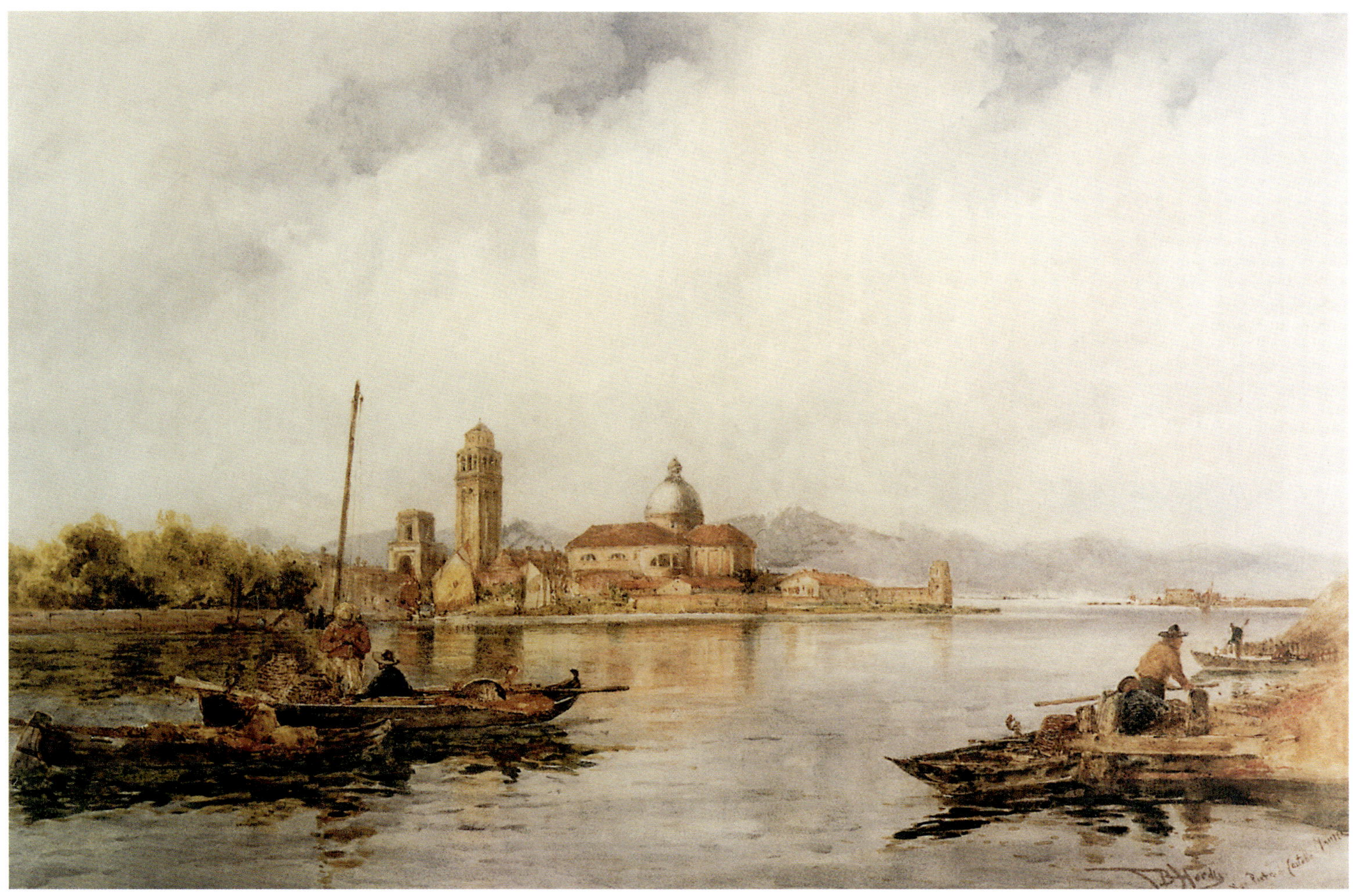

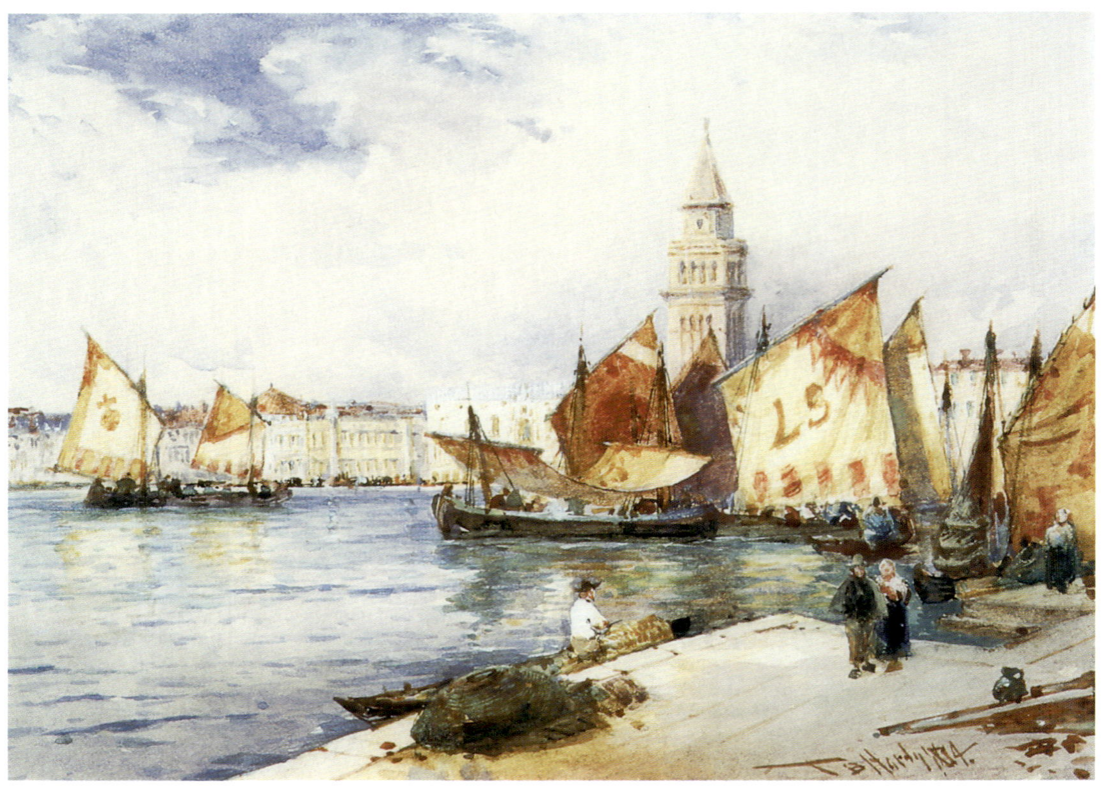

One of a pair of brilliant little watercolours by Hardy, showing a number of fishing boats and gondolas competing for berths on the Riva degli Schiavoni, one of Venice's most popular promenades. The Campanile and Ducal Palace are partly obscured by coloured sails, the Zecca and Columns of San Marco and Teodoro are just visible on the left. In the foreground a gondolier is seeking custom, so far without success, but the sun is shining and the woman, who appears to be arguing with her husband, may still get her way. A large wicker basket painted blue, of the type used for keeping fish alive, has been dumped on the jetty.

Above. Plate 6.39. **Basin of St Mark's.** *Signed and dated 1884. 12 x 17 cm (4¾ x 6¾ in.)*

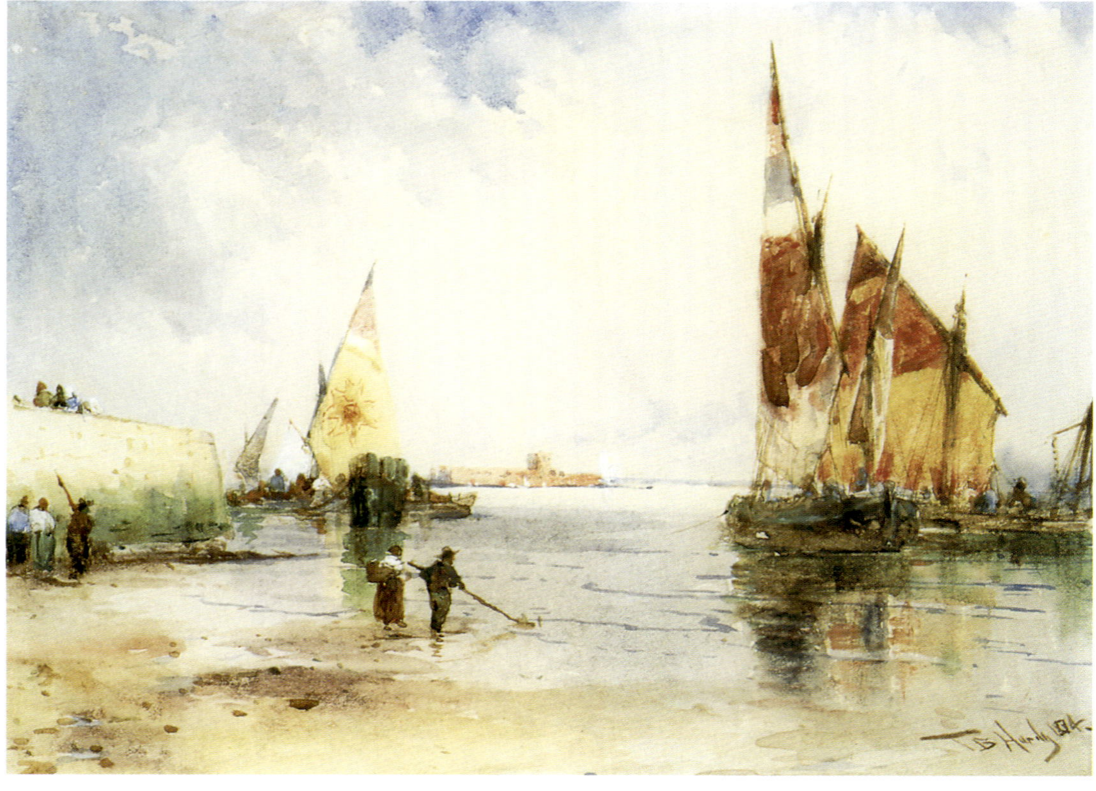

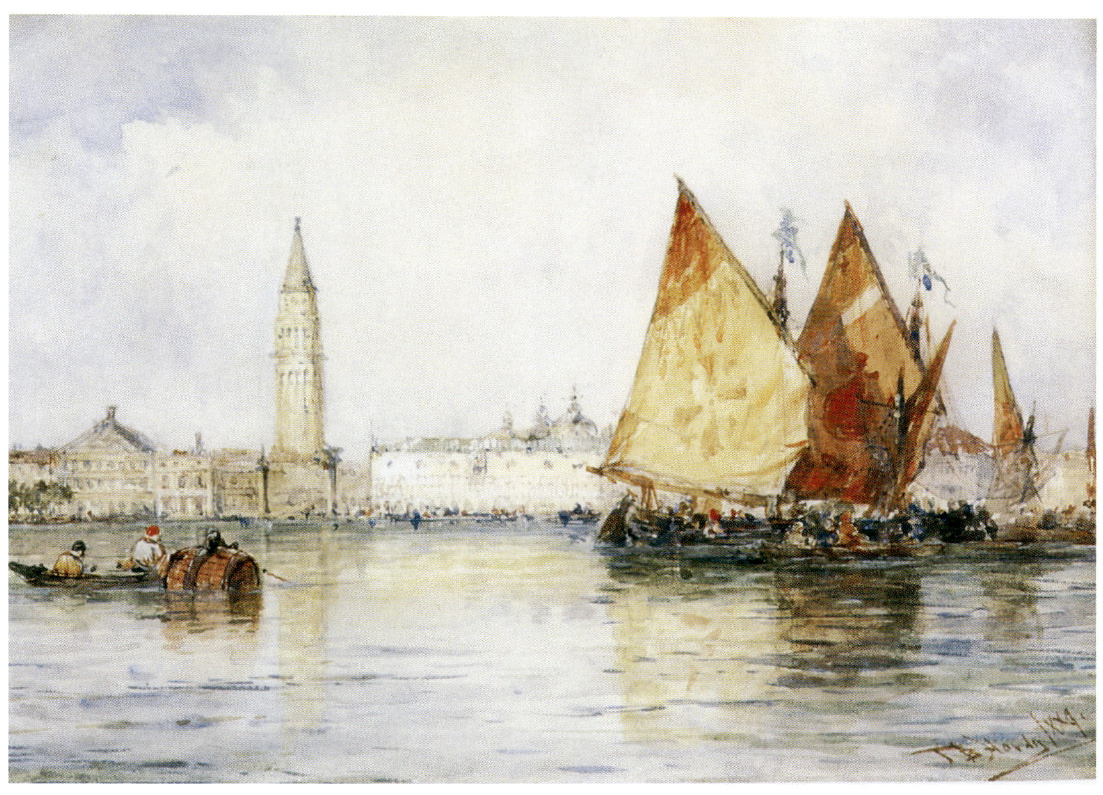

Plate 6.41. **The Basin of St Mark's.** *Signed and dated 1889. 12 x 17.5cm (4¾ x 6⅞ in.)*

Hardy understandably painted many views of the main buildings of St Mark's from various vantage points on the Riva degli Schiavoni and from boats moored in the Basin. This is one of the latter and the figure in the gondola wearing a red hat could well be a self-portrait. The gondola and buoy also provide balance to an image which might otherwise be too heavily weighted on the right where *deojozzi* are jostling for position on the jetty. This is quite a late watercolour in the chronography of his smaller Venetian paintings but rates very highly for all-round quality.

Opposite below. Plate 6.40. **Low Water in the Lagoon.** *Signed and dated 1884. 12 x 17cm (4¾ x 6¾ in.)*

Pair to Plate 6.39, this very accomplished watercolour shows us a beach on one of the outlying islands in the Lagoon. While the larger boats prepare for a day's fishing, some family members occupy themselves shrimping and gathering fresh bait. It is a fine, warm day and a most colourful scene, the sails reflecting beautifully in the gently rippling Lagoon. No doubt these people go through hard times but, for the onlooker, there seem to be many compensations.

Chapter 6 – Venice

This colourful watercolour shows two fishing boats that have just passed under the bridge spanning the Rio Ponte Lungo into the Canale della Giudecca. It takes a matter of seconds to re-step their masts and spread their sails. It would seem that the two boats are working in tandem with a sail stretched out ahead of them to provide shade and anti-glare when hunting fish feeding near the surface. On the left is a *deojozza* moored or drifting slowly down the canal, while further up on the right is Guidecca's principal monument, Palladio's church of Il Redentore, built between 1577 and 1592 in thanksgiving for the end of the 1576 plague which wiped out a third of the city's population.

Plate 6.42. **The Giudecca, Venice.** *Signed, inscribed and dated 1891. 17 x 24cm (6¾ x 9½in.)*

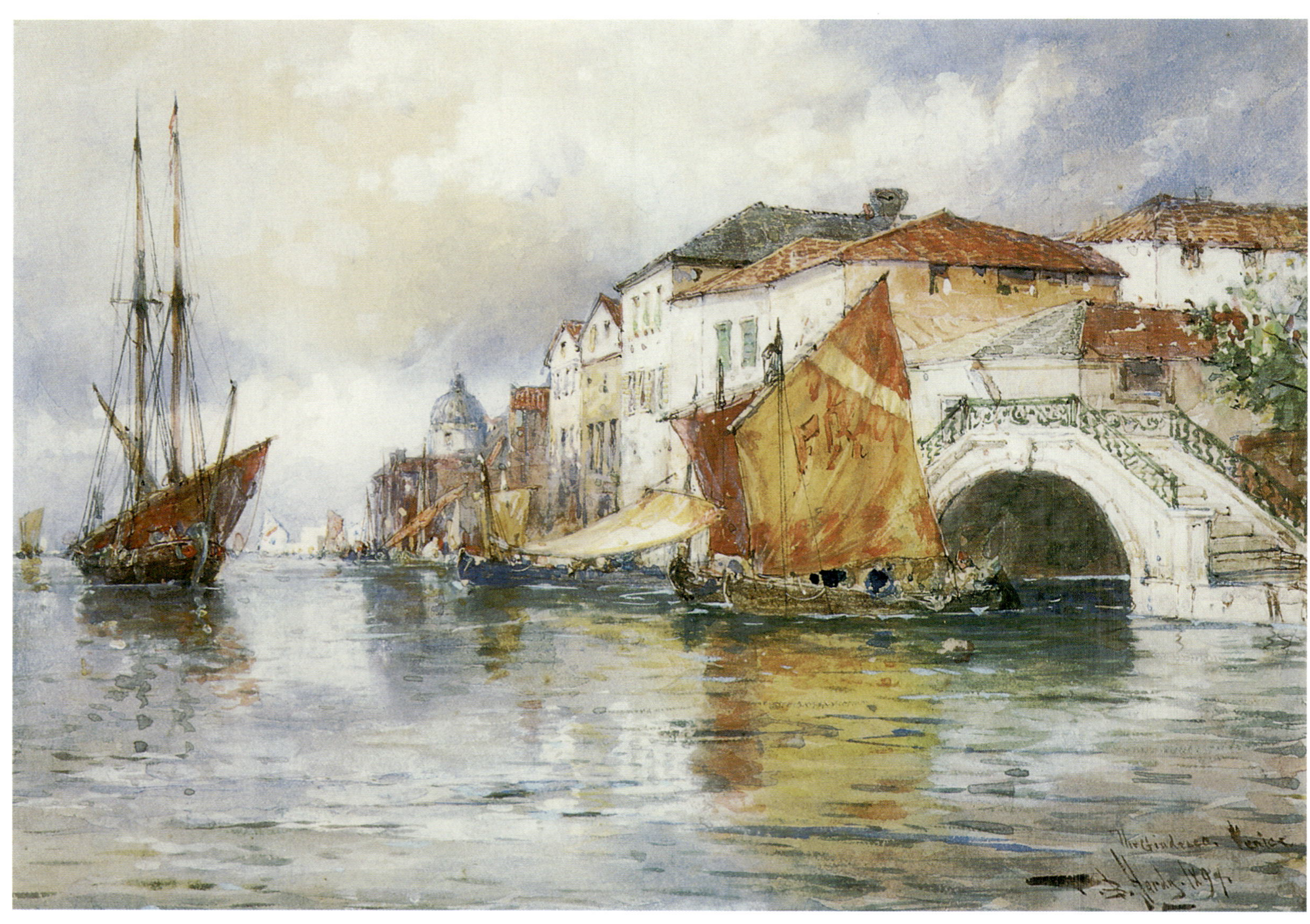

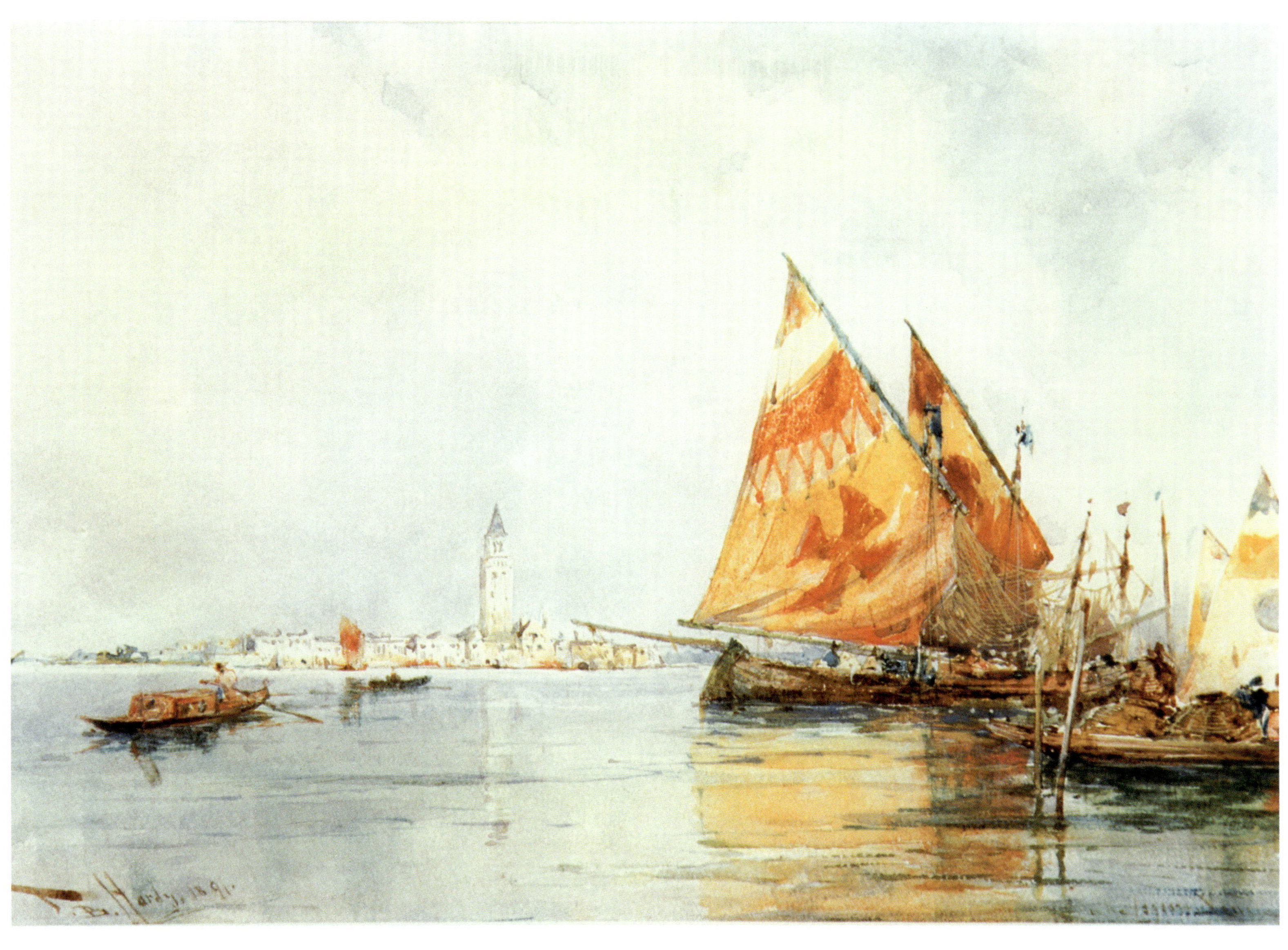

Plate 6.43. **The Lagoon, Venice.** *Signed and dated 1891. 18 x 26cm (7 x 10¼in.)*

Similar to many other views from or close to the Riva degli Schiavoni, Hardy is evidently looking towards the island of San Giorgio Maggiore. Perhaps wisely, except for the campanile, he has left the background indistinct. Artistically, the vast majority of Hardy's Venetian paintings are delightful and, where fishing boats and gear are concerned, accurate. However, his geography can sometimes be puzzling. In the examples illustrated in this chapter there are several instances of 'artistic licence' – campaniles, domes and Palladian features that have been 'borrowed' to embellish or balance a picture. Few artists have been completely innocent in this respect. When back in England, for Hardy to get every detail correct in a finished painting, based on sketches alone, would be remarkable. Once he had been recognised as an artist, Turner never bothered about detail. Hardy did, but was never obsessed by it. Creating a well-executed, emotion-inspiring picture that captured the atmosphere of the subject was the aim for which most artists strived. On the whole, Hardy succeeded.

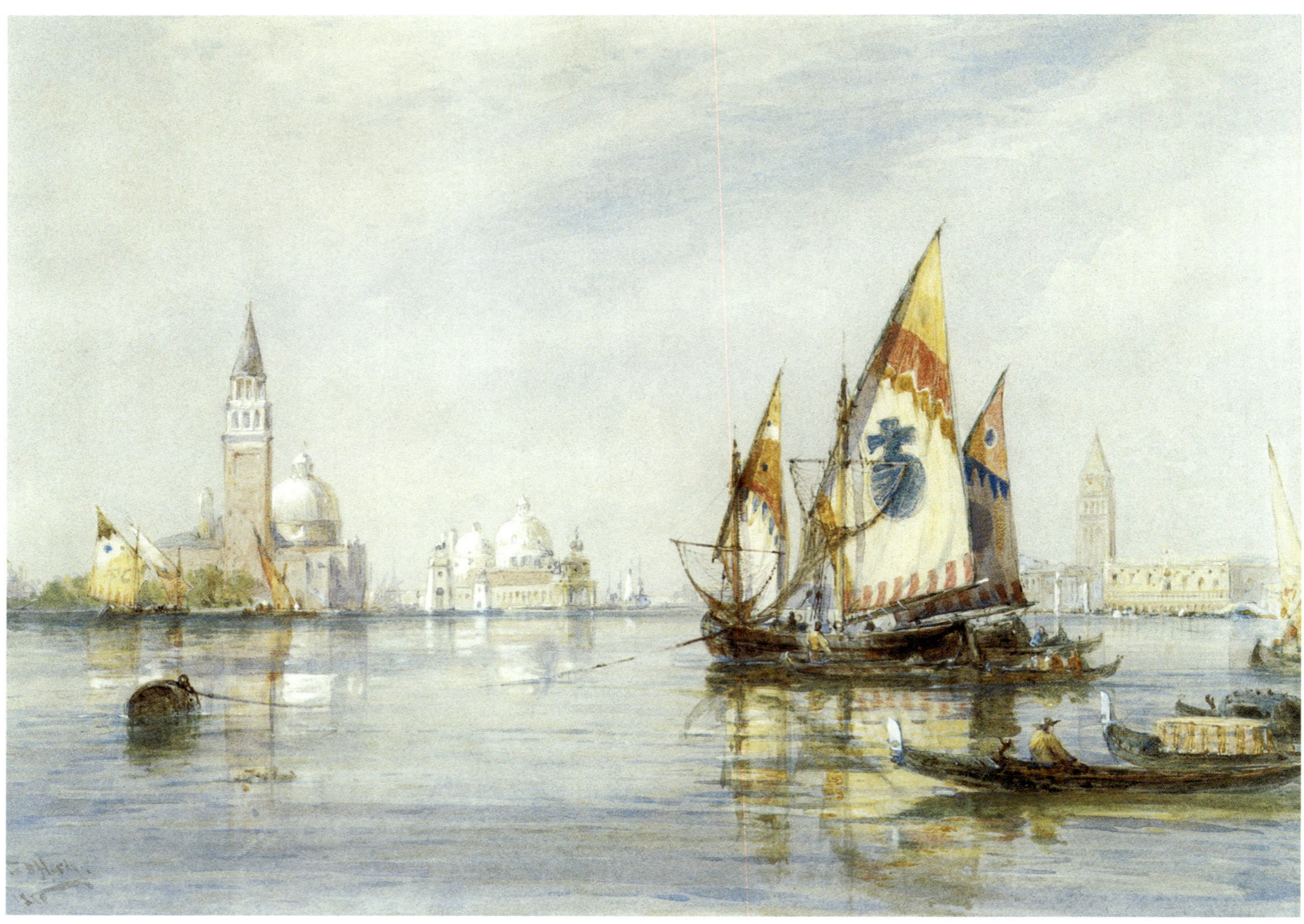

Here, in just the right amount of detail, Hardy has managed to give us San Giorgio Maggiore, the Basilica Santa Maria della Salute, the Campanile and the Palazzo Ducale as background to a group of fishing boats with their wonderfully coloured sails. All on a summer's day! Somehow, perhaps by his skilful painting of reflections in the peaceful waters of the Lagoon, Hardy has added an extraordinary feeling of timelessness and tranquillity to a man-made scene of consummate beauty.

Plate 6.44. **Venice.** *Signed and dated 1880. 24 x 34.5cm (9½ x 13⅝in.)*

So, the end of the Venetian chapter brings us to the end of our journey through Hardy's painting travels. The theme common to so much of his work – including his earliest paintings – is his portrayal of everyday life of fisherfolk and their craft. Whilst Hardy certainly painted to achieve an income, he also painted with love of his subject matter. Few nineteenth century artists have achieved the depth of understanding of light, translucency, tide and wind, cloud and sun. We are fortunate that so many of his great works survive to tell their story to this and future generations of lovers of marine watercolour art.

The final chapter introduces some of Hardy's contemporaries – any of whom might have been influenced by or in turn influenced Hardy himself.

Chapter 6 – Venice

This must qualify as one of the best watercolours that Hardy ever painted. He was, by general consent, at the summit of his prowess as an artist during the 1880s, and Venice always gave him additional inspiration, but this is indeed a most beautiful painting. A wonderful sunny day, a light breeze ruffling the surface of the water and filling out the sails of the fishing boats and, in the background, the historic panorama of San Marco – what more could an artist want, and Hardy made the most of it. There is plenty of activity too – Hardy has painted both fishermen and gondoliers hard at work, all contributing to the bright and colourful atmosphere. It is a fascinating composition with a lot of movement in the foreground as boats glide in and out of view. Many thousands of artists have painted this scene and, if global warming allows, many more will do so. Few will ever achieve this degree of excellence.

Plate 6.45. **Venice.** *Signed and dated 1887. 32 x 50cm (12⅝ x 19⅝in.)*

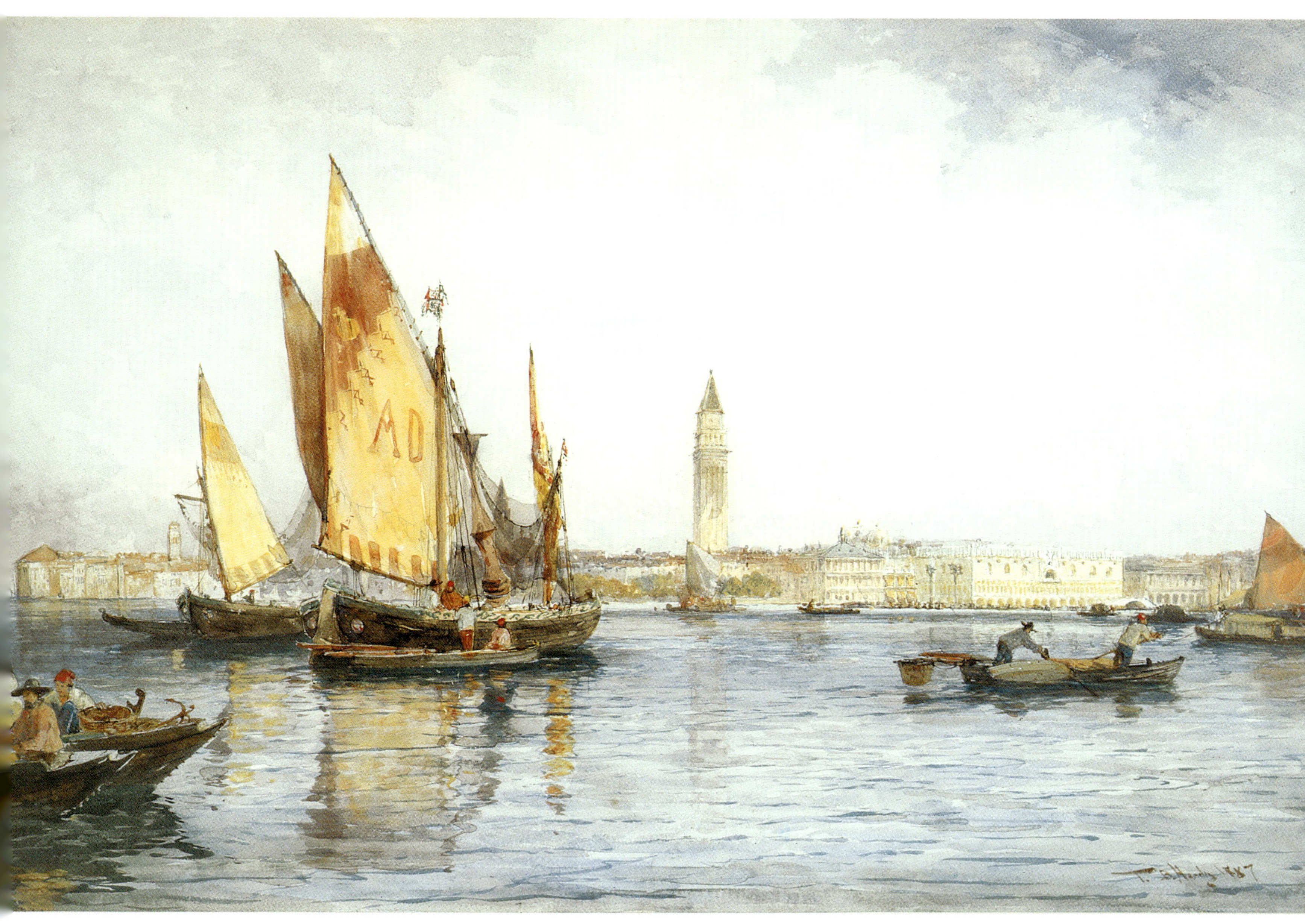

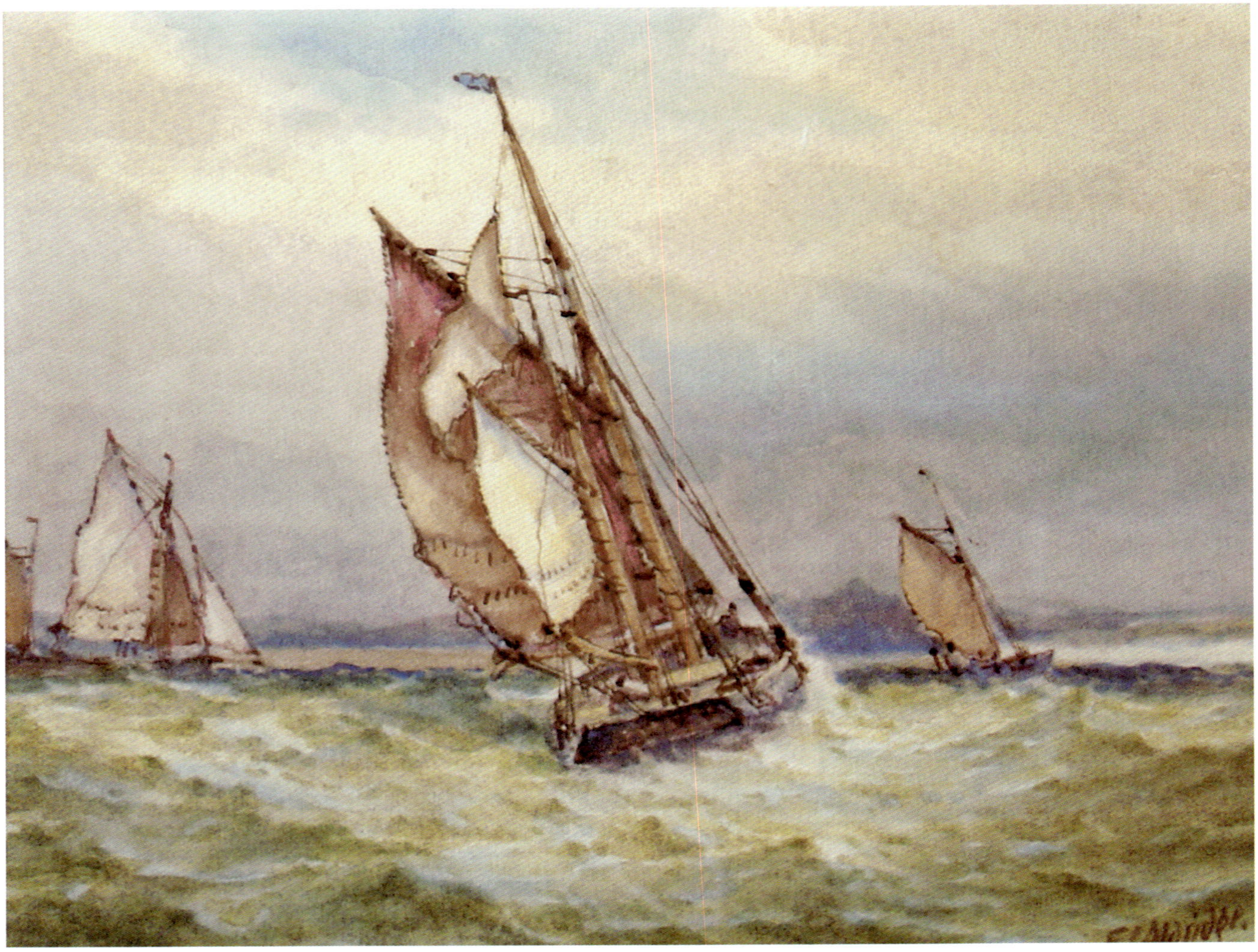

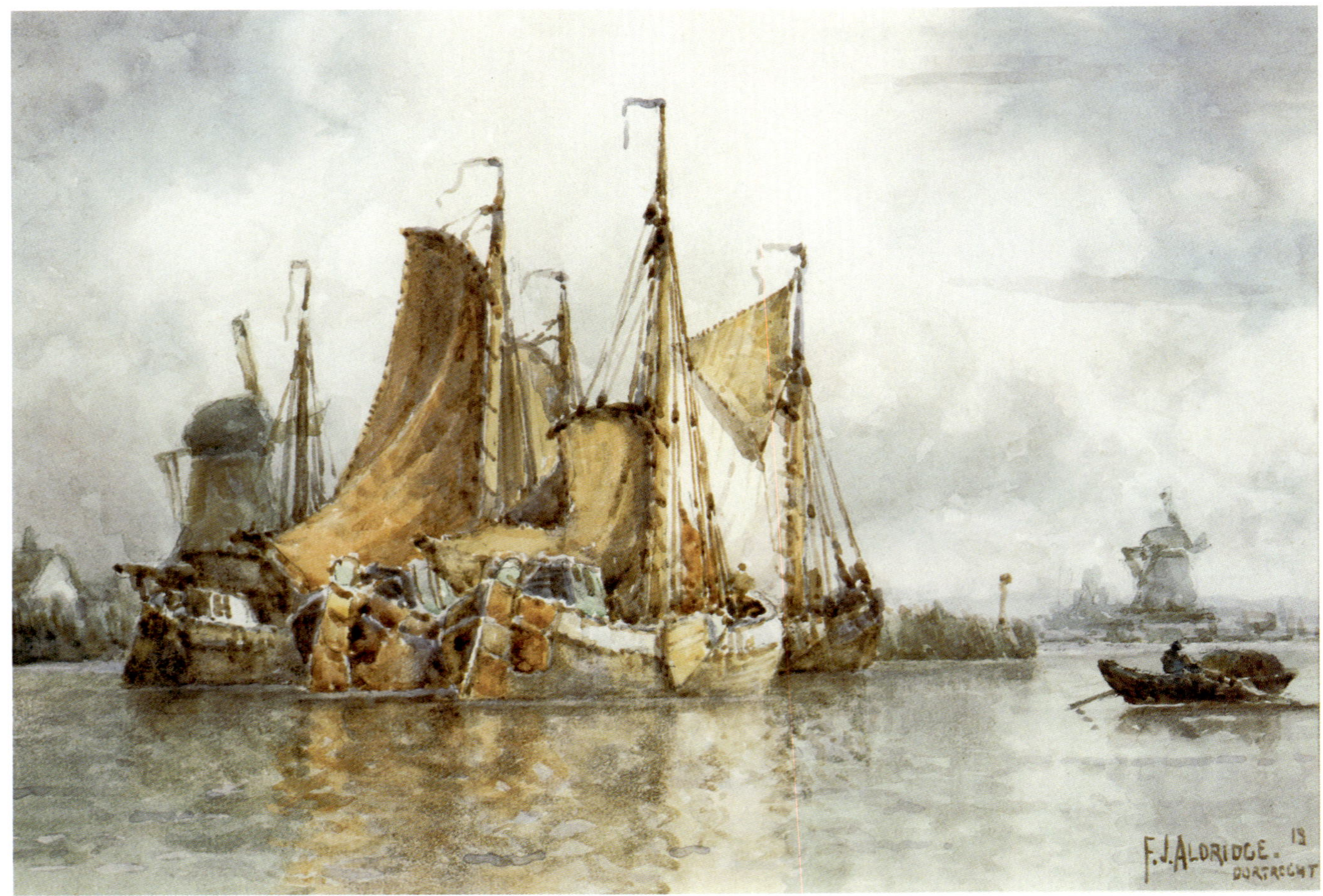

Hardy's Contemporaries

Mention has already been made of several early nineteenth century marine artists who were born and made their name many years before Hardy appeared on the scene. Works by Turner, Owen, Atkins, Bonington, Bentley, Carmichael, Chambers, Clarkson Stanfield, Cooke, Copley Fielding and the Joy brothers could be seen in museums, public art galleries and private collections. More importantly, a selection of these paintings were being reproduced in books and for hanging on the wall by a variety of printing techniques in both monochrome and colour.

So, for a budding artist in the 1860s there was an abundance of inspiration available from the past. There were also a large number of competent artists who made a living out of teaching the essentials, some of whom, like William Callow and William Leighton Leitch, were brilliant. Hardy is believed to have been self-taught but there must have been some interplay and exchange of ideas between him and those artists with whom he came into contact. The artists identified in the following pages are those with whom Hardy probably had some connection.

Frederick James ALDRIDGE (1850-1933)

A popular artist on the South Coast for many years, Aldridge lived most of his life in Worthing where, in due course, he set up a gallery which continued to bear his name until the late twentieth century. He painted many local coastal scenes, especially Shoreham and Littlehampton, and covered the southern coastline between Maldon to the east and Dartmouth to the west (Plate 7.1). He also painted the Dutch beaches (Plate 7.2) and,

Opposite above. Plate 7.1.
Frederick James Aldridge.
Fishing Smacks returning to Harbour, Rye beyond. Signed but undated, c.1910

Opposite below. Plate 7.2.
Frederick James Aldridge.
Dordrecht. Signed and inscribed but undated, c.1910

This is a very typical watercolour, an excellent example of how Aldridge painted the local fishing boats and the shallow waters through which they were sailing. The boats are all hard on the wind, a brisk north-easterly, which is whipping up a moderately rough sea. It is a well-balanced, attractive painting of an offshore scene that could be almost anywhere off the coast between Portsmouth and Dover. Aldridge has chosen Rye as the background recognising, perhaps, that its days as a fishing port were fast vanishing as the sea continued its retreat.

An example of Aldridge's inshore work showing his ability to paint reflections in calm water.

probably his most sought-after works, the Venetian waterways. He concentrated on watercolours of fishing boats in much the same way as Hardy, who clearly influenced him a great deal. His style is much looser than Hardy's and, in shallow waters, his palette is dominated by brown ochre and yellow green shades. Aldridge had talent enough to make a good living and his work still sells well, but his achievements were limited.

William Roxby BEVERLEY (1811-1889)

William was the son of a northern family of actors called Roxby who added the surname Beverley after enjoying their way of life in the East Riding of Yorkshire county town. In keeping with family theatrical tradition, Beverley's painting talents were utilised in scenery painting and design, culminating in his appointment as scenic director at Covent Garden from 1853 to 1884. Privately he also became a successful marine artist and exhibited twenty-five watercolours at the Royal Academy between 1865 and 1880. Never over-concerned with detail, he displayed great skill in achieving a warmth and serenity in his coastal scenes. Among these were a number of beach scenes of Scarborough (Plate 7.3) where, in all probability, he met Hardy and other local artists.

William Thomas Nicholas BOYCE (1858-1911)

Born in Blakeney, Norfolk, he moved with his family to South Shields where his father ran a small fleet of collier brigs. Destined to be a joiner, Boyce gave up his apprenticeship and worked for many years in a drapery store before spending the last ten years of his life as a full-time marine artist. Although accepted and successful in the North East, he never attempted to exhibit in London. Uninfluenced by others, he created and developed his own style of realistic and well-drawn seascapes featuring the shipping of the day plying its trade up the North East Coast. Being half a generation younger, he would probably have met Hardy when the latter was painting in the Tyneside area in the late '70s and '80s. Hardy would have approved of his straightforward, no-nonsense approach to marine painting but would not have felt threatened by the competition.

Plate 7.3. **William Roxby Beverley.** *Off Scarborough*

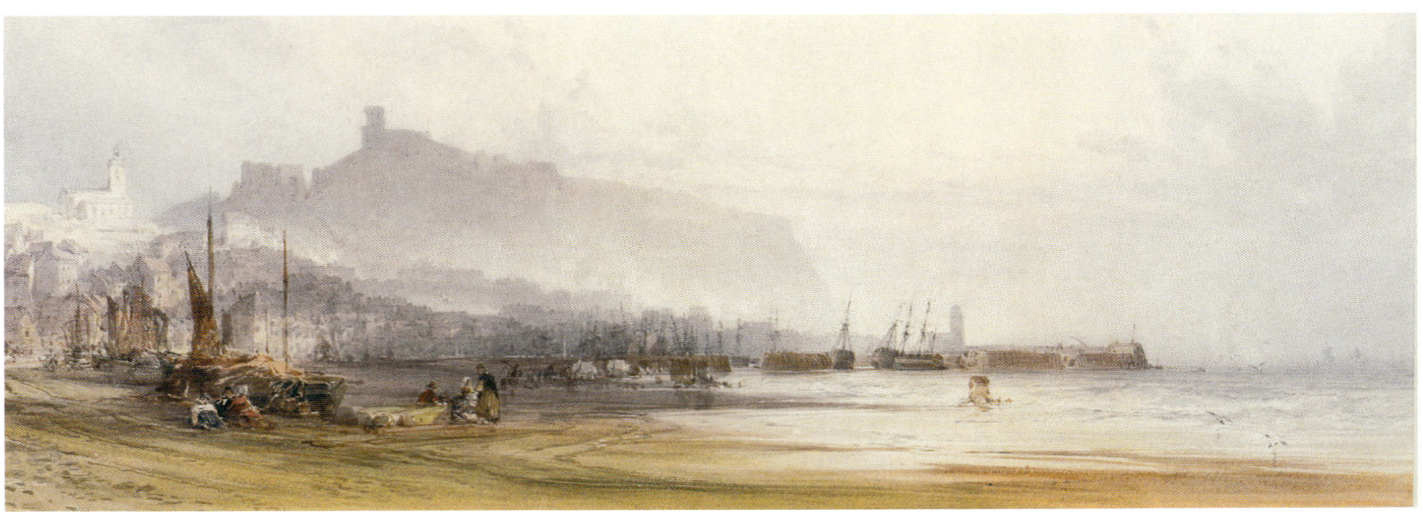

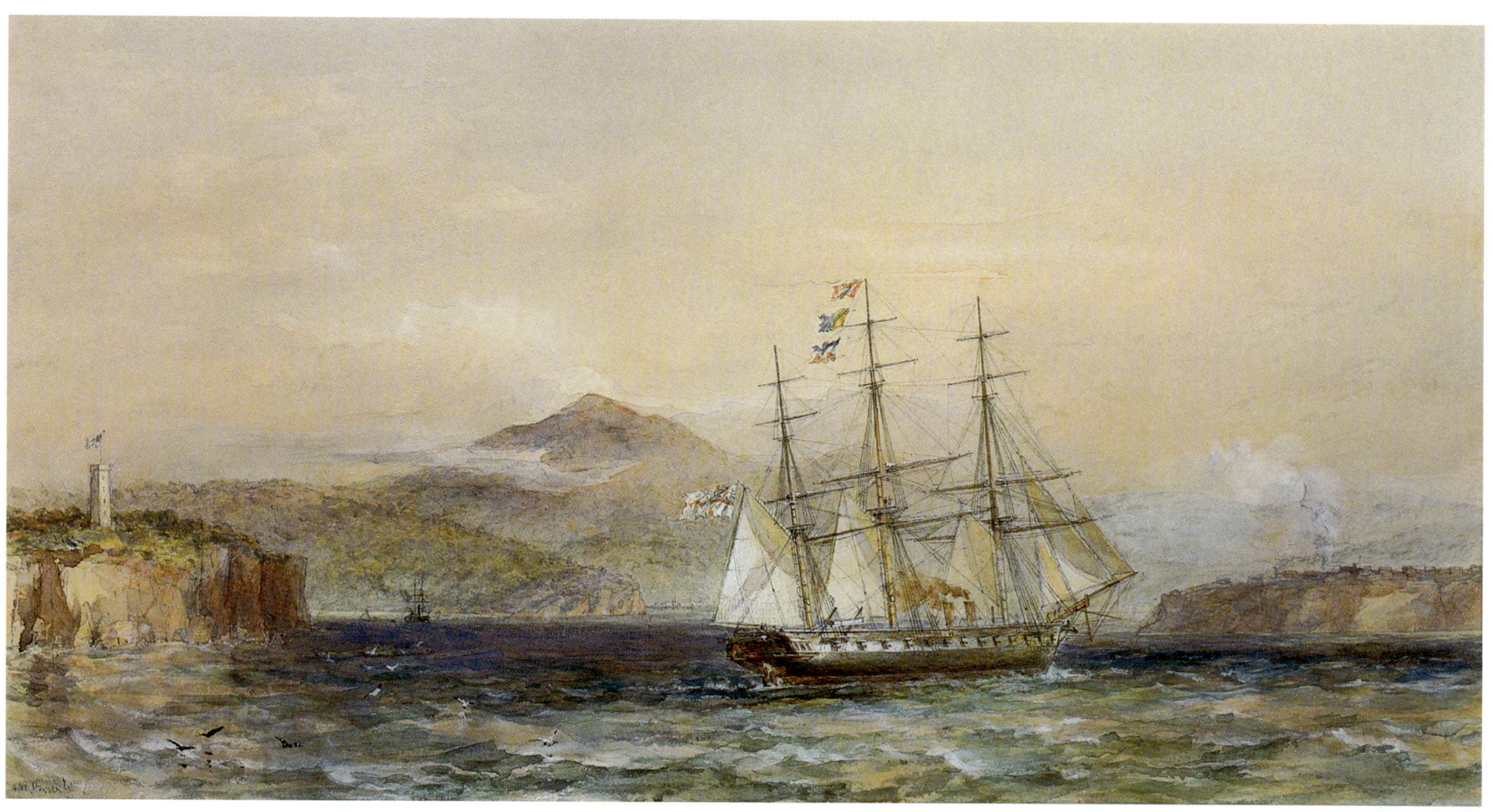

Plate 7.4. **Sir Oswald Walters Brierly,** *HMS* Galatea *(HRH Duke of Edinburgh) off Twofold Bay, New South Wales, standing in to communicate estimated time of arrival Sydney*

Sir Oswald Walters BRIERLY, RWS, FRGS (1817-1894)

Brierly was unquestionably the most widely travelled artist of the nineteenth century. He went out to Australia and New Zealand in 1841, making two surveying cruises on the Australian coast before returning to England in 1851. From 1854 to 1856 he was embarked in Captain Keppel's flagship in both the Baltic and Black Sea campaigns of the Crimean War and, with John Wilson Carmichael, could claim to be one of the first recorded war artists. His relationship with the Royal Navy continued when he accompanied the Duke of Edinburgh, Queen Victoria's youngest son, in two of his early commands, first in the frigate HMS *Racoon*, serving on the Home and Mediterranean stations in 1864, followed by a round-the-world voyage in HMS *Galatea* in 1867-8 (Plate 7.4). The latter included the first Royal visit to Australia, first to Adelaide and then to Sydney where the Duke was shot in the back by an Irish dissident. (He survived to continue a distinguished naval career, attaining the rank of Admiral of the Fleet.) Brierly was appointed Marine Painter in Ordinary to Queen Victoria in 1874 and was knighted in 1885. Elected to the Royal Society of Painters in Watercolours in 1872, he was a prolific artist whose paintings, often reproduced as lithographs and etchings, were eagerly sought after by the Victorian householder.

Chapter 7 – Hardy's Contemporaries

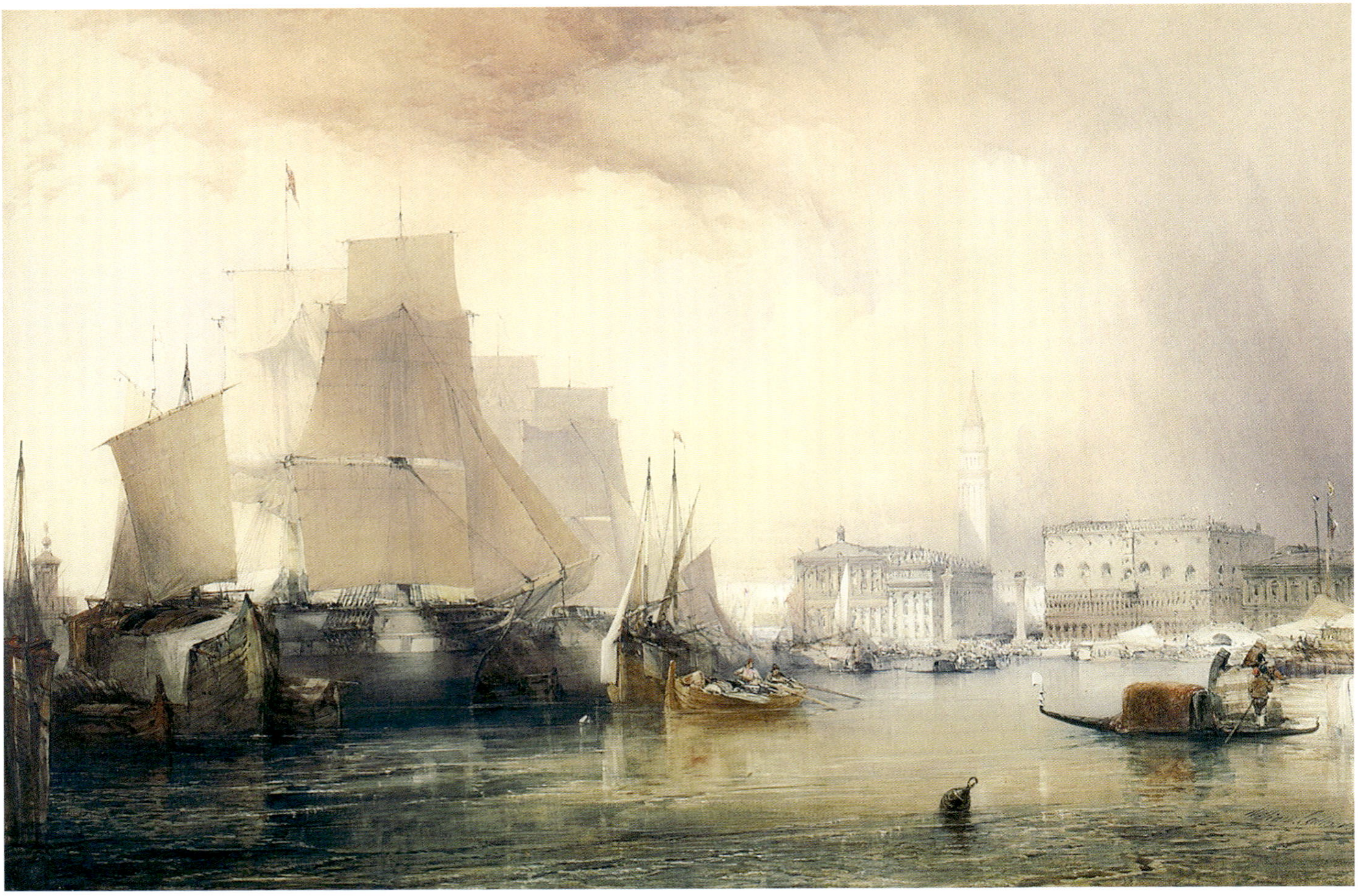

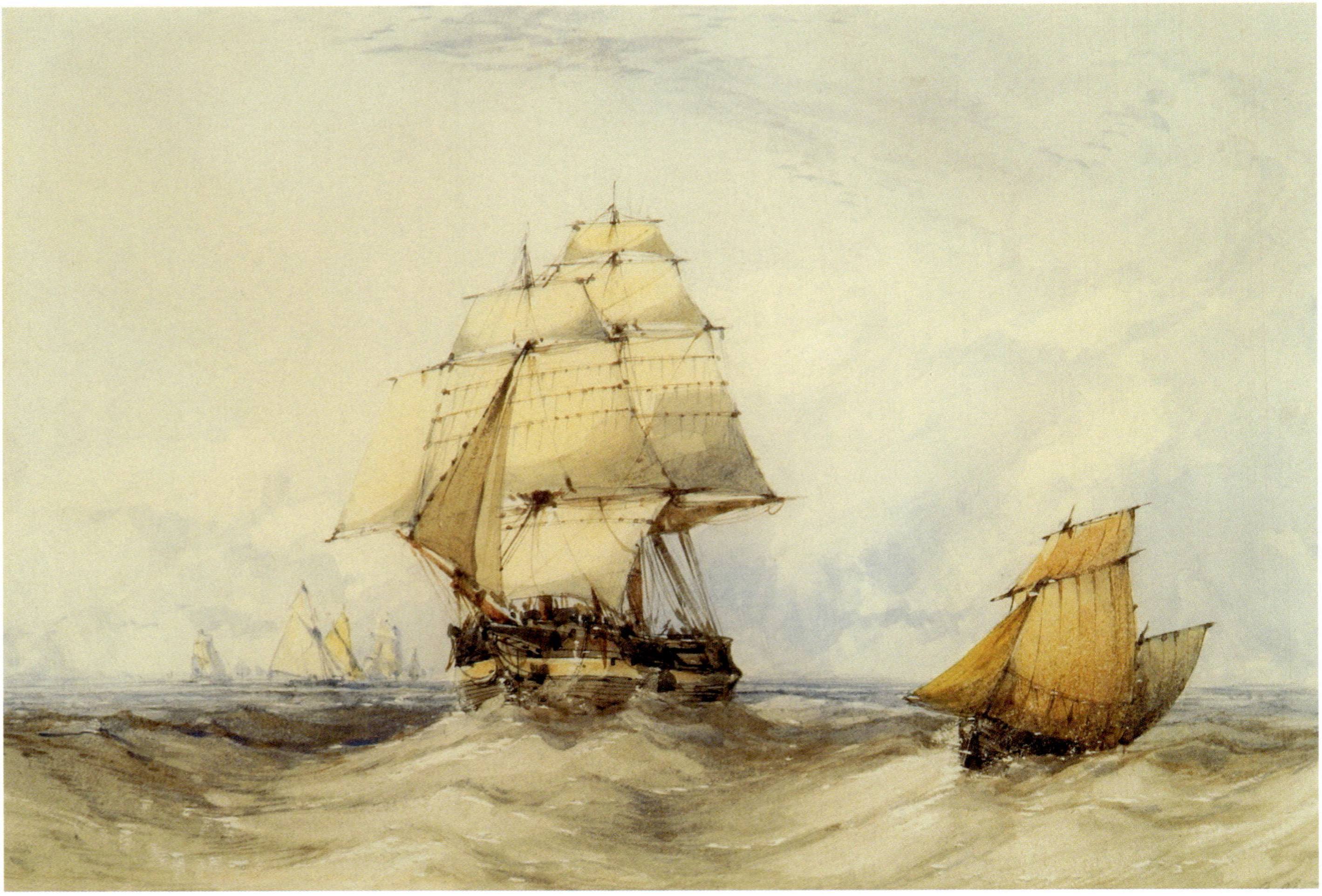

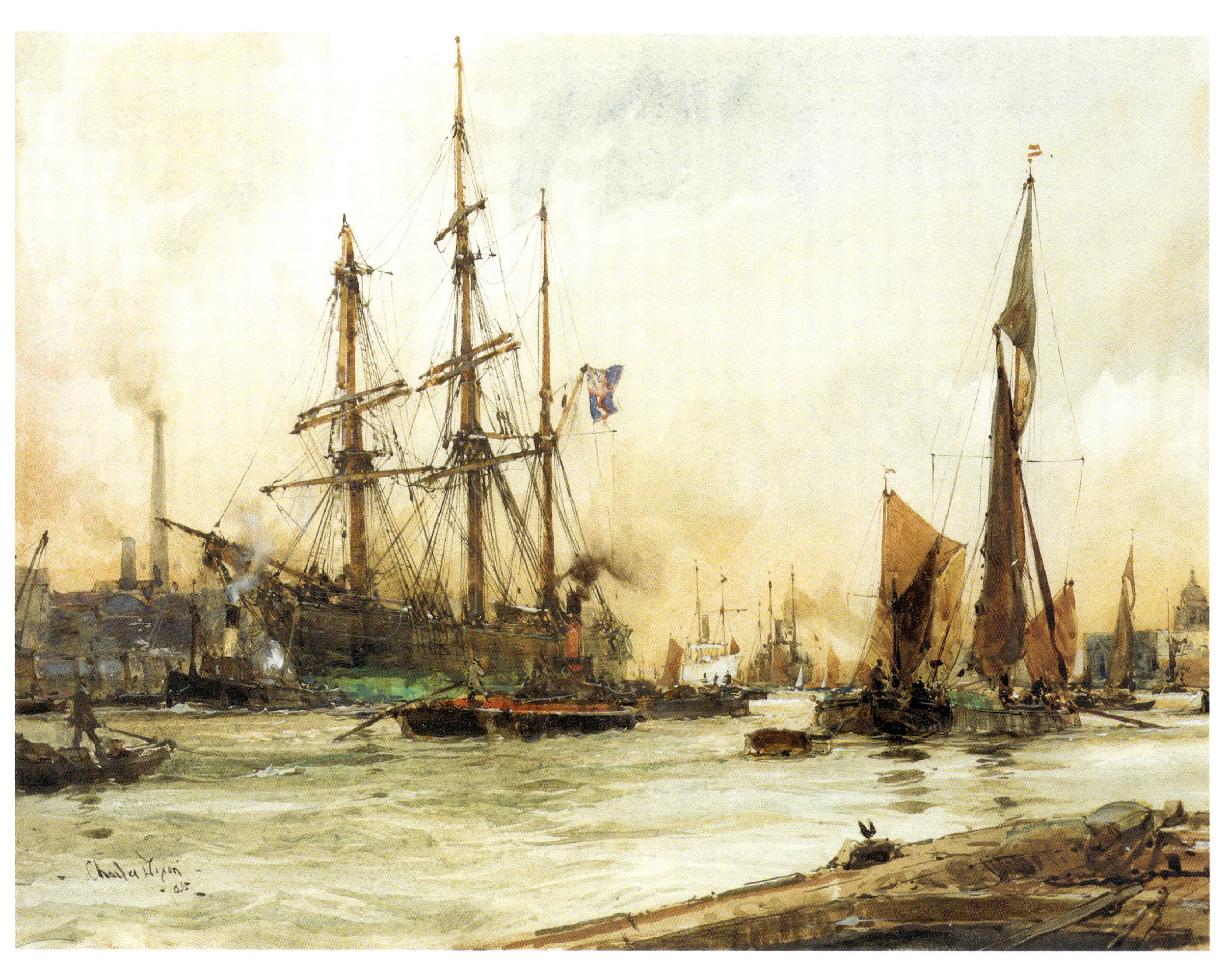

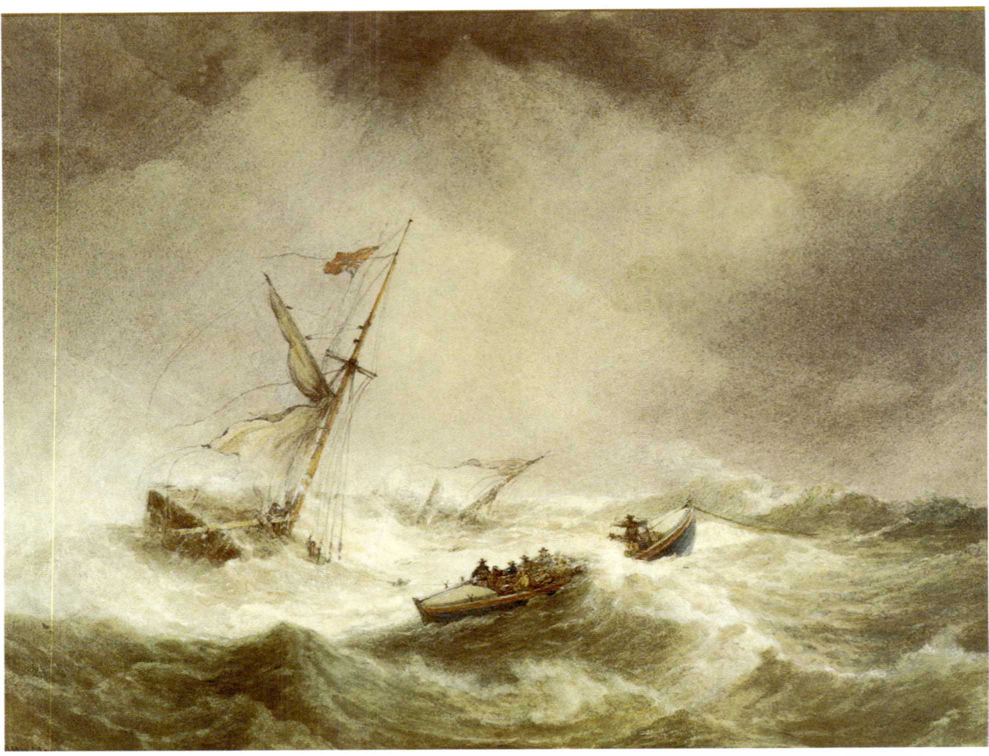

This is a fine example of Duncan's ability to paint a lifeboat rescue in all its dramatic realism. A two-masted brig has already lost its foremast, has broached to and is being swamped by heavy seas. The lifeboat has dropped a sea anchor and has just succeeded in getting a lifeline to one of the survivors. Duncan probably never went to sea with the lifeboatmen on a rescue mission but would have witnessed many from the shore and, like his present-day descendants, would have had great admiration for the RNLI.

Plate 7.8. **Edward Duncan.** *An RNLI Lifeboat attempting a Rescue.* Signed and dated 1872

Edward DUNCAN, RWS (1803-1882)

The son-in-law of William John Huggins, a well-known ship portraitist holding the appointment of Marine Artist to William IV, Duncan served his apprenticeship as an engraver of coaching and marine prints, later concentrating on painting watercolours, usually of marine and coastal subjects. Although he was born nearly forty years before Hardy, Duncan produced some particularly fine marine watercolours during his late sixties and seventies when Hardy was making his name. Interestingly, Duncan exhibited ten marine watercolours at Suffolk Street (The Royal Society of British Artists) between 1876 and 1882, when Hardy had exactly the same number of paintings accepted for exhibition. Hardy was elected RBA two years later and went on to exhibit just under a hundred watercolours in all between 1871 and 1896. Living part of the year on the Gower peninsula, Duncan had first-hand knowledge of stormy weather and the many occasions when ships were wrecked on the Mumbles. There can be no doubt that the two met and that Hardy was influenced by Duncan's immensely powerful portrayal of storms, disasters and rescues at sea (Plate 7.8).

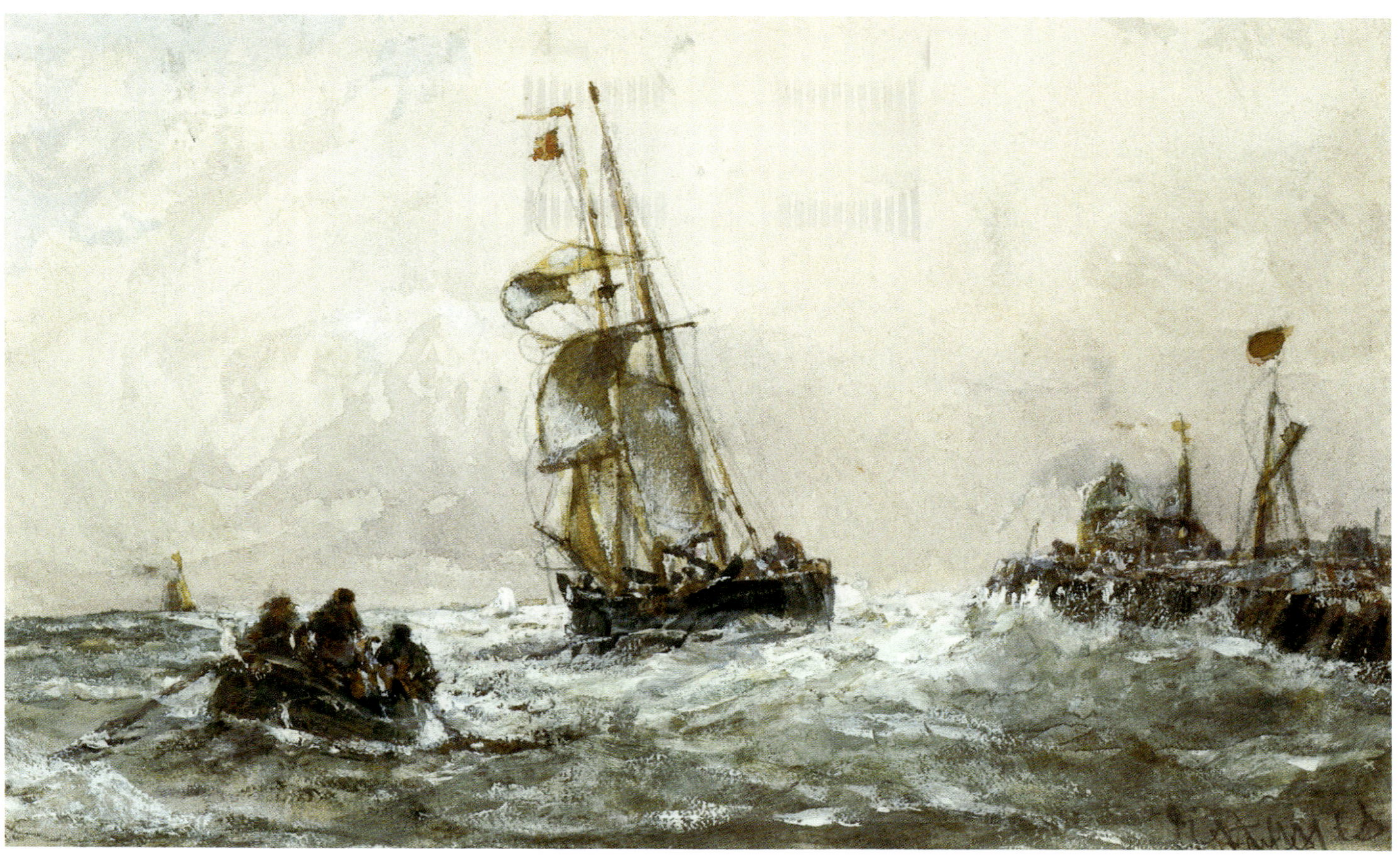

Plate 7.9. **Edwin Hayes.**
Leaving the Pier in a Strong Blow. Signed

A typical example of his work, demonstrating his use of bodycolour and innate ability to paint a realistic sea. Nothing is still in this watercolour – wind, waves, fishing boats and their crews are all, at this moment, restless and agitated. This artist understands the elements of marine painting.

Edwin HAYES, RHA, RI (1820-1904)

Born in Bristol, Hayes went to Dublin at an early age and studied art at the RDS Schools. After spending his early twenties at sea, he returned to work for ten years in Dublin, exhibiting at the Royal Hibernian Academy from 1842. He came to London in 1852, where he painted scenery at the Adelphi and elsewhere, and soon started exhibiting at the major societies and galleries, quickly gaining a reputation as a skilful marine artist in both oils and watercolours. He visited France, Spain and Italy, but most of his subjects were taken from the eastern and southern coasts of England.

Many connoisseurs believed he had few equals at painting the sea (Plate 7.9), especially a rough sea, and his small, quickly and loosely drawn sketches have always been greatly admired. He tended to use a lot of bodycolour, rather more than Hardy, but that aside the two artists had much in common.

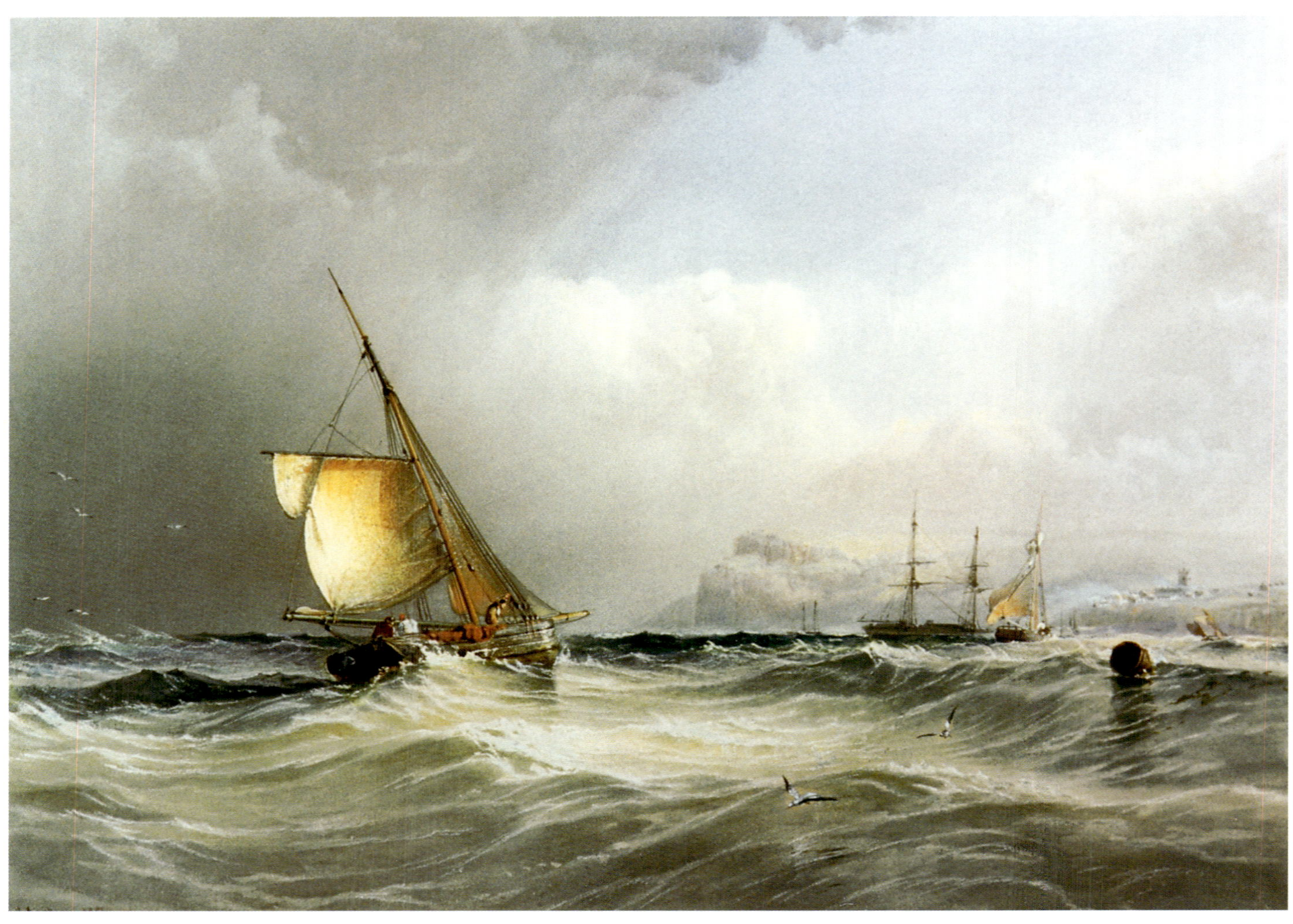

Samuel Phillips JACKSON, RWS (1830-1904)

The son and pupil of Samuel Jackson, the father figure of the Bristol School, he began by exhibiting oil paintings in London in his early twenties. Having been elected as an Associate Member of the Old Watercolour Society in 1853, from then on he concentrated almost exclusively on watercolours. His earlier subjects were found in and around the coasts of Devon and Cornwall and the Bristol Channel. He also visited and painted in the Channel Islands and briefly on the North-east coast. Two of his marine studies were praised by Ruskin: '…the breaking of the waves as true as can be and both pictures are as delicate and earnest in perception of sea and sky'. He was evidently well known for his handling of cloudy, misty and hazy atmosphere (Plates 7.10 and 7.11). After 1870, when living in Henley, most of his subjects were taken from the Thames Valley, but it is for some of his very competent coastal scenes that he will be chiefly remembered.

Opposite above. Plate 7.10.
Samuel Phillips Jackson.
Shipping off the Coast. Signed
and dated 1856

A convincing offshore scene.

Plate 7.11. **Thomas Bush
Hardy.** *A Misty Morning after
S.P.Jackson.* Signed with
monogram

This interesting watercolour is rare proof that, from time to time, Hardy and his contemporaries had a go at copying each other's works or styles or both. This was a genuine attempt by Hardy to copy, on a small scale, an actual S.P.Jackson watercolour and he was meticulous about the inscription 'after'. He also signed with a monogram rather than a full signature, again an extremely unusual practice for Hardy. The question remains – to whom was this watercolour presented? More than likely, to Jackson himself!

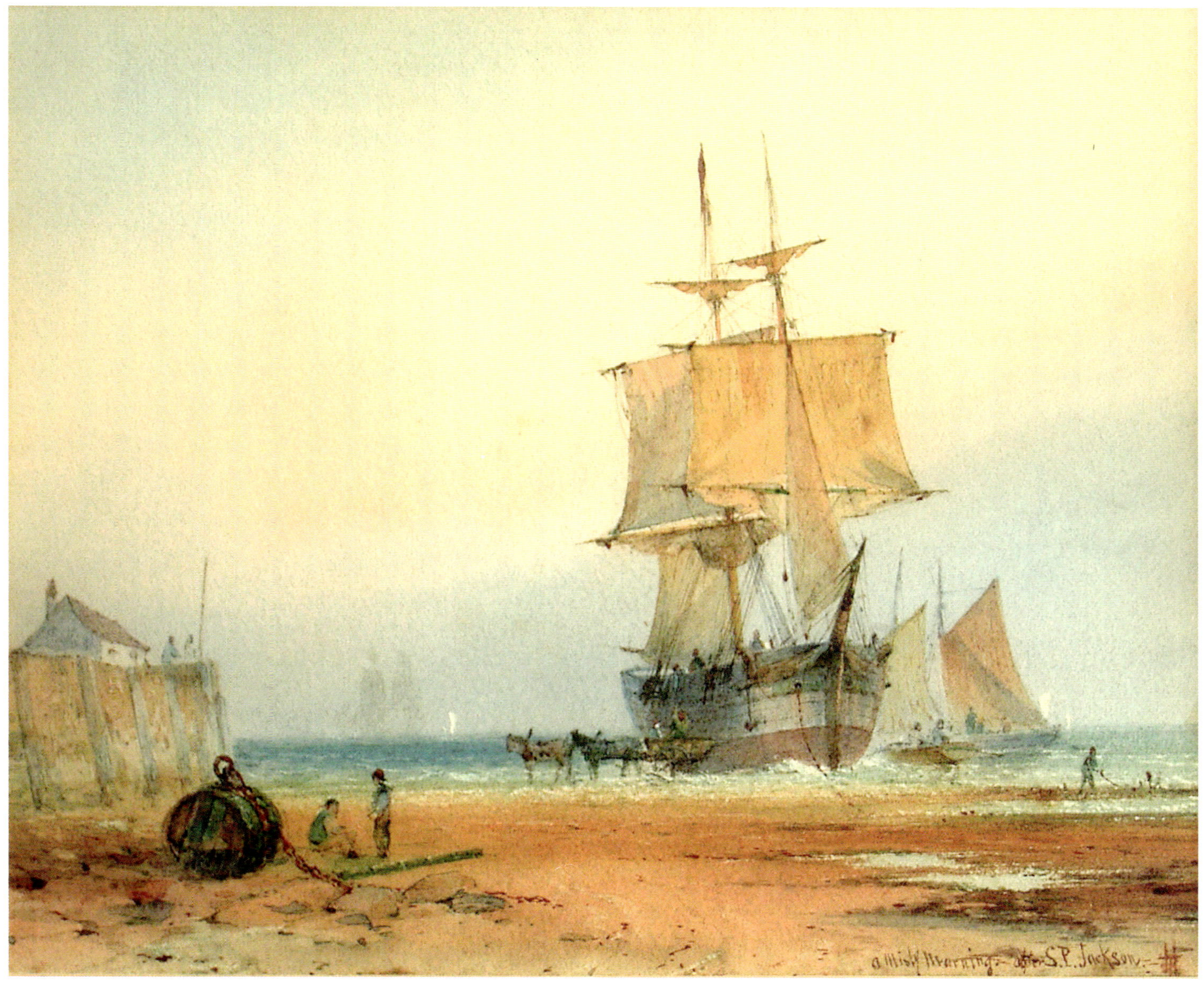

William Leighton LEITCH, RI (1804-1883)

Leitch was primarily a landscape painter who, after spending many years travelling in Europe, settled down in London as a drawing master. His ability to teach soon came to the notice of Queen Victoria who, for many years, employed him as her personal tutor. It is very doubtful that Hardy ever met Leitch but more than possible that he saw and was influenced by some of his watercolour views of Venice.

A well-composed watercolour of San Giorgio de Maggiore viewed from moorings close to the Arsenale. Leitch has captured the warmth and tranquillity of a calm summer's afternoon; very little activity as most of the fishermen would be resting beneath their jury awnings. The sky holds out some hope of an evening breeze, but that can wait.

Plate 7.12. **William Leighton Leitch**. *Venice.* Signed and inscribed.

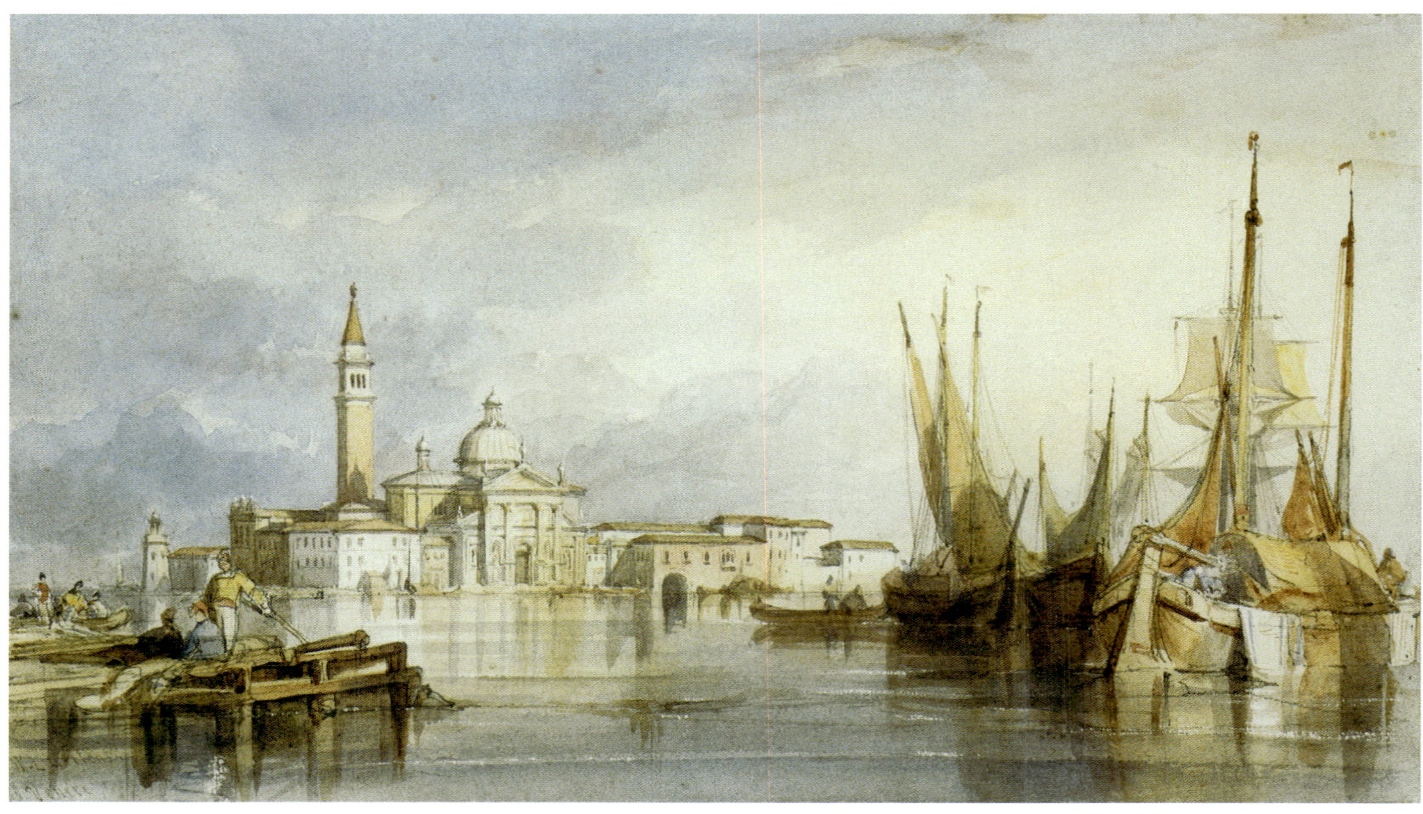

Robert Malcolm LLOYD (fl.1879-1900

Lloyd was a very competent marine and coastal artist working towards the end of the nineteenth century whose ability has not yet been fully recognised. Living nearly all of his life in Kent he made the most of his easy access to the Thames Estuary and the Channel coasts. Although there is no evidence to support the belief that he met Hardy, his paintings of the sea in anything above a moderate breeze suggests that he was very much influenced by Hardy's work in the late 1870s. Whilst recognising his artistic talents, he seldom travelled far from home, which greatly limited his choice of subject, and his colouring and feel for 'light' generally is open to criticism.

Plate 7.13. **Robert Malcolm Lloyd**. *In the Channel.* Signed and inscribed.

This watercolour is a good example of Lloyd at his best. The fishing smack on a broad reach in the foreground makes a fine sight. A stiff southerly breeze is blowing and the sea is beginning to get quite rough: no need to reduce sail at present but it will need watching. Sail and steam and the sea are well drawn – everything moves!

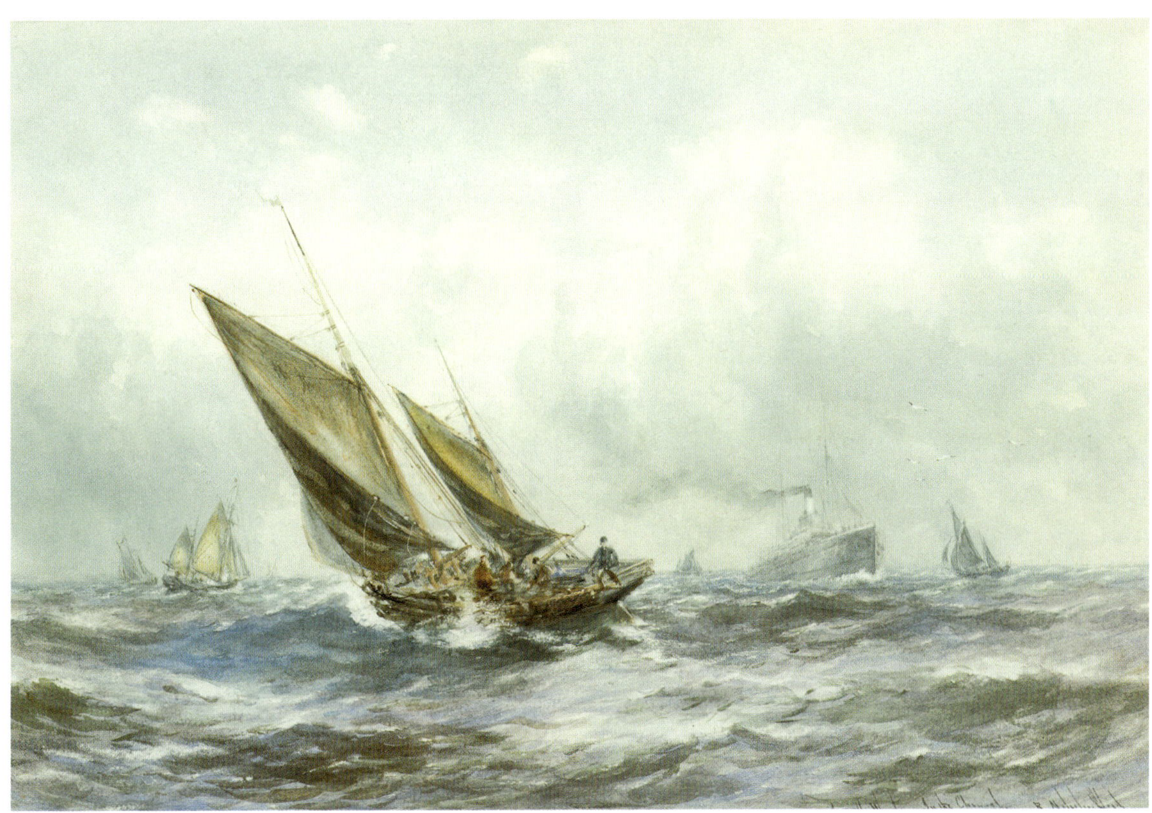

Frank Henry MASON RI, RBA (1876-1965)

Educated in the Training Ship *Conway,* Mason spent his early years at sea before becoming an engineer in shipbuilding. In his mid-twenties he took up marine painting, mainly in watercolour, and before long was exhibiting at many galleries including the Royal Academy. During the First World War he served in the Royal Naval Volunteer Reserve as a Lieutenant and, in addition to his work as a 'war artist', was involved in introducing 'dazzle' camouflage for both warships and merchant ships to confuse U-Boats – with great success. After the war he continued illustrating books and became well known for his posters advertising railway, shipping and cigarette companies. He continued painting in both watercolours and oils throughout the Second World War and into the 1950s. Prior to 1914, when he 'mixed and matched' sail and steam vessels with different coastline backgrounds, his watercolour technique gave his seas a remarkable impression of fluidity and movement.

Mason obviously visited Venice between the wars and, like all artists, was captivated by its beauty. Here he has shown a number of fishing boats under way but making very slow progress in the light airs. But, with the white dome of the Santa Maria della Salute in the background, glinting in the sunlight, they make a fine picture.

Plate 7.14. **Frank Henry Mason.** *Santa Maria della Salute, Venice.* Signed.

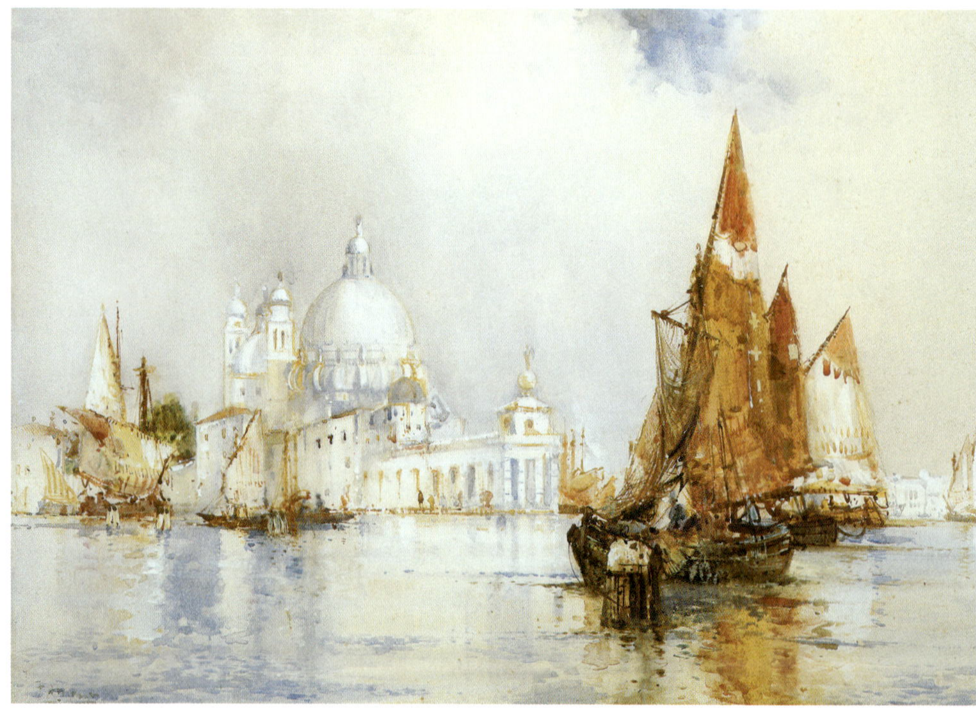

Chapter 7 – Hardy's Contemporaries

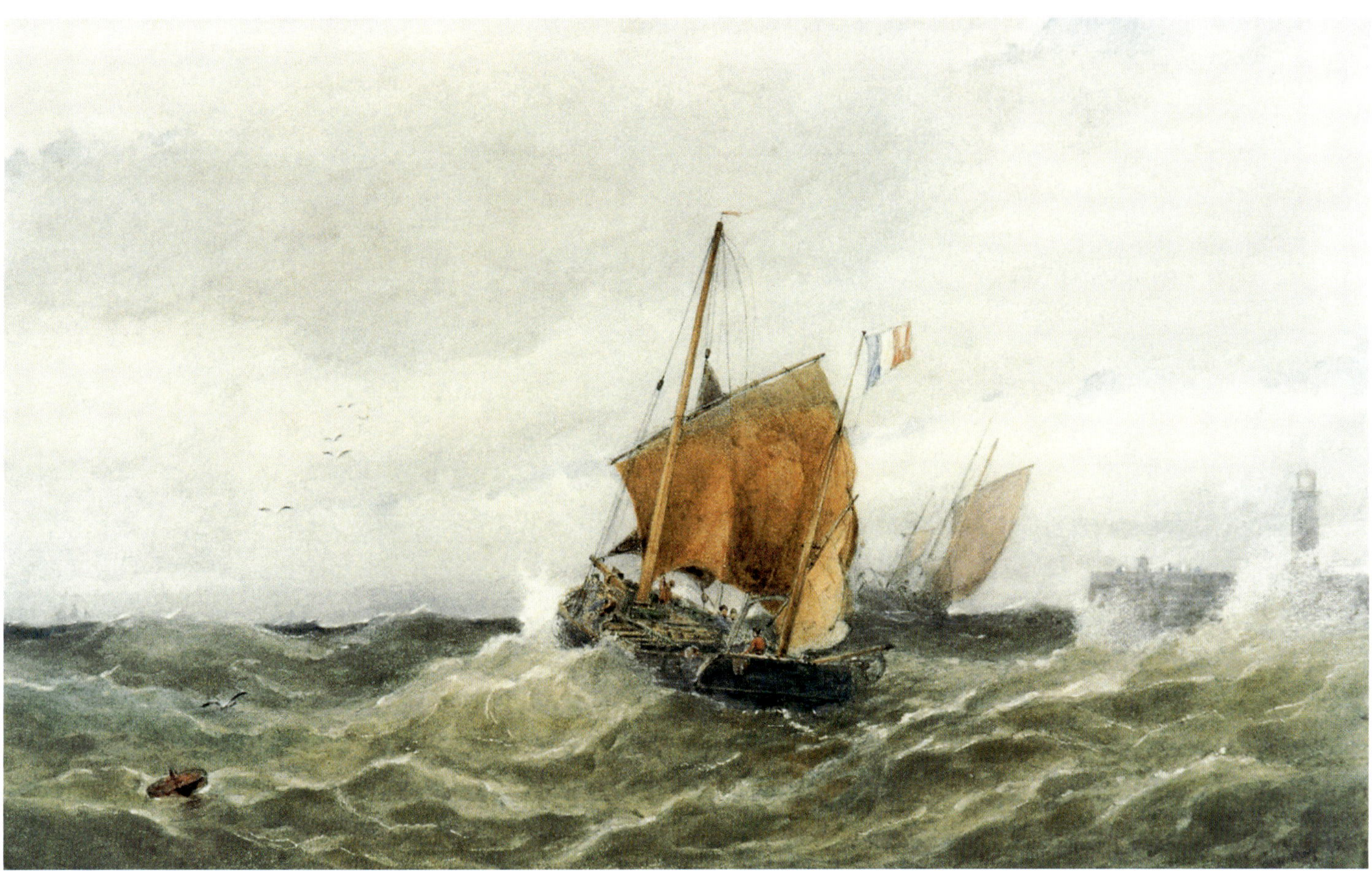

Plate 7.15. **Walter William May.** *French Fishing Vessels Offshore in a Lively Sea.* Signed and dated (18)75

Leaving harbour in a fresh sou'westerly, this large lugger is experiencing a short, steep sea off the pierhead. Captain May has applied all his knowledge and skill in creating a most realistic scene. Bearing in mind the date and location of this watercolour, it is almost inconceivable that May never met Hardy. There is much to admire here and many similarities in colouring and technique. May was the older man by ten years and could have passed on some very useful tips. He had already established a reputation – Hardy would have been happy to accept his advice.

Walter William MAY, RI (1831-1896)

Born in London, May served in the Royal Navy from 1850 to 1870, retiring as a captain. He began exhibiting marine watercolours in 1859, many of them drawing on his experience at sea visiting Scandinavia, the Baltic and the Mediterranean. Like Hardy, he also painted coastal, river and lake scenes in the United Kingdom, France, Holland and Venice. His paintings were tidy and well constructed and the detail always correct – doubtless due to his naval training where officers were required to produce accurate drawings of coastlines and navigational hazards. Although he seemed to prefer painting calm and tranquil scenes, Plate 7.15 shows that, as a seagoing naval officer, he not only had considerable experience of stormy seas, but also knew how to paint them.

Henry MOORE, RA, RWS (1831-1895)

The ninth of thirteen sons of William Moore, a portrait painter, Henry was trained by his father, the York School of Design and, from 1853, at the RA Schools. Until 1857 he painted landscapes from many parts of England and from Switzerland; thereafter he was better known for his marine paintings, in particular those resulting from painstaking pencil studies of the movement of ships in differing sea, swell and wave conditions. His use of colour, reflecting the ever-changing sky, ranged from cold greys to deep blues and greens. Invariably the sea was, in his view, of infinitely greater importance than the ships upon it. Emphasising this, he would often reduce the images and place them on or near the horizon. Some of his watercolours were exceptionally good – he was, after all, a Royal Academician – others a dismal failure. Hardy too experimented from time to time, also with mixed results.

Richard Henry NIBBS (1816-1893)

Nibbs was born in Brighton and died there. His first career was as a musician, where he taught the violin and 'cello and played with the Brighton Theatre Royal Orchestra. An inheritance allowed him the freedom to pursue a career in painting and, for most of his life, this self-taught artist found suitable marine and coastal subjects within fifty miles of Brighton where he continued to keep a studio. He also painted some coastal views and landscapes in France, Holland and Germany. His colouring was a little drab but his overall technique and sensible choice of subject brought him success.

Arthur Wilde PARSONS (1854-1951)

Living in Bristol, Parsons was a prolific painter of shipping in the Bristol Channel, some in fairly muted colours, albeit realistic. Following visits to Italy and Venice, and inspired by the clear light and strong blues of the Mediterranean, he developed a much more colourful approach to all his work. He exhibited eighteen paintings at the Royal Academy between 1867 and 1904. Unless they met in Venice, it is unlikely that Hardy had any close contact with Parsons. So far as is known, Hardy never availed himself of the four hour journey from Paddington to Bristol on Brunel's broad gauge Great Western Railway.

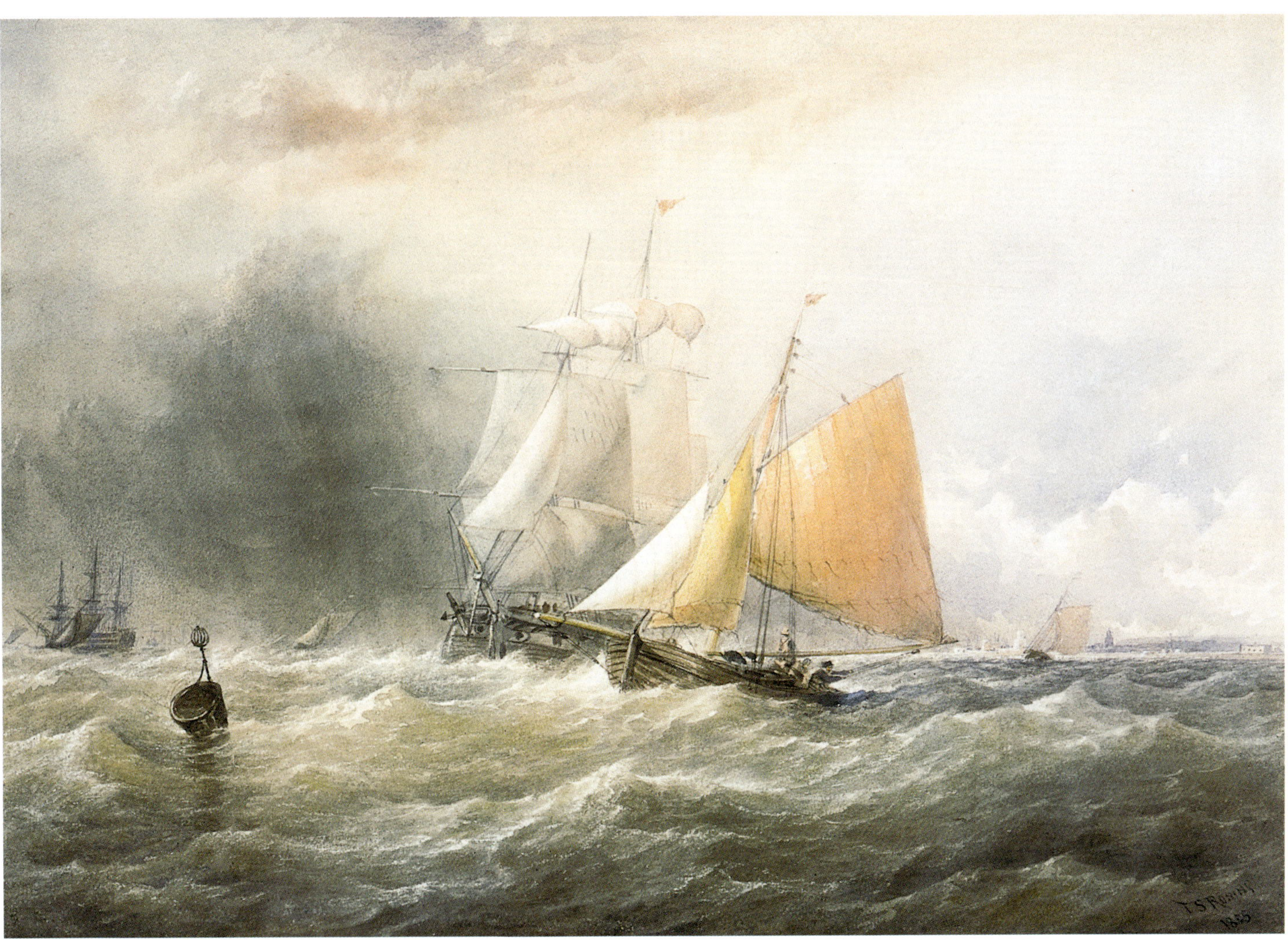

Plate 7.16. **Thomas Sewell Robins.** *Square-Riggers and other Vessels in a Squall Offshore.* Signed and dated 1855

A typical T.S. Robins marine watercolour showing his attention to detail in this drawing of sailing vessels and, above all, his brilliant portrayal of the sea and sky in a sudden squall.

Thomas Sewell ROBINS (1814-1880)

Living in London, Robins studied at the Royal Academy Schools where he attended lectures on perspective given by J.M.W. Turner. As a marine and coastal artist he painted with great technical accuracy and showed a marked aptitude for giving his works 'atmosphere'. He was probably at his best in the 1850s and 1860s when he was travelling widely on the English and Dutch coasts. During this period his watercolour paintings of the sea in all types of climatic condition was masterly (Plate 7.16); he and Edwin Hayes set the standard which few of their contemporaries reached. He was very prolific and had no less than 317 works exhibited at the New Watercolour Society alone. In his early years in London Hardy would have met and been influenced by Robins, by this time an eminent artist in the same specialisation.

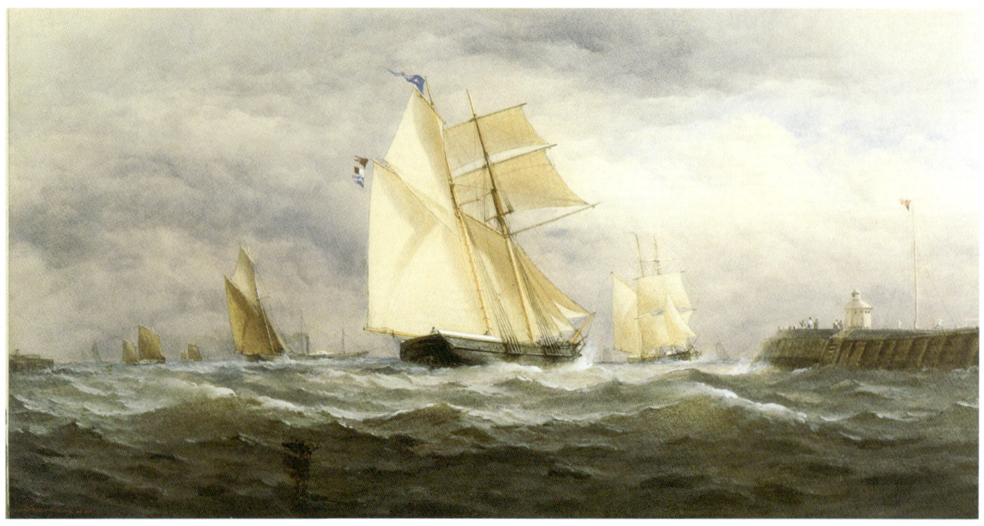

A more cloudy and windswept day than normal but, predictably, Taylor has placed a fine schooner in a convenient shaft of sunlight and transformed what might have been a rather pedestrian picture into a strikingly good marine watercolour.

Plate 7.17. **Charles Taylor Jnr.** *Shipping beyond the Harbour Mouth.* Signed. 41 x 77cm (16⅛ x 30¼ in.)

Charles TAYLOR Jnr (fl.1841-1883)

The son of Charles Taylor who was also a marine artist. The majority of his subjects were taken from the East Coast and Thames Estuary. Painting in watercolour, often on a large scale, his paintings are artistically attractive and historically interesting as they cover, in authentic detail, the transition between sail and steam. His seas and skies are well painted if a bit repetitive. Look for the patch of blue sky and a fluffy white cloud in an otherwise grey sky and the dark shadowed foreground of the sea.

He is also an absolute expert at portraying a ray of sunlight falling on a well-filled sail (Plate 7.17). Hardy may well have picked up a trick or two from this accomplished artist.

George Stanfield WALTERS, RBA (1838-1924)

The son of Samuel Walters, a well-known marine artist in oils, he was born in Liverpool and moved to London in his twenties. His first exhibited watercolour in 1862 at the Royal Society of British Artists led to his very early election to the Society. The quality of his watercolours in the '60s, mainly realistically coloured river and landscape subjects painted in great detail, was undeniable. Soon he began to experiment with harbour and coastal views, again paying great attention to detail, and these were equally popular (Plate 7.18). Like Hardy, he visited many ports on the English and Dutch coasts and among his most successful paintings were some delightful scenes of Venice, usually on a small scale (Plate 7.19). In his coastal paintings he developed a technique

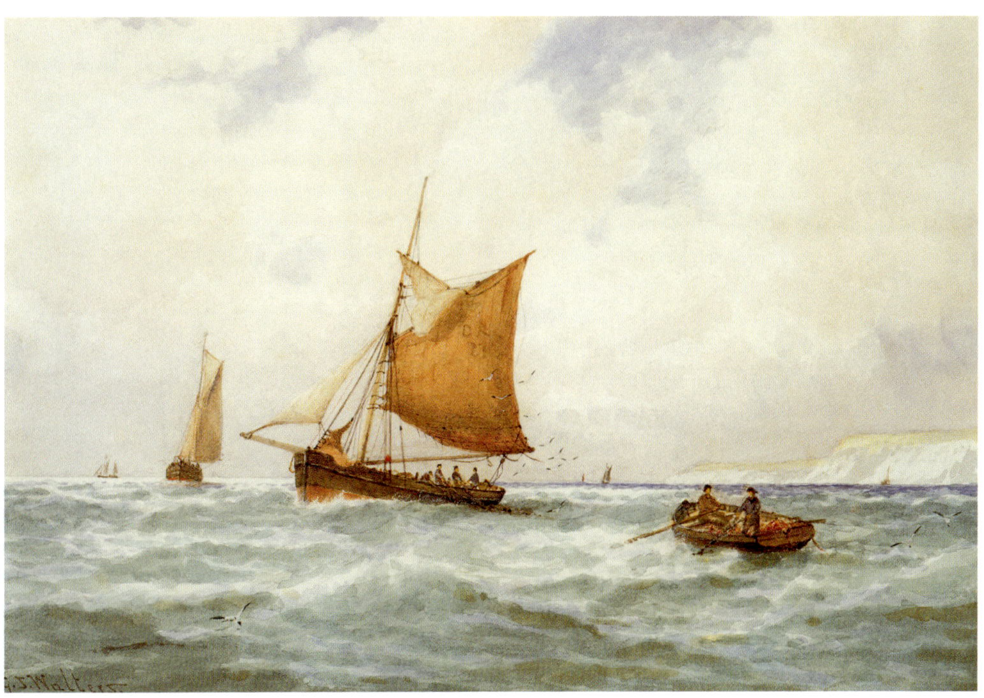

Plate 7.18. **George Stanfield Walters.** *Fishing off the South Coast.* Signed.

There is nothing outstanding about this G.S. Walters watercolour showing a number of fishing boats offshore in the vicinity of Beachy Head. A fine, sunny, breezy day and a blue sea with gently breaking waves which sailors like and the artist has painted well.

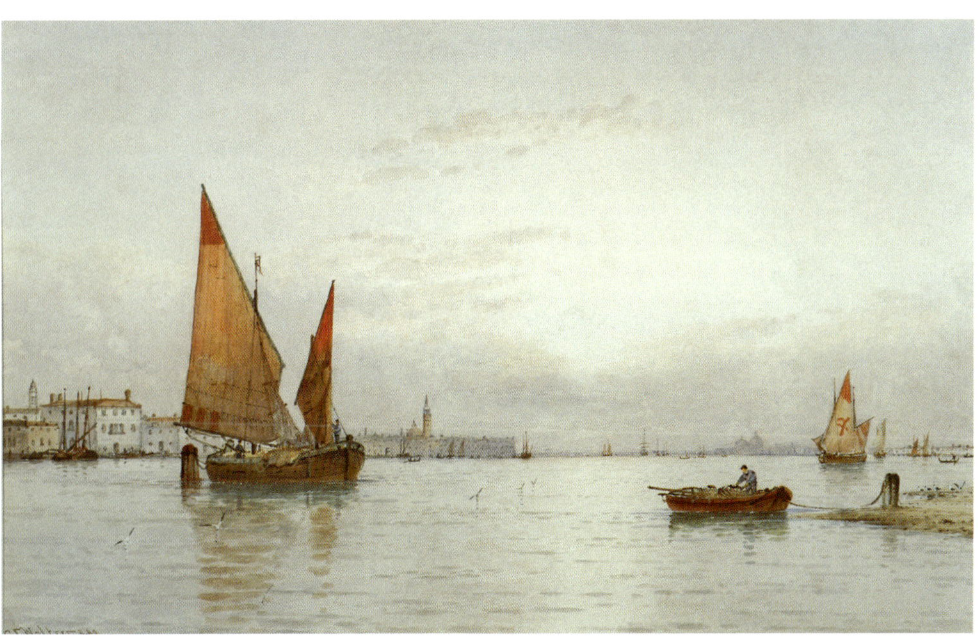

Plate 7.19. **George Stanfield Walters.** *The Lagoon, Venice.* Signed.

A pleasant, calm day on the Lagoon with a few fishermen working and a finely-detailed background of the main islands. Drawing, colour and composition all good.

for depicting the sea reflecting sunlight, usually shortly after sunrise or before sunset. In the '70s and '80s he was producing some very lovely calm seas, ruffled by a light breeze, which shone and sparkled with reflected light. His boats and larger sailing vessels were meticulously drawn. Most unfortunately, many of his later paintings were no more than weak caricatures of his former works. For no obvious reason, Walters, in complete denial of his talent and potential, put commercial output above quality. Thereafter, with few exceptions, his watercolours were unworthy of such an artist.

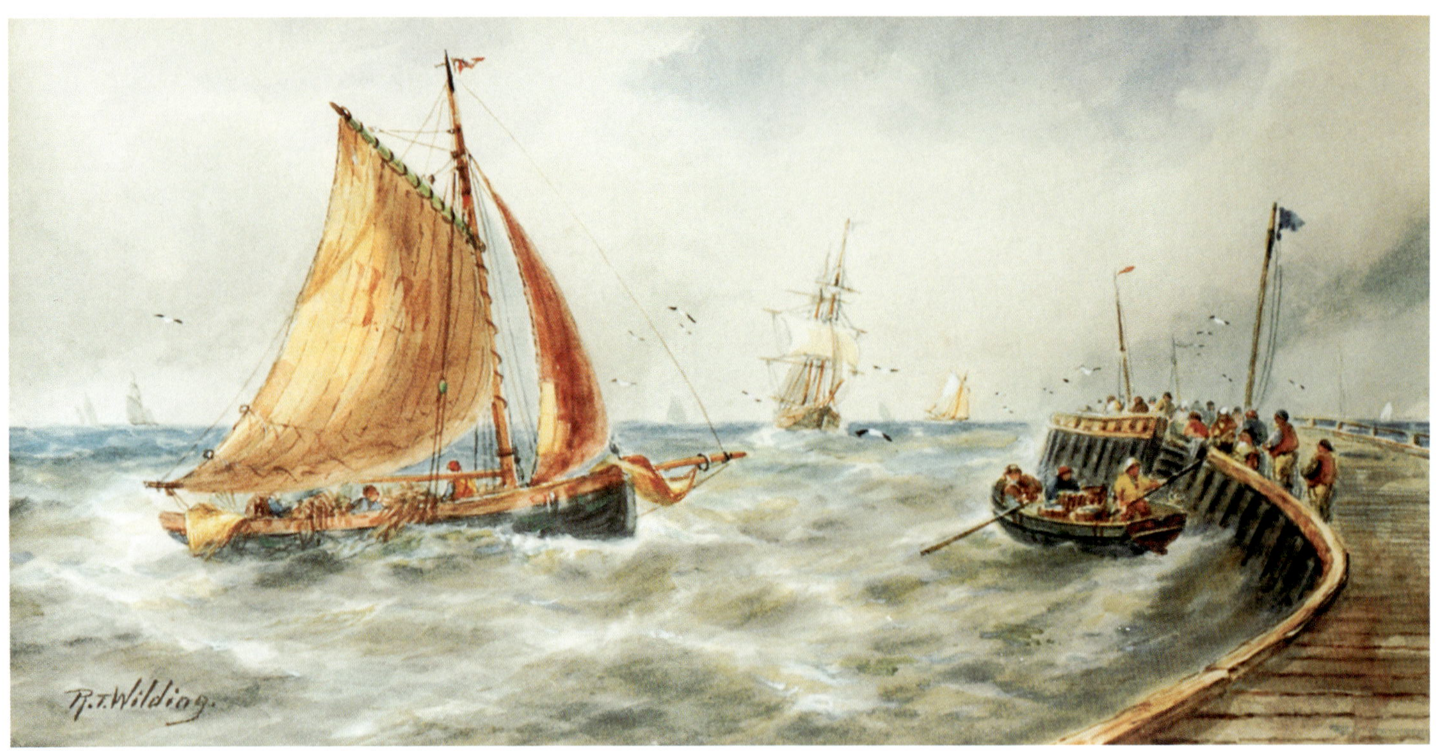

This watercolour shows how much Wilding had learned from Hardy during his apprenticeship. It also shows the marked difference in the colours they used to portray very similar maritime scenes.

Plate 7.20. **Robert Thornton Wilding.** *Fishing Boat approaching the Pier.* Signed.

Robert Thornton WILDING (late 19th-early 20th century)

It is generally believed that Wilding was one of Hardy's young students during the last five or six years of his life. The fact is that a large number of watercolours, with a signature purporting to be Hardy's, were sold during Hardy's lifetime and thereafter which are clearly not by Hardy but are almost certainly by Wilding. Wilding was a reasonable artist himself, painting very much in the style of Hardy and confining himself to subjects in the Portsmouth area and the Channel coastline. Genuine Wildings are all signed, often dated between 1910 and 1920, and turn up at auction fairly frequently. They are pleasant enough coastal scenes, usually small fishing boats at sea in close proximity to shoreside quays and buildings. They have one important feature in common with the fake Hardys – the artist's palette, which bore no relation whatever to Hardy's! Nor, in fairness, did Wilding possess the experience, imagination, technique or sheer skill of his tutor. But good luck to him once he had the self-belief to sign his own name!

William Lionel WYLLIE RA, RI (1851-1931)

Nine years younger than Hardy, Wyllie had his first painting accepted by the Royal Academy as Hardy embarked on his artistic career. Primarily a watercolourist, Wyllie first worked as a maritime illustrator for the *Graphic,* painting historical and contemporary naval subjects and London river scenes. He also painted in oils, several of which are exhibited in national art galleries. His final and greatest work was the huge Panorama of the Battle of Trafalgar permanently on display at the Naval Museum in Portsmouth Historical Dockyard. Today he is probably best known for his very popular black and white etchings of yachting, naval and Thames scenes. His watercolours of similar subjects are also widely collected.

Plate 7.21. **William Lionel Wyllie.** *The Solent Channel.* Signed and inscribed.

This is a typical if rather unexciting watercolour by Wyllie showing two ships out of Southampton passing down the Solent towards Portsmouth and the open sea with many yachts on either beam. Once installed in his house in the shelter of the Round Tower at the entrance to Portsmouth Harbour, Wyllie would have been able to see and sketch many similar scenes.

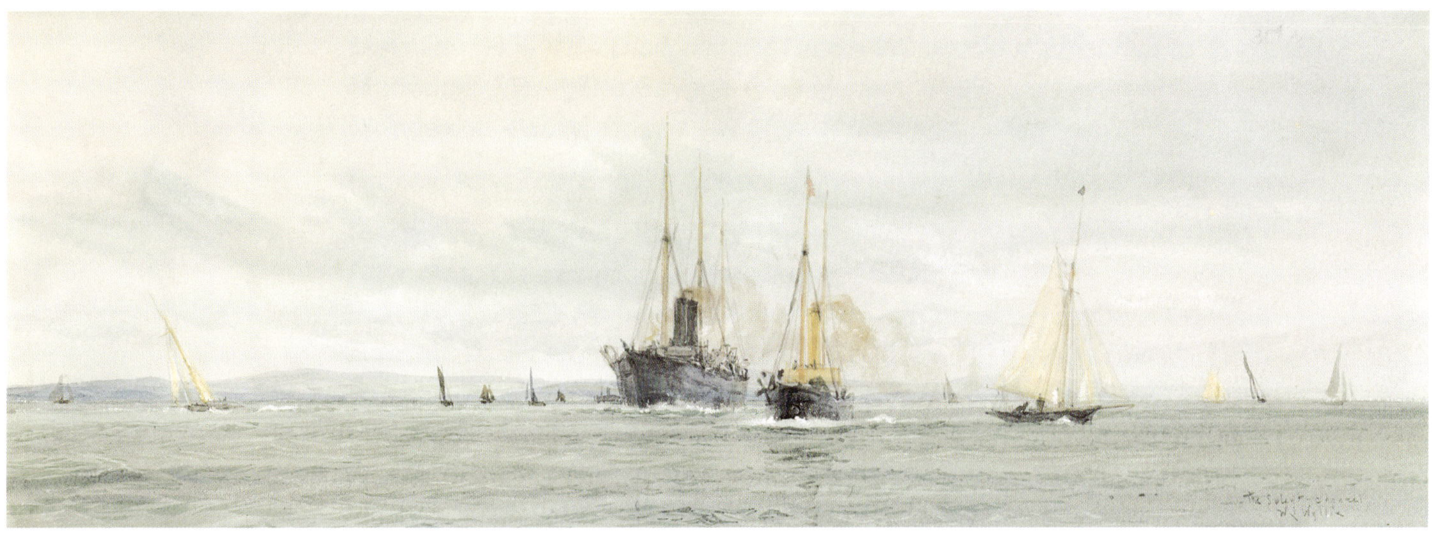

Appendix I

EXTRACTS OF SKETCHBOOK NO 8 DATED 1876

This sketchbook, measuring 4½ x 7⅛in. (11.5 x 18cm) comprises forty pages, of which four are blank and, apart from a further four pages, only the right page is used.

The inside cover has notes written by Hardy that he needed half a dozen HB pencils, two red sable brushes and half a pint of turps. A note reminds him to *'make careful sketches of women's costume'*.

Another amusing note says *'pay for 1½ doz soda and ½ doz brandy and corks waxed and stamped'*.

Some of the more interesting drawings appear as follows:

1876

28 September	Boulogne
28 September	Boulogne, houses
28 September	Boulogne, towards Rue de' l'Ecul
2 October	Quayside activity
2 October	Low tide
2 October	Low tide – study of figures
3 October	Boulogne – Pier study and people
3 October	Noting *'pale sky' light, not quite blue'*
3 October	Stone pier noting *'mud, slime, yellow, black'*
4 October	Fishing boats moored together
4 October	Figures on board the various boats
4 October	Boulogne pier
4 October	Low tide
10 October	3 seascapes, looking south west

The back page notes *'purpose shawls, purple and black striped dress, blue rather light and full apron over black dress'*.

Appendix II

PAINTINGS EXHIBITED AT THE ROYAL ACADEMY

1872 (S)	Off Scarborough blowing fresh from the South East
	Scheveningen, Holland – tide coming in
	Dutch Pinks coming in with the Tide, Scheveningen, Holland
1873	The Strand, Scheveningen
1874 (S)	Dutch Pinks coming in with the Tide, Scheveningen
	(29½ x 49½in./75 x 126cm)
	Margate Harbour
	Gathering Bait, Broadstairs
1875	Flood tide, Scheveningen
	Dutch Pinks leaving Katwyk for the Dogger Bank
1876	A Lazy morning, Scheveningen
	Wind against tide
1877	Caught by the gale
1878	Unloading fishing boats on Boulogne Quay – rain clearing off
1880	A Dutch village
1881	Broadstairs
1882	Too late!
1883	On the Maas
	At Anchor
	Pincks, on the saw hills
	The village of Scheveningen
1884	A cloudy day
	On the sands – Katwijk-oan-Zee
1886	At Shoreham, Essex
	Margate Pler
1887	A Winter's Harvest – Picardy
1888	In the North Sea
	The rough heaving deep expects the storm
1889	The first boat in from the mackerel fishing – Boulogne Harbour
	A change of wind – Boulogne Harbour
1890	Her Majesty's Customs, London
1891 (S)	Her Majesty's Tower
1893	Venice
1894	A haven once for British heroes
1895	A channel port
1897	Home from India

(S) = also exhibited at Suffolk Street

Appendix III

**PAINTINGS EXHIBITED AT
ROYAL INSTITUTE OF PAINTERS IN WATER COLOURS**

1883	Greenwich Pier, Stormy Weather
1885	San Pietro in Volta
	Homeward Bound
1886	Beaching a Pinck, Katwcyk going for a rope
1887	HMS Jenna entering Portsmouth July 1885
	A Hazy Morning Scheveningen Beach
1888	St Valery-sur-Somme
	Katwizk Sands
1889	The Queen of the Adriatic
	A Sussex Mill
1890	End of the Day – Etaples

Appendix IV

PAINTINGS EXHIBITED AT SUFFOLK STREET

		£	s
1871	Robin Hood's Bay, Yorkshire	15	15
	Vessel in Distress off Criacaiett, Wales	12	12
1872	Off Scarborough Harbour	10	10
	Scheveningen Beach – Boats coming in	15	15
	Dutch Pincks, off Scheveningen	15	15
	Tide coming in, Scheveningen	12	12
	The Sand Hill, Scheveningen	10	10
1873	Scheveningen Beach – Nearing Sunset	36	15
	Dutch Pincks coming in with the Tide, Scheveningen	120	-
	On the Dutch Coast – Tide coming in	25	-
1874	On the Medway – Barges in a calm	120	-
	The Thames, London Bridge	52	10
	On the Hague Canal, Holland	42	-
	The Village of Scheveningen, Holland	42	-

		£	s
1875	Calais Harbour	31	10
	Calais Pier – Evening	15	15
	Off Calais	63	-
	Dutch Pincks preparing for sea – Scheveningen	42	-
	The Close of Day – Scheveningen	26	5
1876	Waiting the turn of the tide, Cafecure, pas de Calais	63	-
& 7	Off Treport, a hazy morning		
	The Mouth of the Habour	10	10
1878	The End of the Voyage	26	5
	On the Quay, Boulogne	28	-
	Berck Fishing Boats, off Boulogne	32	-
1879	A Misty Day, Rochester	26	5
	On the Grand Canal, Venice	26	5
	The Dogana and Ducal Palace, Venice	14	14
	Chioggia Boats off San Giorgio, Venice Pair		
	Clearing a Wreck, Bamborough, Northumberland	105	-
	The Dutch Herring Fleet Preparing for Sea, Scheveningen	35	-
	North Sunderland	12	12
	Greenwich Hospital	63	-
1885/6	Entrance to Portsmouth Harbour	84	-
	Church of San Michele, Venice	35	-
	Near Etaples, Pas-de-Calais	25	-
	A Quiet Day, Noordwyk, Holland	16	16
1886	Arrival of the Fish Herring Boats, Katwyk-All-Zee	73	10
1886/7	A fishing village, Picardy	63	-
	At Sea	8	8
1887	'And the long mountains ended in a coast of ever-shifting sand and far away The Phantom Circle of a Morning Sea'	13	10

		£	s
1887/8	The Resting-Place of a Crimean Veteran	21	-
	A beach in Picardy	63	-
1888	At Anchor	12	-
	Near Ambleteuse, Picardy	21	-
	Boulogne Pier	14	14
	On Katwijk Beach	10	-
	A Fishing Village, Picardy	7	7
	The Mouth of the Harbour, Portsmouth	36	15
	Toilers of the Sea, Equiten	42	-
	Ebb Tide, Etaples, Picardy	21	-
	The Church of Saint Michele, Venice	12	12
1889	The Old Water – Gateat Hoorn, on the		
	Zuider Zee	40	-
	A barque on Shore, Ambleteuse, Pas-de-Calais	31	10
1890	Thames Tunnel Pier – An April Day	42	-
	A fresh breeze on the Medway	63	-
	On the French Coast, Low Tide	10	10
	Entrance to Calais Harbour	12	12
	Fishing boats, Venice	5	5
	Venice from the Public Gardens	15	15
	Boulogne Harbour – First Boat in with Mackerell	15	15
	Fishing Boats – Chioggia	10	10
	Clearing Off: A Study from Boulogne Pier	10	10
	Rain Clearing Off: Venice	10	10
	A Kentish Bay: Low Tide (A Study from Nature)	52	10
	Haarlem: Holland	10	10
	A Wet Afternoon: Vencie	6	6
	By the Road Side: Etaples	15	15
	Will She Do It	125	-
	Scarborough Pier	15	15
1891	A Wet Morning, Scarborough Landing Fish	84	-
	On Katwyk Sands	21	-
	Off the French Coast	14	14
	A gale from the North East – Scarborough	35	-
	The Battle of Yarmouth Road, June 3rd, 1653	10	10

		£	s
	Off Scarborough	14	14
	The Doge's Palace, Venice	15	15
	The Murky Tyne	125	-
1892	Her Majesty's Tower	262	10
	Boulogne Pier	6	6
	Katwik Sands	10	10
	1892 Castaway	31	10
	A Summer's Afternoon, Katwick	10	10
	Unloading a Pinck, Scheveningen	10	10
	Tynemouth Castle, Northumberland	15	15
	Flamborough Head, Yorkshire	21	-
1893	On the French Coast	10	10
	Off Ambleteuse	12	12
	The Doge's Palace, Venice	10	10
	Approach to Venice From Adriatic	105	-
	At the Tail of the Goodwins	21	-
	Scheveningen Beach	10	10
	Outward Bound	21	-
	Carnarvon Castle	10	10

13. Clearing a Wreck, Ambleteuse   46.4 x 71.2cm (18¼ x 27⅞in.)
    Signed and dated 1877

14. A Boat with Faggots in the Giudecca, Venice
                                          36.2 x 53.3cm (14¼ x 21in.)
    Signed and dated IXX4 (1884)

15. North Shields on Tyne   64.2 x 107.4cm (25¼ x 42¼in.)
    Signed and inscribed

16. Sea Piece   27.4 x 34.9cm (10¾ x 13¾in.)
    Signed

17. Shore Scene   14.6 x 11.4cm (5¾ x 4½in.)
    Signed

18. Habledown Church, Near Canterbury   25.4 x 39.1cm (10 x 15⅜in.)
    Initialled and inscribed

19. Italian Lake Scene (Plate 6.27)   37 x 60cm (14½ x 23⅝in.)
    Signed and dated 1889

20. Seascape Oil   38.2cm x 43.3cm (15 x 17in.)
    Signed and dated 1887

21. On the Rocks Oil (Plate 3.41)   49.5 x 75cm (19½ x 29½in.)
    Signed and dated 1880

22. Dutch Trawlers   45.1 x 70.8cm (17¾ x 27⁷⁄₃₂in.)
    Signed, inscribed and dated 1874

23. Villa San Clemente (Plate 6.13)   17 x 50cm (6¾ x 19⅝in.)
    Signed and dated 1880

24. Venice   16 x 49.5cm (6¼ x 19½in.)
    Signed, inscribed and dated 1889

25. Rochester   12.2 x 16.3 cm (4¾ x 6⅜in.)
    Signed, inscribed and dated 1879

26. Katwijk   11.2 x 16.8cm (4⅜ x 6⅝in.)
    Signed, inscribed and dated 1879

27. The Dogana and Santa Maria Della Salute, Venice (Plate 6.3)
                                         43.5 x 63cm (17⅛ x 24¾in.)
    Signed, inscribed and dated 1879

28. Off Boulogne   40.6 x 71.2cm (16 x 28in.)
    Signed, inscribed 1878

29. Scheveningen – Getting underway (Plate 4.15)
                                         31.7 x 49.5cm (12½ x 19½in.)
    Signed, inscribed and dated 1879

30. Sea Piece   31.7 x 49.5cm (12½ x 19½in.)
    Signed and dated 1879

31. The Mouth of the Harbour   21.9 x 56.2cm (8⅝ x 22⅛in.)
    Signed and inscribed

32. Boulogne Pier   22.2 x 55.9cm (8¾ x 22in.)
    Signed and inscribed

33. Calais   21 x 23.9cm (8¼ x 9⅜in.)
    Signed and inscribed

34. Scheveningen Beach   23.8 x 34.3cm (9⅜ x 13½in.)
    Signed and inscribed

35. Scheveningen (Plate 4.14)   24.2 x 34.3cm (9½ x 13½in.)
    Signed and inscribed

36. Seascape (Plate 3.40)   14 x 28cm (5½ x 11in.)
    Signed and dated 1882

37. San Giorgio, Venice (Plate 6.5)   24 x 35cm (9½ x 13¾in.)
    Signed, inscribed and dated 1879

38. Hartland Point   28 x 75cm (11 x 29½in.)
    Signed, inscribed and dated 1890

39. Bamburgh Castle (Plate 3.20)   28.5 x 75.5cm (11¼ x 29¾in.)
    Signed and dated 1894

40. Near Torquay (Plate 3.54)   44 x 77cm (17⅜ x 30¼in.)
    Signed, inscribed and dated 1895

41. Chioggia, Venice (Plate 6.8)   34.9 x 52.1cm (13¾ x 20½in.)
    Signed, inscribed and dated 1879

42. Off the Mumbles, Near Swansea (Plate 3.53) 45 x 77.5cm (17¾ x 30½in.)
    Signed, inscribed and dated 1894

43. Doge's Palace and St Mark's Venio   24.1 x 34.9cm (9½ x 13¾in.)
    Signed, inscribed and dated 1870

44. Wind against the Tide, Scheveningen (Plate 4.26)
                                              54 x 94.5cm (21¼ x 37¼in.)
    Signed, inscribed and dated 1883

45. Coming Ashore Oil (Plate 3.42)   46.5 x 99cm (18¼ x 39in.)
    Signed

Notes

1. All are watercolours, with the exception of No. 1 which is charcoal; No. 16 which is an oil on board
    and 20 and 21 which are oil on canvas.
2. Nos. 25, 26, 27, 37, 41 and 43 were bequeathed in 1928 by E.G. Wragg.
3. Nos. 28, 30, 31, 32, 40 and 42 were bequeathed by H.H. Andrew in November 1904.
4. Nos. 38 and 39 were bequeathed by Bertha Annie Sykes.

Appendix VI – Paintings Owned by Sheffield Galleries & Museums Trust

Index

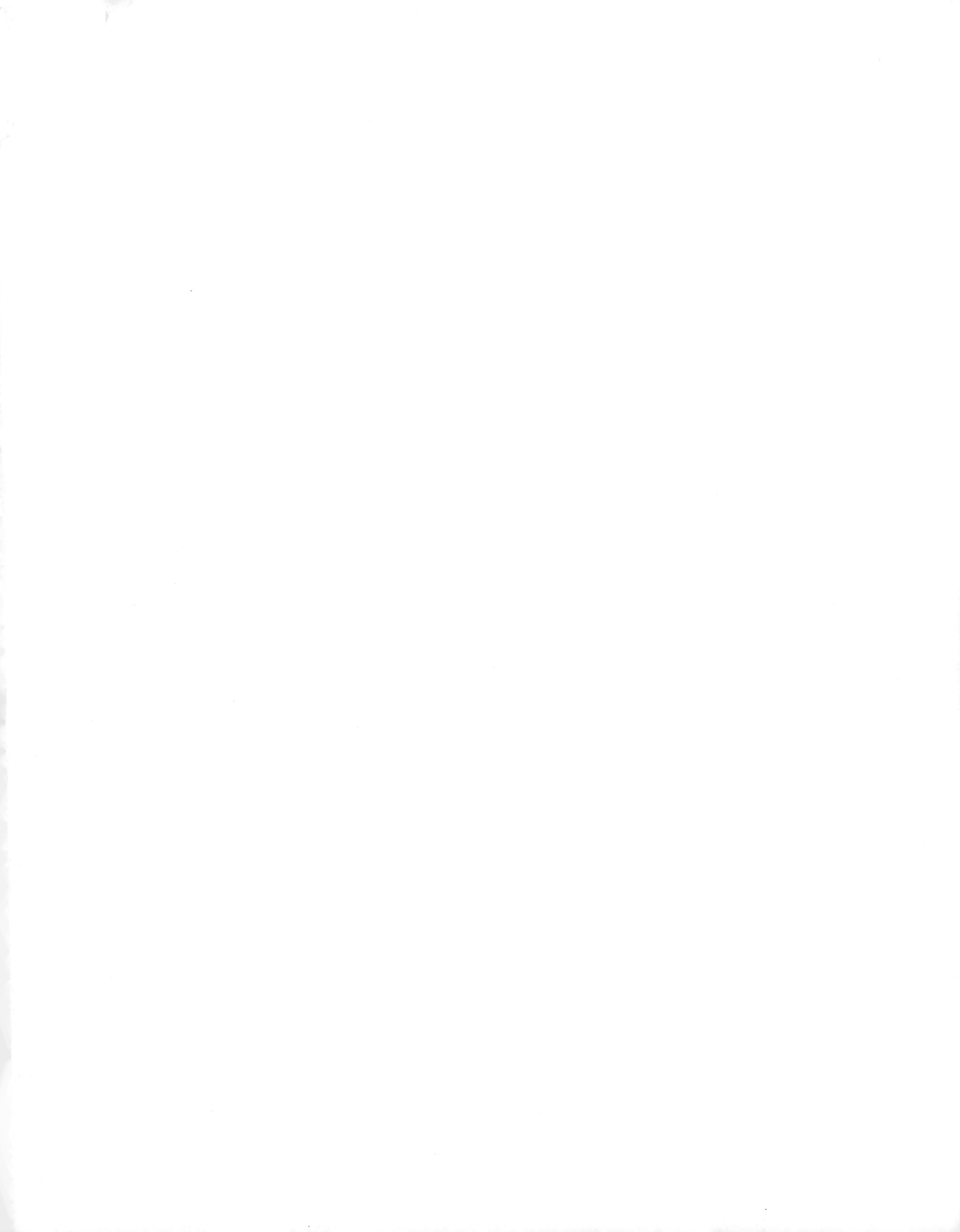

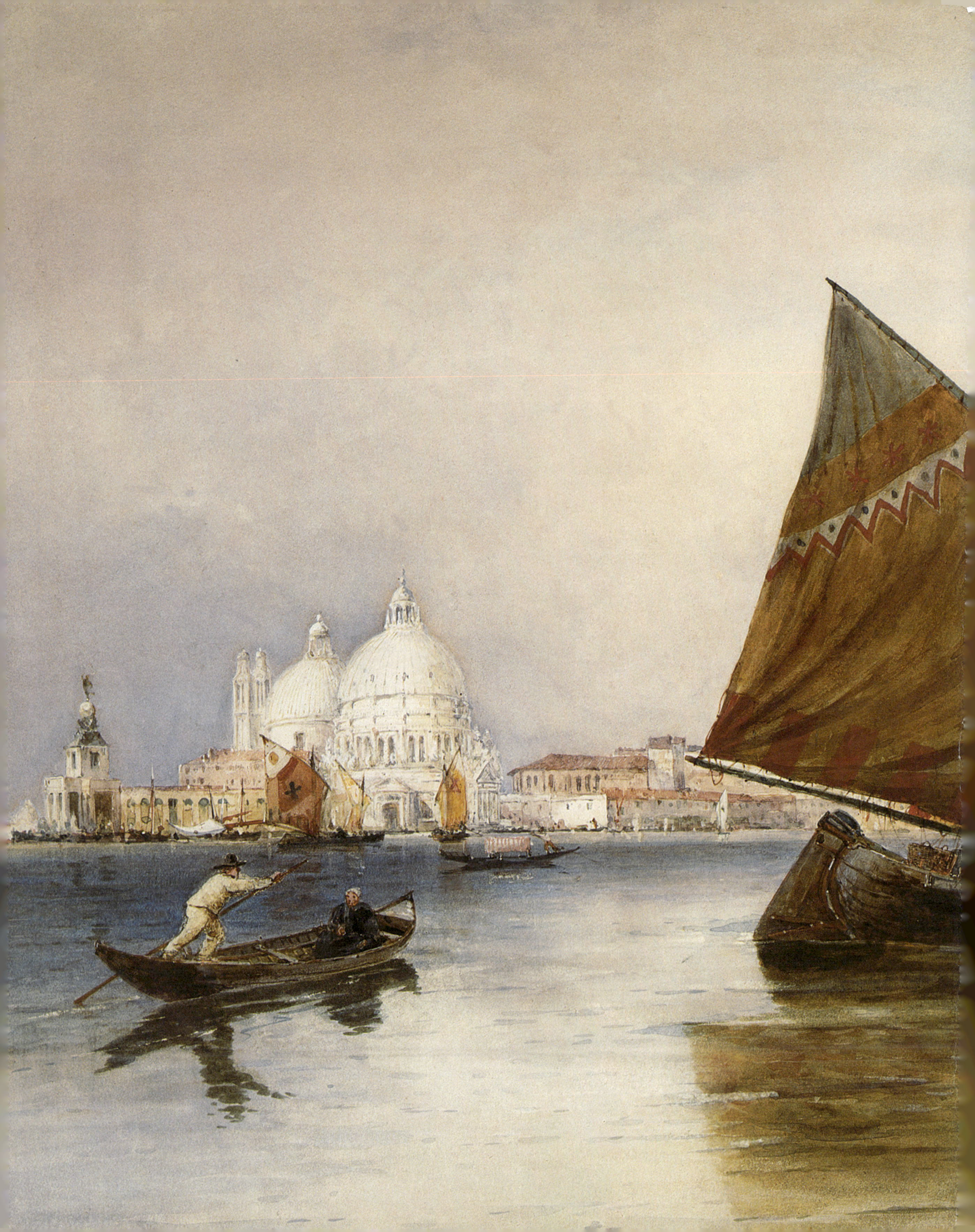